Rick Steves'

BEST OF
EASTERN
EUROPE

2007

Rick Steves & Cameron Hewitt

S0-ARN-171

PRAGUE

1. Archbishop's Palace
2. Basilica of St. George and Convent
3. Bethlehem Chapel
4. Black Light Theater (3)
5. Castle Square
6. Ceremonial Hall
7. Changing of the Guard
8. Charles Bridge
9. Charles University
10. Church of St. Mary the Victorious
11. Church of St. Nicholas (in Little Quarter)
12. Church of St. Nicholas (in Old Town)
13. Convent of St. Agnes of Bohemia
14. To Dancing House
15. Estates Theatre
16. Golden Lane
17. Havelská Market
18. Jewish Quarter
19. Kampa Island
20. Karlova Street
21. Klaus Synagogue
22. Klementinum
23. Lennon Wall
24. To Loreta Church
25. Lucerna Gallery
26. Maisel Synagogue
27. Monument to Victims of Communism Who Survived
28. Mucha Museum
29. Municipal House
30. Mus. of Applied Arts
31. Mus. of Communism
32. Museum of Czech Cubism (in Black Madonna House)
33. Na Příkopě Street
34. Náprsteks Museum of Asian, African & American Cultures
35. National Gallery in Sternberg Palace
36. National Museum
37. National Theatre
38. Nerudova Street
39. Old Jewish Cemetery
40. Old Royal Palace
41. Old Town Hall, Astronomical Clock, Tower & Chapel
42. Old Town Square & Jan Hus Memorial
43. Old-New Synagogue
44. Petřín Tower & Mus. of Jára Cimrman
45. Pinkas Synagogue
46. Powder Tower
47. Prague Castle
48. Royal Gardens
49. Royal Summer Palace
50. Schwarzenberg Palace
51. Spanish Synagogue
52. St. Martin in the Wall
53. St. Vitus Cathedral
54. St. Wenceslas Statue
55. To Strahov Monastery & Library
56. Terraced Gardens
57. Torture Museum
58. Toy and Barbie Museum
59. Týn Church
60. Ungelt Courtyard and House at the Golden Ring Gallery
61. Vrtba Garden
62. Wallenstein Palace & Garden
63. Wenceslas Square

BUDAPEST

- Pedestrian-Friendly Area
- **M** **M** **M** Major Metro Stops
- Landmark or Point of Interest
- **i** Tourist Information Offices

0 m ————— 400 m

0 mi ————— 400 yds

MARGARET ISLAND

To Óbuda & Szentendre

SZENT ISTVÁN PARK

Margitszigit Centrum

MARGIT HÍD

BUDA

Mammut Dep't. Store

Moszkva tér **M**

VÉRMEZŐ

Déli pályaudvar **M**

Déli (Southern) Station

Hadtörténeti Múzeum

VÍZIVÁROS

HÉV Station (to Óbuda & Szentendre)

Halászbástya

Mátyás Templom

Szentháromság tér

Budai Vigadó

Corvin tér

CASTLE HILL

Royal Palace

TABÁN

VÉRMEZŐ

Ádám Clark tér

SZÉCHENYI LÁNCHÍD

Danube

Országház

Kossuth tér

Néprajzi Múzeum

Szabadság tér

Roosevelt tér

Eötvös tér

József Nádor tér

Erzsébet tér

Vigadó tér

Pesti Vigadó

VÁCI UTCA

BELGRÁD RAKPART

GELLÉRT HILL

Rudas Baths

Citadella

Citadella sétány

JUBILEUMI PARK

Szikla-templom

Hotel Gellért

ERZSÉBET HÍD

BUDA

1. Budapest History Museum
2. Cave Church
3. Chain Bridge
4. Citadella
5. Fishermen's Bastion
6. Funicular to Castle Hill
7. Gellért Baths
8. Hilton Hotel (Church Ruins)
9. Hungarian National Gallery
10. Labyrinth Entrance
11. Matthias Church
12. Museum of Military History
13. St. Mary Magdalene Church Remains
14. Turul Bird Statue

PEST

1. Commerce & Catering Museum
2. Franz Liszt Square (Eateries)
3. Great Market Hall
4. Great Synagogue and Jewish Museum
5. Heroes' Square and Millennium Monument
6. To Holocaust Memorial Center
7. House of Terror Museum
8. Hungarian National Museum
9. Legenda Cruise Boats
10. Museum of Ethnography
11. Museum of Fine Arts
12. Opera House
13. Palace of Art
14. Parliament
15. Párisi Udvar Gallery
16. Postal Museum
17. St. István's Basilica
18. Széchenyi Baths
19. Vajdahunyad Castle
20. Vörösmarty Square, Gerbeaud Pastry Shop, and Start of Váci utca Pedestrian Street
21. Zoo

Rick Steves'®

BEST OF
EASTERN
EUROPE

2007

Rick Steves & Cameron Hewitt

AVALON
TRAVEL

CONTENTS

Top Destinations in Eastern Europe

INTRODUCTION

Until 1989, Eastern Europe was a foreboding place—a dark and gloomy corner of the "Evil Empire." But now the obligatory grays and preachy reds of communism live on only in history books, museums, and kitschy theme restaurants. Today's Eastern Europe is a traveler's delight, with low prices, friendly locals, lively squares, breathtaking sights, fascinating history, and a sense of pioneer excitement.

This book breaks Eastern Europe into its top big-city, small-town, and back-to-nature destinations. It then gives you all the information and suggestions necessary to wring the maximum value out of your limited time and money. If you're planning for a month or less in this region, this book is all you need.

Experiencing Europe's culture, people, and natural wonders economically and hassle-free has been my goal for three decades of traveling, tour guiding, and writing. With this book, I pass on to you all of the lessons I've learned, updated for 2007.

You'll wander among Prague's dreamy, fairy-tale spires, bask in the energy of Kraków's Main Market Square, and soak with chess players in a Budapest bath. Ponder Europe's most moving Holocaust memorial at Auschwitz. Enjoy nature as you stroll on boardwalks through the Plitvice Lakes' waterfall wonderland or glide across Lake Bled to a church-topped island in the shadow of the Julian Alps. Taste a proud Hungarian vintner's wine and say, *"Egészségedre!"* (or stick with "Cheers!").

I've been selective, including only the top destinations and sights. For example, Poland has dozens of medieval castles—but Malbork is a cut above the rest.

The best is, of course, only my opinion. But after spending half my adult life researching Europe, I've developed a sixth sense for what travelers enjoy. Just thinking about the places featured in this book makes me want to polka.

This Information Is Accurate and Up-to-Date

This book is updated every year. Most publishers of guidebooks that cover a region from top to bottom can afford an update only every two or three years (and even then, it's often by e-mail or phone). Since this book is selective, it's possible to update it in person each summer. The prices and hours of sights listed in this book are accurate as of mid-2006—but, especially in fast-changing Eastern Europe, understand that guidebooks begin to yellow even before they're printed. Still, if you're traveling with the current edition of this book, you're using the most up-to-date information available in print (for the latest, see www.ricksteves.com/update). Also at our Web site, you'll find a valuable list of reports and experiences—good and bad—from fellow travelers who have used this book (www.ricksteves.com/feedback).

Use this year's edition. People who try to save a few bucks by traveling with an old book learn the seriousness of their mistake... in Eastern Europe. Your trip costs about $10 per waking hour. Your time is valuable. This guidebook saves lots of time.

About This Book

Rick Steves' Best of Eastern Europe is a personal tour guide in your pocket. Better yet, it's actually two tour guides in your pocket: The co-author of this book is Cameron Hewitt, who edits guidebooks and leads Eastern Europe tours for my travel company, Rick Steves' Europe Through the Back Door. Inspired by his Polish roots and by the enduring charm of the Eastern European people, Cameron has spent the last six years closely tracking the exciting changes in this part of the world. Together, Cameron and I keep this book up-to-date and accurate. For simplicity, we've shed our respective egos for this book and have become "I."

This book is organized by destination. Each destination is covered as a mini-vacation on its own, filled with exciting sights and convenient, affordable places to stay and eat. In each chapter, you'll find:

Planning Your Time contains a suggested schedule, with thoughts on how to best use your limited time.

Orientation includes tourist information, city transportation, and an easy-to-read map designed to make the text clear and your arrival smooth.

Sights are rated:

▲▲▲—Worth getting up early and skipping breakfast for;

▲▲—Worth getting up early for;

▲—Worth seeing if it's convenient;

No rating—Worth knowing about.

Sleeping and **Eating** feature descriptions and contact information for my favorite hotels and restaurants.

    Transportation Connections explains how to reach nearby destinations by train, bus, or boat.

    Country Introductions give you an overview of each country's culture, customs, money, history, current events, cuisine, language, and other useful practicalities.

    The chapter on **Understanding Yugoslavia,** which sorts out the various countries and conflicts, gives you a good picture of why Yugoslavia was formed, and why it broke up.

    The **appendix** is a traveler's tool kit, with telephone tips, a climate chart, a list of festivals and national holidays, tips on metric conversion, and a list of US embassies.

    Browse through this book, choose your favorite destinations, and link them up. Then have a great trip! Traveling like a temporary local, you'll get the most out of every mile, minute, and dollar. As you travel the route I know and love, I'm happy you'll be meeting some of my favorite Europeans.

PLANNING

Trip Costs

Traveling in Eastern Europe is a great value. While these countries are Westernizing at an astonishing rate, they remain at the poorer (and cheaper) end of the European scale. Things that natives buy—such as food and transportation—are in line with the local economy (that is, inexpensive). Hotels can be surprisingly expensive, but if you use my listings to find the best accommodations deals, a trip to these countries is substantially cheaper than visiting Italy, Germany, or France.

    Five components make up your trip cost: airfare, surface transportation, room and board, sightseeing and entertainment, and shopping and miscellany. The prices I've listed below are more or less average for all of the destinations in this book. Prices are generally lower in Poland and Slovakia, and higher in Slovenia, Croatia, and Vienna; the Czech Republic and Hungary are in between. Of course, big cities (such as Prague and Budapest) are much more expensive than smaller towns (like Český Krumlov and Eger).

    Airfare: Don't try to sort through the mess. Get and use a good travel agent. A basic round-trip flight from the US to Prague should cost $700 to $1,200 (even cheaper in winter), depending on where you fly from and when. Always consider saving time and money in Europe by flying "open jaw" (into one city and out of another). The additional cost of flying into Prague and out of Dubrovnik is almost certainly cheaper than the added expense (and wasted time) of a two-day overland return trip to Prague.

    Surface Transportation: For the three-week whirlwind trip

What is "Eastern Europe"?

"Eastern Europe" means different things to different people. To most Americans, Eastern Europe includes any place that was once behind the Iron Curtain, from the former East Germany to Moscow. But people who actually live in many of these countries consider themselves "Central Europeans." (To them, "Eastern Europe" is really eastern: Russia, Ukraine, Belarus, and Romania.)

In this book, I use the term "Eastern Europe" the way most Americans do—to describe the **Czech Republic, Slovakia, Poland, Hungary, Slovenia,** and **Croatia.** I've also thrown in a chapter on **Vienna.** This "gateway city" feels more Western than Eastern, but it has important historical ties to the region, and splices neatly into an Eastern European itinerary.

So what do my six core "Eastern European" countries have in common? All of these destinations fell under communist control during the last half of the 20th century. More importantly, for centuries leading up to World War I, they were all part of the Austrian Hapsburg Empire. Before the Hapsburgs, the kings and emperors of these countries also frequently governed their neighbors. And all of these countries (except Hungary) are populated by people of Slavic heritage.

I hope that natives, sticklers, and historians will understand the liberties I've taken with the title of this book. But, after all, would you buy a book called *Rick Steves' Best of the Former Hapsburg Empire?*

described on page 6, allow $300 per person for public transportation (train, bus, and boat tickets). Train travelers will probably save money by simply buying tickets along the way, rather than purchasing a railpass (see "Transportation," page 22). A basic car rental costs about $250 per person per week (based on two people splitting the cost of the car, tolls, gas, and insurance). Long-term car rental is cheapest when arranged in advance from the US, but exorbitant fees for dropping off in a different country can make car rental prohibitively expensive for a multi-country itinerary (see "Car Rental," page 28).

Room and Board: You can thrive in Eastern Europe on an average of $80 a day per person for room and board. An $80-a-day budget per person allows $10 for lunch, $15 for dinner, and $55 for lodging (based on two people splitting the cost of a $110 double room that includes breakfast). That's doable. Students and tightwads do it on $40 a day ($20 per hostel bed, $20 for meals).

Sightseeing and Entertainment: Sightseeing is cheap here. Major sights generally cost $3 to $6, with some more expensive sights at around $10. Figure $10 to $25 for splurge experiences (e.g., going to concerts, taking a twilight cruise on the Danube, watching Slovenia's Lipizzaner stallions, or soaking in a Budapest bath). You can hire your own private guide for four hours for about $80–100—a great value when divided among two or more people. An overall average of $20 a day works for most. Don't skimp here. After all, this category is the driving force behind your trip—you came to sightsee, enjoy, and experience Eastern Europe.

Shopping and Miscellany: Figure $1 per postcard, coffee, beer, and ice-cream cone. Shopping can vary in cost from nearly nothing to a small fortune. Good budget travelers find that this category has little to do with assembling a trip full of lifelong and wonderful memories.

When to Go

The "tourist season" runs roughly from May through September.

Summer has its advantages: the best weather, very long days (light until after 21:00), and the busiest schedule of tourist fun.

In spring and fall—May, June, September, and early October—travelers enjoy fewer crowds, milder weather, and the ability to grab a room almost whenever and wherever they like. Cities are great at this time of year, but some small towns—especially resorts on the Croatian coast—are deserted and disappointing in May and October.

Winter travelers find concert season in full swing, with absolutely no tourist crowds (except in always-packed Prague), but some accommodations and sights are either closed or run on a limited schedule. Croatian coastal towns are completely dead in winter. Confirm your sightseeing plans locally, especially when traveling off-season. The weather can be cold and dreary, and night will draw the shades on your sightseeing before dinnertime. You may find the climate chart in the appendix helpful.

Sightseeing Priorities

Depending on the length of your trip, here are my recommended priorities. Assuming you're traveling by public transportation, I've taken geographical proximity into account.

3 days:	Prague
5 days, add:	Budapest
7 days, add:	Kraków and Auschwitz
9 days, add:	Český Krumlov
12 days, add:	Ljubljana and Bled
16 days, add:	Dubrovnik and Split
22 days, add:	Plitvice Lakes, Eger, Korčula

With more time or a special interest, choose among Vienna, Gdańsk, Pomerania, Toruń, Warsaw, the Danube Bend, Zagreb,

Eastern Europe: Best Three-Week Trip by Train

Day	Plan	Sleep in
1	Arrive in Prague	Prague
2	Prague	Prague
3	Prague; night train to Kraków	Night train
4	Kraków	Kraków
5	Kraków, day trip to Auschwitz	Kraków
6	Kraków, maybe day trip to Wieliczka Salt Mine; night train to Eger	Night train
7	Eger	Eger
8	Early to Budapest	Budapest
9	Budapest	Budapest
10	Budapest	Budapest
11	To Ljubljana (catch early, direct 7.75-hr train; no handy night-train option)	Ljubljana
12	Ljubljana	Ljubljana
13	To Bled	Bled
14	Rent car for day trips around Julian Alps	Bled
15	To Zagreb, sightseeing, then early evening bus to Plitvice Lakes National Park	Plitvice
16	Plitvice hike in morning, then afternoon bus to Split	Split
17	Split	Split
18	Boat to Korčula	Korčula
19	Korčula	Korčula
20	Boat or bus to Dubrovnik	Dubrovnik
21	Dubrovnik	Dubrovnik
22	Dubrovnik and fly home	

This ambitious, speedy, far-reaching itinerary works best by public transportation. Most of the time, you'll take the train. There are a few exceptions: Bled and Ljubljana are better connected by bus. To get from Bled to Plitvice, take the bus to Ljubljana, the train to Zagreb, and then the bus to Plitvice. To get from Plitvice to the coast, take the bus to Split. The Dalmatian Coast destinations are best connected to each other by boat or bus (no trains).

By **car,** this itinerary is exhausting, with lots of long road days. Instead, connect long-distance destinations by night train (e.g., Prague to Kraków, Kraków to Eger/Budapest), then strategically rent cars for a day or two in areas that merit having wheels (e.g., the Czech or Slovenian countryside).

Vienna: The Austrian capital is a likely gateway between Western and Eastern Europe, but it's out of the way for the above itinerary. If you really want to see Vienna, give it two days between Budapest and Ljubljana (it also makes sense if you're going directly between Budapest and Prague).

Slovakia's Spiš Region, and Bratislava.

(The map on page 7 and the three-week itinerary on page 6 include most of the stops in the first 22 days.)

Travel Smart

Your trip to Europe is like a complex play—easier to follow and really appreciate on a second viewing. While no one does the same trip twice to gain that advantage, reading this book's chapters on your intended destinations before your trip accomplishes much the same thing. As a practical matter (to avoid redundancy), many cultural or historical details are explained for one sight and not repeated for another—even if they would increase your understanding and appreciation of that second sight.

As you read through this book, note days of festivals, market days, and when sights are closed. When setting up your itinerary, anticipate problem days. Most museums throughout Eastern Europe close on Mondays, and they almost always stop admitting people 30 minutes before closing time. Hotels in tourist areas are most crowded on Fridays and Saturdays. Saturdays in Europe are virtually weekdays with earlier closing hours. Sundays have the same pros and cons as they do for travelers in the US: Sightseeing attractions are generally open, shops, banks, and markets are closed, and city traffic is light. Rowdy evenings are rare on Sundays.

Be sure to mix intense and relaxed periods in your itinerary. Plan ahead for banking, laundry, picnics, post-office chores, and Internet stops. Every trip (and every traveler) needs at least a few slack days. Pace yourself. Assume you will return.

Reread this book as you travel and visit local tourist information offices. Upon arrival in a new town, lay the groundwork for a smooth departure—write down the schedule for the train or bus you'll take when you depart. Buy a phone card and use it for reservations and reconfirmations. Enjoy the hospitality of Eastern Europeans. Slow down and ask questions. Most locals are eager to point you in their idea of the right direction. Wear your money belt, familiarize yourself with the local currency, and learn a simple formula to quickly estimate rough prices in dollars. Keep a notepad in your pocket for organizing your thoughts. Those who expect to travel smart, do.

Attitude Adjustment

Americans approach Eastern Europe expecting grouchy service, crumbling communist infrastructure, and grimy, depressing landscapes. Many Westerners think that independent travel in the East is reckless—or even dangerous. But those who visit are pleasantly surprised at the beauty, friendliness, safety, and ease of travel here.

Travel in Eastern Europe today is nearly as smooth as travel in the West. The natives speak excellent English and are forever scrambling to impress their guests. Any remaining rough edges simply add to the charm and carbonate the experience.

The East-West stuff still fascinates us, but to locals, the Soviet regime is old news, Cold War espionage is the stuff of movies, and oppressive monuments to Stalin are a distant memory. More than a decade and a half after the fall of the Iron Curtain, Eastern Europeans (or, as they prefer to be called, *Central* Europeans) think about communism only when tourists bring it up. Freedom is a generation old, and—for better or for worse—McDonald's, MTV, and mobile phones are every bit as entrenched here as anywhere else in Europe. Five of the six countries in this book are already part of the European Union, the sixth (Croatia) is on track to join soon...and all of them are looking optimistically to the future.

RESOURCES

Tourist Offices

In the US

Each country's national tourist office in the US is a wealth of information. Before your trip, get the free general information packet, and request any specifics you may want (such as regional and city maps and festival schedules).

Czech Tourism Office: Basic information and a map are free; additional materials are $4 (prepaid by check). Call 212/288-0830 or visit www.czechtourism.com/usa (info-usa@czechtourism.com).

Polish National Tourist Office: Ask for Warsaw and Kraków information, regional brochures, maps, and more. Call 201/420-9910 or visit www.polandtour.org (pntonyc@polandtour.org).

Hungarian National Tourist Office: Request the *Budapest Cityguide* and any specifics (such as horseback-riding info or "Routes to your Roots" booklet for those of Hungarian descent). Call 212/695-1221 or visit www.gotohungary.com (info @gotohungary.com).

Slovak Tourist Office: Call 212/679-7045 or visit www.cometoslovakia.com (slovakoffice@nyc.rr.com).

Slovenian Tourist Office: They have a *Welcome to Slovenia* brochure, map, and information on various regions, hiking, biking, winter travel, and tourist farms. From the US, call Slovenian tel. 011-386-1-560-8823 or visit www.slovenia.info (info@slovenia.info).

Croatian National Tourist Office: Ask for their free brochures and maps. Call 800-829-4416 or visit http://us.croatia.hr (cntony@earthlink.net).

Austrian Tourist Office: Request their *Austria Kit*, maps, and

EU Enlargement and the "New Europe"

On May 1, 2004, the Czech Republic, Slovakia, Poland, Hungary, Slovenia, and five other countries joined the European Union. Though EU membership—and investment—should ultimately benefit everybody, old members and new members have both had their doubts.

For example, new EU member Poland survived the communist era without having to collectivize its small family farms. But now that they've joined the EU, collectivization is mandatory. Traditional Czech cuisine is also in jeopardy. EU hygiene standards dictate that cooked food can't be served more than two hours old. My Czech friend complained, "This makes many of our best dishes illegal." Czech specialties, often simmered, taste better the next day.

Even when the news is good, it's bad. Slovakia, one of the poorest new EU members, suffered from sky-high unemployment and a rusting armaments industry that was abandoned when the Soviets left. Foreign companies are taking advantage of Slovakia's prime location and cheap labor by building several new car factories—turning Slovakia into what *The New York Times* called "the European Detroit." It's a boost to the economy, sure—but as the poor Slovaks become the exploited workforce of wealthy Europe, is it truly good for Slovakia?

A wise Czech grandmother put it best. In her lifetime, she had lived in a country ruled from Vienna (Hapsburgs), Berlin

information on cities and, if pertinent, hiking. Call 212/944-6880 or visit www.austria.info (travel@austria.info).

In Europe

The local tourist information office is your best first stop in any new city. In this book, I'll refer to a tourist information office as a **TI**. Throughout Eastern Europe, you'll find TIs are usually well-organized and always have an English-speaking staff. Try to arrive, or at least telephone, before it closes. Have a list of questions ready, and pick up maps, brochures, and walking-tour information. Most local tourist offices in Eastern Europe are run by the government, which means their information isn't colored by a drive for profit.

Unlike in Western Europe, TIs often don't have a room-booking service—though they can almost always give you a list of local hotels, and if they're not too busy, can call around for you to check on availability. Every town has at least one travel agency with a room-booking service. Even if there's no "fee," you'll pay more for the room than if you book direct, using the listings in this book.

(Nazis), and Moscow (communists). She said, "Now that we're finally ruled from Prague, why would we want to turn our power over to Brussels?"

For their part, longstanding EU members have been skeptical about taking on more countries. Wealthy nations have already spent huge fortunes to improve the floundering economies of poorer member countries (like Portugal, Greece, and Ireland). Most of the new members expect a similar financial-aid windfall. Also on the financial front, Westerners are fretting about an influx of cheap labor from the East (see "The Polish Plumber Syndrome," page 14). Finally, Western Europeans worry about their political power being diluted. When the 10 new nations joined the EU, the geographical center of Europe shifted from Brussels to Prague. In this "New Europe," Poland or the Czech Republic might emerge with a leading role. The East eagerly embraces the future, intent on distancing itself from its painful recent history, while the West tentatively clings to the past, when its power was at its peak (and French, not English, was the world's language).

As the "New Europe" takes shape, players on both sides will continue to define their new roles and seek compromise. So far, the general consensus in the East is that joining Europe was the right move. In a few years, the Slovenes, Poles, Czechs, and their neighbors will all be working harder than ever and enjoying more coins jangling in their pockets...and those coins will be euros.

Rick Steves' Guidebooks, Public Television Show, and Radio Show

With the help of my staff, I produce materials to help you plan your trip and travel smoothly.

Guidebooks: This book is one of a series of 30+ books on European travel that includes country guidebooks, city and regional guidebooks, and my budget-travel skills handbook, *Rick Steves' Europe Through the Back Door*. All are annually updated. My phrase books—for Italian, French, German, Spanish, and Portuguese—are practical and budget-oriented. My other books include *Europe 101* (a crash course on art and history), *European Christmas* (on traditional and modern-day celebrations), and *Postcards from Europe* (a fun memoir of my travels over 25 years). For a complete list of my books, see the inside of the last page of this book.

Public Television and Radio Shows: My television series, *Rick Steves' Europe*, covers European destinations. My weekly public radio show, *Travel with Rick Steves*, features interviews with travel experts from around the world. All the TV scripts and radio shows are at www.ricksteves.com. Listen to the shows at any time—or download them onto your MP3 player to take along on your trip.

Other Guidebooks

Especially if you'll be traveling beyond my recommended destinations, you may want some supplemental information. When you consider the improvements they'll make in your $3,000 vacation, $30 for extra maps and books is money well spent. Especially for several people traveling by car, the weight and expense are negligible. One budget tip can save the price of an extra guidebook. Note that none of the following guidebooks (except mine) are updated annually—check the publication date before you buy.

The Rough Guides, which individually cover the countries in this book, are packed with historical and cultural insight. The Lonely Planet guides are similar, but are designed more for travelers than for intellectuals. If choosing between these two titles, I buy the one that was published most recently. Lonely Planet's fat, far-ranging *Eastern Europe* overview book gives you little to go on for each destination, though their country- and city-specific guides are more thorough.

Students, backpackers, and nightlife-seekers should consider the Let's Go guides (by Harvard students, have the best hostel listings). Dorling Kindersley publishes snazzy Eyewitness Guides covering Prague, the Czech Republic, Slovakia, Budapest, Kraków, Warsaw, Poland, Dubrovnik and the Dalmatian Coast, Croatia, and Vienna. While pretty to look at, these books weigh a ton and are skimpy on actual content.

In Your Pocket publishes regularly updated magazines on major Eastern European cities (including Prague, Budapest, Kraków, Warsaw, Gdańsk, and Zagreb). These handy guides are especially good for their up-to-date hotel, restaurant, and nightlife recommendations (available locally, usually for a few dollars, but often free; condensed versions available free online at www.inyourpocket.com).

For more extensive coverage of the Eastern Adriatic, bring along *Rick Steves' Croatia & Slovenia 2007*. If your Czech travels include destinations outside Prague and Český Krumlov, pick up *Rick Steves' Prague & the Czech Republic 2007*. And for travels in Austria beyond Vienna, consider *Rick Steves' Germany & Austria 2007*. Like the book you're holding now, all of these titles are updated annually in person.

More Recommended Reading and Movies

For information on Eastern Europe past and present, consider these books and films:

Non-Fiction: Lonnie Johnson's *Central Europe: Enemies, Neighbors, Friends* is the best history overview of the countries in this book. Rebecca West's classic, bricklike *Black Lamb and Grey Falcon* is the definitive travelogue of the Yugoslav lands (written during a journey between the two World Wars). For a more recent take, Croatian journalist Slavenka Drakulić has written a trio of insightful essay collections from a woman's perspective: *Café Europa: Life After Communism; The Balkan Express;* and *How We Survived Communism and Even Laughed.* Timothy Garton Ash has written several good "eyewitness account" books analyzing the transition in Eastern Europe over the last two decades, including *History of the Present* and *The Magic Lantern.* For information on Eastern European Roma (Gypsies), consider the textbook-style *We Are the Romani People* by Ian Hancock, and the more literary *Bury Me Standing* by Isabel Fonseca. Tina Rosenberg's dense but thought-provoking *The Haunted Land* asks how those who actively supported communism in Eastern Europe should be treated in the post-communist age.

Fiction: The most prominent works of Eastern European fiction have come from the Czechs. These include *I Served the King of England* (Bohumil Hrabal), *The Unbearable Lightness of Being* (Milan Kundera), and *The Good Soldier Švejk* (Jaroslav Hašek). The Czech existentialist writer Franz Kafka wrote many well-known novels, including *The Trial* and *The Metamorphosis.* Bruce Chatwin's *Utz* is set in communist Prague. James Michener's *Poland* is a hefty look into the history of the Poles. Joseph Roth's *The Radetzky March* details the decline of an aristocratic family in the Austro-Hungarian Empire. *Zlateh the Goat* (Isaac Bashevis Singer) includes seven folktales of Jewish Eastern Europe.

Films: Czech Republic—*Kolya* (1996); *The Trial* (1993); *Kouř* (*Smoke,* 1991); *The Unbearable Lightness of Being* (1988); *The Firemen's Ball* (1967); *Closely Watched Trains* (1966); *The Loves of a Blonde* (1965). Poland—*Karol: A Man Who Became Pope* (2005); *The Pianist* (2002, multiple-Oscar winner); *Schindler's List* (1993, multiple-Oscar winner); *The Wedding* (1972). Hungary—*Kontroll* (2003); *Csinibaba* (1997); *Time Stands Still* (1981); *The Witness* (1969). Croatia—*How the War Started on My Island* (1996); *Underground* (1995); *Tito and Me* (1992); *When Father Was Away on Business* (1985). Slovenia—*No Man's Land* (2002, Slovenian-produced, but deals with Bosnian war; Oscar winner for Best Foreign Film). The BBC produced a remarkable (but difficult-to-find) six-hour documentary series called *The Death of Yugoslavia,* featuring interviews with all of the key players. For a funny and nostalgic look at Eastern Europe's fitful transition to capitalism, the 2003 German film *Good Bye Lenin!* can't be beat.

The Polish Plumber Syndrome

You'll likely enjoy a taste of Eastern European culture on your next trip...to London or Dublin. When Eastern European countries joined the European Union in 2004, three EU members immediately welcomed their new comrades to work without a visa: Great Britain, the Republic of Ireland, and Sweden. This sparked a wave of immigration into these wealthy counties, as Eastern Europeans flocked to the land of plenty to find work. Many ended up in the hospitality industry. A few days before Poland joined the EU, one Kraków hotel manager was already packing his bags. He explained to me, "If I stay here, I can expect only a modest raise every year. But I've got a wife, a kid, and lots of debt. If I move to England, I can get paid in pound sterling instead of złoty for doing the same work—I'll be rich!"

The result has been mixed in each region. Those who have moved are enjoying more money and an irreplaceable cross-cultural experience. But Eastern Europe has seen a somewhat alarming "brain drain," as many of its youngest and most westward-thinking residents have rushed away. And in Britain and Ireland, tourists are encountering desk clerks who don't quite speak fluent English.

The other Western European countries are contemplating opening their borders, but it's controversial. One popular symbol—invented by a right-wing French politician in the summer of 2005—was an invading "Polish plumber" who'd put French plumbers out of a job. The Polish tourist board countered by putting up clever ads in France featuring an alluring Polish hunk stroking a pipe wrench, saying, "I'm staying in Poland...come visit me!"

This is just one more step in the Europe-wide process of integration. Europeans in their twenties have been dubbed the "Erasmus Generation"—after the Erasmus Student Network, an EU organization that fosters study-abroad opportunities within Europe. As European twentysomethings have grown up accustomed to attending universities in other counties, it seems natural for them to identify as "Europeans" rather than as Spaniards, Slovenes, or Swedes. Multilingualism, international résumés, and cross-cultural marriages are the norm.

As with all aspects of the EU enlargement, the resettlement of Poles, Czechs, and Hungarians to the bogs of Ireland will most likely ultimately be good for everyone, despite a few growing pains. It's just one more step in the evolution of a truly united Europe.

Maps

The black-and-white maps in this book, drawn by Dave Hoerlein, are concise and simple. Dave, who is well-traveled in Europe, designed the maps to help you locate recommended places and get to the local TIs, where you can pick up a more in-depth map (usually free) of the city or region. Better maps are sold at newsstands and bookstores—take a look before you buy to be sure the map has the level of detail you want. For drivers, I'd recommend a 1:200,000- or 1:300,000-scale map for each country. Train travelers can usually manage fine with the freebies they get at the local tourist offices.

PRACTICALITIES

Red Tape: Currently, Americans and Canadians need only a passport, but no visa or shots, to travel in the countries covered in this book. Make sure your passport is good for at least 90 days after your ticketed date of return to the US. It's also a good idea to pack a photocopy of your passport in your luggage in case the original is lost or stolen.

Borders: Even though most of these countries are in the EU, they've not yet joined the open-borders Schengen Agreement. That means that for now, you'll still have to show your passport when you cross a border. Americans get needlessly edgy at Eastern European borders, their imaginations fueled by years of Cold War espionage flicks. But scary border delays have long since gone the way of the hammer and sickle. Borders, whether by car or by train, are generally a non-event—flash your passport, maybe wait a few minutes, and move on. You'll be quickly checked as many as four times—by the customs and immigration officers of the country you're leaving and, sometimes after continuing ahead a few yards, the one you're entering. On international night trains, you'll likely be woken up at each border (though sometimes your conductor will take your passport overnight to handle the red tape for you).

The procedure at each border is different. Usually, it's just a quick glance at the passport, the clunk of a stamp, and you're on your way. Since these countries are trying to convince their neighbors to let them open their borders, they're keeping a close eye on corruption—and bribery is a thing of the past. If there is some sort of delay, the worst thing you can do is get impatient or pushy. The angrier you get, the longer it'll take. A polite smile is your best tool to speed things along.

Even as borders fade, when you change countries, you must still change telephone cards, postage stamps, and underpants.

Time: The countries listed in this book are six/nine hours ahead of the East/West Coasts of the US. In Europe—and

Begin Your Trip at www.ricksteves.com

At our travel Web site, you'll find a wealth of **free information** on destinations covered in this book, including fresh monthly news and helpful tips from thousands of fellow travelers.

Our online Travel Store offers travel bags and accessories specially designed by Rick Steves to help you travel smarter and lighter. These include Rick's popular carry-on bags (wheeled and rucksack versions), money belts, totes, toiletries kits, adapters, other accessories, and a wide selection of guidebooks, planning maps, and DVDs.

Choosing the right railpass for your trip—amidst hundreds of options—can drive you nutty. We'll help you choose the best pass for your needs, plus give you a bunch of free extras.

Travel agents will tell you about mainstream tours of Europe, but they won't tell you about **Rick Steves' tours.** Rick Steves' Europe Through the Back Door travel company offers more than two dozen itineraries and 400+ departures reaching the best destinations in this book...and beyond. You'll enjoy great guides, a fun bunch of travel partners (with small groups of generally around 25), and plenty of room to spread out in a big, comfy bus. You'll find European adventures to fit every vacation length. To get our Tour Catalog and a free *Rick Steves Tour Experience* DVD (filmed on location during an actual tour), visit www.ricksteves.com.

throughout this book—you'll be using the 24-hour clock. After 12:00 noon, keep going—13:00, 14:00, and so on. For anything over 12, subtract 12 and add p.m. (14:00 is 2:00 p.m.).

Metric: Get used to metric. A liter is about a quart, four to a gallon. A kilometer is six-tenths of a mile. I figure kilometers to miles by cutting them in half and adding back 10 percent of the original (120 km: 60 + 12 = 72 miles, 300 km: 150 + 30 = 180 miles). For more on metric conversions, see the appendix.

Watt's Up? If you're bringing electrical gear, you'll need a two-prong adapter plug (sold cheap at travel stores in the US) and a converter (to convert the voltage from European to US). Travel appliances often have convenient built-in converters that "auto-sense" the proper voltage. On others, you may have to turn a voltage switch, marked 120V (US) and 240V (Europe).

News: Big cities (such as Prague and Budapest) have weekly English-language newspapers. For international news, Americans keep in touch with the *International Herald Tribune* (published almost daily throughout Europe). Every Tuesday, the European editions of *Time* and *Newsweek* hit the stands with articles of particular interest to European travelers. Sports addicts can get their fix from *USA Today*. News in English will be sold only where there's enough demand: in big cities and tourist centers. Good Web sites include www.europeantimes.com and http://news.bbc.co.uk.

Museum Tips: Eastern Europe's dusty museums don't quite rank with the Louvre or the Prado. The best attractions here are new, modern museums that chronicle the communist regime and celebrate its demise (like Budapest's House of Terror and Statue Park, and Gdańsk's "Roads to Freedom" exhibit at the Solidarity shipyard). But some of the old-fashioned art and history museums are surprisingly good. Generally, you'll follow a confusing, one-way tour route through a maze of rooms with squeaky parquet floors, monitored by grumpy grannies who listlessly point you in the right direction. While many museums label exhibits in English, most don't post full explanations; you'll have to buy a book or borrow laminated translations. In some cases, neither option is available. Audioguides are just catching on.

Discounts: While discounts for sightseeing and transportation are not listed in this book, youths (under 18) and students (only with International Student Identity Cards) sometimes get discounts—but only by asking.

MONEY

Exchange Rates

Most of the countries in this book still use their traditional currencies...for now. In 2007, only Slovenia and Austria officially use the euro currency, but within a few years, the rest will also adopt it.

In countries that don't officially use the euro, many businesses (especially hotels) quote prices in euros anyway. For maximum accuracy, I generally list the prices they gave me—so you'll notice that throughout this book, some prices are in euros while others are in the local currency. Even if places list prices in euros, they'll happily accept the local currency. In fact, if you pay in euros, you'll usually get bad rates and your change back in the local currency.

1 euro (€), used in Slovenia and Austria = about $1.20
22 Czech crowns (*koruna*, Kč) = about $1
30 Slovak crowns (*koruna*, Sk) = about $1
3 Polish złoty (zł, or PLN) = about $1
200 Hungarian forints (Ft, or HUF) = about $1
6 Croatian kuna (kn, or HRK) = about $1

To roughly convert prices in euros to dollars, add 20 percent: €20 is about $24, €50 is about $60, and so on. To convert prices in Czech crowns into dollars, multiply by four and drop the last two digits (e.g., 1,000 Kč = about $40). For Slovak crowns, divide by three and drop the last digit (e.g., 750 Sk = about $25). To go from Hungarian forints into dollars, divide by two and drop the last two digits (e.g., 10,000 Ft = about $50). To convert Polish prices into dollars, divide by three (e.g., 80 zł = about $25). To convert Croatian kuna into dollars, divide by six (e.g., 70 kn = about $11).

So, that 20-zł Polish woodcarving is about $6, the 5,000-Ft Hungarian dinner is about $25, and the 2,000-Kč taxi ride through Prague is...uh-oh.

Banking

Bring plastic (ATM, credit, or debit cards) along with a few hundred dollars in hard cash as an emergency backup. Traveler's checks are a waste of time (waiting at banks) and a waste of money (paying to purchase and then cash checks).

The best and easiest way to get local cash is to use the omnipresent bank machines (always open, low fees, and quick processing). The universal word for "cash machine" in all of these countries is *Bankomat*. To withdraw cash, you'll need a card that can withdraw money from your bank account, plus a PIN code (note that European keypads show only numbers, no letters). Before you go, verify with your bank that your card will work, and inquire about "international transaction" fees (which can be up to $5 plus 5 percent per transaction). Alert your bank that you'll be making withdrawals in Europe; otherwise, the bank may not approve transactions if they perceive unusual spending patterns. Bring two cards in case one gets demagnetized or eaten by a temperamental machine. Since certain fees are charged per exchange, and most ATM screens top out at a certain amount, try to minimize "per visit" fees by pushing the "other amount" button and asking for a higher amount (though this is not always possible, especially in Poland and Croatia).

Bank machines often dispense high-denomination bills, which can be difficult to break (especially at odd hours). My strategy: Request an odd amount of money from the ATM (such as 2,800 Kč instead of 3,000 Kč); or, if that doesn't work, go as soon as possible to a bank or a large store (such as a supermarket) to break the big bills.

Visa and MasterCard are more commonly accepted than American Express. Just like at home, credit or debit cards work easily at larger hotels, restaurants, and shops, but smaller businesses prefer payment in local currency.

Because each country still has its own currency, and you'll likely be crossing several borders throughout your trip, you may wind up with leftover cash from a previous stop. Coins can't be exchanged in other countries, so try to spend them before you cross the border.

Damage Control for Lost or Stolen Cards

If you lose your credit, debit, or ATM card, you can stop people from using your card by reporting the loss immediately to the respective global customer-assistance centers. If you promptly report your card lost or stolen, you typically won't be held responsible for any unauthorized transactions on your account, although many banks charge a liability fee. Call these 24-hour US numbers collect: Visa (tel. 410/581-9994), MasterCard (tel. 636/722-7111), and American Express (tel. 336/393-1111).

At a minimum, have the following information ready: the name of the financial institution that issued you the card, along with the type of card (classic, platinum). Ideally, plan ahead: Pack photocopies of the backs of your cards (with the collect-call numbers), and write down your card numbers on a separate piece of paper that doesn't have your name on it. Providing the following information will allow for a quicker cancellation of your missing card: full card number, whether you are the primary or secondary cardholder, the cardholder's name exactly as printed on the card, billing address, home phone number, circumstances of the loss or theft, and identification verification (such as your birthdate, your mother's maiden name, or your Social Security number—memorize this, don't carry a copy). If you are the secondary cardholder, you'll also need to provide the primary cardholder's identification verification details. You can generally receive a temporary card within two or three business days in Europe.

But bills are easy to convert to the "new" country's currency.

Regular banks have the best rates for changing currency or traveler's checks (except in Poland, where *kantors,* or money-changing kiosks, generally offer good rates—check several to find the best). Post offices and train stations usually change money if you can't get to a bank.

You should use a money belt (a pouch with a strap that you buckle like a belt and wear under your clothes). Thieves target tourists. A money belt provides peace of mind, allowing you to carry lots of cash safely. Don't be petty about taking out money. Withdraw a week's worth of cash, stuff it in your money belt, and travel!

Tips on Tipping

A decade ago, tipping was unheard of in Eastern Europe. But then came the tourists. Today, especially in big cities such as Prague and Budapest, waiters and taxi drivers are beginning to expect Yankee-sized tips when they spot an American. Tipping the appropriate amount—without feeling stingy, but also avoiding contributing to the overtipping epidemic—is nerve-wracking to conscientious visitors. Relax! Many locals still don't tip at all, so any tip is appreciated. As in the US, the proper amount depends on your resources, tipping philosophy, and the circumstances, but the following guidelines should help you out.

Restaurants: Tipping is an issue only at restaurants that have table service. If you order your food at a counter, don't tip. At Eastern European restaurants that have a waitstaff, round up the bill 5–10 percent after a good meal. My rule of thumb is to estimate about 10 percent, then round down slightly to reach a convenient total (for a 370-Kč meal, I pay 400 Kč—a tip of 30 Kč, or about 8 percent). I'm a little more generous in Hungary, where a minimum 10 percent tip is expected (I'll hand over 4,000 Ft for a 3,600-Ft bill—that's a 400-Ft tip, or 11 percent). A 15 percent tip is overly generous, verging on extravagant, anywhere in Eastern Europe. At some greedy tourist-oriented restaurants, especially in Prague and Budapest, a 10 or 15 percent "service charge" may be added to your bill, in which case an additional tip is not necessary. (More commonly, menus or bills remind you that the tip is *not* included.) Look at your bill carefully. If you're not sure whether it includes the tip, just ask.

Taxis: To tip the cabbie, round up about five percent (e.g., for a 71-kn fare, pay 75 kn). If the cabbie hauls your bags and zips you to the airport to help you catch your flight, you might want to toss in a little more. But if you feel like you're being driven in circles or otherwise ripped off, skip the tip.

Hotels: I don't tip at hotels, but if you do, give the porter the local equivalent of $0.50 for carrying bags, and, at the end of your stay, leave a dollar's worth of local cash for the maid if the room was kept clean.

Special Services: Tour guides at public sites sometimes hold out their hands for tips after they give their spiels. If I've already paid for the tour, I don't tip extra. In general, if someone in the service industry does a super job for you, a small tip (the equivalent of a dollar) is appropriate...but not required.

When in doubt, ask: If you're not sure whether (or how much) to tip for a service, ask your hotelier or the TI; they'll fill you in on how it's done on their turf.

VAT Refunds for Shoppers

Wrapped into the purchase price of your souvenirs is a Value Added Tax (VAT) that varies per country. If you spend a minimum amount—which also differs per country—at a store that participates in the VAT refund scheme, you're entitled to get most

VAT Rates and Minimum Purchases Required to Qualify for Refunds

Country of Purchase	VAT Standard Rate*	Minimum in Local Currency	Approx. Min. in US Dollars
Austria	20%	€75.01	$100
Croatia	18.5%	501 kn	$90
Czech Republic	19%	2,000 Kč	$95
Hungary	25%	45,000 Ft	$230
Poland	22%	200 zł	$70
Slovakia	19%	5,000 Sk	$185
Slovenia	20%	€63	$85

* The VAT Standard Rates listed above—while listed as exact amounts—are intended to give you an idea of the rates and minimums involved. But VAT rates fluctuate based on many factors, including what kind of item you are buying. Your refund will also likely be less than the above rate, especially if it's subject to processing fees.

of that tax back (see chart for VAT rates and minimum amounts). Personally, I've never felt that VAT refunds are worth the hassle, but if you do, here's the scoop.

Ideally, the merchant will subtract the tax when you make your purchase (this is more likely to occur if the store ships the goods to your home). Otherwise, you'll need to do all this:

• **Get the paperwork.** Show the merchant your passport, and he or she will fill out the necessary refund document, called a "cheque."

• **Get your stamp at the border or airport.** Process your cheque(s) at your last stop in the country with the customs agent who deals with VAT refunds. It's best to keep your purchases in your carry-on for viewing, but if they're too large or dangerous (such as knives) to carry on, have them inspected before you check your bag. To qualify, your purchased goods should be unused. If you show up at customs wearing your chic Czech shirt, officials might look the other way—or deny you a refund.

• **Collect your refund.** You'll need to return your stamped documents to the retailer or its representative. Many merchants work with a service that has offices at major airports, ports, and border crossings, such as Global Refund (www.globalrefund.com) or Premier Tax Free (www.premiertaxfree.com). These services, which extract a 4 percent fee, usually can refund your money immediately in your currency of choice or credit your card (within two billing cycles). If you have to deal directly with the retailer, mail the store your stamped documents and then wait. It could take months.

Customs Regulations

You can take home $800 in souvenirs per person duty-free. The next $1,000 is taxed at a flat 3 percent. After that, you pay the individual item's duty rate. You can also bring in duty-free a liter of alcohol (slightly more than a standard-sized bottle of wine), a carton of cigarettes, and up to 100 cigars. As for food, anything in cans or sealed jars is acceptable. Don't bring back meat (even if it's dried and cured), cheeses, and fresh fruits and veggies. (Hungarian paprika is OK as long as it's in a sealed container.) To check customs rules and duty rates, visit www.customs.gov.

TRANSPORTATION

In Eastern Europe, I travel mostly by public transportation. For long distances between big cities (such as Prague to Kraków, Warsaw to Budapest, or Vienna to Dubrovnik), I prefer to take a cheap flight or a night train. For shorter distances (like Gdańsk to Warsaw or Ljubljana to Zagreb), I take a daytime train or bus. In areas with lots of exciting day-trip possibilities, such as the Czech or Slovenian countryside, I rent a car for a day or two—or hire a local tour guide with a car to drive me around (which can be cheaper than you might think; I recommend several drivers in this book).

If you're debating between public transportation and car rental, consider these factors: Trains and buses are best for single travelers; those who'll be spending more time in big cities; those with an ambitious, multi-country itinerary; and those who don't want to drive in Europe. While a car gives you more freedom—enabling you to search for hotels more easily and carrying your bags for you—trains and buses zip you effortlessly from city to city, usually dropping you in the center, near the tourist office. Cars are great in the countryside, but a worthless headache in places like Prague, Budapest, and Dubrovnik. If you're lacing the big cities together, the last thing you want is a car.

Public Transportation

Trains

Trains are punctual and cover cities well, but frustrating schedules make a few out-of-the-way recommendations difficult—or impossible—to reach (usually the bus will get you there instead; see "Buses" on page 27). For timetables, the first place to check

Public Transportation in Eastern Europe

Eastern Europe Railpasses

Prices listed are for 2007 and are subject to change. For the latest prices, details, and train schedules (and easy online ordering), see my comprehensive *Guide to Eurail Passes* at www.ricksteves.com/rail.

Map key: Approximate point-to-point one-way second-class rail fares in US dollars. First class costs 50 percent more. Add up fares for your itinerary to see if a railpass will save you money.

EUROPEAN EAST PASS

	1st Class	2nd Class
5 days in 1 month	$257	$180
Extra rail days (max 5)	30	24

Covers Austria, Czech Republic, Slovakia, Hungary, and Poland. The fare for children 4–11 is half the fare. Kids under age 4 travel free.

CZECH PASS

	1st Class	2nd Class
3 out of 15 days	$117	$81
Extra rail days (max 5)	16	12

The fare for children 6–12 is half the fare. Kids under age 6 travel free.

HUNGARY PASS

	Individual 1st Class	Saver 1st Class	Youth 2nd Class
5 out of 15 days	$91	$80	$68
10 days in 1 month	130	116	86

"Saver" prices are per person for two or more people traveling together. "Youth" means under age 26. The fare for children 6–14 is half the individual fare or Saver fare. Huns go free.

POLAND PASS

	Adult 1st Class	Adult 2nd Class	Youth 1st Class	Youth 2nd Class
5 days in 1 month	$140	$107	$98	$75
8 days in 1 month	198	154	140	108
10 days in 1 month	224	172	158	121
15 days in 1 month	310	238	219	167

"Youth" means under age 26. The fare for children 4–11 is half the adult fare. Kids under age 4 travel free.

SELECTPASS

This pass covers travel in three adjacent countries such as Germany, Austria and Hungary. Can also choose Slovenia/Croatia as one "country." Please visit **www.ricksteves.com/rail** for four- and five-country options.

	Individual 1st Class	Saver 1st Class	Youth 2nd Class
5 days in 2 months	$405	$344	$263
6 days in 2 months	444	379	292
8 days in 2 months	530	450	344
10 days in 2 months	611	519	397

"Saver" prices are per person for two or more people traveling together. "Youth" means under age 26. The fare for children 4–11 is half the adult individual fare or Saver fare. Kids under age 4 travel free.

HUNGARY-SLOVENIA-CROATIA

	Individual 1st Class	Saver 1st Class	Youth 2nd Class
5 days in 2 months	$228	$194	$159
6 days in 2 months	251	214	180
8 days in 2 months	296	251	214
10 days in 2 months	340	292	236

"Saver" prices are per person for two or more people traveling together. "Youth" means under age 26. The fare for children 4–11 is half the adult individual fare or Saver fare. Kids under age 4 travel free.

AUSTRIA-CZECH REPUBLIC
or AUSTRIA-HUNGARY

	Individual 1st Class	Saver 1st Class	Youth 2nd Class
4 days in 2 months	$224	$190	$154
Extra rail days (max 6)	33	28	23

"Saver" prices are per person for two or more people traveling together. "Youth" means under age 26. The fare for children 4–11 is half the adult individual fare or Saver fare. Kids under age 4 travel free.

AUSTRIA-SLOVENIA-CROATIA

	Individual 1st Class	Saver 1st Class	Youth 2nd Class
4 days in 2 months	$246	$214	$180
Extra rail days (max 6)	38	33	26

"Saver" prices are per person for two or more people traveling together. "Youth" means under age 26. The fare for children 4–11 is half the adult individual fare or Saver fare. Kids under age 4 travel free.

is Germany's excellent all-Europe timetable at http://bahn.hafas.de/bin/query.exe/en. Individual countries also have their own train timetable Web sites:

- **Czech Republic:** www.vlak-bus.cz
- **Slovakia:** www.cp.sk
- **Poland:** http://rozklad.pkp.pl/bin/query.exe/en
- **Hungary:** www.elvira.hu
- **Slovenia:** www.slo-zeleznice.si
- **Croatia:** www.hznet.hr
- **Austria:** www.oebb.at

You'll rarely need a reservation, except for night trains.

Night Trains: To cover the long distances between the major destinations in this book, consider using night trains (or taking an inexpensive flight—see "Cheap Flights"). Remember, each night on the train saves a day for sightseeing. Fortunately, most of Eastern Europe's big cities are connected by night trains. I love the convenience of night trains, and take them routinely. Still, some of my readers have complained that Eastern European night trains aren't as plush, comfy, and smooth as those they've used in the West. Also, realize that you may be woken up to show your passport each time the train crosses a border (unless the conductor offers to take your passport to deal with the border checks while you sleep). This can be especially frustrating on the train from Kraków to Eger or Budapest, which goes through Slovakia...and crosses the border twice. In general, if you're accustomed to a higher degree of comfort, fly or take a day train.

One more thing: No matter how many times you hear "totally true" stories of train cars being "gassed" with a sleep-inducing drug by thieves, it's an urban legend, most likely invented by travelers who felt foolish for sleeping through a theft. But as on Western European night trains, thefts do occur, so lock the door and secure your belongings (to make it difficult—or at least noisy—for thieves to rip you off). When sleeping on a night train, I wear my money belt.

Railpasses: While railpasses can be a good deal in Western Europe, they usually aren't the best option in the East for two reasons: Point-to-point tickets are cheap and simple here, and most railpasses don't conveniently combine Eastern European countries. For example, with the Eurail Selectpass, you can buy unlimited travel for up to 15 travel days (within a two-month period) in three, four, or five adjacent countries; but of the countries in this book, only Hungary, Austria, and Slovenia/Croatia are eligible. Another option is the European East Pass, covering the Czech Republic, Hungary, Poland, Slovakia, and Austria—but not Slovenia or Croatia. The Czech Republic, Hungary, and Austria have their own individual railpasses, valid for trips only within their country. And three different combo-passes combine various countries: one for Austria and the Czech Republic; another for Austria, Slovenia, and Croatia; and another for Hungary, Slovenia, and Croatia. Again, none of these passes is likely to save you much money, but if a pass matches your itinerary, give it a look and crunch the numbers. For all of the options, see the charts on pages 24 and 25, or visit our Railpass Guide online at www.ricksteves.com/rail.

Language Barrier: For tips on buying train tickets from monolingual staff in Eastern European stations, see "Hurdling the Language Barrier" on page 32.

Buses

While the train can get you most places faster than a bus can, there are a few areas where buses are worth considering. For example, Ljubljana and Lake Bled are connected by both train and bus—but the bus station is right in the town center of Bled, while the train station is a few miles away. And a few destinations, including Croatia's Plitvice Lakes National Park and many of the sights in Slovenia's Karst region, are accessible only by bus. In general, trains are best in Poland and Hungary; buses are often better in Slovakia and Croatia; and it's a toss-up in the Czech Republic and Slovenia. Throughout this book, I'll suggest whether trains or buses are better for a particular destination (in the "Transportation Connections" section in each chapter). When in doubt, ask at the local TI for advice.

Boats

Once you get to the Croatian coast, boats can be your best option. For details, see "Getting Around the Dalmatian Coast" on page 610.

Cheap Flights

Low-cost airlines have arrived in Eastern Europe, allowing you to cheaply connect many of the destinations in this book. One of the biggest Eastern Europe–based budget airlines, **SkyEurope** (www .skyeurope.com), has hubs in Budapest, Kraków, Warsaw, Košice (eastern Slovakia), and Bratislava, with flights to various destinations in both Eastern Europe (including Prague, Dubrovnik, and Split) and Western Europe. **Wizz Air** (www.wizzair.com) has hubs in Budapest, Warsaw, and Katowice (near Kraków), but most of their flights go to Western Europe rather than destinations within Eastern Europe. **Smart Wings** (www.smartwings.net), based in Prague and Budapest, has flights to Western Europe. And LOT, Poland's biggest carrier, has a low-cost subsidiary called **Centralwings** (www.centralwings.com).

Several of the more established Western European budget airlines are expanding their offerings eastward. For example, **easyJet** (www.easyjet.com) now flies from Western hubs to several major

Eastern European cities (including Prague, Kraków, Warsaw, Budapest, Bratislava, and Ljubljana). **Ryanair** (www.ryanair.com) has flights to many Polish cities (including Kraków, Warsaw, and Gdańsk). And **Air Berlin** (www.airberlin.com) connects Budapest and Vienna to the West.

As with all no-frills airlines, be aware of trade-offs for cheap flights: minimal customer service, non-refundable tickets, and strict restrictions on the amount of baggage you're allowed to check without paying extra. In general, you'll be nickel-and-dimed every step of the way (e.g., no free drinks). Also note that you'll sometimes fly out of less convenient, secondary airports. For example, Wizz Air's flights from "Kraków" actually depart from Katowice, 50 miles away (see page 220). And SkyEurope implies they fly from "Vienna," but the airport is actually in Bratislava, Slovakia—nearby, but in a different country (see page 179). Finally, be warned that many no-frills airlines save money by scheduling flights on the same plane extremely close together—so they can pack more flights into one day. But this means that a delay early in the day can trickle down and cause major delays later. While some of the upstarts have improved, newer airlines (which haven't yet worked out the kinks) can be subject to late departures and arrivals.

Now that the established airlines in Eastern Europe face more competition, they've been forced to adapt. Many national carriers sell a handful of seats on certain flights at super-cheap promotional rates, which sell out quickly. In 2006, I flew from Budapest to Kraków on Poland's national airline, LOT, for less than a night-train ticket (www.lot.com). Croatia Airlines (www.croatiaairlines .com) and Slovenia's Adria Airways (www.adria-airways.com) often have similar deals—but only if you book early.

Finally, **Europe by Air** continues to offer their Flight Pass, charging $99 per leg (plus taxes and airport fees) for flights within Europe. They partner with various well-established airlines, providing good coverage for low prices (most useful for Croatia Airlines flights to and from the Dalmatian Coast; tickets can be purchased only in the US, www.europebyair.com, US tel. 888-321-4737).

Driving

Car Rental

It's cheaper to arrange long-term European car rentals in the US than in Europe. For short rentals of a day or two, I usually have no problem finding an affordable car on the spot (I've listed car-rental companies in this book)—but if your itinerary is set, it doesn't hurt to book ahead. All of the big American companies have offices throughout Eastern Europe. Comparison-shop on the Web to find the best deal, or ask your travel agent.

Allow about $750 per person (based on two people sharing

Driving: Distance and Time

Map detail below

m = miles
h = hours
····· = car ferry
Note: Your times may vary based on traffic, construction, and road conditions.

the car) to rent a small economy car for three weeks with unlimited mileage, including gas, parking, and insurance. I normally rent a small, inexpensive model like a Ford Fiesta or Škoda Fabia. You'll pay extra for collision damage waiver (CDW) insurance (described below). Be warned that dropping a car off in a different country—say, picking up in Prague and dropping in Croatia—can be prohibitively expensive (depends on distance, but the extra fee averages a few hundred dollars, and can exceed $1,000). If you're doing a multi-country trip by car, find out what the international drop-off fee will be. If it's exorbitant, consider doing a round-trip itinerary instead...or using public transportation. Again, I prefer to connect long distances by train, then rent cars for a day or two where they're most useful (I've noted these places throughout this book).

As a rule, always tell your car-rental company up front exactly which countries you'll be entering. Some companies levy extra insurance fees for trips taken with certain types of cars (such as BMWs, Mercedes, and convertibles) in certain countries. More importantly, as you cross borders you may need to show the proper paperwork, such as proof of insurance (often called a "green card"). Double-check with your rental agent that you have all the documentation you need before you drive off. For more on borders, see "Borders," page 15.

For driving in Eastern Europe, it's wise to get an International Driving Permit ahead of time at your local AAA office ($10 plus two passport-type photos, www.aaa.com).

Insurance: For peace of mind, I spring for the Collision Damage Waiver insurance (CDW, about $15–25 per day), which limits my financial responsibility in case of an accident. Unfortunately, CDW now has a high deductible hovering at about $1,000–1,500. When you pick up your car, many car-rental companies will try to sell you "super CDW" at an additional cost of $7–15 per day to lower the deductible to zero. Consider the following alternatives.

Some credit cards offer zero-deductible collision coverage (similar to CDW) for no charge to their customers. Quiz your credit-card company on the worst-case scenario. You have to choose either the coverage offered by your car-rental company or by your credit-card company. This means that if you go with the credit-card coverage, you'll have to decline the CDW offered by the car-rental company. In this situation, some car-rental companies put a hold on your credit card for the amount of the full deductible (which can equal the value of the car). This is bad news if your credit limit is low—particularly if you plan on using that card for other purchases during your trip.

Another alternative is buying CDW insurance from Travel Guard ($9/day plus a one-time $3 service fee covers you up to

$35,000, $250 deductible, US tel. 800-826-4919, www.travelguard .com). It's valid throughout Europe, but some car-rental companies refuse to honor it (mainly in Italy and Ireland). Oddly, residents of Washington State are not allowed to buy this coverage.

In summary, buying CDW from the car-rental company—along with the supplemental insurance to buy down the deductible, if you choose—is the easiest but priciest option. Using the coverage that comes with your credit card is cheaper, but can involve more hassle. If you're taking a short trip, an easy solution is to buy Travel Guard's very affordable CDW. For longer trips, consider leasing.

Leasing: If you'll be renting for three weeks or more, look into leasing (either through your travel agent or by going online to check the major companies' Web sites). Leasing allows you to avoid insurance costs and taxes, but you may have to pick up and drop off the car in Germany or Austria.

Driving Tips

During the communist era, Eastern Europe's infrastructure lagged far behind the West's. Now that the Iron Curtain is long gone, superhighways are being rolled out like crazy. Since construction is ongoing, it's not unusual to discover that a not-yet-finished expressway ends, requiring a transfer to an older, slower road. Likewise, you'll sometimes discover that a much faster road has been built between major destinations since your three-year-old map was published. (This is another good reason to travel with the most up-to-date maps available and study them before each drive.) New superhighways recently opened between Dresden and Prague (A17), and from Zagreb to Budapest (to the north) and Zagreb to Split (to the south). As soon as a long-enough section is completed, the roads are opened to the public.

Occasionally backcountry roads are the only option (as with part of the trip between Prague and Kraków, or from Kraków to Hungary through Slovakia). These can be bumpy and slow, but they're almost always paved (or, at least, they once were). In Poland, where the network of new expressways is far from complete, locals travel long distances on two-lane country roads. Since each lane is about a lane and a half wide, passing is commonplace. Slower drivers should keep to the far-right of their lane, and not be surprised when faster cars zip past them.

Tolls: In many countries, driving on highways requires a toll sticker (generally available at the border, post offices, gas stations, and sometimes car-rental agencies): the **Czech Republic** (*dálniční známka*, 200 Kč/15 days, 300 Kč/2 months); **Slovakia** (*úhrada*, 100 Sk/15 days); **Hungary** (*autópálya matrica*, 1,170–1,520 Ft/4 days depending on season, 2,500 Ft/week, 4,200 Ft/month, www .motorway.hu); and **Austria** (*Vignette*, €8/10 days, €22/2 months).

Fines for not having a toll sticker can be stiff. Note that you don't need a toll sticker if you'll be dipping into the country on minor roads—only for major highways. Your rental car may already come with the necessary sticker—ask. In **Slovenia** and **Croatia**, you'll take a toll-ticket as you enter the expressway, then pay when you get off, based on how far you've traveled (very roughly, figure about 5 cents per kilometer). In **Poland**, drivers also pay tolls to use completed expressway segments.

STOP AND LEARN THESE ROAD SIGNS

Speed Limit (km/hr)	Yield	No Passing	End of No Passing Zone
One Way	Intersection	Main Road	Freeway
Danger	No Entry	No Entry for cars	All Vehicles Prohibited
Parking	No Parking	Customs	Peace

   Parking: Parking is a costly headache in big cities. You'll pay about $10–15 a day to park safely. Rental-car theft can be a big problem in cities, especially Prague. Ask at your hotel for advice.

   Laws and Regulations: Learn the universal road signs (see sidebar). Seat belts are required, and two beers under those belts are enough to land you in jail. (In Croatia, you're legally not allowed to have any alcohol in your system at all if you're driving.)

   More and more European countries—such as Slovenia and the Czech Republic—require you to have your headlights on any time you're driving, even in broad daylight. Many cars are rigged to have lights go on and off automatically when you start and stop the engine. Be sure to ask about this regulation, and how your car's lights work, when you pick up your rental car.

COMMUNICATING

Hurdling the Language Barrier

The language barrier in Eastern Europe is no bigger than in the West. In fact, I find that it's much easier to communicate in Hungary or Croatia than in Italy or Spain. Immediately after the Iron Curtain fell in 1989, English speakers were rare. But today, you'll find that most people in the tourist industry—and virtually all young people—speak excellent English.

   Of course, not *everyone* speaks English. You'll run into the most substantial language barriers in situations when you need

Europe's Best Linguists

Why do Eastern Europeans speak English so well—especially since it wasn't commonly taught in schools before the last 18 years?

Residents of big, powerful Western countries, like Germany or France, might think that foreigners should learn their language. But Eastern Europeans are as practical as Westerners are stubborn. They realize that it's unreasonable to expect an American to learn Hungarian (with only 12 million speakers worldwide), Croatian (5 million), or Slovene (2 million). When only a few million people on the planet speak your language, it's essential to find a common language with the rest of the world—so they learn English early and well. In Croatia, for example, all schoolchildren start learning English in the third grade. (I've had surprisingly eloquent conversations with Croatian grade-schoolers.)

Many times, I've heard a French person and a Hungarian conversing in English—a reminder that as Americans, we're lucky to speak the world's new lingua franca.

to deal with a lesser-educated clerk or service person (train stations and post office counters, maids, museum guards, bakers, and so on). Be reasonable in your expectations. Hungarian museum ticket-sellers are every bit as friendly and multilingual as they are in the US. Luckily, it's relatively easy to get your point across in these places. I've often bought a train ticket simply by writing out the name of my destination (preferably with the local spelling—for example, "Praha" instead of "Prague"); the time I want to travel (using the 24-hour clock); and, if necessary, the date I want to leave (day first, then month as a Roman numeral, then year). Here's an example of what I'd show a ticket-seller at a train station: "Warszawa, 17:30–15.VII.07."

Eastern Europeans, realizing that their language intimidates Americans, often invent easier nicknames for themselves—so Šárka goes by "Sara," András becomes "Andrew," and Jaroslav tells you, "Call me Jerry."

Most of the destinations in this book—the Czech Republic, Slovakia, Poland, Slovenia, and Croatia—speak Slavic languages. These languages are closely related to each other and to Russian, and are, to varying degrees, mutually intelligible (though many spellings change—for example, Czech *hrad*, or "castle," becomes Croatian *grad*). Slavic languages have simple vocabularies but are highly inflected—that is, the meaning of a sentence depends on complicated endings that are tacked on to the ends of the words (as in Latin).

Slavic words are notorious for their seemingly unpronounceable, long strings of consonants. Slavic pronunciation can be tricky. In fact, when the first Christian missionaries, Cyril and Methodius, came to Eastern Europe a millennium ago, they invented a whole new alphabet to represent these strange Slavic sounds. The Cyrillic alphabet is still used today in the eastern Slavic countries (such as Serbia and Russia).

Fortunately, the destinations covered in this book all use the same Roman alphabet we do, but they add lots of different diacritics—little markings below and above letters—to represent a wide range of sounds (for example, č, ą, ó, đ, ł). I explain each of these diacritics in this book's various country introductions.

Hungarian is another story altogether—it's completely unrelated to Slavic languages, German, or English. For more on the challenging Magyar tongue, see page 400.

German is spoken in Vienna. As part of the same language family as English, German sounds noticeably more familiar to American ears than the Slavic languages. Throughout Eastern Europe, German can be a handy second language (especially in Croatia, which is popular among German-speaking tourists). And a few words of Italian can come in handy in Slovenia and Croatia.

There are certain universal English words all Eastern Europeans know: hello, please, thank you, super, pardon, stop, menu, problem, and no problem. Another handy word that people throughout the region will understand is *Servus* (SEHR-voos)—the old-fashioned greeting from the days of the Austro-Hungarian Empire. If you draw a blank on how to say hello in the local language, just offer a cheery, "*Servus!*"

Learn the key phrases (see each country introduction) and travel with a phrase book. Consider Lonely Planet's good *Eastern Europe Phrasebook*, which covers all of the destinations in this book (except Vienna).

Don't be afraid to interact with locals. Eastern Europeans can seem shy or even brusque—a holdover from the closed communist society—but often a simple smile is the only icebreaker you need to make a new friend. You'll find that doors open a little more quickly when you know a few words of the language. Give it your best shot. The locals will appreciate your efforts.

Telephones

Smart travelers learn the phone system and use it daily to reserve or reconfirm rooms, get tourist information, reserve restaurants, confirm tour times, or phone home.

Types of Phones

You'll encounter various kinds of phones in your European travels.

Pay phones—in booths, free-standing, or fixed to a wall—line the streets of Europe. Most are no longer coin-operated; you have to buy an insertable phone card, or use an international phone card (both options described under "Paying for Calls").

Hotel room phones are fairly cheap for local calls, but pricey for international calls, unless you use an international phone card.

American mobile phones work in Europe if they're GSM-enabled, tri-band (or quad-band), and on a calling plan that includes international calls. T-Mobile and Cingular have the best deals. For example, with a T-Mobile phone, you can roam all over Europe using your home number, and pay about $1 per minute for making or receiving calls. This option is the most convenient—and can be the most expensive.

Some travelers buy a **European mobile phone** in Europe (but if you're on a strict budget, skip mobile phones and use phone cards instead). The cheapest new phones cost around $75, plus $20–50 for the necessary "SIM card" to make it work (includes some prepaid calling time). A cheapie phone is often "locked" to work affordably only in the country where you buy it, but can also roam (for high rates) in other countries. For around $25 more, you can buy an "unlocked" phone that allows you to use different SIM cards in different countries—which saves money if you'll be making lots of calls. If you're interested, stop by any European shop that sells mobile phones; you'll see prominent store window displays. You aren't required to (and shouldn't) buy a monthly contract—buy prepaid calling time instead. As you use it up, buy additional minutes at newsstands or mobile-phone shops.

Paying for Calls

You can spend a fortune making phone calls in Europe...but why would you? Here's the skinny on different ways to pay, including the best deals.

European phone cards come in two types: official phone cards that you insert into a pay phone, and international phone cards that can be used from virtually any phone.

• **Insertable phone cards** can be purchased at post offices, newsstands, and tobacco shops. Simply take the phone off the hook, insert the prepaid card, wait for a dial tone, and dial away. The price of the call (local or international) is automatically deducted while you talk. These cards only work in the country where you buy them (so your Czech phone card is worthless in Poland). Insertable phone cards are a good deal for calling within Europe, but it's cheaper to make your overseas calls with an international phone card.

• **International phone cards** allow you to call home cheaply (generally around $0.25–0.50 per minute). Unlike the official phone cards, an international phone card is *not* inserted into the phone. Instead, you dial the toll-free number listed on the card, reaching an automated operator. When prompted, you dial in a scratch-to-reveal code number, also written on the card. Then dial your number. Since these cards are not insertable, you can use them from any phone—including the one in your hotel room (if your phone is set on "pulse," switch it to "tone"). These cards are not quite as cheap as similar cards in Western Europe, but they're catching on fast—so rates are sure to drop as more choices become available. (Ah, capitalism.) Look for fliers advertising long-distance rates, or ask about the cards at Internet cafés, news-stands, souvenir shops, and youth hostels. There are many different brands. Simply request an international telephone card, tell the vendor where you'll be making most calls ("to America"), and he'll select the brand with the best deal. Make sure the access number you dial is toll-free, not a local number (or else you'll be paying for a local call *and* deducting time from your calling card). These cards usually work only in the country where you buy them, but some brands work internationally. Buy a lower denomination in case the card is a dud.

Dialing direct from your hotel room without using an international phone card is usually quite expensive for international calls, but it's convenient. Always ask first how much you'll be charged. Keep in mind that you have to pay for local and occasionally even toll-free calls.

Receiving calls in your hotel room is often the cheapest way to keep in touch with the folks back home—especially if your family has an inexpensive way to call you (either a good deal on their long-distance plan, or a prepaid calling card with good rates to Europe). Give them a list of your hotels' phone numbers before you go. As you travel, send your family an e-mail or make a quick pay-phone call to set up a time for them to call you, and then wait for the ring.

Metered phones are available in phone offices and sometimes in bigger post offices. You can talk all you want, then pay the bill when you leave—but be sure you know the rates before you have a lengthy conversation.

Coin-operated phones, while rare, still exist in some areas. If making a call, have a bunch of coins handy—they go fast.

VoIP (Voice over Internet Protocol), which is an option only for those traveling with a laptop computer, allows VoIP users to talk with each other for free via their computers over a fast Internet connection. Look into Skype (www.skype.com) and Google Talk (www.google.com/talk).

US calling cards (such as the ones offered by AT&T, MCI, or Sprint) are the worst option. You'll nearly always save a lot of money by paying for your call in any of the other ways described above.

How to Dial

Calling from the US to Europe, or vice versa, is simple—once you break the code. The European calling chart on page 820 will walk you through it. Remember that European time is six/nine hours ahead of the East/West Coasts of the US.

Making Calls Within a European Country: About half of all European countries use area codes; the other half uses a direct-dial system without area codes.

In countries that use area codes (such as Slovakia, Hungary, Slovenia, Croatia, and Austria), you dial the local number when calling within a city, and you add the area code if calling long distance within the same country. For example, Dubrovnik's area code is 020, and the number of one of my recommended Dubrovnik hotels is 453-834. To call the hotel within Dubrovnik, just dial 453-834. To call it from Split, dial 020/453-834. Hungary is a special case: For domestic long distance, you have to dial "06" before the number. For example, to call an Eger hotel, I'd dial 411-711 if I'm calling from within Eger; but from Budapest, I have to dial 06, then 36 (Eger's area code), then 411-711. For more on the confusing Hungarian phone system, see page 390.

To make calls within a country that uses a direct-dial system (such as the Czech Republic or Poland), you dial the same number whether you're calling across the country or across the street.

Making International Calls: You always start with the international access code (011 if you're calling from the US or Canada, or 00 from Europe). If you see a phone number that begins with +, you have to replace the + with the international access code.

Once you've dialed the international access code, dial the country code of the country you're calling (see chart in appendix).

What you dial next depends on the phone system of the country you're calling. If the country uses area codes, drop the initial zero of the area code, then dial the rest of the number. To call the Dubrovnik hotel from Prague, dial 00, 385 (Croatia's country code), 20/453-834 (omitting the initial zero in the area code). Countries that use direct-dial systems (no area codes) vary in how they're accessed internationally by phone. If you're making an international call to the Czech Republic, simply dial the international access code, country code, and phone number. But if you're calling Poland, drop the initial zero of the phone number.

To call my office from Europe, I dial 00 (Europe's international access code), 1 (US's country code), 425 (Edmonds' area code), and 771-8303.

Don't be surprised that in some countries, local phone numbers have different numbers of digits within the same city, or even the same hotel (e.g., a hotel can have a 6-digit phone number, a 7-digit mobile phone number, and an 8-digit fax number).

E-mail and Mail

E-mail: These days, almost every hotel has an e-mail address and Web site (included in this book). In fact, most hoteliers prefer to receive your booking online rather than by fax or phone. Some family-run pensions can become overwhelmed by the volume of e-mail they receive, so be patient if you don't get an immediate response.

Many hotels have an Internet terminal in the lobby for guests (which I've noted in this book)—sometimes free, sometimes for a fee. I've also listed some Internet cafés, but your hotelier or TI can steer you to the nearest Internet access point.

If you're traveling with a laptop, you'll find that wireless Internet access, or Wi-Fi (sometimes called "WLAN" in Europe), is gradually being installed in hotels and progressive B&Bs. Some charge by the minute, while others are free. On a typical trip with my laptop, I can get online at about half of my hotels.

Mail: You can get stamps at the neighborhood post office, at newsstands inside fancy hotels, and at some mini-marts and card shops. While you can arrange for mail delivery to your hotel (allow 10 days for a letter to arrive), phoning and e-mailing are so easy that I've dispensed with mail stops altogether.

SLEEPING

Much of Eastern Europe simply doesn't have the quaint little family-run pensions and B&Bs that I like to list for other destinations. So, in this book, I've focused my listings on small hotels. I prefer options that are friendly, comfortable, professional-feeling, centrally located, English-speaking, and family-run. Obviously, a place meeting every criterion is rare, and all of my recommendations fall short of perfection—sometimes miserably. But I've listed the best values for each price category, given the above criteria. I've also thrown in a few hostels, private rooms, and other cheap options for budget travelers.

Prices in Eastern Europe are generally low compared to the West...except for beds. You can uncover some bargains, but I think it's worth paying a little more for comfort and a good location. You can find a central, comfortable double for $100 just about anywhere. Plan on spending $90 to $130 per double in big cities, and $60 to $90 in smaller towns.

Sleep Code

I've divided the rooms into three categories, based on the price for a standard double room with bath:

$$$ **Higher Priced**
$$ **Moderately Priced**
$ **Lower Priced**

To save space while giving specific information, I've described my recommended hotels with a standard code. Prices listed are per room, not per person. When a range of prices is listed for a room, the price fluctuates with room size or season. You can assume a hotel takes credit cards unless you see "cash only" in the listing. Unless I note otherwise, the cost of a room includes a buffet breakfast. Virtually all of my recommended accommodations are run by people who speak English; if they don't, I mention it in the listing.

  S = Single room (the price for one person in a double is often slightly more).
  D = Double or twin.
  T = Triple (often a double bed with a single bed moved in).
  Q = Quad (an extra child's bed is usually cheaper).
  b = Private bathroom with toilet and shower or tub.

According to this code, a couple staying at a "Db-2,700 Kč" hotel in Prague would pay a total of 2,700 Czech crowns (about $123) for a double room with a private bathroom. English is spoken, and credit cards are accepted.

While most hotels listed in this book cluster at about $80 to $110 per double, they range from $15 bunks to $250-plus splurges (maximum plumbing and more). Three or four people can save money by requesting one big room. Traveling alone can be expensive: A single room is often only 20 percent cheaper than a double.

Remember that some hotels quote their rates in euros, while others use the local currency. For maximum accuracy, I generally list the prices they gave me.

For environmental reasons, towels are often replaced in hotels only when you leave them on the floor. In cheaper places, they aren't replaced at all, so hang them up to dry and reuse. The cord that dangles over the tub or shower in big Croatian and Slovenian resort hotels is not a clothesline—you pull it if you've fallen and can't get up.

If asked whether they have non-smoking rooms, most hotels in Eastern Europe will say yes. When pressed, they'll sheepishly admit, "Well, *all* of our rooms are non-smoking"...meaning they air them out after a smoker has stayed there. I've described hotels as "non-smoking" only if they have specially designated rooms for this purpose. Be specific and assertive if you need a strictly non-smoking room.

Before accepting a room, confirm your understanding of the complete price. Pay your bill the evening before you leave to avoid the time-wasting crowd at the reception desk in the morning, especially if you need to rush off to catch your train.

The only tip my recommended hotels would like is a friendly, easygoing guest. And, as always, I appreciate feedback on your hotel experiences.

Private Rooms

A cheap option in Eastern Europe (especially in Croatia) is a room in a private home (*sobe* in Slovenia and Croatia; the German word *Zimmer* works there, too, and throughout Eastern Europe). These places are inexpensive, at least as comfortable as a cheap hotel, and a good way to get some local insight. The boss changes the sheets, so people staying several nights are most desirable—and those who stay less than three nights are often charged a lot more (up to 30 percent). For more on Croatian *sobe*, see page 608.

Hostels

For $15 to $20 a night, travelers of any age can stay at a youth hostel. While official hostels admit nonmembers for an extra fee, it's best to join the club and buy a youth hostel card before you go (call Hostelling International at 202/783-6161 or order online at www.hiayh.org). To increase your options, consider the many independent hostels that don't require a membership card (www.hostels.com). Cheap meals are sometimes available, and kitchen facilities are usually provided for do-it-yourselfers. Expect crowds in the summer, snoring, and lots of youth groups giggling and making rude noises while you try to sleep. Family rooms and doubles are often available on request, but it's basically boys' dorms and girls' dorms. Many hostels are locked up from about 10:00 until 17:00, and a 23:00 curfew is often enforced. Hosteling is ideal for those traveling single: prices are per bed, not per room, and you'll have an instant circle of friends. More and more hostels are getting their business acts together, taking credit card reservations over the phone and leaving sign-in forms on the door for each available room. If you're serious about traveling cheaply, get a card, carry your own sheets, and cook in the members' kitchens.

Making Reservations

It's possible to travel at any time of year without reservations (especially if you arrive early in the day). But given the erratic accommodations values and the quality of the gems I've found for this book, I'd highly recommend that you book rooms ahead as soon as your itinerary is set—or at least call ahead for rooms a day or two in advance as you travel. Even if a hotel clerk says the hotel is fully booked, you can try calling between 9:00 and 10:00 on the day you plan to arrive. That's when the hotel clerk knows who'll be checking out and just which rooms will be available. I've taken great pains to list telephone numbers with long-distance instructions (see "Telephones," earlier in this chapter and in the appendix). Use the telephone and the convenient phone cards. Most hotels listed are accustomed to English-only speakers. A hotel receptionist will trust you and hold a room until 16:00 (4:00 p.m.) without a deposit, though some will ask for a credit-card number. Honor (or cancel by phone) your reservations. Long distance is cheap and easy from public phone booths. Don't let these people down—I promised you'd call and cancel if for some reason you won't show up. Don't needlessly confirm rooms through the tourist office; they'll take a commission.

If you know exactly which dates you need and really want a particular place, reserve a room well in advance before you leave home. To reserve from home, e-mail, call, or fax the hotel. Phone and fax costs are reasonable, e-mail is a steal, and simple English is usually fine. To fax, use the form in the appendix (or find it online at www.ricksteves.com/reservation). A two-night stay in August would be "2 nights, 16/8/07 to 18/8/07." (Europeans write the date in this order—day/month/year—and hotel jargon counts your stay from your day of arrival through your day of departure.)

If you e-mail or fax a reservation request and receive a response with rates stating that rooms are available, this is not a confirmation. You must confirm that the rates are fine and that indeed you want the room for the agreed-upon dates. (Don't just assume you can extend upon arrival; take the time to consider in advance how long you'll stay.) You'll often receive a response requesting one night's deposit. A credit-card number and expiration date will usually work. Be sure to fax your card number (rather than e-mail it) to keep it private, safer, and out of cyberspace. If you use your credit card for the deposit, you can pay with your card or cash when you arrive; if you don't show up, you'll be billed for one night. Ask about the cancellation policy when you reserve; sometimes you may have to cancel as much as two weeks ahead to avoid paying a stiff penalty. Reconfirm your reservations several days in advance for safety.

EATING

Eastern Europe offers good food for very little money—especially if you venture off the main tourist trail. This is affordable sightseeing for your palate.

Slavic cuisine has a reputation for being heavy and hearty, with lots of pork, potatoes and cabbage...which is true. But the food here is also delicious, and there's a lot more diversity from country to country than you might expect. Tune in to the regional and national specialties and customs (see each country's introduction in this book for details).

Ethnic restaurants provide a welcome break from Slavic fare. Seek out vegetarian, Italian, Indian, Chinese, and other similar places. They're especially good in big cities such as Prague, Budapest, or Kraków (I've listed a few tasty options). Hungarian cuisine is rich and spicy (think paprika), while Slovenia and Croatia have delectable seafood and lots of Italian-style dishes (pastas and pizzas).

When restaurant-hunting, choose a spot filled with locals, not the place with the big neon signs boasting, "We Speak English and Accept Credit Cards." Incredible deals abound in Eastern Europe, where locals can't afford more than $5 for a fine dinner. Venturing even a block or two off the main drag leads to local, higher-quality food for less than half the price of the tourist-oriented places. Most restaurants tack a menu onto their door for browsers and have an English menu inside. Only a rude waiter will rush you. Good service is relaxed (slow to an American).

When you're in the mood for something halfway between a restaurant and a picnic meal, look for take-out food stands, bakeries (with sandwiches and small pizzas to go), delis with stools or a table, department-store cafeterias, salad bars, or simple little eateries for fast and easy sit-down restaurant food.

The Czech Republic is beer country, with Europe's best and cheapest brew. Poland also has fine beer, but the national drink is *wódka*. Hungary, Slovenia, and Croatia are known for their wines. Each country has its own distinctive liqueur, most of them a variation on *slivovice* (SLEE-voh-veet-seh)—a plum brandy so highly valued that it's the de facto currency of the Carpathian Mountains (often used for bartering with farmers and other mountain folk). Menus list drink size by the tenth of a liter, or deciliter (dl).

> ## How Was Your Trip?
>
> Were your travels fun, smooth, and meaningful? If you'd like to share your tips, concerns, and discoveries, please fill out the survey at www.ricksteves.com/feedback or e-mail me at rick @ricksteves.com. I personally read and value your feedback. Thanks in advance—it helps a lot.

TRAVELING AS A TEMPORARY LOCAL

We travel all the way to Europe to enjoy differences—to become temporary locals. You'll experience frustrations. Certain truths that we find "God-given" or "self-evident"—like cold beer, ice in drinks, bottomless cups of coffee, hot showers, cigarette smoke being irritating, and bigger being better—are suddenly not so true. One of the benefits of travel is the eye-opening realization that there are logical, civil, and even better alternatives. A willingness to go local ensures that you'll enjoy a full dose of local hospitality.

Fortunately for you, hospitality is a local forte. The friendliness of the Eastern Europeans seems to have only been enhanced during the communist era: Tangible resources were in short supply, so an open door and a genial conversation were all that people had to offer. For many Eastern Europeans, the chance to chat with an American is still a delightful novelty. Even so, some people—hardened by decades of being spied on by neighbors and standing in long lines to buy food for their family—seem brusque at first. In my experience, all it takes is a smile and a little effort to befriend these kind, gentle residents of the former "Evil Empire."

If there is a negative aspect to the European image of Americans, we can appear loud, aggressive, impolite, rich, and a bit naive. While Europeans look bemusedly at some of our Yankee excesses—and worriedly at others—they nearly always afford us individual travelers all the warmth we deserve.

While updating this book, I heard over and over again that my readers are considerate and fun to have as guests. Thank you for traveling as temporary locals who are sensitive to the culture. It's fun to follow you in my travels.

Judging from all the positive comments I receive from travelers who have used this book, it's safe to assume you'll enjoy a great, affordable vacation—with the finesse of an experienced, independent traveler.

Thanks, and happy travels!

BACK DOOR TRAVEL PHILOSOPHY
From *Rick Steves' Europe Through the Back Door*

Travel is intensified living—maximum thrills per minute and one of the last great sources of legal adventure. Travel is freedom. It's recess, and we need it.

Experiencing the real Europe requires catching it by surprise, going casual..."Through the Back Door."

Affording travel is a matter of priorities. (Make do with the old car.) You can travel—simply, safely, and comfortably—anywhere in Europe for $100 a day plus transportation costs. In many ways, spending more money only builds a thicker wall between you and what you came to see. Europe is a cultural carnival, and, time after time, you'll find that its best acts are free and the best seats are the cheap ones.

A tight budget forces you to travel close to the ground, meeting and communicating with the people, not relying on service with a purchased smile. Never sacrifice sleep, nutrition, safety, or cleanliness in the name of budget. Simply enjoy the local-style alternatives to expensive hotels and restaurants.

Extroverts have more fun. If your trip is low on magic moments, kick yourself and make things happen. If you don't enjoy a place, maybe you don't know enough about it. Seek the truth. Recognize tourist traps. Give a culture the benefit of your open mind. See things as different but not better or worse. Any culture has much to share.

Of course, travel, like the world, is a series of hills and valleys. Be fanatically positive and militantly optimistic. If something's not to your liking, change your liking. Travel is addictive. It can make you a happier American as well as a citizen of the world. Our Earth is home to six and a half billion equally important people. It's humbling to travel and find that people don't envy Americans. Europeans like us, but, with all due respect, they wouldn't trade passports.

Globe-trotting destroys ethnocentricity. It helps you understand and appreciate different cultures. Regrettably, there are forces in our society that want you dumbed down for their convenience. Don't let it happen. Thoughtful travel engages you with the world—more important than ever these days. Travel changes people. It broadens perspectives and teaches new ways to measure quality of life. Rather than fear the diversity on this planet, travelers celebrate it. Many travelers toss aside their hometown blinders. Their prized souvenirs are the strands of different cultures they decide to knit into their own character. The world is a cultural yarn shop, and Back Door travelers are weaving the ultimate tapestry. Join in!

CZECH REPUBLIC

CZECH REPUBLIC

(Česká Republika)

 Despite their difficult 20th-century experience, the Czechs managed to preserve their history. In Czech towns and villages, you'll find a simple joy of life—a holdover from the days of the Renaissance. The deep spirituality of the Baroque era still shapes the national character. The magic of Prague, the beauty of Český Krumlov, and the lyrical quality of the countryside relieve the heaviness caused by the turmoil that passed through here. Get beyond Prague and explore the country's medieval towns. These rugged woods and hilltop castles will make you feel like you're walking through the garden of your childhood dreams.

Of the Czech Republic's three main regions—Bohemia, Moravia, and small Silesia—the best known is Bohemia. It has nothing to do with beatnik bohemians, but with the Celtic tribe of Boheia that inhabited the land before the coming of the Slavs. A long-time home of the Czechs, Bohemia is circled by a naturally fortifying ring of mountains and cut down the middle by the Vltava River, with Prague as its capital. The wine-growing region of Moravia (to the east) is more hilly, Slavic, and colorful.

Tourists often conjure up images of Bohemia when they think of the Czech Republic. But the country consists of more than rollicking beer halls and gently rolling landscapes. It's also about dreamy wine cellars and fertile Moravian plains, with the rugged Carpathian Mountains on the horizon. Politically and geologically, Bohemia and Moravia are two distinct regions. The soils and climates in which the hops and wine grapes grow are very different...and so are the two regions' mentalities. The boisterousness of the Czech polka contrasts with the melancholy of the Moravian ballad; the politics of the Prague power-broker is at odds with the spirituality of the Moravian bard.

Only a tiny bit of Silesia—around the town of Opava—is part of the Czech Republic today; the rest of the region is in Poland and Germany. (The Hapsburgs lost traditionally Czech Silesia to Prussia in the 1740s, and 200 years later, Germany in turn ceded most of it to Poland.) People in Silesia speak a wide variety of dialects that mix Czech, German, and Polish. Perhaps due to their diverse genes and cultural heritage, women from Silesia are famous for being intelligent and beautiful.

Since 1989, when the Czechs won their independence from Soviet control, more Czechs have been traveling. People are working harder—but the average monthly wage is still only about $800. Roads have been patched up, facades have gotten facelifts, and neighborhood grocery stores have been pushed out by supermarkets.

Most young Czechs are caught up in the new freedom. Everyone wants to travel—to the practical West to study law, or to the mystical East to learn to speak Tamil. They want to work for big bucks at a multinational investment bank, or for a meager salary at a non-profit organization operating in Afghanistan. With so many material dreams suddenly within reach, fewer Czechs are having children. In the 1990s, the birth rate fell dramatically, but since 2001 it has been slowly rising again.

Yet, even faced with a bright future, some locals maintain a healthy dose of pessimism and are reluctant to dive headlong into the Western rat race. Things still go a little slower here, and people find pleasure in simple things.

Czech children, adults, and grandparents delight in telling stories. In Czech fairy tales, there are no dwarfs and monsters. To

Czech Republic Almanac

Birth of Two Nations: The nation of Czechoslovakia—formed after World War I, and dominated by the USSR after World War II—split on January 1, 1993, into two separate nations: the Czech Republic (Česká Republika) and Slovakia.

Population: 10 million people. About 95 percent are ethnic Czechs, who speak Czech. Unlike some of their neighbors (including the very Catholic Poles and Slovaks), Czechs are inclined to be agnostic: One in four is Roman Catholic, but the majority (60 percent) list their religion as unaffiliated.

Latitude and Longitude: 50°N and 15°E (similar latitude to Vancouver, BC).

Area: 31,000 square miles (similar to South Carolina or Maine).

Geography: The Czech Republic is made up of three regions—Bohemia (Čechy), Moravia (Morava), and a small slice of Silesia (Slezsko). The climate is generally cool and cloudy.

Biggest Cities: Prague (the capital, 1.2 million), Brno (380,000), Ostrava (318,000), and Plzeň (165,000).

Economy: The Gross Domestic Product is $200 billion (similar to Indiana). The GDP per capita is $19,500 (less than half that of the average American). Some major money makers for the country are machine parts, cars and trucks, and beer (including Pilsner Urquell and the original Budweiser—called "Czechvar" in the US).

experience the full absurdity and hilarity of Czech culture, you need a child's imagination and the understanding that the best fun comes from being able to laugh at yourself. Czech writers invented the robot, the pistol, and Black Light Theater (an absurd show of illusion, puppetry, mime, and modern dance—see page 123). Literature and film are the most transparent windows into the Czech soul.

The most famous Czech literary figure is the title character of Jaroslav Hašek's *Good Soldier Švejk*, who frustrates the WWI Austro-Hungarian army he serves by cleverly playing dumb. Other well-known Czech writers include Václav Havel (playwright who went on to become Czechoslovakia's first post-communist president; he authored many essays and plays, including *The Garden Party*); Milan Kundera (author of *The Unbearable Lightness of Being*, set during the "Prague Spring" uprising); Bohumil Hrabal (stream-of-consciousness writer who captures the Czech spirit in *I Served the King of England* and *Too Loud a Solitude*); and Karel Čapek (novelist and playwright who created the robot in the play *R.U.R.*). But the most famous Czech writer of all is the existentialist great, Franz Kafka—a Prague Jew who wrote in German about people

More than a third of trade is with next-door-neighbor Germany. Privatization of formerly government-run industries goes on.

Currency: 22 Czech crowns (*koruna*, Kč) = about $1.

Government: Until 1989, Czechoslovakia was a communist state under Soviet control. Today, the Czech Republic is a member of the European Union (since 2004) and a vibrant democracy, with 68 percent of its eligible population voting in the 2006 election. Its parliament is made up of 200 representatives elected every four years and 81 senators elected for six years. No single political party dominates. The two big parties—the conservative Civic Democrats and the left-of-center Social Democrats—each won just a third of the vote in the 2006 election. The other three parties—the Communists, Christian Democrats, and the Greens—hold enough sway that the leader of the winning party typically heads a coalition government. The president (currently Václav Klaus, a conservative) is selected every five years by the legislators.

Flag: The Czech flag is red (bottom), white (top), and blue (a triangle along the hoist side).

The Average Czech: The average Czech has 1.2 kids (rising again, after the sharp decline that followed the end of communism), will live 76 years, and has one television in the house.

turning into giant cockroaches *(The Metamorphosis)* and urbanites being pursued and persecuted for crimes they know nothing about *(The Trial)*.

Ninety percent of the tourists who visit the Czech Republic see only Prague. But if you venture outside the capital, you'll enjoy traditional towns and villages, great prices, a friendly and gentle countryside dotted by nettles and wild poppies, and almost no Western tourists. Since the time of the Hapsburgs, fruit trees have lined the country roads for everyone to share. Take your pick.

Practicalities

Telephones: Dial 112 for emergencies, 158 for police. If an 0800 number doesn't work, replace the 0800 with 822. The basic, insertable Český Telecom phone card works well.

To make phone calls anywhere within the Czech Republic, dial the entire nine-digit number. To call the Czech Republic from another country, first dial the international access code (00 if calling from Europe or 011 from the US or Canada), then 420 (the Czech Republic's country code), then the nine-digit number. To call out of the Czech Republic, dial 00, the country code of the country you're calling (see chart in appendix), the area code if the country's phone system uses area codes (note that sometimes the initial zero is dropped depending on the country), and the local number.

Red Tape: Anyone planning to bring a rental car into the Czech Republic should check with their car-rental company first (see page 28). To drive on Czech highways, you'll need a toll sticker *(dálniční známka),* sold at borders, post offices, and gas stations (200 Kč/15 days, 300 Kč/2 months).

Transportation: If you have a Eurailpass, note that it doesn't cover the Czech Republic; you'll need to buy point-to-point train tickets for your travels to and from Prague (see page 24).

Czech History

The Czechs have always been at a crossroads of Europe—between the Slavic and Germanic worlds, between Catholicism and Protestantism, and between the Cold War East and West. As if having foreseen all of this, the mythical founder of Prague—the beautiful princess Libuše—named her city "Praha" (meaning "threshold" in Czech). Despite these strong external influences, the Czechs have retained their distinct culture...and a dark, ironic sense of humor to keep them laughing through it all.

Charles IV and the Middle Ages

Prague's castle put Bohemia on the map in the ninth century. About a century later, the region was incorporated into the German Holy Roman Empire. Within a couple hundred years, Prague was one of Europe's largest and most highly cultured cities.

The 14th century was Prague's Golden Age, when Holy Roman Emperor Charles IV ruled from here. Born to a German nobleman and a Czech princess, Charles IV was a dynamic man on the cusp of

the Renaissance. He spoke five languages, counted Petrarch as a friend, imported French architects to make Prague a grand capital, founded the first university north of the Alps, and invigorated the Czech national spirit. (He popularized the legend of the good king Wenceslas to give his people a near mythical, King Arthur–type cultural standard-bearer.) Much of Prague's history and architecture (including the famous Charles Bridge, Charles University, and St. Vitus Cathedral) can be traced to this man's rule. Under Charles IV, the Czech people gained esteem among Europeans.

Jan Hus and Religious Wars

Jan Hus (c. 1370–1415) was a local preacher and professor who got in trouble with the Vatican a hundred years before Martin Luther. Like Luther, Hus preached in the people's language rather than Latin. To add insult to injury, he complained about Church corruption. Tried for heresy and burned in 1415, Hus became both a religious and a national hero. While each age has defined Hus to its liking, the way he challenged authority while staying true to himself has always inspired and rallied the Czech people. (For more on Hus, see the sidebar on page 79.)

Inspired by the reformist ideas of Jan Hus, the Czechs rebelled against both the Roman Catholic Church and German political control. This burst of independent thought led to a period of religious wars, and ultimately the loss of autonomy to Vienna. Ruled by the Hapsburgs of Austria, Prague stagnated—except during the rule of King Rudolf II (1552–1612), a Holy Roman Emperor. With Rudolph living in Prague, the city again emerged as a cultural and intellectual center. Astronomers Johannes Kepler and Tycho de Brahe and other scientists flourished, and much of the inspiration for Prague's great art can be attributed to the king's patronage.

Not long after, Prague entered one of its darkest spells. The Thirty Years' War (1618–1648) began in Prague when Czech Protestant nobles, wanting religious and political autonomy, tossed two Catholic Hapsburg officials out of the window of the castle. (This was one of Prague's many defenestrations—a uniquely Czech solution to political discord in which offending politicians are thrown out the window.) The Czech Estates Uprising lasted for two years, ending in a crushing defeat of the Czech army in the Battle of White Mountain (1620), which marked the end of Czech freedom. Twenty-seven leaders of the uprising were executed (today commemorated by crosses on Prague's Old Town Square—see page 81), most of the old Czech nobility was dispossessed, and Protestants had to leave the country or convert to Catholicism. Often called "the first world war" because it engulfed so many nations, the Thirty Years' War was particularly tough on Prague. During this period, its population dropped from 60,000 to 25,000. The result of this war was 300 years of Hapsburg rule from afar, as Prague became a German-speaking backwater of Vienna.

Czech Nationalist Revival

The end of Prague as a "German" city came gradually. As the Industrial Revolution attracted Czech farmers and peasants into the cities, the demographics of the Czech population centers began to shift. Between 1800 and 1900, though it remained part of the Hapsburg Empire, Prague went from being an essentially German town to a predominantly Czech one. Like in the rest of

Notable Czechs

St. Wenceslas (907–935): Bohemian duke who allied the Czechs with the Holy Roman Empire. He went on to become the Czech Republic's patron saint, and is memorialized as a "good king" in the Christmas carol. For more on Wenceslas, see page 96.

Jan Hus (1370–1415): Proto-Protestant Reformer who was burned at the stake (see page 79).

Comenius (1592–1670): "Teacher of Nations" and Protestant exile whose ideas paved the way for modern education.

Antonín Dvořák (1841–1904): Inspired by a trip to America, he composed his *New World Symphony*.

Jára Cimrman (1853–1914): Illustrious fictional inventor, explorer, philosopher, and all-around genius. Despite being overwhelmingly voted the "Greatest Czech of All Time" in a recent nationwide poll, he was not awarded the title; for details on the controversy, see page 110.

Alfons Mucha (1860–1939): You might recognize his turn-of-the-century Art Nouveau posters of pretty girls entwined in vines. Visit his museum in Prague (see page 99) and marvel at his stained-glass window in St. Vitus Cathedral (page 118).

Franz Kafka (1883–1924): While working for a Prague insurance firm, he wrote (in German) *The Metamorphosis* (man awakes as a cockroach), *The Trial,* and other psychologically haunting stories and novels.

Milan Kundera (1929–): Wrote the novel *The Unbearable Lightness of Being* (which became a film).

Václav Havel (1936–): The country's first post-Soviet president, who's also known as a playwright and philosopher.

Martina Navrátilová (1956–): Tennis star of the 1980s. For more on Czech sports, see page 54.

Europe, the 19th century was a time of great nationalism, as the age of divine kings and ruling families came to a fitful end. The Czech spirit was stirred by the completion of Prague's St. Vitus Cathedral, the symphonies of Antonín Dvořák, and the operas of Bedřich Smetana performed in the new National Theatre.

After the Hapsburgs' Austro-Hungarian Empire suffered defeat in World War I, their vast holdings broke apart and became independent countries. Among these was a union of Bohemia, Moravia, and Slovakia, the brainchild of a clever politician named Tomáš Garrigue Masaryk (see page 116). The new nation, Czechoslovakia, was proclaimed in 1918, with Prague as its capital.

Troubled 20th Century

Independence lasted only 20 years. In the notorious Munich Agreement of September 1938—much to the dismay of the Czechs and Slovaks—Great Britain and France peacefully ceded to Hitler the so-called "Sudetenland" (a fringe around the edge of Bohemia, populated mainly by people of German descent). It wasn't long before Hitler seized the rest of Czechoslovakia...and the Holocaust began.

For centuries, Prague's cultural make-up consisted of a rich mix of Czech, German, and Jewish people—historically about evenly divided. But only 5 percent of the Jewish population survived the Holocaust. After World War II ended, the three million people of Germanic descent who lived in Czechoslovakia were pushed into Germany. This forced resettlement—which led to the deaths of untold tens of thousands of Germans—was the idea of Czechoslovak President Edvard Beneš, who had been ruling from exile in London throughout the war (see page 154). As a result of both of these policies (the Holocaust and the expulsion of Germans), today's Czech Republic is largely homogenous—about 95 percent Czechs.

Although Prague escaped the bombs of World War II, it went directly from the Nazi frying pan into the communist fire. A local uprising freed the city from the Nazis on May 8, 1945, but the Soviets "liberated" them on May 9.

Most of the communist chapter (1948–1989) was grim. The "Prague Spring" uprising—initiated by a young generation of reform-minded communists in 1968—was crushed. The charismatic leader, Alexander Dubček, was exiled (and made a forest ranger in the backwoods), and the years following the unsuccessful revolt were particularly disheartening. In the late 1980s, the communists began constructing Prague's huge TV tower (now the city's tallest structure)—not only to broadcast Czech TV transmissions, but also to jam Western signals. The Metro, built around the same time, was intended for mass transit, but was also designed to be a giant fallout shelter for protection against capitalist bombs.

But the Soviet empire crumbled. Czechoslovakia regained its freedom in the student- and artist-powered 1989 "Velvet Revolution" (so called because there were no casualties...or even broken windows). Václav Havel, a writer who had been imprisoned by the communist regime, became Czechoslovakia's first post-communist president. In 1993, the Czech and Slovak Republics agreed on the "Velvet Divorce" and became two separate countries (see sidebar on page 172).

Havel ended his second (and, constitutionally, last) five-year term in 2003. While he's still admired by Czechs as a great thinker, writer, and fearless leader of the opposition movement during the

Czech Sports

Prague's top sports are soccer (called "football" here) and hockey. Surprisingly, the Czechs are a world power in both.

The Czech **soccer** team reached the finals and semi-finals of the last three European Cups. In 2006, they made it to Round One of the World Cup, defeating the United States 3-0 before being eliminated with 0-2 defeats to Ghana and Italy. They are currently the eighth-ranked team in the world. Within the Czech Republic, the two oldest and by far most successful soccer clubs are the bitter Prague rivals, Sparta and Slavia. Slavia has always been the better team, while Sparta has merely harvested more trophies. Sparta's stadium at Letná (behind the metronome ticking above the river) is easier to get to.

The Czech national **hockey** team won four out of the last eight world championships. In 2006, the Czech team lost to Sweden in the final. There are more than a hundred Czech players in the United States' NHL. Think Jaromír Jágr, one of the NHL's leading scorers. Sparta and Slavia also have hockey teams, but the rivalry is less jaded, as the teams from smaller towns are more than their equals. Slavia plays in the brand-new, state-of-the-art Sazka Arena built for the 2004 world hockey championships in Prague (right at the Českomoravská Metro stop).

Back in the old days, ice hockey was the only battleground on which Czechoslovaks could seek revenge on their Russian oppressors. To this day, the hockey rink is where Czechs are proudest about their nationality. If you are in Prague in May during the hockey championships, join locals cheering their team in front of a giant screen on the Old Town Square (and other main squares around the country).

Ice hockey is also the most popular sport in Slovakia. To understand the friendly relationship between Czechs and Slovaks after their Velvet Divorce in 1989 (see sidebar on page 172), just walk into any Czech or Slovak pub during the hockey championships. Unless the two teams are playing each other, all Czechs passionately support the Slovak team, and vice versa.

communist days, many consider him less successful as a president. Some believe that the split of Czechoslovakia was partly caused by Havel's initial insensitivity to Slovak demands. The current president, Václav Klaus, was the pragmatic author of the economic reforms in the 1990s. Klaus' election in 2003 symbolized a change from revolutionary times, when philosophers became kings, to humdrum politics, when offices are gained by bargaining with the opposition (Communist votes in the Parliament were the decisive factor in Klaus' election). A major turning point occurred on May 1, 2004, when the Czech Republic joined the European Union.

Today, while not without its problems, the Czech Republic is enjoying a growing economy (up 5 percent in 2006) and a strong democracy, and Prague has emerged as one of the most popular tourist destinations in Europe.

Czech Food

Czech cuisine is heavy, hearty, and tasty. Expect lots of meat, potatoes, and cabbage. Still, there's more variety than you might expect. Ethnic restaurants provide a welcome break from Slavic fare. Seek out vegetarian, Italian, or Chinese (I've recommended several options).

After a sip of beer, ask for the *jídelní lístek* (menu). *Polévka* (soup) is the most essential part of a meal. The saying goes: "The soup fills you up, the dish plugs it up." Some of the thick soups for a cold day are *zelná* or *zelňačka* (cabbage), *čočková* (lentil), *fazolová* (bean), and *dršťková* (tripe—delicious if fresh, chewy as gum if not). The lighter soups are *hovězí* or *slepičí vývar s nudlemi* (beef or chicken broth with noodles), *pórková* (leek), and *květáková* (cauliflower). *Pečivo* (bread) is either delivered with the soup or you need to ask for it; it's always charged separately depending on how many *rohlíky* (rolls) or slices of *chleba* (yeast bread) you eat.

Main dishes are divided into *hotová jídla* (quick, ready-to-serve standard dishes, in some places available only during lunch hours, 11:30–14:30) and the more specialized *jídla na objednávku* or *minutky* (plates prepared when you order). Even the supposedly quick *hotová jídla* will take longer than fast food you're used to back home.

A Czech restaurant is a social place where people come to relax. Tables are not private. You can ask to join someone and will most likely make some new friends. Instead of worrying about how much sightseeing you're missing during your two-hour lunch, appreciate the opportunity to learn more about Czech culture.

Hotová jídla (ready-to-serve dishes) come with set garnishes. The standard menu across the country includes *smažený řízek s bramborem* (fried pork fillet with potatoes), *svíčková na smetaně s knedlíkem* (beef tenderloin in cream sauce with dumplings), *vepřová s knedlíkem a se zelím* (pork with dumplings and cabbage), *pečená kachna s knedlíkem a se zelím* (roasted duck with dumplings and cabbage), *maďarský guláš s knedlíkem* (the Czech version of Hungarian goulash), and *pečené kuře s bramborem* (roasted chicken with potatoes). In this landlocked country, fish options are limited to *kapr* (carp) and *pstruh* (trout), prepared in a variety of ways and served with potatoes or fries. Vegetarians can go for the delicious *smažený sýr s bramborem* (fried cheese with potatoes) or default for *čočka s vejci* (lentils with fried egg). If you're spending the evening out with friends, have a beer and feast on the huge *vepřové koleno s hořčicí a křenem* (pork knuckle with mustard and horseradish sauce) with *chleba* (yeast bread).

The range of the *jídla na objednávku* (meals prepared to order) depends on the chef. You choose your starches and garnishes, which are charged separately.

Šopský salát, like a Greek salad, is usually the best salad option (a mix of tomatoes, cucumbers, peppers, onion, and feta cheese with vinegar and olive oil). The waiter will bring it with the main dish, unless you specify that you want it before.

For *moučník* (dessert), there are *palačinka* (crêpes served with fruit or jam), *lívance* (small pancakes with jam and curd), or *zmrzlinový pohár* (ice-cream sundae). Many restaurants will offer different sorts of *koláče* (pastries) and *štrůdl* (apple strudel), but it's much better to get these directly from a bakery.

No Czech meal is complete without a cup of strong *turecká káva* (Turkish coffee—finely ground coffee that only partly dissolves, leaving "mud" on the bottom, drunk without milk). Although espressos and instant coffees have made headway in the past few years, many Czechs regard them as a threat to their culture.

A good alternative to a beer is *minerálka* (mineral water). These healthy waters have a high mineral content. They're naturally carbonated because they come from the springs in the many Czech spas (Mattoni, the most common brand, is from Carlsbad). If you want plain water, ask for *voda bez bublinek* (water without bubbles). Tap water is generally not served. Water comes bottled and generally costs more than beer.

Bohemia is beer country (see sidebar, next page), with Europe's best and cheapest brew. Locals also like the herb liquor *becherovka*. Moravians prefer wine and *slivovice* (SLEE-voh-veet-seh)—a plum brandy so highly valued that it's the de facto currency of the Carpathian Mountains (often used for bartering with farmers and other mountain folk). *Medovina* ("honey wine") is mead.

In bars and restaurants, you can go wild with memorable liqueurs, most of which cost about a dollar a shot. Experiment. *Fernet,* a bitter drink made from many herbs, is the leading Czech apéritif. *Absinthe,* made from wormwood and herbs, is a watered-down version of the hallucinogenic drink that's illegal in the US and much of Europe. It's famous as the muse of many artists (including Henri de Toulouse-Lautrec in Paris more than a century ago). *Becherovka,* made of 13 herbs and 38 percent alcohol, was used to settle upset aristocratic tummies and as an aphrodisiac. This velvety drink remains popular today. *Becherovka* and tonic mixed together is nicknamed *beton* ("concrete"). If you

Czech Beer

Czechs are among the world's most enthusiastic beer *(pivo)* drinkers—adults drink an average of 80 gallons a year. The pub is a place to have fun, complain, discuss art and politics, talk hockey, and chat with locals and visitors alike. The *pivo* that was drunk in the country before the Industrial Revolution was much thicker, providing the main source of nourishment for the peasant folk. Even today, it doesn't matter whether you're in a *restaurace* (restaurant), a *hostinec* (pub), or a *hospoda* (bar)—a beer will land on your table upon the slightest hint

to the waiter, and a new pint will automatically appear when the old glass is almost empty. (You must tell the waiter *not* to bring more.) Order beer from the tap (*točené* means "draft," *sudové pivo* means "keg beer"). A *pivo* is large (0.5 liter, or 17 oz); a *malé pivo* is small (0.3 liter, or 10 oz). Men invariably order the large size. *Pivo* for lunch has me sightseeing for the rest of the day on Czech knees.

The Czechs invented lager in nearby Plzeň ("Pilsen" in

German), and the result, Pilsner Urquell, is on tap in many local pubs. But be sure to venture beyond this famous beer. The Czechs produce plenty of other good beers, including Krušovice, Gambrinus, Staropramen, and Kozel. Budvar, from the town of Budějovice ("Budweis" in German), is popular with Anheuser-Busch's attorneys. (The Czech and the American breweries for years disputed the "Budweiser" brand name. The solution: The Czech Budweiser is sold under its own name in Europe, China, and Africa, while in America it is marketed as Czechvar.)

The big degree symbol on bottles does not indicate the percentage of alcohol content. Twelve degrees is about 4.2 percent alcohol, 10 degrees is about 3.5 percent alcohol, and 11 and 15 degrees are dark beers.

Each establishment has only one kind of beer on tap; to try a particular brand, look for its sign outside. A typical pub serves only one brand of 10-degree beer, one brand of 12-degree beer, and one brand of dark beer. Czechs do not mix beer with anything, and do not hop from pub to pub (in one night, it is said, you must stay loyal to one woman and to one beer).

Key Czech Phrases

English	Czech	Pronounced
Hello. (formal)	*Dobrý den.*	DOH-bree dehn
Hi. / Bye. (informal)	*Ahoj.*	AH-hoy
Do you speak English?	*Mluvíte anglicky?*	MLOO-vee-teh ANG-lits-kee
Yes. / No.	*Ano. / Ne.*	AH-no / neh
Please. / You're welcome. / Can I help you?	*Prosím.*	PROH-zeem
Thank you.	*Děkuji.*	DYACK-quee
I'm sorry. / Excuse me.	*Promiňte.*	PROH-meen-teh
Good.	*Dobře.*	DOHB-zhay
Goodbye.	*Na shledanou.*	nah SKLEH-dah-now
one / two	*jeden / dva*	YAY-dehn / dvah
three / four	*tři / čtyři*	tree / chuh-TEE-ree
five / six	*pět / šest*	pyeht / shehst
seven / eight	*sedm / osm*	SEH-dum / OH-sum
nine / ten	*devět / deset*	DEHV-yeht / DEH-seht
hundred	*sto*	stoh
thousand	*tisíc*	TYEE-seets
How much?	*Kolik?*	KOH-leek
local currency	*koruna (Kč)*	koh-ROO-nah
Where is...?	*Kde je...?*	gday yeh
...the toilet	*...vécé*	vayt-SAY
men	*muži*	MOO-zhee
women	*ženy*	ZHAY-nee
water / coffee	*voda / káva*	VOH-dah / KAH-vah
beer / wine	*pivo / víno*	PEE-voh / VEE-noh
Cheers!	*Na zdraví!*	nah zdrah-VEE
The bill, please.	*Účet, prosím.*	OO-cheht PROH-zeem

drink three, you'll find out why.

You can stay in a pub as long as you want—no one will bring you an *účet* (bill) until you ask for it: *"Pane vrchní, zaplatím!"* ("Mr. Waiter, now I pay!").

Czech Language

Czech, a Slavic language closely related to its neighbors' Polish and Slovak, bears little resemblance to Western European languages. These days, English is commonly spoken, and you'll find the language barrier minimal. Among older people, German is a common second language.

An acute accent *(á, é, í, ó, ú, ý)* means you linger on that vowel. The letter *c* always sounds like "ts" (as in "cats"). The little accent *(háček)* above the *č, š,* or *ž* makes it sound like "ch," "sh", or "zh" (as in "leisure"), respectively. A *háček* above *ň* makes it sound like "ny" (as in "canyon"), and over *ě* makes it sound like "yeh." Czech has one sound that occurs in no other language: *ř* (as in "Dvořák"), which sounds like a cross between a rolled "r" and "zh."

PRAGUE

(Praha)

It's amazing what nearly two decades of freedom can do. Prague has always been historic. Now it's fun, too. No other place in Europe has become so popular so quickly. And for good reason: Prague—the only Central European capital to escape the bombs of the last century's wars—is one of Europe's best-preserved cities. It's filled with sumptuous Art Nouveau facades, offers tons of cheap Mozart and Vivaldi, and brews the best beer in Europe. Beyond its architecture and traditional culture, it's an explosion of pent-up entrepreneurial energy jumping for joy after 40 years of communist rule. Its low prices can cause you to jump for joy, too.

Planning Your Time

Prague demands a minimum of two full days (with 3 nights, or 2 nights and a night train). From Budapest, Warsaw, or Kraków, it's a handy night train. From Munich, Berlin, and Vienna, Prague is about a six-hour train ride by day (you also have the option of a longer night train from Munich).

With two days in Prague, I'd spend a morning seeing the castle and a morning in the Jewish Quarter. Use your afternoons for loitering around the Old Town, Charles Bridge, and the Little Quarter, and split your nights between beer halls and live music. Keep in mind that Jewish Quarter sights close on Saturday.

ORIENTATION

Locals call their town "Praha" (PRAH-hah). It's big, with 1.2 million people, but focus on its relatively compact old center during a quick visit. As you wander, take advantage of brown street signs

directing you to tourist landmarks. Self-deprecating Czechs note that while the signs are designed to help tourists (locals never use them), they're only printed in Czech. Still, thanks to the little icons, the signs can help smart visitors who are sightseeing on foot.

The Vltava River divides the west side (Castle Quarter and Little Quarter) from the east side (New Town, Old Town, Jewish Quarter, Main Train Station, and most of the recommended hotels).

Prague addresses come with references to a general zone. Praha 1 is in the old center on either side of the river. Praha 2 is in the new city, southeast of Wenceslas Square. Praha 3 and higher indicate a location farther from the center. Virtually everything I list is in Praha 1 (unless noted otherwise).

Tourist Information

TIs are at several key locations: **Old Town Square** (in the Old Town Hall, just to the left of the Astronomical Clock; Easter–Oct Mon–Fri 9:00–19:00, Sat–Sun 9:00–18:00; Nov–Easter Mon–Fri 9:00–18:00, Sat–Sun 9:00–17:00; tel. 224-482-018), **Main Train Station** (generally same hours as Old Town Square TI, but closed Sun), and the castle side of **Charles Bridge** (Easter–Oct daily 10:00–18:00, closed Nov–Easter). For general tourist information in English, dial 12444 (Mon–Fri 8:00–19:00) or check the TIs' useful Web site: www.prague-info.cz.

The TIs offer maps, phone cards, a useful transit guide, information on guided walks and bus tours, and bookings for private guides, concerts, hotel rooms, and rooms in private homes.

Several monthly events guides—all of them packed with ads—include the *Prague Guide* (29 Kč), *Prague This Month* (free), and *Heart of Europe* (free, summer only). The English-language weekly *Prague Post* newspaper is handy for entertainment listings and current events (sold cheap at newsstands).

Arrival in Prague

Upon arrival, be sure to buy a city map, with trams and Metro lines marked and tiny sketches of the sights for ease in navigating (30–70 Kč, many different brands; sold at kiosks, exchange windows, or tobacco stands). It's a mistake to try doing Prague without a good map—you'll refer to it constantly. The *Kartografie Praha* city map, which shows all the tram lines and major landmarks, includes a castle diagram and a street index. It comes in two versions: 1:15,000 covers the city center, and 1:25,000 includes the whole city. The city center map is easier to navigate and sufficient unless you're staying in the suburbs.

Prague Landmarks

English	Czech	Pronounced
Main Train Station	Hlavní Nádraží	hlav-nee nah-drah-zhee
Old Town	Staré Město	stah-reh myehs-toh
Old Town Square	Staroměstské Náměstí	star-roh-myehst-skeh nah-myehs-tee
New Town	Nové Město	noh-vay myehs-toh
Little Quarter	Malá Strana	mah-lah strah-nah
Jewish Quarter	Josefov	yoo-zehf-fohv
Castle Quarter	Hradčany	hrad-chah-nee
Charles Bridge	Karlův Most	kar-loov most
Wenceslas Square	Václavske Náměstí	vaht-slahf-skeh nah-myehs-tee
Vltava River	Vltava	vul-tah-vah

By Train

Prague has two train stations. The Main Station (Hlavní Nádraží) serves all trains from Kraków, Frankfurt, Munich, and Salzburg; some trains from Budapest and Vienna; and most trains within the Czech Republic. The secondary station (Nádraží Holešovice) handles all trains from Berlin, some trains from Vienna and Budapest, and the high-speed SC Pendolino train to the eastern Czech Republic.

Upon arrival, get money. The stations have ATMs (best rates) and exchange bureaus (rates are generally bad, but can vary—compare by asking at two windows what you'll get for $100, but keep in mind that many of the windows are run by the same company). Then buy your map and confirm your departure plans. Those arriving on an international train may be met at the tracks by room hustlers, trying to snare tourists for cheap rooms. These can be a good value.

Main Station (Hlavní Nádraží): This station's low-ceilinged hall contains a fascinating mix of travelers, kiosks, gamblers, loitering teenagers, and older riffraff. The creepy station ambience is the work of communist architects, who expanded a classy building to make it just big, painting it the compulsory dreary gray with reddish trim. An ATM is near the subway entrance. The station's baggage-storage counter is reportedly safer than the lockers.

At the Wasteels travel office, Jaroslav and Jaromír offer a helpful and friendly service. You can drop by here upon arrival to get a transit ticket without using the ATM (they take euro coins) and

Rip-Offs in Prague

Prague's new freedom comes with new scams. There's no particular risk of violent crime, but green, rich tourists do get taken by con artists. Simply be on guard, particularly when traveling on trains (thieves thrive on overnight trains), changing money (tellers with bad arithmetic and inexplicable pauses while counting back your change), dealing with taxis (see "By Taxi," page 70), paying in restaurants (see "Eating," page 135), and in seedy neighborhoods.

Anytime you pay for something, make a careful note of how much it costs, how much you're handing over, and how much you expect back. Count your change. Someone selling you a phone card marked 190 Kč might first tell you it's 790 Kč, hoping to pocket the difference. If you call her bluff, she'll pretend it never happened.

Plainclothes policemen "looking for counterfeit money" are con artists. Don't show them any cash or your wallet. If you're threatened with an inexplicable fine by a "policeman," conductor, or other official, you can walk away, scare him away by saying you'll need a receipt (which real officials are legally required to provide), or ask a passerby if the fine is legit. On the other hand, do not ignore the plainclothes inspectors on the Metro and trams who have shown you their badges.

Pickpockets can be little children, or adults dressed as professionals or even as tourists. They target Western visitors. Many thieves drape jackets over their arms to disguise busy fingers.

confirm and buy your outbound train tickets. They can help you figure out train connections, and sell train tickets to anywhere in Europe—with domestic stopovers if you like—along with tickets for fast local trains and cheap phone cards (no commission; Mon–Fri 9:00–17:00 or later, Sat 9:00–16:00, closed Sun, tel. 972-241-954, www.wasteels.cz). You can even leave your bags here for a short time.

The information office for Czech Railways (downstairs on the left) is less helpful, and the ticket windows downstairs don't give schedule information. The windows marked *vnitrostátní* sell tickets within the Czech Republic.

The AVE office on the main floor books rooms in hotels and pensions, and sells taxi vouchers for trips into town at double the fair rate (daily 6:00–23:00; with your back to the tracks, walk down to the orange ceiling and past the "Meeting Point"—their office is in the left corner by the exit to the taxis; tel. 251-551-011, fax 251-555-156, www.avetravel.cz, ave@avetravel.cz).

If you're killing time at the station (or for a wistful glimpse of

Thieves work the crowded and touristy places in teams. They use mobile phones to coordinate their bumps and grinds. Be careful if anyone creates a commotion at the door of a Metro or tram car (especially around the Národní Třída and Vodičkova tram stops, or on the made-for-tourists trams #22 and #23)—it's a smoke-screen for theft.

Car theft is also a big problem in Prague (many Western European car-rental companies don't allow their rentals to cross the Czech border). Never leave anything valuable in your car—not even in broad daylight on a busy street.

The sex clubs on Skořepka street, just south of Havelská Market, routinely rip off naive tourists and can be dangerous. They're filled mostly with Russian prostitutes and German and Asian guys. Lately this district has become the rage for British "stag" parties (happy to take cheap airline flights to get to cheap beer and cheap thrills).

This all sounds intimidating. But Prague is safe. It has its share of petty thieves and con artists, but very little violent crime. Don't be scared—just be alert.

a more genteel age), go upstairs into the Art Nouveau hall. Here, under an elegant dome, you can sip coffee, enjoy music from the 1920s, watch boy prostitutes looking for work, and see new arrivals spilling into the city.

The station was originally named for Emperor Franz Josef. Later, it was renamed for President Woodrow Wilson (see the commemorative plaque in the main exit hall leading away from the tracks), because his promotion of self-determination led to the creation of the free state of Czechoslovakia in 1918. Under the communists (who weren't big fans of Wilson), it was bluntly renamed simply Hlavní Nádraží—"Main Station."

Even though the Main Station is basically downtown, it can be a little tricky to get to your hotel. The biggest challenge is that the **taxi** drivers at the train station are a gang of no-neck mafia thugs who wait around to charge an arriving tourist five times the regular rate. To get an honest cabbie, I'd walk a few blocks and hail one off the street; pay a premium for a voucher at the AVE office (see above); or call AAA Taxi (tel. 233-113-311). A taxi should get you to your hotel for no more than 200 Kč (see "Getting Around Prague," page 68). A better option may be to take the **Metro**. It's dirt-cheap and easy, with very frequent departures. Once you're on the Metro, you'll wonder why you'd bother with a taxi (inside the train station arrival hall, look for the red *M* with two directions: Háje or Ládví). To get to hotels in the Old Town, catch a Háje-bound train to the Muzeum stop, then transfer to the green line (direction: Dejvická) and get off at either Můstek or Staroměstská; these stops straddle the Old Town. Or, if your hotel is close enough, consider **walking** (Wenceslas Square, a downtown landmark, is less than a 10-minute walk away: Turn left out of the station and follow Wilsonova street to the huge National Museum).

Holešovice Station (Nádraží Holešovice): This station, slightly farther from the center, is suburban mellow. The main hall has all the services of the Main Station in a more compact area. On the left are international and local ticket windows (open 24 hours), an information office, and an AVE office for last-minute accommodations (daily 12:00–20:00, tel. 972-224-660). On the right is a little-frequented café with Internet access (1 Kč/min, daily 8:00–19:30). Two ATMs are immediately outside the first glass doors, and the Metro is 50 yards to the right (follow signs toward *Vstup*, which means "entrance"; it's three stops to Hlavní Nádraží—the Main Station—or four stops to the city-center Muzeum stop). Taxis and trams are outside to the right (allow 200 Kč for a cab to the center). The airport bus (45 Kč, 2/hr) is outside to the left.

By Plane

Prague's modern, tidy, low-key **Ruzyně Airport,** located 12 miles (about 30 min) west of the city center, is as user-friendly as any airport in Western Europe or the US. The airport has ATMs (avoid the change desks); desks promoting their transportation service (such as city transit and shuttle buses); kiosks selling city maps and phone cards; and a tourist service with few printed materials. Airport info: tel. 220-113-314, operator tel. 220-111-111.

Getting to and from the airport is easy. Leaving the airport, you have four options:

Dirt Cheap: Take bus #119 to the Dejvická Metro station, or #100 to the Zličín Metro station (20 min), then take the Metro into the center (20 Kč, info desk in airport arrival hall).

Cheap: Take the Čedaz minibus shuttle to Náměstí Republiky, across from Kotva department store (daily 5:30–21:30, 2/hr, pay 90 Kč directly to driver, info desk in arrival hall).

Moderate: Take a Čedaz minibus directly to your hotel, with a couple of stops likely en route (480 Kč for a group of up to 4 to the same hotel, tel. 220-114-286).

Expensive: Catch a taxi. Cabbies wait at the curb directly in front of the arrival hall. Airport taxi cabbies are honest but more expensive. Carefully confirm the complete price before getting in. It's a fixed rate of 600–700 Kč, with no meter.

Helpful Hints

Medical Help: A **24-hour pharmacy** is at Palackého 5 (a block from Wenceslas Square, tel. 224-946-982). There are two state **hospitals** in the center: the **General Hospital** (open daily 24 hours, right above Karlovo Náměstí at U Nemocnice 2, Praha 2, use entry G, tel. 224-962-564); and the **Na Františku Hospital** (on the embankment next to Hotel InterContinental, Na Františku 1, go to the main entrance, for English assistance call Mr. Hacker between 8:00–14:00, tel. 222-801-278 or tel. 222-801-371—serious problems only). The reception staff may not speak English, but doctors do. For better-than-standard assistance in English (including dental service), consider the top-quality **Hospital Na Homolce** (less than 1,000 Kč for an appointment, from 8:00–16:00 tel. 252-922-146; for after-hours emergencies tel. 257-211-111; bus #167 from Anděl Metro station, Roentgenova 2, Praha 5).

Internet Access: Internet cafés are well-advertised and scattered through the Old and New Towns. Consider **Bohemia Bagel** near the Jewish Quarter (see page 141). **Káva Káva Káva Coffee,** on the boundary between the Old and New Towns, is in the Platýz courtyard off Národní 37.

Bookstores: Prague has several enjoyable bookshops with English titles. **Anagram Bookshop,** in the Ungelt courtyard behind the Týn Church, sells books in English on a wide range of topics (Mon–Sat 10:00–20:00, Sun 10:00–19:00, Týn 4, tel. 224-895-737). **V Ráji,** next to Maisel Synagogue in the Jewish Quarter, is the flagship store of a small publishing house dedicated to books about Prague. They offer an assortment of photo publications, fairy tales, and maps (Maiselova 12, tel. 222-326-925). **Kiwi Map Store,** near Wenceslas Square, is one of Prague's best sources for maps (Mon–Fri 9:00–19:00, Sat 9:00–14:00, closed Sun, Jungmanova 23, tel. 224-948-455).

Laundry: A full-service laundry near most of the recommended hotels is at Karolíny Světlé 10 (200 Kč/8-pound load, wash and dry in 2 hours, Mon–Fri 7:30–19:00, closed Sat–Sun, 200 yards from Charles Bridge on Old Town side). Or surf the Internet while your undies tumble-dry at Korunní 14 (160 Kč/load wash and dry, Internet access-2 Kč/min, daily 8:00–20:00, near Náměstí Míru Metro stop, Praha 2).

Local Help: Magic Praha is a tiny travel service run by hardworking Lída Jánská. A charming Jill-of-all-trades who takes her clients' needs seriously, she's particularly helpful with accommodations and transfers throughout the Czech Republic, private tours, and side-trips to historic towns (tel. 235-325-170, mobile 604-207-225, www.magicpraha.cz, magicpraha @magicpraha.cz).

Car Rental: All of the biggies have offices in Prague (check each company's Web site, or ask at the TI). For a local alternative, consider **Alimex,** which features a wide variety of new vehicles (tel. 233-350-001, toll-free tel. 800-150-170, www .alimexcr.cz). The cheapest model, a Škoda Fabia, is a great value (450 Kč/day with basic insurance, plus 238 Kč/day for full theft and damage insurance; additional fees: 500-Kč tax for airport pickup, 357 Kč for delivery to your hotel; discounts if you book online, smart to reserve up to a week ahead in peak season). Note that the cheapest cars sometimes have giant ads pasted on the side. They have branches at the airport (daily 8:00–22:00) and near the Holešovice Station (daily 8:00–18:00).

Best Views: Enjoy the "Golden City of a Hundred Spires" during the early evening, when the light is warm and the colors are rich. Good viewpoints include the terrace at the Strahov Monastery (above the castle), the top of St. Vitus Cathedral (at the castle), the top of either tower on Charles Bridge, the Old Town Square clock tower (has an elevator), the Restaurant u Prince Terrace (see page 141), and the steps of the National Museum overlooking Wenceslas Square.

Getting Around Prague

You can walk nearly everywhere. But after you figure out the public transportation system, the Metro is slick, the trams fun, and the taxis quick and easy. For details, pick up the handy transit guide at the TI. City maps show the tram, bus, and Metro lines.

By Metro and Tram

Affordable and excellent public transit is perhaps the best legacy of the communist era (locals ride all month for 460 Kč). The three-line Metro system is handy and simple, but doesn't always get you right to the tourist sights (landmarks such as the Old Town Square and Prague Castle are several blocks from the nearest Metro stops). The trams rumble by every two or three minutes and take you just about anywhere.

Tickets: The trams and Metro work on the same cheap tickets:

- 20-minute basic ticket with limited transfer options *(základní s omezenou přestupností)*—14 Kč. With this ticket, no transfers

Prague Metro

Line A (GREEN) – – –
Line B (YELLOW) ·······
Line C (RED) ———

NOT TO SCALE

DCH

are allowed on trams and buses, but on the Metro you can go up to five stops with one transfer (not valid for night trams or night buses).

- 75-minute transfer ticket with unlimited transfers *(základní přestupní)*—20 Kč.
- 24-hour pass *(jízdenka na 24 hodin)*—80 Kč.
- 3-day pass *(jízdenka na 3 dny)*—220 Kč.
- 7-day pass *(jízdenka na 7 dní)*—280 Kč.

Buy tickets from your hotel, at newsstand kiosks, or from automated machines (select ticket price, then insert coins). For convenience, buy all the tickets you think you'll need—but estimate conservatively. Remember, Prague is a great walking town, so unless you're commuting from a hotel far outside the center, you will likely find that individual tickets work best. Be sure to validate your ticket on the tram, bus, or Metro by sticking it in the machine (which stamps a time on it—watch locals and imitate). Inspectors routinely ambush ticketless riders (including tourists) and fine them 500 Kč on the spot.

Tips: Navigate by signs listing end stations. When you come to your stop, push the yellow button if the doors don't automatically open. Although it seems that all Metro doors lead to the neighborhood of Výstup, that's simply the Czech word for "exit." When a tram pulls up to a stop, two different names are announced: first, the name of the stop you're currently at, followed by the name of the stop that's coming up next. Confused tourists, thinking they've heard their stop, are notorious for rushing off the tram one stop too soon. Trams run every 5–10 minutes in the daytime (a schedule is posted at each stop). The Metro closes at midnight, and the nighttime tram routes (identified with white numbers on blue backgrounds at tram stops) run all night at 30-minute intervals. There's more information and a complete route planner at www.dp-praha.cz.

Handy Trams: Trams #22 and #23 are practically made for sightseeing, using the same route to connect the New Town with the Castle Quarter (find the line marked on the color map at beginning of this book). The trams use some of the same stops as the Metro (making it easy to get to—or travel on from—the tram route). Of the many stops these trams make, the most convenient are two in the New Town (Národní Třída Metro stop, between the bottom of Wenceslas Square and the river; and Národní Divadlo, at the National Theatre), one stop in the Little Quarter (Malostranská Metro station), and three stops above Prague Castle (Královský Letohrádek, Pražský Hrad, and Pohořelec; for details, see "Getting to Prague Castle—By Tram" on page 109).

By Taxi

Prague's taxis—notorious for hyperactive meters—are being tamed. New legislation is in place to curb crooked cabbies, and police will always take your side in an argument. Many cabbies are crooks who consider it a good day's work to take one sucker for a ride. You'll make things difficult for a dishonest cabbie by challenging an unfair fare.

While most hotel receptionists and guidebooks advise avoiding taxis, I find Prague to be a great taxi town and use them routinely. With the local rate, they're cheap (read the rates on the door: drop charge—36 Kč; per-kilometer charge—25 Kč; and waiting time per minute—5 Kč). Tourists overestimate how much a typical taxi trip should cost. Before getting in, ask the cabbie for a rough estimate, which shouldn't exceed 200 Kč for a long ride anywhere in the center. (If he quotes a price higher than this, he's probably a crook.) Then be sure the cabbie turns on the meter at the #1 tariff (look for the word *sazba,* meaning "tariff," on the meter). Avoid cabs waiting at tourist attractions and train stations. To improve your odds of getting a fair meter rate—which starts only when you take off—call for a cab (or have your hotel or restaurant call one for you). **AAA Taxi** (tel. 233-113-311) and **City Taxi** (tel. 257-257-257) are the most likely to have English-speaking staff—and honest cabbies. I also find that hailing a passing taxi usually gets me a decent price.

If a cabbie surprises you at the end with an astronomical fare, simply pay 200 Kč, then go into your hotel. On the miniscule chance he follows you, the receptionist will back you up.

TOURS

Walking Tours—Many small companies offer walking tours of the Old Town, the castle, and more. For the latest, pick up the walking tour fliers at the TI. Since guiding is a routine side-job for local university students, you'll generally get hardworking young guides at good prices. While I'd rather go with my own private guide (below), public walking tours are cheaper, cover themes you might not otherwise consider, connect you with other English-speaking travelers, and allow for spontaneity. **Prague Walks** is as good as any (250–1,000 Kč, 1.5–6 hrs, tel. 222-322-309, fax 261-214-603, mobile 603-271-911, www.praguewalks.com, pwalks @comp.cz). Consider their clever Good Morning Walk, which starts at 8:00 (April–Aug only), before the crowds hit.

▲▲**Private Guides**—In Prague, hiring a local guide is particularly smart—they're twice as helpful for half the price compared to guides in Western Europe. Because prices are usually per hour (not per person), small groups can inexpensively use a guide for several days. Guides meet you wherever you like and tailor the tour to your interests. Visit their Web sites in advance for details on various walks, airport transfers, countryside excursions, and other services offered, and then make arrangements by e-mail.

Katka Svobodová, an anthropologist and historian, is a hardworking guide who know her stuff, speaks excellent English, and enjoys showing individuals and small groups around (400 Kč/hr, 3-hour minimum, mobile 603-181-300, www.praguewalker.com, katerina@praguewalker.com). **Šárka Pelantová** and her team of guides get beyond the dates and famous buildings to provide insight into the culture, and are eager to build a walk around your interests (400 Kč/hr for 1 or 2 people, 600 Kč/hr for 3 or more, mobile 777-225-205, www.prague-guide.info, saraguide@volny.cz).

Prague at a Glance

In the Old Town

▲▲▲**Old Town Square** Colorful, magical main square of Old World Prague, with dozens of colorful facades, the dramatic Jan Hus Memorial, looming Týn Church, and fanciful Astronomical Clock. **Hours:** Týn Church open 10:00–13:00 & 15:00–17:00; clock strikes on the hour 8:00–21:00, until 20:00 in winter.

▲▲▲**Charles Bridge** Atmospheric, statue-lined bridge connecting the Old Town to the Little Quarter and Prague Castle. **Hours:** Always open.

▲▲▲**Jewish Quarter** The best Jewish sight in Europe, featuring various synagogues and an evocative cemetery. **Hours:** Sun–Fri 9:00–18:00, closed Sat.

▲▲**Museum of Medieval Art** The best Gothic art in the land, displayed at St. Agnes Convent. **Hours:** Tue–Sun 10:00–18:00, closed Mon.

▲**Havelská Market** Colorful open-air market selling crafts and produce. **Hours:** Daily 9:00–18:00.

Museum of Czech Cubism Exhibit of early-20th-century Czech artistic school, in the Old Town's interesting Black Madonna House. **Hours:** Tue–Sun 10:00–18:00, closed Mon.

Klementinum The Czech National Library, an oasis of tranquil courtyards next to Charles Bridge and touristy Karlova street. **Hours:** Courtyards always open.

In the New Town

▲▲**Wenceslas Square** Lively boulevard at the heart of modern Prague. **Hours:** Always open.

▲▲**Mucha Museum** Likeable collection of Art Nouveau works by Czech artist Alfons Mucha. **Hours:** Daily 10:00–18:00.

▲▲**Municipal House** Pure Art Nouveau architecture, including Prague's largest concert hall and several eateries. **Hours:** Daily 10:00–18:00.

▲▲**Museum of Communism** The rise and fall of the regime, from start to Velvet finish. **Hours:** Daily 9:00–21:00.

Dancing House Frank Gehry–designed building on the Vltava riverbank. **Hours:** Always viewable.

In the Little Quarter
Church of St. Nicholas Jesuit centerpiece of Little Quarter Square, with ultimate High Baroque decor and a climbable bell tower. **Hours:** Church—daily 9:00–17:00; tower—April–Oct daily 10:00–18:00, closed Nov–March.

Petřín Hill Little Quarter hill with public art, a funicular, a replica of the Eiffel Tower, and the quirky museum of a nonexistent Czech hero. **Hours:** Funicular—daily 8:00–22:00; tower and museum—daily 10:00–22:00.

In the Castle Quarter
▲▲▲**St. Vitus Cathedral** The Czech Republic's most important church, featuring a climbable tower and a striking stained-glass window by Art Nouveau artist Alfons Mucha. **Hours:** Daily April–Oct 9:00–17:00, Nov–March 9:00–16:00, but closed Sunday mornings year-round for Mass.

▲▲**Prague Castle** Traditional seat of Czech rulers, with St. Vitus Cathedral, Old Royal Palace, Basilica of St. George, shop-lined Golden Lane, and lots of crowds. **Hours:** Castle sights—daily April–Oct 9:00–17:00, Nov–March 9:00–16:00; castle grounds—daily 5:00–23:00.

▲**Strahov Monastery and Library** Baroque center of learning, with ornate reading rooms and old-fashioned science exhibits. **Hours:** Daily 9:00–12:00 & 13:00–17:00.

Loreta Church Baroque church featuring what's supposedly the actual house of the Virgin Mary. **Hours:** Tue–Sun 9:00–12:15 & 13:00–16:30, closed Mon.

Toy and Barbie Museum Several centuries of toys, starring an army of Barbies. **Hours:** Daily 9:30–17:30.

My readers have also recommended **Renata Blažková** (tel. 222-716-870, mobile 602-353-186, blazer@volny.cz) and **Martin Bělohradský** (martinb@uochb.cas.cz).

The **TI** also has plenty of private guides (rates for a 3-hour tour: 1,200 Kč/1 person, 1,400 Kč/2 people, 1,600 Kč/3 people, 2,000 Kč/4 people; desk at Old Town Square TI, arrange and pay in person at least 2 hours in advance, tel. 224-482-562, guides@pis.cz). For a listing of more private guides, see www.guide-prague.cz.

Jewish-Themed Walks: Silvie Wittmann, a native Czech Jew, has developed a diverse group of knowledgeable guides who aspire to bring Jewish traditions back to life in Prague. Consider her three-hour walking tour of the Jewish Quarter (630 Kč includes entry to the Jewish Museum, May–Oct Sun–Fri at 10:30 and 14:30, Nov–April Sun–Fri at 10:30 only, no tours on Sat) or her six-hour trip to Terezín Concentration Camp (1,150 Kč includes transportation and all entries, departs May–Oct daily at 10:00; mid-March–April and Nov–Dec no Mon, Wed, or Fri tours; Jan–mid-March by appointment only). All tours require prior reservation and meet in front of Hotel InterContinental at the end of Pařížská Street (tel. & fax 222-252-472, mobile 603-168-427, www.wittmann-tours.com, sylvie@wittmann-tours.com).

Outside Prague: To get beyond Prague, call Thomas Zahn, who runs **Pathways Guided Travel.** Thomas, an American who married into the Czech Republic, specializes in helping Americans of Czech descent find their roots. He also organizes and leads creative, affordable (mostly one- and two-day) excursions from Prague. Hiking, biking, horseback riding, or canoeing, you'll explore the unknown charms of the region with a small group and a committed guide. Explore Thomas' Web site for ways to connect with the rural Czech countryside and experience more than Prague on your visit (tel. 257-940-113, mobile 603-758-983, www.pathfinders.cz).

Bus Tours—While I generally recommend cheap big-bus orientation tours for an efficient, once-over-lightly look at great cities, Prague just isn't built for bus tours. In fact, most bus tours of the city are walking tours that use buses for pick-ups and transfers. The sightseeing core (Castle Quarter, Charles Bridge, and the Old Town) is not accessible by bus. So if you insist on a bus, you're playing basketball with a catcher's mitt.

Bus tours make more sense for day trips out of Prague. Several companies have kiosks on Na Příkopě where you can comparison-shop. **Premiant City Tours** offers 20 different tours, including Terezín Concentration Camp, Karlštejn Castle, and Český Krumlov (1,750 Kč, 10 hrs), and a river cruise. The tours feature live guides and depart from near the bottom of Wenceslas Square at Na Příkopě 23. Get tickets at an AVE travel agency, your hotel, on the bus, or at Na Příkopě 23 (tel. 224-946-922, mobile 606-600-123, www.premiant.cz). Tour salespeople are notorious for telling you anything to sell a ticket. Some tours, especially those heading into the countryside, can be in as many as four different languages. Hiring a private guide, many of whom can drive you around in their car, can be a much better value (see above).

Cruises—Prague isn't ideal for a boat tour. Still, the hour-long Vltava River cruises, which leave from near the castle end of Charles Bridge about hourly, are scenic and relaxing, though not informative (100–150 Kč).

▲**Paddleboat Cruises**—Renting a rowboat or paddleboat on Slovanský Island (by the National Theatre) is a better way to enjoy the river. You'll float at your own pace among the swans and local lovers in their own paddleboats (about 80 Kč/hr, bring photo ID for deposit).

SIGHTS

I've arranged these sights according to which of Prague's four towns you'll find them in (see sidebar on following page): Old Town, New Town, Little Quarter, or Castle Quarter.

The Old Town (Staré Město)

From Prague's dramatic centerpiece, the Old Town Square, sight-seeing options fan out in all directions. Get oriented on the square before venturing onward. You can find out about Jewish heritage in the Jewish Quarter (Josefov), a few blocks from the Old Town Square. Closer to the square, you'll find the quaint and historic Ungelt courtyard and Celetná street, which leads to the Museum of Czech Cubism and the landmark Estates Theatre. Nearby, Karlova street funnels all the tourists to the famous Charles Bridge. All of the sights described here are within a five-minute walk of the magnificent Old Town Square.

Old Town Square (Staroměstské Náměstí)

The focal point for most visits, Prague's Old Town Square is well worth ▲▲▲. This has been a market square since the 11th century. It became the nucleus of the Old Town (Staré Město) in the 13th century, when its Town Hall was built. Today, the old-time market stalls have been replaced by cafés, touristy horse buggies, and souvenir hawkers. But under this shallow surface the square hides a magic power to evoke the history that has passed through here.

• *Gawk your way to the square's centerpiece, the...*

Jan Hus Memorial: This monument, erected in 1915 (500 years after the Czech reformer's martyrdom by fire), symbolizes the long struggle for Czech freedom (see sidebar on page 79). Walk

Prague's Four Towns

Until about 1800, Prague was actually four distinct towns with four town squares, all separated by fortified walls. Each town had a unique character, which came from the personality of the people who initially settled it. Today much of Prague's charm survives in the distinct spirit of each of its towns.

Castle Quarter (Hradčany): Since the ninth century, when the first castle was built on the promontory overlooking a ford across the Vltava River, Castle Hill has been occupied by the ruling class. When Christianity arrived in the Czech lands, this hilltop—oriented along an east–west axis—proved a perfect spot for a church and, later, the cathedral (which, according to custom, must be built with the altar pointing east). Finally, the nobles built their representative palaces in proximity to the castle to compete with the Church for influence on the king. Even today, you feel like clip-clopping through this neighborhood in a fancy carriage. The Castle Quarter—which hosts the offices of the president and prime minister—has high art and grand buildings, little commerce, and few pubs.

Little Quarter (Malá Strana): This Baroque town of fine palaces and gardens rose from ashes of a merchant settlement that burned in the 1540s. The Czech and European nobility who settled here took pride in the grand design of their gardens. In the 1990s, after decades of decay, the gardens were carefully restored. While some are open only to the successors of the former nobility—including the Czech Parliament and the American, German, and Polish Embassies—many are open to visitors.

Old Town (Staré Město): The Charles Bridge connects the Little Quarter with the Old Town. A boomtown since the 10th century, this has long been the busy commercial quarter—filled with merchants, guilds, and supporters of Jan Hus (folks who wanted a Czech-style Catholicism). Trace the walls of this town in the modern road plan (the Powder Tower is a remnant of a wall system that completed a fortified ring, half provided by the river). The marshy area closest to the bend—least inhabitable and therefore allotted to the Jewish community—became the ghetto (today's Josefov, or Jewish Quarter).

New Town (Nové Město): The New Town rings the Old Town—cutting a swath from riverbank to riverbank—and is fortified with Prague's outer wall. In the 14th century, the king created this town, tripling the size of what would become Prague. Wenceslas Square was once the horse market of this busy working-class district. Even today, the New Town is separated from the Old Town by a "moat" (the literal meaning of the street called

Prague Overview

Na Příkopě). As you cross bustling Na Příkopě, you leave the glass and souvenir shops behind and enter a town of malls and fancy shops that cater to locals and visitors alike.

The Royal Way: Cutting through the four towns—from St. Vitus Cathedral down to the Charles Bridge, and then from the bridge to the Powder Tower—is the Royal Way (Královská Cesta), the ancient path of coronation processions. Today this city spine is marred by tacky trinket shops and jammed by tour groups. Use it for orientation only—try to avoid it if you want to see the real Prague.

Prague's Old Town

M - Metro Stop   **T** - Tram Stop   ::: - Pedestrian Passageway

1. Church of St. Nicholas
2. Ungelt Courtyard & House at the Golden Ring
3. Church of St. James
4. St. Agnes Convent & Museum of Medieval Art
5. Museum of Czech Cubism in the Black Madonna House
6. Estates Theatre
7. Havelská Market
8. Bethlehem Chapel
9. Charles University
10. Klementinum (National Library)

Jan Hus and Martin Luther

The word *catholic* means "universal." The Roman Catholic Church—in many ways the administrative ghost of the Roman Empire—is the only organization to survive from ancient times. For more than a thousand years, it enforced its notion that the Vatican was the sole interpreter of God's word on earth, and the only legitimate way to be a Christian was as a Roman Catholic. Jan Hus (c. 1369–1415) lived and preached a century before Martin Luther. Both were college professors, as well as priests. Both drew huge public crowds as they preached in their university chapels. Both promoted a local religious autonomy. Both helped establish their national languages. (Hus gave the Czechs their unique accent marks to enable the letters to fit the sounds.) And both got in big trouble. While Hus was burned, Luther survived. Living after Gutenberg, Luther was able to spread his message more cheaply and effectively, thanks to the new printing press. Since Luther was high-profile and German, killing him would have caused major political complications. While Hus may have loosened Rome's grip on Christianity, Luther orchestrated the Reformation that finally broke it. Today, both are honored as national heroes as well as religious reformers.

around the memorial. Jan Hus stands tall between two groups of people: victorious Hussite patriots and Protestants defeated by the Hapsburgs. One of the patriots holds a chalice (cup); in the

medieval Church, only priests could drink the wine at Communion. Since the Hussites fought for their right to take both the wine and the bread, the cup is their symbol. Hus looks proudly at the Týn Church (described later in this sec-

tion), which became the headquarters and leading church of his followers. A golden chalice once filled the now-empty niche under the gold bas-relief of the Virgin Mary on the church's facade. After the Hapsburg (and, therefore, Catholic) victory over the Czechs in 1620, the Hussite chalice was melted down and made into the image of Mary that shines from that spot high over the square today.

Behind the statue of Jan Hus, the bronze statue of a mother with her children represents the ultimate rebirth of the Czech nation. Because of his bold stance for independence in the way

Prague's Old Town Square

common people worship God, Hus was excommunicated and burned in Germany a century before the age of Martin Luther.

• *Standing by Jan Hus, get oriented with a...*

Spin-Tour: Whirl clockwise to get a look at Prague's diverse architectural styles: Gothic, Renaissance, Baroque, Rococo, and Art Nouveau. Start with the green domes of the Baroque **Church of St. Nicholas.** Originally Catholic, now Hussite, this church is a popular venue for concerts. (There's another green-domed Church of St. Nicholas—also popular for concerts—by the same architect across the Charles Bridge in the Little Quarter.) The Jewish Quarter (Josefov) is a few blocks behind the church, down the uniquely tree-lined Pařížská—"Paris street." (For more on the Jewish Quarter, see page 89.) Pařížská, an eclectic cancan of mostly Art Nouveau facades, leads to a bluff that once sported a 100-foot-tall stone Stalin. Demolished in 1962 after Khrushchev exposed Stalin's crimes, it was replaced in 1991 by a giant ticking **metronome**—partly to commemorate Prague's centennial exhibition (the 1891 exhibition is remembered by the Little Quarter's

Eiffel-esque Petřín Tower), and partly to send the message that for every power, there's a time to go.

Spin to the right, past the Hus Memorial and the fine yellow Art Nouveau building. The large Rococo palace on the right is part of the **National Gallery;** the temporary exhibits here are often the best in town.

To the right, you can't miss the towering, Gothic **Týn Church** (pronounced "teen"), with its fanciful spires flanking the gold bas-relief of Mary. For 200 years after Hus' death, this was Prague's leading Hussite church (described in more detail later in this section). A narrow lane leading to the church's entrance passes the **Via Musica,** the most convenient ticket office in town (see page 123). Behind the Týn Church is a gorgeously restored medieval court-yard called **Ungelt** (see page 83). The row of pastel houses in front of Týn Church has a mixture of Gothic, Renaissance, and Baroque facades.

To the right of these buildings, shop-lined **Celetná street** leads to a square called Ovocný Trh (with the Estates Theatre and Museum of Czech Cubism—see page 85), and beyond that, to the Powder Tower and Municipal House in the New Town (see page 100).

Continue spinning right—with more gloriously colorful archi-tecture—until you reach the pointed 250-foot-tall spire marking the 14th-century **Old Town Hall** (which has the only elevator-accessible tower in town—see below). The chunk of pink building attached to the tower of the Neo-Gothic City Hall is the town's memorial to bad losers. The building once stretched all the way to the Church of St. Nicholas. Then, in the last days of World War II (May of 1945), German tanks knocked off this landmark—to the joy of many Prague citizens who considered it an ugly, oversized 19th-century stain on the medieval square. Across the square from the Old Town Hall (opposite the Astronomical Clock), touristy **Melantrichova street** leads directly to the New Town's Wenceslas Square (see page 94), passing the craft-packed Havelská Market (see page 85) along the way.

• *Now wander across the square, toward the Old Town Hall Tower. Embedded in the pavement at the base of the tower (near the snack stand), you'll see...*

Twenty-Seven Crosses: These white inlaid crosses mark the spot where 27 Protestant nobles, merchants, and intellectuals were beheaded in 1621 after rebelling against the Catholic Hapsburgs. The execution ended Czech independence for 300 years—and it's still one of the grimmest chapters in their history. Until recently, Czechs walked around this sacred spot, avoiding stepping on it, and many would stop to pay their respects. But today the sacred soil is home to a hot-dog vendor, and few notice the crosses in the pavement.

• *Looming behind the crosses is the Old Town Hall. Near the base of the tall tower, around the corner to the left, is Prague's famous...*

Astronomical Clock: Join the gang for the striking of the hour on the Old Town Hall clock, worth ▲▲ (daily 8:00–21:00, until 20:00 in winter). As you wait, see if you can figure out how the clock works.

With revolving disks, celestial symbols, and sweeping hands, this clock keeps several versions of time. Two outer rings show the hour: Bohemian time (gold Gothic numbers on black background, counts from sunset—find the zero, between 23 and 1...supposedly the time of tonight's sunset) and modern time (24 Roman numerals, XII at the top being noon, XII at the bottom being midnight). Five hundred years ago, everything revolved around the earth (the fixed middle background—with Prague marking the center, of course).

To indicate the times of sunrise and sunset, arcing lines and moving spheres combine with the big hand (a sweeping golden sun) and the little hand (a moon that spins to show various stages). Look for the orbits of the sun and moon as they rise through day (the blue zone) and night (the black zone).

If this seems complex to us, it must have been a marvel 500 years ago. Because the clock was heavily damaged during World War II, a lot of what you see today is a reconstruction. The circle below (added in the 19th century) shows the signs of the zodiac, scenes from the seasons of a rural peasant's life, and a ring of saints' names—one for each day of the year, with a marker showing today's special saint (at top).

Four statues flanking the clock represent the 15th-century outlook on time. A Turk with a mandolin symbolizes hedonism, a Jewish moneylender is greed, and the figure staring into a mirror stands for vanity. All these worldly goals are vain in the face of Death, whose hourglass reminds us that our time is unavoidably running out.

At the top of the hour (don't blink—the show is pretty quick): First, Death tips his hourglass and pulls the cord, ringing the bell; then the windows open and the 12 apostles parade by,

acknowledging the gang of
onlookers; then the rooster
crows; and then the hour is
rung. The hour is often off
because of daylight saving
time (completely sense-
less to 15th-century clock-
makers). At the top of the
next hour, stand under the
tower—protected by a line

of banner-wielding, powdered-wigged concert salespeople—and
watch the tourists.

• *To the left of the clock is Prague's main TI, which has an information
desk and sells tickets for a pair of activities...*

Tower Climb and Old Town Hall Tour: In good weather, zip
up the Old Town Hall tower via elevator for some of Prague's best
views (50 Kč, daily 9:00–18:00). Slightly less interesting is the 45-
minute tour of the Old Town Hall, which includes a Gothic chapel and a close-up look at the inner workings of the Astronomical
Clock (plus its statues of the 12 apostles; 50 Kč, 2/hr).

• *Now that you're oriented, you can use this delightful square as your
launchpad for the rest of Prague's Old Town sights.*

Týn Church

While this church, rated ▲, has a long history, it's most notable for
its 200-year-stint as the leading church of the Hussite movement
(generally open daily 10:00–13:00 & 15:00–17:00). It was Catholic
before the Hussites, and returned to Catholicism after the Hussites
were defeated. As if to insult Hus and his doctrine of simplicity, the
church's once elegant and pure Gothic columns are now encrusted
with noisy Baroque altars. While Gothic, the church interior is
uncharacteristically bright because of its Baroque-age clear win-
dowpanes and whitewash. Read the church's story (posted in
English, rear-left side) for a Catholic spin on the church's story—
told with barely a mention of Hus. The fine 16th-century, carved
John the Baptist altar (right aisle) is worth a look.

Outside, on the side of the church facing Celetná street, find a
statue of St. Mary resting on a temporary column against the wall.
The Catholics are still waiting for a chance to reinstall St. Mary in
the middle of the Old Town Square, where she used to stand more
than a century ago.

Behind Týn Church

▲Ungelt Courtyard (Týnský Dvůr)—Ever since the Old Town
was established, the Ungelt courtyard—located directly behind
the Old Town Square's Týn Church—has served as a hostel for

foreign merchants, much like a Turkish caravanserai. Here the merchants (usually German) would store their goods and pay taxes before setting up stalls on the Old Town Square. Notice there are only two entrances into the complex—guaranteeing the safety of goods and merchants. After decades of disuse, the courtyard had fallen into such disrepair by the 1980s that authorities considered demolishing it. Marvelously restored a few years ago, the Ungelt courtyard is now the most pleasant area in the Old Town for an outdoor coffee (such as at Ebel Coffee House—see page 143), sorting through wooden crafts, and paging through English books (at Anagram Bookshop, described on page 67).

Church of St. James (Kostel Sv. Jakuba)—Perhaps the most beautiful church in the Old Town, the Church of St. James is just behind Ungelt courtyard. The Franciscan Order has occupied this church and the adjacent monastery nearly as long as merchants occupied Ungelt. A medieval city was a complex phenomenon: side-by-side, there existed commerce, brothels, and a life of contemplation. (I guess it's not that much different from today.) Artistically, St. James (along with the church at Strahov Monastery—see page 113) is a stunning example of how simple Gothic spaces could be transformed into sumptuous feasts of Baroque decoration. The blue light in the altar highlights one of Prague's most venerated treasures—the bejeweled Madonna Pietatis. Above the *pietà*, as if held aloft by hummingbird-like angels, is a painting of the martyrdom of St. James (free, daily 9:30–12:00 & 14:00–16:00).

As you leave, find the black and shriveled-up arm with clenched fingers (15 feet above and to the left of the door). According to legend, a thief attempted to rob the Madonna Pietatis from the altar, but his hand was frozen the moment he touched the statue. The monks had to cut off the arm in order for it to let go. The dried-up arm now hangs here as a warning—and the entire delightful story is posted nearby in English.

North of the Old Town Square, near the River
▲▲Museum of Medieval Art—The Museum of Medieval Art in Bohemia and Central Europe (1200–1550) is housed in the St. Agnes Convent. The 14th century was Prague's Golden Age, and the religious art displayed in this Gothic space is a testament to the rich cultural life of the period. Each exquisite piece is well-lit and thoughtfully described in English. Follow the arrows on a chronological sweep through Gothic art history. The various Madonnas and saints were gathered here from churches all over Central Europe (100 Kč, Tue–Sun 10:00–18:00, closed Mon, two blocks northeast of the Spanish Synagogue, along the river at Anežská 12).

On Celetná Street, Toward the New Town

Celetná, a pedestrian-only street, is a convenient and relatively untouristy way to get from the Old Town Square to the New Town (specifically the Powder Tower and Municipal House, described on page 100). Along the way, at the square called Ovocný Trh, you'll find these sights.

Museum of Czech Cubism—Cubism was a potent force in Prague in the early 20th century. The fascinating Museum of Czech Cubism

in the Black Madonna House (Dům u Černé Matky Boží) offers the complete Cubist experience: Cubist architecture (stand back and see how masterfully it makes its statement while mixing with its neighbors...then get up close and study the details), a great café (upstairs), a ground-floor shop, and, of course, a museum. On three floors, you'll see paintings, furniture, graphics, and architectural drafts by Czech Cubists. This building is an example of what has long been considered the greatest virtue of Prague's architects: the ability to adapt their grandiose plans to the existing cityscape (museum entry-100 Kč, Tue–Sun 10:00–18:00, closed Mon, corner of Celetná and Ovocný Trh at Ovocný Trh 19, tel. 224-301-003). If you're not interested in touring the museum itself, consider a drink in the similarly decorated upstairs Grand Café Orient (see page 142).

Estates Theatre (Stavovské Divadlo)—Built by a nobleman in the 1770s, this classicist building—gently opening its greenish walls onto Ovocný Trh—was the prime opera venue in Prague at a time when an Austrian prodigy was changing the course of music. Wolfgang Amadeus Mozart premiered *Don Giovanni* in this building, and personally directed many of his works here. Prague's theater-goers would whistle arias from Mozart's works on the streets the morning after they premiered here. Today part of the National Theatre group, the Estates Theatre continues to produce *The Marriage of Figaro*, *Don Giovanni*, and occasionally *The Magic Flute*. For a more intimate encounter with Mozart, go to Villa Bertramka (see page 125).

On Melantrichova Street

▲**Havelská Market**—Skinny, tourist-clogged Melantrichova street leads directly from the Old Town Square's Astronomical Clock to the bottom of Wenceslas Square. But even along this most crowded of streets, a genuine bit of Prague remains: Havelská Market, offering crafts and produce. The open-air market was set up in the 13th century for the German trading community. Though heavy on souvenirs these days, the market still keeps hungry locals and vagabonds fed cheaply. It's ideal for a healthy snack; merchants are happy to sell a single vegetable or piece of fruit; and you'll find a washing fountain and plenty of inviting benches midway down the street. The market is also a fun place to browse for crafts. It's a homegrown, homemade kind of place; you'll often be dealing with the actual artist or farmer (market open daily 9:00–18:00, produce best on weekdays; more souvenirs, puppets, and toys on weekends). The many cafés and little eateries circling the market offer a fine and relaxing vantage point from which to view the action.

From Old Town Square to Charles Bridge

Karlova Street—Karlova street winds through medieval Prague from the Old Town Square to the Charles Bridge (it zigzags...just follow the crowds). This is a commercial gauntlet, and it's here that the touristy feeding-frenzy of Prague is most ugly. Street signs keep you on track, and *Karlův most* signs point to the bridge. Obviously, you'll find few good values on this drag. Two favorite places providing a quick break from the crowds are just a few steps off Karlova on Husova street: **Cream and Dream Ice Cream** (Husova 12) and **U Zlatého Tygra,** a colorful pub serving great, cheap beer in a classic and untouristy setting (Husova 17; see page 138).

Klementinum—The Czech Republic's massive National Library borders touristy Karlova street. The contrast could not be starker—step out of the most souvenir-packed stretch of Eastern Europe, into the meditative silence of Eastern Europe's biggest library. The Klementinum was built to house a college in the 1600s by the Jesuits, who had been invited to Prague by the Catholic Hapsburgs to offset the influence of the predominantly Protestant Charles University nearby. The building was transformed into a library in the early 1700s, when the Jesuits took firm control of the university. Their books, together with the collections of several noble families (written in all possible languages...except Czech), form the nucleus of what is now the six-million-volumes-strong National and University Library. (Note that the Klementinum's Chapel of Mirrors is a popular venue for evening concerts.)

Charles Bridge (Karlův Most)

Among Prague's defining landmarks, this much-loved bridge offers one of the most pleasant and entertaining quarter-mile strolls in Europe. It's well worth ▲▲▲. Enjoy the bridge at different times of day. The bridge is most memorable early—before the crowds—and late, during that photographers' "magic hour" when the sun is low in the sky.

At the Old Town end of the bridge, in a little square, is a statue of the bridge's namesake, **Charles IV.** This Holy Roman Emperor

Charles Bridge Reconstruction

Talked about for decades, the long-overdue reconstruction of the Charles Bridge finally began in the fall of 2006. In the first stage, the entire bridge will be reinforced with a steel frame on the inside. Then the deteriorated sandstone pieces will be replaced by new ones. In the past, builders often chose poor-quality sandstone, and this is precisely the mistake current workers want to avoid—in fact, as of this writing they're still debating which quarry they're going to use.

Don't worry about not being able to cross this most characteristic of Prague's landmarks. Aware of the blow that closing the entire bridge would deal to the tourist industry, the city of Prague chose a plan that will keep at least one side of the bridge open throughout the reconstruction. To minimize impact on the nearby areas, all of the building material will be transported by river. A completion date has not yet been set, but it seems likely that for years to come, the project will give visitors a rare chance to peek into the entrails of the centuries-old structure.

(*Karlo Quatro*—the guy on the 100-Kč bill) ruled his vast empire from Prague in the 14th century. He's holding a contract establish-

ing Prague's university, the first in Northern Europe. This statue was erected in 1848 to celebrate the university's 500th birthday. The women around Charles' pedestal symbolize the university's four subjects: the arts, medicine, law, and theology. (From the corner by the busy street, many think the emperor's silhouette makes it appear that he's peeing on the tourists.)

Bridges had been built on this spot before, as the remnant tower from the Judith Bridge (the smaller of the two bridge towers at the far end) testifies. All were washed away by floods. After a major flood in 1342, Emperor Charles IV decided to commission an entirely new structure rather than repair the old one. Until the 19th century, this was Prague's only bridge crossing the river.

How do you make a bridge last seven centuries? Back in the 1300s, they believed in the magic of time and numbers. The founding stone was laid in 1357, on the 9th of July at 5:31 (it's a palindrome: 135797531). On the Old Town bank, a spot was chosen for the ending of the bridge that lined up perfectly with the tomb of St. Vitus (in the cathedral across the river) and the setting sun at summer solstice.

This magical spot is now occupied by the **bridge tower,** considered one of the finest Gothic gates anywhere. Contemplate the fine sculpture on the Old Town side of the tower, showing the 14th-century hierarchy of kings, bishops, and angels. Climbing the tower rewards you with wonderful views over the bridge (40 Kč, daily 10:00–19:00, as late as 22:00 in summer).

In the 17th century, there were no statues on the bridge—only a **cross,** which you can still see as part of the third sculpture on the right. The gilded Hebrew inscription celebrating Christ was paid by a fine imposed on a Jew for mocking the cross.

The bronze Baroque statue depicting **John of Nepomuk**—a saint of the Czech people—draws a crowd (look for the guy with the five golden stars around his head, near the Little Quarter end of the bridge on the right). John of Nepomuk was a 14th-century priest to whom the queen confessed all her sins. According to a 17th-century legend, the king wanted to know his wife's secrets, but Father John dutifully refused to tell. He was tortured and eventually killed by being tossed off the bridge. When he hit the water, five stars appeared. The shiny plaque at the base of the statue depicts the heave-ho. Devout pilgrims—from Mexico and Moravia alike—touch the engraving to

make a wish come true. You get only one chance in life for this wish, so think carefully before you touch the saint. Notice the date on the inscription: This oldest statue on the bridge was unveiled in 1683, on the supposed 300th anniversary of the martyr's death. You'll find statues like this one on squares and bridges throughout the country. The actual spot of the much-talked about heave-ho is a few steps farther away from the castle—find the five points of the Orthodox cross between two statues on the bridge railing.

Most of the other Charles Bridge statues date from the late 1600s and early 1700s. Today half of them are replicas—the originals are in city museums, out of the polluted air.

At the far end of Charles Bridge, you reach the **Little Quarter.** For sights in this neighborhood, see page 104.

Prague's Jewish Quarter

Jewish Quarter (Josefov)

Prague's Jewish Quarter neighborhood and its well-presented, profoundly moving museum tell the story of this region's Jews. For me, this is the most interesting collection of Jewish sights in Europe, well worth ▲▲▲. The Jewish Quarter is an easy walk from Old Town Square, up delightful Pařížská street (next to the green-domed Church of St. Nicholas).

As the Nazis decimated Jewish communities in the region, Prague's Jews were allowed to collect and archive their treasures here. While the archivists were ultimately killed in concentration camps, their work survives. Seven sights scattered over a three-block area make up the tourists' Jewish Quarter. Six of the sights—all except the Old-New Synagogue—are called "The Museum" and are covered by one admission ticket. Your ticket comes with a map locating the sights and listing admission appointments—the times you'll be let in if it's very busy. (Ignore the times unless it's really crowded.) You'll notice plenty of security (stepped up since 9/11).

Cost, Hours, Tours: To visit all seven sights, you'll pay 500 Kč (300 Kč for the six sights that make up The Museum, plus 200 Kč for the Old-New Synagogue; all sights open Sun–Fri April–Oct 9:00–18:00 , Nov–March 9:00–16:30, closed Sat—the Jewish Sabbath—and on Jewish holidays). Each sight is thoroughly and thoughtfully described in English, making a guided tour unnecessary for most visitors. Occasional guided walks in English start at the Maisel Synagogue (50 Kč, 3 hours, tel. 222-317-191).

Cemetery: The Old Jewish Cemetery—with its tightly packed tombstones—is, for many, the most evocative part of the experience. Unfortunately, there's no ticket just to see the cemetery, and they've closed off most free viewpoints into the cemetery. If the 300-Kč museum ticket is too steep for you and you just want a free peek at the famous cemetery, climb the steps to the covered porch of the Ceremonial Hall (but don't rest your chin on the treacherous railing).

Planning Your Time: The most logical start (if you'll be seeing everything) is to buy your ticket at Pinkas Synagogue and visit this most powerful memorial of the museum complex first. From there, walk through the Old Jewish Cemetery, which leads to the Ceremonial Hall and Klaus Synagogue. After visiting those, head over to the Old-New Synagogue, have a coffee break (Pekařství bakery or Franz Kafka Café, both described on page 141, are nearby). Next, visit the museum-like Maisel Synagogue, and finally the Spanish Synagogue. (Note that Prague's fine Museum of Medieval Art in Bohemia and Central Europe, described on page 84, is only a few blocks from the Spanish Synagogue.)

Art Nouveau and the New Josefov: Going from sight to sight in the Jewish Quarter, you'll walk through perhaps Europe's finest Art Nouveau neighborhood. Make a point to enjoy the circa-1900 buildings with their marvelous trimmings and oh-wow entryways. While today's modern grid plan has replaced the higgledy-piggledy medieval streets of old, Široká ("Wide Street") was and remains the main street of the ghetto.

Pinkas Synagogue (Pinkasova Synagóga)—A site of Jewish worship for 400 years, today this synagogue is a poignant memorial to the victims of the Nazis. The walls are covered with the handwritten names of 77,297 Czech Jews who were sent from here to the gas chambers at Auschwitz and other camps. (As you ponder this sad sight, you'll hear the somber reading of the names alternating with a cantor singing the Psalms.) Hometowns are in gold and family names are in red, followed in black by the individual's first name, birthday, and last date known to be alive. Notice that families generally perished together. Extermination camps are listed on the east wall. Climb eight steps into the women's gallery. When the communists moved in, they closed the synagogue and erased virtually everything. With freedom, in 1989, the Pinkas Synagogue was reopened and the names were rewritten. (The names in poor condition near the ceiling are original.) Note that large tour groups may disturb this small memorial's compelling atmosphere between 10:00 and 12:00.

Prague's Jewish Heritage

The Jewish people from the Holy Land (today's Israel) were dispersed by the Romans 2,000 years ago. Over the centuries, their culture survived in enclaves throughout the world: "The

Torah was their sanctuary which no army could destroy." Jews first came to Prague in the 10th century. The Jewish Quarter's main intersection (Maiselova and Široká streets) was the meeting point of two medieval trade routes.

During the Crusades in the 12th century, the pope declared that Jews and Christians should not live together. Jews had to wear yellow badges, and their quarter was walled in. It became a ghetto. In the 16th and 17th centuries, Prague had one of the biggest ghettos in Europe, with 11,000 inhabitants. Within its six gates, Prague's Jewish Quarter was a gaggle of 200 wooden buildings. It was said that "Jews nested rather than dwelled."

The "outcasts" of Christianity relied mainly on profits from money-lending (forbidden to Christians) and community solidarity to survive. While their money bought them protection (the kings highly taxed Jewish communities), it was often also a curse. Throughout Europe, when times got tough and Christian debts to the Jewish community mounted, entire Jewish communities were evicted or killed.

In the 1780s, Emperor Josef II, motivated more by economic concerns than philanthropy, eased much of the discrimination against Jews. In 1848, the Jewish Quarter's walls were torn down, and the neighborhood—named Josefov in honor of the emperor who provided this small measure of tolerance—was incorporated as a district of Old Town.

In 1897, ramshackle Josefov was razed and replaced by a new modern town—the original 31 streets and 220 buildings became 10 streets and 83 buildings. This is what you'll see today: an attractive neighborhood of pretty, mostly Art Nouveau buildings, with a few surviving historic Jewish structures. By the 1930s, Prague's Jewish community was hugely successful. But of the 120,000 Jews living in the area in 1939, just 10,000 survived the Holocaust to see liberation in 1945. Today only a few thousand Jews remain in Prague...but the legacy of their ancestors lives on.

Upstairs is the **Terezín Children's Art Exhibit** (very well-described in English), displaying art drawn by Jewish children who were imprisoned at Terezín Concentration Camp and later perished. Terezín makes an emotionally moving day trip from Prague (get details from TI).

Old Jewish Cemetery (Starý Židovský Hřbitov)—From the Pinkas Synagogue, you enter one of the most wistful scenes in

Europe—Prague's Old Jewish Cemetery. As you wander among 12,000 evocative tombstones, remember that from 1439 until 1787, this was the only burial ground allowed for the Jews of Prague. Because of limited space, the Jewish belief that the body should not be moved once buried, and the sheer number of graves, tombs were piled atop each other. With its many layers, the cemetery became a small plateau. And as things settled over time, the tombstones got crooked. The Hebrew word for cemetery means "House of Life." Many Jews believe that death is the gateway into the next world. Pebbles on the tombstones are "flowers of the desert," reminiscent of the old days when rocks were placed upon the sand gravesite to keep the body covered. Wedged under some of the pebbles are scraps of paper containing prayers.

Ceremonial Hall (Obřadní Síň)—Leaving the cemetery, you'll find a Neo-Romanesque mortuary house built in 1911 for the purification of the dead (on left). It's filled with a worthwhile exhibition, described in English, on Jewish medicine, death, and burial traditions. A series of crude but instructive paintings (hanging on walls throughout the house) show how the "burial brotherhood" took care of the ill and buried the dead. As all are equal before God, the rich and poor alike were buried in embroidered linen shrouds similar to the one you'll see on display.

Klaus Synagogue (Klauzová Synagóga)— This 17th-century synagogue (also near the cemetery exit) is the final wing of a museum devoted to Jewish religious practices. Exhibits on the ground floor explain the Jewish calendar of festivals. The central case displays a Torah (the first five books of the Bible) and solid silver pointers used when reading—necessary since the Torah is not to be touched. Upstairs is an exhibit on the rituals of Jewish life (circumcision, bar and bat mitzvah, weddings, kosher eating, and so on).

Old-New Synagogue (Staronová Synagóga)—For more than 700 years, this has been the most important synagogue and the central building in Josefov. Standing like a bomb-hardened bunker, it feels like it has survived plenty of hard times. Stairs take you down to the street level of the 13th century and into the Gothic interior. Built in 1270, it's the oldest synagogue in Eastern Europe (separate 200-Kč admission includes worthwhile 10-minute tour—ask about it, Sun–Thu 9:30–18:00, Fri 9:30–17:00, closed Sat). Snare an attendant who likely loves to show visitors around. The steep admission keeps many away, but even if you decide not to pay, you can see the exterior and a bit of the interior. (Go ahead...pop in and crane your cheapskate neck.)

The lobby (down the stairs, where you show your ticket) has two fortified old lockers—in which the most heavily taxed community in medieval Prague stored its money in anticipation of the taxman's arrival. As 13th-century Jews were not allowed to build, the synagogue was erected by Christians (who also built the St. Agnes Convent nearby). The builders were good at four-ribbed

vaulting, but since that resulted in a cross, it wouldn't work for a synagogue. Instead, they made the ceiling using clumsy five-ribbed vaulting.

The interior is pure 1300s. The Shrine of the Ark in front is the focus of worship. The holiest place in the synagogue, it holds the sacred scrolls of the Torah. The old rabbi's chair to the right remains empty (notice the thin black chain) out of respect. The red banner is a copy of the one the Jewish community carried through town during medieval parades. Notice the yellow-pointed hat within the Star of David (on the banner), which the pope ordered all Jewish men to wear in 1215. Twelve is a popular number (e.g., windows) because it symbolizes the 12 tribes of Israel. The horizontal slit-like windows are an 18th-century addition, allowing women to view the male-only services.

Maisel Synagogue (Maiselova Synagóga)—This synagogue was built as a private place of worship for the Maisel family during the 16th-century Golden Age of Prague's Jews. Maisel, the financier of the Hapsburg king, had lots of money. The synagogue's interior is decorated Neo-Gothic. In World War II, it served as a warehouse for the accumulated treasures of decimated Jewish communities that Hitler planned to use for his "Museum of the Extinct Jewish Race." The one-room exhibit shows a thousand years of Jewish history in Bohemia and Moravia. Well-explained in English, topics include the origin of the Star of David, Jewish mysticism, discrimination, and the creation of Prague's ghetto. Notice the eastern wall, with the holy ark containing the scroll of the Torah. The central case shows the silver ornamental Torah crowns that capped the scroll.

Spanish Synagogue (Španělská Synagóga)—Jewish history continues through the 18th, 19th, and tumultuous 20th centuries in this ornate, Moorish-style synagogue built in the 1800s. The upstairs is particularly intriguing, with circa-1900 photos of Josefov, an exhibit on the fascinating story of this museum and its relationship with the Nazi regime, and life in Terezín. The Winter Synagogue (also upstairs) shows a trove of silver worship aids gathered from depopulated Jewish neighborhoods in the countryside in the early 1940s, and gives a sense of what the Nazis stockpiled.

The New Town (Nové Město)

Enough of medieval Prague—let's leap into the modern era. The New Town, with Wenceslas Square as its focal point, is today's urban Prague. This part of the city offers bustling boulevards and interesting neighborhoods. The New Town is the best place to view Prague's remarkable Art Nouveau art and architecture and to learn more about its recent communist past.

Wenceslas Square (Václavské Náměstí)

More a broad boulevard than a square (until recently, trams rattled up and down its parklike median strip), this ▲▲ city landmark is named for King Wenceslas—featured both on the 20-Kč coin and the equestrian statue that stands at the top of the boulevard. Wenceslas Square (Václavské Náměstí) functions as a stage for modern Czech history: The creation of the Czechoslovak state was celebrated here in 1918; in 1968, the Soviets put down huge popular demonstrations here; and, in 1989, more than 300,000 Czechs and Slovaks converged here to claim their freedom.

• *Start near the Wenceslas statue at the top (Metro: Muzeum). Look to the building crowning the top of the square.*

National Museum (Národní Muzeum): While its collection is dull, this building offers a powerful view, and the interior is richly decorated in the Czech Revival Neo-Renaissance style that heralded the 19th-century rebirth of the Czech nation. The light-colored patches in the museum's columns fill holes where Soviet bullets hit during the crackdown against the 1968 "Prague Spring" uprising. Lowly masons—defying their communist bosses, who wanted the

Prague's New Town

1. Grand Hotel Evropa
2. Lucerna Gallery
3. Franciscan Garden
4. Museum of Communism
5. Dvořák Museum
6. State Opera
7. Grand Café Slavia

damage to be forgotten—showed their Czech spirit by intentionally mismatching their patches (80 Kč, daily May–Sept 10:00–18:00, Oct–April 9:00–17:00, halls of Czech fossils and animals).

• *To the left of the National Museum (as you face it) is an ugly...*

Communist-Era Building: This housed the rubber-stamp Parliament back when they voted with Moscow. A Social Realist statue showing triumphant work- ers still stands at its base. It's now home to Radio Free Europe. After communism fell, RFE lost its funding and could no longer afford its Munich headquarters. In gratitude for its broadcasts—which kept the people of Eastern Europe in touch with real news—the cur- rent Czech government now rents the building to RFE for 1 Kč a year. (As RFE energetically beams its American message deep into Islam from here, it has been threatened recently by Al-Qaeda, and a plan is underway to move it to an easier-to-defend locale in the suburbs.)

• *In front of the National Museum is the equestrian...*

Statue of St. Wenceslas: Wenceslas (Václav) is the "good king" of Christmas-carol fame. He was the wise and benevolent 10th-century duke of Bohemia. A rare example of a well-educated and liter- ate ruler, King Wenceslas I was cred- ited by his people for Christianizing his nation and lifting up the culture. He astutely allied the Czechs with Saxony, rather than Bavaria, giving the Czechs a vote when the Holy Roman Emperor was selected (and therefore more political clout). After his murder in 929, Wenceslas was canonized as a saint. He became a symbol of Czech nationalism and statehood—and remains an icon of Czech unity whenever the nation has to rally. Supposedly, when the Czechs face their darkest hour, Wenceslas will come riding out of Blaník Mountain (east of Prague) with an army of knights to rescue the nation. In 1620, when Austria stripped Czechs of their independence, many people went to Blaník Mountain to see whether it had opened up. They did the same at other critical points in their history (in 1938, 1948, and 1968)—but Wenceslas never emerged. Although now safely part of NATO and the EU, Czechs remain pessimistic: If Wenceslas hasn't come out yet, the worst times must still lie ahead.

Study the statue. Wenceslas is surrounded by the four other Czech patron saints. Notice the focus on books. A small nation without great military power, the Czech Republic chose national heroes who enriched the culture by thinking, rather than fighting. This statue is a popular meeting point. Locals say, "I'll see you under the horse's...tail."

• *Thirty yards below the big horse is a small garden with a low-key...*

Memorial: This commemorates victims of communism, such as Jan Palach. In 1969, a group of patriots decided that an act of self-immolation would stoke the fires of independence. Jan Palach, a philosophy student who loved life, but wanted it with freedom, set himself on fire on the steps of the National Museum for the cause of Czech independence and died a few days later in a hospital ward. Czechs are keen on anniversaries. Huge demonstrations swept the city on the 20th anniversary of Palach's death. These led, 10 months later, to the overthrow of the Czech communist government in 1989.

This grand square is a gallery of modern **architectural styles.** As you wander downhill, notice the fun mix, all post-1850: Romantic Neo-Gothic, Neo-Renaissance, and Neo-Baroque from the 19th century; Art Nouveau from around 1900; ugly Functionalism from the mid-20th century (the "form follows function" and "ornamentation is a crime" answer to Art Nouveau); Stalin Gothic from the 1950s "communist epoch" (a good example is the Jalta building, halfway downhill on the right); and the glass-and-steel buildings of the 1970s.

• *Walk a couple of blocks downhill through the real people of Prague (not tourists) to **Grand Hotel Evropa**, with its hard-to-miss, dazzling Art Nouveau exterior and plush café interior full of tourists. Stop for a moment to ponder the events of...*

November of 1989: This huge square was filled every evening with more than 300,000 ecstatic Czechs and Slovaks believing freedom was at hand. Assembled on the balcony of the building opposite Grand Hotel Evropa (look for the *Marks & Spencer* sign) were a priest, a rock star (famous for his unconventional style, which constantly unnerved the regime), Alexander Dubček (hero of the 1968 revolt), and Václav Havel (the charismatic playwright, newly released from prison, who was every freedom-loving Czech's Mandela). Through a sound system provided by the rock star, Havel's voice boomed over the gathered masses, announcing the resignation of the politburo and saying that the Republic of Czechoslovakia's freedom was imminent. Picture that cold November evening, with thousands of Czechs jingling their keychains in solidarity, chanting at the government, "It's time to go now!" (To quell this revolt, government tanks could have given it the Tiananmen Square treatment—which spilled lots of patriotic blood in China just six months earlier. Locals believe Gorbachev must have made a phone call recommending that blood not be shed over this.) For more on the events leading up to this climactic rally, see "Národní Třída and the Velvet Revolution" on page 101.

• *Immediately opposite Grand Hotel Evropa is the Lucerna Gallery (use entry marked* Palác Rokoko *and walk straight in).*

Lucerna Gallery: This grand mall retains some of its Art Deco glamour from the 1930s, with shops, theaters, a ballroom in the basement, and the fine Lucerna Café upstairs. You'll see a sculpture—called *Wenceslas Riding an Upside-Down Horse*—hanging like a swing from a glass dome. David Černý, who created the statue in 1999, is the Czech Republic's most original contemporary artist. Always aspiring to provoke controversy, Černý has painted a menacing Russian tank pink, attached crawling babies to the rocket-like Žižkov TV tower, defecated inside the National Gallery to protest the policies of its director, and sunk a shark-like Saddam Hussein inside an aquarium for a 2005 exhibition. Inside are also a **Ticketpro box office** (with all available tickets, daily 9:30–18:00) and a lavish 1930s Prague cinema (under the upside-down horse, shows artsy films in Czech with English subtitles, or vice versa, 110 Kč).

Directly across busy Vodičkova street (with a handy tram stop) is the Světozor mall. Inside you'll find the **World of Fruit Bar Světozor;** it's every local's favorite ice-cream joint. True to its name, the bar tops its ice cream with every variety of fruit. They sell cakes and milkshakes, too. Ask at the counter for an English menu.

• *Farther down the mall on the left is the entrance to the peaceful...*

Franciscan Garden (Františkánská Zahrada): Its white benches and spreading rosebushes are a universe away from the fast beat of the city that throbs behind the buildings surrounding the garden.

Back on Wenceslas Square, if you're in the mood for a mellow hippie teahouse, consider a break at **Dobrá Čajovna** ("Good Teahouse") near the bottom of the square (#14—see page 143). Or, if you'd like an old-time wine bar, pop into the plain **Šenk Vrbovec** (nearby at #10); it comes with a whiff of the communist days, embracing the faintest bits of genteel culture from an age when refinement was sacrificed for the good of the working class.

They serve traditional drinks, Czech keg wine, Moravian wines (listed on blackboard outside), *becherovka* (the 13-herb liqueur), and—only in autumn—*burčák* (young wine that tastes like grape juice halfway to wine).

The bottom of Wenceslas Square is called **Můstek,** which means "Bridge"; a bridge used to cross a moat here, allowing entrance into the Old Town (you can still see the original Old Town entrance down in the Metro station).

• *Running to the right from the bottom of Wenceslas Square is the street called...*

Na Příkopě: Meaning "On the Moat," this busy boulevard follows the line of the Old Town wall, leading to one of the wall's former gates, the Powder Tower. Along the way, it passes the Museum of Communism (see page 101) and a couple of Art Nouveau sights. City tour buses (see page 74) leave from along this street, which offers plenty of shopping temptations (such as these malls: Slovanský Dům at Na Příkopě 22, and Černá Růže at Na Příkopě 12, next door to Mosers, with a crystal showroom upstairs).

Na Příkopě: Art Nouveau Prague

Stroll up Na Příkopě to take in two of Prague's best Art Nouveau sights. The first one is on the street called Panská (turn right up the first street you reach as you walk up Na Příkopě from Wenceslas Square); the second is two blocks farther up Na Příkopě, next to the big, Gothic Powder Tower.

▲▲**Mucha Museum**—This is one of Europe's most enjoyable little museums. I find the art of Alfons Mucha (MOO-kah, 1860–1939) insistently likeable. See the crucifixion scene he painted as an eight-year-old boy. Read how this popular Czech artist's posters, filled with Czech symbols and expressing his people's ideals and aspirations, were patriotic banners that aroused the national spirit. And check out the photographs of his models. With the help of this abundant supply of slinky models, Mucha was a founding father of the Art Nouveau movement. Partly overseen by Mucha's grandson, the museum is two blocks off Wenceslas Square and wonderfully displayed on one comfortable floor (120 Kč, daily 10:00–18:00, well-described in English, Panská 7, tel. 224-233-355, www.mucha.cz). The included 30-minute video is definitely worthwhile (in English, generally at :15 and :45 past the hour—ask for the starting time); it describes the main project of Mucha's life—the *Slavic Epic,* now on display in Moravský Krumlov (a small town in the eastern Czech Republic).

• *Coming back to Na Příkopě and continuing toward the Powder Tower, notice the Neo-Renaissance* **Živnostenská Banka** *building on the corner of Nekázanka. It houses a modern bank with classy circa-1900 ambience*

Art Nouveau

Prague is the best Art Nouveau town in Europe, with fun-loving facades gracing streets all over town. Art Nouveau, born in Paris, is "nouveau" because it wasn't inspired by Rome. It's neo-nothing...a fresh answer to all the revival styles of the later 19th century and an organic response to the Eiffel Tower art of the Industrial Age. The style liberated the artist in each architect. Notice the unique curves and motifs on each Art Nouveau facade, which express originality. Artists such as Alfons Mucha believed that the style should include all facets of daily life. They designed everything from buildings and furniture to typefaces and cigarette packs.

Prague's three top Art Nouveau architects are Jan Koula, Josef Fanta, and Osvald Polivka, whose last name means "soup" in Czech (think "Cola, Fanta, and Soup"—easy to remember and impress your local friends).

Prague's Art Nouveau highlights include the facades lining the streets of the Jewish Quarter, the Mucha window in St. Vitus Cathedral, and Grand Hotel Evropa on Wenceslas Square. The top two sights for Art Nouveau fans are the Mucha Museum and the Municipal House.

(enter and peek into the main hall upstairs).

At the end of Na Příkopě, you'll arrive at the...

▲▲**Municipal House (Obecní Dům)**—The Municipal House is the "pearl of Czech Art Nouveau." Financed by cultural and artistic leaders, it was built (1905–1911) as a ceremonial palace to reinforce the self-awareness of the Czech nation. It features Prague's largest concert hall, a recommended Art Nouveau café (Kavárna Obecní Dům, see page 143), and two other restaurants. Pop in and wander around the lobby of the concert hall. Walk through to the ticket office on the ground floor. For the best look, including impressive

halls and murals you won't otherwise see, take one of the regular hour-long **tours** (open daily 10:00–18:00; tours—150 Kč, generally at 10:15, 12:00, 14:00, and 16:00, in English 2/day, buy ticket from ground-floor shop where tour departs; tel. 222-002-101).

Standing in front of the Municipal House, you can survey four different styles of architecture. First, enjoy the pure Art Nouveau of the Municipal House itself. Featuring a goddess-like Praha presiding over a land of peace and high culture, the *Homage to Prague* mosaic on the building's striking facade stoked cultural pride and nationalist sentiment. Across the street, the classical fixer-upper from 1815 was the customs house (currently being renovated). The stark national bank building (Česká Národní Banka) is textbook Functionalism from the 1930s. Across the square, former barracks are making way for Prague's biggest shopping mall, which promises none of its neighbors' elegance.

Powder Tower: The big, black Powder Tower (not worth touring inside) was the Gothic gate of the town wall, built to house the city's gunpowder. The decoration on the tower, portraying Czech kings, is the best 15th-century sculpture in town. If you go through the tower, you'll reach Celetná street, which leads past a few sights (described on page 85) to the Old Town Square.

Národní Třída: Communist Prague

From Můstek at the bottom of Wenceslas Square, you can head west on Národní Třída (in the opposite direction from Na Příkopě and the Art Nouveau sights) for an interesting stroll through urban Prague to the National Theatre and the Vltava River. But first, consider dropping into the Museum of Communism, a few steps down Na Příkopě (on the right).

▲▲**Museum of Communism**—This museum traces the story of communism in Prague: the origins, dream, reality, and nightmare; the cult of personality; and finally, the Velvet Revolution (see sidebar on page 102). Along the way it gives a fascinating review of the Czech Republic's 40-year stint with Soviet economics, "in all its dreariness and puffed-up glory." You'll find propaganda posters, busts of communist all-stars (Marx, Lenin, Stalin), and a photograph of the massive stone Stalin that overlooked Prague until 1962. Slices of communist life are re-created here, from a bland store counter to a typical classroom (with textbooks using Russia's Cyrillic alphabet—no longer studied here—and a poem on the chalkboard extolling the virtues of the tractor). Don't miss the Jan Palach exhibit and the 20-minute video (plays continuously, English subtitles) showing how the Czech people chafed under the big red yoke from the 1950s through 1989 (180 Kč, daily 9:00–21:00, Na Příkopě 10, above a McDonald's and next to a casino—Lenin is turning over in his grave, tel. 224-212-966, www.museumofcommunism.com).

• *Now head for the river (with your back to Wenceslas Square, go left down 28 Října to Národní Třída). Along the way, Národní Třída has a story to tell.*

Národní Třída and the Velvet Revolution—Národní Třída ("National Street") is where you feel the pulse of the modern city. The street, which connects Wenceslas Square with the National

The Velvet Revolution of 1989

On the afternoon of November 17, 1989, 30,000 students gathered in Prague's New Town to commemorate the 50th anniversary of the suppression of student protests by the Nazis, which had led to the closing of Czech universities through the end of World War II. The 1989 demonstration—initially planned by the Communist Youth as a celebration of the communist victory over fascism—spontaneously turned into a protest *against* the communist regime. "You are just like the Nazis!" shouted the students. The demonstration was planned to end in the National Cemetery at Vyšehrad (the hill just south of the New Town). But when the planned events concluded in Vyšehrad, the students decided to march on towards Wenceslas Square to make history.

As they worked their way north along the Vltava River towards the New Town's main square, the students were careful to keep their demonstration peaceful. Any hint of violence, the demonstrators knew, would incite brutal police retaliation. In fact, as the evening went on, the absence of police became conspicuous. (In the 1980s, the police never missed a chance to participate in any demonstration...preferably outnumbering the demonstrators). At about 20:00, as the students marched down this very stretch of street towards Wenceslas Square, three rows of policemen suddenly blocked the demonstration at the corner of Národní and Spálená streets. A few minutes later, military vehicles with fences on their bumpers (having crossed the bridge by the National Theatre) appeared behind the marching students. This new set of cops compressed the demonstrators into the stretch of Národní Třída between Voršilská and Spálená. The end of Mikulandská street was also blocked, and policemen were hiding inside every house entry. The students were trapped.

At 21:30, the "Red Hats" (a special anti-riot commando force known for its brutality) arrived. The Red Hats lined up on both sides of this corridor. To get out, the trapped students had to run through the passageway as they were beaten from the left and right. Police trucks ferried captured students around the corner to the headquarters of the secret police (on Bartolomějská) for interrogation.

The next day, university students throughout Czechoslovakia decided to strike. Actors from theaters in Prague and Bratislava joined the student protest. Two days later, the students' parents—shocked by the attacks on their children—marched into Wenceslas Square. The wave of peaceful demonstrations sparked by the events of November 17, 1989, ended later that year on December 29 with the election of Václav Havel as the president of a free Czechoslovakia.

Theatre and the river, is a busy thoroughfare running through the heart of urban Prague. In 1989, this unassuming boulevard played host to the first salvo of a Velvet Revolution that would topple the communist regime.

Make your way down Národní Třída until you hit the tram tracks (just beyond the Tesco department store). On the left, look

for the photo of Bill Clinton playing saxophone, with Václav Havel on the side (this is the entrance to Reduta, Prague's best jazz club; next door are two recommended eateries, Café Louvre and Le Patio—see page 140). Just beyond that, you'll come to a short corridor with white arches. Inside this arcade is a simple memorial to the hundreds of students injured here by the police on November 17, 1989 (see sidebar).

Along the Vltava River

I've listed these sights from north to south, beginning at the grand, Neo-Renaissance National Theatre, which is five blocks south of Charles Bridge and stands along the riverbank at the end of Národní Třída.

National Theatre (Národní Divadlo)—Opened in 1883 with Smetana's opera *Libuše*, this theater was the first truly Czech venue in Prague. From the very start, it was nicknamed the "Cradle of Czech Culture." The building is a key symbol of the Czech national revival that began in the late 18th century. In 1800, "Prag" was predominantly German. The Industrial Revolution brought Czechs from the countryside into the city, their new urban identity defined by patriotic teachers and priests. By 1883, most of the city spoke Czech, and the opening of this theater represented the birth of the modern Czech nation. It remains an important national icon: The state annually pours more subsidies into this theater than into all of Czech film production. It's the most beautiful venue in town for opera or ballet, often with world-class singers (see page 124).

Next door (just inland, on Národní Třída) is the boxy, glassy facade of the **Nová Scéna.** This "New National Theatre" building, dating from 1983 (the 100th anniversary of the original National Theatre building), reflects the bold and stark communist aesthetic. The Nová Scéna hosts Laterna Magica Black Light Theater performances, among other events (see page 124).

Across the street from the National Theatre is the former haunt of Prague's intelligentsia, **Grand Café Slavia,** a Viennese-style coffeehouse that makes a fine stop for a meal or drink with a view of the river (see page 142).

•Just south of the National Theatre in the Vltava are...

Prague's Islands—From the National Theatre, the Legions' Bridge (Most Legií) leads across the island called **Střelecký Ostrov.** Covered with chestnut trees, this island boasts Prague's best beach (on the sandy tip that points north to Charles Bridge). You might see a fisherman pulling out trout from a river that's now much cleaner than it used to be. Bring a swimsuit and take a dip just a stone's throw from Europe's most beloved bridge. In summer, the island hosts open-air movies (most in English or with English subtitles, nightly mid-July–early Sept at around 21:00, www.strelak.cz).

In the mood for boating instead of swimming? On the next island down, **Slovanský Ostrov,** you can rent a paddleboat (40 Kč/hr for rowboats, 60 Kč/hr for paddleboats, bring a picture ID as deposit). A lazy hour paddling around Střelecky Ostrov, or just floating sleepily in the middle of the river surrounded by this great city's architectural splendor, is a delightful experience on a sunny day. It's cheap, easy, fun—and it's good for you.

• A 10-minute walk (or one stop on tram #17) from the National Theatre, beyond the islands, is Jirásek Bridge (Jiráskův Most), where you'll find the...

Dancing House (Tančící Dům)—If ever a building could get your toes tapping, it would be this one, nick-named "Fred and Ginger" by American architecture buffs. This metallic samba is the work of Frank Gehry (who designed the equally striking Guggenheim Museum in Bilbao, Spain, and Seattle's Experience Music Project). Eight-legged Ginger's wispy dress and Fred's metal mesh head are easy to spot. The building's top-floor restaurant, La Perle de Prague, is a fine place for a fancy French meal (VIPs often eat and drink here, reservation needed even to get into the elevator, tel. 221-984-160).

The Little Quarter (Malá Strana)

This charming neighborhood, huddled under the castle on the west bank of the river, is low on blockbuster sights but high on ambience. The most enjoyable approach from the Old Town is across Charles Bridge. From the end of the bridge (TI in tower), Mostecká street leads two blocks up to Little Quarter Square (Malostranské Náměstí) and the huge Church of St. Nicholas. But before you head up there, consider a detour to Kampa Island (all described below).

Prague's Little Quarter

Legend:

⌐ – VIEW

★ LITTLE QUARTER SQUARE

Ⓜ – METRO STOP

Ⓣ – TRAM #22 + #23 STOPS

200 YARDS

200 METERS

1. Old Mill Water Wheel
2. Lennon Wall
3. Church of St. Nicholas
4. Wallenstein Palace
5. Wallenstein Garden Entrance
6. Vrtba Garden
7. Church of St. Mary the Victorious
8. Monument to Victims of Communism Who Survived
9. Hungry Wall
10. Petřín Tower & Museum of Jára Cimrman
11. Mirror Maze
12. US Embassy

Between Charles Bridge and Little Quarter Square

Kampa Island—One hundred yards before the castle end of the Charles Bridge, stairs on the left lead down to the main square of

Kampa Island (mostly created from the rubble of the Little Quarter, which was destroyed in a 1540 fire). The island features relaxing pubs, a breezy park, hippies, lovers, a fine contemporary art gallery, and river access. From the main square, Hroznová lane (on the right)

leads to a bridge. Behind the old mill wheel, notice the high-water marks from the flood of 2002. The water wheel is the last survivor of many that once lined the canal here. Each mill once had its own protective water spirit *(vodník)*. Today only one wheel—and one spirit (Mr. Kabourek)—remains.

• *Fifty yards beyond the bridge (on the right, under the trees) is the...*

Lennon Wall (Lennonova Zeď)—While Lenin's ideas hung like a water-soaked trench coat upon the Czech people, the rock singer John Lennon's ideas gave many locals hope and a vision. When Lennon was killed in 1980, a memorial wall covered with graffiti spontaneously appeared. Night after night, the police would paint over the "All You Need Is Love" and "Imagine" graffiti. And day

after day, it would reappear. Until independence came in 1989, travelers, freedom-lovers, and local hippies gathered here. Silly as it might seem, this wall is remembered as a place that gave hope to locals craving freedom. Even today, while the tension and danger associated with this wall is gone, people come here to imagine. *"John žije"* is Czech for "John lives."

• *From here, you can continue up to Little Quarter Square.*

On or near Little Quarter Square

The focal point of this neighborhood, Little Quarter Square (Malostranské Náměstí) is dominated by the huge Church of St. Nicholas. Note that there's a handy Via Musica ticket office across from the church.

Church of St. Nicholas (Kostel Sv. Mikuláše)—When the Jesuits came to Prague, they found the perfect piece of real estate for their church and its associated school—right on Little Quarter Square.

The church (built 1703–1760) is the best example of High Baroque in town. It's giddy with curves and illusions. The altar features a lavish gold-plated Nicholas flanked by the two top Jesuits: the founder, St. Ignatius Loyola and his missionary follower, St. Francis Xavier. Climb up the **gallery** through the staircase in the left transept for a close-up look at a collection of large canvases and illusionary frescoes by Karel Škréta, the greatest Czech Baroque painter. Notice that at first glance, the canvases are utterly dark. But as sunbeams shine through the window, various parts of the painting brighten up. Like a looking glass, it reflects the light, creating a play of light and darkness. This painting technique reflects a central Baroque belief: The world is full of darkness, and the only hope that makes it come alive comes from God. The church walls seem to nearly fuse with the sky, suggesting that happenings on earth are closely connected to heaven. Find St. Nick with his bishop's miter in the center of the ceiling, on his way to heaven (60 Kč, church open daily 9:00–17:00, opens at 8:30 for prayer).

Tower Climb: For a good look at the city and the church's 250-foot dome, climb 215 steps up the bell tower (50 Kč, April–Oct daily 10:00–18:00, closed Nov–March, tower entrance is outside the right transept).

Concerts: The church is also an evening concert venue; tickets are generally on sale at the door (450 Kč, generally nightly except Tue at 18:00, www.psalterium.cz).

• *From here, you can hike 10 minutes uphill to the castle (and five more minutes to the Strahov Monastery). For information on these sights, see "The Castle Quarter" on page 109. If you're walking up to the castle, consider going via...*

Nerudova Street—This steep, cobbled street, leading from Little Quarter Square to the castle, is named for Jan Neruda, a gifted 19th-century journalist (and somewhat less talented fiction writer). It's lined with old buildings still sporting the characteristic doorway signs (e.g., the lion, three violinists, house of the golden suns) that once served as street addresses. The surviving signs are carefully restored and protected by law. They represent the family name, the occupation, or the various passions of the people who once inhabited the houses. (If you were to replace your house number with a symbol, what would it be?) In 1777, in order to collect taxes more effectively, Hapsburg empress Maria Theresa decreed that numbers be used instead of these quaint house names. This neighborhood is filled with old noble palaces, now generally used as foreign embassies and offices of the Czech parliament.

South of Little Quarter Square, to Petřín Hill

Karmelitská street, leading south (along the tram tracks) from Little Quarter Square, is home to these sights.

Church of St. Mary the Victorious (Kostel Panny Marie Vítězné)—This otherwise ordinary Carmelite church displays Prague's most worshipped treasure, the Infant of Prague (Pražské Jezulátko). Kneel at the banister in front of the tiny, lost-in-gilded-Baroque altar, and find the prayer in your language (of the 13 in the folder).

Brought to Czech lands during the Hapsburg era by a Spanish noblewoman who came to marry a Czech nobleman, the Infant has become a focus of worship and miracle tales in Prague and Spanish-speaking countries. South Americans come on pilgrimage to Prague just to see this one statue. An exhibit upstairs shows tiny embroidered robes given to the Infant, including ones from Maria Theresa of Austria (1754) and Vietnam (1958), and a video showing a nun lovingly dressing the doll-like sculpture (free, Mon–Sat 9:30–17:30, Sun 13:00–17:00, English-language Mass Sun at 12:00, Karmelitská 9, www.pragjesu.com).

• *Continue a few more blocks down Karmelitská to the south end of the Little Quarter (where the street is called Újezd, roughly across the Legions' Bridge from the National Theatre). Here you find yourself at the base of...*

Petřín Hill—This hill, topped by a replica of the Eiffel Tower, features several unusual sights.

The figures walking down the steps in the hillside make up the **Monument to Victims of Communism Who Survived.** The monument's figures are gradually atrophied by the totalitarian regime. They do not die, but slowly disappear, one limb at a time. The statistics say it all: In Czechoslovakia alone, 205,486 people were imprisoned, 248 were executed, 4,500 died in prison, 327 were shot attempting to cross the border, and 170,938 left the country. To the left of the monument is the **Hungry Wall,** the 14th-century Charles IV's equivalent of FDR's work-for-food projects. On the right (50 yards away) is the base of a handy **funicular**—hop on to reach Petřín Tower (uses 20-Kč tram/Metro ticket, runs daily 8:00–22:00, every 10–15 min).

The summit of Petřín Hill is considered the best place in Prague to take your date for a romantic city view. Built for an exhibition in 1891, the 200-foot-tall **Petřín Tower** is a fifth the height of its Parisian big brother built two years earlier. Climbing the 400 steps rewards you with amazing views over the city. Local wives drag their men to Petřín Hill each May Day to reaffirm their love with a kiss under a blooming sour-cherry tree.

In the tower's basement is the funniest sight in Prague, the **Museum of Jára Cimrman, Genius Who Did Not Become Famous.** The museum traces Cimrman's (fictional) life, including pictures and English descriptions of the thinker's overlooked inventions (50 Kč includes tower and Cimrman museum, daily

10:00–22:00). For more on the mysterious Cimrman, see the side-bar on page 110.

The **mirror maze** next door is nothing special, but fun to quickly wander through since you're already here (50 Kč, daily 10:00–22:00).

The Castle Quarter (Hradčany)

Looming above Prague, dominating its skyline, is the Castle Quarter. Prague Castle and its surrounding sights are packed with Czech history as well as with tourists. In addition to the castle itself, I enjoy visiting the nearby Strahov Monastery—which has a fascinating old library and beautiful views over all of Prague.

Castle Square (Hradčanské Náměstí)—right in front of the castle gates—is at the center of this neighborhood. Stretching along the promontory away from the castle is a regal neighborhood that ends at the Strahov Monastery. Above the castle are the Royal Gardens, and below the castle are more gardens and lanes leading down to the Little Quarter.

Getting to Prague Castle

If you're not up for a hike, the tram offers a sweat-free ride up to the castle. Taxis are expensive, as they have to go the long way around (200 Kč).

By Foot: Begin in the Little Quarter, just across Charles Bridge from the Old Town. Hikers can follow the main cobbled road (Mostecká) from Charles Bridge to Little Quarter Square, marked by the huge, green-domed Church of St. Nicholas. (The nearest Metro stop is Malostranská, from which Valdštejnská street leads down to Little Quarter Square.) From Little Quarter Square, hike uphill along Nerudova street (described on page 107). After about 10 minutes, a steep lane on the right leads to the castle. (If you continue straight, Nerudova becomes Úvoz and climbs to the Strahov Monastery.)

By Tram: Trams #22 and #23 take you up to the castle. While you can catch the tram in various places, these three stops are particularly convenient: at the Národní Třída Metro stop (between Wenceslas Square and the National Theatre in the New Town); in front of the National Theatre (Národní Divadlo, on the riverbank in the New Town); and at Malostranská (the Metro stop in the Little Quarter). After rattling up the hill, these trams make three stops near the castle: Get off at **Královský Letohrádek** for the scenic approach to the castle (through the Royal Gardens—free entry, open April–Oct daily 10:00–18:00, closed Nov–March); or stay on one more stop to get off at **Pražský Hrad** (most direct but least interesting—simply walk along U Prašného Mostu over the bridge into the castle); or go yet one more stop to **Pohořelec** to

Jára Cimrman: When Optimists Should Be Shot

"I am such a complete atheist that I am afraid God will punish me." Such is the pithy wisdom of Jára Cimrman, the man overwhelmingly voted the "Greatest Czech of All Time" in a nationwide poll in 2005. Who is Jára Cimrman? A philosopher? An explorer? An inventor? He is all of these things, yes, and much more. Today a museum celebrates his life (see listing on page 108).

Born in the mid-19th century to a Czech tailor of Jewish descent and an Austrian actress, Cimrman studied in Vienna before starting off on his journeys around the world. He traversed the Atlantic by a steamboat he designed himself, taught drama to peasants in Peru, and drifted across the Arctic Sea on an iceberg. Other astounding feats soon followed. Cimrman was the first to come within 20 feet of the North Pole. He was the first to invent the light bulb (unfortunately, Edison beat him to the patent office by five minutes). It was he who suggested to the Americans the idea for a Panama Canal, though, as usual, he was never credited. Indeed, Cimrman surreptitiously advised many of the world's greats: Eiffel on his tower, Einstein on his theories of relativity, Chekhov on his plays. ("You can't just have *two* sisters," Cimrman told the playwright. "How about three?") In 1886, long before the world knew of Sartre or Camus, Cimrman was writing tracts such as *The Essence of the Existence*, which would become the foundation for his philosophy of "Cimrmanism," also known as "Non-Existentialism." (Its central premise: "Existence cannot not exist.")

This man of unmatched genius would have won the honor of "Greatest Czech of All Time" if not for the bureaucratic narrow-mindedness of the poll's sponsors, who had a single objection to Cimrman's candidacy: "He's not real." Jára Cimrman is the brainchild of two Czech humorists—Zdeněk Svěrák and Jiří Šebánek—who brought their patriotic Renaissance man to life in 1967 in a satirical radio play. So, even though Cimrman handily won the initial balloting in January, Czech TV officials—blatantly biased against his non-existentialism—refused to let him into the final rounds of the competition.

How should we interpret the fact that the Czechs would

visit the Strahov Monastery before hiking down to the castle (to get to the monastery from this tram stop, follow tram tracks uphill for 50 yards, enter fancy gate on left near red-brick wall, you'll see twin spires of monastery).

Tram Tips: When you're choosing which of the castle's three tram stops to get off at, consider the time of day. The castle is plagued with crowds. If visiting in the morning, use the Pražský Hrad tram stop for the quickest commute to the castle. Be at the rather choose a fictional character as their greatest countryman over any of their flesh-and-blood national heroes—say, Charles IV (the 14th-century Holy Roman Emperor who established Prague as the cultural and intellectual capital of Europe), Jan Hus (the 15th-century religious reformer who challenged the legitimacy of the Catholic Church), Comenius (the 17th-century educator and writer considered one of the fathers of modern education), or Martina Navrátilová (someone who plays a sport with bright green balls)? The more cynically inclined—many Czechs among them—might point out that the Czech people have largely stayed behind their mountains for the past millennia, with little interest in, or influence on, happenings elsewhere in the world. Perhaps Cimrman is so beloved because he embodies that most prickly of ironies: a Czech who was greater than all the world's greats, but who for some hiccup of chance has never been recognized for his achievements.

Personally, I like to think that the vote for Cimrman says something about the country's rousing enthusiasm for blowing raspberries in the face of authority. Throughout its history—from the times of the Czech kings who used crafty diplomacy to keep the German menace at bay, to the days of Jan Hus and his questioning of the very legitimacy of any ruler's power, to the flashes of anti-communist revolt that at last sparked the Velvet Revolution in 1989—the Czechs have maintained a healthy disrespect for those who would tell them what is best or how to live their lives. Other countries soberly choose their "Greatest" from musty tomes of history, but the Czechs won't play this silly game. Their vote for a fictional personage, says Cimrman's co-creator Svěrák, says two things about the Czech nation: "That it is skeptical about those who are major figures and those who are supposedly 'the Greatest.' And that the only certainty that has saved the nation many times throughout history is its humor."

Cimrman would agree. A man of greatness, he was always a bit skeptical of those who saw themselves as great, or who marched forward under the banner of greatness. As Cimrman liked to say, "There are moments when optimists should be shot."

door of St. Vitus Cathedral when it opens at 9:00 (because just 10–15 minutes later, it'll be swamped with tour groups). See the castle sights quickly, then move on to the Strahov Monastery. I'd avoid the castle entirely mid-morning, but by mid-afternoon, the tour groups are napping and the grounds are (relatively) uncrowded. If going in the afternoon, take the tram to the Pohořelec stop, see the Strahov Monastery, then wander down to the castle.

Prague's Castle Quarter

1. Castle Square & Plague Column
2. Schwarzenberg Palace
3. Archbishop's Palace
4. Sternberg Palace
5. Castle Gate
6. Tickets & Information
7. St. Vitus Cathedral
8. Old Royal Palace
9. Basilica of St. George
10. Golden Lane
11. Toy & Barbie Museum
12. Steps to Terraced Gardens
13. Royal Gardens
14. Royal Summer Palace
15. Loreta Church
16. Strahov Monastery & Library
17. Museum of Miniatures
18. Černín Palace
19. Klášterní Pivovar (Brewery)
20. Restaurace Nad Úvozem
21. Hostinec u Černého Vola Pub
22. Malý Buddha Veggie Rest.
23. Espresso Kajetánka
24. Na Baště Café

Ⓜ = Metro Stop
Ⓣ = Tram #22 + #23 Stops
⁻¡ = View

200 YARDS
200 METERS

Strahov Monastery and Library

Twin Baroque domes high above the castle mark the Strahov Monastery. Worth ▲, this complex is best reached from the Pohořelec stop on tram #22 or #23 (from the stop, go up the red-railed ramp and through the gate into the monastery grounds). If you're coming on foot from the Little Quarter, allow 15 minutes for the uphill hike. After seeing the monastery, hike down to the castle (a 5-min walk).

Monastery: The monastery (Strahovský Klášter Premonstrátů) had a booming economy of its own in its heyday, with vineyards and the biggest beer hall in town—still open. Its main church, dedicated to the Assumption of St. Mary, is an originally Romanesque structure decorated by the monks in textbook Baroque (usually closed, but look through the window inside the front door to see its interior).

Library: The adjacent library (Strahovská Knihovna) offers a peek at how enlightened thinkers in the 18th century influenced learning (80 Kč, daily 9:00–12:00 & 13:00–17:00). Cases in the library gift shop show off illuminated manuscripts (described in English). Some are in old Czech, but these are rare. Because the Enlightenment believed in the universality of knowledge, there was little place for vernaculars—therefore, few books here are in the Czech language. Two rooms (seen only from the door) are filled with 10th- to 17th-century books under elaborately painted ceilings. The theme of the first and bigger hall is philosophy, with the history of man's pursuit of knowledge painted on the ceiling. The other hall focuses on theology. Notice the gilded locked case containing the *libri prohibiti* (prohibited books) at the end of the room. Only the abbot had the key, and you had to have his blessing to read these books—by writers such as Nicolas Copernicus and Jan Hus, even including the French encyclopedia. As the Age of Enlightenment began to take hold in Europe at the end of the 18th century, monasteries still controlled the books. The hallway connecting these two library rooms was filled with cases illustrating the new practical approach to natural sciences. Find the baby dodo bird (which became extinct in the 17th century).

Nearby Views: Just downhill from the monastery, past the venerable linden trees (a symbol of the Czech people) and through the gate, the views from the **monastery garden** are among the best in Prague. From the public perch below the tables, you can see St. Vitus Cathedral (the heart of the castle complex), the green dome of the Church of St. Nicholas (marking the center of the Little Quarter), the two dark towers fortifying both ends of Charles Bridge, and the fanciful black spires of the Týn Church (marking the Old Town Square). On the horizon is the modern **Žižkov TV and radio tower** (conveniently marking the liveliest nightlife zone in town). Begun in the 1980s, it was meant to jam Radio Free Europe's broadcast from Munich. By the time it was finished, communism was dead and Radio Free Europe's headquarters had actually moved to Prague.

To reach the castle from Strahov Monastery, take Loretánská (the upper road, passing Loreta Square—see below); this is more interesting than going on the lower road, Úvoz, which takes you steeply downhill, below Castle Square (see map on page 112).

On Loreta Square, Between Strahov Monastery and Castle Square

From the monastery, take Loretánská street to Loreta Square (Loretánské Náměstí). As you wander this road, you'll pass several mansions and palaces, and an important pilgrimage church.

Loreta Church—This church has been a hit with pilgrims for centuries, thanks to its dazzling bell tower, peaceful yet plush cloister, sparkling treasury, and much-venerated "Holy House" (90 Kč, Tue–Sun 9:00–12:15 & 13:00–16:30, closed Mon).

Once inside the entry, follow the one-way clockwise route. Strolling along the cloister, notice that the ceiling is painted with the many places Mary has miraculously appeared to the faithful in Europe.

In the garden-like center of the cloister stands the ornate **Santa Casa** (Holy House), considered by some pilgrims to be part of Mary's home in Nazareth. Because many pilgrims returning from the Holy Land docked at the Italian port of Loreto, it's called the Loreta Shrine. The Santa Casa is the "little Bethlehem" of Prague. It is the traditional departure point for Czech pilgrims setting out on the long, arduous journey to Europe's most important pilgrimage site, Santiago de Compostela, in northwest Spain. Inside, on the left wall, hangs what some consider to be an original beam from the house of Mary. It's overseen by a much-venerated statue of the "Black Virgin." The Santa Casa itself might seem like a bit of a letdown, but consider that you're entering the holiest spot in the country for generations of believers.

The small Baroque church behind the Santa Casa is one of the most beautiful in Prague. The decor looks rich—but the marble and gold is all fake (tap the columns). From the window in the back, you can see a stucco relief on the Santa Casa showing angels rescuing the house from a pagan attack in Nazareth, and making a special delivery to Loreto in Italy.

Continue around the cloister. In the last corner is St. Bearded Woman (Svatá Starosta). This patron saint of unhappy marriages is a woman whose family arranged for her to marry a pagan man. She prayed for an escape, sprouted a beard...and the guy said, "No way." While she managed to avoid the marriage, it angered her father, who crucified her. The many candles here are from people suffering through unhappy marriages.

Take a left just before the exit and head upstairs, following signs to the treasury—a room full of jeweled worship aids (well-described in English). The highlight here is a monstrance (Communion wafer holder) from 1699, with over 6,000 diamonds.

Enjoy the short carillon concert at the top of the hour; from the lawn in front of the main entrance, you can see the racks of bells being clanged. (At the exit, you'll see a schedule of English Masses and upcoming *poutní*—pilgrimages—departing from here.)

Castle Square (Hradčanské Náměstí)

This is the central square of the Castle Quarter. Enjoy the awesome city view and the two entertaining bands that play regularly at the gate. (If the Prague Castle Orchestra is playing, say hello to friendly, mustachioed Josef, and consider getting the group's terrific CD.) A café with dramatic city views called Espresso Kajetánka hides a few steps down, immediately to the right as you face the castle (see page 145). From here, stairs lead into the Little Quarter.

Castle Square was a kind of medieval Pennsylvania Avenue—the king, the most powerful noblemen, and the archbishop lived here. Look uphill from the gate. The Renaissance **Schwarzenberg Palace** (on the left, with the big rectangles scratched on the wall, now under renovation) was where the Rožmberks "humbly" stayed when they were in town from their Český Krumlov estates. The Schwarzenberg family inherited the Krumlov estates and aristocratic prominence in Bohemia, and stayed in the palace until the 20th century.

The archbishop still lives in the yellow Rococo **palace** across the square (with the three white goose necks in the red field—the coat of arms of Prague's archbishops).

Through the portal on the left-hand side of the palace, a lane leads to the **Sternberg Palace** (Šternberský Palác), filled with the National Gallery's skippable collection of European paintings—including minor works by Albrecht Dürer, Peter Paul Rubens, Rembrandt, and El Greco (100 Kč, Tue–Sun 10:00–18:00, closed Mon).

The black Baroque sculpture in the middle of the square is a **plague column,** erected as a token of gratitude to the saints who saved the population from the epidemic, and an integral part of the main square of many Hapsburg towns.

The statue marked *TGM* honors **Tomáš Garrigue Masaryk** (1850–1937), a university professor and a pal of Woodrow Wilson. At the end of World War I, Masaryk united the Czechs and the Slovaks into one nation and became its first president (see sidebar on page 116).

Tomáš Garrigue Masaryk
(1850–1937)

Masaryk was the George Washington of Czechoslovakia. He founded the first democracy in Eastern Europe at the end of World War I, uniting the Czechs and the Slovaks to create Czechoslovakia. Like Václav Havel 70 years later, Masaryk was a politician whose vision extended far beyond the mountains enclosing the Bohemian basin.

Masaryk was born into a poor servant family in southern Moravia. After finishing high school, the village boy set off to attend university in Vienna. Masaryk earned his Ph.D. in sociology just in time for the opening of the Czech-language university in Prague. By that time, he was already married to an American music student named Charlotta Garrigue, who came from a prominent New York family. (The progressive Tomáš actually took her family name as part of his own.) Charlotta opened the doors of America's high society to Masaryk. Among the American friends he made was a young Princeton professor named Woodrow Wilson.

Masaryk was greatly impressed with America, and his admiration for its democratic system became the core of his gradually evolving political creed. He traveled the world and went to Vienna to serve in the parliament. By the time World War

Prague Castle (Pražský Hrad)

For more than a thousand years, Czech leaders have ruled from Prague Castle. Today Prague's Castle is, by some measures, the biggest on earth. A visit here is worth ▲▲. Four stops matter, and all are explained here: St. Vitus Cathedral, Old Royal Palace, Basilica of St. George, and the Golden Lane.

Hours: Castle sights are open daily April–Oct 9:00–17:00, Nov–March 9:00–16:00, last entry 15 minutes before closing; grounds are open daily 5:00–23:00. St. Vitus Cathedral is closed Sunday mornings for Mass. Be warned that the cathedral can be unexpectedly closed due to special services—consider calling ahead to confirm (tel. 224-373-368 or 224-372-434). If you're not interested in entering the museums, you could try a nighttime visit—the castle grounds are safe, peaceful, floodlit, and open late.

Tickets: The **cathedral** requires its own ticket (100 Kč, free for pilgrims accompanied by their priest). For the other castle

I broke out in 1914, Masaryk was 64 years old and—his friends thought—ready for retirement. But while most other Czech politicians stayed in Prague and supported the Hapsburg Empire, Masaryk went abroad in protest and formed a highly original plan: to create an independent, democratic republic of Czechs and Slovaks. Masaryk and his supporters recruited an army of 100,000 Czech and Slovak soldiers willing to fight with the Allies against the Hapsburgs...establishing a strong case to put on his friend Woodrow Wilson's Oval Office desk.

On the morning of October 28, 1918, news of the unofficial capitulation of the Hapsburgs reached Prague. Local supporters of Masaryk's idea quickly took control of the city and proclaimed the free republic. As the people of Prague tore down double-headed eagles (a symbol of the Hapsburgs), Czechoslovakia was born.

On November 11, 1918, four years after he had left the country as a political nobody, Masaryk arrived in Prague as the greatest Czech hero since the revolutionary priest Jan Hus. The dignified old man rode through the masses of cheering Czechs on a white horse. He told the jubilant crowd, "Now go home—the work has only started." Throughout the 1920s and 1930s, Masaryk was Europe's most vocal defender of democratic ideals against the rising tide of totalitarian ideologies.

In 2001, the US government honored Masaryk's dedication to democracy by erecting a monument to him in Washington, D.C.—he is one of only three foreign leaders (along with Gandhi and Churchill) to have a statue in the American capital.

sights, rather than the comprehensive long tour ticket (350 Kč), I recommend buying the short tour ticket (250 Kč, covers the Old Royal Palace, Basilica of St. George, and the Golden Lane at peak hours, buy in palace or in basilica). If you want to save time and money, skip the Golden Lane during the day and return at night for a romantic, crowd-free visit (free in the morning and evening).

Tours: Hour-long tours in English depart from the main ticket office about three times a day, but cover only the cathedral and Old Royal Palace (90 Kč plus ticket, tel. 224-373-368). Consider the worthwhile **audioguide** (250 Kč/2 hrs, 300 Kč/3 hrs, must leave ID). You can rent the audioguide for 200 Kč all day by picking it up at the main desk in the TI across from the cathedral entrance, and showing this book (this rate was promised to me through 2007 by the manager there). Leave your ID with them, and instead of exiting the castle from the bottom, you'll need to hike back up to the entry point to retrieve your ID (desk closes at 17:00).

Crowd-Beating Tips: Huge throngs of tourists turn the castle grounds into a sea of people during peak times (9:15–15:00). St. Vitus Cathedral is the most crowded part of the castle complex. If visiting in the morning, ideally be at the cathedral entrance promptly at 9:00, when the doors open. For 10 minutes, you'll have the sacred space for yourself (after about 9:15, tour guides jockeying unwieldy groups from tomb to tomb turn the church into a noisy human traffic jam). Late afternoon is least crowded.

Castle Gate and Courtyards—Begin at Castle Square. From here, survey the castle—the tip of a 1,500-foot-long series of courtyards, churches, and palaces. The guard changes on the hour (5:00–23:00), with the most ceremony and music at noon.

Walk under the fighting giants, under an arch, through the passageway, and into the courtyard. The modern green awning with the golden-winged cat (just past the ticket office) marks the offices of the Czech president. The current president, Václav Klaus, is popular with members of the older generation (who like consistency)—but is bitterly resented by younger people, many of whom see him as incapable of considering points of view other than his own. Outside the Czech Republic, Klaus is chiefly known for his unconstructive criticism of the European Union.

As you walk through another passageway, you'll find yourself facing...

▲▲▲St. Vitus Cathedral (Katedrála Sv. Víta)—The Roman Catholic cathedral symbolizes the Czech spirit—it contains the tombs and relics of the most important local saints and kings, including the first three Hapsburg kings.

Cathedral Facade: Before entering, check out the facade.

What's up with the guys in suits carved into the facade below the big round window? They're the architects and builders who finished the church. Started in 1344, construction was stalled by wars and plagues. But, fueled by the 19th-century rise of Czech nationalism, Prague's top church was finished in 1929 for the 1,000th anniversary of the death of St. Wenceslas. While it looks all Gothic, it's actually two distinct halves: the original 14th-century

Gothic around the high altar, and the modern Neo-Gothic nave. For 400 years, a temporary wall sealed off the functional, yet unfinished, cathedral.

Mucha Stained-Glass Window: Go inside, buy your ticket, show your ticket at the fenced-off area, and find the third window on the left. This masterful 1931 Art Nouveau window is by Czech artist Alfons Mucha (if you like this, you'll love the Mucha Museum in the New Town—see page 99). Notice Mucha's stirring nationalism: Methodius and Cyril, widely considered the fathers of Slavic-style Christianity, are top and center. Cyril—the monk in black holding the Bible—brought the word of God to the Slavs. They had no written language in the ninth century—so he designed the necessary alphabet (Glagolitic, which later developed into Cyrillic). Methodius, the bishop, is shown baptizing a mythic, lanky, long-haired Czech man—a reminder of how he brought Christianity to the Czech people. Scenes from the life of Cyril on the left and scenes from the life of Methodius on the right bookend the stirring and epic Slavic scene. In the center are a kneeling boy and a prophesying elder—that's young St. Wenceslas and his grandmother, St. Ludmila. In addition to being specific historical figures, these characters are also symbolic: The old woman, with closed eyes, stands for the past and memory, while the young boy, with a penetrating stare, represents the hope and future of a nation. Notice how master designer Mucha draws your attention to these two figures through the use of colors—the dark blue on the outside gradually turns into green, then yellow, and finally the gold of the woman and the crimson of the boy in the center. In Mucha's color language, blue stands for the past, gold for the mythic, and red for the future. Besides all the meaning, Mucha's art is simply a joy to behold. (And on the bottom, the tasteful little ad for *Banka Slavie*, which paid for the work, is hardly noticeable.)

Relief of Prague: Continue circulating around the apse. As you walk around the high altar, study the fascinating carved-wood relief of Prague. It depicts the victorious Hapsburg armies entering the castle after the Battle of White Mountain, while the Protestant king Frederic escapes over the Charles Bridge (before it had any statues). Carved in 1630, 10 years after the famous event occurred, the relief also gives you a peek at Prague in 1620, stretching from the Týn Church to the cathedral (half-built at that time, up to where you are now). Notice that back then, the Týn Church was

Hussite, so the centerpiece of its facade is not the Virgin Mary—but a chalice, symbol of Jan Hus' ideals. The old city walls—now replaced by the main streets of the city—stand strong. The Jewish Quarter (the slummy, muddy zone along the riverside below the bridge on the left) fills land no one else wanted.

Apse: Circling around the high altar, you pass graves of bishops, including the tomb of St. Vitus (behind the chair of the bishop). The stone sarcophagi are kings from the Přemysl dynasty (12th–14th centuries). Locals claim the gigantic, shiny tomb of St. John of Nepomuk has over a ton of silver (for more on St. John of Nepomuk, see page 88). After the silver tomb, look up at the royal box from where the king would attend Mass in his jammies (an elevated corridor connected his private apartment with his own altar-side box pew).

Look for the finely carved wood panel that gives a Counter-Reformation spin on the Wars of Religion. It shows the "barbaric" Protestant nobles destroying the Catholic icons in the cathedral after their short-lived victory.

Wenceslas Chapel: A fancy roped-off chapel (right transept) houses the tomb of St. Wenceslas, surrounded by precious 14th-century murals showing scenes of his life, and a locked door leading to the crown jewels. The Czech kings used to be crowned right here in front of the coffin, draped in red. The chapel is roped off because the wallpaper is encrusted with precious and semi-precious stones. (Lead us not into temptation.) You can view the chapel from either door (if the door facing the nave is crowded, duck around to the left to find a generally open door).

Spire: You can climb 287 steps up the spire for one of the best views of the whole city (included in cathedral ticket, April–Oct daily 9:00–17:00 except Sun morning, last entry 45 minutes before closing, closes at 16:00 Nov–March).

Back Outside the Cathedral: Leaving the cathedral, turn left (past the public WC). The **obelisk** was erected in 1928—a single piece of granite celebrating the 10th anniversary of the establishment of Czechoslovakia. It was originally much taller, but broke in transit—an inauspicious start for a nation destined to last only 70 years. Up in the fat, green tower of the cathedral is the Czech Republic's biggest bell, nicknamed "Zikmund." In June of 2002, it cracked—and two months later, the worst flood in recorded history hit the city. As a nation sandwiched between great powers, Czechs are deeply superstitious. Often feeling unable to influence the course of their own history, they helplessly look at events as we might look at the weather and other natural phenomena—trying to figure out what fate has in store for them next.

Find the 14th-century **mosaic** of the Last Judgment outside on the right transept. It was commissioned Italian-style by King Charles IV, who was modern, cosmopolitan, and ahead of his time. Jesus oversees the action, as some go to heaven and some go to hell. The Czech king and queen kneel directly below Jesus and the six patron saints. On coronation day, they would walk under this arch, which would remind them (and their subjects) that even those holding great power are not above God's judgment. The royal crown and national jewels are kept in a chamber (see the grilled windows) above this entryway, which was the cathedral's main entry for centuries while the church remained uncompleted.

Across the square and 20 yards to the right, a door leads into the Old Royal Palace (in the lobby, there's a WC with a window shared by the men's and women's sections—meet your partner to enjoy the view).

Old Royal Palace (Starý Královský Palác)—This was the seat of the Bohemian princes starting in the 12th century. While exten-

sively rebuilt, the **large hall** is late Gothic, designed as a multipurpose hall for the old nobility. It's big enough for jousts—even the staircase was designed to let a mounted soldier gallop in. It was filled with market stalls, giving nobles a chance to shop without actually going into town. In the 1400s, the nobility met here to elect their king. This tradition survived until modern times, as the parliament crowded into this room until the late 1990s to elect the Czechoslovak (and later Czech) president. (The last two elections happened in another, far more lavish hall in the castle.) Look up at the flower-shaped, vaulted ceiling.

On your immediate right, enter the two small Renaissance rooms known as the **"Czech Office."** From these rooms (empty today except for their 17th-century porcelain heaters), two governors used to oversee the Czech lands for the Hapsburgs in Vienna. In 1618, angry Czech Protestant nobles poured into these rooms and threw the two Catholic governors out of the window. An old law actually permits defenestration—throwing people (usually bad politicians) out of windows when necessary. Old prints on the wall show the second of Prague's many defenestrations. The two governors landed—fittingly—in a pile of horse manure. Even though they suffered only broken arms and bruised egos, this event kicked off the huge and lengthy Thirty Years' War.

As you exit through the side door, notice how the halls are big enough to accommodate knights on horseback. Before you gallop out, pause at the door to consider the subtle yet racy little Renaissance knocker. Go ahead—play with it for a little sex in the palace (be gentle).

Across from the palace exit is the...

Basilica of St. George (Bazilika Sv. Jiří)—Step into the beautifully lit Basilica of St. George to see Prague's best-preserved Romanesque church. St. Wenceslas' mother, St. Ludmila, was reburied here in 973. The first Bohemian convent was established here near the palace.

Today, the **convent** next door houses the National Gallery's Collection of Old Masters, featuring the best Czech paintings from the Mannerist and Baroque periods (100 Kč, Tue–Sun 10:00–18:00, closed Mon).

Continue walking downhill through the castle grounds. Turn left on the first street, which leads into the...

Golden Lane (Zlatá Ulička)—During the day, this street of old buildings, which originally housed goldsmiths, is jammed with tourists and lined with overpriced gift shops. Franz Kafka lived briefly at #22. There's a deli/bistro at the top. The tiny street is free, empty, and evocative in the morning (before 9:00) and at night (after 17:00 in summer, 16:00 in winter). Exit the lane through a corridor at the last house (#12).

Toy and Barbie Museum (Muzeum Hraček)—At the bottom of the castle complex, just after leaving the Golden Lane, a long, wooden staircase leads to two entertaining floors of old toys and dolls thoughtfully described in English. You'll see a century of teddy bears, 19th-century model train sets, and an incredible Barbie collection (the entire top floor). Find the buxom 1959 first edition, and you'll understand why these capitalistic sirens of material discontent weren't allowed here until 1989 (60 Kč, 120 Kč per family, not included in any castle tickets, daily 9:30–17:30, WC next to entrance).

After Your Castle Visit: Tourists squirt slowly through a fortified door at the bottom end of the castle. From there, you can follow the steep lane directly back to the riverbank (and the Malostranská Metro station).

Or you can take a hard right and stroll through the long, delightful park. Along the way, notice the modernist design of the **Na Valech Garden,** which was carried out by the "court architect" of the 1920s, Jože Plečnik of Slovenia (see page 541).

Halfway through the long park is a viewpoint overlooking **terraced gardens;** you can zigzag down through these gardens into the Little Quarter (80 Kč, April–Oct daily 10:00–18:00, closed Nov–March).

If you continue through the park all the way to Castle Square, you'll find two more options: a staircase leading down into the Little Quarter, or a cobbled street taking you to historic Nerudova street (described on page 107).

Congratulations. You've conquered the castle.

ENTERTAINMENT

Prague booms with live and inexpensive theater, classical music, jazz, and pop entertainment. Everything's listed in several monthly

cultural events programs (free at TI) and in the *Prague Post* newspaper.

You'll be tempted to gather fliers as you wander through the town. Don't bother. To really understand all your options (the street Mozarts are pushing only their concerts), drop by a **Via Musica** box office. There are two: One is next to Týn Church on the Old Town Square (daily 10:30–19:30, tel. 224-826-969), and the other is in the Little Quarter across from the Church of St. Nicholas (daily 10:30–18:00, tel. 257-535-568). The event schedule posted on their wall clearly shows everything that's playing today and tomorrow, including tourist concerts, Black Light Theater, and marionette shows, with photos of each venue and a map locating everything (www.viamusica.cz).

Ticketpro sells tickets for the serious concert venues and most music clubs (daily 8:00–12:00 & 12:30–16:30, Rytířská 31, between Havelská Market and Estates Theatre; also has a booth in Tourist Center at Rytířská 12, daily 9:00–20:00; English-language reservations tel. 296-329-999).

Consider buying concert tickets directly from the actual venues. You won't save money, but more of your money will go to the musicians.

Black Light Theater—A kind of mime/modern dance variety show, Black Light Theater has no language barrier and is, for many, more entertaining than a classical concert. Unique to Prague (though somewhat comparable to a very low-budget Cirque du Soleil), Black Light Theater originated in the 1960s as a playful and mystifying theater of the absurd. These days, some aficionados lament that it's becoming a cheesy variety show, while others are uncomfortable with the sexual flavor of some acts. Still, it's an unusual theater experience that most enjoy. Shows last about 90 minutes. Avoid the first four rows, which get you so close that it ruins the illusion. Each theater has its own personality:

Ta Fantastika is traditional and poetic, with puppets and a little artistic nudity (*Aspects of Alice* nightly at 21:30, 620 Kč, reserved seating, near east end of Charles Bridge at Karlova 8, tel. 222-221-366, www.tafantastika.cz). **Image Theatre** has more mime and absurd, with shows including *Clonarium, Fiction,* and *The Best of Image:* "It's precisely the fact that we are all so different that unites us" (shows nightly at 18:00 and 20:00, 400 Kč, open seating—arrive early to grab a good spot, just off Old Town Square at Pařížská 4, tel. 222-314-448, www.imagetheatre.cz). **Laterna Magica,** in the big, glassy Nová Scéna building next to the National Theatre, mixes black-light techniques with film projection into a multi-media performance that draws Czech audiences (*Wonderful Circus, Rendezvous, Graffiti,* shows Mon–Sat at 20:00, no shows on Sun, 680 Kč, tel. 224-931-482, www.laterna.cz). The other Black Light Theaters advertising around town aren't as good.

Tourist Concerts—Each day, six to eight classical concerts designed for tourists fill delightful Old World halls and churches with music of the crowd-pleasing sort: Vivaldi, Best of Mozart, Most Famous Arias, and works by the famous Czech composer Antonín Dvořák. Concerts typically cost 400–1,000 Kč, start anywhere from 13:00 to 21:00, and last about an hour. Common venues are two buildings on Little Quarter Square (the Church of St. Nicholas and the Prague Academy of Music in Liechtenstein Palace); in the Klementinum's Chapel of Mirrors; at the Old Town Square (in a different Church of St. Nicholas); and in the stunning Smetana Hall in the Municipal House (see page 100). The artists vary from excellent to amateur.

A sure bet is the jam session held every Monday at 17:00 at **St. Martin in the Wall,** where Prague's best professional musicians gather to tune in and chat with each other (400 Kč, Martinská street, just north of the Tesco department store in the Old Town).

Serious Concerts—True music-lovers should consider Prague's top symphonic venue, the **Rudolfinum** (featuring the Czech Philharmonic, on Palachovo Náměstí, in Jewish Quarter on the Old Town side of Mánes Bridge). Concerts in the large Dvořák Hall or the small Suk Hall usually start at 19:30 (also afternoons on weekends). The ticket office is on the right side, under the stairs (250–1,000 Kč, open until just before the show starts, tel. 227-059-352).

The **National Theatre** (Národní Divadlo, on the New Town side of Legií Bridge)—with a must-see Neo-Renaissance interior (see page 103)—is best for opera and ballet (shows from 19:00, 300–1,000 Kč, tel. 224-912-673, www.nationaltheatre.cz). The **Estates Theatre** (Stavovské Divadlo) is where Mozart premiered and per-sonally directed many of his most beloved works (see page 85). *Don Giovanni, The Marriage of Figaro,* and *The Magic Flute* are on the program a couple of times each month (shows from 20:00, 800–1,400 Kč, between the Old Town Square and the New Town on a square called Ovocný Trh, tel. 224-214-339, www.estatestheatre.cz). The ticket office for both of these theaters is in the little square (Ovocný Trh) behind the Estates Theatre.

The **State Opera** (Státní Opera) focuses on Verdi (shows at 19:00 or 20:00, 400–1,200 Kč, buy tickets at the theater, on 5 Května—the busy street between the Main Train Station and Wenceslas Square, see map on page 95, tel. 224-227-693, www.opera.cz).

During his frequent visits to Prague, Mozart stayed with his friends in the beautiful, small, Neoclassical **Villa Bertramka,** now the Mozart Museum. Surrounded by a peaceful garden, the villa preserves the time when the Salzburg prodigy felt more appreciated in Prague than in Austria. Intimate concerts are held some afternoons and evenings, either in the garden or the small concert hall (110 Kč, daily April–Oct 9:30–18:00, Nov–March 9:30–17:00, Mozartova 169, Praha 5; from Metro: Anděl, it's a 10-min walk—head to Hotel Mövenpick and then go up alley behind hotel; tel. 257-317-465, www.bertramka.cz).

World-class musicians are in town during these musical festivals: **Prague Spring** (mid-May–early June, www.festival.cz) and **Prague Autumn** (mid-Sept–mid-Oct, www.pragueautumn.cz).

For any of these concerts, locals dress up, but many tourists wear casual clothes—as long as you don't show up in sneakers and ripped jeans, you'll be fine.

SHOPPING

Prague's entire Old Town seems designed to bring out the shopper in visitors. Puppets, glass, and ceramics are traditional. Shop your way from the Old Town Square up Celetná to the Powder Tower, then along Na Příkopě to the bottom of Wenceslas Square (Václavské Náměstí). The city center is tourist-oriented—most locals do their serious shopping in the suburbs.

Celetná is lined with big stores selling all the traditional Czech goodies. Tourists wander endlessly here, mesmerized by the window displays. Celetná Crystal, about midway down the street, offers the largest selection of affordable crystal. You can have the glass safely shipped home directly from the shop (for purchases over 2,000 Kč, you can get a refund of the VAT tax—see page 20).

Na Příkopě has a couple of good modern malls. The best is Slovanský Dům (daily 10:00–20:00, Na Příkopě 22), where you wander deep past a 10-screen multiplex into a world of classy restaurants and designer shops surrounding a peaceful, park-like inner courtyard. Another modern mall is Černá Růže (daily

10:00–20:00, Na Příkopě 12). Next door is Mosers, which has a museum-like crystal showroom upstairs.

Národní Třída (National Street) is less touristy and lined with some inviting stores. The big Tesco department store in the middle sells anything you might need, from a pin for a broken watchband to a swimsuit (generally daily 9:00–21:00, Národní Třída 26).

Crystal: Along with shops on Celetná and Na Příkopě, a small square just off the Old Town Square, Malé Náměstí, is ringed by three major crystal retailers (generally open daily 10:00–20:00): Mosers, Rott Crystal, and Crystalex (which claims to have "factory-direct" prices, at #6 on the square).

SLEEPING

Peak season for hotels in Prague is late April, May, June, September, and early October. Easter and Christmas are the most crowded times, when prices are jacked up a bit. I've listed peak-time prices—if you're traveling in July or August, you'll find rates generally 15 percent lower, and from November through March, about 30 percent lower.

Room-Booking Services

Prague is awash with fancy rooms on the push list; private, small-time operators with rooms to rent in their apartments; and roving agents eager to book you a bed and earn a commission. You can save about 30 percent by showing up in Prague without a reservation and finding accommodations upon arrival. It is, however, a hustle and you will not necessarily get your choice. If you're coming in by train or car, you'll encounter booking agencies. They can virtually always find you a reasonable place and, if it's a private guest house, your host can even come and lead you to the place.

Athos Travel has a line on 200 properties (ranging from hostels to 5-star hotels), 90 percent of which are in the historical center. To book a room, call them or use their handy Web site, which allows you to search for a room based on various criteria (best to arrange in advance during peak season, can also help with last-minute booking off-season, tel. 241-440-571, fax 241-441-697, www.a-prague.com, info@a-prague.com). Readers report that Athos is aggressive with its business policies—while there's no fee to cancel well in advance, they strictly enforce penalties on cancellations within 48 hours.

AVE, at the Main Train Station (Hlavní Nádraží), is another booking service (daily 6:00–23:00). With the tracks at your back, walk down to the orange ceiling and past the "Meeting Point" (don't go downstairs)—their office is in the left corner by the exit to the rip-off taxis. Their display board shows discounted hotels,

---

Sleep Code

(22 Kč = about $1, country code: 420)
S = Single, **D** = Double/Twin, **T** = Triple, **Q** = Quad, **b** = bathroom,
s = shower only. Unless otherwise noted, credit cards are accepted, and breakfast and tax are included. Everyone listed here speaks English.

To help you sort easily through these listings, I've divided the rooms into three categories based on the price for a standard double room with bath:

$$$ Higher Priced—Most rooms 4,000 Kč or more.
$$ Moderately Priced—Most rooms between 3,000–4,000 Kč.
$ Lower Priced—Most rooms 3,000 Kč or less.

---

and they have a slew of hotels and small pensions available (2,000-Kč pension doubles in old center, 1,500-Kč doubles a Metro ride away). You can reserve by e-mail using your credit card as a deposit (tel. 251-551-011, fax 251-555-156, www.avetravel.cz, ave@avetravel .cz), or just show up at the office and request a room. Be clear on the location before you make your choice.

For a more personal touch, Lída Jánská's **Magic Praha** helps with accommodations (tel. 235-325-170, mobile 604-207-225, www.magicpraha.cz, magicpraha@magicpraha.cz; see "Helpful Hints," page 67). Lída rents a well-located apartment with a river view near the Jewish Quarter.

Web-booking services, such as Priceline.com and Biddingfortravel.com, enable budget travelers to snare fancy rooms on the push list for half the rack rate. It's not unusual to find a room in a four-star hotel for 1,300 Kč—but keep in mind that many of these international business-class hotels are far from the city center.

Old Town Hotels and Pensions

You'll pay higher prices to stay in the Old Town, but for many travelers, the convenience is worth the expense. These places are all within a 10-minute walk of the Old Town Square.

$$$ Hotel Maximilian is a sleek, mod, 70-room place with Art Deco black design, big, plush living rooms, and all the business services and comforts you'd expect in a four-star hotel. It faces a church on a perfect little square just a short walk from the action (Db-4,500 Kč, extra bed-1,500 Kč, their "preferred rate" gives you a 14 percent discount if you lock in a reservation with no cancellation option, check online for lower rates, Haštalská

Hotels in Prague's Old Town

M - METRO STOP   **Ⓣ** - TRAM STOP   ═══ - PEDESTRIAN PASSAGEWAY

❶ Hotel Maximilian
❷ Residence Řetězová
❸ Hotel Haštal
❹ Pension u Medvídků
❺ Green Garland Pension
❻ Hotel u Klenotníka
❼ Old Prague Hostel
❽ Hostel Týn

14, tel. 225-303-111, fax 225-303-110, www.maximilianhotel.com, reservations@maximilianhotel.com).

$$$ Residence Řetězová is on a central but delightfully quiet cobbled lane. Its medieval shell has been remodeled into nine elegant, plush, and spacious apartments—each one is unique. You can enjoy the mystery and ambience of old Prague with all the modern comforts (Db-4,500–5,600 Kč, check online for lower rates and to choose your room, free Internet access, Řetězová 9, tel. & fax 222-221-800, www.residenceretezova.com, info@residenceretezova .com).

$$ Hotel Haštal, next to Hotel Maximilian (listed above) on the same quiet, hidden square in the Old Town, was a popular hotel back in the 1920s. Newly renovated, its Art Nouveau style was preserved to complement the neighborhood's vibrant circa-1900 architecture. Its 24 rooms are comfortable, but the walls are a bit thin (Sb-2,900 Kč, Db-3,600 Kč, extra bed-550 Kč, 20 percent discount when booking online, air-con, Haštalská 16, tel. 222-314-335, www.hastal.com, info@hastal.com). The hotel's small restaurant is understandably popular with locals for its reasonably priced lunch specials and draft beer.

$$ Pension u Medvídků has 31 comfortably renovated rooms in a big, rustic, medieval shell with dark wood furniture. Upstairs, you'll find lots of beams—or, if you're not careful, they'll find you (Sb-2,300 Kč, Db-3,500 Kč, Tb-4,500 Kč, extra bed-500 Kč, "historical" rooms 10 percent more, apartment for 20 percent more, manager Vladimír promises readers of this book a 10 percent discount with cash if you book direct in 2007, Internet access, Na Perštýně 7, tel. 224-211-916, fax 224-220-930, www .umedvidku.cz, info@umedvidku.cz). The pension runs a popular beer-hall restaurant with live music most Fridays and Saturdays until 23:00—request an inside room for maximum peace.

$$ Green Garland Pension (U Zeleného Věnce), on the same quiet pedestrian street as Residence Řetězová, has a warm and personal feel rare in the Old Town. Located in a thick 14th-century building with open beams, it has a blond-hardwood charm decorated with a woman's touch. Its nine rooms are clean and simply furnished (big Sb-2,900 Kč, Db-3,400 Kč, bigger Db-3,700 Kč, Tb-4,400 Kč, 10 percent discount with cash, family suite, Řetězová 10, tel. 222-220-178, fax 224-248-791, www.uzv.cz, pension@uzv.cz).

$$ Hotel u Klenotníka ("At the Jeweler"), with 11 modern, comfortable rooms in a plain building, is three blocks off the Old Town Square (Sb-2,500 Kč, small double-bed Db-3,300 Kč, bigger twin-bed Db–3,800 Kč, Tb-4,500 Kč, Marie and Helena promise 10 percent off when booking direct with this book in 2007, Rytířská 3, tel. 224-211-699, fax 224-221-025, www.uklenotnika .cz, info@uklenotnika.cz).

Under the Castle, in the Little Quarter

The first three listings are buried on quiet lanes deep in the Little Quarter among cobbles, quaint restaurants, rummaging tourists, and embassy flags. The last is a 10-minute walk up the river on a quiet and stately street with none of the intense medieval cityscape of the others.

Hotels and Restaurants in the Little Quarter

🗼 – VIEW

★ LITTLE QUARTER SQUARE

Ⓜ – METRO STOP

Ⓣ – TRAM #22 + #23 STOPS

200 YARDS

200 METERS

❶ Dům u Velké Boty
❷ Hotel Sax
❸ Dům u Žluté Boty
❹ Hostel Sokol
❺ Hotel Julián
❻ U Sedmi Švábů Rest. & U Osla v Kolébce Pub

❼ U Hrocha Pub
❽ Restaurace Rybářský Klub
❾ Restaurace David & Baráčnická Rychta Club
❿ Malostranská Beseda Club

$$$ Dům u Velké Boty ("House at the Big Boot"), in front of the German Embassy, is the quintessential family hotel in Prague—homey, comfy, and extremely friendly. Charlotta, Jan, and their two sons treat every guest as a (thirsty) friend, and the wellspring of their stories never runs dry. Each of their 12 rooms is uniquely decorated, most in tasteful 19th-century Biedermeier style (tiny S-2,100 Kč, two D rooms that share a bathroom-3,550 Kč each, Db-4,780 Kč, extra bed-725 Kč, prices can be soft when slow, cash only, free Internet access and Wi-Fi, Vlašská 30, tel. 257-532-088, www.bigboot.cz, info@bigboot.cz). While they don't include tax or breakfast in their rates, I've included them in the prices above for easy comparison. There's no hotel sign on the house—look for the splendid geraniums that Jan nurtures in the windows.

$$$ Hotel Sax will delight the artsy yuppie with its 22 business-style rooms, fruity atrium, and modern, stylish decor (Sb-4,100 Kč, Db-4,400 Kč, Db suite-5,100 Kč, extra bed-1,000 Kč, elevator, Jánský Vršek 3, tel. 257-531-268, fax 257-534-101, www.sax.cz, hotel@sax.cz).

$$$ Dům u Žluté Boty ("House at the Yellow Boot"), perhaps the most charming small hotel in Prague, is well-run by sisters Jana and Jiřina. Each of its seven rooms is unique: Some preserve the 16th-century wooden ceilings, some feel like mountain lodges, and others are a bit marred by an insensitive 1970s adaptation (Sb-3,800 Kč, Db-4,300 Kč, Tb-5,000 Kč, extra bed-900 Kč, 15 percent discount with cash and this book if you book direct in 2007, some thin walls, Jánský Vršek 11, tel. 257-532-269, fax 257-534-134, www.zlutabota.cz, hotel@zlutabota.cz).

$$ Hotel Julián is an oasis of professional, predictable decency in a quiet, untouristy neighborhood. Its 32 spacious, fresh, well-furnished rooms and big, homey public spaces hide behind a noble Neoclassical facade. The staff is friendly and helpful (Sb-3,680 Kč, Db-3,980 Kč, Db suite-4,800 Kč, extra bed-900 Kč, discount for booking online, 5 percent discount off best quoted rate with this book in 2007, free tea and coffee in room, air-con, elevator, plush and inviting lobby, parking lot; Metro: Andel, then an 8-min walk; or take tram #6, #9, #12, #20, or #58 for two stops; Elišky Peškové 11, Praha 5, reservation tel. 257-311-150, reception tel. 257-311-145, fax 257-311-149, www.julian.cz, casjul@vol.cz). Free lockers and a shower are available for those needing to check out early but stay until late (for example, for an overnight train). Mike's Chauffeur Service, based here, is reliable and affordable (see page 146).

Away from the Center

Moving just outside central Prague saves you money—and gets you away from the tourists and into some more workaday residential neighborhoods. The following listings (great values compared to the downtown hotels) are all within a five- to 15-minute tram or Metro ride from the center.

Beyond Wenceslas Square

These hotels are in urban neighborhoods on the outer fringe of the New Town, beyond Wenceslas Square. But they're still within several minutes' walk of the sightseeing zone, and are well-served by trams.

$$$ Sieber Hotel, with 20 rooms, is a quality, four-star, business-class hotel in an upscale residential neighborhood near the former royal vineyards (Vinohrady). They do a good job of being homey and welcoming (Sb-4,480 Kč, Db-4,780 Kč, extra bed-990 Kč, fourth night free, 30 percent discount for last-minute reservations, air-con, elevator, Internet access, 3-min walk to Metro: Jiřího z Poděbrad, or tram #11, Slezská 55, Praha 3, tel. 224-250-025, fax 224-250-027, www.sieber.cz, reservations@sieber.cz).

$$ Hotel Anna, with 24 bright, pastel, and classically charming rooms, is a bit closer in—just 10 minutes by foot east of Wenceslas Square (Sb-2,400 Kč, Db-3,300 Kč, Tb-4,000 Kč, non-smoking rooms, elevator, Budečská 17, Praha 2, Metro: Náměstí Míru, tel. 222-513-111, fax 222-515-158, www.hotelanna.cz, reception@hotelanna.cz). They run a similar hotel (same standards and prices) nearby.

$$ Hotel 16 is a sleek and modern business-class place with an intriguing Art Nouveau facade, polished cherry-wood elegance, high ceilings, and 14 fine rooms (Sb-2,800 Kč, Db-3,500 Kč, bigger Db-3,700 Kč, Tb-4,700 Kč, 10 percent discount with this book in 2007, triple-paned windows, back rooms facing the garden are quieter, air-con, elevator, Internet access, 10-min walk south of Wenceslas Square, Metro: I. P. Pavlova, Kateřinská 16, Praha 2, tel. 224-920-636, fax 224-920-626, www.hotel16.cz, hotel16@hotel16 .cz, Frantisek).

The Best Values, Farther from the Center

These accommodations are a 10- to 20-minute tram ride from the center, but once you make the trip, you'll see it's no problem—and you'll feel pretty smug saving $50–100 a night per double by not sleeping in the Old Town. These hotels are within a stone's throw of peaceful Vyšehrad park, with a legendary castle on a cliff overlooking the Vltava River.

$ Dům u Šemíka, a friendly hotel named for a heroic mythical horse, offers 25 rooms in a quiet residential neighborhood just below Vyšehrad Castle, a 10-minute tram ride south of the Old Town (Sb-1,900 Kč, Db-2,500 Kč, apartment-2,700–5,000 Kč for 2–4 people, extra bed-790 Kč, ask for the "direct booking"

Hotels and Restaurants in the New Town and Beyond

① To Sieber Hotel
② Hotel Anna
③ Hotel 16
④ To Hostel Elf
⑤ Restaurace u Pinkasů
⑥ Hospoda u Nováka
⑦ Le Patio & Café Louvre
⑧ Dobrá Čajovna Teahouse
⑨ Restaurant Červená Tabulka

Rick Steves discount; from the center, take trams #3, #17, or #21 to Výtoň, go under rail bridge, and walk 3 blocks uphill to Vratislavova 36; Praha 2, tel. 224-920-736, fax 224-911-602, www .usemika.cz, usemika@usemika.cz).

$ Guest House Lída, with 12 homey and spacious rooms, fills a big house in a quiet residential area farther inland, a 15-minute tram ride from the center. Jan, Jiří, and Jitka Prouza, who run the place, are a wealth of information and know how to make people feel at home (Sb-1,380 Kč, small Db-1,440 Kč, Db-1,760 Kč, Tb-2,110 Kč, Qb-2,530 Kč, cash only, family rooms, top-floor family suite with kitchenette, Internet access, parking garage-200 Kč/day, Metro: Pražského Povstání; exit Metro and turn left on Lomnického between the Metro station and big blue-glass ČSOB building, follow Lomnického for 500 yards, then turn left on Lopatecká, go uphill and ring bell at Lopatecká #26, no sign outside; Praha 4, tel. & fax 261-214-766, www.lidabb.eu, lidabb @seznam.cz). The Prouza brothers also rent four apartments across the river, an equal distance from the center (Db-1,500 Kč, Tb-1,920 Kč, Qb-2,100 Kč).

Hostels in the Center

It's tough to find a double for under 3,000 Kč in the old center. But Prague has an abundance of fine hostels—each with a distinct personality, and each excellent in its own way for anyone wanting a 400-Kč dorm bed or an extremely simple, twin-bedded room for around 1,300 Kč.

$ Old Prague Hostel is a small and very friendly place with 70 beds on the second and third floors of an apartment building on a back alley near the Powder Tower. The spacious rooms were once apartment bedrooms, so it feels less institutional than most hostels. Hanging out in the comfy TV lounge/breakfast room, you'll feel like part of an international family. Older travelers would feel comfortable in this mellow place (six D-1,360 Kč, bunk in 3–8-person room-450–530 Kč; includes breakfast, sheets, towels, lockers, and Internet access; reserve ahead, Benediktská 2, see map on page 128 for location, tel. 224-829-058, fax 224-829-060, www .oldpraguehostel.com, oldpraguehostel@seznam.cz).

$ Hostel Týn is hidden in a silent courtyard two blocks from the Old Town Square. Because the management is aware of its value, they don't bother being too friendly (D-1,200 Kč, T-1,350 Kč, bunk in 4–5-bed co-ed room-400 Kč, lockers, reserve ahead, Týnská 19, located on map on page 128, tel. 224-828-519, mobile 776-122-057, www.hostel-tyn.web2001.cz, backpacker@razdva.cz).

$ Hostel Elf, a 10-minute walk to both the Main Train Station and the Florenc bus station, is fun-loving, ramshackle, covered with noisy, self-inflicted graffiti, and the wildest of these hostels. They offer cheap, basic beds, a helpful staff, and lots of creative services—kitchen, free luggage room, laundry, no lockout, free tea, cheap beer, a terrace, and lockers (120 beds, D-900 Kč, bunk in 6–11-person room-320 Kč, includes sheets and breakfast, cash only, next to tracks heading into Main Train Station but noise isn't a problem, Husitská 11, Praha 3, tel. 222-540-963, www .hostelelf.com, info@hostelelf.com).

$ Hostel Sokol, plain and institutional with 100 beds, is peacefully located just off park-like Kampa Island in the Tyrš House buildings (the seat of the Czech Sokol Organization). Big WWI hospital-style rooms are lined with single beds and lockers (bunk in 8–14-person room-350 Kč, cash only, no breakfast, easy to reserve without deposit by phone or e-mail, open 24/7, kitchen, Nosticova 2, see map on page 130 for location, tel. 257-007-397, fax 257-007-340, www.sokol-cos.cz/index_en.htm, hostel@sokol-cos .cz). From the Main Train Station, ride tram #9 to Újezd. From the Holešovice station, take tram #12 to Hellichova. From either tram stop, walk 200 yards to the hostel.

EATING

A big part of Prague's charm is found in wandering aimlessly through the city's winding old quarters, marveling at the architecture, watching the people, and sniffing out fun restaurants. You can eat well here for very little money. What you'd pay for a basic meal in Vienna or Munich will get you a feast in Prague. In addition to meat-and-potatoes Czech cuisine (see "Czech Food," page 55), you'll find trendy, student-oriented bars and lots of fine ethnic eateries. For ambience, the options include traditional, dark Czech beer halls; elegant Art Nouveau dining rooms; and hip and modern cafés.

Watch out for scams. Many restaurants put more care into ripping off green tourists (and even locals) than in their cooking. Tourists are routinely served cheaper meals than what they ordered, given a menu with a "personalized" price list, charged extra for things they didn't get, or shortchanged. Speak Czech. Even saying "Hello" in Czech (see phrases on page 58) will get you better service. Avoid any menu without clear and explicit prices. Be careful of waiters padding the tab. Carefully examine your itemized bill and understand each line (a 10 percent service charge is sometimes added—in that case, there's no need to tip extra). Tax is always included in the price, so it shouldn't be tacked on later. Part with very large bills only if necessary, and deliberately count your change. Never let your credit card out of your sight. Make it a habit to get cash from an ATM to pay for your meals. (Credit cards can cost merchants as much as 10 percent.) Remember, there are two parallel worlds in Prague: the tourist town and the real city. Generally, if you walk two minutes away from the tourist flow, you'll find better value, ambience, and service.

I've listed these eating and drinking establishments by neighborhood (see "Prague's Four Towns," page 76). The most options—and highest prices—are in the Old Town. If you want a memorable splurge, see "Dining with Style" on page 145. For a light meal, consider one of Prague's many cafés (see "Cafés" on page 142). Many of the places listed here are handy for an efficient lunch, but may not offer fine evening dining. Others make less sense for lunch but are great for a slow, drawn-out dinner. Read the descriptions to judge which is which.

Fun, Touristy Neighborhoods: Several areas are pretty and well-situated for sightseeing, but lined only with touristic restaurants. While these places are not necessarily bad values, I've listed only a few of your many options—just survey the scene in these spots and choose whatever looks best. Kampa Square, just off the Charles Bridge, feels like a small-town square. Havelská Market is surrounded by colorful little eateries, any of which give a fine perch for viewing the market scene while you munch. The grand Old Town Square is *the* place to nurse a drink or enjoy a meal while watching the tide of people, both tourists and locals, sweep back and forth. There's often some event on the main square, and its many restaurants provide tasty and relaxing vantage points.

Dining with a View: For great views, consider these options: **U Prince** (rooftop dining above a fancy hotel, completely touristy but awesome views, recommended and described below); the **Bellavista Restaurant** at Strahov Monastery; **Petřínské Terasy** and **Nebozízek** next to the funicular stop halfway up Petřín Hill; and the many overpriced but elegant places serving scenic meals along the riverbanks. For the best cheap riverside dinner, have a picnic on a paddleboat (see page 75). There's nothing like drifting down the middle of the Vltava River as the sun sets while munching your picnic and sipping your beer with your favorite travel partner.

In or near the Old Town

While most of these eateries are in the Old Town proper, some are a few steps into the New Town.

Characteristically Czech Places

With the inevitable closing of cheap student pubs (replaced by shops and hotels that make more money), it's getting difficult to find a truly Czech pub in the historic city center. Most Czechs no longer go to "traditional" eateries, preferring the cosmopolitan taste of the world to the mundane taste of sauerkraut. As a result,

Prague Restaurants

M - Metro Stop   **T** - Tram Stop   ::: - Pedestrian Passageway

1. Plzeňská Rest. u Dvou Koček
2. Restaurace u Provaznice
3. U Medvídků Beer Hall
4. U Zlatého Tygra Pub
5. Restaurace u Betlémské Kaple
6. Česká Kuchyně
7. Restaurace Mlejnice
8. Country Life Veggie Restaurant
9. Lehká Hlava Veggie Restaurant
10. Klub Architektů
11. Dahab
12. Chez Marcel
13. Beas
14. Orange Moon
15. Molly Malone's Irish Pub
16. Bohemia Bagel
17. Rest. u Prince Terrace
18. Municipal House Eateries
19. Grand Café Slavia
20. Grand Café Orient
21. Café Montmartre
22. Ebel Coffee House
23. Havelská Market

ancient institutions with "authentic" Czech ambience have become touristy—but they're still great fun, a good value, and respected by Czechs. Expect wonderfully rustic spaces, smoke, surly service, and reasonably good, inexpensive food. Understand every line on your bill.

Plzeňská Restaurace u Dvou Koček ("By the Two Cats") is a typical Czech pub with cheap, no-nonsense, hearty Czech food and beer. Sandwiched between the two red-light-district streets, and filled now with tourists rather than Czechs, the restaurant somehow maintains its charm (200 Kč for three courses and beer, serving original Pilsner Urquell with accordion music nightly until 23:00, under an arcade, facing a tiny square between Perlová and Skořepka streets).

Restaurace u Pinkasů, with a menu that reads like a 19th-century newspaper, is a Prague institution, founded in 1843. It's best in summer, when you sit in the garden behind the building in the shade of the Gothic buttresses of the St. Mary of the Snows Church. But beware—its waiters could win the award for the rudest service in town (daily 9:00–24:00, tucked in a courtyard near the bottom of Wenceslas Square, on the border between Old and New Towns, located on map on page 133, Jungmannovo Náměstí 16, tel. 221-111-150).

Restaurace u Provaznice ("By the Ropemaker's Wife") has all the Czech classics, peppered with the story of a once-upon-a-time-faithful wife. (Check the menu for details of the gory story.) It's less touristed and less expensive than the other restaurants in this area. Natives congregate here for their famously good "pig leg" with horseradish and Czech mustard (daily 11:00–24:00, a block into the Old Town from the bottom of Wenceslas Square at Provaznická 3, tel. 224-232-528).

U Medvídků ("By the Bear Cubs"), which started out as a brewery in 1466, is now a flagship beer hall of the Czech Budweiser. The ambience of the one large room is bright, noisy, pretty touristy, and a bit smoky (daily 11:30–23:00, a block toward Wenceslas Square from Bethlehem Square at Na Perštýnì 7, tel. 224-211-916). The small beer bar next to the restaurant (daily 16:00–3:00 in the morning) is used by university students during emergencies—such as after most other pubs have closed.

U Zlatého Tygra ("By the Golden Tiger") has long embodied the proverbial Czech pub, where beer turns strangers into kindred spirits who cross the fuzzy line between memory and imagination as they tell their hilarious life stories to each other. Today "the Tiger" is a buzzing shrine to one of its longtime regulars, the writer Bohumil Hrabal, whose fictions immortalize many of the colorful characters that once warmed the wooden benches here (daily 15:00–23:00, often jam-packed, just south of Karlova at Husova 17).

Hospoda u Nováka, behind the National Theatre (i.e., not so central), is emphatically Czech, with few tourists. It takes good care of its regulars (you'll see the old monthly beer tabs in a rack just inside the door). Nostalgic communist-era signs are everywhere. During that time, pubs like this were close-knit communities where regulars escaped from the depression of daily life. Today the Nováka is a bright and smoky hangout where you can still happily curse whatever regime you happen to live under. While the English menu lists the well-executed Czech classics, it doesn't list the cheap daily specials (daily 10:00–23:00, V Jirchářích 2, tel. 224-930-639).

Restaurace u Betlémské Kaple, behind Bethlehem Chapel, is not "ye olde" Czech. It has light wooden decor, cheap lunch deals, and fish specialties that attract natives and visitors in search of a good Czech bite for Czech prices (daily 11:00–23:00, Betlémské Náměstí 2, tel. 222-221-639).

Česká Kuchyně ("Czech Kitchen") is a blue-collar cafeteria serving steamy old Czech cuisine to a local clientele. It's fast, practical, cheap, and traditional as can be. There's no English inside, so—if you want apple charlotte, but not tripe soup—be sure to review the small English menu in the window outside before entering. Note the numbers of your preferred dishes because they correspond to the Czech menu you'll see inside. Pick up your tally sheet as you enter, grab a tray, point liberally to whatever you'd like, and keep the paper to pay as you exit. It's extremely cheap... unless you lose your paper (daily 9:00–20:00, very central, across from Havelská Market at Havelská 23, tel. 224-235-574).

Restaurace Mlejnice ("The Mill") is a fun little pub strewn with farm implements and happy eaters, located just out of the tourist crush two blocks from the Old Town Square. They serve hardy traditional and modern Czech plates for 150–180 Kč (daily 11:00–24:00, reservations smart in evening, between Melantrichova and Železná at Kožná 14, tel. 224-228-635).

Hip Restaurants

Country Life Vegetarian Restaurant is a bright, easy, non-smoking cafeteria with a well-displayed buffet of salads and hot veggie dishes. It's midway between the Old Town Square and the bottom of Wenceslas Square. They're serious about their vegetarianism, serving only plant-based, unprocessed, and unrefined food. Its dining area is quiet and elegantly woody for a cafeteria, with three tables and wicker chairs outside in the courtyard (Sun–Thu 9:00–20:30, Fri 9:00–17:00, closed Sat, through courtyard at Melantrichova 15/Michalská 18, tel. 224-213-366).

Lehká Hlava ("Clear Head") Vegetarian Restaurant, tucked away on a cul-de-sac, has a mission to provide a "clear atmosphere for enjoying food." Sitting as if in an enchanted forest, diners enjoy dishes from around the world (100–150-Kč plates, two-course 90-Kč daily special, no eggs, no smoke, lots of vegan dishes, daily 11:30–23:30, reservations smart in the evening, between Bethlehem Chapel and the river at Boršov 2, tel. 222-220-665).

Klub Architektů, next to Bethlehem Chapel, is a modern hangout in a medieval cellar serving excellent original dishes, hearty salads, Moravian wines, and Slovak beer. The friendly waiters make the atmospheric subterranean space into one of most welcoming places in the Old Town (daily, Betlémské Náměstí 169, tel. 224-401-214).

At **Le Patio,** on the big and busy Národní Třída, the first thing you'll notice are the many lanterns suspended from the ceiling—and the big ship moored out back (okay, just its hulking bow). Le Patio has a hip, continental feel to it, but for a place that also sells furniture (head straight back, and down the stairs), they definitely need comfier dining chairs. The atmosphere is as pleasant and carefully designed as the dishes, with international fare from India, France, and points in between. There's always a serious vegetarian option available (200–350-Kč plates, daily 8:00–23:00, Národní 22, tel. 224-934-375). Diners enjoy live music Friday and Saturday nights (19:30–22:30).

Ethnic Eateries on or near Dlouhá Street

Dlouhá, the wide street leading away from the Old Town Square behind the Jan Hus monument (left of Týn Church), is lined with ethnic restaurants catering mostly to cosmopolitan locals. Within a couple of blocks, you can eat your way around the world. From Dlouhá, wander the Rámová/Haštalská Masná area to survey a United Nations of eateries: You'll find Moroccan (**Dahab,** with some interesting hubbly-bubbly action at Dlouhá 33), Spanish, French (**Chez Marcel** at Haštalská 12 is understandably popular—with a fun-loving waitstaff), Afghan, Italian, and these four, which deserve special consideration:

Indian: **Beas** is a cheap vegetarian restaurant ruled by a Punjabi chef who concocts mild *thalis* (mixed platters) in the style of northern Indian plains and *dosas* of the southern Indian variety. Tucked away in a courtyard behind the Týn Church, this place is popular with university students (Mon–Sat 9:30–20:00, Sun 10:00–18:00, Týnská 19).

Thai: **Orange Moon** specializes in Thai curries, but you'll also find dishes from Myanmar (Burma) and India served in a space delightfully decorated with artwork from Southeast Asia. This restaurant attracts a mixture of locals, expats, and tourists (daily 11:30–23:30, reservations recommended, Rámová 5, tel. 222-325-119).

Irish: **Molly Malone's Irish Pub** may seem a strange recommendation in Prague—home of the world's best beer—but this is the kind of ambience locals (and not tourists) seek out. Having a drink here will likely put you in touch with a fun Czech crowd. This has been the expat and local favorite for Guinness ever since the Velvet Revolution enabled the Celts to return to one of their homelands. Worn wooden floors, dingy walls, and the Irish manager transport you right into the heart of blue-collar Dublin (which is, after all, a popular place for young Czechs to find jobs in the high-tech industry). Hidden in a forgotten corner of Josefov, Molly Malone's is a destination for those who have adopted Prague and aren't just passing through (Sun–Thu 11:00–1:00 in the morning, Fri–Sat 11:00–2:00 in the morning, U Obecního Dvora 4, tel. 224-818-851).

American: **Bohemia Bagel** is hardly authentic—exasperated Czechs insist that bagels have nothing to do with Bohemia. Owned by an American, this practical café caters mostly to youthful tourists, with good sandwiches (100–125 Kč), a little garden out back, and Internet access (1.50 Kč/min). If homesick, you'll love the menu, with everything from Philly cheesesteak to bacon and eggs (daily 7:00–24:00, Masná 2, tel. 224-812-560).

In the Jewish Quarter

These three eateries are well-located to break up a demanding tour of the Jewish Quarter—all within two blocks of each other on or near Široká (see the map on page 89).

Kolkovna is big and woody, yet modern, serving a fun mix of Czech and international cuisine—ribs, salads, cheese plates, and good beer (a bit overpriced but good energy, daily 11:00–24:00, across from Spanish Synagogue at V Kolkovně 8, tel. 224-819-701).

Franz Kafka Café, with a cool, dark, and woody interior strewn with historic photos of the ghetto and a few good sidewalk tables, is great for a relaxing salad, sandwich, snack, or drink (150-Kč salads, daily 10:00–21:00, a block from the cemetery at Široká 12).

Pekařství ("Bakery") is a little deli with fresh sandwiches, greasy microwavable meat pies, tempting cakes, yogurt, and a cooler full of drinks. It's self-serve and dirt-cheap, with plain circa-1960 linoleum loft seating upstairs (daily 7:00–22:30, Široká 10, near the Pinkas Synagogue). Head upstairs to see the insane director of the National Gallery throwing paint on a nude woman.

Dining with an Old Town Square View

Restaurant u Prince Terrace, in the five-star U Prince Hotel facing the Astronomical Clock, is designed for foreign tourists. A sleek elevator takes you to its rooftop, where every possible inch is used to serve good food (international with plenty of fish) from their open-air grill. The view is arguably the best in town—especially at sunset. The menu is a fun but overpriced mix, with photos to make ordering easy. Being in such a touristy spot, waiters are experts at nicking you with confusing menu charges; don't be afraid to confirm exact prices before ordering. This place is also great for just a drink at sunset or late at night (fine salads, 240–300-Kč plates, daily until 24:00, brusque staff, outdoor heaters when necessary, Staroměstské Náměstí 29, tel. 224-213-807—but no reservations possible).

Cafés

These places—dripping with history—are as much about the ambience as they are about the coffee. Most cafés also serve sweets and light meals.

Grand Café Slavia, across from the National Theatre (facing the Legions Bridge on Národní street), is a fixture in Prague, famous as a hangout for its literary elite. Today, it's tired and clearly past its prime, with an Art Deco interior, lousy piano entertainment, and celebrity photos on the wall. But its iconic status makes it a fun stop for a coffee—skip the food (daily 8:00–23:00, sit as near the river as possible). Notice the *Drinker of Absinthe* painting on the wall (and on the menu for 55 Kč)—with the iconic Czech writer struggling with reality.

Café Louvre is a longtime elegant favorite (opened in 1902) that still draws an energetic young crowd. From the big and busy Národní street, you walk upstairs into a venerable world of newspapers on sticks (including English) and waiters in vests and aprons. The back room has long been the place for billiard tables (100 Kč/hr). An English flier tells its history (200-Kč plates, 120-Kč two-course lunch offered 11:00–15:00, open daily 8:00–23:30, Národní 22, tel. 224-930-949).

Grand Café Orient is just two flights up off busy Celetná street, yet a world away from the crush of tourism below. Located in the Black Madonna House, the café is upstairs from the Museum of Czech Cubism (see page 85) and, fittingly, decorated with a Cubist flair. With its stylish old circa-1910 decor toned to dark green, this space is full of air and light—and a good value, to boot (salads, sandwiches, great balcony seating, Mon–Fri 9:00–22:00, Sat–Sun 10:00–22:00, Ovocný Trh 19, at the corner of Celetná near the Powder Tower, tel. 224-224-240).

Café Montmartre, on a small street parallel to Karlova, combines Parisian ambience with unbeatable Czech prices. Dreamy Czech minds have found their asylum here after Grand Café Slavia (see above) and other long-time favorites have either closed down or become stuck in their past. The main room is perfect for discussing art and politics, while the intimate room behind the courtyard is where you recite poetry to your date (Mon–Fri 10:00–23:00, Sat–Sun 12:00–23:00, Řetězová 7, tel. 222-221-244).

Ebel Coffee House, in the Ungelt courtyard behind the Týn Church, is the local Starbucks—priding itself on the wide assortment of fresh coffee grounds from every coffee-growing country in the world, inviting cakes, and a colorful setting that delights the mind as much as the caffeine does (daily 9:00–22:00, Týn 1, tel. 224-895-788).

Teahouses

Many Czech people are bohemian philosophers at heart and prefer the mellow, smoke-free environs of a teahouse to the smoky, traditional beer hall. Young Czechs are much more interested in traveling to exotic destinations like Southeast Asia, Africa, or Peru than to Western Europe, so the Oriental teahouses set their minds in vacation mode.

While there are teahouses all over town, a fine example in a handy locale is Prague's original one, established in 1991. **Dobrá Čajovna** ("Good Teahouse"), just a few steps off the bustle of Wenceslas Square, takes you into a very peaceful world that elevates tea to an almost religious ritual. At the desk you'll be given an English menu and a bell. Grab a seat and study the menu, which lovingly describes each tea. The menu lists a world of tea (very fresh, prices by the small pot), "accompaniments" (such as Exotic Miscellany), and light meals "for hungry tea drinkers." When you're ready to order, ring your bell to beckon a tea monk—likely a member of the "Lovers of Tea Society" (Mon–Sat 10:00–21:30, Sun 14:00–21:30, near the base of Wenceslas Square, opposite McDonald's at Václavské Náměstí 14, www.cajovna.com).

Art Nouveau Splendor

The **Municipal House** (Obecní Dům), the sumptuous Art Nouveau concert hall, has three restaurants: a café, a French restaurant, and a beer cellar (all at Náměstí Republiky 5). The dressy café, Kavárna Obecní Dům, is drenched in chandeliered, Art Nouveau elegance and offers the best value and experience here (light, pricey meals and drinks with great atmosphere and bad service, 250-Kč three-course special daily for lunch or dinner, open daily 7:30–23:00, live piano or jazz trio 16:00–20:00, tel. 222-002-763). The fine and formal French restaurant in the next wing oozes Mucha elegance (700–1,000-Kč meals, daily 12:00–16:00 and 18:00–23:00, tel. 222-002-777). For the location, see the map on page 133.

In the Little Quarter

These characteristic eateries are handy for a bite before or after your Prague Castle visit. For locations, see the map on page 130.

U Sedmi Švábů ("By the Seven Roaches") is a touristy den where even the cuisine is medieval. Since America was not yet discovered in the Middle Ages, you won't find any corn, potatoes, or tomatoes on the menu. The salty yellow things that come with the Krušovice beer are chickpeas. Carnivores thrive here: Try the skewered meats *(špíz u Sedmi Švábů)*, flaming beef *(flambák)*, or pork knuckle (daily 11:00–23:00, Janský Vršek 14, tel. 257-531-455).

U Osla v Kolébce ("By the Donkey in the Cradle") fills a peaceful courtyard just a minute off the touristy hubbub of Nerudova. The laid-back scene consists of two restaurants with nearly identical simple menus, dominated by tasty sausages and salads (daily 10:00–22:00, Jánský Vršek 8, below Nerudova, next door to U Sedmi Švábů, tel. 731-407-036).

U Hrocha ("By the Hippo"), a very authentic little pub packed with beer-drinkers and smoke, serves simple, traditional meals— basically meat starters with bread. Just below the castle near Little Quarter Square (Malostranské Náměstí), it's actually the haunt of many members of Parliament, which is located just around the corner (daily 12:00–23:00, chalkboard lists daily meals in English, Thunovská 10).

Restaurace Rybářský Klub, on Kampa Island overlooking the river, is run by the Society of Czech Fishermen and serves one of the widest and tastiest selections of freshwater fish in Prague at reasonable prices. Dine on fish-cream soup, pike, trout, carp, or catfish under the imaginative artwork of Little Quarter painter Mr. Kuba. On warm evenings, late May through October, they fill their dock with tables and offer my choice for the best riverside dining in town (three-course meal for around 400 Kč, riverside menu not as extensive as indoor restaurant menu, daily 12:00–23:00, U Sovových Mlýnů 1, tel. 257-534-200).

In the Castle Quarter

To locate the following restaurants, see the map on page 112.

Klášterní Pivovar ("Monastery Brewery") was founded by an abbot in 1628. The brewery closed down in 1907, but it finally re-opened in 2004 after meticulous restoration in two large rooms and a pleasant courtyard. The wooden decor and circa-1900 newspaper clippings (including Hapsburg Emperor Franz Josef's "Proclamation to My Nations," announcing the beginning of World War I), bring you to the heart of the best in Czech pub dining. Beer-flavored cheese served on toasted black-yeast bread is a must starter for any meal here. Both locally brewed beer and Czech Budweiser flows liberally (daily 10:00–22:00, Strahovské Nádvoří 301, tel. 233-353-155, www.klasterni-pivovar.cz). It's directly across from the entrance to the Strahov library (not to be confused with the enormous, group-oriented Klášterní Restaurace next door, to the right).

Restaurace Nad Úvozem is hidden in the middle of a staircase that connects Loretánská and Úvoz streets. This secret spot, which boasts super views of Prague, offers excellent food for surprisingly low prices, given its location. Try the roast beef in plum sauce (170 Kč). The service is slower when the restaurant is full, as the kitchen has limited space (daily 12:00–21:00; as you go down Loretánská watch for pans, scoops, and spoons hanging on chains on your right at #15; tel. 220-511-532). To discourage pub-goers from mingling with diners, the beer here is terribly overpriced (69 Kč).

Hostinec u Černého Vola ("By the Black Ox") is a smoky, dingy old-time pub—its survival in the midst of all the castle splendor and tourism is a marvel. It feels like a kegger on the banks of the river Styx, with classic bartenders serving up Kozel beer (traditional "goat" brand with excellent darks) and beer-friendly light meals. The pub is located on Loretánská (no sign outside, sniff for cigarette smoke and look for the only house on the block without an arcade—or see map on page 112, daily 10:00–22:00, English menu on request).

Malý Buddha ("Little Buddha") serves delightful food—especially vegetarian—and takes its theme seriously. You'll step into a mellow, low-lit escape of bamboo and peace to be served by people with perfect complexions and almost no pulse (Tue–Sun 13:00–22:30, closed Mon, non-smoking, between the castle and Strahov Monastery at Úvoz 46, tel. 220-513-894).

Espresso Kajetánka, just off Castle Square, has magnificent city views. It's a good, if overpriced, place for a drink or snack as you start or end your castle visit (daily 10:00–20:00, Ke Hradu, tel. 257-533-735).

Na Baště, more convenient but not as scenic, is in a garden through the gate to the left of the main castle entry. The outdoor seating, among Jože Plečnik's ramparts and obelisks, is the castle at its most peaceful (Sun–Thu 11:00–23:00, Fri–Sat 11:00–24:00, tel. 281-933-010).

Dining with Style

In Prague, a fancy candlelit dinner with fine wines and connoisseur-approved dishes costs more than most locals can afford—but it's still a bargain in comparison to similar restaurants in Paris or Dallas. I list only two such splurges: one aristocratic, Old World, under the castle; one more modern, untouristy, and near the Old Town Square.

Restaurace David, with two little 18th-century rooms hiding on a small cobblestone street opposite the American Embassy in the Little Quarter, is my choice for a romantic splurge. The exquisite cuisine, a modern incarnation of traditional Czech, with

French and European influences, ranges from game to roasted duck and liver. Your meal comes with the gourmet quotient of knives and fancy glasses, and graceful waiters serve you like an aristocrat—appropriately, considering the neighborhood (most meals 600–1,000 Kč, open daily, reservations recommended, Tržiště 21, tel. 257-533-109).

Restaurant Červená Tabulka ("Red Chalkboard") is in a low, nondescript townhouse in a quiet neighborhood outside of the tourist circus. Sit in the dressy candlelit interior or on the quiet and breezy cobbled courtyard. Either way, there's not a dumpling in sight. The menu features modern international dishes with a focus on fish (fine 300-Kč plates and gourmet presentation). The wines are excellent and a great value (daily 11:30–23:00, Lodecká 4, tel. 224-810-401). To get to the restaurant from the Municipal House, cross Náměstí Republiky and turn right onto Truhlářská; it's 200 yards down the street on the corner of quiet Petrské Náměstí square.

TRANSPORTATION CONNECTIONS

Getting to Prague: Centrally located Prague is a logical gateway between Western and Eastern Europe. If you're coming from the West and using a Eurailpass, you must purchase tickets to cover the portion of the journey from the Czech border into Prague (buy at the train station before you board the train for Prague—it's only about $12 from the border to Prague). From the East, Prague is connected by convenient night trains with Budapest, Kraków, and Warsaw.

You'll find handy Czech train and bus schedules at www .vlak-bus.cz (train info tel. 221-111-122, little English spoken). Remember that for all train connections, it's important to confirm which of Prague's stations to use.

From Prague by Train to: Český Krumlov (8/day, 1/day direct, 4 hrs), **Budapest** (every 2 hours, 7–8.5 hrs; 1 direct night train, 9 hrs), **Kraków** (3/day with changes, 7.5–8 hrs; 1 direct night train/day, 8.5 hrs), **Warsaw** (2/day direct including 1 night train, more with changes, 8.5–9.5 hrs), **Vienna** (7/day, 4–6 hrs), **Berlin** (7/day, 5 hrs), **Munich** (3/day with changes, 6 hrs; 1 direct night train), **Frankfurt** (4/day, 7 hrs).

By Bus to: Terezín (hourly, 1 hr), **Český Krumlov** (7/day, 3.5 hrs, from Florenc station; an easy direct 3-hr bus leaves at about 9:00).

By Car with a Driver: Mike's Chauffeur Service is a reliable family-run company with fair and fixed rates around town and beyond. Friendly Mike's motto is, "We go the extra mile for you" (round-trip fares with waiting time included, guaranteed through

2007 with this book: Český Krumlov-3,800 Kč, Terezín-1,700 Kč, Karlštejn-1,500 Kč, minivan with plenty of room for up to 4 people, minibus also available, tel. 241-768-231, mobile 602-224-893, www.mike-chauffeur.cz, mike.chauffeur@cmail.cz). On the way to Krumlov, Mike will stop at no extra charge at Hluboká Castle or České Budějovice, where the original Bud beer is made. Mike offers a "Panoramic Transfer to Vienna" for 7,000 Kč (depart Prague at 8:00, arrive Český Krumlov at 10:00, stay up to 6 hrs, 1-hr scenic Czech riverside-and-village drive, then a 2-hr autobahn ride to your Vienna hotel, maximum 4 people). Mike also offers a similar "Panoramic Transfer to Budapest" for 10,000 Kč (2 hrs to Český Krumlov, then 1-hr scenic drive to Linz, followed by 5–6 hrs on expressway to Budapest).

ČESKÝ KRUMLOV

Lassoed by its river and dominated by its castle, this enchanting town feels lost in a time warp. While Český Krumlov is the Czech Republic's answer to Germany's Rothenburg, it has yet to be turned into a medieval theme park. When you see its awe-inspiring castle, delightful Old Town of shops and cobbled lanes, characteristic little restaurants, and easy canoeing options, you'll understand why having fun is a slam dunk here.

Český Krumlov (CHESS-key KROOM-loff) means, roughly, "Czech Bend in the River." Calling it "Český" for short sounds silly to Czech speakers (since dozens of Czech town names begin with "Český"). "Krumlov" for short is okay.

Since Krumlov is the second-most-visited town (1.5 million visits annually) in the Czech Republic, there's enough tourism to make things colorful and easy—but not so much that it tramples the place's charm. This town of 15,000 attracts a young, bohemian crowd, drawn here for its simple beauty, cheap living, and fanciful bars.

Planning Your Time

Because the castle and theater can be visited only with a guide (and English tours are offered just a few times a day), serious sightseers should reserve both tours first thing in the morning in person at the castle and theater (or call the castle), and then build their day around the tour times. Those who hate planning ahead on vacation can join a Czech tour anytime with an English information sheet.

A paddle down the river to Zlatá Koruna Abbey is a highlight (3 hrs, see "Canoeing and Rafting the Vltava," page 159), and a 20-minute walk up to the Křížový Vrch ("Hill of the Cross") rewards

Český Krumlov

TO ČESKÉ
BUDĚJOVICE
& PRAGUE

TO TRAIN
STATION

100 YARDS
100 METERS

CHVALŠINSKÁ SILNICE

MAIN ROAD

CITY GATE

MONASTERY

PIVOVARSKÁ

BAROQUE THEATER

CASTLE

FOOT-BRIDGE

LATRAN

NOVE MESTO

CASTLE GARDENS

DLOUHA

RADNIČNÍ

BARBER'S BRIDGE

BREWERY

EGON SCHIELE ART CENTER

ŠIROKÁ

SOUKEN.

PARKÁN

MUSEUM OF REGIONAL HISTORY

BUS STN.

VLTAVA

KÁJ.

KOST.

HORNI

BRIDGE

HORNI

ROOSEVELTOVA

KAPLICKÁ

ST. VITUS RIVER

HOTEL RŮŽE

DCH

RYBÁŘ.

LINECKÁ

MĚSTSKÝ PARK

MAIN ROAD

P – PARKING
★ = MAIN SQUARE
(NÁMĚSTÍ SVORNOSTI)

TO STATIONS OF THE CROSS

① Castle View Apts.
② Pension Olšakovský
③ Pension Sladová
④ Lobo Pension & Pension Danny
⑤ Little Pension Teddy
⑥ Pension Myší Díra & Maleček Boat Rental
⑦ Pension Anna

⑧ Hostel 99 & Hospoda 99 Rest.
⑨ Krumlov House Hostel
⑩ Na Louži Restaurant
⑪ Krčma u Dwau Maryí
⑫ Cikánská Jizba Tavern
⑬ Rest. u Dobráka
⑭ Rest. u Města Vídně
⑮ Laibon Restaurant

⑯ Rybářská Rest.
⑰ Rest. Barbakán
⑱ Dobrá Čajovna Teahouse
⑲ Start Short River Float
⑳ End Short River Float & Start Zlatá Koruna Float

you with a fine view of the town and its unforgettable riverside setting (see "Hiking," page 160). Other sights are quick visits and worthwhile only if you have a particular interest (Egon Schiele, puppets, torture, and so on).

The town itself is the major attraction. Evenings are for atmospheric dining and drinking. Sights are generally open 10:00–17:00 and closed on Monday.

ORIENTATION

Český Krumlov is extremely easy to navigate. The twisty Vltava River, which makes a perfect S through the town, ropes the Old Town into a tight peninsula. Above the Old Town is the Castle Town. Český Krumlov's one main street starts at the isthmus and heads through the peninsula. It winds through town and continues across a bridge before snaking through the Castle Town, the castle complex (a long series of courtyards), and the castle gardens high above. The main square, Náměstí Svornosti—with the TI, ATMs, and taxis—dominates the Old Town and marks the center of the peninsula. All recommended restaurants and hotels are within a few minutes' walk of this square. No sight in town is more than a five-minute stroll away.

Tourist Information

The helpful TI is on the main square (daily 9:00–19:00, July–Aug until 20:00, shorter hours in winter, tel. 380-704-622, www .ckrumlov.cz). Pick up the free city map. The 129-Kč *City Guide* explains everything in town and includes a fine town and castle map in the back. The TI can check train, bus, and flight schedules. Ask about concerts, city walking tours in English, and canoe trips on the river. A second, less-crowded "TI"—actually a private business—is just below the castle (daily 9:00–19:00, tel. 380-725-110).

Arrival in Český Krumlov

By Train: The train station is a 15-minute walk from town (turn right out of the station, then walk downhill onto a steep cobbled path leading to an overpass into the town center). Taxis are standing by to zip you to your hotel (about 100 Kč).

By Bus: The bus station is just three blocks away from the Old Town (from the bus station lot, drop down to main road and turn left, then turn right at Potraviny grocery store to reach the center). Figure on 60 Kč for a taxi from the station to your hotel.

Helpful Hints

Internet Access: Fine Internet cafés are all over town and in many of the accommodations. The TI on the main square has several fast, cheap, stand-up stations. Perhaps the best cybercafé is behind the TI by the castle (tel. 380-725-117). **Pension Teddy** has Internet access in its bar (1 Kč/min, open long hours daily, Rooseveltova street).

Bookstore: Shakespeare and Sons is a good little English-language bookstore (daily 11:00–20:00, a block below the main square at Soukenická 44, tel. 380-711-203).

Laundry: Pension Lobo runs a self-service launderette under the castle. Since there are only a few machines, you may have to wait (140 Kč/load, daily 9:00–20:00, Latrán 73).

Festivals: Locals drink oceans of beer and celebrate their medieval roots at big events such as the Celebration of the Rose (Slavnosti Růže), where blacksmiths mint ancient coins, jugglers swallow fire, mead flows generously, and pigs are roasted on open fires (June 22–24 in 2007). The summer also brings a top-notch international jazz and alternative music festival to town, performed in pubs, cafés, and the castle gardens (July 20–Aug 25 in 2007). During the St. Wenceslas celebrations, the square becomes a medieval market and the streets come alive with theater and music (Sept 28). Reserve a hotel well in advance if you'll be in town for these events (for more details, see www.ckrumlov.cz).

TOURS

Walking Tours—Since the town itself, rather than its sights, is what it's all about here, taking a guided walk is key for a meaningful visit. The TI sponsors three different guided walks. They are cheap, in English, and time well-spent. All meet in front of the TI on the main square. No reservations are necessary—just drop in and pay the guide. The **Historic Town Walk** offers the best general town introduction and is most likely to run (225 Kč, daily at 10:00, 90 min). The **Rose Tour** covers Renaissance and town architecture (160 Kč, daily at 14:00, 60 min). The **Brewing History Tour,** which is the most intimate of the many brewery tours in this land that so loves its beer, takes you through the Eggenberg Brewery (150 Kč, daily at 12:30, 90 min). For a self-guided town walk, consider renting an **audioguide** from the TI (60 Kč/hr).

Local Guides—**Oldřiška Baloušková** is a hardworking, excellent, young English-speaking guide who can show you around her hometown (400 Kč/hr, mobile 737-920-901, krumlovguide @hotmail.com). **Jiří (George) Václavíček,** a gentle and caring man who perfectly fits mellow Český Krumlov, is a joy to share this town with (350 Kč/hr, tel. 380-726-813, mobile 603-927-995, jiri.vaclavicek@seznam.cz). **Karolína Kortušová** is an enthusiastic young woman with great organizational skills. Her company,

Český Krumlov History

With the natural moat provided by the sharp bend in the Vltava, it's no wonder this has been a choice spot for eons. Celtic tribes first settled here a century before Christ. Then came German tribes. The Slavic tribes arrived in the ninth century. The Rožmberks—Bohemia's top noble family—ran the city from 1302 to 1602. You'll see their rose symbol all over town. In many ways, the 16th century was the town's Golden Age, when Český Krumlov hosted artists, scientists, and alchemists from all over Europe. In 1588, the town became home to an important Jesuit college. The Hapsburgs bought the region in 1602, ushering in a more Germanic period. (After that, as many as 75 percent of the town's people were German—until 1945 when most Germans were expelled.)

The rich mix of Gothic, Renaissance, and Baroque buildings is easy to under-appreciate. As you wander, look up...notice the surviving details in the stonework. Step into shops. Snoop into back lanes and tiny squares. Gothic buildings curve with the winding streets. Many precious Gothic and Renaissance frescoes were whitewashed in Baroque times (when the colorful trimmings of earlier times were way out of style). Today these precious frescoes are being rediscovered and restored.

With its rich German heritage, it was easy for Hitler to claim that this region—the Sudetenland—was rightfully part of

Krumlov Tours, can set you up with a good local tour guide, palace and theater admissions, river trips, and more (guides-400 Kč/hr, mobile 723-069-561, www.krumlovtours.com, info@krumlovtours .com).

SELF-GUIDED WALK

Welcome to Český Krumlov

The town's ▲▲▲ sight is its cobbled cityscape, surrounded by its babbling river and capped by a dramatic castle. All of Český Krumlov's meager sights are laced together in this charming walk from the top of the Old Town, down its spine, across the river, and up to the castle.

• Start at the bridge over the isthmus, once the fortified grand entry gate to the town.

Horní Bridge: From this "Upper Bridge," note the natural fortification provided by the tight bend in the river. The last building in town (just over the river) is the Eggenberg Brewery (with daily tours—see "Tours," above). Behind that, on the horizon, is a pile of white apartment high-rises—built in the last decade of

Germany, and in 1938, the infamous Munich Agreement made it his. Americans liberated the town in 1945. Due to Potsdam Treaty–approved ethnic cleansing, three million Germans in Czech lands were sent west to Germany. Emptied of its German citizenry, Český Krumlov turned into a ghost town, partially inhabited by Roma (Gypsies).

In the post-WWII world planned by Stalin and FDR, the border of the Soviet and American spheres of influence fell about here. While the communist government established order, the period from 1945 to 1989 was a smelly time capsule, as the town was infamously polluted. Its now-pristine river was foamy with pollutants from the paper mill just upstream, while the hills around the town were marred with blocks of prefabricated concrete. The people who moved in never fully identified with the town—in Europe, a place without ancestors is without life-giving roots. But the bleak years of communism paradoxically provided a cocoon to preserve the town. There was no money, so little changed, apart from a build-up of grime.

Today, with its new prosperity, Český Krumlov looks like a fairy-tale town. In fact, movie producers consider it ideal for films. *The Adventures of Pinocchio,* starring Jonathan Taylor Thomas, was filmed right here in 1995, as was the opening sequence for the 2006 film *The Illusionist.*

the communist era and considered the worst places in town to call home. Left of the brewery stands the huge monastery (not generally open to the public). Behind that on Kleť, the highest hilltop, stands a TV tower that locals say was built to jam Voice of America broadcasts. Facing the town, on your left, rafters take to the river for the sloppy half-hour float around town to the take-out spot just on your right.

• *A block downhill on Horní (Upper) street is the...*

Museum of Regional History: This small museum gives you a quick look at regional costumes, tools, and traditions. When you pay, pick up the English translation of the displays (it also includes a lengthy history of Krumlov). Start on the top floor, where you'll see a Bronze Age exhibit, old paintings, a glimpse of noble life, and a look at how the locals rafted lumber from Krumlov all the way to Vienna. Don't miss the fun-to-study ceramic model of Český Krumlov in 1800 (note the extravagant gardens high above the town). The lower floor comes with fine folk costumes and domestic art (50 Kč, daily 10:00–17:00, until 18:00 in July–Aug, Horní 152, tel. 380-711-674).

• *Below the museum, a little garden overlook affords a fine castle view.*

Edvard Beneš and the German Question

Czechoslovakia was created in 1918, when the vast, multi-ethnic Hapsburg Empire broke into smaller nations after losing World War I. The principle that gave countries such as Poland, Czechoslovakia, and Romania independence was called "self-determination": Each nation had the right to its own state within the area where its people were in the majority. But the peoples of Eastern Europe had mixed over the centuries, making it impossible to create functioning states based purely on ethnicity. In the case of Czechoslovakia, the borders were drawn along historical rather than ethnic boundaries. While the country was predominantly Slavic, there were also areas with overwhelmingly German and Hungarian majorities. One of these areas—a fringe around the western part of the country, mostly populated by Germans—was known as the Sudetenland.

At first, the coexistence of Slavs and Germans in the new republic worked fine. German parties were important power brokers and participated in almost every coalition government. Hitler's rise to power, however, led to the growth of German nationalism, even outside Germany. Soon 70 percent of Germans in Czechoslovakia voted for the Nazis. In September 1938, the Munich Agreement ceded the Sudetenland to Germany—and the Czech minority had to leave.

Edvard Beneš was the first Czechoslovak secretary of state (1918–1934) and later became the country's second president (1934–1948). Beneš led the Czechoslovak exile government in London during World War II. Like most Czechs and Slovaks, Beneš believed that after the hard feelings produced by the Munich Agreement, peaceful coexistence of Slavs and Germans in a single state was impossible. His postwar solution: Move the Sudeten Germans to Germany, much as the Czechs had been forced out of the Sudetenland before. Through skillful diplomacy, Beneš got

Immediately across the street, notice the Renaissance facade of...

Hotel Růže: This former Jesuit college hides a beautiful courtyard. Pop inside to see a couple of bronze busts that stand like a shrine to the founders of Czechoslovakia. The one on the right, dedicated by the Czech freedom fighters, commemorates the first Czechoslovak president, Tomáš Garrigue Masaryk (in office 1918–1934; see sidebar on page 116). The bust on the left recalls Masaryk's successor, Edvard Beneš (in office 1934–1948; see sidebar above).

• *Walk another block down the main drag, until you reach steps on the left leading to the...*

Church of St. Vitus: Český Krumlov's main church was built as a bastion of Catholicism in the 15th century, when the Roman the Allies to sign on to this idea.

Shortly after the end of World War II, three million people of German ancestry were forced to leave their homes. Millions of Germanic people in Poland, Romania, Ukraine, and elsewhere met with a similar fate. Many of these families had been living in these areas for centuries. The methods employed to expel them included murder, rape, and plunder. (Today we'd call it "ethnic cleansing.")

In 1945, Český Krumlov lost 75 percent of its population, and Czechs moved into vacated German homes. Having easily acquired the property, the new residents didn't take much care of the houses. Within a few years, the once-prosperous Sudetenland was reduced to shabby towns and uncultivated fields—a decaying, godforsaken region. After 1989, displaced Sudeten Germans—the majority of whom now live in Bavaria—demanded that the Czechoslovak government apologize for the violent way in which the expulsion was carried out. Some challenged the legality of the decrees, and for a time the issue threatened otherwise good Czech-German relations.

Although no longer such a hot-button diplomatic issue, the so-called Beneš Decrees remain divisive in Czech politics. While liberals consider the laws unjust, many others—especially the older generations—see them as fair revenge for the behavior of the Sudeten Germans prior to the war. In the former Sudetenland, where Czech landowners worry that the Germans will try to claim back their property, Beneš is a hugely popular figure. His bust in Český Krumlov's Hotel Růže is one of the first memorials to Beneš in the country. The bridge behind the Old Town has been named for Beneš since the 1990s. The main square—the center of a thriving German community 70 years ago—is now ironically called "Square of Concord."

Catholic Church was fighting the Hussites. The 17th-century Baroque high altar shows a totem of religious figures: the Virgin Mary (crowned in heaven), St. Vitus (above Mary), and way up on top, St. Wenceslas, the patron saint of the Czech people—long considered their ambassador in heaven. The canopy in the back, while empty today, once supported a grand statue of a Rožmberk atop a horse. The statue originally stood at the high altar. Too egotistical for Jesuits, it was later moved to the rear of the nave, and then lost for good. As you listen to the river, notice the empty organ case. While the main organ is out for restoration, the cute little circa-1716 Baroque beauty is getting plenty of use (see photos of the restoration work on the far wall, church open daily 10:00–19:00, Sunday Mass at 9:30, tel. 380-711-336).

• *Continuing on Horní street, you'll come to the...*

Main Square (Náměstí Svornosti): Lined by a mix of Renaissance and Baroque homes of burghers (all built upon 12th-century Gothic foundations), the main square has a grand charm. There's continuity here. Lékárna, with the fine, red, Baroque facade on the lower corner of the square, is still a pharmacy, as it has been since 1620. McDonald's tried three times to get a spot here but was turned away. The Town Hall flies the Czech flag and the town flag, which shows the rose symbol of the Rožmberk family, who ruled the town for 300 years.

Imagine the history this square has seen: In the 1620s, the rising tide of Lutheran Protestantism threatened Catholic Europe. Krumlov was a seat of Jesuit power and learning, and the intellectuals of the Roman church allegedly burned books on this square. Later, when there was a bad harvest, locals blamed witches—and burned them, too. Every so often, terrible plagues rolled through the countryside. In a nearby village, all but two residents were killed by a plague.

But the plague stopped before devastating the people of Český Krumlov, and in 1715—as a thanks to God—they built the plague monument that stands on the square today. Much later, in 1938, Hitler stood right here before a backdrop of long Nazi banners to celebrate the annexation of the Sudetenland. And in 1968, Russian tanks spun their angry treads on these same cobblestones to intimidate locals who were demanding freedom. Today, thankfully, this square is part of an unprecedented peace and prosperity for the Czech people.

• *The following three museums are grouped around the main square.*

Puppet Museum: You'll see fascinating displays in three small rooms of more than 300 movable creations (overwhelmingly of Czech origin, but also some from Burma and Rajasthan). At the model stage, children of any age can try their hand at pulling the strings on their favorite fairy tale (80 Kč, daily 10:00–21:00, Radniční 29, tel. 380-713-422, www.inspirace.krumlov.cz).

Torture Museum: This is just a lame haunted house: dark, with sound effects, cheap modern models, and prints showing off the cruel and unusual punishments of medieval times (80 Kč, daily 9:00–20:00, English descriptions, Náměstí Svornosti 1, tel. 380-766-343).

Egon Schiele Art Center: This classy contemporary art gallery has temporary exhibits, generally featuring 20th-century Czech artists. The top-floor permanent collection celebrates the Viennese artist Egon Schiele (pronounced "Sheila"), who once spent a few weeks here during a secret love affair. A friend of Gustav Klimt and an important figure in the Secessionist movement in Vienna, Schiele lived a short life (1890–1918). His cutting-edge lifestyle and harsh art of graphic nudes didn't always fit the conservative, small-town style of Český Krumlov, but townsfolk are happy enough today to charge you to see this relatively paltry collection (180 Kč, daily 10:00–18:00, Široká 70, tel. 380-704-011). The Schiele collection in Vienna's Belvedere Palace is far better (see page 777).

• *From the main square, walk up Radniční street and cross the...*

Barber's Bridge (Lazebnicky Most): This wooden bridge, decorated with two 19th-century statues, connects the Old Town and the Castle Town. In the center stands a statue of St. John of Nepomuk, who's also depicted in a prominent statue on Prague's Charles Bridge (see page 86). Among other responsibilities, he's the protector against floods. In the great floods of August 2002, the angry river submerged the bridge (but removable banisters minimized the damage). Stains just above the windows of the adjacent building show how high the water rose.

• *After crossing the bridge, hike on up the hill. Your next stop is Krumlov Castle.*

SIGHTS

Krumlov Castle (Krumlovský Zámek)

No Czech town is complete without a castle—and now that the nobles are gone, their mansions are open to us common folk. The Krumlov Castle complex, worth ▲▲, includes bear pits, the castle itself, a rare Baroque theater, and groomed gardens.

Round Tower (Zámecká Věž)—The strikingly colorful round tower marks the location of the first castle, built here to guard the medieval river crossing. With its 16th-century Renaissance paint job colorfully restored, it looks exotic, featuring fancy astrological decor, terracotta symbols of the zodiac, and a fine arcade. Climb its 162 steps for a great view (30 Kč, daily 9:00–18:00, last entry 17:30).

Bear Pit—At the site of the castle drawbridge, the bear pit holds a family of European brown bears, as it has since the Rožmberks added bears to their coat of arms in the 16th century to demonstrate their (fake) blood relation to the distinguished Italian family of Orsini (the name means "bear-like").

Castle—The immense castle is a series of courtyards with shops, contemporary art galleries, and tourist services. The interior is accessible only by tour, which gives you a glimpse of the places where the Rožmberks, Eggenbergs, and Schwarzenbergs dined, studied, worked, prayed, entertained, and slept. (By European standards, the castle's not much, and the tours move slowly.) Imagine being an aristocratic guest here, riding the dukes' assembly line of fine living: You'd promenade through a long series of elegant spaces and dine in the sumptuous dining hall before enjoying a concert in the Hall of Mirrors, which leads directly to the Baroque Theater (described below). After the play, you'd go out into the château garden for a fireworks finale.

Cost, Hours, and Tours: To see the interior, you must take a 60-minute escorted tour: Tour I (Gothic and Renaissance rooms, of the most general interest) or Tour II (19th-century castle life). Tours run June–Aug Tue–Sun 9:00–12:00 & 13:00–18:00, spring and fall until 17:00, closed Mon and Nov–March. Tours in Czech cost 90 Kč, leave regularly, and include an adequate flier in English containing about half the information imparted by the guide (generally a student who's just memorized the basic script). English tours are preferable, but cost more (160 Kč), run less frequently, and are often booked solid. Make your reservation when you arrive in town; just walk up to the castle office. Or you can call 380-704-721, though the number is often busy. You'll be issued a ticket with your tour time printed on it. Be in the correct courtyard at that time, or you'll be locked out.

▲▲**Baroque Theater (Zámecké Divadlo)**—Europe once had several hundred fine Baroque theaters. Using candles for light and fireworks for special effects, most burned down. Today only two survive in good shape and are open to tourists: one at Stockholm's Drottningholm Palace, and one here, at Krumlov Castle. During the 45-minute tour, you'll sit on benches in the theater and then go under the stage to see the wood-and-rope contraptions that enabled scenes to be scooted in and out within seconds (while fireworks and smoke blinded the audience). Due to the theater's fragility, the number of visitors is strictly regulated. There are only five English tours a day, limited to 25 people per group and generally sold out in advance. While it's a lovely little theater with an impressive 3-D effect that makes the stage look deeper than it really is, I wouldn't bother with the tour unless you can snare a spot on an English one. The theater is used only once a year for an actual performance, with attendance limited to Baroque theater enthusiasts. You can call 380-704-721 to establish English-language tour times and reserve a space; but as with the castle tour, you will likely do best by visiting the ticket office in person (180 Kč, tours daily May–Oct only; English departures at 10:00, 11:00, 13:00, 14:00, 15:00, and

16:00; buy theater tour tickets at castle ticket office).

Castle Gardens—This 2,300-foot-long garden crowns the castle complex. It was laid out in the 17th century, when the noble family would light it with 22,000 oil lamps, torches, and candles for special occasions. The lower part is geometrical and symmetrical—French-style. The upper is rougher—English-style (free, May–Sept daily 8:00–19:00, April and Oct daily 8:00–17:00, closed Nov–March).

Near Český Krumlov

Zlatá Koruna Abbey—Directly above the river at the end of a three-hour float by raft or canoe (see "Activities," below), this abbey was founded in the 13th century by the king to counter the growing influence of the Vítek family, the ancestors of the mighty Rožmberks. As you enter the grounds, notice the central linden tree, with its strange, cape-like leaves; it's said to have been used by the anti-Catholic Hussites when they hanged the monks. The short, guided abbey tour takes you through the rare two-storied Gothic Chapel of the Guardian Angel, the main church, and the cloister. After the order was dissolved in 1785, the abbey functioned briefly as a village school before being turned into a factory during the Industrial Revolution. Damage from this period is visible on the cloister's crumbling arches. The abbey was restored in the 1990s and opened to the public only few years ago (85 Kč, tours in Czech run every 45 minutes, Tue–Sun 9:00–15:15, until 16:15 June–Aug, closed Mon and Oct–March, call 380-743-126 to arrange an English tour, access via river float).

ACTIVITIES

Český Krumlov lies in the middle of a valley popular for canoeing, rafting, hiking, and horseback riding. Boat-rental places are convenient to the Old Town, and several hiking paths start right in town.

Canoeing and Rafting the Vltava

Splash a little ▲▲▲ river fun into your visit by renting a rubber raft or hard plastic canoe for a quick 30-minute spin around Český Krumlov. Or go for a three-hour float and paddle through the Bohemian forests and villages of the nearby countryside. You'll end up at Zlatá Koruna Abbey (described above), where the rafting company will shuttle you back to town—or provide you with a bicycle to pedal back on your own along a bike path. This is a great hot-weather activity. Though the river is far from treacherous, be prepared to get wet.

On any trip, you'll encounter plenty of inviting pubs and cafés for breaks along the way. There's a little whitewater, but the river is so shallow that if you tip, you simply stand up and climb back in. (When that happens, pull the canoe up onto the bank to empty it, since you'll never manage to pour the water out while still in the river.)

Choose from a kayak, a canoe (fastest, less work, more likely to tip), or an inflatable raft (harder rowing, slower, but very stable). Prices are per boat (2–6 people) and include a map, a waterproof container, and transportation to or from the start and end points. Here are your options:

Quickie Circle-the-Town Float: The easiest half-hour experience is to float around the city's peninsula, starting and ending at opposite sides of the tiny isthmus. Heck, you can do it twice (350 Kč for 1 or 2 people in a canoe or raft).

Three-Hour Float to Zlatá Koruna Abbey: This is your best basic trip, with pastoral scenery, a riverside pub on the left after two hours, and a beautiful abbey as your destination (about 9 miles, 700 Kč for 1 or 2 people). From there you can bike back or catch a shuttle bus home—simply arrange a return plan with the rental company.

Longer and Faster Trips: If you start upriver from Krumlov (direction: Rožmberk), you'll go faster with more whitewater, but the river parallels a road so it's a little less idyllic. Longer trips in either direction involve lots of paddling even though you're going downstream. Rafting companies can review the many day-trip options with you.

Rental Companies: Several companies offer this lively activity. Perhaps the handiest are **Půjčovna Lodí Maleček Boat Rental** (open long hours daily April–Oct, closed Nov–March, at recommended Pension Myší Díra, Rooseveltova 28, tel. 380-712-508, www.malecek.cz, lode@malecek.cz) and **Cestovní Agentura Vltava** (April–Oct daily 9:00–18:00, closed Nov–March, in Pension Vltava at Kájovská 62, tel. 380-711-988, www.ckvltava.cz). Vltava also rents mountain bikes (320 Kč per day) and can bring a bike to the abbey for you to ride back.

Hiking

For an easy 20-minute hike to Křížový Vrch (Hill of the Cross), walk to the end of Rooseveltova street, cross at the traffic light, then head straight for the first (empty) chapel-like Station of the Cross. Turning right, it's easy to navigate along successive Stations of the Cross until you reach the white church on the hill (closed), set in the middle of wild meadows. Looking down into the valley at the medieval city nestled within the S-shaped river, framed by the rising hills, it's hard to imagine any town with a more powerful *genius loci* (spirit of the place). The view is best at sunset.

SLEEPING

Krumlov is filled with small, good, family-run pensions offering doubles with baths from 1,000–1,500 Kč and hostel beds for 300 Kč. Summer weekends and festivals (see page 151) are busiest and most expensive; reserve ahead when possible. Hotels (not a Krumlov forte) speak some English and accept credit cards; pensions rarely do either. While you can find a room upon arrival here, it's better to book at least a few days ahead if you want to stay in the heart of town. Cars are not very safe overnight—locals advise paying for a garage.

In the Old Town
$$$ Castle View Apartments, run by local guide Jiří Václavíček, rents seven apartments. These are the plushest and best-equipped rooms I found in town—the bathroom floors are heated, all come with kitchenettes, and everything's done just right. Their Web site describes each of the stylish apartments (1,800–4,000 Kč depending on size, view, and season; the big 4,000-Kč apartment sleeps up to six, complex pricing scheme, reserve direct with this book in 2007 to claim a 10 percent discount off their online prices, fourth night free, non-smoking, voucher for breakfast at next-door Grand Hotel, Šatlavská 140, tel. 380-726-813, www.castleview.cz, info @castleview.cz).

On Parkán Street, Below the Square
Secluded Parkán street, which runs along the river below the square, has a row of pensions with three to five rooms each. These places have a family feel and views of the looming castle above.

$$ Pension Olšakovský has an unbeatable breakfast area on a terrace next to the river. The owner's father, a professional musician, can teach you classical dance or piano (Db-1,050–1,250 Kč, includes parking, Parkán 114, tel. & fax 380-714-333, mobile 604-430-181, www.ckrumlov.cz/penzionekolsakovsky, j.olsakovsky @post.cz).

$ Pension Sladová is a standard family operation on the town side of Parkán street (Sb-800 Kč, Db-990 Kč, Tb-1,360 Kč, Parkán 125, mobile 602-363-049, fax 380-712-781, www.ckrumlov .cz/sladova, hana.sladova@seznam.cz).

Sleep Code

(22 Kč = about $1, country code: 420)
S = Single, **D** = Double/Twin, **T** = Triple, **Q** = Quad, **b** = bathroom,
s = shower only. Unless otherwise noted, prices include breakfast.

To help you sort easily through these listings, I've divided the rooms into three categories based on the price for a standard double room with bath:

$$$ Higher Priced—Most rooms 1,500 Kč or more.
$$ Moderately Priced—Most rooms between
                            1,000–1,500 Kč.
$ Lower Priced—Most rooms 1,000 Kč or less.

On Latrán Street, at the Base of the Castle

A quiet, cobbled pedestrian street (Latrán) runs below the castle just over the bridge from the Old Town. It's a 10-minute walk downhill from the train station. Lined with characteristic shops, the street has a couple of fine little family-run, eight-room pensions.

$$ Lobo Pension fills a modern, efficient, concrete building with eight fresh, spacious rooms (Db-1,100 Kč, Tb-1,500 Kč, includes parking, Latrán 73, tel. & fax 380-713-153, www.pensionlobo.cz, pensionlobo@cmail.cz).

$ Pension Danny is a little funkier, with homier rooms and a tangled floor plan above a restaurant (Db-890 Kč, apartment Db-1,190 Kč, breakfast in room, Latrán 72, tel. 380-712-710, www.pensiondanny.cz, pensiondanny@tiscali.cz).

On Rooseveltova Street, Between the Bus Station and the Old Town

Rooseveltova street, midway between the bus station and the Old Town (a four-minute walk from either), is lined with several fine little places, each with easy free parking. The key here is tranquility—the noisy bars of the town center are out of earshot.

$$ Little Pension Teddy has seven decent riverview rooms sharing a common balcony (Db-1,200 Kč with this book in 2007, cash only, a bit smoky, Internet access in the bar—1 Kč/min, Rooseveltova 38, tel. 380-711-595, www.teddy.cz, info@teddy.cz).

$$ Pension Myší Díra ("Mouse Hole") hides eight sleek, spacious, bright, and woody Bohemian contemporary rooms overlooking the Vltava River just outside the Old Town (Db-1,000–1,690 Kč, bigger deluxe riverview Db-1,200–1,990 Kč, prices depend on day and season—Fri–Sat most expensive, breakfast in your room, Rooseveltova 28, tel. 380-712-853, fax 380-711-900, www.malecek.cz). The no-nonsense reception, which closes at 20:00, also runs the recommended boat-rental company (Půjčovna Lodí Maleček, at same address), as well as the similar Pension Vok by the river, a five-minute walk away.

$$ Pension Anna is well-run, with two doubles, five apartments, and a restful little garden. Its apartments are spacious suites, with a living room and stairs leading to the double-bedded loft (Db-1,250 Kč, Db apartment-1,550 Kč, extra bed-400 Kč, Rooseveltova 41, tel. & fax 380-711-692, pension.anna@quick.cz). If you book a standard Db and they bump you up to an apartment, don't pay more than the Db rate.

Hostels

There are several hostels in town. Hostel 99 (closest to the train station) is clearly the high-energy, youthful party hostel. Krumlov House (closer to the bus station) is more mellow. Both are well-managed and each is a five-minute walk from the main square.

$ Hostel 99's picnic-table terrace looks out on the Old Town. While the gentle sound of the river gurgles outside your window, late at night you're more likely to hear a youthful international crowd having a great time. The hostel caters to its fun-loving young guests, offering free inner tubes for river floats, rental bikes, and a free keg of beer each Wednesday. The adjacent and recommended Hospoda 99 restaurant serves good, cheap soups, salads, and meals (65 beds in 4- to 10-bed coed rooms-300 Kč, D-700 Kč, T-900 Kč, use the lockers, no curfew or lockout, 10-min downhill walk from train station or two bus stops to Spicak, Vezni 99, tel. & fax 380-712-812, www.hostel99.com, hostel99@hotmail.com).

$ Krumlov House Hostel is take-your-shoes-off-at-the-door, shiny, hardwood-with-throw-rugs mellow. Efficiently run by a Canadian, it has a hip and trusting vibe and feels welcoming to travelers of any age (24 beds, 6 beds in two dorms-300 Kč per bed, Db-800 Kč, 3-person apartment-900 Kč, family room, no breakfast but there is a guests' kitchen, DVD library, laundry facilities, Rooseveltova 68, tel. 380-711-935, www.krumlovhostel.com).

EATING

Krumlov, with a huge variety of creative little restaurants, is a fun place to eat. In peak times, the good places fill fast, so make reservations or eat early.

Na Louži seems to be everyone's favorite little Czech bistro, with 40 seats in one 1930s-style room decorated with funky old advertisements. They serve inexpensive, tasty Czech cuisine and hometown Eggenberg beer on tap. If you've always wanted to play the piano for an appreciative Czech crowd in a colorful little tavern...do it here (daily, Kájovská 66, tel. 337-711-280).

Krčma u Dwau Maryí ("Tavern of the Two Marys") is a characteristic old place with idyllic riverside picnic tables, serving ye olde Czech cuisine and drinks. The fascinating menu explains the history of the house and makes a good case that the food of the poor medieval Bohemians was tasty and varied. Buck up for buckwheat, millet, greasy meat, or the poor-man's porridge (daily 11:00–23:00, Parkán 104, tel. 337-717-228).

Cikánská Jizba is a Roma (Gypsy) tavern filling one den-like, barrel-vaulted room. The Roma staff serves Slovak-style food as if it's Roma. Krumlov has a big Roma history, and even today 1,000 Roma people live on the edge of town. While this rustic little restaurant—which packs its 10 tables under a mystic-feeling Gothic vault—won't win any cuisine awards, you never know what festive and musical activities will erupt (daily, 2 blocks toward castle from main square at Dlouhá 31, tel. 380-717-585).

Restaurace u Dobráka ("Good Man") is like eating in a medieval garage with a giant poster of Karl Marx overseeing the action. Lojza, who's been tossing steaks on his open fire for years, makes sure you'll eat well. Locals know it as the best place for steak and fish—expect to pay 350 Kč for a full meal. He charges too much for his beer to keep the noisy beer-drinkers away (open from Easter until Lojza "has a shoebox full of money," Široká 74, tel. 380-717-776).

Restaurace u Města Vídně ("City of Vienna"), attached to a business-class hotel and the only dressy place in town, is where VIPs invariably end up. While there's hardly a hint of Český Krumlov in the dining room, the ambience is elegant, the presentation classy, and the French and international cuisine as close to gourmet as you'll find in town. Dine under a medieval vault or in the courtyard (allow 1,000 Kč per meal, a short walk beyond the castle at Latrán 77, tel. 380-720-180).

Laibon is the modern vegetarian answer to the carnivorous Middle Ages. Settle down inside or head out onto the idyllic river terrace, and lighten up your pork-loaded diet with soy goulash or Mútábúr soup (daily 11:00–23:00, Parkán 105).

Rybářská Restaurace ("Fisherman's Restaurant") doesn't look particularly inviting from outside, but don't get discouraged. This is *the* place in town to taste freshwater fish you've never heard of (and never will again). Try eel, perch, shad, carp, trout, and more. Choose between indoor tables under fishnets or riverside picnic benches outside (daily 11:00–22:00, on the island by the mill-wheel).

Restaurace Barbakán is built into the town fortifications, with a terrace hanging high over the river. It's a good spot for old-fashioned Czech cooking and beer at the top of town near the recommended Rooseveltova street accommodations (open long hours daily, reasonable prices, Horní 26, tel. 380-712-679).

Hospoda 99 Restaurace serves good and cheap soups, salads, and meals. It's the choice of hostelers and locals alike for its hamburgers, vegetarian food, Czech dishes, and cheap booze (meals served 10:00–22:00, bar open until 24:00, at Hostel 99, Vezni 99, tel. 380-712-812). This place is booming until late, when everything else is hibernating.

Dobrá Čajovna is a meditative teahouse. While directly across from the castle entrance, it's a world away from the touristic hubbub. As is so often the case, if you want to surround yourself with locals, don't go to a traditional place...go ethnic. With its meditative karma inside and a peaceful terrace facing the monastery out back, it provides a relaxing break (daily 13:00–22:00, Latrán 54, mobile 777-654-744).

TRANSPORTATION CONNECTIONS

Virtually all trains to and from Český Krumlov require a transfer in the city of České Budějovice, a transit hub just to the north. České Budějovice's bus and train stations are next to each other.

From Český Krumlov by Train to: České Budějovice (6/day, 1 hr), **Prague** (7/day, change usually required, 4 hrs—bus is faster, cheaper, and easier), **Vienna** (4/day, with at least one change, 6–7 hrs), **Budapest** (4/day with at least one change, 11–13 hrs).

From Český Krumlov by Bus to: Prague (7/day, 3.5 hrs, 180 Kč; 2 of the daily departures—12:00 and 16:45—can be reserved and paid for at TI, or simply buy tickets from driver), **České Budějovice** (transit hub for other destinations; about 2/hr, 30–50 min, 30 Kč). The Český Krumlov bus station, a five-minute walk out of town, is just a big parking lot with numbered stalls for various buses (bus info tel. 380-711-190, timetables online at http://jizdnirady.atlas.cz).

By Shuttle Bus or Private Car to Linz and Beyond: If you get to Linz, Austria by bus or car, you'll have your choice of fast trains that run hourly from Linz to Munich, Salzburg, and Vienna. **Pension Lobo** in Český Krumlov runs a shuttle bus service to Linz (600 Kč, 90 min, departs daily at 11:00, 2 people minimum, tel. 380-713-153). A taxi to Linz costs 2,000 Kč (sometimes less). If money is no object, hiring a private car can be efficient, especially to Budapest (the TI has referrals).

SLOVAKIA

SLOVAKIA

(Slovensko)

Slovakia is the West Virginia of Central Europe—poor, relatively undeveloped, but spectacularly beautiful in its own rustic way. Sitting quietly in the very center of Central Europe, wedged between stronger and more prosperous nations (the Czech Republic, Hungary, and Poland), Slovakia was brutally disfigured by the communists, then overshadowed by the Czechs. But in recent years, this fledgling republic has begun to find its wings. Thanks to EU funding and international business investment, Slovakia is on the verge of an economic boom. Today two very different Slovakias are emerging: the modern, industrialized, relatively affluent west, centered on the capital of Bratislava; and the remote, rustic, poorer east, with high unemployment and more traditional lifestyles.

Slovakia is far more ethnically diverse than its neighbors. Among Slovakia's large minority groups are Hungarians, many of whom still cling to the century-old glory days when this was called Upper Hungary and ruled from Budapest. Many Slovaks resent the cultural chauvinism of Hungarians, and still harbor hard feelings toward their former oppressors. Another large group is the Roma (Gypsies; see page 190). Rounding out the cultural cocktail are Czechs, Ruthenians (Carpathian Mountain peasants of Ukrainian origin), and a smattering of Germans.

Though the Slovaks are more closely associated with their former countrymen, the Czechs, they actually have more culturally in common with their other neighbors, the Poles. While the Czechs take pride in a marked agnosticism, the Slovaks tend to be more devout Catholics. Also like the Poles, the Slovaks have a strong agricultural (rather than industrial) heritage. And the

Slovak and Polish languages are surprisingly similar.

There are two schools of thought on Slovakia. Some people

love the country for its stark natural beauty and because it's an exciting cultural detour off the prettified tourist mainstream. Slovakia gives more adventurous travelers the opportunity to feel the pulse of a nation that's still struggling to transition into democracy—and yet is stable and safe enough to be comfortable. These people enjoy hiking along Slovakia's glorious mountain trails, driving through its humble villages, interacting with its kind and simple people, and pondering the blemish that communism has left on its pastoral landscape.

Other people can't wait to leave Slovakia, turned off by its drab industrial skeletons, relative poverty, and dearth of must-see sights compared to the rest of Eastern Europe. Tourists focusing on pretty-as-a-postcard Eastern Europe will want to spend more time elsewhere...and should.

What is clear is that Slovakia is not your standard European country. With lots of pleasant surprises, Slovakia is worth a peek for more adventurous travelers.

The country's capital, Bratislava, is perfectly situated at the western tip of the country, right on the train line between Budapest and Vienna. Up in the north—not far from the Polish border—is the most beautiful part of this mountainous nation: the rolling hills of the Spiš Region and jagged peaks of the High Tatras.

Practicalities

Telephones: Insertable telephone cards, sold at newsstands and kiosks everywhere, get you access to the modern public phones.

When calling locally, dial the number without the area code. To make a long-distance call within the country, start with the area code (which begins with 0). To call a Slovak number from abroad,

Slovakia Almanac

Official Name: Slovenská Republika, though locals call it Slovensko. The nation is the eastern half of the former Czechoslovakia (split peaceably in 1993).

Population: 5.4 million people. The majority are native Slovaks who are Roman Catholic and speak Slovak. But one in 10 has Hungarian roots, and an estimated one in 10 is Roma (Gypsy).

Latitude and Longitude: 48°N and 20°E (similar latitude to Paris or Vancouver, BC).

Area: 19,000 square miles (the size of Massachusetts and New Hampshire put together).

Geography: The northeastern half of Slovakia features the beautiful rolling hills and spiky, jagged peaks of the Carpathian Mountains. The southwestern half is quite flat—a continuation of the Hungarian Plain. The climate is generally cool and cloudy.

Biggest Cities: Only two cities have more than 100,000 inhabitants: Bratislava in the west (the capital, 450,000) and Košice in the east (235,000).

Economy: The Gross Domestic Product is $88 billion (less than half that of the Czech Republic), and the GDP per capita is $16,300 (less than the average Czech and roughly half that of the average German). Despite a recent economic upturn, unemployment hovers at about 12 percent.

dial the international access number (00 if calling from Europe, 011 from the US or Canada), followed by 421 (Slovakia's country code), then the area code (without the initial 0) and the number. To call out of Slovakia, dial 00, the country code of the country you're calling (see chart in appendix), the area code if applicable (you may need to drop initial zero), and the local number.

Information: For more in-depth information about Slovakia, pick up a copy of *Spectacular Slovakia*, an excellent annual magazine produced by the English-language newspaper in Bratislava (www.spectacularslovakia.sk).

Slovak History

Even though it's more recently associated with the Czech Republic, Slovakia was for centuries ruled from Budapest and known as Upper Hungary. While the Ottomans occupied most of Hungary in the 16th and 17th centuries, the Hungarians moved their capital to Bratislava. But even throughout the long era of Hungarian domination, most people living in Slovakia were Slavs.

Czechoslovakia was formed at the end of World War I, when the Austro-Hungarian Empire was splitting into pieces. During

Currency: 30 Slovak koruna (Sk) = about $1.

Government: President Ivan Gašparovič heads a government that isn't dominated by any single political party. Slovakia also has a 150-seat National Council (like a parliament). Slovakia joined the European Union in 2004.

Flag: Horizontal bands of white, blue, and red with a shield bearing a "patriarchal cross" (with two crossbars instead of one) atop three humps. The three humps represent three historic mountain ranges of Slovakia: Mátra (now in northern Hungary, near Eger), Fatra, and Tatra. The double-barred cross represents St. Stephen (István) of Hungary, commemorating the many centuries that Slovakia was part of Hungary.

Slovaks You May Recognize: Andy Warhol (American Pop Artist who gained more than his 15 minutes of fame; born to Slovak immigrants), Martina Hingis (Swiss tennis player born in Slovakia), Štefan Bani (emigrated to America and invented the parachute).

this flurry of new nation-building, a small country of 10 million Czechs or five million Slovaks was unlikely to survive. The Czechs were concerned about the huge number of Germans in their territory (the Sudetenland), while the Slovaks—who had endured relatively oppressive conditions under the Hungarian half of the empire—were unsure of their ability to steer their own nation.

And so these two Slavic peoples decided there was safety in numbers. (It was a delicate balance—there were more Sudeten Germans in Czechoslovakia than there were Slovaks.) The union was logical enough—especially in the eyes of Tomáš Masaryk, Czechoslovakia's first president (and a buddy of Woodrow Wilson's from Princeton). Masaryk was from the border of the two regions and spoke a dialect that mixed elements of Czech and Slovak. Czechoslovakia was born.

The Czechs and the Slovaks were constantly reminded that they were countrymen in name only. In a prelude to World War II, these two peoples were again split along the cultural fault that always divided them: Today's Czech Republic was absorbed into Germany, while much of the Slovak land went to Nazi-allied Hungary.

It's Not You, It's Me: The Velvet Divorce

In the autumn of 1989, hundreds of thousands of Czechs and Slovaks streamed into Prague to demonstrate on Wenceslas Square. Their "Velvet Revolution" succeeded, and Czechoslovakia's communist regime peacefully excused itself.

Almost immediately, the union began to splinter. Ever since they joined with the Czechs in 1918, the Slovaks felt they were ruled from Prague (unmistakably the political, economic, and cultural center of the country) rather than from their own capital. And the Czechs, for their part, resented the financial burden of their poorer neighbors to the east. In the post-communist world, the Czechs found themselves with a 10 percent unemployment rate...compared to 20 or 30 percent unemployment in the Slovak lands. In this new world of flux and freedom, long-standing tensions came to a head.

The dissolution of Czechoslovakia began over a hyphen, as the Slovaks wanted to rename the country Czecho-Slovakia. Ideally, this symbolic move would come with a redistribution of powers: two capitals and two UN reps, but one national bank and a single currency. The Slovaks were also less enthusiastic about abandoning the communist society altogether, since the Soviet regime had left them with a heavily industrialized economy that depended on a socialist element for survival.

Initially, many Czechs couldn't understand the Slovaks' demands. The first post-communist president of Czechoslovakia,

During the communist era, the regime decided to convert the Slovak economy from a low-key agricultural model to a base of heavy industry. But the industry was centrally planned for communist purposes (relying on raw materials imported from elsewhere within the Eastern Bloc)—so it made sense only as a cog in the communist machine. Many of Slovakia's factories built heavy arms, making the country the biggest producer of tanks in the world. Slovakia became one of the ugliest and most polluted corners of Eastern Europe. The Slovak environment—and economy—are still recovering.

When the wave of uprisings spread across Eastern Europe in 1989, Czechoslovakia peacefully achieved its own freedom with the Velvet Revolution. Then, on January 1, 1993, Czechoslovakia amicably split into two nations: the Czech and Slovak Republics (see sidebar above). At first, many Slovaks weren't sure this was so wise. But more recently, it seems that the Czechs and Slovaks are getting along better than ever—by choice, not because they're compelled to. Czechs root for the Slovak hockey team, and Slovaks cheer on the Czech soccer powerhouse...unless, of course, their the Czech Václav Havel, made matters worse when he took a rare trip to the Slovak half of his country in 1990. In a fit of terrible judgment, Havel boldly promised he'd close the ugly, polluting Soviet factories in Slovakia...seemingly oblivious to the fact that many Slovaks still depended on these factories for survival. Havel left in disgrace and visited the Slovak lands only twice more in the next two and a half years.

In June 1992, the Slovak nationalist candidate Vladimír Mečiar fared surprisingly well in the elections—suggesting that the Slovaks were serious about secession. The politicians plowed ahead, getting serious about the split in September 1992. The transition took only three months, from start to finish.

The people of Czechoslovakia never actually voted on the separation; in fact, public opinion polls in both regions were two-thirds *against* the split. This makes Slovakia quite possibly the only country in the history of the world to gain independence... even though they didn't want it.

The Velvet Divorce became official on January 1, 1993, and each country ended up with its own capital, currency, and head of state. The Slovaks let loose a yelp of excitement, and the Czechs emitted a sigh of relief. The divorce dissolved the tensions, and a decade and a half later, most Czechs and Slovaks still feel closer to each other than to any other nationality.

teams are playing against each other.

After the so-called Velvet Divorce, the first president of Slovakia was a former boxer named Vladimír Mečiar, whose authoritarian rule was not much better than the communists'. Mečiar was frequently accused of corruption (including pulling issues off the ballot when they seemed to be going against him), and people suspect he was involved in the kidnapping, torture, and humiliation of one of his political opponent's sons in 1995. He was also notorious for making offensive statements about his country's substantial Hungarian and Roma minorities. Mečiar drew criticism from neighboring Eastern and Western European nations, as well as the US. He was finally defeated at the polls in 2000, but—like a bad penny—he kept turning up, nearly winning elections in 2002 and 2004. And now, once again, Mečiar plays a minor role in government, as leader of a small fringe party that has a share in Slovakia's current government coalition.

But, as Mečiar (and his voting base) gets along in years, Slovakia appears to be turning to more mainstream politics. Slovakia joined the European Union in May of 2004—a monumental

Key Slovak Phrases

English	Slovak	Pronounced
Hello. (formal)	Dobrý deň.	DOH-bree dyehn
Hi. / Bye. (informal)	Ahoj.	AH-hoy
Do you speak English?	Hovoríte po anglicky?	hoh-VOH-ree-teh poh ANG-lits-kee
Yes. / No.	Áno. / Nie.	AH-no / nyeh
Please. / You're welcome. / Can I help you?	Prosím.	PROH-seem
Thank you.	Ďakujem.	DYAH-koo-yehm
I'm sorry. / Excuse me.	Prepáčte.	preh-PAHCH-teh
Good.	Dobro.	DOH-broh
Goodbye.	Do videnia.	doh vih-DAY-neeah
one / two	jeden / dva	YAY-dehn / dvah
three / four	tri / štyri	tree / SHTEE-ree
five / six	päť / šesť	peht / shehst
seven / eight	sedem / osem	SEH-dyehm / OH-sehm
nine / ten	deväť / desať	DYEH-veht / DYEH-saht
hundred	sto	stoh
thousand	tisíc	TYEE-seets
How much?	Koľko?	KOHL-koh
local currency	koruna (Sk)	koh-ROO-nah
Where is...?	Kde je...?	gday yeh
...the toilet	...záchod	ZAH-khohd
men	muži	MOO-zhee
women	ženy	ZHAY-nee
water / coffee	voda / káva	VOH-dah / KAH-vah
beer / wine	pivo / víno	PEE-voh / VEE-noh
Cheers!	Na zdravie!	nah ZDRAH-vyeh
the bill	účet	OO-cheht

step forward. Still, the Slovaks are slow to embrace these changes. In the EU parliamentary elections held a few months after they joined, Slovakia had the lowest voter turnout of all the EU nations.

As one of the poorest EU members, Slovakia has a lot to gain from its membership—and, in fact, the country has already made some huge advances. Low labor costs and an unbeatable location have attracted many foreign automakers to build plants here, leading the *New York Times* to dub Slovakia "the European Detroit." In 2007, Slovakia will become the world's biggest car producer... per capita, of course. Ireland's "Celtic Tiger" economic boom has led people to make comparisons with Slovakia, even predicting the coming of a "Tatra Tiger" (named for the Slovak mountain range). Inspired by the model of Ireland—another poor, "backward" country that has enjoyed phenomenal economic growth since joining the EU—Slovaks seem poised to pounce on the future.

Slovak Food

Slovak cuisine is similar to Czech cuisine—with lots of starches and gravy, and plenty of pork, cabbage, and potatoes (see "Czech Food," page 55). If there's anything distinctive about Slovak food, it's the slight Hungarian influence—Slovaks use more paprika than their Czech cousins. Slovakia also has a strong tradition of grilling pickled meats. Also keep an eye out for Slovakia's national dish, *bryndzové halušky* (small potato dumplings with sheep's cheese and bits of bacon). Like the Czechs, the Slovaks produce fine beer *(pivo)*. One of the top brands is Zlatý Bažant ("Golden Pheasant").

Slovak Language

Many people assume Slovak is virtually the same as Czech. To be sure, there are similarities—but they're hardly identical.

Slovak is handy as a sort of a lingua franca of Slavic tongues. Czechs can understand Poles, but not Slovenes; Poles can understand Croatians, but not Czechs. But Slovak speakers generally find they can understand—and be understood in—any of these languages.

Slovak's similarity to Czech was exaggerated during the 75 years that they shared a country. Soccer games would be broadcast with two commentators—one spoke Czech, and the other spoke Slovak. Anyone growing up in this era grew comfortable using the languages interchangeably. But today's teenagers—who have only spoken exclusively Czech or Slovak—find they have trouble understanding each other.

BRATISLAVA

For centuries, Bratislava—known as "Pressburg" to its German inhabitants—was a complex and beautiful city, with deep roots in many different cultures: Slovak, German/Austrian, Hungarian, Jewish, Romanian, and Roma (Gypsy). The Hungarians used the city—which they called "Poszony"—as their capital during the century and a half that Buda and Pest were occupied by Ottoman invaders. Later, Bratislava was one of Hapsburg empress Maria Theresa's favorite places. Everyone from Hans Christian Andersen to Casanova sang the wonders of this bustling burg on the Danube. When Czechoslovakia was formed at the end of World War I, the city shed its German and Hungarian names, proudly taking the new Slavic name "Bratislava"—meaning roughly "City of Brotherly Love."

In the 20th century, Bratislava became the textbook example of a historic city whose multilayered charm and delicate cultural fabric were destroyed and shrouded in gray by the communist regime. The communists were more proud of their ultramodern suspension bridge, New Bridge (Most SNP), than of the historic Jewish quarter they razed to make way for it. Now the bridge and its highway slice through the center of the Old Town, and the heavy traffic rattles the stained-glass windows of St. Martin's Cathedral.

But the latest chapter in Bratislava's story is one of great success. Over the last decade, the city has gone from being a desolate, gloomy victim of communism to a thriving economic center and social hub. Its population of 450,000 includes some 70,000 students (at the city's six universities), creating an atmosphere of youthful energy and optimism. The increasingly rejuvenated Old

Town is traffic-free, giving it an almost Mediterranean ambience on sunny summer days, when Bratislava's outdoor cafés hum with life.

Planning Your Time

Bratislava is blessed with a priceless location on the Danube (and the tourist circuit), smack-dab between Budapest and Vienna. On the plus side, the ambience in the Old Town is enjoyable. On the other hand, actual sightseeing options are disappointing, and a busy traveler—one more interested in seeing museums than in sipping coffee—gets bored here quickly. On my list of priorities, time spent in Budapest and Vienna is more precious. But if you're passing through and you're curious, Bratislava merits a quick sightseeing sprint. Head straight for the Old Town, wander through to the river, and—if time allows—hike up to the castle.

I've listed no hotels in Bratislava; beds are better in nearby Vienna and Budapest.

ORIENTATION

(area code: 02)

Bratislava, with nearly half a million residents, is Slovakia's capital and biggest city. It has a small, colorful Old Town (Staré Mesto) surrounded by the ugly communist sprawl of the New Town and suburbs. The Old Town and the castle above it are the only parts of Bratislava worth visiting.

Bratislava's grim Stalinist vibe isn't all bad. It offers hardy travelers an opportunity for a cultural scavenger hunt deep into the guts of apartment-block neighborhoods, where the average Josefs of the "Evil Empire"—from here to Vladivostok—eked out their lives. Across the river from the Old Town, the suburb called Petržalka is gloomy and harrowing, in a *1984*-comes-to-life sort of way.

Beware: Bratislavans in the tourist zone sometimes try to short-change and otherwise rip off their city's visitors as brazenly as their Prague cousins do. Check your bill and count your change carefully.

Tourist Information

The TI, called the Bratislava Culture and Information Centre, has two branches in the heart of the city. There's a small window in the **train station** (June–Sept Mon–Fri 8:00–19:30, Sat–Sun 8:00–16:30; Oct–May Mon–Fri 8:30–17:00, closed Sat–Sun; tel. 02/5249-5906). The **main branch** is across the square from the back of the Old Town Hall on Primaciálne Námestie (June–Sept Mon–Fri 8:30–19:00, Sat 9:00–16:00, Sun 10:00–15:00; Oct–May Mon–Fri 8:30–18:00, Sat 9:00–14:00, closed Sun; Klobučnícka 2, tel. 02/5443-3715, www.bkis.sk and www.bratislava.sk). Pick up the free map and browse their brochures; they can also help you find a room for a modest fee.

The main TI shares an office with the Bratislava **tour guide association** (tel. 02/5443-4059, guides@bkis.sk). They offer a one-hour Old Town walking tour in English every day at 14:00 (400 Sk, 2-person minimum, call ahead to confirm). The **Bratislava City Card,** sold by the TI for just 200 Sk for one day, includes free passage on this tour—essentially cutting the price in half, and adding sightseeing and transportation benefits to boot.

For a more extensive (and expensive) look at the city, join a longer **Bratislava Sightseeing** city tour. There are three itineraries: Discover Bratislava (1,290 Sk, 4 hours, almost daily, minibus tour to outlying sights, then walking tour of Old Town), Communist Bratislava (1,150 Sk, 3 hours, 1/week, sights from the Red old days), and Little Carpathians (1,980 Sk, 5 hours, 2/week, wine road and other sights in the countryside). All tours depart from the Carlton Hotel (near National Theater on long, skinny Hviezdoslavovo Square, look for fliers locally for schedule, or visit www.visitbratislava.info; best to reserve in advance).

Martin Sloboda, one of Bratislava Sightseeing's owners, is a can-do entrepreneur who writes local guidebooks and runs his own guiding agency. Martin can set you up with a good local guide (€120/3 hours, €150/4 hours), and can help you track down your Slovak roots (tel. 02/5464-1467, www.msagency.sk, info @msagency.sk).

Arrival in Bratislava

By Train: Bratislava's Main Train Station, called Bratislava Hlavná Stanica, is about a half-mile north of the Old Town. As you emerge from the tracks, the TI is down the hall to your left, and the luggage check desk is to your right (look for *ú schovňa batožín;* there are no lockers, and the check desk usually closes for 30-min lunch and dinner breaks—try to confirm that they'll be there when you get back if you'll be rushing to catch a train).

It's an easy 15-minute **walk** to the center. Leave through the front door and head along the communist-style arcade (to the right) past the buses to the busy street. Take the overpass across the street, and continue straight on Štefánikova. This formerly elegant old street is lined with rotting facades from Bratislava's high-on-the-hog Hapsburg era. After about 10 minutes, you'll pass the nicely manicured presidential gardens on your left, then the Grassalkovich Palace, Slovakia's "White House." Continue straight through the busy intersection, and head for the green onion-domed steeple. This is St. Michael's Gate, at the start of the Old Town (described below).

Bratislava

200 YARDS
200 METERS

★ **MAIN SQUARE**

TO TRAIN STATION

PRESIDENTIAL GARDENS

GRASSALKOVICH PALACE

ŠTEFÁNIKOVA

PALISADY

ULICA

KOZIA UL.

STAROMESTSKÁ

SVORADOVA

PILÁRIKOVA

ŽIDOVSKÁ

SUCHÉ MÝTO

NÁM. 1 MÁJA

OBCHODNA

ST. MICHAEL'S GATE

NÁMESTIE SNP

POST

KAPU.

BASTOVA

ZÁMOČ

MICHALSKÁ

BIELA

SED

PRIMATE'S HOUSE

OLD

ZÁMOCKÁ UL.

CASTLE

STAIRS

PREPOŠT

ST. MARTINS

ZELENA

PÁNSKÁ

RYBÁRSKA BRÁNA

STR.

LAURINSKA

GORKÉHO

JESENSKÉHO

MEDENÁ

OLD TOWN HALL

TOWN

NATIONAL THEATER

KUPELNÁ

PARLIA-MENT

VODNY VRCH

ZÁM. SCHODY

HVIEZDOSLAVOVO NÁM.

PAUL

U.S. EMBASSY

VAJANSKÉHO

NABR. ARM. GEN. L. SVOBODU

RYBNÉ NÁM.

RÁZU

SOVO

NEW BRIDGE→

NATIONAL GALLERY

HYDROFOIL TERMINAL

D A N U B E   R I V E R

TO PETRŽALKA

If you want to shave a few minutes off the trip, you can go part of the way by **tram** (from train station's main hall, with tracks at your back, look for signs to *električky* on left; take escalator down, buy a 14-Sk "basic ticket" from the machine, and hop on tram #1).

By Plane: Some budget carriers—especially SkyEurope—fly into Bratislava Airport (Letisko Bratislava, airport code: BTS, www.letiskobratislava.sk). This airport is marketed as "Vienna-Bratislava," thanks to its proximity to both capitals. Located six miles northeast of downtown Bratislava, the airport is officially named for Milan Rastislav Štefánik, who worked toward the creation of Czechoslovakia at the end of World War I. The airport has easy bus connections into Bratislava's Main Train Station (bus #61, 6/hr in peak time, 3/hr in slow times, trip takes 30 min; to reach the bus stop, exit straight out of the arrivals hall, cross the street, buy a ticket at the kiosk, and look for the bus stop on your right). To get to Vienna, catch one of the buses coordinated to meet SkyEurope flights (€10–15, trip takes about 90 min), or take a taxi (figure €60–90, depending on whether you use a cheaper Slovak or more expensive Austrian cab). SkyEurope's Web site has more details (www.skyeurope.com).

SIGHTS

On a short visit, it's enough to simply wander the Old Town, enjoy a drink at an outdoor café, and soak in Slovakia. If you need more diversion than that, you can hike up to the castle. More low-impact sightseeing options include a pair of dusty, sleepy museums in the heart of the Old Town (described below). If you're interested in museums beyond the ones I mention, check out www.snm.sk.

▲**Old Town Wander**—This self-guided stroll takes you through the heart of old Bratislava. If you're coming from the station, make your way toward the green onion-domed steeple of St. Michael's Gate (explained in "Arrival in Bratislava," above). Before going through the passage into the Old Town, peek over the railing on your left to the inviting garden below—once part of the city moat.

Step through the passageway into the delightfully traffic-free **Old Town.** Pretty as it is now, the Old Town was a decrepit ghost town during the communist era. Locals avoided this desolate corner of the city, preferring to spend time in the Petržalka suburb across the river. But after the fall of communism, city leaders decided to revitalize this zone, in an effort to make it the place to see and be seen once again. They replaced all of the cobbles, spruced up the public buildings, and encouraged the new private owners of other buildings to invest in careful restoration. It worked: Today the Old Town is gleaming, and packed with locals and tourists alike.

Continue through the onion-domed **St. Michael's Gate** (Michalská Brána), the last remaining tower of the city wall. As you pass under the gate, notice the "kilometer zero" plaque in the ground, marking the point from which distances in Slovakia are measured.

Coming through the gate, you're at the head of **Michalská**

street. The cafés and restaurants that line this street are inviting, especially in summer. But if you don't look beyond the facades and outdoor tables, you'll miss much of Bratislava's charm. Courtyards and galleries burrow through the city's buildings, most of them open to the public. For example, just inside St. Michael's Gate on the right, the gallery at #7 is home to several fashion designers.

As you stroll down Michalská, think about which of these places you'd like to circle back to later for a drink or a meal. The **chocolate shop** at #6 (on the left) is highly regarded among locals. Look above the shop's entrance and find the cannonball embedded in the wall above the seal. This commemorates the fact that Napoleon laid siege to the city twice, causing massive devastation—even worse than the city suffered during World War II. Keep an eye out for these cannonballs all over town...somber reminders of one of Bratislava's darkest times.

Noticing a lot of skin? Slovak women are known for their provocative dress. When pressed for a reason for this, locals smirk and say, "That's just the way it is."

Two blocks down from St. Michael's Gate, the name of this main drag changes to Ventúrska, the street jogs to the right, and the café scene continues. This is a good time for you to detour left (along Sedlárska) and head for the **Main Square** (Hlavné Námestie)—the bustling centerpiece of Old World Bratislava. Virtually every building around this square dates from a different architectural period, from Gothic (the yellow tower) to Art Nouveau (the fancy facade facing it from across the square). When these buildings were restored a few years ago, great pains were taken to achieve authenticity—each one even matches the color most likely used when it was originally built.

Peering over one of the benches is a cartoonish statue of **Napoleon** (notice the French flag marking the embassy right behind him). With bare feet and a hat pulled over his eyes, it's hardly a flattering portrait—you could call it the Slovaks' revenge for the difficulties they faced at his armies' hands. Napoleon is just the first we'll see of many whimsical statues that dot Bratislava's Old Town. Most of these date from the late 1990s, when city leaders wanted to entice locals back into the newly prettied-up Old Town.

At the top of the Main Square is the impressive **Old Town Hall** (Stará Radnica), marked by a bold yellow tower. Near the bottom of the tower, notice the cannonball embedded in the facade—yet another reminder of Napoleon's impact on Bratislava. Over time, the Old Town Hall gradually grew, annexing the buildings next to it—creating a mishmash of architectural styles along this side of the square. Step through the passageway into the Old Town Hall's gorgeously restored courtyard with Renaissance arcades.

The Old Town Hall houses a ho-hum **City History Museum** (Mestské Múzeum), with a tower you can climb and a museum on torture (a.k.a. "feudal justice") in the basement (50 Sk, Tue–Fri 10:00–17:00, Sat–Sun 11:00–18:00, closed Mon).

On the other side of the Old Town Hall is Bratislava's most interesting museum, the **Primate's House** (Primaciálny Palác, 40 Sk, Tue–Fri 10:00–17:00, Sat–Sun 11:00–18:00, closed Mon). This grand mansion, gradually expanded and glorified over several centuries by a series of archbishops who lived here, features fancy apartments, a Mirror Hall for concerts and meetings, a striking marble chapel, and a series of six English tapestries.

Backtrack to the Main Square. Facing the Old Town Hall, go down the street at the bottom of the square to your right (Rybárska Brána). A block down this street, you'll come to a jovial chap doffing his top hat. This is a statue of **Schöner Náci,** who lived in Bratislava until the 1960s. This eccentric old man, a poor carpet cleaner, would dress up in his one black suit and top hat, and go strolling through the city, offering gifts to the women he fancied. (He'd often whisper *"schön"*—German for "pretty"—to the women, which is how he got his nickname.) After spending his life cheering up the gloomy streets of communist Bratislava, Schöner Náci gets to spend eternity greeting visitors in front of his favorite café.

As a sad epilogue, Schöner Náci's arm was broken off recently by a bunch of drunks. As Prague gets more expensive, Bratislava is becoming the cheaper alternative for weekend "stag parties," popular with Brits lured here by cheap flights and cheap beer. Locals hope this is a short-lived trend, and that those rowdy louts will move farther east before long.

Continue down Rybárska. A block farther on, at the intersec-tion of Panská and Rybárska, keep an eye out for **Čumil** ("the Peeper"), grinning at passersby from a manhole. This was the first and still the favorite of Bratislava's statues. There's no story behind this one—the artist simply wanted to create a fun icon, and let the townspeople make up their own tales. Čumil has survived being driven over by a truck—twice—and he's still grinning.

Continuing past Čumil, you'll reach the long, skinny square called **Hviezdoslavovo Námestie**—another part of Bratislava that has undergone much-needed rejuvenation recently. The landscaped park in the center is particularly inviting, with more fun sculptures (including, at the far end, Hans Christian Andersen) and a life-size chessboard. At this end of the square is the impressive, silver-topped Slovak National Theater (Slovenské Národné Divadlo)—evidence of Bratislava's strong theatrical tradition.

Right in front of the theater (by the McDonald's), look down into the glass **display case** to see the foundation of the one-time Fishermen's Gate into the city. Surrounding the base of the gate is water. This entire square was once a tributary of the Danube, and the Carlton Hotel across the way was a series of inns on different islands. The buildings along the Old Town side of the square mark where the city wall once stood.

From here, it's just a block to the Danube—passing the Slovak National Gallery, for those fascinated by Slovak art (big green building)—and a good look at the communists' pride and joy, the **New Bridge** (Nový Most, a.k.a. Most SNP). As with many Soviet-era landmarks around Eastern Europe, many locals aren't crazy about this structure—not only for the questionable starship *Enterprise* design, but also because of the oppressive regime it represents. However, the restaurant and observation deck up top—long a stale holdover from communist times—was recently renovated into a posh eatery with see-through tables.

If you follow the Danube toward the bridge, before long you'll spot big **St. Martin's Cathedral** (Dóm Sv. Martina) on the right.

This historic church isn't looking too sharp these days—and the highway thundering a few feet in front of its door (courtesy of the Soviets) doesn't help matters. If it were any closer, the off-ramp would go through the nave. Sad as it is now, the cathedral has been party to some pretty important history. While Buda and Pest were occupied by Ottomans for a century and a half, Bratislava was the capital of Hungary. Many Hungarian kings and queens were crowned in this church. A replica of the Hungarian crown still tops the steeple.

If you walk under the highway, then start climbing the stairs marked *Zámocké Schody*, you'll wind up at...

Bratislava Castle (Bratislavský Hrad)—This imposing fortress, nicknamed the "upside-down table," is the city's most prominent landmark. The castle saw its finest days when Hapsburg empress

Maria Theresa took a liking to Bratislava in the 18th century, and decided she wanted to have a nice place to hold court here. But M.T.'s castle burned to the ground in an 1811 fire, and it was left as a ruin for a century and a half—not reconstructed until 1953. The communist rebuild—especially inside the courtyard, which feels like a prison exercise yard—is drab and uninviting. The castle houses a few dull museums (history, musical instruments) and the chance to toss a coin down an incredibly deep well (280 feet before you hear the plop—the same distance as to the Danube; find entrance at far left corner as you enter main courtyard). But the best reason to visit the castle is for the views—especially of the New Bridge and the endless communist apartment blocks of the Petržalka suburb across the river.

By the way, the huge, pointy monument back toward the train station is **Slavín,** where more than 6,800 Soviet soldiers who fought to liberate Bratislava from the Nazis are buried. A nearby church had to take down its steeple so as not to draw attention away from the huge Soviet soldier on top of the monument.

TRANSPORTATION CONNECTIONS

From Bratislava by Train to: Vienna (about hourly, 1 hr), **Budapest** (4/day direct, 2.25–4 hrs), **Prague** (3/day direct, 4.25–5.5 hrs).

You can also connect to both Budapest and Vienna by **boat** (see page 480 and 784, respectively).

THE SPIŠ REGION

The most beautiful part of Slovakia is the mountainous north-central region, comprising the jagged High Tatras and the Spiš Region. The dramatic Carpathian Mountains slice through Eastern Europe here, dividing the Poles and Czechs in the north from the Hungarians and Yugoslavs in the south. With these Carpathian peaks as a backdrop, this region offers fine high-mountain scenery; easy river-rafting trips with fun-loving guides through a breathtaking gorge; a classic, Old World walled town with one of Europe's finest Gothic altarpieces; a glimpse at Slovakia's complicated ethnic mix; and treacherous but legendary hiking trails in a place so pretty, they call it "paradise."

Planning Your Time

The Spiš Region is a handy place for drivers to break up the long journey between Kraków and Hungary—Levoča is worth an overnight to recharge and get a taste of rural Slovakia. But unless you have a special interest, don't go out of your way to reach this area. Train travelers or those on a speedy itinerary should skip it (sleep through Slovakia on the night train, and wake up in Eger or Budapest).

Getting to the Spiš Region

Seeing the Spiš Region is a real headache without a car. You'll take the bus to get to Levoča. If you're going between Kraków and Hungary (Eger or Budapest), the train line veers around Levoča far to the east, through Košice. From Košice, trains will get you to Prešov or Spišská Nová Ves, and the bus will take you the rest of the way to Levoča. From the west, buses run between Bratislava

The Spiš Region

and Levoča (though it's often faster to take the train to Poprad, then bus to Levoča). For specific schedules, see www.cp.sk.

Levoča

Levoča (LEH-voh-chah) is a diamond in the rough. If you can look past the crumbling facades and potholed roads, you'll see Slovakia's finest small town—with a mostly intact medieval wall, a main square ringed by striking Renaissance facades, and one of the greatest Gothic altarpieces in all of Europe.

Levoča boomed in the Middle Ages, when trade between Hungary and Poland brought abundant merchant traffic through

History of the Spiš Region

The Spiš (pronounced "speesh") region is one of the most historic and scenic corners of Slovakia. The area was named Szepes ("beautiful") by the Hungarians, who controlled this area in the Middle Ages. After the Tatars swept through in the 13th century, decimating the local population, the Hungarians invited Saxons (from the region of today's Germany around Dresden) to come and resettle the land. Silver, copper, and iron ore were discovered, and the Spiš became a prosperous mining region, with 24 bustling, richly decorated Saxon towns (including Levoča). The region became a showcase of Gothic and, later, Renaissance architecture.

For centuries, the Spiš was populated by a colorful mix of Saxons, Jews, and Slovaks. But after World War II, Czechoslovakia forced out people of German heritage—including descendents of those Saxon settlers who arrived here centuries before. Spiš was abandoned, and many towns were repopulated by Slovaks, while others were settled by Roma (Gypsies; see page 190).

Today's Spiš, while still suffering from economic ills, is emerging as a popular tourist destination.

its gates. In the 15th century, the town's centerpiece was built: St. James Church. A local woodcarver named Master Pavol packed the church with one of the most impressive collections of altar-pieces in the world—including the pièce de résistance, an exquisite 60-foot-high altar.

In the 19th century, Levoča vied with a neighboring town, Spišská Nová Ves (eight miles south), to host a station on an important rail line that was being built. S.N.V. won, and became a transportation hub for the region. While unfortunate for Levoča's economy at the time, this lack of train access has allowed Levoča to remain a wonderfully well-preserved Old World village of 10,000. If all of this makes Levoča feel off the beaten track, so much the better.

ORIENTATION

(area code: 053)

Levoča is small—you can walk from one end of the walled burg to the other in 15 minutes—and all roads lead to the town's main square, which is named for the important woodcarver, Master Pavol (Námestie Majstra Pavla).

The **TI**, like most everything else of interest, is on the main square (tel. 053/451-3763, www.levoca.sk). You can hire your own

local guide for 500 Sk per hour. This is a cheap way to maximize your sightseeing time...and get to know a local (TI can help you arrange).

SIGHTS AND ACTIVITIES

▲**Church of St. James (Chrám Sv. Jakuba)**—This huge Gothic church, dominating Levoča's main square, contains 11 ornately decorated altars—including the tallest wooden altarpiece in the world.

The church dates from the 14th century. In the late 15th century, neighboring VIPs visited here. The greatest Hungarian king, Mátyás Corvinus, came in 1474 (for more on Corvinus, see sidebar on page 426). Two decades later, representatives of Poland's powerful Jagiellonian dynasty paid a visit. These important guests—both commemorated inside the church—are a reminder that Slovakia has long been at a crossroads of Eastern Europe.

In the early 16th century, the great sculptor Master Pavol left his mark on the church. Master Pavol's unique, almost cartoonish style features figures with too-big heads, strangely weepy eyes, and honest-to-goodness personalities. Pavol's masterpiece is the church's single most impressive sight: the 60-foot-tall **main altar,** carved out of linden wood and bathed in gold paint. The large central figures represent Mary and the Baby Jesus, flanked by St. James (the church's namesake, on left) and St. John the Evangelist (on right). The four panels surrounding these figures depict scenes from James' and John's lives and deaths. Beneath them is a depiction of the Last Supper. Unusual in Gothic art, each apostle has his own individual features (based on the local merchants who financed the work). With this and his other carvings, Master Pavol was knocking on the door of the Renaissance.

The nave is lined with several other altarpieces—some by Master Pavol, some by others. At the front of the right nave (right-hand corner), look for the altar depicting the **Passion of Christ,** carved for the 1474 visit of Hungarian King Mátyás Corvinus. Jesus looks like Mátyás, Mary resembles his Italian wife, and the altar was supposed to bring the couple good luck in having a child.

To the left as you view the main altar, notice the interesting medieval **frescoes** on the wall (splotchy from a bad 19th-century renovation). The frescoes on the left depict the life of St. Dorothy. On the right are two strips. The upper strip shows a couple performing good deeds (feeding the hungry, visiting prisoners, burying the dead, and so on). In the lower strip, they sit on animals representing the mortal sins.

As you leave, at the back of the left nave, look for another Master

Pavol altar with an iconic statue of **Mary.** When the Reformation swept Europe in the 16th century, locals hid statues such as Mary (who was tucked away in the Town Hall) to protect them from iconoclasts who destroyed religious symbols to unclutter their communion with God. Two centuries later, the long-forgotten statues were miraculously discovered and brought back to the church...for you to enjoy. (Slovaks love this emotive depiction of Mary so much, they put her on the 100-Sk note.)

Cost, Tours, Hours: The cost is 50 Sk, and you can visit only at the times posted on the door of the church office, across the street from the church entrance (on the north side of the church, facing the top of the square). You'll be accompanied by a guide, but you don't have to listen to her spiel (usually Slovak only—but ask for English). Use the above information to appreciate the church, or find the talking box in the back of the nave and insert a coin for English. The church is open July–Aug Tue–Sat 9:00–17:00, Sun 13:00–17:00, Mon 11:00–17:00, tours every 30 min; Sept–Oct and Easter–June Tue–Sat 8:30–16:00, Sun 13:00–16:00, Mon 11:30–16:00, tours roughly hourly, though not always at the top of the hour; Nov–Easter Tue–Sat 8:30–16:00, closed Sun–Mon, tours roughly hourly. Tel. 053/451-2347, mobile 0907-521-673, www .chramsvjakuba.sk.

House of Master Pavol—The downside of the Church of St. James is that you can see the breathtaking altarpieces only from a distance, so you can't get a sense of what made Pavol the Master. At this museum, replicas of the statues allow you to look Pavol's creations right in their big, weepy eyes (30 Sk, daily 9:00–17:00, tel. 053/451-2786).

Levoča Town Hall (Radnica v Levoči)—The huge, Renaissance-

style building behind the Church of St. James used to be the Town Hall; now it's a museum featuring the town and region's history and colorful folk cultures. You'll watch a movie in English before wandering though a grand, wood-carved meeting hall (with a beautifully painted ceiling) and rooms of maps of historic Levoča and the Spiš Region (30 Sk, skimpy English information, daily 9:00–17:00, tel. 053/451-2786).

Mariánska Hora—This humble church, overlooking Levoča from a perch on a nearby hill, has been an important site for pilgrimages for centuries. Every year, on the first weekend of July, hundreds of thousands of Slovaks flock to the hill from the surrounding countryside—many walking as far as 30 miles. In 1995, Pope John Paul

The "Gypsy Question"

Eastern Europe is home to a silent population—mostly in Romania, Bulgaria, Hungary, and this part of Slovakia—of millions of dark-skinned people who speak an Indian-based dialect and follow their own, decidedly non-European culture. The most common name for Europe's overlooked culture, "Gypsy," is a holdover from the time when these people were thought to have come from Egypt. While the term isn't overtly offensive to most, it's both geographically mistaken and politically incorrect. (It's also taken on a negative connotation—as with the ethnic slur, "I've been gypped!") Today's preferred term for these people is "Roma."

The Roma most likely originated in today's India. In fact, the language still spoken by about two-thirds of today's European Roma—called Romany—is related to contemporary Indian languages. The Roma migrated into Europe through the Ottoman Empire (today's Turkey), arriving in the Balkan Peninsula in the 1300s. Traditionally, Roma earned their livelihood as entertainers (fortune telling, music and dancing, horse shows, dancing bears); as thieves; and as metalworkers (which is why they tended to concentrate in mining areas, like Slovakia and Kosovo).

Roma were initially not allowed to enter Austrian territory, but as the Hapsburgs recaptured lands once controlled by the Ottomans (like Slovakia and Hungary), they permitted the Roma already living there to stay. In the 18th and 19th centuries, as "Gypsy music" funneled into the theaters of Vienna and Budapest, a romantic image of the Roma emerged: a happy-go-lucky nomadic lifestyle; intoxicating music, with dancers swirling around a campfire; mystical, or even magical, powers over white Europeans; and alluring, sultry women. But white Europe's image of the Roma also had a sinister side. Even today, Europeans and Americans alike might warn their children, "If you don't behave, I'll sell you to the Gypsies!" This widespread bigotry culminated in the Holocaust—when half a million Roma people were murdered in Nazi concentration camps.

Today's Roma are Europe's forgotten population—estimates range from 6 to 12 million throughout the Continent. Many Roma do their best to integrate with their white neighbors. But Roma who hold down jobs and send their kids to school often find themselves shunned both by their fellow Roma, and by the white Europeans they're emulating. Other Roma resist assimilation. For example, in the Spiš Region, some Roma live in small, remote, self-contained villages—a long walk up a dirt road away from the mainstream "civilization." Polygamy is not uncommon, and girls marry and begin having children at a very early age. Most children start attending school, but a high percentage drop out after just a few years.

Largely because of their unconventional lifestyle, Roma are subject to a pervasive prejudice unparalleled in today's Europe. Local news anchors—hardly fair or balanced—pointedly scapegoat the Roma for problems. A small town in the Czech Republic tried to build a wall between its wealthy neighborhood and the Roma ghetto. Schools are sometimes carefully segregated, with signs reading, "Whites Only." And recently, obstetricians in the Czech Republic have been accused of sterilizing their female Roma patients without their informed consent.

It's easy to criticize these seemingly closed-minded attitudes. But, in the eyes of white Europeans, the Roma's poor reputation is at least partly deserved. While many Roma are upstanding citizens, others do turn to thievery for survival. The tour-guide refrain, "Watch out for Gypsy thieves!" might seem racist—but it's also good advice. Many visitors have learned the hard way that it's downright foolish not to keep a close eye on a Roma person loitering in a tourist zone.

The large Roma population also puts an enormous strain on the already overtaxed social-welfare networks in these countries. Unemployment in the Spiš Region is near 30 percent—but among Roma, it's more like 50 percent in the summer (when some seasonal work is available) to 80 percent in the winter. To a white Slovak struggling to succeed in the tough times of post-communist Eastern Europe, Roma people are often seen as freeloaders.

What emerges is a seemingly unsolvable problem—a fundamental cultural misunderstanding, tinged with racist undertones, that separates the people of this region. So far, the Roma haven't produced a Martin Luther King, Jr., to mobilize the culture and demand equal rights—and many experts think they likely never will. The greatest "crossover" success stories are musicians and artists, with no political aspirations.

But the white European community is beginning to take note. The Decade of Roma Inclusion—launched in 2005 by Hungarian-American businessman George Soros—is an initiative being undertaken by eight Eastern European countries to better address the human rights of their Roma citizens (www .romadecade.org). Many are hopeful, too, that with the EU's increased focus on cooperation and human rights, the Roma will find a welcome home in the new, united Europe.

II made a pilgrimage here, saying Mass in front of some 650,000 people.

Near Levoča

Spiš Castle (Spišský Hrad)—Just a few miles from Levoča lies one of Europe's largest castles. Spiš Castle watches over the region from high on a bluff, overlooking a desolate terrain. Though there have been castles on this strategic spot for as long as people have lived here, the current version was built during the 15th century. Since its destruction in 1781, only

evocative, photogenic ruins remain. Hollywood recently paid Spiš Castle a visit to film the 2007 epic *The Last Legion*.

The interior is tourable, though anyone you ask will tell you it's pretty dull in there (100 Sk, daily May–Sept 8:30–19:00, Oct 8:30–18:00, last entry 45 min before closing, closed Nov–April, tel. 053/454-1336, www.spisskyhrad.sk). However, views of the castle from the surrounding countryside are majestic.

Spiš Castle is the centerpiece of a cluster of interesting sights. The town just below the castle is **Spišské Podhradie** ("Under the Spiš Castle"). On a ridge opposite Spiš Castle is **Spišská Kapitula,** the site of the Spiš Region's cathedral, surrounded by a modest village and an imposing 14th-century wall. And tucked behind Spiš Castle is **Žehra,** a village with a simple, onion-domed church that contains some 13th- to 15th-century wall paintings.

Getting There: From Levoča, take the main road (E50) east. After 7.5 miles, you'll see the first turnoff, which takes you scenically past Spišská Kapitula and through Spišské Podhradie (park near town and hike all the way up, or cut through town back to the main road and wind around to the second exit). To get to the castle more directly, stay on E50 past the first exit, and go another two miles, where there'll be another turnoff to the right leading up to the parking lot behind the castle.

Slovak Paradise (Slovenský Raj)—Outdoors enthusiasts from all over Eastern Europe flock to this national park, and for good reason—it features steep river gorges lined with waterfalls, and plateaus pocked by caves, offering some of the most enjoyable hikes this side of the Plitvice Lakes (see page 708). The Slovak Paradise is known for its seemingly treacherous trails—one often-photographed stretch features ladders laid at sharp uphill angles, spanning a gaping gorge. The faint of heart should steer clear of these more challenging hikes; in other parts of the park, you'll find trails suitable for any hiker (www.slovenskyraj.sk). Spišská Nová

Ves is the handiest gateway, on the northeastern fringe of the park (and with a convenient train station).

River Rafting in the Pieniny—A few miles north of Levoča, at the border with Poland, is the Pieniny region (www.pieniny.sk). Here, the Dunajec (DOO-nah-yets) River flows through a dramatic gorge in the shadow of sheer limestone cliffs, with Poland

on one bank and Slovakia on the other—like a set from *The Lord of the Rings.*

The best way to experience the Pieniny is on a boat cruise. You'll board a *plt'*—a strange, pontoon-type raft made up of five canoe-like skiffs lashed together and bridged with long benches— and ply the waters of the Dunajec River. Your lively conductor is dressed in the traditional costume of the Góral folk who populate this region. The trip is generally smooth—no whitewater to speak of—and offers a lazy chance to enjoy the scenery.

Rafting trips go roughly from early May through late October, weather permitting (daily 8:30–17:00, until 15:00 Sept–Oct, about 250 Sk per person, float lasts about 1 hour). The best stretch of river is 5.5-mile-long, U-shaped **Dunajec Canyon,** that begins near the town of **Červený Kláštor** ("Red Cloister"—this old building is near the town itself) and ends at the town of **Lesnica.** Hop on at a raft landing—marked as *prístav plt'í* on signs and maps. When you reach Lesnica, catch the bus back to your starting point...or hike the three miles back to Červený Kláštor.

SLEEPING

All of the presidents of Central European countries converged on Levoča for a conference in 1998, and you'll see photos of many of them decorating the few proud hotels in town. All of these hotels are right on the main square, Námestie Majstra Pavla.

$$ Hotel Satel is a plush, swanky place that caters to tour groups. Its 23 frou-frou rooms are all pastel pinks, spread around a beautifully restored inner courtyard (Sb-€50, Db-€75, 40 percent cheaper Oct–April, breakfast-€4, elevator to some rooms, Námestie Majstra Pavla 55, tel. 053/451-2943, fax 053/451-4486, www.hotelsatel.com, satel-le@hotelsatel.com).

$ Hotel Barbakan, near the top of the main square, feels traditional. Though its 15 rooms are dark, it's a decent option for the price (Sb-€35, Db-€46, suite-€52, 15 percent cheaper Oct–April, extra bed-€12, breakfast-€5, lots of stairs with no elevator,

---

Sleep Code

(30 Sk = about $1, €1 = about $1.20, country code: 421, area code: 053)

S = Single, **D** = Double/Twin, **T** = Triple, **Q** = Quad, **b** = bathroom, **s** = shower only. Credit cards are accepted and English is spoken at each place. For the convenience of their international guests, Levoča's hotels generally quote prices in euros. These rates do not include breakfast.

To help you sort easily through these listings, I've divided the rooms into two categories, based on the price for a standard double room with bath:

$$ Higher Priced—Most rooms €50 or more.
$ Lower Priced—Most rooms less than €50.

Košická 15, tel. 053/451-4310, fax 053/451-3609, www.barbakan.sk, recepcia.hot@barbakan.sk).

$ Hotel Arkada, popular with tours, has 32 nondescript rooms (Sb-€30, Db-€45, lavish suite-€50, 10 percent cheaper Oct–April, extra bed-€10, breakfast-€4, Námestie Majstra Pavla 26, tel. 053/451-2372, fax 053/451-2255, www.arkada.sk, arkada @stonline.sk).

EATING

Hotel Satel and **Hotel Barbakan,** listed above, both have restaurants. But **Reštaurácia u 3 Apoštolov** ("Three Apostles"), also right on the square, is a cut above, serving tasty Slovak cuisine. The decor is nothing special, but the food is delicious and cheap: pungent garlic soup, excellent trout, and the tasty "Apostle Specialty"—sautéed beef and vegetables in a spicy sauce, wrapped in a potato pancake (main dishes about 150 Sk, long hours daily, Námestie Majstra Pavla 11, tel. 053/451-2302).

The High Tatras
(Vysoké Tatry)

While not technically in the Spiš Region, Slovakia's most breathtaking mountain range is nearby. The High Tatras mountain range is small but mighty—dramatic, nearly 9,000-foot-tall granite peaks spike up from the plains, covering an area of only about 100 square miles. The High Tatras are the northernmost and highest part of the Carpathian Mountains, which stretch across the heart of Eastern Europe all the way to Romania. These cut-glass peaks have quickly become legendary among hardy, in-the-know travelers for their remarkably inexpensive hiking and skiing opportunities.

The High Tatras make up the Polish-Slovak border. Without a car, the most accessible approach is from the Polish resort town of **Zakopane** (an easy 1.5-hour bus or train connection from Kraków). But for more rugged beauty, head to the southern part of the range, in Slovakia.

The mid-sized city of **Poprad**—located on a plain about 10 miles from the mountains—is the most convenient launchpad for venturing into Slovakia's High Tatras. Along the base of the High Tatras are various modest resort towns (including the biggest, Starý Smokovec). There's no shortage of scenic hikes all over the region (good maps and guidebooks available locally). The best no-sweat high-altitude option is to take the **cable car** from the resort village of Tatranská Lomnica up to the viewpoint at Lomnický Štít (8,640 feet; popular and crowded, so visit early).

By car, take road 537 along the base of the High Tatras to connect the various towns. By public transportation, you'll commute by electric trains *(električky)* from Poprad into Starý Smokovec. (There are also direct, one-hour buses from Levoča to Starý Smokovec.) From Starý Smokovec, you can continue by electric train on to Tatranská Lomnica and other villages. Each town has its share of simple resort-type hotels, but serious hikers enjoy staying in the High Tatras' many *chaty* (mountain huts). For more details on the High Tatras, visit www.tanap.sk or www.tatry.net. *Spectacular Slovakia* magazine, mentioned on page 170, also has good coverage of the region (www.spectacularslovakia.sk).

POLAND

POLAND

(Polska)

Americans who think of Poland as run-down—full of rusting factories, smoggy cities, and gloomy natives—are speechless when they step into Kraków's vibrant main square, Gdańsk's colorful pedestrian drag, or Warsaw's lively Old Town. While parts of the country are still cleaning up the industrial mess left by the Soviets, Poland also has some breathtaking medieval cities that show off its warm and welcoming people, dynamic history, and unique cultural fabric.

The Poles are a proud people—as moved by their spectacular failures as by their successes. Their quiet elegance has been tempered by generations of abuse by foreign powers. The Poles place a lot of importance on honor, and you'll find fewer scams and con artists here than in other countries.

In a way, there are two Polands: lively, cosmopolitan urban centers, and hundreds of tiny farm villages in the countryside. City-dwellers often talk about the "simple people" of Poland—those descended from generations of farmers, working the same plots for centuries and living an uncomplicated, traditional lifestyle. This large contingent of old-fashioned, salt-of-the-earth folks—who like things the way they are—is a major reason why Poland was so hesitant to join the European Union (see page 208).

Poland is the poorest of the countries that joined the European Union in 2004. While the most important tourist centers have been prettied up admirably, you only need venture a few blocks, or drive through the countryside, to see unmistakable signs of poverty. It's the little things that aren't quite up to Western snuff: parks with patches of mud instead of grass, ramshackle farmhouses with overgrown yards, and rough-around-the-edges infrastructure (rusted railings, pot-holed roads, and so on). These finer points are expensive to cultivate—unnecessary niceties that the Poles simply can't afford yet. But with the Poles' ambitious spirit and new EU investment, it shouldn't be long before Poland starts to look more like the wealthy West.

Poland is one of Europe's most devoutly Catholic countries. Catholicism defines these people, holding them together through times when they had little else. Squeezed between Protestant Germany (originally Prussia) and Orthodox Russia, Poland wasn't even a country for generations (1795–1918). Its Catholicism helped keep it alive. In the last century, while "under communism" (as that age is referred to), Poles found their religion a source of strength as well as rebellion—they could express dissent by going to church. Some of Poland's best sights are churches, usually filled with locals praying silently. While these church interiors are worth a visit, be especially careful to show the proper respect (maintain silence, keep a low profile, and snap pictures discreetly).

Visitors are surprised at how much of Poland's story is a Jewish story. Before World War II, 80 percent of the world's Jews lived in Poland. Warsaw was the world's second-largest Jewish city (after New York) with 380,000 Jews (out of a total population of 1.2 million). Poland was a magnet for Jews because of its relatively welcoming policies. Still, Jews were forbidden from owning land; that's why they settled mostly in the cities. But the Holocaust (and a later Soviet policy of sending "troublemaking" Jews to Israel) decimated the Jewish population. This tragic chapter, combined with postwar border shifts and population movements, made

Poland Almanac

Official Name: Rzeczpospolita Polska (Republic of Poland), or Polska for short.

Snapshot History: This thousand-year-old country has been dominated by foreigners for much of the last two centuries, finally achieving true independence (from the Soviet Union) in 1989.

Population: Nearly 39 million people, slightly more than California. About 97 percent are ethnically Polish and speak Polish. Three out of every four Poles is a practicing Catholic. The population is younger than most European countries, with an average age of 37 (Germany's is 42).

Latitude and Longitude: 52°N and 20°E (similar latitude to Berlin, London, and Edmonton, Alberta).

Area: 122,000 square miles, the same as New Mexico (or Illinois and Iowa put together).

Geography: Because of its overall flatness, Poland has been a corridor for invading armies since its infancy. The Vistula River (680 miles) runs south-to-north up the middle of the country, passing through Kraków and Warsaw, and emptying into the Baltic Sea at Gdańsk. Poland's climate is generally cool and rainy—40,000 storks love it.

Biggest Cities: Warsaw (the capital, 1.7 million), Łódź (790,000), and Kraków (757,000).

Economy: The Gross Domestic Product is $505 billion (a little more than the state of Ohio), but the GDP per capita is $13,100—less than a third what the average Ohioan makes. The 1990s saw an aggressive—and very successful—transition from state-run socialism to privately-owned capitalism. Still, Poland's traditional potato-and-pig-farming society is behind the times, with 16 percent of the country's workers producing less than 3 percent of its GDP. One in five Poles is unemployed, and nearly one in five lives in poverty. Poland's entry into the European Union in 2004 brought substantial financial aid that should improve things.

Currency: 1 złoty (zł, or PLN) = 100 groszy (gr) = about 30 cents; 3 zł = about $1.

Poland one of Europe's most ethnically homogenous countries. Today, virtually everyone in the country speaks Polish, and only a few thousand Polish Jews remain.

Poland is historically extremely pro-American. Of course, their big neighbors (Russia and Germany) have been their historic enemies. And when Hitler invaded in 1939, the Poles felt let down by their supposed European friends (France and Britain), who declared war on Germany but provided virtually no military

Real Estate: A typical, one-bedroom apartment in Warsaw (250 square feet) rents for roughly $600 a month.

Government: Poland's president selects the prime minister and Cabinet, with legislators' approval. They govern along with a two-house legislature (Sejm and Senat) of 560 seats. Currently Poland is ruled by the Kaczyński brothers, co-founders of the conservative "Law and Justice" party—Lech Kaczyński is president, and Jarosław Kaczyński is prime minister. These former child actors (no joke) are leading Poland in a decisively right-wing, anti-EU direction. For more on the Kaczyński brothers, see page 209.

Flag: The upper half is white, and the lower half is red—the traditional colors of Poland. Poetic Poles claim the white represents honor, and the red represents the enormous amounts of blood spilled by the Poles to honor their nation. The flag sometimes includes a coat of arms with a crowned eagle (representing Polish sovereignty). Under Poland's many oppressors (including the Soviets), the crown was removed from the emblem, and its talons were trimmed. On regaining its independence, Poland coronated its eagle once more.

The Average Pole: New prosperity aside, the average Pole spends just 4 percent of what a German spends on personal consumption. One in four Poles uses the Internet, and the average Pole will live to about age 75. The average woman gets married at 24 and will have 1.25 children.

Not-so-Average Poles: Despite the many "Polack jokes" you've heard (and maybe repeated), you actually know of many famous Polish intellectuals—you just don't realize they're Polish. The "Dumb Polack" Hall of Fame includes Karol Wojtyła (Pope John Paul II), Mikołaj Kopernik (Nicolas Copernicus), composer Fryderyk Chopin, scientist Marie Curie (née Skłodowska), writer Teodor Józef Korzeniowski (better known as Joseph Conrad, author of *Heart of Darkness*), filmmaker Roman Polański *(Chinatown, The Pianist)*, politician Lech Wałęsa...and one of this book's co-authors.

support. America has always been regarded as the big ally from across the ocean. In 1989, when Poland finally won its freedom, many Poles only half-joked that they should apply to become the 51st state of the United States.

On my first visit to Poland, I had a poor impression of Poles, who seemed brusque and often elbowed ahead of me in line. I've since learned that all it takes is a smile and a cheerful greeting—preferably in Polish—to break through the thick skin that helped these kind people survive the difficult communist times. With a friendly hello *(Dzień dobry!)*, you'll turn any grouch into a new friend.

Practicalities

Restroom Signage: To confuse tourists, the Poles have devised a secret way of marking their WCs. You'll see doors marked with *męska* (men) and *damska* (women)—but even more often, you'll simply see a triangle (for men) or a circle (for women). Likewise, a sign with a triangle, a circle, and an arrow is directing you to the closest WCs.

Pay to Pee: To irritate tourists, Polish bathrooms often charge a small fee. Sometimes you'll even be charged at a restaurant where you're paying to dine. Sadly, many American visitors let this minor inconvenience interfere with their enjoyment of the trip. My advice: You don't have to like it, but get used to it—it's a hassle, but it's cheap (usually around 1 zł).

Train Station Lingo: "PKP" is the abbreviation for Polish National Railways ("PKS" is for buses). In larger towns with several train stations, you'll usually use the one called Główny (meaning "Main"—except in Warsaw, where it's Centralna). Underneath the stations are often mazes of walkways—lined with market stalls—that lead to platforms *(peron)* and exits *(wyjście)*. Most stations have several platforms, each of which has two tracks *(tor)*. Departures are generally listed by the *peron*, so keep your eye on both tracks for your train. Arrivals are *przyjazdy*, and departures are *odjazdy*. Left-luggage counters or lockers are marked *przechowalnia bagażu*. *Kasy* are ticket windows. "Information" windows are more often than not staffed by monolingual grouches. Smile sweetly, write down your destination and time, and hang on to your patience. The line you choose will invariably be the slowest one—leave plenty of time to buy your ticket before your train departs (or, if you're running out of time, buy it on board for a few dollars extra). To get into town, follow signs for *wyjście do centrum* or *wyjście do miasta*.

Museum Tips: Virtually every museum in Poland is closed on Monday. The ticket window for any museum closes a half-hour before the museum's closing time, and this last-entry deadline is strictly enforced. Poland's museums are notorious for constantly tweaking their opening times. I've tried to list the correct hours, but be aware that they're virtually impossible to predict—try to confirm locally if you have your heart set on a particular place.

Polish Artists: Though Poland has produced world-renowned scientists, musicians, and writers, the country isn't known for its artists. Polish museums greet foreign visitors with fine artwork by unfamiliar names. If you're planning to visit any museums in

---

Top 10 Dates That Changed Poland

A.D. 966—The Polish king, Mieszko I, is baptized a Christian, symbolically uniting the Polish people and founding the nation.

1385—The Polish queen (called a "king" by sexist aristocrats of the time) marries a Lithuanian duke, starting the two-century reign of the Jagiełło family.

1410—Poland defeats the Teutonic Knights at the Battle of Grunwald, part of a Golden Age of territorial expansion and cultural achievement.

1572—The last Jagiellonian king dies, soon replaced by bickering nobles and foreign kings. Poland declines.

1795—In the last of three partitions, the country is divvied up by its more-powerful neighbors: Russia, Prussia, and Austria.

1918—Following World War I, Poland gets back its land and sovereignty.

1939—Gdańsk (then called Danzig) is invaded by Nazi Germany, starting World War II. At war's end, the country is "liberated" (i.e., occupied) by the Soviet Union.

1980—Lech Wałęsa leads a successful strike, demanding more freedom from the communist regime.

1989—The Berlin Wall falls, and Poland soon gains independence under its first president...Lech Wałęsa.

2004—Poland joins the European Union, pedaling fast to catch up to its more-prosperous neighbors.

Poland, there are two artists worth remembering: **Jan Matejko,** a 19th-century positivist who painted grand historical epics (see page 307); and one of his students, **Stanisław Wyspiański,** a painter and playwright who led the charge of the Młoda Polska movement (the Polish answer to Art Nouveau—see page 231) in the early 1900s.

Telephones: Insertable telephone cards, sold at newsstands and kiosks everywhere, get you access to the modern public phones. Cheap international phone cards for calling the US have only recently begun to appear (often sold at Internet cafés or youth hostels; see page 35 for details).

In an emergency, dial 112; to summon the police, call 997. Remember these prefixes: 0800 is toll-free, and 0700 is expensive (like phone sex). Many Poles use mobile phones (which come with 060 and 050 prefixes).

Poland uses a direct-dial system, which means you call the same number whether dialing across the street or across the country. To call Poland from another country, first dial the international access number (00 if you're calling from Europe, or 011 from the US and Canada), followed by 48 (Poland's country code), then the number (without the initial 0). To call out of Poland, dial 00, the country code of the country you're calling (see chart in appendix), the area code if applicable (may need to drop initial zero), and the local number (see page 35 for details).

Polish History

Poland is flat. Take a look at a topographical map of Europe, and you can see the Poles' historical dilemma: The path of least resistance from northern Europe to Russia is right through Poland. Over the years, many invaders— from Napoleon to Hitler—have taken advantage of Poland's strategic location. The country is nicknamed "God's playground" for the many wars that have rumbled through its territory. Poland has been invaded by Soviets, Germans, French, Austrians, Russians, Prussians, Swedes, Teutonic Knights, Tatars, Bohemians, Magyars—and, about 1,300 years ago, Poles.

Medieval Greatness

The first Poles were a tribe called the Polonians ("people of the plains"), a Slavic band that showed up in these parts in the eighth century. In 966, Mieszko I, Duke of the Polonian tribe, adopted Christianity and founded the Piast dynasty (which would last for more than 400 years). Poland was born.

Poland struggled with two different invaders in the 13th century: the Tatars (Mongols who ravaged the south) and the Teutonic Knights (Germans who conquered the north—see page 368). But despite these challenges, Poland persevered. The last king of the Piast dynasty was also the greatest: Kazimierz the Great, who famously "found a Poland made of wood and left one made of brick and stone"—bringing Poland (and its capital, Kraków) to international prominence (see page 228). The progressive Kazimierz also invited Europe's much-persecuted Jews to settle here, establishing Poland as a haven for the Jewish people—which it would remain until the Nazis arrived.

Kazimierz the Great died at the end of the 14th century without a male heir. His grand-niece, Jadwiga, became "king" (the Poles weren't ready for a "queen") and married Lithuanian Prince Władysław Jagiełło, uniting their countries against a common enemy, the Teutonic Knights. Their marriage marked the beginning of the Jagiellonian dynasty and set the stage for Poland's

Golden Age. With territory spanning from the Baltic Sea to the Black Sea, Poland flourished.

Foreign Kings and Partitions

When the Jagiellonians died out in 1572, political power shifted to the nobles. Poland became a nation governed by its wealthiest 10 percent—the *szlachta,* or nobility, who elected a series of foreign kings. Many of these kings made bad diplomatic decisions and squandered the country's resources. To make matters worse, the Polish Parliament *(Sejm)* introduced the concept of *liberum veto,* whereby any measure could be vetoed by a single member of parliament. This policy—which effectively demanded unanimous approval for any law to be passed—paralyzed the *Sejm*'s waning power.

By the late 18th century, Poland was floundering—and surrounded by three land-hungry empires (Russia, Prussia, and Austria). Over the course of less than 25 years, these countries divided Poland's territory among themselves in a series of three partitions. In 1795, "Poland" (nicknamed "the cake of kings"—to be sliced and eaten at will) disappeared from Europe's maps, not to return until 1918.

Even though Poland was gone, the Poles wouldn't go quietly. As the partitions were taking place, Polish soldier Tadeusz Kościuszko (a hero of the American Revolution) returned home to lead an unsuccessful military resistance against the Russians. After another failed uprising against Russia in 1830, many of Poland's top artists and writers fled to Paris—including pianist Fryderyk Chopin and Romantic poet Adam Mickiewicz (whose statue adorns Kraków's main square and Warsaw's Royal Way). These Polish artists tried to preserve the nation's spirit with music and words; those who remained in Poland continued to fight with swords and fists. By the end of the 19th century, the image of the Pole as a tireless, idealistic insurgent emerged. During this time, some Romantics—with typically melodramatic flair—dubbed Poland "the Christ of nations" for the way it was misunderstood and persecuted by the world.

At the end of World War I, Poland finally regained its independence...but the peace didn't last long.

Saddle on a Cow: World War II and Communism

In the early 20th century, Poland enjoyed an exhilarating ethnic mix—including Germans, Russians, Ukrainians, Lithuanians, and an enormous Jewish minority. A third of Poland spoke no Polish. But then, on September 1, 1939, Hitler began World War II by attacking the Baltic port city of Gdańsk. With six million deaths in the next six years, Poland suffered the worst per-capita WWII

The Heritage of Communism

While Poland has been free, democratic, and capitalist since 1989, even young adults carry lots of psychological baggage from living under communism. Although the young generally embrace the fast new affluence with enthusiasm, many older people tend to be nostalgic about that slower-paced time that came with more security. And even young professionals, with so much energy and hope now, don't condemn everything about that stretch of history. A friend who was 13 in 1989 recalled those days this way:

"My childhood is filled with happy memories. Under communism, life was family-oriented. Careers didn't matter. There was no way to get rich, no reason to rush, so we had time. People always had time.

"But there were also shortages—many things were 'in deficit.' Sometimes my uncle would bring us several toilet paper rolls, held together with a string—absolutely the best gift anyone could give. I remember my mother and father had to 'organize' for special events...somehow find a good sausage and some Coca-Cola.

"Boys in my neighborhood collected pop cans. Since drinks were very limited in Poland, cans from other countries represented a world of opportunities beyond our borders. Parents could buy their children these cans on the black market, and the few families who were allowed to travel returned home with a treasure trove of cans. One boy up the street from me went to Italy, and proudly brought home a Pepsi can. All of the boys in the neighborhood wanted to see it—it was a huge status symbol. But a month later, communism ended, you could buy whatever you wanted, and everyone's can collections were worthless.

"We had real chocolate only for Christmas. The rest of the year, for treats we got something called 'chocolate-like product'—it was sweet, dark, and smelled vaguely of chocolate. And we had oranges from Cuba for Christmas, too. Everybody was excited when the newspapers announced, 'The boat with the oranges from Cuba is just five days from Poland.' We waited with excitement all year for chocolate and those oranges. The smell of Christmas was so special. Now we have that smell every day. Still, my happiest Christmases were under communism."

losses of any nation. At the war's end, as the victorious Allies shifted Poland's borders significantly westward, a massive movement of populations took place: Germans from western Poland were forced into Germany, and Poles from what would become Ukraine were transplanted to Poland proper. After millions died in the war, millions more were displaced from their ancestral homes. When the dust settled, Poland was in rubble...and almost exclusively Polish.

Poland was arguably hit harder by the Soviet regime than the other countries in this book. As conditions worsened in the 1970s, food shortages were the norm. Stores were marked by long lines stretching around the block. Poles were issued ration coupons for food staples, and cashiers clipped off a corner when a purchase was made...assuming, of course, the item was in stock. It often wasn't.

The little absurdities of communist life—which today seem almost comical—made every day a struggle. For years, every elderly woman in Poland had hair the same strange magenta color. There was only one color of dye available, so the choice was simple: Let your hair grow out (and look clownishly half red and half white), or line up and go red.

During these difficult times, the Poles often rose up—staging major protests in 1956, 1968, 1970, and 1976. Stalin famously noted that introducing communism to the Poles was like putting a saddle on a cow.

When an anti-communist Polish cardinal named Karol Wojtyła was elected Pope in 1978, it was a sign to his countrymen that change was in the air. (For more on Pope John Paul II, see page 234.) In 1980, Lech Wałęsa, an electrician at the shipyards in Gdańsk, became the leader of the Solidarity movement, the first workers' union in communist Eastern Europe. After an initial 18-day strike at the Gdańsk shipyards, the communist regime gave in, legalizing Solidarity (for more on Solidarity, see page 343).

But the union grew too powerful, and the communists felt their control slipping away. On Sunday, December 13, 1981, Poland's head of state, General Wojciech Jaruzelski, declared martial law in order to "forestall Soviet intervention." (Whether the Soviets actually would have intervened remains a hotly debated issue.) Tanks ominously rolled through the streets of Poland on that snowy December morning, and the Poles were terrified.

Martial law would last until 1983. Each Pole has his or her own chilling memories of this frightening time. During riots, the people would flock into churches—the only place they would be safe from the ZOMO, or riot police. But Solidarity struggled on, going underground and becoming a united movement of all demographics, 10 million members strong (more than a quarter of the population).

Polish Jokes

Through the dreary communist times, the Poles managed to keep their sense of humor. A popular target of jokes was the riot police, or ZOMO. Here are just a few of the things Poles said about these unpopular cops:

- It's better to have a sister who's a whore than a brother in the ZOMO.
- ZOMO police are hired based on the 90-90 principle: They have to weigh at least 90 kilograms (200 pounds), and their I.Q. must be less than 90.
- ZOMO would be dispatched in teams of three: one who could read, one who could write, and a third to protect those other two smart guys.
- A ZOMO policeman was sitting on the curb, crying. Someone came up to him and asked what was wrong. "I lost my dog!" he said. "No matter," the person replied. "He's a smart police dog. I'm sure he can find his way back to the station." "Yes," the ZOMO said. "But without him, *I* can't!"

The communists gave their people no options at elections: If you voted, you voted for the regime. Poles liked to joke that in some ways, this made communists like God—who created Eve, then said to Adam, "Now choose a wife." The communists could run a pig as a candidate, and it would still win. A popular symbol of dissent became a pig painted with the words, "Vote Red."

There were even jokes about jokes. Under communism, Poles noted that there was a government-sponsored prize for the funniest political joke: 15 years in prison.

In July 1989, the ruling Communist Party agreed to hold open elections (reserving 65 percent of representatives for themselves). Their goal was to appease Solidarity, but the plan backfired: Communists didn't win a single seat. These elections helped spark the chain reaction across Eastern Europe that eventually tore down the Iron Curtain. Lech Wałęsa became Poland's first post-communist president. (For more on Lech Wałęsa, see page 344.)

Poland in the 21st Century: The European Union

When 10 new countries joined the European Union in May 2004, Poland was the most ambivalent of the bunch. After centuries of being under other empires' authority, the Poles were hardly eager to relinquish some of their hard-fought autonomy to Brussels. Some Poles see the EU as an unstoppable monster, but most believe their country had to join to survive in today's Europe. Many Poles thought that EU membership would make things worse (higher prices, a loss of traditional lifestyles) before they got better. But now, a few years later, most begrudgingly acknowledge that the benefits of EU membership have outweighed the drawbacks.

While other countries were planning their fireworks displays to celebrate EU enlargement on May 1, 2004, Poland was seized by a strange sort of mass hysteria. The country buzzed with rumors of increased prices. When the news reported that sugar would be subject to a higher tax rate, there was a run on the stores, as the Poles bought up as much sugar as they could stockpile. The result? A shortage of sugar...and higher prices, even before May 1. (If this sounds like a bad Polack joke come to life, remember the days after September 11, 2001, when US stores ran out of tarp, duct tape, and bottled water.)

The most obvious impact of EU membership so far has been the tremendous migration of young Poles seeking work in other EU countries (mostly Britain, Ireland, and Sweden, which waive visa requirements for Eastern European workers). Many of them find employment at hotels and restaurants. Visitors to London and Dublin are noticing a surprising language barrier at the front desks of hotels, and Polish expat newspapers are joining British gossip rags on newsstands. Those who remain in Poland are becoming concerned about the "brain drain" of bright young people flocking out of their country. For more on this phenomenon, see "The Polish Plumber Syndrome" on page 14.

Poland is by far the most populous of the new EU members, with 39 million people (about the same as Spain, or about half the size of Germany). This makes Poland the sixth-largest of the 27 EU member states—giving it serious political clout, which it has already asserted in shaping a new EU constitution. As the EU learns to live with its new Eastern European comrades, Poland looks poised to take a leading role in the "New Europe."

The Kaczyński Brothers:
Those Two Who Would Lead Poland

Poland's political process took a surprising turn in the 2005 presidential election, won by Lech Kaczyński and his conservative "Law and Justice" party. The party's platform is pro–tax cuts, fiercely Euroskeptic (anti-EU), and very Catholic. This suits the Poles fine. Like a nation of Newt Gingriches, Poles are phobic when it comes to "big government," since they've been subjugated and manipulated so much by foreign oppressors over the centuries. This is partly why the infrastructure here still lags somewhat behind other Eastern European countries (lower taxes = less investment in roads). In general, Poland may be the most politically conservative country in Europe (though still to the left of the US).

In a queasy twist, several months after his election, President

Lech Kaczyński took the controversial step of appointing his identical twin brother (and Law and Justice party co-founder) Jarosław as Poland's prime minister. The Kaczyński brothers were child actors who appeared in several popular movies together—their biggest hit was a flick titled *Those Two Who Would Steal the Moon*. As teenagers, they would switch identities and take tests for each other. Today the 45-minute-older, unmarried, and slightly more handsome Jarosław, who still lives with the twins' mother, is considered one of Poland's most eligible bachelors. (You can't make this stuff up.)

Love them or hate them, these pudgy, baby-faced twin brothers are leading Poland into the 21st century.

Polish Food

Polish food is hearty and tasty. Since Poland is north of the Carpathian Mountains, its weather tends to be chilly, which limits the kinds of fruits and vegetables that flourish here. Like other northern European countries (such as Russia or Scandinavia), dominant staples include potatoes, dill, berries, beets, and bread. Much of what you might think of as Jewish food turns up on Polish menus (gefilte fish, potato pancakes, chicken soup, and so forth)—not necessarily because either group influenced the other, but because they lived in the same area for centuries under the same climatic and culinary influences.

Polish soups are a highlight. The most typical are *żurek* and *barszcz*. *Żurek* (often translated as "sour soup" on menus) is a light-colored soup made from a sourdough base, usually containing a hard-boiled egg and pieces of *kiełbasa* (sausage). *Barszcz*, better known to Americans as borscht, is a savory beet soup. There are various types of borscht: *Barszcz czerwony* (red borscht) is a broth with a deep red color, sometimes containing dumplings or a hard-boiled egg. *Barszcz ukraiński* (Ukrainian borscht) is similar, but has vegetables mixed in (usually cabbage, beans, and carrots). In summer, try the "Polish gazpacho"—*chłodnik*, a cream soup with beets, onions, and radishes that's served cold.

Another familiar Polish dish is pierogi. These ravioli-like dumplings come with various fillings. The most traditional are minced meat, sauerkraut, mushroom, cheese, and blueberry, but many restaurants experiment with more exotic fillings. Pierogi are often served with specks of fatty bacon to add flavor. Pierogi are a budget traveler's dream: Restaurants serving them are everywhere, and they're generally cheap, filling, and tasty.

Bigos is a rich and delicious sauerkraut stew cooked with meat, mushrooms, and whatever's in the pantry. *Gołąbki* is cabbage leaves stuffed with minced meat and rice in a tomato or mushroom sauce. *Kotlet schabowy* (fried pork chops)—once painfully scarce

Bar Mleczny (Milk Bar)

Eating at a *bar mleczny* is an essential Polish sightseeing expe-rience. These cafeterias, which you'll see all over the country, are an incredibly cheap way to get a good meal...and, with the right attitude, a fun cultural experience.

In the communist era, the government subsidized the food at milk bars, allowing lowly workers to enjoy a meal out. The tradition continues, and today, Poland still foots the bill for most of your milk-bar meal. Prices are astoundingly low—my bill for a full meal usually comes to about $4—and, while communist-era fare was gross, today's milk-bar cuisine is usually quite tasty.

Milk bars usually offer many of the traditional tastes listed in this section. Common items are soups (like *żurek* and *barszcz*), a variety of cabbage-based salads, *kotlet* (fried pork chops), pierogi (like ravioli, with various fillings), and *naleśniki* (pancakes). You'll often see glasses of juice and (of course) milk, but most milk bars also stock bottles of water and Coke.

There are two general types of milk bars: updated, mod-ern cafeterias that cater to tourists (English menus), add some modern twists to their traditional fare, and charge about 50 percent more; and time-machine dives that haven't changed for decades. At truly traditional milk bars, the service is aimed at locals—no English menu and a confusing ordering system.

Every milk bar is a little different, but here's the general procedure: Head to the counter, wait to be acknowledged, and point to what you want. Handy vocabulary: *to* (sounds like "toe") means "that"; *i* (pronounced "ee") means "and."

If the milk-bar lady asks you any questions, you have three options: nod stupidly until she just gives you something; repeat one of the things she just said (assuming she's asked you to choose between two options, like meat or cheese in your pierogi); or hope that a kindly English-speaking Pole in line will leap to your rescue. If nothing else, ordering at a milk bar is an adventure in gestures. Smiling seems to slightly extend the patience of milk-bar staffers.

Once your tray is all loaded up, pay the cashier, do a double-take when you realize how cheap your bill is, then find a table. After the meal, it's generally polite, if not expected, to bus your dishes (watch locals and imitate).

in communist Poland—remain a local favorite to this day. *Kaczka* (duck) is popular, as is fish: Look for *pstrąg* (trout), *karp* (carp, beware of bones), and *węgorz* (eel). Poles eat lots of potatoes, which are served with nearly every meal. The bagel-like rings you'll see on the street, *obwarzanki*, are fresh, tasty, and cheap.

Poland has excellent pastries. A *piekarnia* is a bakery specializing in breads. But if you really want something special, look for a *cukiernia* (pastry shop). The classic Polish treat is *pączki*, glazed jelly doughnuts. They can have different fillings, but most typical is a wild-rose jam. *Szarlotka* is apple cake—sometimes made with chunks of apples (especially in season), sometimes with apple filling. *Sernik* is cheesecake, and *makowiec* is poppy-seed cake. *Winebreda* is an especially gooey Danish. *Babeczka* is like a cupcake filled with pudding. You may see *jabłko w cieście*—slices of apple cooked in dough, then glazed. *Napoleonka* is a French-style treat with layers of crispy wafers and custard.

Lody (ice cream) is popular. The most beloved traditional candy is *ptasie mleczko* (birds' milk), which is like a semi-sour marshmallow covered with chocolate. E. Wedel is the country's top brand of chocolate, with outlets in all the big cities (see page 321).

Thirsty? *Woda* is water, *woda mineralna* is bottled water (*gazowana* is with gas/carbonation, *niegazowana* is without), *kawa* is coffee, *herbata* is tea, *sok* is juice, and *mleko* is milk. Żywiec and Okocim are the best-known brands of *piwo* (beer).

Wódka (vodka) is a Polish staple—the name means, roughly, "precious little water." Żubrówka, the most famous brand of vodka, comes with a blade of grass from the bison reserves in eastern Poland (look for the bottle with the bison). The bison "flavor" the grass...then the grass flavors the vodka. Poles often mix Żubrówka with apple juice, and call this cocktail *szarlotka* ("apple cake"). For "Cheers!" say, "*Na zdrowie!*" (nah ZDROH-vyeh).

Unusual drinks to try if you have the chance are *kwas* (a cold, fizzy, Ukrainian-style non-alcoholic beverage made from day-old rye bread) and *kompot* (a hot drink made from stewed berries). Poles are unusually fond of carrot juice (often cut with fruit juice); Kubuś is the most popular brand.

"Bon appétit" *is* "*Smacznego*" (smatch-NEH-goh). To pay, ask for the *rachunek* (rah-KHOO-nehk) or say, "*Płacę*" (PWOTS-eh, "I'll pay").

Polish Language

Polish is closely related to its neighboring Slavic languages (Slovak and Czech), with the biggest difference being that Polish has lots of fricatives (hissing sounds—"sh" and "ch"—often in close proximity). Consider the opening line of Poland's most famous tongue-twisting nursery rhyme: *W Szczebrzeszynie chrzaszcz brzmi*

Key Polish Phrases

English	Polish	Pronounced
Hello. (formal)	*Dzień dobry.*	jehn DOH-bree
Hi. / Bye. (informal)	*Cześć.*	cheshch
Do you speak English? (asked of a man)	*Czy Pan mówi po angielsku?*	chee pahn MOO-vee poh ahn-GYEHL-skoo
Do you speak English? (asked of a woman)	*Czy Pani mówi po angielsku?*	chee PAH-nee MOO-vee poh ahn-GYEHL-skoo
Yes. / No.	*Tak. / Nie.*	tahk / nyeh
Please. / You're welcome. / Can I help you?	*Proszę.*	PROH-sheh
Thank you.	*Dziękuję.*	jehn-KOO-yeh
I'm sorry. / Excuse me.	*Przepraszam.*	pzheh-PRAH-shahm
Good.	*Dobrze.*	DOHB-zheh
Goodbye.	*Do widzenia.*	doh veed-ZAY-nyah
one / two	*jeden / dwa*	YEH-dehn / dvah
three / four	*trzy / cztery*	tzhee / chuh-TEH-ree
five / six	*pięć / sześć*	pyench / sheshch
seven / eight	*siedem / osiem*	SYEH-dehm / OH-shehm
nine / ten	*dziewięć / dziesięć*	JEH-vyench / JEH-shench
hundred	*sto*	stoh
thousand	*tysiąc*	TEE-shanch
How much?	*Ile?*	EE-leh
local currency	*złoty (zł)*	ZWOH-tee
Where is...?	*Gdzie jest...?*	gdzeh yehst
...the toilet	*...toaleta*	toh-ah-LEH-tah
men	*męska*	MEHN-skah
women	*damska*	DAHM-skah
water / coffee	*woda / kawa*	VOH-dah / KAH-vah
beer / wine	*piwo / wino*	PEE-voh / VEE-noh
Cheers!	*Na zdrowie!*	nah ZDROH-vyeh
the bill	*rachunek*	rah-KHOO-nehk

w trzcinie ("In Szczebrzeszyn, a beetle is heard in the reeds"—pronounced vuh shih-chehb-zheh-shee-nyeh khzhahshch bzh-mee vuh tzhuh-cheen-yeh...or something like that).

Polish intimidates Americans with long, difficult-to-pronounce words. But if you take your time and sound things out, you'll quickly develop an ear for it. First of all, the stress is always on the next-to-last syllable. The letter *c* always sounds like "ts" (as in "cats"). The letter combinations *ć, ci,* and *cz* all sound like "ch"; *ś, si,* and *sz* all sound like "sh"; and *ż, zi,* and *rz* all sound like "zh" (as in "leisure"). The letter *ń* and the combination *ni* sound like "ny" (as in "canyon").

Some Polish vowels have a nasalized sound, like in French. If you see *ę* or *ą,* pronounce them as "en" or "an."

One of the trickiest changes to get used to: *w* sounds like "v," and *ł* sounds like "w." So, "Lech Wałęsa" isn't pronounced "lehk wah-LEH-sah," as Americans tend to say—but "lehkh vah-WEHN-sah."

As you're tracking down addresses, these words will help: *miasto* (town), *plac* (square), *rynek* (big market square), *ulica* (road), *aleja* (avenue), and *most* (bridge).

KRAKÓW

Kraków is the Boston of Poland: a beautiful, old-fashioned city buzzing with history, enjoyable sights, tourists, and college students. Even though the country's capital moved from here to Warsaw 400 years ago, Kraków remains Poland's cultural and intellectual center. Of all of the Eastern European cities laying claim to the boast "the next Prague," Kraków is for real. Now's the time to visit: just as the tourist infrastructure ramps up, but before it's swamped with crowds.

Kraków grew wealthy from trade in the late 10th and early 11th centuries. Traders who passed through were required to stop here for a few days and sell their wares at a reduced cost. Local merchants turned around and sold those goods with big price hikes...and Kraków thrived. In 1038, it became Poland's capital.

Tatars invaded in 1241, leaving the city in ruins. Krakovians took this opportunity to rebuild their streets in a near-perfect grid, a striking contrast to the narrow, mazelike lanes of most medieval towns. The destruction also paved the way for the spectacular Main Market Square—still Kraków's best attraction.

King Kazimierz the Great sparked Kraków's Golden Age in the 14th century (see page 228). In 1364, he established the university that still defines the city (and counts Copernicus and Pope John Paul II among its alumni).

But Kraków's power waned as Poland's political center shifted to Warsaw. In 1596, the capital officially moved north. At the end of the 18th century, three neighboring powers—Russia, Prussia, and Austria—partitioned Poland, annexing all of its territory and dividing it among themselves. Warsaw ended up as a satellite of oppressive Moscow, and Kraków became a poor provincial

Kraków's Old Town

- ① Bike Rental
- ② Trams #3, #13 & #34 to Kazimierz
- ③ Minibuses to Wieliczka Salt Mine (Confirm at TI)
- ④ To Warszawska St. & Minibuses to Auschwitz (Confirm at TI)

backwater of Vienna. But despite Kraków's reduced prominence, Austria's comparatively liberal climate helped turn the city into a haven for intellectuals and progressives (including a young revolutionary thinker from Russia named Vladimir Lenin).

Kraków emerged from World War II virtually unscathed. But when the communists took over, they decided to give intellectual (and potentially dissident) Kraków an injection of good Soviet values—in the form of heavy industry. They built Nowa Huta, an enormous steelworks and planned town for workers, on Kraków's outskirts—dooming the city to decades of smog. Thankfully,

Kraków Essentials

English	Polish	Pronounced
Main Train Station	Kraków Główny	KROCK-oof GWOHV-nee
Old Town	Stare Miasto	STAH-reh mee-AH-stoh
Main Market Square	Rynek Główny	REE-nehk GWOHV-nee
Cloth Hall	Sukiennice	soo-kyeh-NEET-seh
Floriańska Street	Ulica Floriańska	OOH-leet-suh floh-ree-AHN-skah
Park around the Old Town	Planty	PLAHN-tee
Castle Hill	Wawel	VAH-vehl
Jewish Quarter	Kazimierz	kah-ZHEE-mehzh
Vistula River	Wisła	VEES-wah
Salt Mine	Wieliczka	vee-LEECH-kah
Planned Communist Suburb	Nowa Huta	NOH-vah HOO-tah

Kraków is now much cleaner than it was 15 years ago.

Pope John Paul II was born (as Karol Wojtyła) in nearby Wadowice, and served as archbishop of Kraków before being called to Rome. Poland is devoutly Catholic; make sure to visit a few of Kraków's many churches. University life, small but thought-provoking museums, great restaurants, sprawling parks, and Jewish history round out the city's appeal.

Over the last few years, I've watched the number of visitors to Kraków skyrocket. The city has come to life at a speed paralleled only by Prague's transition a decade ago. Yet despite its overwhelming popularity, competition keeps prices delightfully low.

Planning Your Time

Kraków and its important side-trips deserve at least two full days on the busiest itinerary. Most people can easily fill three days. The city's sights are quickly exhausted, but more than any town in Europe, Kraków is made for aimless strolling.

Ideally, spend two full days in Kraków itself, plus a visit to Auschwitz (either as a side-trip on the third day, or en route to or from Kraków). In a pinch, spend one day sightseeing in Kraków, another at Auschwitz, and two evenings on the Main Market Square.

With only one full day in Kraków, follow this plan: Take

my self-guided walk of Kraków's Royal Way to cover the city's core. Visit any Old Town museums that interest you (Wyspiański Museum, Czartoryski Museum, Jagiellonian University Museum), and have lunch on or near the Main Market Square. Spend the afternoon at Wawel Castle (note that many castle sights close at 15:00). Savor the Square over dinner or a drink, or enjoy traditional Jewish music and cuisine in Kazimierz.

With more time in Kraków, explore Kazimierz, the former Jewish Quarter—a must for those interested in Jewish heritage, and illuminating for anyone. Or, if you're intrigued by the architecture of the communist era, head for the Nowa Huta suburb.

Auschwitz, an essential side-trip, requires the better part of a day for a round-trip visit (see next chapter). If you have more time, the Wieliczka Salt Mine nearby makes another good day trip. It's conceivably possible to fit Auschwitz and Wieliczka into the same day, especially with an early start and a local driver—but it's far more reasonable to do them on separate days.

ORIENTATION

(area code: 012)
Kraków (KROCK-oof, sometimes spelled "Cracow" in English) is mercifully compact, flat, and easy to navigate. While the urban sprawl is big (with about 757,000 people), the tourist's Kraków feels small. You can walk from the northern edge of the Old Town to the southern edge (Wawel Hill) in about 15 minutes.

Most sights—and almost all recommended hotels and restaurants—are in the Old Town (Stare Miasto), which is surrounded by a greenbelt called the Planty. In the center of the Old Town lies the Main Market Square (Rynek Główny). From the Main Market Square, the Main Train Station is a 15-minute walk to the northeast; Kazimierz (the Jewish quarter) is a 20-minute walk to the southeast; and Wawel Hill (with a historic castle, museums, and Poland's national church) is a 10-minute walk south. Just beyond Wawel is the Vistula River.

Tourist Information

Kraków has several TIs. The handiest for travelers are in the **Planty** park, between the Main Train Station and Main Market Square (June–Sept Mon–Sat 9:00–19:00, Sun 9:00–17:00; Oct–May daily 9:00–17:00; in round kiosk at ulica Szpitalna 25, tel. 012-432-0110); just north of the Main Market Square on **ulica Św. Jana** (Mon–Sat 10:00–18:00, closed Sun, at #2, tel. 012-421-7787); and in the **Town Hall Tower** right on the Main Market Square (daily June–Sept 9:00–19:00, Oct–May 9:00–17:00, tel. 012-433-7310). Other branches are in **Kazimierz** (Mon–Fri 10:00–16:00, closed

Sat–Sun, ulica Józefa 7, tel. 012-422-0471), **Nowa Huta** (Tue–Sat 10:00–16:00, closed Sun–Mon, os. Słoneczne 16, tel. 012-643-0303), and the **airport** (daily 9:00–17:00, tel. 012-285-5341). The Web site for all TIs is www.krakow.pl.

At any TI, ask what's new in fast-changing Kraków, browse the brochures, and pick up the free one-page map and the *Kraków Tourist Compendium* booklet. The TIs also offer a free room-finding service.

I'd skip the **Kraków Tourist Card,** which covers public transportation in Kraków, admission to several city museums, and moderate discounts to outlying sights and tours (45 zł/2 days, 65 zł/3 days). Since public transportation is mostly unnecessary and museums are so cheap, this card doesn't make sense for most visitors.

Arrival in Kraków

By Train: Kraków's Main Train Station (called "Kraków Główny") is just northeast of the Old Town. The area around the station has recently undergone a lengthy and desperately needed reconstruction project. Now the station area feels modern and slick, with a brand-new bus station (behind the train tracks—see below) and the massive, futuristic Galeria Krakowska shopping mall (sharing a broad plaza with the train station).

Taxis from the station are cheap and easy (from the tracks, take the elevator or stairs to the rooftop above you, where you'll find a giant parking lot where taxis wait; the fair metered rate to downtown is a reasonable 10–15 zł).

Most hotels are within easy walking distance. It's about a 15-minute stroll to the Main Market Square—look for signs to the center *(wyjście do centrum or dojście do centrum).* From the tracks, you'll first walk down some stairs and pass through a tunnel, then turn left, head back up to ground level, and walk under a long green canopy. (Don't try to detour through the Galeria Krakowska shopping mall, which you can enter directly from the tunnel—once inside the enormous mall, it's confusing to find your way back out the other end.) At the end of the green canopy, you'll go through the main terminal building and exit on the other side, where you'll emerge into a brand-new, wide-open plaza (plac Dworcowy) fronted by the Galeria Krakowska mall and a yellow post office. Continue straight out of the station and bear left around the post office. Several flights of stairs feed into a pedestrian underpass beneath the busy ring road; as you emerge from this underpass, bear right (following signs for *Rynek Główny/Main Market*) and head into the Planty park. You'll see the round TI kiosk on your left, and the Main Market Square is a few blocks straight ahead.

By Bus: The brand-new bus station is right behind the train station. To get into town, use the tunnel that takes you under the train tracks (following signs for *PKP*—the train station—and *centrum*). Once at the train station, follow the directions above.

You're more likely to be going *to* the bus station (to catch a bus to Auschwitz). To get to the bus station from the Old Town, first head to the train station (go through the Planty park and use the underpass). From the train station's main arrivals hall, walk under the long green canopy to the train platforms. Use the pedestrian underpass to go under the tracks (following signs for *dojście do dworca autobusowego*); when you emerge on the other side, the bus station is the blocky, modern, poorly marked building on your left. Inside are the standard amenities (lockers and toilets), domestic and international ticket windows, and an electronic board showing the next several departures. Bus departures marked in red leave from the upper *(gorná)* stalls, which are designated with a *G* (you see these out the window). Bus departures marked in green leave from the lower *(dolna)* stalls, which are designated with a *D;* to find these, go down the easy-to-miss stairs (marked *zejście na dolna płytę*) on the left just beyond the ticket windows.

By Car: *Centrum* signs lead you into the Old Town—you'll know you're there when you hit the ring road that surrounds the Planty park. Your hotel can advise you on directions and parking. The most central parking lot is on ulica Szczepańska, a block west of the Main Market Square.

By Plane: The small, modern **John Paul II Kraków-Balice Airport** is about 10 miles west of the center. A brand-new train station near the airport allows you to zip quickly downtown (catch the blue shuttle bus in front of the terminal, which will take you to the station nearby; then buy the 4-zł ticket on the train for the 15-min trip to Kraków's Main Train Station—see arrival instructions above). You can also catch the Radtur bus in front of the airport to Kraków's main bus station (7 zł, may not run in the winter, see bus station arrival instructions above). Or, for door-to-door service, catch a cab from the taxi stand in front of the terminal (around 50 zł, more expensive at night, about 30 min). Airport info: tel. 012-285-5120, www.lotnisko-balice.pl.

Note that many budget flights—including those on Wizz Air, SkyEurope, Centralwings, easyJet, and Ryanair—use the **International Airport Katowice in Pyrzowice** (Międzynarodowy Port Lotniczy Katowice w Pyrzowicach, www.gtl.com.pl). This airport serves the city of Katowice, about 50 miles west of Kraków. Direct buses run sporadically between Katowice Airport and Kraków's Main Train Station (50 zł, about 4/day, trip takes 1.75 hrs, www.axet.com.pl). You can also take the bus from Katowice Airport into the Katowice train station, then take the train to Kraków (hourly, 1.5 hrs). Wizz Air's Web site is useful for figuring out your connection: www.wizzair.com.

Helpful Hints

Sightseeing Schedules: Most museums are closed Monday, and many are free one day a week. Hours at museums tend to change frequently; carefully confirm the opening times of sights at the TI.

Internet Access: Kraków's many Internet cafés—it seems there's one on every corner—charge around 1 zł for 15 min.

Post Office: The main post office (Poczta Główna) is at the intersection of Starowiślna and the Westerplatte ring road, a few blocks east of the Main Market Square.

Bookstore: For used English books, try **Massolit Books,** just west of the Old Town (Sun–Thu 10:00–20:00, Fri–Sat 10:00–22:00, ulica Felicjanek 4, tel. 012-432-4150).

Laundry: Doing laundry in Kraków is frustrating. There's no good self-service launderette in the center, unless you're staying at a hostel. Your hotel can do your wash, but it's expensive. If you must have something laundered, a central option is **Betty Clean** (about 10 zł per shirt, 15 zł for pants, takes 24 hours, pay 50 percent more for express 3-hour service, Mon–Fri 7:30–19:30, Sat 8:00–15:30, closed Sun, just outside the Planty park at ulica Zwierzyniecka 6, tel. 012-423-0848).

Travel Agencies: Orbis, at the top of the Main Market Square, books bus tours, changes money, and sells train tickets (May–Sept Mon–Fri 9:00–19:00, Sat 9:00–15:00, closed Sun, closes 1 hour earlier Oct–April, Rynek Główny 41, www.orbis .krakow.pl, tel. 012-619-2449). The agency posts a handy complete train schedule in their window. Buy your train tickets in this central location (no fee, English spoken) to avoid the trip to (and often long lines at) the station.

Also on the Square—right in the Cloth Hall—is **MCIT** (Małopolskie Centrum Informacji Turystycznej), which sells maps and guidebooks, books tours, arranges transportation and car rentals, and has a room-finding service (generally open summer Mon–Fri 9:00–20:00, Sat 9:00–18:00, Sun 9:00–16:00; winter Mon–Fri 9:00–17:00, Sat 9:00–14:00, usually closed Sun in winter; in middle of Cloth Hall facing St. Mary's Church at Rynek Główny 1–3, tel. 012-421-7706, www.mcit.pl).

Getting Around Kraków

Kraków's top sights and best hotels are easily accessible by foot. You'll only need wheels if you're going to the Kazimierz Jewish quarter or the Nowa Huta suburbs.

By Public Transit: Trams and buses zip around Kraków's urban sprawl. While most trams are new and modern, a few rickety old trams with big windows (dubbed "aquariums" by locals)

Kraków at a Glance

Be Warned: Kraków's museum hours tend to fluctuate. If you want to be sure to get into a certain sight, confirm the hours in advance.

▲▲▲**Main Market Square** Stunning heart of Kraków and a people magnet any time of day. **Hours:** Always open.

▲▲**Planty** Once a moat, now a scenic park encircling the city. **Hours:** Always open.

▲▲**St. Mary's Church** Landmark church with extraordinary wood-carved Gothic altarpiece. **Hours:** Mon–Sat 11:30–18:00, Sun 14:00–18:00.

▲▲**Cloth Hall** Fourteenth-century market hall with 21st-century souvenirs. **Hours:** Summer Mon–Fri 9:00–18:00, Sat–Sun 9:00–15:00, sometimes later; winter Mon–Fri 9:00–16:00, Sat–Sun 9:00–15:00.

▲▲**St. Francis' Basilica** Lovely Gothic church with some of Poland's best Art Nouveau. **Hours:** Open long hours daily.

▲▲**Wawel Cathedral** Poland's splendid national church, with tons of tombs, a crypt, and a climbable tower. **Hours:** Ticket sales for crypt and tower May–Sept Mon–Sat 9:00–17:15, Sun 12:15–17:15; Oct–April Mon–Sat 9:00–15:45, Sun 12:15–15:45.

▲▲**Wawel Castle Grounds** Historic hilltop with views, castle, cathedral, courtyard with chakras, and a passel of museums. **Hours:** Grounds open daily May–Sept 6:00–20:00, Oct–April 6:00–17:00.

also rattle around the city.

The trams you're most likely to use are #4 to Nowa Huta, and #3, #13, and #34 to Kazimierz. The same tickets are used for both trams and buses, and can be purchased at kiosks marked *RUCH*, or—for 0.50 zł extra—from the driver. There are three kinds of tickets: A *bilet jednoprzejazdowy* (basic single ticket, no transfers) costs 2.50 zł at a kiosk. Technically, if you're using this cheap ticket, you have to buy a separate ticket for your bag (or risk a fine). So you might as well get a *bilet godzinny*—good for an hour, and allowing transfers and luggage (3.10 zł). Always validate your ticket when you board the bus or tram.

You can also get longer-term tickets for 24 hours (10.40 zł), 48 hours (18.80 zł), and 72 hours (25 zł). These must be validated the

▲▲**Jewish Cemeteries** Two touching burial sites—the Old (1552–1800) and New (post-1800)—in Kazimierz. **Hours:** Old Cemetery—May–Oct Sun–Fri 9:00–17:30, Nov–April until 15:30, closes at sundown on Fri, always closed Sat; New Cemetery—Sun–Fri 8:00–18:00, until 16:00 in winter, closed Sat.

▲**Czartoryski Museum** Varied collection, with European paintings (da Vinci and Rembrandt) and Polish armor, handicrafts, and decorative arts. **Hours:** May–Oct Tue and Thu 10:00–16:00, Wed and Fri–Sat 10:00–19:00, Sun 10:00–15:00, closed Mon; Nov–April Tue, Thu, and Sat–Sun 10:00–15:30, Wed and Fri 10:00–18:00, closed Mon.

▲**Wyspiański Museum** Art by the talented leader of the Młoda Polska Art Nouveau movement. **Hours:** May–Oct Wed and Sat 10:00–19:00, Thu–Fri 10:00–16:00, Sun 10:00–15:00; Nov–April Wed–Thu and Sat–Sun 10:00–15:30, Fri 10:00–18:00; closed Mon–Tue year-round.

▲**Isaac Synagogue** Kazimierz house of worship showing evocative historical movies of the Jewish Quarter. **Hours:** Sun–Fri 9:00–19:00, July–Aug until 20:00, closed Sat, closes at sundown on winter Fri—as early as 15:00 in Dec.

▲**Polish Folk Museum** Traditional rural Polish life on display—an open-air museum moved inside. **Hours:** May–Sept Mon and Wed–Fri 10:00–17:00, Sat–Sun 10:00–14:00, closed Tue; Oct–April Mon 10:00–18:00, Wed–Fri 10:00–15:00, Sat–Sun 10:00–14:00, closed Tue.

first time you use them, and can only be purchased at special MPK ticket booths (the handiest is in the Planty park near the TI).

By Taxi: Just as in other big Eastern European cities, only take cabs that are clearly marked with a company logo and telephone number. Kraków taxis start at 5 zł and charge 2–3 zł per kilometer. Rides are very short and generally run less than 10 zł. You're more likely to get the fair metered rate by calling or hailing a cab, rather than taking one waiting at tourist spots. To call a cab, try **Radio Taxi** (tel. 012-9191).

By Buggy: Romantic, horse-drawn buggies trot around Kraków from the Main Market Square. The going rate is a hefty 100 zł for a 30-minute tour.

By Bike: Wypożyczalnia Rowerów Rent-a-Bike, half a block off the Main Market Square, is run by easygoing Michał Bisping. Biking the Planty park and along the riverside promenades gives your trip a great extra dimension and gets you out of the prettied-up Old Town to see a slice of untouristy Kraków (5 zł/hr, 35 zł/day, April–Oct daily 9:00–dusk, closed Nov–March, ulica Św. Anny 4, mobile 0501-745-986, www.bikes-rental.prv.pl).

TOURS

Local Guides—Kraków has several affordable guides. I've enjoyed working with two in particular, both of whom have cars (for driving you to Auschwitz or on other day trips, or for taking you into the countryside to help you track down your Polish roots): **Marta Chmielowska** (250 zł/half-day, 300 zł with her car, full day just a little more, 500 zł to Auschwitz, mobile 0603-668-008, martachm @op.pl) and **Anna Gega** (by foot: 250 zł/4 hrs, 350 zł/day; by car: 300 zł/4 hrs, 450 zł/day; mobile 0604-151-293, leadertour@wp.pl).

Walking Tours—Various companies run city walking tours in English daily in summer. Most do a 2.5-hour tour of the Old Town as well as a 2.5-hour tour of Kazimierz, the Jewish district (40–60 zł per tour, depending on company). Because the scene is continually evolving, it's best to pick up fliers locally (at the TI or your hotel) and choose the one that fits your interests and schedule. Four people can hire their own great local guide for about the same amount of money.

Crazy Guides—This irreverent company offers tours to the communist suburb of Nowa Huta and other outlying sights. For details, see page 255.

Bus Tours—Various tour companies run bus-plus-walking itineraries (each of them around 120–130 zł), including a general city overview (3 hrs), Auschwitz (6 hrs), Wieliczka Salt Mine (4 hrs), and other regional side-trips. Get information at the TI.

Golf-Cart Tours—Several outfits based on the Main Market Square offer tours on a golf cart with recorded commentary (prices are for up to 4 people: 100 zł for half-hour tour of Old Town or Kazimierz, 170 zł for hour-long tour of both the Old Town and Kazimierz).

SIGHTS

Kraków's Royal Way Walk

Most of Kraków's major sights are conveniently connected by this self-guided walking tour. This route is known as the "Royal Way" because the king used to follow this same path when he returned to Kraków after a journey. After the capital moved to Warsaw, most kings were still coronated and buried in Wawel Cathedral at the far end of town—and they followed this same route for both occasions. You could sprint through this three-part walk in under an hour (less than a mile altogether), but it's much more fun if you take it slow.

Royal Way Walk Part 1: Barbican to Main Market Square

Begin the walk at the north end of the Old Town, at the barbican.

▲Barbican (Barbakan), Florian Gate (Brama Floriańska), and City Walls—Tatars invaded Kraków three times in the 13th century. After the first attack destroyed the city in 1241, Krakovians built this wall. The original rampart had 47 watchtowers and eight gates. The big, round defensive fort standing outside the wall is a barbican. Structures like this provided extra fortification to weak sections. Imagine how it looked in 1500, when this barbican stood outside the town moat with a long bridge leading to the Florian Gate—the city's main entryway. Today you can pay 5 zł to scramble along the passages and fortifications of the barbican (daily 10:30–18:00). There's little to see inside...except for once a month in the summer, when a battle of knights is staged here (get details at TI).

• Before entering the Old Town, look to the left and right of the barbican to see the...

▲▲Planty—By the 19th century, Kraków's no-longer-necessary city wall had fallen into disrepair. Krakovians decided to tear down what remained, fill in the moat, and plant trees. (The name comes not from the English "plant," but from the Polish plantovac, or "flat"—since they flattened out this area to create it.) Today, the Planty is a beautiful park that stretches 2.5 miles around the entire perimeter of Kraków's Old Town.

• Go through the Florian Gate into the Old Town. Inside the gate, notice the little chapel with a replica of the famous Black Madonna of Częstochowa, a town just north of here. Once through the gate, you're standing at the head of Kraków's historic (and now touristic) gamut...

▲Floriańska Street (Ulica Floriańska)—On the inside of the city wall, you'll see a makeshift **art gallery,** where starving students hawk the works they've painted at the Academy of Fine Arts (across the busy street from the barbican). Portraits, still lifes, landscapes, local scenes, nudes...this might just be Kraków's best collection of art. If you were to detour along the gallery (to the left as you face the gate), in a block you'd arrive at another fine collection—the eclectic Czartoryski Museum, home to a rare Leonardo da Vinci oil painting (see "National Museum Branches," page 242).

Walking down Floriańska street, you can't miss the **McDonald's** on the left. When renovating this building, they discovered a Gothic cellar—so they excavated it and added seating.

Today, you can super-size your ambience by dining on a Big Mac and fries under a medieval McVault.

Cukiarnia Jama Michalika (farther down on left, at #45)—a dark, atmospheric café popular with locals for its coffee and pastries—began in 1895 as a simple bakery in a claustrophobic back room. A brothel upstairs scared off respectable patrons, so the owner attracted students by creating a cabaret act called "The Green Balloon." To this day, the cabaret—political satire set to music—still runs (in Polish only). Around the turn of the 20th century, this was a hangout of the Młoda Polska (Young Poland) movement—the Polish answer to Art Nouveau (explained on page 231). The walls are papered with sketches from poor artists who couldn't pay their tabs. Poke around inside, and see how many green balloons you can spot. Consider having coffee and dessert here (Sun–Thu 9:00–22:00, Fri–Sat 9:00–23:00). Expect a grouchy greeting and a fee for the coat-check and miserable bathrooms.

Two blocks ahead on the left (at #3, 50 yards before the big church), you'll see **Jazz Club u Muniaka.** In the 1950s, Janusz Muniak was one of the first Polish jazzmen. Now he owns this place, and jams regularly here in a cool cellar surrounded by jazzy art. If you hang around the bar before the show, you might find yourself sitting next to Janusz himself, smoking his pipe... and getting ready to smoke on the saxophone (for details, see "Entertainment" on page 258).

• *Continue into the Main Market Square, where you'll run into...*

▲▲St. Mary's Church (Kościół Mariacki)—A church has stood on this spot for 800 years. The original church was destroyed by the first Tatar invasion in 1241, but all subsequent versions—including the current one—have been built on the same foundation. You can look down the sides to see how the Main Market Square has risen about seven feet over the centuries.

How many church towers does St. Mary's have? Technically, the answer is one. The shorter tower belongs to the church; the taller one is a municipal watchtower, from which you'll hear a bugler playing the hourly *hejnał* song. According to Kraków's favorite legend, during that first Tatar invasion, a town watchman saw the enemy approaching and sounded the alarm. Before he could finish the tune, an arrow pierced his throat—which is why, even today, the *hejnał* stops *subito* partway through. Today's buglers—12 in all—are firemen first, musicians second. Each one works a 24-hour shift up there, playing the *hejnał* on the hour, every hour (broadcast on national

Polish radio at noon). Sometimes in the summer, you can actually climb up all those stairs to visit them (ask at the wooden kiosk in front of the church, or check with the TI).

The church's front door is open 14 hours a day and is free to those who come to pray. Tourists use the door around the right side (4 zł, Mon–Sat 11:30–18:00, Sun 14:00–18:00). The rusty neck-stock (behind the tourists' left door) was used for public humiliation until the 1700s. The church's highlight, its wooden altarpiece, is open daily between noon and 18:00. Try to be here by 11:45 for the ceremonial opening or at 18:00 for the closing.

Inside, you're drawn to one of the most impressive medieval woodcarvings in existence—the exquisite, three-part Gothic **altarpiece** by German Veit Stoss (Wit Stwosz in Polish). Carved in 12 years and completed in 1489, it's packed with emotion rare in Gothic art. Stoss used oak for the structural parts and linden trunks for the figures. When the altar doors are closed, you see scenes from the lives of Mary and Jesus. The open altar depicts the Dormition (death) of the Virgin. The artist catches the apostles (11, without Judas) around Mary, reacting in the seconds after she collapses. Mary is depicted in three stages: dying, being escorted to heaven by Jesus, and (at the very top) being crowned in heaven (flanked by two Polish saints—Adalbert and Stanisław). The six scenes on the sides are the Annunciation, birth of Jesus, visit by the Three Magi, Jesus' Resurrection, his Ascension, and Mary becoming the mother of the apostles at Pentecost.

There's more to St. Mary's than the altar. While you're admiring this church's art, notice the flowery Neo-Gothic painting covering the choir walls. Stare up into the starry, starry blue ceiling. As you wander around, consider that the church was renovated a century ago by three Polish geniuses from two very different artistic generations: the venerable positivist Jan Matejko and his Art Nouveau students, Stanisław Wyspiański and Józef Mehoffer (we'll learn more about these two later on our walk). The huge silver bird under the organ loft in back is a crowned eagle, the symbol of Poland.

▲▲▲**Main Market Square (Rynek Główny)**—Kraków's marvelous Square, one of Europe's most gasp-worthy public spaces, bustles with street musicians, colorful flower stalls, cotton-candy vendors, loitering teenagers, businesspeople commuting by foot, gawking tourists, and the lusty coos of pigeons. This Square is where Kraków lives. On my last visit, local teens practiced break-dancing moves at one end of the Square while activist types protested Poland's EU membership at the other.

The Square was established in the 13th century, when the city had to be rebuilt after being flattened by the Tatars. At the time, it was the biggest square in medieval Europe. It was illegal to sell

Kazimierz the Great
(1333–1370)

Out of the many centuries of Polish kings, only one earned the nickname "great," and he's the only one worth remembering: Kazimierz the Great.

K. the G., who ruled Poland from Kraków in the 14th century, was one of those larger-than-life medieval kings who left his mark on all fronts—from war to diplomacy, art patronage to womanizing. His scribes bragged that Kazimierz "found a Poland made of wood, and left one made of brick and stone." He put Kraków on the map as a major European capital. He founded many villages (some of which still bear his name) and replaced wooden structures with stone ones (such as Kraków's Cloth Hall). Kazimierz also established the Kraków Academy (today's Jagiellonian University), the second-oldest university in Central Europe. And to protect all these new building projects, he heavily fortified Poland by building a series of imposing forts and walls around its perimeter.

Most of all, Kazimierz is remembered as a progressive, tolerant king. In the 14th century, other nations were deporting—or even interning—their Jewish subjects, who were commonly scapegoated for anything that went wrong. But the enlightened and kindly Kazimierz actively encouraged Jews to come to Poland by granting them special privileges, often related to banking and trade—establishing the country as a safe haven for Jews in Europe.

Kazimierz the Great was the last of Poland's long-lived Piast dynasty. Although he left no male heir—at least, no legitimate one—Kazimierz's advances set the stage for Poland's Golden Age (14th–16th centuries). After his death, Poland united with Lithuania (against the common threat of the Teutonic Knights), the Jagiellonian dynasty was born, and Poland became one of Europe's mightiest medieval powers.

anything on the street, so everything had to be sold here on the Main Market Square. It was divided into smaller markets, such as the butcher stalls, the ironworkers' tents, and the Cloth Hall (see below). Recent work to renovate the Square's pavement has revealed a wealth of remains from previous structures. In 2007, they hope to open an "underground museum" beneath the Cloth Hall to show off their excavations.

The statue in the middle of the Square is of Romantic poet **Adam Mickiewicz** (1789–1855). His epic masterpiece, *Pan Tadeusz*, is still regarded as one of the greatest works in Polish, and Mickiewicz is considered the "Polish Shakespeare." A wistful, nostalgic tale of Polish-Lithuanian nobility, *Pan Tadeusz* stirred patriotism in a Poland that had been dismantled by surrounding empires.

Near the end of the Square, you'll see the tiny **Church of St. Adalbert,** the oldest church in Kraków (10th century). This Romanesque structure predates the Square. Like St. Mary's (described above), it seems to be at an angle because it's aligned east–west, as was the custom when it was built. (In other words, the churches aren't crooked—the Square is.)

Drinks are reasonably priced at cafés on the Square (most around 10 zł). Find a spot where you like the view and the chairs, then sit and sip. Enjoy the folk band. Tip them, and you can photograph their traditional Kraków garb up close. (A big tip gets you *The Star-Spangled Banner.*)

As the Square buzzes around you, imagine this place before 1989. There were no outdoor cafés, no touristy souvenir stands, and no salesmen hawking cotton candy. The communist government shut down all but a handful of the businesses. They didn't want people to congregate here—they should be at home, resting, because "a rested worker is a productive worker." The buildings were covered with soot from the nearby Lenin Steelworks in Nowa Huta. (The communists denied the pollution, and when the student "Green Brigades" staged a demonstration in this Square to raise awareness in the 1970s, they were immediately arrested.)

Now imagine the Square two years ago, during Pope John Paul II's illness and death in the spring of 2005. News trucks sat anx-

iously around the perimeter of the Square, and TV cameramen jockeyed for position on temporary platforms. After the Pope died, huge banners—red and white (for Poland) and yellow and white (for the Vatican), both with black bands—were draped from the towers of St. Mary's Church. An enormous photograph of the Pope was displayed atop the Town Hall Tower, and makeshift memorials filled window displays around the city. On April 4, two nights after the Pope died, a memorial service took place at a soccer stadium south of the Old Town. Throughout the day, Kraków's students—communicating by e-mail and mobile phone text messages—coordinated a huge, spontaneous memorial parade. As the sun set, tens of thousands of young Krakovians marched silently into one end of this Square, around the Cloth Hall, and out the other end, toward the stadium.

• *The huge, yellow building right in the middle of the Square is the...*

▲▲**Cloth Hall (Sukiennice)**—In the Middle Ages, this was the place that cloth-sellers had their market stalls. Kazimierz the

Great turned the Cloth Hall into a permanent structure in the 14th century. In 1555, it burned down, and was replaced by the current building. The letter *S* (above the entryway) stands for King Sigismund the Old, who commissioned this version of the hall. As Sigismund fancied all things Italian (including women—he married an Italian princess), this structure is in the Italianate Renaissance style. We'll see more works by Sigismund's imported Italian architects at Wawel Castle.

The Cloth Hall is still a functioning market—mostly souvenirs, including wood carvings, chess sets, jewelry (especially amber), painted boxes, and trinkets (summer Mon–Fri 9:00–18:00, Sat–Sun 9:00–15:00, sometimes later; winter Mon–Fri 9:00–16:00, Sat–Sun 9:00–15:00). Cloth Hall prices are slightly inflated, but still cheap by American standards. You're paying a little extra for the convenience and the atmosphere, but you'll see locals buying gifts here, too.

WCs and telephones are at each end of the Cloth Hall. The upstairs of the Cloth Hall has traditionally housed the very good Gallery of 19th-Century Polish Art. But since the gallery is under renovation for the next several years, the paintings are on display elsewhere—in a castle inconveniently far from the city center (see page 245).

• *Browse through the Cloth Hall passageway. As you emerge into the other half of the Square, the big tower on your left is the...*

Town Hall Tower—This is all that remains of a Town Hall building from the 14th century—when Kraków was the powerful capital of Poland. After the 18th-century partitions of Poland, Kraków's prominence took a nosedive. By the 19th century, Kraków was Nowheresville. As the town's importance crumbled, so did its Town Hall. It was cheaper to tear down the building than to repair it, and all that was left standing was this nearly 200-foot-tall tower. In summer, you can climb the tower, stopping along the way to poke around an exhibit on Kraków history—but the views from up top are disappointing (5 zł, May–Oct daily 10:30–14:00 & 14:30–18:00, closed Nov–April). In the bottom of the tower is a TI, where you buy your ticket for the tower.

The **gigantic head** you may see at the base of the Town Hall Tower is a sculpture by contemporary artist Igor Mitoraj, who studied here in Kraków. Typical of Mitoraj's works, the head is an empty shell that appears to be wrapped in cloth. It was originally

Młoda Polska (Young Poland)

Polish art in the late 19th century was ruled by positivism, a school with a very literal, straightforward focus on Polish history (Jan Matejko led the charge; see page 307). But when the new generation of Kraków's artists came into their own in the early 1900s, they decided that the old school was exactly that. Though moved by the same spirit and goals as the previous generation—evoking Polish patriotism at a time when their country was being occupied—these new artists used very different methods. They were inspired by a renewed appreciation of folklore and peasant life. Rather than being earnest and literal (an 18th-century Polish war hero on horseback), the new art was playful and highly symbolic (the artist frolicking in a magical garden in the idyllic Polish countryside). This movement became known as Młoda Polska (Young Poland)—Art Nouveau with a Polish accent.

Stanisław Wyspiański (vees-PAYN-skee, 1869–1907) was the leader of Młoda Polska. He produced beautiful artwork, from simple drawings to the stirring stained-glass images in Kraków's St. Francis' Basilica. Wyspiański was an expert at capturing human faces with realistic detail, emotion, and personality. The versatile Wyspiański was also an accomplished stage designer and writer. His patriotic play *The Wedding*—about the nuptials of a big-city artist and a peasant girl—is regarded as one of Poland's finest dramas. The largest collection of Wyspiański's art is in Kraków's Wyspiański Museum, but you'll also see examples in Kraków's St. Francis' Basilica and Warsaw's National Museum.

Józef Mehoffer (may-HOH-fehr), Wyspiański's good friend and rival, was another great Młoda Polska artist. Mehoffer's style is more expressionistic and abstract than Wyspiański's, often creating an otherworldly effect. See Mehoffer's work in Kraków's St. Francis' Basilica and at the artist's former residence; and in Warsaw, at the National Museum.

Other names to look for include **Jacek Malczewski** (mahl-CHEHV-skee), who specialized in self-portraits, and **Olga Boznańska** (bohz-NAHN-skah), the movement's only prominent female artist. Both are featured in Warsaw's National Museum.

intended to be placed near the train station (where they might have moved it, if you don't see it here). But because of construction delays at the station, it found a home here on the Square. While some locals enjoy having a work by their fellow Krakovian in such a prominent place, others disapprove of its sharp contrast with the Square's genteel Old World ambience.

• *There are plenty of diversions to keep you busy here on the Square (including some good restaurants; see "Eating," page 265). When you're ready to continue down the Royal Way, follow Part 2 of the walk.*

Royal Way Walk Part 2:
Main Market Square to Wawel Castle

After the king passed through the grand Main Market Square, he'd continue on to his castle. We'll take a one-block detour from his route to introduce you to one of Kraków's best churches. Leave on the street in the middle of the bottom of the Square. Ulica Bracka leads one long block (and across the busy Franciszkańska street) directly to the side door of a big red-brick church. Go ye.

▲▲**St. Francis' Basilica (Bazylika Św. Franciszka)**—This beautiful Gothic church, which was Pope John Paul II's home church while he was archbishop of Kraków, features some of Poland's best Art Nouveau *in situ* (in the setting for which it was intended). After an 1850 fire, it was redecorated by the two leading members of the Młoda Polska (Young Poland) movement: Stanisław Wyspiański and Józef Mehoffer. These two talented and fiercely competitive Krakovians were friends who apprenticed together under Poland's greatest painter, Jan Matejko. The glorious decorations of this church are the result of their great rivalry run amok. (For more Wyspiański or Mehoffer, visit their museums—see "National Museum Branches," page 242.)

Highlights include:

1. Paintings and stained-glass windows by **Stanisław Wyspiański.** The windows flanking the high altar represent the Blessed Salomea (left, the church's founder, buried in a side chapel) and St. Francis (right, the church's namesake). Salomea was a medieval Polish woman who became queen of Hungary, but later returned to Poland and entered a convent after her husband's death. Notice she's dropping a crown—repudiating the earthly world and giving herself over to the simple, stop-and-smell-God's-roses lifestyle of St. Francis. As you face the back of the church, look at the window in the rear of the nave: *God the Father Let It Be*, Wyspiański's finest masterpiece. The colors beneath the Creator change from yellows and oranges (fire) to soothing blues (water), depending on the light. Wyspiański was supposedly inspired by Michelangelo's vision of God in the Sistine Chapel, though he used a street beggar to model the specific features of God. Wyspiański

also painted the delightful floral designs decorating the walls of the nave—fitting for a church dedicated to a saint so famous for his spiritual connection to nature. (For more on Wyspiański, see page 231.)

2. The chapel on the right side of the nave (as you face the back of the church) contains some evocative Stations of the Cross. This is **Józef Mehoffer**'s response to Wyspiański's work. The centerpiece of the room is a replica of the Shroud of Turin—which, since it touched the original shroud, is also considered a holy relic.

3. The modern painting (with an orange background, midway up the nave on the left as you face the back of the church) depicts **St. Maksymilian Kolbe,** the Catholic priest who traded his own life to save a fellow inmate at Auschwitz (see his story on page 279). Kolbe is particularly beloved here, as he actually served at this church.

4. Just before going out the back door (below Wypiański's stained-glass window), find the **silver plate** labeled "Jan Paweł II" on the second pew from the last (on right); this was Pope John Paul II's favorite place to pray when he lived in the Archbishop's Palace across the street.

• *Stepping outside (through the back door), look to the right. The light-yellow building across the street is the...*

Archbishop's Palace—This building (specifically, the window over the stone entryway) was Pope John Paul II's residence when he was the archbishop of Kraków. When he became Pope, it remained his home-away-from-Rome for visits to his hometown. After a long day of saying formal Mass during his visits to Kraków, he'd wind up here. Weary as he was, before going to bed he'd stand in the window for hours, chatting casually with the people assembled below—about religion, but also about sports, current events, and whatever was on their minds. In 2005, when the Pope's health deteriorated, this street filled with his supporters, even though the Pope was in Rome. For days, somber locals focused their vigil on this same window, their eyes fixed on a black crucifix that had been placed here. At 21:37 on the night of April 2, 2005, the Pope passed away in Rome. Ten thousand Krakovians were in this street, under this window, listening to a Mass broadcast on loudspeakers from the church. When the priest announced the Pope's death, every single person simultaneously fell to their knees in silence. For the next several days, thousands of the faithful continued to stand in this street, staring intently at the window where they last saw the man they considered to be the greatest Pole.

• *Now turn right, walk along the side of the church, cross the little square, and turn right again down busy Grodzka street. You're back on the Royal Way proper. After two blocks, on the right (at #45), you'll see a...*

Karol Wojtyła (1920–2005):
The Life and Death of the Greatest Pole

Karol Wojtyła was born to a humble family in the town of Wadowice (near Kraków) on May 18, 1920. Karol's mother died when he was a young boy. When he was older, he moved with his father to Kraków to study philosophy and drama at Jagiellonian University. Young Karol was gregarious and athletic—an avid skier, hiker, swimmer, and soccer goalie. During the Nazi occupation in World War II, he was forced to work in a quarry. In defiance of the oppressive Nazis, he secretly studied theology and appeared in illegal underground theatrical productions. When the war ended, he resumed his studies, this time at the theology faculty.

After graduating in 1947, Wojtyła swiftly rose through the ranks of the Catholic Church hierarchy. By 1964, he was archbishop of Kraków, and just three years later, he became the youngest cardinal ever in the Roman Catholic Church. Throughout the 1960s, he fought an ongoing battle with the regime when they refused to allow the construction of a church in the Kraków suburb of Nowa Huta. After years of saying Mass for huge crowds in open fields, Wojtyła finally convinced the communists to allow the construction of the Lord's Ark Church in 1977 (see page 257). A year later, just as Poland was facing its darkest hour, Karol Wojtyła was called to the papacy—the first non-Italian pope in more than four centuries.

Imagine you're Polish in the 1970s. Your country was devastated by World War II, and has struggled under an oppressive regime ever since. Food shortages are epidemic. Lines stretch around the block even to buy a measly scrap of bread. Life is bleak, oppressive, and hopeless. Then someone who speaks your language—someone you've admired your entire life, and one of the only people you've seen successfully stand up to the regime—becomes one of the world's most influential people. A Pole like you is the leader of a billion Catholics. He makes you believe that the impossible can happen. He says to you again and again: *"Nie*

Milk Bar *(Bar Mleczny)*—These government-subsidized cafeterias are the locals' choice for a quick, cheap, filling, lowbrow lunch. Prices are deliriously cheap (soup costs less than a dollar), and the food isn't bad. If you're ready for lunch, three handy milk bars are within a few steps of here (listed under "Eating"). For more on milk bars, see page 211.

• *Just a block ahead—after passing another milk bar (Bar Grodzki)—the square on your right is...*

Mary Magdalene Square (Plac Św. Marii Magdaleny)—Back when Kraków was just a village, this was its main square. Today *lękajcie się"*—"Have no fear." And you begin to believe it.

In addition to encouraging his countrymen, the Pope had a knack for challenging the communists. He'd push at them strongly enough to get his point across, but never went so far as to jeopardize the stature of the Church in Poland. Gentle but pointed wordplay was his specialty. The inspirational role he played in the lives of Lech Wałęsa and the other leaders of Solidarity gave them the courage to stand up to the communists (for more on Solidarity, see page 343). Many people (including Mikhail Gorbachev) credit Pope John Paul II for the collapse of Eastern European communism.

Even as John Paul II's easy charisma attracted new worshippers to the Church (especially young people), his conservatism on issues such as birth control, homosexuality, and female priests pushed away many Catholics. Under his watch, the Church struggled with embarrassing pedophilia scandals in the US. By the end of his papacy, John Paul II's failing health and old-fashioned politics had caused him to lose stature in worldwide public opinion. And yet, approval of the Pope never waned in Poland. His countrymen—even the relatively few atheists and agnostics—saw John Paul II both as the greatest hero of their people...and as a member of the family, like a kindly grandfather.

When Pope John Paul II died on April 2, 2005, the mourning in Poland was deep and sustained. Though the Pope's passing was hardly unexpected, it created an overwhelming wave of grief that flooded the country for weeks. Musical performances of all kinds were cancelled for a week after his death, and the irreverent MTV-style music channel simply went off the air out of respect.

Karol Wojtyła has already been fast-tracked for sainthood. Out of 265 popes, only two have been given the title "great." There's already talk in Rome of increasing that number to three. Someday soon we may speak of this remarkable soul as "John Paul the Great." His countrymen already do.

it offers a great visual example of Krakow's religious nature. In the Middle Ages, Kraków was known as "Small Rome" for its many churches. Today, there are 142 churches and monasteries within the city limits (32 in the Old Town alone)—more per square mile than anywhere outside Rome. You can see several of them from this spot: The nearest, with the picturesque white facade and red dome, is the **Church of Saints Peter and Paul** (Kraków's first Baroque church). The statues lining this church's facade are the 11 apostles (minus Judas), plus Mary Magdalene—hence the name of the square. The next church to the right, with the twin towers, is the Romanesque **St. Andrew's** (now with a Baroque interior). According to legend, a spring inside this church provided water to citizens who holed up here during Tatar invasions in the 13th century. If you look farther down the street, you can see three more churches. And the square next to you used to be a church, too—it burned in 1855, and only its footprint survives.

• *Go through the square (admiring the sculpture on the column that won Kraków's distinguished "ugliest statue" award in 2002), and turn left down...*

Kanonicza Street (Ulica Kanonicza)—With so many churches around here, the clergy had to live somewhere. Many lived on this well-preserved street—supposedly the oldest street in Kraków. As you walk, look for the cardinal hats over three different doorways. The Hotel Copernicus, on the left, has hosted visitors both famous (Copernicus himself) and infamous (George W. Bush). Find the yellow house on the right (#19), where Karol Wojtyła lived for 10 years after World War II—long before he became Pope John Paul II. Today this building houses Kraków's only museum dedicated to its favorite son, worth visiting if you're a fan of the late pontiff (for more on the museum, see page 247).

• *At the end of Kanonicza street, a ramp leads up to the most important piece of ground in all of Poland.*

Royal Way Walk Part 3: Wawel Hill

Wawel (VAH-vehl), a symbol of Polish royalty and independence, is sacred territory to every Polish person. A castle has stood here since the beginning of recorded history. Today, Wawel—awash in tourists—is the most visited sight in the country. Crowds and an overly complex admissions system for the hill's many historic sights can be exasperating. Thankfully, a stroll through the cathedral and around the castle grounds requires no tickets, and—with the help of the following self-guided commentary—is enough. The many museums on Wawel (described below) are mildly interesting, but can be skipped (grounds open daily May–Sept 6:00–20:00, Oct–April 6:00–17:00).

Walk up the long ramp to the castle entry. When Kraków was part of the Hapsburg Empire in the 19th century, the Austrians turned this castle complex into a fortress—destroying much of its delicate beauty. When Poland regained its independence after World War I, the castle was returned to its former glory. The bricks you see on your left as you climb the ramp bear the names of Poles from around the world who donated to the cause.

The jaunty equestrian statue ahead is **Tadeusz Kościuszko** (1746–1817)—a familiar name to American history buffs. Kościuszko was a hero of the American Revolution and helped design West Point. When he returned to Poland, he fought bravely but unsuccessfully against the Russians (during the partitions that would divide Poland's territory among three neighboring powers).

• *Hiking through the Heraldic Gate next to Kościuszko, you pass the ticket office (if you'll be going into the museums, use the other ticket office, with shorter lines, on top of the hill—see "Tickets and Reservations," page 242). As you crest the hill, on your left is...*

▲▲**Wawel Cathedral**—Poland's national church is its Westminster Abbey. While the history buried here is pretty murky to most Americans, to Poles, this church is *the* national mausoleum. It holds the tombs of nearly all of Poland's most important rulers and greatest historical figures.

Exterior: Go around to the far side of the cathedral to take in its profile. This uniquely eclectic church is the product of centuries of haphazard additions...yet somehow, it works. It began as a simple, stripped-down Romanesque church in the 12th century. (The white base of the nearest tower is original. In fact, anything at Wawel that's made of white limestone like this was probably part of the earliest Romanesque structures.) Kazimierz the Great and his predecessors gradually surrounded the cathedral with some 20 chapels, which were further modified over the centuries—making this beautiful church a happy hodgepodge of styles. To give you a sense of the historical sweep, scan the chapels from left to right: 14th-century Gothic, 12th-century Romanesque (the base of the tower), 17th-century Baroque (the inside is Baroque, though the exterior is a copy of its Renaissance neighbor), 16th-century Renaissance, and 18th- and 19th-century Neoclassical. (This variety in styles is even more evident in the chapels' interiors.)

Pay attention to the two particularly interesting domed chapels to the right of the tall tower. The gold one is the Sigismund's Chapel, housing memorials to the Jagiellonian kings—including Sigismund the Old, who was responsible for Kraków's Renaissance renovation in the 16th century. Poles consider this chapel, made with 80 pounds of gold, to be the finest Renaissance chapel north of the Alps. The green chapel next to it, home to the Swedish Waza dynasty, resembles its neighbor (but it's a copy built 150 years later, and without all that gold). The tallest tower, called the Sigismund Tower, has a clock with only an hour hand.

Go back around and face the front entry for more architectonic silliness. You see Gothic chapels flanking the door, a Renaissance ceiling, lavish Baroque decoration over the door, and some big bones (thought to come from extinct animals). Years ago, these were taken for the bones of giants and put here as an oddity to be viewed by the public. (Back then, there were no museums, so notable items like these were used to lure people to the church.) It's said that as long as the bones hang here, the cathedral will stand. The door is the original from the 14th century, with fine wrought-iron work. The *K* with the crown stands for Kazimierz the Great. The black marble frame is made of Kraków stone from nearby quarries.

For a quick peek at the interior, step inside. (If you want to visit the other interior sights described below—a crypt and a tower climb to a big bell—first buy a 10-zł ticket in the building across the street.)

Interior: The cathedral interior is slathered in Baroque memorials and tombs. The silver tomb under a canopy in the center is that of the first Polish saint, Stanisław (dating from the 15th century, and inspired by the one in St. Peter's at the Vatican). Circling around to the right, you'll find the sarcophagus of St. Jadwiga (behind the main altar, with a dog at her feet). This 14th-century "King of Poland" helped Christianize Lithuania, fought the Teutonic Knights, kicked off the grand Jagiellonian dynasty, and was sainted by Pope John Paul II in 1997. (The sexist big-wigs of the time begrudgingly allowed her to take the throne, but refused to call her "Queen.") All the flowers here prove she's popular with Poles today. Across from Jadwiga, the 16th-century Sigismund Chapel—with its silver altar—is the gold-roofed one you just saw from the outside. Farther back on the left is The Great One—Kazimierz, of course (look for *Kazimierz Wielki*). Poke into the choir for a look at the high altar. For 200 years, the colorful chair on the right has been the seat of Kraków's arch-bishops, including Karol Wojtyła, who served here for 14 years before becoming pope. Near the main door (on the left as you face outside), peek into the Gothic chapel with its Russian Orthodox–style 14th-century frescoes.

For most visitors, that's everything worth seeing in the cathedral. But if you're a fan of big bells and the tombs of VIPs (Very Important Poles), you can see—with a 10-zł ticket—the...

Bell, Crypt, and Tombs: Claustrophobic wooden stairs lead up to the 11-ton **Sigismund Bell** and pleasant views of the steeples and spires of Kraków. Then, descend into the little **crypt** (with a rare, purely Romanesque interior), which houses the remains of Adam Mickiewicz—the Romantic poet whose statue dominates the Main Market Square. Finally, when you're ready to leave (since you'll exit outside the church), head through the chapel in the back-right corner to find the door down to the **royal tombs.** The first room houses Poland's greatest war heroes: Kościuszko (of American Revolution fame), Jan III Sobieski (who successfully defended Vienna from the Ottomans; in the simple black coffin with the gold inscription *J III S*), Sikorski, Poniatowski, and so on. Then you'll wander through several rooms of second-tier Polish kings, queens, and their kids. Marshal Józef Piłsudski, the WWI hero who ruled Poland from 1926 to 1935, has the last grave (in the room on the right, just before you exit). His tomb was moved here so the rowdy soldiers who came to pay their respects wouldn't disturb the others.

Cost and Hours: While most of the cathedral is free, you'll need a ticket to climb down through the royal tombs or up the tower to see the bell (10 zł, tickets sold across from entrance, May–Sept Mon–Sat 9:00–17:15, Sun 12:15–17:15; Oct–April Mon–Sat 9:00–15:45, Sun 12:15–15:45).

Cathedral Museum—This small museum, with various holy robes and replicas of what's buried with the kings, plus the Sigismund Bell's original clapper, is across from the cathedral's main entry (5 zł, Tue–Sun 10:00–15:00, closed Mon).

• *When you're finished in the cathedral, stroll around the...*

▲▲**Wawel Castle Grounds**—This hill has seen lots of changes over the years. Kazimierz the Great turned a small fortress into a mighty Gothic castle in the 14th century. Today, you'll see the cathedral and a castle complex, but little remains of Kazimierz's grand fortress, which burned to the ground in 1499. In the grassy field across from the cathedral, you'll see the foundations of two Gothic churches that were destroyed when the Austrians took over Wawel in the 19th century and needed a parade ground for their troops. (They built the red-brick hospital building beyond the field, now used by Wawel administration.)

Behind the cathedral, a grand green entryway leads into the palace's Renaissance courtyard. If the design seems to have

echoes of Florence, that's because it was designed and built by young Florentines after Kazimierz's original castle burned down. Notice the three distinct levels: The ground floor housed the private apartments of the higher nobility (governors and castle administrators); the middle level held the private apartments of the king; and the top floor—much taller, to allow more light to fill its impressive spaces—were the public state rooms of the king. The ivy-covered wing to the right of where you entered served as the headquarters of the notorious Nazi governor of German-occupied Poland, Hans Frank. (He was tried and executed in Nürnberg after the war.) The wall at the far end of the courtyard is a false wall, designed to create a pleasant Renaissance symmetry, and also to give the illusion that the castle is bigger than it is. Looking through the windows, notice that there's nothing but air on the other side. When foreign dignitaries visited, these windows could be covered to complete the illusion. The entrances to most Wawel museums are around this courtyard, and some believe that you'll find something even more special: chakra.

Adherents to the Hindu concept of **chakra** believe that a powerful energy field connects all living things. Mirroring the seven chakra points on the body (from head to groin), there are seven points on the surface of the earth where this energy is most concentrated: Delhi, Delphi, Jerusalem, Mecca, Rome, Velehrad... and Wawel Hill—specifically over there in the corner (immediately to your left as you enter the courtyard). Look for peaceful people (here or elsewhere on the castle grounds) with their eyes closed. One thing's for sure: They're not thinking of Kazimierz the Great. The smudge marks on the wall are from people pressing up against this corner, trying to absorb some good vibes from this chakra spot.

The Wawel administration seems creeped out by all this. They've done what they can to discourage this ritual (such as putting up information boards right where the power is supposedly most focused), but believers still gravitate from far and wide to hug the wall. Give it a try...and let the Force be with you. (Just for fun, ask a Wawel tour guide about the chakra, and watch her squirm—they're forbidden from talking about it.)

If you plan to visit some of the castle museums, now's the time (see "Wawel Castle Museums"). But if you're looking for a scenic wrap-up to this royal ramble, leave the courtyard the way you came in, and keep going straight toward the opening in the wall. You'll be rewarded with a beautiful view over the Vistula River and Kraków's outskirts. Directly below you, along the riverbank, is a fire-belching monument to the **dragon** that was instrumental in the founding of Kraków...

Once upon a time, a prince named Krak founded a town on Wawel Hill. It was the perfect location—except for the fire-breathing dragon who lived in the caves under the hill and terrorized the town. Prince Krak had to feed the dragon all of the town's livestock to keep the monster from going after the townspeople. But Krak, with the help of a clever shoemaker, came up with a plan. They stuffed a sheep's skin with sulfur and left it outside the dragon's cave. The dragon swallowed it, and before long, developed a terrible case of heartburn. To put the fire out, the dragon started drinking water from the Vistula. He kept drinking and drinking until he finally exploded. The town was saved, and Kraków thrived.

Our walking tour is finished. If you want to head down to see the Vistula and the dragon close up, take a shortcut through the nearby **Dragon's Den** (Smocza Jama). It's just a 135-step spiral staircase and a few underground caverns—worthwhile only as a quick way to get from the top of Wawel down to the banks of the Vistula (3 zł, pay at machine—coins only, April–Oct daily 10:00–17:00, July–Aug until 18:00, closed Nov–March, enter around corner from bookstore on courtyard overlooking river).

Wawel Castle Museums—There are five museums and exhibits in Wawel Castle (not including the cathedral and Cathedral Museum). Each has its own admission (hours for all museums, unless otherwise noted: April–Oct Sun 10:00–15:00, Mon 9:30–12:00, Tue and Fri 9:30–16:00, Wed–Thu and Sat 9:30–15:00; Nov–March Sun 10:00–15:00, Tue–Sat 9:30–15:00, closed Mon, tel. 012-422-5155, ext. 219, www.wawel.krakow.pl). Notice that in the high season (April–Oct), visiting on Monday has both advantages (Royal State Rooms, Crown Treasury and Armory, and Lost Wawel are all free) and disadvantages (Royal Private Apartments and Oriental Art are closed, and the rest closes at 12:00). Off-season (Nov–March), everything is closed on Monday—except, mysteriously, the Lost Wawel exhibit.

The **Royal State Rooms** (Komnaty Królewskie), while precious to Poles, are mediocre by European standards. Still, this is the best of the Wawel museums (15 zł, free on Mon April–Oct, free on Sun Nov–March, enter through courtyard). First you'll wander through some ho-hum halls to get to the Throne Room, with 30 carved heads in the ceiling. According to legend, one of these heads got mouthy when the king was trying to pass judgment—so its mouth has been covered to keep it quiet. Then you'll walk along the outdoor gallery (enjoying views down into the courtyard) before heading upstairs. These top-floor rooms are best, with remarkably decorated wooden ceilings, gorgeous "leather tooled" walls, and 16th-century Brussels tapestries (140 of the original series of 300 survive). Wandering these halls (with their period furnishings), you get a feeling for the 16th- and 17th-century glory days of Poland, when it was a leading power in Eastern Europe. The Senate Room, with its throne and fine tapestries, is the climax.

The **Royal Private Apartments** (Prywatne Apartamenty Królewskie) are more of the same, and the only part of the complex that must be visited with a guided tour (20 zł, enter through courtyard; April–Oct closed Mon, English tours Tue–Sun at 10:50, 12:00, and 13:10, often more; Nov–March closed Sun–Mon, English tours Tue–Sat at 12:00, usually plus others).

The **Crown Treasury and Armory** (Skarbiec i Zbrojownia) is a decent collection of swords, saddles, and shields; ornately decorated muskets and crossbows; and cannons in the basement (15 zł, free on Mon April–Oct, closed Sun–Mon Nov–March, enter through courtyard).

The small **Oriental Art** (Sztuka Wschodu) exhibit displays swords, carpets, vases, and remarkable Turkish tents (upstairs, next to the Senate Room) used by the Ottomans during the 1683 Battle of Vienna. These are trophies of Jan III Sobieski, the Polish king who led a pan-European army to victory in that battle (7 zł, tickets sold at the door, closed Mon April–Oct, closed Sun–Mon Nov–March, enter through courtyard, don't miss entry on your way back downstairs from Royal State Rooms).

The **Lost Wawel** (Wawel Zaginiony) exhibit traces the history of this hill and its various churches and castles. The one-way route leads through excavations of a 10th-century church, and exhibits include a model of the cathedral in its original Romanesque form (much simpler, before all the colorful, bulbous domes, chapels, and towers were added). There's also a replica of the entire castle complex in the 18th century (pre-Austrian razing). A display shows fascinating decorative tiles from 16th-century stoves that once heated the place, plus some medieval artifacts (7 zł, tickets sold at door, free on Mon April–Oct, free on Sun Nov–March; Nov–March open Mon but closed Tue, enter near snack bar across from side of cathedral).

Tickets and Reservations: Tickets are sold at several points around the Wawel grounds. Most people line up at the top of the entry ramp, but it's faster to buy tickets at the "Tourist Centre" at the far corner of the castle grounds (across the field from the cathedral, near the café). You can buy tickets for the Oriental Art and Lost Wawel exhibits at the main ticket windows or at the door. Tickets are limited—and sold only at the main ticket windows—for the Royal State Rooms, Crown Treasury and Armory, and Royal Private Apartments (which can be visited only with a tour). Boards show how many tickets for each of these are still available on the day you're there. Tickets come with an assigned entry time (though you can usually sneak in before your scheduled appointment). In the summer, ticket lines can be long, and sights can sell out by midday. You can reserve tickets ahead for the tour of the Royal Private Apartments (no fee) and the Royal State Rooms and the Crown Armory and Treasury (16-zł reservation fee for up to 9 people; tel. 012-422-1697). Frankly, the sights aren't worth all the fuss—if they're sold out, you're not missing much.

National Museum Branches

Kraków's **National Museum** (Muzeum Narodowe) is made up of a series of small but interesting museums scattered throughout the city. Oddly enough, the main branch (Gmach Główny) is the least worth visiting, with 20th-century Polish art and temporary exhibits (west of Main Market Square at aleja 3 Maja 1). I've listed the best of the National Museum's branches below.

All of the branches are covered by a single 25-zł **"Jubilee Ticket."** This ticket isn't worth it unless you're going to at least three branches (which most tourists won't).

Be warned: The **hours** of these museums can be maddeningly sporadic. If you have your heart set on a particular museum, confirm the opening times carefully before you visit.

▲**Czartoryski Museum (Muzeum Czartoryskich)**—This eclectic collection, displaying armor, handicrafts, decorative arts, and paintings, is one of Kraków's best-known (and most overrated) museums. While it's mostly just dull historical bric-a-brac, two world-class paintings—a da Vinci and a Rembrandt—make it worth ▲▲ for art-lovers (9 zł, more for special exhibits, permanent collection likely free on Thu in summer and on Sun in winter, decent 10-zł audioguide helps make things meaningful; May–Oct Tue and Thu 10:00–16:00, Wed and Fri–Sat 10:00–19:00, Sun 10:00–15:00, closed Mon; Nov–April Tue, Thu, and Sat–Sun 10:00–15:30, Wed and Fri 10:00–18:00, closed Mon; last entry 30 min before closing, no photos allowed, 2 blocks north of the Main Market Square at ulica Św. Jana 19, tel. 012-422-5566). A warning: The museum's major attractions are often not displayed (on loan to other museums), and this disappointing fact isn't well-advertised before you buy your ticket. Try to confirm that the two famous paintings are actually there before you enter.

Inspired by Poland's 1791 constitution (Europe's first), Princess Izabela Czartoryska began collecting bits of Polish history and culture. She fled with the collection to Paris after the 1830 insurrection, and 45 years later, her grandson returned it to its present Kraków location. When he ran out of space, he bought part of the monastery across the street, joining the buildings with a fancy passageway. The Nazis took the collection to Germany, and although most of it has been returned, some pieces are still missing.

Buy your ticket and walk up to the second floor. You'll wander through rooms of armor (the ceremonial Turkish tent—from the 1683 siege of Vienna—and feathered Hussar armor are impressive), tapestries, treasury items, majolica, Meissen porcelain figures, and paintings.

The third floor is devoted to European art. After a few halls of also-rans, you'll come to the museum's prize possessions. First is *Lady with an Ermine,* by Leonardo da Vinci. This small (21" x 16"), simple portrait of a teenage girl is one of the most influential paintings in art history and a rare surviving work by one of history's greatest minds. The girl is likely Cecilia Gallerani, the young mistress of the Duke of Milan, Leonardo's employer. The ermine (white during winter) suggests several overlapping meanings, including a symbol of chastity (thus praising Cecilia's questioned virtue) and a naughty reference to the Duke's nickname, "Ermellino"—notice that his mistress is sensually, um, "stroking the ermine"...

Painted before the *Mona Lisa*, the portrait was immediately recognized as revolutionary. Cecilia turns to look off-camera at someone, catching her in an unguarded moment, a behind-the-scenes look unheard of in the days of the posed, front-facing formal portrait. Her simple gestures and faraway gaze speak volumes about her inner thoughts and personality. Leonardo tweaks the generic Renaissance "pyramid" composition by turning it to three-quarters angle and softening it with curved lines—from her eyes, down her cheek and sloping shoulders, then doubling back across her folded arms.

Lady with an Ermine is one of only three surviving oil paintings by Leonardo. It's better preserved than her famous cousin in Paris *(Mona Lisa)*, and—many think—simply more beautiful. Can we be sure it's really by the enigmatic Leonardo? Well, recently they found the master's fingerprint—literally—pressed into the paint.

On the wall opposite the lady and her ermine, notice the empty frame with a print of a Rembrandt portrait inside. This is one of the pieces the Nazis didn't give back.

In the next room is the museum's other highlight, Rembrandt's **Landscape with the Good Samaritan.** This small, remarkably detailed painting depicts the popular parable. On the right, see the Samaritan help the wounded man onto his horse (as a little boy watches). To the left, much farther down the road (just beyond the waterfall), find the two tiny figures walking—the priest and the Levite who passed the injured man by.

Back on the second floor and across the passageway, in the former monastery, is the rest of the collection: more armor (with some beautifully ornate saddles), Czartoryski family portraits, and ancient art.

▲**Wyspiański Museum (Muzeum Wyspiańskiego)**—If you enjoyed Stanisław Wyspiański's stained glass and wall paintings in St. Francis' Basilica, visit the museum that collects his work. Housed in a renovated mansion, this museum traces the personal history and artistic development of the Młoda Polska poster boy (7 zł, more for special exhibits, permanent collection likely free on Thu in summer and on Sun in winter, dry 15-zł English audioguide basically repeats the good English descriptions posted in most rooms; May–Oct Wed and Sat 10:00–19:00, Thu–Fri 10:00–16:00, Sun 10:00–15:00, closed Mon–Tue; Nov–April Wed–Thu and Sat–Sun 10:00–15:30, Fri 10:00–18:00, closed Mon–Tue; 1 block northwest of the Main Market Square at ulica Szczepańska 11, tel. 012-292-8183).

The museum layout is frequently rearranged, so keep your eyes open for the highlights. There's often a display of Wyspiański's precocious childhood sketchbooks, as well as works from his youthful collaboration with his teacher Jan Matejko and his friend Józef Mehoffer as they renovated St. Mary's Church (including designs for beautiful stained-glass windows). You may also see the design for the dramatic stained-glass *Apollo*, which hangs in the House of the Medical Society (which, unfortunately, is closed to the public). In the stairwell are more stained-glass designs, this time for Wyspiański's masterpiece, *God the Father Let It Be*, from St. Francis' Basilica. Find the model of the elaborate acropolis Wyspiański planned for the top of Wawel Hill, with a domed palace, an amphitheater, and a circus maximus. Filling another room are portraits of Wyspiański's family—including his daughter Helenka just waking up, and his wife breast-feeding their son Staś. Helenka circles around to get good views of both of them, appearing twice in the painting. Rounding out the collection are more portraits and self-portraits, serene landscapes, the costumes and sets Wyspiański designed for his own plays, and copies of Wyspiański's printed works (which he also designed himself).

Gallery of 19th-Century Polish Art (Galeria Sztuki Polskiej XIX Wieku)—This surprisingly enjoyable collection of works by obscure Polish artists, which is usually displayed on the upper level of the Cloth Hall, has been relocated to a village 12 miles away during the Cloth Hall Gallery renovation. It's probably not worth the trek out there to see, unless you're a Polish painting fanatic (8 zł, likely open Tue–Sat 10:00–16:00, Sun 10:00–15:00, closed Mon, open later some evenings in summer, shorter hours Nov–April; in the Royal Castle in the village of Niepołomice, 12 miles south of the city center; tel. 012-422-1166).

While you probably won't recognize any of the names in here, some of these paintings are just plain good. The biggest works are by the historical painter Jan Matejko (for more on Matejko, see page 307). One of Matejko's paintings depicts Tadeusz Kościuszko—a hero of the American Revolution, now back in his native Poland fighting the Russians—doffing his hat after his unlikely victory at the battle at Racławice. Another Matejko painting shows the last Grand Master of the fearsome Teutonic Knights swearing allegiance to the Polish king in 1525. This historic ceremony took place in the Main Market Square of the capital at the time, Kraków. Notice the Cloth Hall and the spires of St. Mary's Church in the background. Matejko has painted his own face on one of his favorite historical figures, the jester Stańczyk (at the foot of the throne; for more on Stańczyk, see page 308).

Other excellent, but more obscure, painters are also represented. Find Józef Chełmoński's energy-charged *Four-in-Hand* (depicting a Ukrainian horseman giving a lift to a pipe-smoking nobleman) and misty *Cranes*. And my favorite: Władysław Podkowiński's gripping *Frenzy*, with a pale, sensuous woman clutching an all-fired-up black stallion. The painting caused a frenzy indeed at its 1894 unveiling—leading the unbalanced artist to attack his creation with a knife.

More National Museum Branches—You can also check out the museum of Wyspiański's friend and rival, the **Józef Mehoffer House** (Dom Józefa Mehoffera, 6 zł, ulica Krupnicza 26, tel. 012-421-1143), and the former residence of their mentor, the **Jan Matejko House** (Dom Jana Matejki, 6 zł, ulica Floriańska 41, tel. 012-422-5926). Both are usually open the same hours as the Wyspiański Museum.

Other Museums

The following sights, while not part of the National Museum and therefore not covered by the combo-ticket, are worth considering if you're looking to fill out your Kraków sightseeing experience.

Jagiellonian University Museum: Collegium Maius—Kraków had the second university in Central Europe (after Prague), boasting over the centuries such illustrious grads as Copernicus and Pope John Paul II. This city is still very much a university town, and Jagiellonian University proudly leads tours of its historic oldest building, the 15th-century Collegium Maius (1 block west of the Main Market Square at ulica Jagiellońska 15). In the Middle Ages, professors were completely devoted to their scholarly pursuits. They were unmarried, and lived, ate, and slept here in an almost monastic environment. They taught downstairs and lived upstairs. In many ways, this building feels more like a monastery than a university.

To visit the interior, you'll choose between two different guided tours. The shorter 30-minute "main exhibition" route includes the library, refectory, treasury, assembly hall, and an exhibit of Copernicus' original instruments (12 zł, or 6 zł on Sat, a few tours per day in English, leaves every 20 min Mon–Fri 10:00–14:20, Thu until 17:20, Sat until 13:20, none Sun). The one-hour deluxe version adds some medieval sculptures, a Rubens, a Rembrandt, some old scientific instruments, and Chopin's piano (16 zł, usually in English, Mon–Fri at 13:00, none Sat–Sun). It's always smart to call ahead to find out when the shorter tour is scheduled in English, and to reserve for either tour (tel. 012-663-1521). The shorter tour is especially popular and books up long in advance (20 people maximum), particularly on Saturdays, when it's half-price.

Aside from the courtyard, the only part of the Colleguim Maius you can see without a tour is an interactive exhibit that allows you to tinker with replicas of old scientific tools (7 zł, free on Sat, open Mon–Sat 10:00–14:30, closed Sun).

Before you leave, enjoy a cup of hot chocolate at the chocolate shop—widely regarded as the best in town.

Archdiocesan Museum (Muzeum Archidiecezjalne)—Kraków does not yet have a comprehensive museum devoted to its most famous resident, Pope John Paul II. But this museum, in a building where JPII lived both as a priest and as a bishop, does its best to capture some of his story. The museum consists of several parts: the underwhelming ground-floor collection of sacral art (with altars, paintings, and vestments); various temporary exhibits; and the top-floor museum devoted to John Paul II. Wandering past the scores of paintings and photographs, JPII's cult of personality is almost palpable. Unfortunately, since the collection mostly consists of elaborate gifts received by the Holy Father from around the world, it offers little intimacy or insight into the man himself. Still, it'll be appreciated by JPII admirers (5 zł, Tue–Fri 9:00–16:00, Sat–Sun 10:00–15:00, closed Mon, Kanonicza 19-21, tel. 012-421-8963).

Kazimierz (Jewish Quarter)

The neighborhood of Kazimierz (kah-ZHEE-mezh), 20 minutes by foot southeast of Kraków's Old Town, is the historic heart of Kraków's once-thriving Jewish community. After years of neglect, the district is today being rediscovered by Krakovians and tourists alike. Visitors expecting a polished, touristy scene like Prague's Jewish Quarter will be surprised...and maybe disappointed. This is basically a local-feeling neighborhood with a handful of Jewish cemeteries, synagogues, and restaurants, and often a few pensive Israeli tour groups wandering the streets. But for me, the lack of crowds makes it an even more evocative experience than the Prague alternative.

Getting to Kazimierz: It's about a 20-minute **walk** from the Old Town. From the Main Market Square, walk down ulica Sienna (near St. Mary's Church). At the fork, bear right through the Planty park. At the intersection with the busy Westerplatte ring road, you'll continue straight ahead (bear right at fork) down busy Starowiślna for 15 more minutes. To hop the **tram,** go to the stop on the left-hand side of ulica Sienna (at the intersection with Westerplatte, across the street from the Poczta Główna, or Main Post Office). Catch tram #3, #13, or #34 and go two stops to Miodowa. Walking or by tram, at the intersection of Starowiślna and Miodowa, you'll see a small park across the street and to the right. To reach the heart of Kazimierz—ulica Szeroka—cut through this park. To get back into the Old Town, catch tram #3,

Kazimierz

❶ Hotel Astoria

❷ Karmel Pensjonat

❸ El-jot Art Center Rooms

❹ Tournet Guest House

❺ Restauracja Samoobsługowa Polakowski

❻ Jarden Bookshop & Restauracja Arka Noego

❼ Klezmer-Hois Restaurant

❽ Ariel Restaurant

❾ Pierożki u Vincenta

❿ Bagel Mama

#13, or #34 from the intersection of Starowiślna and Miodowa (kitty-corner from where you got off the tram) and go two stops back to the Poczta Główna stop.

Orientation: Start your visit to Kazimierz on **ulica Szeroka,** which is more of a long, parking-lot square than a street, surrounded by Jewish restaurants, hotels, and synagogues. Check in at the **Jarden Bookshop** at the top of the square (Mon–Fri 9:00–18:00, Sat–Sun 10:00–18:00, ulica Szeroka 2, tel. 012-429-1374, www.jarden.pl, jarden@jarden.pl). It serves as a tourist information center for the neighborhood, and sells a wide variety of books on Kazimierz and Jewish culture in the region (including a good 6-zł Kazimierz map and well-illustrated 17-zł *Jewish Kraków* guidebook). They also run several tours (prices based on the number of people; I've listed the price per person for 2 people): Jewish

Jewish Kraków

After King Kazimierz the Great encouraged Jews to come to Poland in the 14th century (see page 228), a large Jewish community settled in and around Kraków. According to legend, Kazimierz (the king) established Kazimierz (the village) for his favorite girlfriend—a Jewish woman named Ester—just southeast of the city walls. (If you have a 50-zł note, take a look at it: that's Kazimierz the Great on the front, and on the back is his capital, Cracovia, and the most important town he founded, Casmirus.)

It's a cute legend, but the village of Kazimierz didn't really become a Jewish enclave until much later. By the end of the 15th century, there were large Jewish populations in both Kazimierz and in Kraków. Kraków's Jewish community and the university students clashed, and when a destructive fire broke out in 1495, the Jews were blamed. The king at the time forced all of Kraków's Jews to move to Kazimierz.

Kazimierz was an autonomous community, with its own Town Hall, market square, and city walls (though many Jews still commuted into Kraków's Main Market Square to do business). Within Kazimierz, the Christian (west) and Jewish (east) neighborhoods were also separated by a wall. But by 1800, the walls came down, Kazimierz became part of Kraków, and the Jewish community flourished.

By the start of World War II, 65,000 Jews lived in Kraków (mostly in Kazimierz)—making up more than a quarter of the city's population. When the Nazis arrived, they immediately sent most of Kraków's Jews to the ghetto in the eastern Polish city of Lublin. Soon after, they forced Kraków's remaining 15,000 Jews into a walled ghetto at Podgórze, across the river. The Jews' cemeteries were defiled, and their buildings ransacked and destroyed. In 1942, the Nazis began transporting Kraków's Jews to death camps. Many others were worked to death in the Podgórze ghetto. Only a few thousand Kraków Jews survived the war.

Today's Kraków has only about 200 Jewish residents. During the communist era, this waning population was ignored or mistreated. But in recent years, Kazimierz has enjoyed a renaissance of Jewish culture—thanks largely to the popularity of *Schindler's List* (which was partly filmed here). Look for handwritten letters from Steven Spielberg and the cast in local restaurants (such as Ariel) and hotels. These have more recently been joined by autographs from *The Pianist* director Roman Polański. While few Jews live here now, the spirit of the Jewish tradition lives on in the many synagogues, as well as in the soulful cemeteries.

Kazimierz overview (55 zł, 2 hrs, walking tour), Kazimierz and the WWII ghetto (70 zł, 3 hrs, walking, the best overview), *Schindler's List* sights (100 zł, 2 hrs, by car), and Auschwitz-Birkenau (180 zł, 6–7 hrs, by car). Call to reserve ahead, as tours are by appointment only. Tours will run if a minimum of three people sign up, but pairs or singles can join an already scheduled tour.

If you visit on Saturday, you'll find only the Old Synagogue museum and Galicia Jewish Museum open. For hotel and restaurant suggestions, see page 264 of "Sleeping" and page 268 of "Eating." Several recommended restaurants offer live traditional Jewish music nightly in summer.

▲▲**Jewish Cemeteries**—Kazimierz has two Jewish cemeteries, far less touristy and, to me, at least as powerful as the famous one in Prague.

The small **Old Cemetery** (Stary Cmentarz) was used to bury members of the Jewish community from 1552 to 1800. It has been

renovated—so in a way, it actually feels "newer" than the New Cemetery. After the New Cemetery (described in next paragraph) was opened in the 1800, this cemetery gradually fell into disrepair. What remained was further desecrated by the Nazis during World War II. In the 1950s, it was discovered, excavated, and put back together as you see here. Shattered gravestones form a mosaic wall around the perimeter. As in all Jewish cemeteries, you may see small stones stacked on the graves (originally placed over desert graves to cover the body and prevent animals from disturbing it). Behind the little synagogue to the left, the tallest tombstone next to the tree belonged to Moses Isserle (a.k.a. Remu'h), an important 16th-century rabbi. He is believed to be a miracle worker, and his grave was one of the only ones that remained standing after World War II. The knee-high metal receptacle nearby is for written prayers (5 zł, very sporadic hours according to demand—especially outside of peak season—but generally open May–Oct Sun–Fri 9:00–17:30, Nov–April until 15:30, closes at sundown on Fri, always closed Sat, enter through Remu'h Synagogue at ulica Szeroka 40).

The much larger **New Cemetery** (Nowy Cmentarz) has graves of those who died after 1800. Nazis vandalized this cemetery, selling many of its gravestones to stonecutters, and using others as pavement in their concentration camps. Today, many of the gravestones have since been returned to their original positions. Other headstones could not be replaced, and were used to create the moving mosaic wall and Holocaust monument (on the right as you enter). Most gravestones are in one of three languages: Hebrew (generally the oldest, especially if there's no other language); Yiddish (which looks like German); and Polish (from Jews who assimilated into the Polish community). The earliest graves are simple stones, while later ones imitate graves in Polish Catholic cemeteries—larger, more elaborate, and with a long stone jutting out to cover the body. Notice that some new-looking graves have old dates. These were most likely put here well after the Holocaust (or even after communism) by relatives of the dead (free, Sun–Fri 8:00–18:00, until 16:00 in winter, closed Sat, tricky to find—go under railway bridge at east end of ulica Miodowa, jog left as you emerge, cemetery is to your right, enter through gate with small *cmentarz żydowski* sign).

▲**Isaac Synagogue (Synagoga Isaaka)**—This is Kraków's most accessible sight for learning more about the Kazimierz Jewish community. The synagogue, Kraków's biggest, was built in the 17th century. During a recent renovation, they discovered giant wall paintings of prayers (for worshippers who couldn't afford to buy books). In a side room is a powerful display of photographs, and a continuously running 98-minute loop of six different films about the Jewish heritage of Kazimierz (mostly silent, others in Hebrew, Polish, Yiddish, and English). Two of the most important films (lasting a total of 7 min)—showing the town before the Nazis came, and then the forced transition to the Podgórze ghetto—play continuously in the main hall (7 zł, Sun–Fri 9:00–19:00, July–Aug until 20:00, closed Sat, closes at sundown on winter Fri—as early as 15:00 in Dec, a block west of ulica Szeroka at ulica Kupa 18, tel. 012-430-5577).

Other Synagogues—Three synagogues surround Kazimierz's main square, ulica Szeroka. **Remu'h Synagogue,** from 1553, has been carefully renovated and is the only fully active synagogue in Kraków (included in 5-zł entry fee for Old Cemetery, same unpredictable hours as Old Cemetery, ulica Szeroka 40). The **Old Synagogue** (Stara Synagoga), the oldest surviving Jewish building in Poland, is now a three-room museum on local Jewish culture, with English descriptions (7 zł, free on Mon; April–Oct Mon 10:00–14:00, Tue–Sun 10:00–17:00; Nov–March Mon 10:00–14:00, Wed–Thu and Sat–Sun 9:00–16:00, Fri 10:00–17:00, closed Tue; ulica Szeroka 24). The recently renovated **High Synagogue** displays a photo exhibition of the people who lived here before and after the Holocaust (7 zł, daily 9:00–19:00, just around the corner from the Old Synagogue at ulica Józefa 38).

Two other synagogues face each other across ulica Miodowa, three blocks northwest of ulica Szeroka. **Tempel Synagogue** (Synagoga Templu) has the grandest interior—big and dark, with elaborately decorated, gilded ceilings and balconies—and the most lived-in feel of the bunch (5 zł, Sun–Fri 9:00–16:00, closed Sat, corner of ulica Miodowa and ulica Podbrzezie). The smaller **Kupa Synagogue** (Synagoga Kupa) sometimes hosts temporary exhibits (Miodowa 27).

Galicia Jewish Museum (Galicja Muzeum)—This new museum, the brainchild of a visionary English photojournalist named Chris Schwarz, focuses on the present rather than the past. With a series of beautiful photographs displayed around a restored Jewish furniture factory, the exhibit shows today's remnants of yesterday's Judaism in the area around Kraków (a region known as "Galicia"). From forgotten synagogues to old Jewish gravestones flipped over and used as doorsteps, these giant postcards of Jewish artifacts (with good English descriptions) ensure that an important part of this region's heritage won't be forgotten. Complementing this permanent collection are good temporary exhibits (7 zł, daily April–Oct 9:00–19:00, Nov–March 9:00–18:00, 1 block east of ulica Szeroka at ulica Dajwór 18, tel. 012-421-6842, www .galiciajewishmuseum.org). The museum also serves as a sort of cultural center, with a good bookstore, café, and programming that caters to both locals and visitors (from Jewish dancing lessons to Yiddish classes to Jewish karaoke).

Kazimierz Market Square (Plac Nowy)—The natives shop at plac Nowy's market stalls. This is a gritty, factory-workers-on-lunch-break contrast to Kraków's touristy Main Market Square (stalls open Tue–Sun 6:00–14:00, a few also open later, closed Mon). Consider dropping by here for some shopping (sorry, no souvenirs), people-watching, or a quick, cheap, and local lunch (see "Eating," page 268). Other, much trendier restaurants are popping up all around this square.

▲**Polish Folk Museum (Muzeum Etnograficzne)**—This clever and refreshingly good museum hides a few blocks west of the Jewish area of Kazimierz, in the former town hall. The square it's on, plac Wolnica, was Kazimierz's primary market square, once almost as big as Kraków's. Inside the museum, you'll find models of traditional rural Polish homes, as well as musty replicas of the interiors (like an open-air folk museum—but inside). On the second floor are traditional Polish folk costumes, holiday celebrations (including Christmas decorations), and traditional instruments (such as a "Polish bagpipe" you don't have to blow into—no kidding). The top floor features folk art, past and present (6.50 zł, free on Sun; May–Sept Mon and Wed–Fri 10:00–17:00, Sat–Sun 10:00–14:00, closed Tue; Oct–April Mon 10:00–18:00, Wed–Fri 10:00–15:00, Sat–Sun 10:00–14:00, closed Tue; ulica Krakowska 46, tel. 012-430-6023).

Podgórze—This neighborhood, directly across the Vistula from Kazimierz, is where the Nazis forced Kraków's Jews into a ghetto in early 1941. (*Schindler's List* and the films in the Isaac Synagogue depict the sad scene of the Jews loading their belongings onto carts and trudging over the bridge into Podgórze.) The ghetto was surrounded by a wall with a fringe along the top that resembled Jewish gravestones—a chilling premonition of what was to come. A short section of this wall is still standing along Lwowska street.

Ghetto Heroes' Square (plac Bohaterow Getta) is the focal point of the visitor's Podgórze. To get there, continue through Kazimierz on trams #3, #13, or #34 (described under "Getting to Kazimierz" on page 247) to the stop called plac Bohaterow Getta. On the square you'll find the **Pharmacy Under the Eagle** (Apteka pod Orłem), with a modest exhibit about the Jewish experience before and after the ghetto.

Most people coming to Podgórze are actually looking for...
Schindler's Factory—Fans of the Holocaust movie and book—and the compassionate Kraków businessman who did his creative best to save the lives of his Jewish workers—can see Oskar Schindler's actual factory. This is where Schindler worked, and where Spielberg filmed much of *Schindler's List*. After the war, the factory became the Telpod electronics manufacturing plant. But it went bust a few years back, and now most of the buildings are abandoned. The city is gradually converting this facility into a new "Museum of the Place." If you're interested in visiting, inquire at the Kraków TI about what kind of progress they're making. Just inside the main building is a long staircase (immortalized in a scene from *Schindler's List*) to Oskar Schindler's office. Gestapo agents and other Nazi troops were also stationed in this building to keep an eye on Schindler and his workers. Just behind that are crumbling factory buildings (also slated for future reconstruction).

Getting There: From Ghetto Heroes' Square (plac Bohaterow Getta), it's about a five-minute walk: Head up Kącik street (to the left of the big, glass skyscraper), go under the railroad underpass marked *Kraków-Zabłocie*, and continue two blocks to the second big building on the left (ulica Lipowa 4).

Closer to the center, **Schindler's apartment** is a block from Wawel Castle at ulica Straszewskiego 7 (unmarked and not available for tours).

Wieliczka Salt Mine (Kopalnia Soli Wieliczka)

Wieliczka (vee-LEECH-kah), 10 miles southeast of Kraków, is beloved by Poles. Though it's a bit overrated, most visitors find it's worth ▲▲.

This remarkable mine has been producing salt since at least

the 11th century. Under Kazimierz the Great, one-third of Poland's income came from these precious deposits. Wieliczka miners spent much of their lives underground, leaving for work before daybreak and returning after sundown, rarely emerging into daylight. To pass the time, and to immortalize their national pride and religiosity in art, 19th-century miners began to carve figures, chandeliers, and eventually even an elaborate chapel out of the salt. Until a few years ago, the mine still produced salt. Today's miners—about 400 of them—work on maintaining the 200 miles of chambers. This entire network is supported by wooden beams (because metal would rust).

From the lobby, your guide leads you 210 feet down a winding staircase. From this spot, you begin a 1.5-mile generally downhill stroll (more than 800 steps down all together) past 20 of the mine's 2,000 chambers (with signs saying when they were dug), finishing 443 feet below the surface. When you're done, an elevator beams you back up.

The tour shows how the miners lived and worked, using horses who spent their whole lives without ever seeing the light of day. It takes you through some impressive underground caverns past subterranean lakes, and introduces you to some of the mine's many sculptures (including one of Copernicus—who actually visited here in the 15th century—as well as an army of salt elves and this region's favorite son, Pope John Paul II). Your jaw will drop as you enter the enormous **Chapel of St. Kinga,** carved over three decades in the early 20th century. Look for the salt-relief carving of the Last Supper (its 3-D details are astonishing, considering it's just six inches deep).

While advertised as two hours, your tour finishes in a deep-down shopping zone 90 minutes after you started (they hope you'll hang out and shop). Note when the next elevator departs (just 3/hr), and you can be outta there on the next lift. Zip through the shopping zone in two minutes, or step over the rope and be immediately in line for the great escape (you'll be escorted 300 yards to the skinny industrial elevator, into which you'll be packed like mine workers).

Cost and Hours: Visits are by tour only (65 zł for a guided tour). English tours are generally daily year-round at 10:00, 11:30, 12:30, 13:45, 15:00, and 17:00; June and Sept also at 9:00; July–Aug every half hour between 8:30 and 18:00. If you miss the English-language tour (or decide to just show up and take whatever's going next), buy the informative guidebook, which narrates the exact route the tours do (daily April–Oct 7:30–19:30, Nov–March 8:00–17:00, ulica Daniłowicza 10, tel. 012-278-7302, www.kopalnia.pl). You'll pay an extra 10 zł for permission to use your camera—but be warned that flash photos often don't turn out, thanks to the irregular reflection of the salt crystals. Dress warmly—the mine is a constant 57 degrees Fahrenheit.

Mine Museum: Your ticket includes a dull mine museum at the end of the tour. It adds an hour to the mine tour and is discouraged by local guides ("1.5 miles more walking, colder, more of the same"). Make it clear when you buy your ticket that you're not interested in the museum.

Getting to Wieliczka: The salt mine, 10 miles from Kraków, is best reached by minibus (3 zł, 4/hr or with demand). These minibuses (with *Wieliczka Soli* sign in window) leave from various points around Kraków, usually near the Main Post Office (Poczta Główna; it's east of Main Market Square, just beyond the Planty park, at the start of Starowiślna street). The departure point changes occasionally—confirm at the TI.

A different minibus, operated by the salt mine, charges more and departs from Royal Hotel on Grodzka street in Kraków (75-zł ticket includes 65 zł for the mine and 10 zł round-trip for the minibus).

Taking a taxi (about 50 zł) is fastest, and taking the train makes no sense.

Nowa Huta

Nowa Huta ("New Steel Works"), an enormous planned workers' town, offers a glimpse into the stark, grand-scale aesthetics of the communists. While it's five miles east of central Kraków, a little tricky to see on your own, and worth only ▲▲ for most visitors, architects and communists may want to make a pilgrimage here.

Getting There: Tram #4 goes from near Kraków's Old Town (catch it on the ring road near Kraków's Main Train Station) along Pope John Paul II Avenue (aleja Jana Pawła II) to Nowa Huta's main square, plac Centralny (about 30 min total). From there, tram #4 continues a few minutes farther to the main gate of the Tadeusz Sendzimir Steelworks, and then it returns to Kraków.

Tours: True to its name, Mike Ostrowski's **Crazy Guides** is a very loosely run operation that takes tourists to Nowa Huta in genuine communist-era vehicles (mostly Trabants and Polski Fiats). While the content is good, be warned that Mike and his comrades are laid-back, very informal, and sometimes crude. If you're offended by a foul-mouthed guide who reminds you of a scruffy college student, or if you don't like the idea of careening down the streets of Kraków in a car that feels like a cardboard box with a lawnmower engine, skip this tour. For the rest of us, it's a fun and convenient way to experience Nowa Huta (119 zł per person for 2.5-hr Nowa Huta tour; 159 zł per person for 4-hr Communism Deluxe tour that also includes their makeshift "museum"—a communist-era apartment that's decorated to give you a taste of the way things were; 159 zł per person for 4-hr "Real Kraków" tour that covers the basic Nowa Huta trip plus other outlying sights; cash only, reserve ahead and they'll pick you up at your hotel, mobile 0500-091-200, www.crazyguides.com, mike @crazyguides.com).

History: Nowa Huta was the communists' idea of paradise. It's one of only three towns outside the Soviet Union that were custombuilt to showcase socialist ideals. (The others are Dunaújváros—once called Sztálinváros—south of Budapest, Hungary; and Eisenhüttenstadt—once called Stalinstadt—near Brandenburg, Germany.) Completed in just 10 years (1949–1959), Nowa Huta was primarily built because the Soviets felt that smart and sassy Kraków needed a taste of heavy industry. Farmers and villagers were imported to live and work in Nowa Huta. Many of the new residents weren't accustomed to city living, and brought along their livestock (who grazed in the fields around unfinished buildings). For commies, it was downright idyllic: Dad would cheerily ride the tram into the steel factory, mom would dutifully keep house, and the kids could splash around at the man-made beach and learn how to cut perfect red stars out of construction paper. But Krakovians had the last laugh: Nowa Huta, along with Lech Wałęsa's shipyard in Gdańsk, was one of the home bases of the Solidarity strikes that eventually brought down the regime. Now, with the communists long gone, Nowa Huta remains a sooty suburb of Poland's cultural capital, with a whopping 200,000 residents.

Sights: Nowa Huta's focal point used to be known simply as **Central Square** (plac Centralny), but in a fit of poetic justice, it was recently renamed for the anti-communist Ronald Reagan (plac Centralny im. Ronalda Reagana). This square is the heart of the planned town. A map of Nowa Huta looks like a clamshell: a semi-circular design radiating out from Central/Reagan Square. Numbered streets fan out like spokes on a wheel, and trolleys zip workers directly to the immense factory.

Believe it or not, the inspiration for Nowa Huta was the Renaissance (which, thanks to the textbook Renaissance design of the Cloth Hall and other landmarks, Soviet architects considered typically Polish). Note the elegantly predictable arches and galleries that would make Michelangelo proud. When first built (before it was layered with grime), Nowa Huta was delightfully orderly, primly painted, impeccably maintained, and downright beautiful... if a little boring. It was practical, too: Each of the huge apartment blocks is a self-contained unit, with its own grassy inner courtyard, school, and shops. Driveways (which appear to dead-end at underground garage doors) lead to vast fallout shelters.

Today's Nowa Huta is a far cry from its glory days. Wander around. Poke into the courtyards. Reflect on what it would be like to live here. It may not be as bad as you imagine. Ugly as they seem from the outside, these buildings are packed with happy little apartments filled with color, light, and warmth.

The wide boulevard running northeast of Central/Reagan Square, Solidarity Avenue (aleja Solidarności, lined with tracks for tram #4), leads to the **Tadeusz Sendzimir Steelworks.** Originally named for Lenin, this factory was supposedly built using plans stolen from a Pittsburgh plant. It was designed to be a cog in the communist machine—reliant on iron ore from Ukraine, and therefore worthless unless Poland remained in the Soviet Bloc. Down from as many as 40,000 workers at its peak, the steelworks now employs only about 10,000. Today there's little to see other than the big sign, stern administration buildings, and smokestacks in the distance. Examine the twin offices flanking the sign—topped with turrets and a decorative frieze inspired by Italian palazzos, these continue the Renaissance theme of the housing districts.

Another worthwhile sight in Nowa Huta is the **Lord's Ark Church** (Arka Pana, several blocks northwest of Central/Reagan Square on ulica Obrońców Krzyża). Back when he was archbishop of Kraków, Karol Wojtyła fought for years to build a church in this most communist of communist towns. When the regime refused, he insisted on conducting open-air Masses before crowds in fields—until the communists finally capitulated. Consecrated on May 15, 1977, the Lord's Ark Church has a Le Corbusier-esque design that looks like a fat, exhausted Noah's Ark resting on Mount Ararat—encouraging Poles to persevere through the floods of communism. While architecturally interesting, the church is mostly significant as a symbol of an early victory of Catholicism over communism.

SHOPPING

Two of the most popular Polish souvenirs—amber and pottery—come from areas far from Kraków. Amber *(bursztyn)* is found on northern Baltic shores (see page 373). "Polish pottery," the distinctive blue-and-white pieces, is made in the region of Silesia, west of Kraków (mostly in the town of Bolesławiec). Because neither of these items actually comes from Kraków, you won't find any great bargains. Somewhat more local are the many wood carvings you'll see.

The **Cloth Hall**, smack-dab in the center of the Main Market Square, is the most convenient place to pick up any Polish souvenirs. It has a great selection, respectable prices, and the city's highest concentration of pickpockets (summer Mon–Fri 9:00–18:00, Sat–Sun 9:00–15:00, sometimes later; winter Mon–Fri 9:00–16:00, Sat–Sun 9:00–15:00).

A small but swanky mall called **Pasaż 13** is a few steps off the southeast corner of the Main Market Square, where Grodzka street enters the Square. Enter the mall under the balcony marked *Pasaż 13* (next to the Benetton store). The bookstore up top offers fine views over the Square (mall open Mon–Sat 9:00–21:00, Sun 9:00–17:00).

Two new, enormous shopping malls lie just beyond the tourist zone. The gigantic **Galeria Krakowska,** with 270 shops, shares a square with the train station (Mon–Sat 9:00–22:00, Sun 10:00–21:00, can't miss it right next to the Main Train Station). Note that nearby landmarks are signposted inside the massive, labyrinthine mall (*PKP/PKS* leads to the train and bus stations; *Stare Miasto* goes to the Old Town). Only slightly smaller is the **Galeria Kazimierz** (Mon–Sat 10:00–22:00, Sun 10:00–20:00, just a few blocks east of the Kazimierz sights, along the river).

ENTERTAINMENT

As a town full of both students and tourists, Kraków has plenty of entertainment options. There's a wide range of **concerts,** from tourist-oriented "Chopin's greatest hits" shows in quaint old ballrooms, to serious philharmonic performances. Some of Kraków's many churches (such as the Church of Sts. Peter and Paul on ulica Grodzka) also serve as concert venues. Because Kraków's live-music scene is continually evolving, it's best to inquire locally about what's on during your visit. Hotel lobbies are stocked with fliers for upcoming concerts. But to get all of your options, visit the TI on ulica Św. Jana, which specializes in cultural events (Mon–Sat 10:00–18:00, closed Sun, just off the Main Market Square at ulica Św. Jana 2, tel. 012-421-7787). They can tell you what's on in Kraków, book tickets for most concerts (no extra fee), and tell you how to get tickets for the others. The monthly *Karnet* cultural events book lists everything (4 zł, half in Polish and half in English, also online at www.karnet.krakow.pl).

For something a little more edgy, delve into Kraków's

thriving **jazz** scene. Several popular clubs hide on the streets surrounding the Main Market Square (most shows start around 21:00). The most famous is Jazz Club u Muniaka, described on my self-guided walk (see page 226; 10–20-zł cover, open nightly 19:00–1:00 in the morning, live music nightly at 21:30, best music Thu–Sat, ulica Floriańska 3, www.umuniaka.krakow.pl). Other options include Harris Piano Jazz Bar (on the Square at #28, www .harris.krakow.pl), Stalowa Magnolia (ulica Św. Jana 15, www .stalowemagnolie.com), and Razzy Dazzy (ulica Św. Tomasza 11a, www.razzydazzyjazz.com).

Finally, consider the nightly **klezmer music** concerts in the Jewish quarter, Kazimierz (described on page 247).

SLEEPING

Healthy competition—with new, cleverly run places cropping up all the time—keeps Kraków's accommodation prices reasonable and makes choosing a hotel fun rather than frustrating. I've focused my accommodations on two areas: in and near the Old Town; and in Kazimierz, which is a local-style, more affordable neighborhood that is home to both the old Jewish quarter and Kraków's most happening nightlife.

Rates are soft. Hoteliers don't need much of an excuse to offer you 10 to 20 percent off, especially on weekends or in the off-season.

In the Old Town

While you could stay away from the center, accommodations values here are so good that there's little sense in sleeping beyond

---

Sleep Code

(3 zł = about $1, €1 = about $1.20, country code: 48)
S = Single, **D** = Double/Twin, **T** = Triple, **Q** = Quad, **b** = bathroom, **s** = shower only. Breakfast is included, credit cards are accepted, and English is spoken (unless otherwise noted). Some hotels quote prices in euros.

To help you sort easily through these listings, I've divided the rooms into three categories, based on the price for a standard double room with bath:

$$$ Higher Priced—Most rooms 400 zł (€105) or more.
$$ Moderately Priced—Most rooms between 300–400 zł (€80–105).
$ Lower Priced—Most rooms 300 zł (€80) or less.

the Planty park. Most of my listings are inside (or within a block or two of) the former city walls.

The Old Town has three basic types of accommodations: small, well-run guest houses (my favorite); big hotels (comfortable but overpriced); and upstart youth hostels. I've listed the best of each type.

Guest Houses

These good-value pensions almost invariably come with lots and lots of stairs, and are run by smart, can-do, entrepreneurial owners. These places book up fast, especially in summer—reserve as far ahead as possible. Don't expect a 24-hour reception desk.

$ At **Pensjonat Trecius,** Michał Palarczyk and his right-hand woman Monika offer surprising class for low prices. Hiding upstairs in a nondescript building overlooking the bustling (and sometimes noisy) Floriańska pedestrian street, its eight rooms are nicely decorated (S-120 zł, Sb-140–220 zł depending on size, D-150 zł, Db-180–300 zł depending on size, extra bed-55 zł, 5 percent cheaper if you pay cash, continental breakfast-8 zł, full breakfast-16 zł, non-smoking, reception open Mon–Fri 8:00–20:00, Sat–Sun 8:00–15:00—but if you're arriving at another time you can arrange later check-in, 2 blocks from the Main Market Square at ulica Św. Tomasza 18, tel. 012-421-2521, fax 012-426-8730, www.trecius .krakow.pl, hotel@trecius.krakow.pl).

$ **La Fontaine B&B,** run by a French family, offers eight rooms and four apartments up several flights of stairs over a cellar restaurant just a few steps off the Main Market Square. Tastefully decorated with French flair, it's cute as a poodle (Sb/Db-€67, extra bed-€15, apartment for up to 4-€115, cheaper off-season, low slanted ceilings, ulica Sławkowska 1, tel. 012-422-6564, fax 012-431-0955, www.bblafontaine.com, biuro@bblafontaine.com).

$ **Globtroter Guest House** offers 15 rustic-feeling rooms with high ceilings and big beams around a serene garden courtyard. Jacek (Jack) conscientiously focuses on value, keeping prices as low as possible by not offering needless extras (June–Aug: Sb-165 zł, Db-270 zł; April–May and Sept–Oct: Sb-150 zł, Db-250 zł; Nov–March: Sb-120 zł, Db-180 zł; 2 people can cram into a single to save money, larger suites for up to 6 also available, cash only, no breakfast at hotel, but you can buy 10–12-zł breakfast from courtyard restaurant, fun 700-year-old brick cellar lounge down below, go down passageway at plac Szczepański 7/15, tel. 012-422-4123, fax 012-422-4233, www.cracow-life.com/globtroter, globtroter @cracow-life.com).

$ **Grodzka Aparthotel** offers eight apartments around a courtyard along one of Kraków's most happening streets, just a few steps off the Square. The studio apartments are as nice as a hotel

Kraków Hotels and Restaurants

1. Pensjonat Trecius
2. La Fontaine B&B
3. Globtroter Guest House
4. Grodzka Aparthotel
5. Bed & Breakfast
6. Hotel Maltański
7. Hotel Pugetów
8. Hotel Gródek
9. Hotel Senacki
10. Hotel Classic
11. Hotel Wawel
12. Hotel Saski
13. Mama's Hostel
14. Nathan's Villa Hostel
15. Rest. pod Aniołami
16. Polskie Smaki
17. Restauracja Farina
18. Miód Malina Rest.
19. Restauracja Jarema
20. Chłopskie Jadło Rest. (3 Locations)
21. Chimera Cafeteria
22. Kwandras Lunch Bar
23. Bar Mleczny & Bar Grodzki
24. Cyklop Pizza
25. Pizzeria Trzy Papryczki
26. Rest. Redolfi
27. Rest. Hawełka & Tetmajerowska
28. Cukiarnia Jama Michalika
29. Jazz Club u Muniaka
30. Massolit Books
31. Launderette

room for a fraction of the price, except that most have only a fold-out sofa bed (studio-220 zł, 1-bedroom-250–280 zł, 2-bedroom-360 zł, prices soft—especially for advance booking, no reception at night, no breakfast but can buy a 15-zł breakfast at nearby café, Grodzka 4, mobile 066-054-1085, www.grodzka.net.pl, info @grodzka.net.pl).

$ Bed & Breakfast is your last resort, with 40 cheap, ram-shackle rooms, a treehouse floor plan, thin walls, and mix-and-match furniture in a great location (S-100 zł, Sb-130 zł, D-180 zł, Db-210 zł, Tb-300 zł, extra bed-70 zł, they'll do your laundry for 15 zł, ulica Wiślna 10, tel. & fax 012-421-9871, www.accommodation .com.pl, wislna@wp.pl).

Hotels

$$$ Donimirski Boutique Hotels, with three different locations in or near Kraków's Old Town, offer the city's best splurge expe-rience (Web site for all: www.donimirski.com). All Donimirski hotels offer my readers a 15 percent discount through 2007. You can expect any of these hotels to have some of the friendliest staff in Kraków and all of the classy little extras that add up to a memo-rable hotel experience (like a fluffy white bathrobe for every guest). **Hotel Maltański**—my home away from home in Kraków—has 16 rooms in the beautifully renovated former royal stables, just out-side the Planty park and only two blocks from Wawel Castle (Sb-560 zł, Db-590 zł, cheaper Nov–March, parking-30 zł/day, ulica Straszewskiego 14, tel. 012-431-0010, fax 012-431-0615, maltanski @donimirski.com). **Hotel Pugetów,** with seven plush rooms and a fun breakfast cellar, is on the other side of town, in a slightly dingy but convenient neighborhood between the Main Market Square and Kazimierz (Sb-350 zł, Db-510 zł, Db suite-890 zł, cheaper Nov–March, ulica Starowiślna 13–15, tel. 012-432-4950, pugetow@ donimirski.com). The new **Hotel Gródek**—by far the fanciest and most central of the bunch—offers 20 rooms a three-minute walk behind St. Mary's Church on a quiet street overlooking the Planty park. This place is easily the best splurge in town, with a wonderful location, gorgeously decorated rooms, and a top-notch breakfast surrounded by a mini-museum of artifacts discovered while they were building the place (Sb-700 zł, Db-740 zł, cheaper Nov–March, Na Gródku, tel. 012-431-9030, grodek@donimirski .com). If you have a car, ask about rooms at their countryside castle, Zamek Korzkiew.

$$$ Hotel Senacki is a business-class place renting 20 tasteful rooms between Wawel Castle and the Main Market Square. Six of the rooms have air-conditioning for no extra charge—if you'll be here in summer, request this when you reserve (Sb-€105, Db-€120–140, lower price is for "attic" rooms with skylight windows and a flight of stairs after the elevator, deluxe Db-€160, extra bed-€25, €10 cheaper Fri–Sun, 15 percent cheaper Nov–March, parking-60 zł/day, non-smoking rooms, elevator—but doesn't go to "attic" rooms, ulica Grodzka 51, tel. 012-421-1161, fax 012-422-7934, www.senacki.krakow.pl, recepcja@senacki.krakow.pl).

$$$ Hotel Classic, a modern home in old Kraków (on a peaceful street just inside the Planty park), has 30 rooms, a sleek marble lobby, professional staff, reasonable prices, and little character (April–Oct: Sb-€110, Db-€120; Nov–March: Sb-€75, Db-€85; manager Katarzyna promises readers of this book a 20 percent discount on weekdays and 25 percent discount Fri–Sun with a 2-night minimum stay in 2007, elevator, ulica Św. Tomasza 32, tel. 012-424-0303, fax 012-429-3680, www.hotel-classic.pl, hotel @hotel-classic.pl).

$$ Hotel Wawel, with a swanky marble lobby and the history of the hotel painted on the walls, has 39 rooms in a good location. Some of the rooms are nicely renovated, and cost the same as the slightly musty older rooms—request a renovated room when you reserve (Sb-260 zł, Db-380 zł, big "retro" Db-370 zł, Tb-450 zł, 30 zł extra for air-con, elevator—but doesn't go to top floor, ulica Poselska 22, tel. 012-424-1300, fax 012-424-1333, www .hotelwawel.pl, hotel@hotelwawel.pl).

$$ Hotel Saski rents 60 high-ceilinged rooms a few steps from the Main Market Square (six of them share institutional-feeling bathrooms down the hall). My other hotel recommendations are modern, but this is your best old-fashioned-feeling option, with a frou-frou lobby, kitschy gift shops, uniformed bellhop, and antique elevator. The rooms have worn furniture and the hotel somehow lacks soul, but it's a decent value for the location (S-235 zł, Sb-295 zł, D-265 zł, Db-360 zł, deluxe Db-450–470 zł, Tb-420 zł, elevator, ulica Sławkowska 3, tel. 012-421-4222, fax 012-421-4830, www.hotelsaski.com.pl, info@hotelsaski.com.pl).

Hostels

New hostels are born—and go extinct—every other day in Kraków. But these two are the real deal. Accept no substitutes. My first listing is just steps off the Main Market Square; the second one is in an up-and-coming neighborhood between Wawel Hill and Kazimierz.

$ Mama's Hostel is ideally located and more dignified than most hostels—like an old apartment taken over by vagabonds with good manners, but who still know how to have a good time (46 beds, 55 zł per person in a 6-bed room, 50 zł in an 8–10-bed room; includes sheets, breakfast, laundry, and lockers; non-smoking, no curfew, ulica Bracka 4, tel. & fax 012-429-5940, www.mamashostel .com.pl, hostel@mamashostel.com.pl).

$ Nathan's Villa Hostel is run by an energetic young Bostonian and his wife. It's loose, easygoing, and fun, with 19 cleverly painted rooms, a bar, a beer garden, an art gallery, and plenty of backpacker bonding. Their advertising promises advice on how to "get hammered"...if that's not your scene, sleep elsewhere (bunk in 4-bed room-65 zł, in 6-bed room-60 zł, in 8-bed room-55 zł, in 10-bed room-50 zł, 5 zł less Nov–Feb; includes breakfast, sheets, laundry facilities, and lockers; free Internet access, non-smoking, no curfew or lockout time, ulica Św. Agnieszki 1, tel. 012-422-3545, www.nathansvilla.com, krakow@nathansvilla.com).

Kazimierz

Sleep in Kazimierz to be close to Kraków's Jewish heart—or simply to experience a cheaper, less touristy, more local-feeling neighborhood outside the Old Town. With the highest concentration of pubs and nightclubs in town, Kazimierz is emerging as *the* spot for nightlife—which means that all of these places can be subject to some noise, especially on weekends. The downside: You are a 20-minute walk from the fairy-tale medieval ambience of Kraków's old center. Some of the klezmer music restaurants listed in "Eating" also rent rooms, but they're generally an afterthought to the food and music, and not a good value. For locations, see the map on page 248.

$$ Hotel Astoria is your best big-hotel option in Kazimierz, even though it lacks character. This hotel, renting 33 comfy rooms a couple of blocks from the center of Kazimierz, is popular with Israeli tour groups (Sb-280 zł, Db-360 zł, Db suite-400 zł, extra bed-70 zł, less on weekends and with an online reservation, free underground parking, air-con, non-smoking floor, elevator, ulica Józefa 24, tel. 012-432-5010, fax 012-432-5020, www.astoriahotel.pl, biuro@astoriahotel.pl).

$ Karmel Pensjonat, with 10 rooms on a pleasant side street near the heart of Kazimierz, feels elegant despite its reasonable prices (Sb-200 zł, twin Db-298 zł, "komfort plus" Db with 1 big bed-360 zł, extra bed-50 zł, 20 percent less Nov–Feb, ulica Kupa 15, tel. 012-430-6697, fax 012-430-6726, www.karmel.com.pl, hotel@karmel.com.pl).

$ El-jot Art Center rents 15 rooms, in addition to running a theater and an art gallery. It's a tasteful mix of old and new (Sb-239 zł, Db-289 zł, Tb-369 zł, 2-room apartment-459 zł, ulica Miodowa 15, tel. & fax 012-421-3326, www.cak.pl, info@cak.pl).

$ Tournet Guest House, well-run by friendly Piotr Działowy, offers 13 cheap, clean, colorful rooms near the edge of Kazimierz toward Wawel Hill. The "basic" rooms don't include breakfast (7 zł extra) or TV sets (basic Sb-100 zł, standard Sb-140 zł, basic Db-120 zł, standard Db-180 zł, Tb-220 zł, extra bed-50 zł, 20 zł less Nov–March—except basic rooms, ulica Miodowa 7, tel. 012-292-0088, fax 012-292-0089, www.accommodation.krakow.pl, tournet@accommodation.krakow.pl).

EATING

Kraków is one of Eastern Europe's best dining towns, with surprising diversity, high quality, and low prices. For Polish food, you have several inexpensive options (plus some splurges) in the Old Town. For Jewish food, head to Kazimierz.

In the Old Town

Kraków's Old Town is littered with great restaurants. Prices are reasonable even on the Main Market Square. And a half-block away, they get even better. All of these eateries (except the milk bars) are likely to be booked up on weekends—always reserve ahead.

Restauracja pod Aniołami ("Under Angels") offers a dressy, candlelit atmosphere outside on a covered patio, or inside in a romantic cellar with rough wood and medieval vaults. The cuisine is traditional Polish, with an emphasis on grilled meats and trout (on a wood-fired grill). Don't go here if you're in a hurry—only if you want to really slow down and enjoy your dinner (main dishes 20–50 zł, daily 13:00–24:00, reservations smart, ulica Grodzka 35, tel. 012-421-3999). If you want a fast, cheap, and tasty lunch, drop by their tiny **sandwich bar** for fun open-faced sandwiches to take away or enjoy on their sidewalk tables (Mon–Sat 9:00–21:00, Sun 11:00–18:00, shorter hours off-season).

Polskie Smaki ("Polish Flavors") is a homey little self-service cafeteria with a surprisingly elegant interior—sort of a dressed-up milk bar. They serve fast, inexpensive, and tasty traditional meals a block off the Main Market Square, with delicious borscht and *gołąbki* (stuffed cabbage rolls) at a fraction of what you'd pay elsewhere (main dishes 6–8 zł, borrow the English menu and/or point to what you want, daily 10:00–22:00, ulica Św. Tomasza 5, tel. 012-422-4822).

Restauracja Farina, with a fish-and-bottles theme, features a welcoming atmosphere, friendly service, and Polish and Mediterranean cuisine with an emphasis on fresh fish (most main dishes 25–45 zł, seafood up to 70 zł, daily 12:00–23:00, 2 blocks north of the Square at ulica Św. Marka 16, at intersection with ulica Św. Jana, tel. 012-422-1680).

Miód Malina ("Honey Raspberry") is a delightful Polish-Italian fusion restaurant well-located on bustling Grodzka street. The menu is half Polish and half Italian—yet, remarkably, they do both cuisines equally well. You can start with borscht and follow it with spaghetti Bolognese, or have a caprese salad before downing a dish of wood-fired pierogi. Sit in the cozy, warmly painted interior, or out in the courtyard (15-zł pierogi, 15–25-zł wood-fired pizzas and main dishes, 25–40-zł pastas, daily 12:00–23:00, ulica Grodzka 40, tel. 012-430-0411).

Restauracja Jarema offers a tasty reminder that Kraków used to rule a large swath of Ukraine and Lithuania. They serve eastern Polish/Ukrainian cuisine amid 19th-century aristocratic elegance— you'll feel like you're dining in an old mansion (main dishes 25–50 zł, daily 12:00–23:00, usually live music from 19:00, reservations wise, across the street from barbican at plac Matejki 5, tel. 012-429-3669).

Chłopskie Jadło ("Peasant Food") is part of a successful chain serving reasonably priced, authentic Polish food (most main dishes 15–40 zł, fish dishes around 45 zł). The peasant theme begins with rustic bread that comes with farmer cheese and lard (*smalec*). It's kitschy—touristy and fun, with "bed board" chairs—but the food is good, and it's packed with foreign visitors, Polish tourists, and locals. As the chain has become more successful, the food quality has gone a little downhill, but it's still a reliable bet for a typical Polish meal. There are two central locations just off the Main Market Square: a smaller one north (daily 12:00–24:00, ulica Św. Jana 3, tel. 012-429-5157), and one to the south with a farmyard patio and a sprawling, labyrinthine series of cellars (daily 12:00–24:00, ulica Grodzka 9, tel. 012-429-6187). A third, less touristy location is between Wawel Hill and Kazimierz (Sun–Thu 12:00–22:00, Fri–Sat 12:00–24:00, ulica Agnieszki 1, tel. 012-421-8520).

Chimera, just off the Main Market Square, is a cafeteria that serves fast traditional meals to a steady stream of students, either outside on their quiet courtyard, or inside in what seems like a fake Old World stage set (good salad buffet: small plate-10 zł, big plate-14 zł, good for vegetarians, daily 9:00–23:00, near university at ulica Św. Anny 3, it's the second restaurant marked *Chimera* as you approach from the Square). I'd skip their expensive full-service restaurant (main dishes 35–60 zł, daily 12:00–24:00, next door and slightly closer to the Square).

Pizza: **Cyklop,** with 10 tables wrapped around the cook and his busy oven, has excellent wood-fired pizzas (1-person pizzas for 15–20 zł, daily 11:30–22:00, near St. Mary's Church at Mikołajska 16, tel. 012-421-6603). **Pizzeria Trzy Papryczki** ("Three Peppers")—also dishing out wood-fired pizzas at similar prices—has better ambience, but the pizza's not quite as good as Cyklop's (daily 11:00–24:00, ulica Poselska 17, tel. 012-292-5532).

Milk Bars on Ulica Grodzka

Ulica Grodzka, the busy street that cuts south from the Main Market Square, has a convenient little pocket of three milk bars within a few steps of each other (all are open daily for lunch and dinner, but only until 19:00 or 20:00, sometimes later in summer). Survey all three options before you dive in. For pointers on eating at a milk bar, review the sidebar on page 211.

Approaching from the Square, the first one you'll come to (on your left, across from recommended Restauracja Pod Aniołami) is the most modern and upscale of the three: **Kwandras Lunch Bar** ("Quarter"—as in, you can eat here in a quarter-hour; pierogi and other dishes for 6–9 zł, full dinner for 12 zł, ulica Grodzka 32, tel. 012-294-2222).

A few steps up the street and on the right is the most basic and traditional, with a blue-and-white sign reading simply **Bar Mleczny** ("Milk Bar"; low-profile sign over the door reads *Restauracja "pod Temidą"*). The next best thing to a time machine to the communist era, this place has grumpy monolingual service, a mostly local clientele, and cheap but good food (4–10-zł mains).

A few more steps down, also on the right (just before the two churches), is **Bar Grodzki,** a single tight little room with shared tables. In addition to the standard milk-bar fare, Bar Grodzki specializes in tasty potato pancake dishes *(placki ziemniaczane)*. I especially like the "Hunter's Delight"—potato pancake with sausage, melted cheese, and spicy sauce for 13 zł. The English menu posted by the counter makes ordering easy (most main dishes 7–14 zł).

Splurging on the Main Market Square

You'll find plenty of traditional, relatively expensive, tourist-oriented Polish food on the Square. The service can be surly and occasionally dishonest (check your bill carefully). While tourists go for the ye olde places, natives hang out at pizza joints (like Sphinx, part of a wildly popular Poland-wide chain). Poles generally afford this zone on their meager incomes by just having a drink on the Square after eating at home.

Restauracja Redolfi comes with my favorite Square view, great salads, French cuisine, and a wide selection of desserts. This place is fine for just a drink or for a full meal (25-zł salads, main dishes 40–50 zł, daily 9:00–24:00, Rynek Główny 38, tel. 012-423-0579).

Restauracja Hawełka, with good seats overlooking the Square's action, serves traditional Polish cuisine. This was a rowdy pub in the communist days, but now the interior has a genteel painting-gallery ambience. They're especially proud of their mushroom soup in a bread bowl (main dishes 25–70 zł, daily 11:00–23:00, near the corner of Szczepańska at Rynek Główny 34).

Tetmajerowska serves up some of the finest cooking in town—game, Polish, and European—in a plush, elegant modernist (c. 1911) interior upstairs from Restauracja Hawełka. The presentation is classy, the service formal, and the ambience as romantic as the piano is live. It's on the Square, but has no view (main dishes 40–70 zł, daily 13:30–23:00, reservations recommended, near the corner of Szczepańska at Rynek Główny 34, tel. 012-422-0631).

Kazimierz

The entire district is bursting with lively cafés and bars—it's a happening night scene. Jewish food is the specialty here. The non-Jewish places I've listed are fast, cheap, and convenient, but not worth going out of your way for. For locations, see the map on page 248.

Klezmer Concerts and Jewish Food: Kazimierz is a hub of Jewish restaurants, featuring cuisine and music that honors the neighborhood's Jewish heritage (and caters to its Jewish visitors). On a balmy summer night, the air is filled with the sound of klezmer music—traditional Jewish music from 19th-century Poland, generally with violin, string bass, clarinet, and accordion. Skilled klezmer musicians can make their instruments weep or laugh like human voices. Several places on ulica Szeroka (Kazimierz's main square) offer klezmer concerts nightly in the summer at 20:00 (unless otherwise noted). Each restaurant has a similar menu, with main dishes for 20–40 zł. You'll pay an additional cover charge just for the music (15–22 zł per person). While it'd be nice to pop into each restaurant to compare the performers, it's customary to reserve ahead at a single place to dine. At **Klezmer-Hois,** which fills a venerable former Jewish ritual bathhouse, you'll feel like you're dining in a rich grandparent's home (22-zł cover, daily 8:00–22:00, music almost nightly year-round, #6, tel. 012-411-1245, www.klezmer.pl). **Restauracja Arka Noego** ("Noah's Ark") has a good reputation for its music (15-zł cover, daily 9:00–2:00 in the morning, music nightly at 20:30 March–Oct, shares building with Jarden Bookshop at #2, tel. 012-429-1528). **Ariel** is a popular restaurant that has gone downhill in recent years, and receives mixed reviews for its food (20-zł cover, daily 10:00–24:00, music in up to 4 different rooms, best upstairs in the larger dining hall, #18, tel. 012-421-7920).

Inexpensive Polish Food: **Restauracja Samoobsługowa Polakowski** is a glorified milk bar with country-kitchen decor and cheap but delicious Polish fare. Curt service...cute hats (main dishes about 6–8 zł, borrow the English menu and/or point to what you want, daily 9:00–22:00, just behind the top of ulica Szeroka at ulica Miodowa 39). **Pierożki u Vincenta** is a tiny, Vincent van Gogh–inspired eatery serving great pierogi (Polish-style ravioli) with both traditional fillings and creative new-fangled versions (7–8 zł, Sun–Thu 12:00–21:00, Fri–Sat 12:00–22:00, ulica Józefa 11, tel. 012-430-6834). The **plac Nowy market** offers a fully authentic, blue-collar Polish experience—join the workers on their lunch break at the little food windows on Kazimierz's market square.

Bagels and Burritos: **Bagel Mama,** run by an American named Nava, offers good 14-zł burritos, plus 9-zł bagels with various spreads. Though the menu's limited, it offers a break from Polish fare (Sun and Tue–Thu 10:00–21:00, Fri–Sat 10:00–20:00, closed Mon; also closed during the French Open, which Nava caters; behind Tempel Synagogue at ulica Podbrzezie 2, tel. 012-431-1942).

TRANSPORTATION CONNECTIONS

For getting between Kraków and **Auschwitz,** see page 282 in the next chapter.

From Kraków by Train to: Warsaw (hourly, 2.75 hrs, see below), **Gdańsk** (2/day direct, 7 hrs; plus 1 direct night train, 10.75 hrs; more with transfer in Warsaw), **Toruń** (1/day direct, 7.75 hrs; better to transfer at Warsaw's Zachodnia station: 4/day, 5.75–6.5 hrs), **Prague** (1 direct night train/day, 8.5 hrs; otherwise transfer in Katowice, Wrocław, or Ostrava-Svinov, 8–11 hrs), **Berlin** (2/day direct, including 1 night train, 9.5–10.5 hrs; otherwise transfer in Warsaw, 9–11 hrs), **Budapest** (1 direct night train/day, 11 hrs; otherwise transfer in Katowice, Poland, or Břeclav, Czech Republic, 9–10 hrs), and **Vienna** (2/day direct, including 1 night train, 6.5–8.25 hrs).

The train to **Warsaw** is particularly pleasant: A speedy 2.75 hours without stopping, from city center to city center. You'll be offered a free drink and snack to nibble on as you enjoy the pastoral scenery.

AUSCHWITZ-BIRKENAU

The unassuming regional capital of Oświęcim (ohsh-VEENCH-im) was the site of one of humanity's most unspeakably horrifying tragedies: the systematic murder of at least 1.1 million innocent people. From 1941 until 1945, Oświęcim was the home of Auschwitz, the biggest, most notorious concentration camp in the Nazi system. Today, Auschwitz is the most poignant memorial anywhere to the victims of the Holocaust.

A visit here is obligatory for Polish 14-year-olds; students usually come again during their last year of school, as well. You'll often see Israeli high school groups walking through the grounds waving their Star of David flags. Many visitors, including Germans, leave flowers and messages. One of the messages reads: "Nations who forget their own history are sentenced to live it again."

ORIENTATION

"Auschwitz" actually refers to a series of several camps in Poland—most importantly Auschwitz I, in the village of Oświęcim (50 miles, or a 75-minute drive, west of Kraków), and Auschwitz II (a.k.a. Birkenau, about 2 miles west of Oświęcim). Those visiting Auschwitz generally see both parts. **Auschwitz I,** where public transportation from Kraków arrives, has the main museum building, the *Arbeit Macht Frei* gate, and indoor museum exhibits in former prison buildings. Then a brief shuttle-bus ride takes visitors to **Birkenau**—on a much bigger scale and mostly outdoors, with the famous guard tower (with another bookshop and more WCs), a vast field with ruins of barracks, a few tourable rough barracks, the notorious "dividing platform," and a giant monument flanked

Why Visit Auschwitz?

Why visit a notorious concentration camp on your vacation? Auschwitz-Birkenau is one of the most moving sights in Europe, and certainly the most important of all the Holocaust memorials. Seeing the camp can be difficult: Many visitors are overwhelmed by a combination of sadness and anger over the tragedy, as well as inspiration at the remarkable stories of survival. But Auschwitz survivors and victims' families want tourists to come here and experience the scale and the monstrosity of the place. In their minds, a steady flow of visitors will ensure that the Holocaust is always remembered—so it never happens again.

Auschwitz isn't for everyone. But I've never met anyone who toured Auschwitz and regretted it. For many, it's a profoundly life-altering experience—and at the very least, it will forever affect the way you think about the Holocaust.

by remains of destroyed crematoria.

Begin at Auschwitz I. The museum's main building has ticket booths (to pay for a tour or to make a donation), bookshops (consider the good 3-zł *Guide-Book* or the 6-zł laminated map), exchange offices, WCs, and eateries. You'll also find maps of the camp (posted on the walls) and a theater that shows a powerful film. A helpful **information desk**—where you can ask questions, buy tickets for the tour (see "Tours"), and find out about bus schedules for the return trip to Kraków—is halfway down the main entrance hall on the right, in the back corner behind the little tables.

Cost, Hours, Information: Entrance to the camp is free, but donations are gladly accepted. The museum opens every day at 8:00, and closes June–Aug at 19:00, May and Sept at 18:00, April and Oct at 17:00, March and Nov–mid-Dec at 16:00, and mid-Dec–Feb at 15:00. Information: tel. 033-844-8100, www .auschwitz.org.pl.

Getting There: For details on getting between Kraków and Auschwitz, see "Transportation Connections" on page 282.

Getting from Auschwitz I to Birkenau: Buses shuttle visitors two miles between the camps nearly hourly (free, leaving Auschwitz I at the bottom of the hour and Birkenau at the top of the hour, times posted at the bus stop outside the main building of each site; very limited departures in winter—Dec–Feb only 1/ day, usually departing Auschwitz I at 13:30). Taxis are also standing by (about 15 zł). Many visitors, rather than wait for the next bus, decide to walk between the camps—offering a much-needed

On the Way to Auschwitz: The Polish Countryside

You'll spend about an hour gazing out the window as you drive or ride to Auschwitz. This may be your only real look at the Polish countryside. Ponder these thoughts about what you're passing...

The small houses you see are traditionally inhabited by three generations at the same time. Nineteenth-century houses (the few that survive) often sport blue stripes. Back then, parents announced that their daughters were now eligible by getting out the blue paint. Once they saw these blue lines, local boys were welcome to come a-courtin'.

Big churches mark small villages. Tiny roadside memorials and crosses indicate places where fatal accidents have occurred.

Polish farmers traditionally had small lots that were notorious for not being very productive. These farmers somewhat miraculously survived the communist era without having to merge their farms. For years, they were Poland's sacred cows: producing little, paying almost no tax, and draining government resources. But since Poland joined the European Union in 2004, they're being forced to get up to snuff...and, in many cases, collectivize their farms after all.

Since most people don't own cars, bikes are common and public transit is excellent. There are lots of bus stops, as well as minibuses that you can flag down anywhere for a 2-zł ride. The bad roads are a legacy of communist construction, exacerbated by heavy truck use and brutal winters.

Poland has more than 2,000 counties, or districts, each with its own coat of arms; you'll pass several along the way. The forests are state-owned, and locals enjoy the right to pick berries in the summer and mushrooms in the autumn (you may see people—often young kids—selling their day's harvest by the side of the road). The mushrooms are dried and then boiled to make tasty soups in the winter.

chance for reflection. Along the way, you'll pass the Judenrampe, a new exhibit featuring an old train car like the ones used to transport prisoners, explained by an informational sign.

Film: The 17-minute movie (too graphic for children) was shot by Ukrainian troops days after the Red Army liberated the camp (3.50 zł, buy ticket on arrival; always in English at 11:00 and 13:00, often also at 15:00, sometimes more—ask when you arrive).

Photography: Taking pictures has recently been banned inside the museum buildings, because shutterbugs were holding up the line of people waiting to see the exhibits. (The buildings are generally designed for a one-way visit, so all visitors follow the same path through the rooms and sometimes-narrow hallways.) You're allowed to take photographs of anything outside, both at Auschwitz I and at Birkenau.

Eating: There's a café and decent cafeteria (Bar Smak) at the main Auschwitz building. More options are in the commercial complex across the street.

TOURS

Round-trip tours from Kraków to Auschwitz take care of transportation for you (see "Tours" in the Kraków chapter, page 224). But with a tour, you pay triple and have to adhere to a strict schedule. The most rewarding way to visit is to go by yourself, take one of the camp's organized tours, and then explore the grounds on your own.

The Auschwitz Museum has a network of excellent guides who are serious and frank, and feel a strong sense of responsibility about sharing the story of the camp. The 3.5-hour **English tour** covers Auschwitz, Birkenau, and the film (26 zł, buy ticket halfway down the main entry hall, on the right, in the back corner behind the tables). There are generally at least three English tours scheduled each day (at 11:00, 13:00, and 15:00, possibly more with demand, but only at 11:00 in winter); try to arrive at least 20 minutes ahead, because if the tour's full, you'll have to wait until the next one.

You can also hire your own **private guide** for the basic 3.5-hour tour of the camp (197 zł), or for a longer six-hour "study tour" (345 zł). This guide service is an exceptional value and worthwhile if you have special interest in the camp (arrange 2 weeks ahead, call 033-844-8100 or e-mail dyspozytornia@pro.onet.pl). Remember, you can also hire your own private guide in Kraków with a car (400–500 zł—see "Tours" in the Kraków chapter, page 224).

Visiting without a guide works just fine, given the abundance of English descriptions and the self-guided tour of both camps described below.

SELF-GUIDED TOUR

Auschwitz I

Before World War II, this camp was a base for the Polish army. When Hitler occupied Poland, he took over these barracks and turned it into a concentration camp for his Polish political enemies. The location was ideal, with a nearby rail junction and rivers providing natural protective boundaries. In 1942, Auschwitz became a death camp for the extermination of European Jews and others

Auschwitz Renovation

In December of 2006, the International Auschwitz Council announced plans to renovate the site over the next several years. The museum at Auschwitz I, widely considered the oldest Holocaust exhibit in the world, has been largely unchanged in the more than 50 years since it opened. Now the museum displays will be modernized, but key elements (such as the displays of human hair, eyeglasses, and suitcases) will still be incorporated. At Birkenau, restorers will build retaining walls to prevent the remains of the huge crematoria—key evidence of Nazi crimes—from slowly sinking into the ground.

Because of the renovation, be aware that the information in this chapter (especially the self-guided tour) is subject to change. Ask about recent developments when you arrive at the camp.

that Hitler considered "undesirable." By the time the camp was liberated in 1945, at least 1.1 million people had been murdered here—approximately 960,000 of them Jewish.

As you exit the entry building's back door and go toward the camp, you see the notorious gate with the cruel message, *Arbeit Macht Frei* ("Work Sets You Free"). Note that the B was welded on upside down by belligerent inmates. On their arrival, new prisoners were told the truth: The only way out of the camp was through the crematorium chimneys.

Just inside the gate and to the right, the camp orchestra (made up of prisoners) used to play marches; having the prisoners march made them easier to count.

The main road leads past the barracks. An average of 14,000 prisoners were kept at this camp at one time. (Birkenau could hold up to 100,000.) The first row of barracks contains the **National Memorials,** created by the home countries of the camps' victims. The most worthwhile are the "Suffering, Struggle, and Destruction of the Jews" exhibit (block 27) and the nearby Roma (Gypsy) exhibit. Most of the other national memorials were created during the communist era, so they have a decidedly socialist spin; some have been updated (including Hungary, block 18, and the Czech and Slovak Republics, block 16).

The most interesting part of the camp is the second row of

Auschwitz I

To OŚWIĘCIM TOWN

To BIELSKO BIAŁA

NOT TO SCALE

MUSEUM ENTRANCE

1. Ticket Desk
2. Arbeit Macht Frei Gate
3. National Memorials
4. Block 4: Extermination
5. Block 5: Evidence of Crimes
6. Block 6: Everyday Life
7. Block 7: Camp Conditions
8. Execution Courtyard
9. Crematorium
10. Gallows
11. Block 11: "Death Block"
12. Camp Commander's Home
13. Theater (Graphic Film)
14. Shuttle Bus to Birkenau

barracks, which holds the museum exhibitions. Blocks 4 and 5 focus on how Auschwitz prisoners were killed. Blocks 6, 7, and 11 explore the conditions for prisoners who survived here a little longer than most.

Block 4 features exhibits on extermination. In the first room is a map showing all of the countries Auschwitz prisoners were brought from—as far away as Norway and Greece. You'll also find an urn filled with ashes, a symbolic memorial to all of the camp's victims. In Room 2, a map shows that victims were transported here from all over Europe. To prevent a riot, the Nazis claimed at first that this was only a transition camp for resettlement in Eastern Europe. Room 3 displays some of the only photos that exist of victims inside the camp—taken by arrogant SS men.

Upstairs in Room 4 is a chilling model of a Birkenau crematorium. People entered on the left, then got undressed in the underground rooms (hanging their belongings on numbered hooks and encouraged to remember their numbers to retrieve their clothes later). They then moved into the "showers" and were killed by Zyklon-B gas. This efficient factory of murder took about 20 minutes to kill 20,000 people in four gas chambers. Elevators brought the bodies up to the crematorium. Members of the *Sonderkommand*—Jewish inmates who were kept isolated and forced by the Nazis to work here—removed the corpses' gold teeth and shaved off their hair (to be sold) before putting the bodies in the ovens. It wasn't unusual for a *Sonderkommand* worker to discover a wife, child, or parent among the dead. A few committed suicide by throwing themselves at electric fences; those who didn't were systematically executed by the Nazis after a two-month shift. Across from the model of the crematorium are canisters of Zyklon-B (hydrogen cyanide), the German-produced cleaning agent that is lethal in high doses. Across the hall in Room 5 is a wall of victims' hair—4,400 pounds of it. Also displayed is cloth made of the hair, used to make Nazi uniforms.

Back downstairs in Room 6 is an exhibit on the plunder of victims' personal belongings. People being transported here were encouraged to bring luggage—and some victims had even paid in advance for houses in their new homeland. After they were killed, everything of value was sorted and stored in warehouses that prisoners named "Canada" (after a country they associated with great wealth). Although the Canada warehouses were destroyed, you can see a few of these items in the next building.

Block 5 focuses on material evidence of the crimes that took place here. It consists mostly of piles of the victims' goods, a tiny fraction of everything the Nazis stole. As you wander through the rooms, you'll see eyeglasses; fine Jewish prayer shawls; crutches and prosthetic limbs (the first people the Nazis ever exterminated were mentally and physically ill German citizens); a seemingly endless mountain of shoes; and suitcases with names of victims—many marked *Kind*, or "child." Visitors often wonder if the suitcase with the name "Frank" belonged to Anne, one of the Holocaust's most famous victims. After being discovered in Amsterdam by the Nazis, the Frank family was transported here to Auschwitz, where they were split up. Still, it's unlikely this suitcase was theirs. Anne Frank and her sister Margot were sent to the Bergen-Belsen camp in northern Germany, where they died of typhus shortly before the war ended. Their father, Otto Frank, survived Auschwitz and

Chilling Statistics: The Holocaust in Poland

The majority of people murdered by the Nazis during the Holocaust were killed right here in Poland. For centuries, Poland was known for its tolerance of Jews, and right up until the beginning of World War II, Poland had Europe's largest concentration of Jews: 3,500,000. Throughout the Holocaust, the Nazis murdered 4,500,000 Jews in Poland (many of them brought in from other countries) at camps, including Auschwitz, and in ghettos such as Warsaw's.

By the end of the war, only 300,000 Polish Jews had survived—less than 10 percent of the original population. Many of these survivors were granted "one-way passports" (read: deported) to Israel by the communist government in 1968 (following a big student demonstration with a strong Jewish presence). Today, only a few thousand Jews live in all of Poland.

was found barely alive by the Russians, who liberated the camp in January of 1945.

Although the purpose of Auschwitz was to murder its inmates, not all of them were killed immediately. After an initial evaluation, some prisoners were registered and forced to work. (This did not mean they were chosen to live—but rather to die later.) In **Block 6,** you see elements of the everyday life of prisoners. The halls are lined with photographs of victims. Notice the dates of arrival *(przybył)* and death *(zmarł)*—those who were registered survived here an average of two to three months. (Flowers are poignant reminders that these victims are survived by loved ones.) Room 1 displays drawings of the arrival process—sketched by survivors of the camp. After the initial selection, those chosen to work were showered, shaved, and photographed. After a while, photographing each prisoner got to be too expensive, so prisoners were tattooed instead (see photographs): on the chest, on the arm, or—for children—on the leg. A display shows the symbols that prisoners had to wear to show their reason for internment—Jew, Roma (Gypsy), homosexual, political prisoner, and so on.

Room 4 shows the starvation that took place. The 7,500 survivors that the Red Army found here when the camp was liberated were living skeletons (the healthier ones had been forced to march to Germany). Of those liberated, 20 percent died soon after of disease and starvation. Look for the prisoners' daily ration (in the glass case): a pan of tea or coffee in the morning; thin vegetable soup in the afternoon; and a piece of bread (often made with sawdust or chestnuts) for dinner. This makes it clear that Auschwitz was never intended to be a "work camp," where people were kept alive, healthy, and efficient to do work. Rather, people were meant to die here—if not in the gas chambers, then through malnutrition and overwork.

You can see scenes from the prisoner's workday (sketched by survivors after liberation) in Room 5. Prisoners worked as long as the sun shone—eight hours in winter, up to twelve hours in summer—mostly on farms or in factories. Room 6 is about Auschwitz's child inmates, 20 percent of the camp's victims. Blond, blue-eyed children—like the girl in the bottom row on the right—were either "Germanized" in special schools or, if younger, adopted by German families. Dr. Josef Mengele conducted experiments on children, especially twins and triplets, to try to figure out ways to increase fertility for German mothers.

Block 7 shows living and sanitary conditions at the camp—which you'll see in more detail later at Birkenau. Blocks 8–10 are vacant (medical experiments were carried out in Block 10). Step into the **courtyard** between Blocks 10 and 11. The wall at the far end is where the Nazis shot several thousand political prisoners, leaders of camp resistance, and religious leaders. Notice that the windows are covered, so that nobody could witness the executions. Also take a close look at the memorial—the back of it is made of a material designed by Nazis to catch the bullets without a ricochet. Inmates were shot at short range—about three feet. The pebbles represent prayers from Jewish visitors.

The most feared place among prisoners was the **"Death Block" (#11),** from which nobody ever left alive. In Room 5, you can see how prisoners lived in these barracks—three-level bunks, with three prisoners sleeping in each bed (they had to sleep on their sides so they could fit). Death here required a trial (the room in which sham trials were held—lasting about 2 minutes each—is on display). In Room 6, people undressed before they were executed. In the basement, you'll see several different types of cells. The Starvation Cell (#18) held prisoners selected to starve to death when a fellow prisoner escaped; Maksymilian Kolbe spent two weeks here to save a man's life (see sidebar). In the Dark Cell (#20), which held up to 30, people had only a small window for ventilation—and if it became covered with snow, the prisoners suffocated. At the end of the hall in Cell 21, you can see where a prisoner scratched a crucifix (left) and image of Jesus (right) on the wall. In the Standing Cells (#22), four people would be forced to stand together for hours at a time (of course, the bricks went all the way to the ceiling then). Upstairs is an exhibit on resistance within the camp.

Before you leave Auschwitz, visit the **crematorium** (from Block 11, exit straight ahead and go past the first row of barracks, then turn right and go straight on the road between the two rows of

St. Maksymilian Kolbe
(1894–1941)

Among the many inspirational stories of Auschwitz is that of a Polish priest named Maksymilian Kolbe. Before the war, Kolbe traveled as a missionary to Japan, then worked in Poland for a Catholic newspaper. While he was highly regarded for his devotion to the Church, some of his writings had an unsettling anti-Semitic sentiment. But during the Nazi occupation, Kolbe briefly ran an institution that cared for refugees—including Jews.

In 1941, Kolbe was arrested and interned at Auschwitz. When a prisoner from Kolbe's block escaped in July of that year, the Nazis punished the remaining inmates by selecting 10 of them to put in the Starvation Cell until they died—based on the Nazi "doctrine of collective responsibility." After the selection had been made, Kolbe offered to replace a man who expressed concern about who would care for his family. The Nazis agreed. (The man Kolbe saved is said to have survived the Holocaust.)

All 10 of the men—including Kolbe—were put into Starvation Cell 18. Two weeks later, when the door was opened, only Kolbe had survived. The story spread through-out the camp, and Kolbe became an inspiration to the inmates. To squelch the hope he had given the others, Kolbe was executed by lethal injection.

In 1982, Kolbe was canonized by the Catholic Church. Some critics—mindful of his earlier anti-Semitic rhetoric—still consider Kolbe's sainthood controversial. But most Poles feel he redeemed himself for his earlier missteps through this noble act at the end of his life.

barracks; pass through the gap in the fence and look for the chimney on your left). People undressed outside, or just inside the door. Up to 700 people at a time could be gassed here. Inside the door, go into the big room on the right. Look for the vents in the ceiling—this is where the SS men dropped the Zyklon-B. Through the door is a replica of the furnace. This facility could burn 340 bodies a day—so it took two days to burn all of the bodies from one round of executions. The Nazis didn't like this inefficiency, so they built four more huge crematoria at Birkenau.

Shortly after the war, camp commander Rudolf Höss was tried, convicted, and sentenced to death. Survivors requested that he be executed at Auschwitz. In 1947, he was hanged. These gallows are preserved behind the crematorium (about a hundred yards from his home where his wife—who loved her years here—read stories to their children, very likely by the light of a human-skin lampshade).

Take your time with Auschwitz I. When you're ready, continue to the second stage of the camp—Birkenau (see "Getting from Auschwitz I to Birkenau," page 271).

Auschwitz II—Birkenau

In 1941, when the original Auschwitz camp got to be too small for the capacity the Nazis envisioned, they began a second camp in some nearby farm fields. The original plan was for a camp that could hold 200,000 people, but at its peak, Birkenau (Brzezinka) held only about 100,000. They were still adding onto it when the camp was liberated in 1945.

Train tracks lead past the main building and into the camp. The first sight that greeted prisoners was the guard tower (familiar to many visitors from the stirring scenes in *Schindler's List*). Climb to the top of the entry building (also houses WCs and bookstore) for an overview of the massive camp. As you look over the camp, you'll see a vast field of chimneys and a few intact wooden and brick barracks. The train tracks lead straight back to the dividing platform, and then dead-end at the ruins of the crematorium and camp monument at the far side.

Some of the barracks were destroyed by Germans. Most were dismantled to be used for fuel and building materials shortly after the war. But the first row has been reconstructed (using components from the original structures). Visit the barracks on the right.

The first of these barrack buildings was the **latrine:** The front half of the building contained washrooms, and the back was a row of toilets. There was no running water; prisoners were in charge of keeping these clean. Because of the unsanitary conditions, the Nazis were afraid to come in here—so it was the heart of the black market and the inmates' resistance movement.

The fourth barrack was a **bunk** building. Each inmate had a personal number, a barrack number, and a bed number. Inside, you can see the beds (angled so that more could fit). An average of 400 prisoners—but up to 1,000—would be housed in each of these buildings. These wooden structures, designed as stables by a German company (look for the horse-tying rings on the wall), came in prefab pieces that made them cheap and convenient. Two chimneys connected by a brick duct provided a little heat. The bricks were smoothed by inmates who sat here to catch a bit of warmth.

Auschwitz II—Birkenau

- PARKING

FORMER

BARRACKS

To AUSCHWITZ I

❶ Guard Tower, Viewpoint,
WC & Bookstore

❷ Latrine & Restored
Barracks

❸ Dividing Platform

❹ Brick Barracks

❺ Crematoria Ruins (4)

❻ "The Sauna"

❼ Monument

❽ Shuttle Bus to
Auschwitz I

Follow the train tracks toward the monument about a half-mile away, at the back end of Birkenau. At the intersection of these tracks and the perpendicular gravel road (halfway to the monument) was the gravel **dividing platform.** A Nazi doctor would stand facing the guard tower and evaluate each prisoner. If he pointed to the right, the prisoner was sentenced to death, and trudged—unknowingly—to the gas chamber. If he pointed to the left, the person would be registered and live a little longer. It was here that families from all over Europe were torn apart forever.

On the left-hand side of the tracks are some **brick barracks.** The supervisors lived in the two smaller rooms near the door. Farther in, most barracks still have the wooden bunks that held about 700 people per building. Four or five people slept on each bunk, including the floor—reserved for new arrivals. There were chamber pots at either end of the building. After a Nazi doctor died of typhus, sanitation improved, and these barracks got running water.

As you walk along the camp's only road, which leads along the tracks to the crematorium, imagine the horror of this place—no grass, only mud, and all the barracks packed with people, with smoke blowing in from the busy crematoria. This was an even worse place to die than Auschwitz I.

The train tracks lead to the camp memorial and crematorium. At the end of the tracks, go 50 yards to the left and climb the three concrete steps to view the ruin of the **crematorium.** This is one of four crematoria here at Birkenau, each with a capacity to cremate more than 4,400 people per day. At the far-right end of the ruins, see the stairs where people entered the rooms to undress. People were given numbered lockers, conning them into thinking they were coming back. (The Nazis didn't want a panic.) Then they piled into the "shower room"—the underground passage branching away from the memorial—and were killed. Their bodies were burned in the crematorium (on the left), giving off a scent of sweet almonds (the Zyklon-B). Beyond the remains of the crematorium is a hole—once a gray lake where tons of ashes were dumped. This efficient factory of death was destroyed by the Nazis as the Red Army approached, leaving today's evocative ruins.

With more time, you could continue deeper into the camp—to the reception and disinfection building that prisoners called **"the sauna,"** and to the remains of the other two destroyed **crematoria.**

The Soviets arrived on January 27, 1945, and the nightmare of Auschwitz was over. The Polish parliament voted to turn these grounds into a museum, so that the world would understand, and never forget, the horror of what happened here. The **monument** at the back of the camp, built in 1967 (by the communist government in its heavy "Social Realist" style), represents gravestones and the chimney of a crematorium. The plaques, written in each of the languages spoken by camp victims (including English, far right), explain that the memorial is "a cry of despair and a warning to humanity."

TRANSPORTATION CONNECTIONS

Remember that the Auschwitz Museum is in the town of Oświęcim, about 50 miles west of Kraków.

From Kraków to Auschwitz

Frequent **buses** connect Kraków and Auschwitz, mostly run by PKS Oświęcim (7 zł, roughly hourly, 1.5 hrs, get the most recent schedule at any Kraków TI, buses depart from Kraków's new bus station behind the train station—see page 219). Buy a one-way ticket to leave your options open for getting home (described below). Once in the town of Oświęcim, buses from Kraków stop first at the train station, then continue on to a low-profile bus stop on the edge of the Auschwitz camp grounds (you'll see a small *Muzeum Auschwitz* sign on the right just before the stop, and a blue *Oświęcim Muzeum PKS* sign on the stop itself). From this bus stop, follow the sign down the road and into the parking lot; the main museum building is across the lot on your left. Note that since most buses don't actually go into the museum's parking lot, the Auschwitz stop can be easy to miss.

Several **minibuses** also head from Kraków directly to the Auschwitz Museum (7 zł, 1.5 hrs). The departure point in Kraków for these minibuses changes frequently. They likely go from a big, dusty parking lot on Warszawska street, beyond the north end of plac Matejki (across the ring road from the Barbican). However, this will likely change in the near future—get the latest details at Kraków's TI.

You could ride the **train** to Oświęcim, but it's less convenient than the bus because it leaves you at the train station, farther from the museum (8/day, 1.25–1.75 hrs, 11 zł).

If you wind up at the Oświęcim **train station,** it's about a 20-minute walk to the camp (turn right out of station, go straight, then turn left at roundabout, camp is several blocks ahead on left). Or you can take a taxi (around 15 zł).

A **taxi** between Kraków and Auschwitz runs about 200 zł one-way. But if you're splurging for a taxi, you might as well pay for a private guide to drive you here, as well as show you around once you arrive (see "Tours" in the Kraków chapter, page 224).

Returning from Auschwitz to Kraków

If you're using public transportation, you'll get the most complete information on the return trip to Kraków at Auschwitz. Upon arrival at Auschwitz I, visit the information window inside the main building (halfway down the main entry hall, on the right, in the back corner behind the tables). They can give you a schedule of departures and explain where the bus or minibus leaves from. Remember to allow enough time to make it back to Auschwitz I from Birkenau to catch your bus.

Most buses and minibuses back to Kraków do not leave from the camp parking lot itself (though some buses do). Instead, you'll most likely catch the bus from the stop on the edge of the Auschwitz I grounds (described previously). To reach this bus stop, leave the Auschwitz I building through the main entry and walk straight along the parking lot, then turn right on the road near the end of the lot. At the dead end, cross the street to the little bus stop (with a blue *Oświęcim Muzeum PKS* sign). Don't be distracted by the ads for a nearby travel agency—you can buy tickets on the bus. Note that there's no public transportation back to Kraków from Birkenau, where most people end their tours; you'll have to take the shuttle bus back to Auschwitz I first.

WARSAW

(Warszawa)

Warsaw (Warszawa, vah-SHAH-vah in Polish) is Poland's capital and biggest city. It's huge, famous, and important...but not particularly romantic. If you're looking for Old World quaintness, head for Kraków. If you're tickled by spires and domes, get to Prague. But if you want to experience a truly 21st-century city, Warsaw's your place.

Like Berlin, Warsaw is modernizing—fast. Mindful of its history, yet optimistic about the future, Warsaw has happily emerged from a long hibernation. Varsovians are embracing their role as the capital city of an influential nation in the "New Europe." The European Union has two universities aimed at educating future political leaders (or "Eurocrats"). One is in Bruges, Belgium, just down the road from the EU capital of Brussels. The other one is right here. Warsaw also has gleaming new skyscrapers and street signs, stylishly dressed locals, cutting-edge shopping malls, swarms of international businesspeople, and a gourmet coffee shop on every corner.

Warsaw has good reason to be a city of the future: The past hasn't been very kind. Since becoming Poland's capital in 1596, Warsaw has seen wave after wave of foreign rulers and invasions—especially during the last hundred years. But in this horrific crucible, the enduring spirit of the Polish people was forged. As one proud Varsovian told me, "Warsaw is ugly because its history is so beautiful."

The city's darkest days came during the Nazi occupation of World War II. First, its Jewish residents were forced into a tiny ghetto. They rose up...and were slaughtered. Then, its Polish residents rose up...and were slaughtered. Hitler sent word to systematically demolish this troublesome city. At the war's end, Warsaw was devastated. An estimated 800,000 residents were dead—almost two out of every three Varsovians.

The Poles almost gave up on what was then a pile of rubble to build a brand-new capital city elsewhere. But ultimately they decided to rebuild, creating a city of contrasts: painstakingly restored medieval lanes, crumbling communist apartment blocks (*bloki* in Polish), and sleek, super-modern, glass-and-steel sky-scrapers. Between the buildings, you'll find fragments of a complex, sometimes tragic, and often inspiring history.

A product of its complicated past, sprinkled with the big-city style and sophistication of the present, while remaining quintes-sentially Polish, Warsaw is a place worth grappling with to under-stand the Poland of today...and the Europe of tomorrow.

Planning Your Time

Though you can get a good taste in a short visit—as a day-trip, or en route elsewhere—it's easy to fill a full day here.

With a few hours, gape at Stalin's towering Palace of Culture and Science, then wander along the Royal Way and through the reconstructed Old Town. With a little more time, relax in Łazienki Park or seek out the sights of whichever topics interest you: art, Holocaust history, the Warsaw Uprising, Polish royalty, or Chopin.

If you're coming from Germany, consider connecting to Warsaw via an overnight train from Berlin. See Warsaw, and then move on to Kraków later that same day (hourly trains, 2.75 hours).

ORIENTATION

(area code: 022)
Warsaw sprawls with 1.7 million residents. Everything is on a big scale—it seems to take forever to walk just a few "short" blocks. Get comfortable with public transportation and plan your sight-seeing wisely to avoid backtracking.

Virtually everything of interest to travelers is on the west bank of the Vistula River. The city's Central Train Station (Warszawa Centralna) is in the shadow of its biggest landmark: the can't-miss-it, skyscraping Palace of Culture and Science. To the east of the station, parallel to the river, runs the "Royal Way" boulevard, con-necting the sights in the north (Old Town and New Town) with

Central Warsaw

the sights in the south (Łazienki Park, and beyond that, Wilanów Palace). Most major sights and recommended hotels and restaurants are along this spine.

Another tip: You'll hear about two distinct uprisings that occurred against the Nazis during World War II. They're easy to confuse, but try to keep them straight: the **Ghetto Uprising** was staged by Warsaw's dwindling Jewish population in the spring of 1943 (see page 311); the **Warsaw Uprising,** a year later, came at the hands of the (mostly non-Jewish) Polish Home Army (see page 314).

Tourist Information

Warsaw's helpful, youthful TI has four offices: on the **Royal Way** near Castle Square (daily May–Sept 9:00–20:00, Oct–April 9:00–18:00, Krakowskie Przedmieście 39), at the **Central Train Station** (daily May–Sept 8:00–20:00, Oct–April 8:00–18:00), and at both terminals at the **airport** (main terminal same hours as Central Train Station TI, Etuda terminal daily 8:00-18:00). The general information number for all TIs is 022-9431 (www.warsawtour.pl). All four branches offer several free, useful materials: a city map (with key phone numbers on the back), a well-produced booklet called *Warsaw: In Short,* and a series of brochures on sights ("city breaks," Jewish heritage, Chopin). The TI also has a free room-booking service.

The **Warsaw Tourist Card,** which covers public transportation and admission to over 20 museums, isn't worth the price for most travelers (35 zł/24 hrs, 65 zł/3 days).

Arrival in Warsaw

By Train: Most trains arrive at the big, dreary Central Train Station (Warszawa Centralna), a communist-era monstrosity next to the Palace of Culture and Science. You'll emerge from your platform *(peron)* into a confusing labyrinth of passageways. At this underground level, you'll find **lockers** near *peron* 4—look for *przechowalnia bagażu.* Emerge into the **main arrival hall** (follow signs to *Hala Główna*) to get your bearings. Lining one wall of this hall are **ticket windows,** some of which are designated for international tickets *(kasa międzynarodowa).* There's also a rail service center in the corner of the main hall (under the big, orange *Apteka Non Stop* sign). If the lines at the main hall ticket windows are way too long, you can find more ticket windows in the maze of corridors under the station. Allow yourself plenty of time to wait in line to buy tickets. Some locals bypass these lines altogether and buy their tickets on the train for an extra charge (about 7 zł extra). Train info: tel. 022-9436.

From the station, **bus #175** takes you right to the Royal

Warsaw Essentials

English	Polish	Pronounced
Warsaw	Warszawa	vah-SHAH-vah
Central Train Station	Warszawa Centralna	vah-SHAH-vah tsehn-TRAHL-nah
Palace of Culture and Science	Pałac Kultury i Nauki (or simply "Pałac")	PAH-wahts nah-OO-kee
New Town	Nowe Miasto	NOH-vay mee-AH-stoh
Old Town	Stare Miasto	STAH-reh mee-AH-stoh
Old Town Market Square	Rynek Starego Miasta	REE-nehk stah-RAY-goh mee-AH-stah
Royal Way	Szłak Królewski	shwock kroh-LEHV-skee
Popular restaurant street on Royal Way	Nowy Świat	NOH-vee SHVEE-aht
Attraction-lined street on Royal Way	Krakowskie Przedmieście	krah-KOHV-skyeh pzhehd-MYESH-cheh
Royal Castle	Zamek Królewski	ZAH-mehk kroh-LEHV-skee
Castle Square	Plac Zamkowy	plahts zahm-KOH-vee
Piłsudski Square	Plac Marszałka Józefa Piłsudskiego	plahts mar-SHAW-kah yoh-ZEH-fah pew-sood-SKYAY-goh
Łazienki Park	Park Łazienkowski	park wah-zhehn-KOV-skee
Vistula River	Wisła	VEES-wah

Way and Old Town in about 10 minutes (see "Getting Around Warsaw"). You can catch this bus—and others going in the same direction—in front of the skyscraper with the LOT airlines office and Hotel Marriott across busy aleja Jerozolimskie from the station. Follow signs to exit at *Al. Jerozolimskie*, near *peron*/platform 1 (the easiest way across this street is via a pedestrian underpass—look for *Hotel Marriott* signs). **Taxis** wait outside the main hall (many are crooked—look for one with a company logo and telephone number, and ask for an estimate up front).

By Car: Warsaw is a stressful city to drive and park in. Arrange parking with your hotel, and get around by foot or public transit. You must pay to park in the city Monday–Friday 8:00–18:00. Park your car (likely on a sidewalk), find the parking pay station, and insert coins until the proper amount of time appears in the left-hand window (about 2 zł/hr). Press the green button, wait for your ticket, and put it on your dashboard. Sometimes public parking areas are monitored by "attendants"—unemployed creeps who kindly help you find a spot, then ask if you want them to "watch your car" for you. Try to avoid parking where you see these crooks, but if you do, 1–2 zł is a small investment to prevent the car from being damaged.

By Plane: Warsaw's **Fryderyk Chopin International Airport** (Port Lotniczy im. Fryderyk Chopina) is about six miles southwest of the center. The various terminals are all close together: The main terminal (called "Terminal 1"), used by LOT and other major carriers, is divided into two sections: international and domestic (you'll walk briefly outside to get between them). A separate terminal, called Etuda, is used by low-cost airlines. (To complicate things, a brand-new Terminal 2 may open in early 2007.)

At both Terminal 1 and the Etuda terminal, you'll find a TI, plus lots of ATMs and exchange offices *(kantor)*. From either terminal, bus #175 runs into the center (Central Train Station, Royal Way, and Old Town; tickets sold for 2.40 zł at kiosk, or 3 zł from driver, 4–6/hr, fewer Sat–Sun, 30 min). The 20-minute taxi ride to the center shouldn't cost you more than 40 zł (though hucksters who approach you offering a ride may try to charge you astronomical rates—ask for an estimate, and if it's more than 40 zł, ask the next guy). The trip into town can take much longer during rush hour, because only one main thoroughfare connects the airport to the center. Airport info: tel. 022-650-4100, www .lotnisko-chopina.pl.

Getting Around Warsaw

By Public Transit: In this big city, it's essential to get a handle on public transportation. Ignore the Metro (which is useless to most tourists), and take advantage of the buses and trams. All three systems use the same tickets. A single ticket costs 2.40 zł (called *bilet jednorazowy,* good for one trip, no transfers); a one-day ticket costs 7.20 zł (*bilet dobowy,* good for 24 hours); and a three-day ticket is 12 zł *(bilet trzydniowy).* Buy your ticket at any kiosk with a *RUCH* sign, and be sure to validate it as you board by inserting it in the little yellow box (24-hour and 3-day tickets need only be validated the first time you ride). You can also buy the basic one-ride tickets from your bus or tram driver for an extra 0.60 zł.

Most of the city's major attractions line up on a single axis, the Royal Way, which is served by several different buses (but no trams). The designed-for-tourists **bus #180** conveniently connects virtually all of the significant sights and neighborhoods: the former Jewish Ghetto, Castle Square/Old Town, the Royal Way, Łazienki Park, and Wilanów Palace (south of the center). This particularly user-friendly bus lists sights in English on the posted schedule inside (other buses don't). **Bus #175** links the airport, the Central Train Station, the Royal Way, and Old Town. Those two buses, as well as buses #116, #122, #195, #503, and #518, go along the most interesting stretch of the Royal Way (between aleja Jerozolimskie and Castle Square in the Old Town). Bus routes beginning with "E" are express, so they go long distances without stopping.

Note that on Saturdays and Sundays in summer (June–Oct), the Nowy Świat section of the Royal Way is closed to buses, so the above buses detour along a parallel street.

By Taxi: As in most big Eastern European cities, it's wise to use only cabs that are clearly marked with a company logo and telephone number (or call your own: Locals like MPT Radio Taxi, tel. 022-9191). All official taxis have similar rates: 6 zł to start, then 2–3 zł per kilometer (more after 22:00 or in the suburbs). The drop fee may be higher if you catch the cab in front of a big, fancy hotel.

TOURS

Various companies offer bus tours (which include some walking) for 120–140 zł (3–4.5 hrs, get information at TI). A tourist train does a 30-minute circuit, leaving from in front of the Royal Castle (20 zł, daily May–Oct, doesn't run Mon Nov–April).

SELF-GUIDED WALK

Warsaw's Royal Way

The Royal Way (Szlak Królewski) is the six-mile route that kings of Poland used to take from their main residence (at Castle Square in the Old Town) to their summer home (Wilanów Palace, south of the center). In the heart of the city, the Royal Way is a busy boulevard with two different names: hip and vibrant **Nowy Świat** (at the south end), which offers a good glimpse at urban Warsaw; and **Krakowskie Przedmieście** (at the north end, ending at the Old Town), lined with historic landmarks and better for sightseeing.

Since this spine connects most hotels, restaurants, and sights, you'll probably use it—on foot or by bus—sometime during your trip (key buses are noted under "Getting Around Warsaw," above).

This ▲▲ self-guided walk should make your commute more interesting. I've focused on the intriguing stretch closest the Old Town, where the street is called Krakowskie Przedmieście. To skip directly to this point ("Part 2"), take the bus to the Uniwersytet stop and backtrack one block. Not counting sightseeing stops, figure about 10 minutes to walk along Nowy Świat ("Part 1"), then another 20 minutes along Krakowskie Przedmieście to the Old Town ("Part 2").

Royal Way Walk Part 1: Nowy Świat

Begin at the head of the boulevard called Nowy Świat, at the intersection with busy **aleja Jerozolimskie** ("Jerusalem Avenue"). This street once led to a Jewish settlement called New Jerusalem. Like so much else in Warsaw, it's changed names many times. Between the World Wars, it became "May 3rd Avenue," celebrating Poland's 1791 constitution (Europe's first). But when the communists took power, they didn't fancy this highly nationalistic name, so they switched it back to "Jerusalem"—strangely disregarding the religious connotations of that name. (Come on, guys—what about a good, old-fashioned "Stalin Avenue"?)

In the middle of aleja Jerozolimskie, notice the giant **palm tree.** When a local artist went to the real Jerusalem, she was struck at how many palm trees she saw there. She decided it was only appropriate that one should grace Warsaw's own little stretch of "Jerusalem." This model palm tree—with a trunk from France and leaves from California, where theme parks abound with such fake trees—went up a few years ago as a temporary installation. It was highly controversial, dividing the neighborhood. One snowy winter day, the pro–palm tree faction—who appreciate the way the tree spices up this otherwise predictable metropolis—camped out here in bikinis and beachwear to show their support. They prevailed, and the tree still stands.

As you face the palm tree, look across the street and up the block to the left to see the **National Museum**—a good place for a Polish art lesson (more interesting than it sounds—see page 306).

To the right of the National Museum, directly across from Nowy Świat ("New World") stands a big, blocky building that used to be the **headquarters of the Communist Party.** A popular communist-era joke: What do you see when you turn your back on the Communist Party? A new world.

Today's Poland is confidently striding into a new world...and so should we. Get marching.

Nowy Świat is a charming shopping boulevard, nicknamed the "Champs-Elysées of Warsaw" by Varsovians. Well, maybe not quite. But, lined with shops, cafés, and restaurants, it's less dreary-urban and more upscale-elegant than other parts of the city. Before

Old Town and Royal Way

1. Duval Apartments
2. Old Town Apts. Office
3. Hotel Harenda
4. To Ibis Warszawa Stare Miasto
5. Dom Przy Rynku Hostel
6. Restauracja pod Samsonem
7. Podwale Piwna Kompania
8. Pierogarnia na Bednarskiej
9. Siedem Grzechów Rest.
10. U Fukiera & Gessler Restaurants
11. Uniwersytecky Milk Bar

World War II, Nowy Świat was Warsaw's most popular neighborhood. And today, once again, rents are higher here than anywhere else in the city. While tourists flock into the Old Town, Varsovians and visiting businesspeople prefer this zone.

Ulica Chmielna, the first street to the left, is an appealing pedestrian boutique street leading to Emil Wedel's chocolate heaven (described on page 321). Between here and the Palace of Culture and Science stretches one of Warsaw's trendiest shopping neighborhoods (culminating in the new Galleria Centrum mall, just across from the Palace).

Across the street from Chmielna (on the right) is the street called **Foksal,** which is emerging as one of Warsaw's most pleasant and trendy dining zones. On a balmy summer evening, this street is filled with chatty al fresco diners, sipping drinks and nibbling at plates of cutting-edge international cuisine.

A few steps down Nowy Świat, on the left, don't miss the **A. Blikle** pastry shop and café—*the* place in Poland to buy sweets. (For more on this popular spot, see page 320.) If you're homesick for Starbucks, drop into one of the many gourmet coffee shops that line this stretch of Nowy Świat—with American-style lattes "to go."

The next three blocks are more of the same. Eat and shop your way up Nowy Świat, until you reach the big Copernicus statue in the middle of the street.

Royal Way Walk Part 2: Krakowskie Przedmieście

The street name changes to Krakowskie Przedmieście (roughly translated as "Suburb in the Direction of Kraków") at the big statue of **Copernicus,** in front of the Polish Academy of Science. Mikołaj Kopernik was born in Toruń (see page 378) and went to college in Kraków. The Nazis stole this statue and took it to Germany (which, like Poland, claims Copernicus as its own). Now it's back where it belongs.

We'll pass many churches along this route, but the **Church of the Holy Cross** is unique (Kościół Św. Krzyża, across from Copernicus). Composer Fryderyk Chopin's heart is inside one of the pillars of the nave (second big pillar on the left, look for the marker). After two decades of exile in France, Chopin's final wish was to have his heart brought back to his native Poland. During World War II, the heart was hidden away in the countryside for safety. Chopin's organs aside, this church feels more alive than most. Locals often drop in. Check out the bright gold chapel, located on the left as you face the altar, at the front of the church. It's dedicated to a saint whom Polish Catholics believe helps them with "desperate and hopeless causes." People praying here are likely dealing with some tough issues. The beads draped from the altarpieces help power their prayers, and the many little brass plaques are messages of thanks for prayers answered.

After leaving the church, continue up the street and take the pedestrian underpass to the other side. You're at the gates to the main campus of **Warsaw University,** founded in 1816. This area is a lively student district with plenty of bookstores and cafés. A few steps back up the street (at #20) is the Uniwersytecky Bar, a classic **milk bar** *(bar mleczny)*—a subsidized government cafeteria filled with students and anyone who wants a bargain (for more about milk bars, see page 211).

The 18th century was a time of great political decline for Poland, as a series of incompetent foreign kings mishandled crises and squandered funds. But ironically, it was also Warsaw's biggest economic boom time. Along this boulevard, aristocratic families of the period built **mansions**—most of them destroyed during World War II and rebuilt since, some with curious flourishes. (Just past the university on the right, look for the doorway supported by four bearded brutes admiring their overly defined abs.) Over time, many of these families donated their mansions to the university.

The yellow church a block up from the university is the Church of the Nuns of the Visitation (Kościół Sióstr Wizytek). The monument in front commemorates **Cardinal Stefan Wyszyński,** who was the Polish primate (the head of the Polish Catholic Church) from 1948 to 1981. He took this post soon after the arrival of the communists, who opposed the Church, but also realized it would be risky for them to shut down the churches in such an ardently religious country. The Communist Party and the Catholic Church coexisted tensely in Poland, and when Wyszyński protested a Stalinist crackdown in 1953, he was arrested and imprisoned. Three years later, in a major victory for the Church, Wyszyński was released. He continued to fight the communists, becoming a great hero of the Polish people in their struggle against the regime.

Farther up, you'll see the elegant **Hotel Bristol,** Warsaw's classiest. Leave the Royal Way briefly to reach Piłsudski Square (a block away on the left, up the street opposite Hotel Bristol).

The vast, empty-feeling **Piłsudski Square** (Plac Marszałka Józefa Piłsudskiego) has been important Warsaw real estate for years, constantly changing with the times. An Orthodox cathedral here was torn down in the 1920s, when anti-Russian passions ran high in newly independent Poland. During the Nazi occupation, it took the name "Adolf-Hitler-Platz." Under the communists, it was Zwycięstwa, meaning "Victory" (of the Soviets over Hitler's fascism). When the regime imposed martial law in 1981, the people of Warsaw silently protested by filling the square with a giant cross made of flowers. The huge plaque in the ground near the road commemorates two monumental communist-era Catholic events

Warsaw at a Glance

▲▲**Old Town Market Square** Recreation of Warsaw's glory days, with lots of colorful architecture. **Hours:** Always open.

▲▲**National Museum** Collection of mostly Polish art, with unknown but worth-discovering works by Jan Matejko and the Młoda Polska (Art Nouveau) crew. **Hours:** Tue–Sun 10:00–16:00, Thu until 18:00, closed Mon.

▲**Castle Square** Colorful spot with whiffs of old Warsaw—Royal Castle (below), monuments, and a chunk of the city wall, with cafés just off the square. **Hours:** Always open.

▲**Royal Castle** Warsaw's best palace, rebuilt after World War II, but stocked with original furnishings (hidden during the war). **Hours:** Various tour routes with different hours. Generally open Tue–Sun 10:00–16:00 or 18:00, summer Mon 11:00–16:00 or 18:00, shorter tours and permanent exhibition closed on Sun, closed Mon in winter.

▲**Chopin Museum** Elegant old mansion with Chopin bric-a-brac and occasional piano concerts. **Hours:** May–Sept Mon, Wed, and Fri 10:00–17:00, Thu 12:00–18:00, Sat–Sun 10:00–14:00, closed Tue; Oct–April Mon–Wed and Fri–Sat 10:00–14:00, Thu 12:00–18:00, closed Sun.

on this square: John Paul II's first visit as pope to his homeland on June 2, 1979; and the funeral on May 31, 1981, of Cardinal Stefan Wyszyński, whom we met across the street.

Stand near this giant plaque, with the Royal Way at your back, for this quick spin-tour orientation: Ahead are the Tomb of the Unknown Soldier and Saxon Garden; to the right is the old National Theater, eclipsed by a modern business center/parking garage; farther to the right is a statue of Piłsudski (which you passed to get here—described below); and to the right of that—past the big gray Polish Ministry of Defense building—is the Victoria Hotel, the ultimate plush, top-of-the-top hotel where all communist-era VIPs stayed. To the right of the hotel, on the horizon, you can see Warsaw's newly emerging skyline. The imposing Palace of Culture and Science, which once stood alone over the city, is being joined by a cluster of brand-new skyscrapers, giving Warsaw a Berlin-esque vibe befitting its important role as a business center of the "New Europe."

Walk to the fragment of colonnade by the park that marks the **Tomb of the Unknown Soldier** (Grób Nieznanego Żołnierza).

▲**Łazienki Park** Lovely, sprawling green space with Chopin statue, peacocks, and Neoclassical buildings. **Hours:** Always open.

▲**Warsaw Uprising Museum** High-tech exhibit tracing the history of the Uprising and celebrating its heroes. **Hours:** Mon, Wed, and Fri 8:00–18:00, Thu until 20:00, Sat–Sun 10:00–18:00, closed Tue.

Warsaw Historical Museum Glimpse of the city before and after World War II, with excellent movie in English. **Hours:** Museum—Tue and Thu 11:00–18:00, Wed and Fri 10:00–15:30, Sat–Sun 10:30–16:30, closed Mon; Movie—Tue–Sat at noon.

Palace of Culture and Science Huge "Stalin Gothic" sky-scraper with a more impressive exterior than interior, housing theaters, multiplex cinema, observation deck, and more. **Hours:** Observation deck—daily June–Sept 9:00–20:00, Fri–Sat until 23:45; Oct–May 9:00–18:00.

Jewish Ghetto: Path of Remembrance Pilgrimage from Ghetto Heroes Square to the infamous Nazi "transfer spot" where Jews were sent to death camps. **Hours:** Always open.

The colonnade was once part of a much larger palace built by the Saxon prince electors (Dresden's Augustus the Strong and his son), who became kings of Poland in the 18th century. After the palace was destroyed in World War II, this fragment was kept to memorialize Polish soldiers. The names of key battles are etched into the columns, urns contain dirt from major Polish battlefields, and the two soldiers are pretty stiff.

Just behind the Tomb is **Saxon Garden** (Ogród Saski)—a favorite park among locals—which was also built by the Saxon kings of Poland. Like most foreign kings, Augustus the Strong and his son cared little for their Polish territory, building gardens like these for themselves instead of investing in more pressing needs. Poles say that foreign kings such as Augustus did nothing but "eat, drink, and loosen their belts" (it rhymes in Polish). According to Poles, these selfish absentee kings are the culprits for Poland's eventual decline.

Walk back out toward the Royal Way, stopping at the statue you passed earlier. In 1995, the square was again re-named—this time for **Józef Piłsudski,** the guy with the big walrus moustache.

Piłsudski (1867–1935) forced out the Russian Bolsheviks from Poland in 1920 in the so-called Miracle on the Vistula. Piłsudski is credited with creating a once-again-independent Poland after over a century of foreign oppression, and he essentially ran Poland after World War I. Of course, under the communists, Piłsudski was swept under the rug, but today he's enjoying a renaissance as Poland's favorite prototype anti-communist hero (his name adorns streets, squares, and bushy-mustachioed monuments all over the country).

Return to Hotel Bristol, turn left, and continue your Royal Way walk. Next door to the hotel, you'll see the huge **Radziwiłł Palace.** The Warsaw Pact was signed here in 1955, officially uniting the Soviet satellite states in a military alliance against NATO. This building also serves as the Polish White House, with the offices of Poland's figurehead president, Lech Kaczyński. For more on Kaczyński—and his identical twin brother Jarosław, Poland's prime minister—see "Those Two Who Would Lead Poland" on page 209.

Beyond Radziwiłł Palace, you'll reach a statue (on a pillar) of **Adam Mickiewicz,** Poland's national poet. Polish high school students have a big formal ball (like a prom) 100 days before graduation. After the ball, if students come here and hop around the statue on one leg, it's supposed to bring them good luck on their finals. Mickiewicz, for his part, looks like he's suffering from a heart attack—perhaps in response to the impressively ugly National Theater and Opera a block in front of him.

Continue to the end of the Royal Way, marked by the big pink palace. For a scenic finale to your Royal Way stroll, climb the 150 steps of the view tower by **St. Anne's Church** (3 zł, sporadic hours but generally open daily 10:00–18:00, until 20:00 in summer, on the right just before Castle Square). You'll be rewarded with a great view of the Old Town, river, and Warsaw's skyline.

From St. Anne's Church, it's just another block—past inviting art galleries and restaurants—to the Castle Square, the TI, and the start of the Old Town.

SIGHTS

The Old Town

In 1945, not a building remained standing in Warsaw's "Old" Town (Stare Miasto). Everything you see is rebuilt, mostly finished by 1956. Some think the Old Town feels artificial and phony, in a Disney World kind of way. For others, the painstaking postwar reconstruction just feels right, with Old World squares and lanes charming enough to give Kraków a run for its money. Before 1989, stifled by communist repression and choking on smog, the Old

Town was an empty husk of its historic self. But now, the market stalls have returned, and the locals and tourists are out strolling.

These sights are listed in order from south to north, beginning at the Castle Square and ending at the entrance to the New Town. For the best route from the Central Train Station to the Old Town, see the "Royal Way" self-guided walk, above.

▲**Castle Square (Plac Zamkowy)**—This lively square is dominated by the big, pink Royal Castle, the historic heart of Warsaw's political power.

After the second great Polish dynasty—the Jagiellonians—died off in 1572, the Republic of Nobles (about 10 percent of the population) elected various foreign kings to their throne. The guy on the 72-foot-tall **pillar** is Sigismund III, the first Polish king from the Swedish Waza family. In 1596, he relocated the capital from Kraków to Warsaw. This move made sense, since Warsaw was closer to the center of 16th-century Poland (which had expanded to the east), and because the city had been gaining political importance as the meeting point of the Sejm, or parliament of nobles, over the preceding 30 years. Along the right side of the castle, notice the two previous versions of this pillar lying on a lawn. The first one, from 1644, was falling apart and had to be replaced in 1887 by a new one made of granite. In 1944, a Nazi tank broke this second pillar—a symbolic piece of Polish heritage—into the four pieces (still pockmarked with bullet holes) that you see here today. As Poland rebuilt, its citizens put Sigismund III back on his pillar.

Across the square from the castle, you'll see the partially reconstructed defensive wall. This rampart once enclosed the entire Old Town. Situated at the crossroads of Eastern Europe, Warsaw—like all of Poland—has seen invasion from all sides.

Explore the café-lined lanes that branch downhill off Castle Square. Street signs (from the early 1950s) indicate the year that each street was originally built.

The first street leading off the square is **ulica Piwna** ("Beer Street"), where you'll find **St. Martin's Church** (Kościół Św. Martina, on the left). Run by Franciscan nuns, this church has a simple, modern interior. Notice the partly destroyed crucifix—all that survived World War II. Across the street and closer to Castle Square, admire the carefully carved doorway of Restauracja pod Gołębiami ("Under Doves")—dedicated to the memory of an old woman who fed birds amidst the Old Town rubble after World War II.

Back on the Castle Square, find the white **plaque** in the middle of the second block (by plac Zamkowy 15/19). It explains that 50 Poles were executed by Nazis on this spot on September 2, 1944. You'll see plaques like this all over the Old Town, each one commemorating victims or opponents of the Nazis. Notice the brick planter under the plaque; it's often filled with fresh flowers to honor the victims.

▲**Royal Castle (Zamek Królewski)**—There has been a castle here since the Mazovian dukes built a wooden version in the 14th cen-

tury. It has shifted shape with the tenor of the times, being rebuilt and remodeled by many different kings. When Warsaw became the capital in 1596, this massive building was used both as the king's residence and as the meeting place of the parliament (Sejm). After it was destroyed in World War II, rebuilding began again in the 1950s and was not completed until the 1970s.

Of all of Warsaw's many castles, this one is most interesting to tour—which isn't saying much. While the exterior is entirely reconstructed, many of the furnishings are original (hidden away when it became clear the city would be demolished). Each room is well-described in English.

The castle makes a great Polish history textbook. In fact, you'll likely see grade-school classes sitting cross-legged on the floors. Watching the teachers quizzing eager young history buffs, you can only imagine what it's like to be a young Pole, with such a tumultuous recent history.

Warning: The information on touring the castle—the castle opening times, tour routes, and castle layout—is maddeningly sporadic. Things frequently change depending on special events, temporary exhibitions, the direction the wind is blowing, and the inexplicable whims of palace administrators.

Touring the Castle: The castle has various parts, each with separate tickets. For a basic visit, you'll choose between two completely different tour routes: **Route I** (10 zł, year-round Tue–Sat 10:00–16:00, mid-April–Sept also open Mon 11:00–16:00); or **Route II,** which is more expensive since it includes a mandatory tour with a Polish-speaking guide (18 zł, mid-April–Sept Tue–Sat 10:00–18:00, Mon 11:00–18:00; Oct–mid-April Tue–Sat 10:00–16:00, closed Mon). On Sundays, a special **Sunday Route** includes the "greatest hits" of both routes (generally free, mid-April–Sept 11:00–18:00, Oct–mid-April 11:00–16:00). The castle may be free one day a week (likely Mon, maybe Sun).

Route I—including the Senators' Chamber and the Matejko rooms—is better. The last entry for either route is one hour before closing.

There's also a **permanent exhibition** that includes decorative arts (17th and 18th centuries), a porcelain gallery, a coin collection, some paintings (including a pair of Rembrandts), and various exhibits of interest only to Polish historians (10 zł, Tue–Sat 10:00–16:00, mid-April–Sept also open Mon 11:00–16:00, always closed Sun). Rounding out the attractions is a series of temporary exhibitions. The palace is at Plac Zamkowy 4 (tel. 022-657-2170, www.zamek-krolewski.com.pl). A public WC is on the courtyard just around the corner of the castle.

Route I Highlights: The **Parliament Chambers** are a reminder that this "castle" wasn't just the king's house, but also the meeting place of the legislature. The grand **Senators' Chamber,** with the king's throne, is surrounded by different coats of arms. Each one represents a region that was part of Poland during its Golden Age, back when it was united with Lithuania and its territory stretched from the Baltic to the Black Sea. In this room, Poland adopted its 1791 constitution. It was the first in Europe, written soon after America's and just months before France's. And, like the Constitution of the United States, it was very progressive, based on the ideals of the Enlightenment. But when the final partitions followed in 1793 and 1795, Poland was divided between neighboring powers and disappeared from the map until 1918—so the constitution was never really put into action. The next room features paintings by **Jan Matejko** that capture the excitement surrounding the adoption of this ill-fated constitution (for more on Matejko, see page 307).

Route II Highlights: Climb the stairs and wander through the ornate rooms. You'll see two different types of royal apartments: public state rooms and private chambers. In the **Throne Room,** note the crowned eagle, the symbol of Poland, decorating the banner behind the throne. The Soviets didn't allow anything royal or aristocratic, so postwar restorations came with crown-less eagles. Only after 1989 were the crowns replaced (in the case of this banner, sewn on). A few rooms later is the **Canaletto Room,** filled with canvases of late-18th-century Warsaw painted in exquisite detail by this talented artist. These paintings came in handy when the city needed to be rebuilt. (This Canaletto, also known for his panoramas of Dresden, was the nephew of another artist with the same nickname, famous for painting Venice's canals.) Continue wandering through the sumptuous halls, saying hello to US Constitution co-signer Ben Franklin (by the door in the Green Room) and gaping at the Marble Room (with portraits of Polish kings around the ceiling—find your favorite).

• *After you finish touring the castle and you're ready to resume exploring the Old Town, turn left at the end of the square onto...*

St. John's Street (Świętojańska)—On the plaque under the street name sign, you can guess what the dates mean, even if you don't speak Polish: This building was constructed 1433–1478, destroyed in 1944, and rebuilt 1950–1953.

• *Partway down the street on the right, you'll come to the big brick...*

Cathedral of St. John the Baptist (Katedra Św. Jana Chrzciciela)—This cathedral-basilica is the oldest (1339) and most important church in Warsaw. Poland's constitution was consecrated here on May 3, 1791. Much later, this church became the final battleground of the 1944 Warsaw Uprising—when a Nazi tank (appropriately named *Goliath*) drove into the church and intentionally exploded, massacring the rebels. You can still see part of that tank's tread hanging on the outside wall of the church (through the passage on the right side, near the end of the church).

Despite the church's historical significance, its interior is pretty dull (free, open long hours daily, closed 13:00–15:00 and during services). Look for the crucifix ornamented with real human hair (chapel left of high altar). The high altar holds a copy of the Black Madonna—proclaimed "everlasting queen of Poland" after a victory over the Swedes in the 17th century. The original Black Madonna is in Częstochowa (125 miles south of Warsaw)—a mecca for Slavic Catholics, who visit in droves in hopes of a miracle.

• *Continue up the street and enter Warsaw's grand...*

▲▲**Old Town Market Square (Rynek Starego Miasta)**—Seventy years ago, this was one of the most happening spots in Central Europe. Sixty years ago, it was rubble. And today, like a phoenix rising from the ashes, it reminds residents and tourists alike of the prewar glory of the Polish capital.

Go to the **mermaid fountain** in the middle of the square. The mermaid is an important symbol in Warsaw—you'll see her

everywhere. Legend has it that a mermaid *(syrenka)* lived in the Vistula River and protected the townspeople. While this siren supposedly serenaded the town, Varsovians like her more for her strength (hence the sword). In fact, the woman who modeled for this sculpture, Krystyna Krahelska, served as a paramedic for the Polish Home Army during the Warsaw Uprising (code name: "Danuta"). On the second day of the fighting, she was shot in the chest and died, becoming a martyr for the Polish people.

Each of the square's four sides is named for a prominent 18th-century Varsovian: Kołłątaj, Dekert, Barss, and Zakrzewski. These men served as "Presidents" of Warsaw (more or less the mayor), and Kołłątaj was also a framer of Poland's 1791 constitution. Take some time to explore the square. Enjoy the colorful architecture. Notice that many of the buildings were intentionally built to lean out into the square—to simulate the old-age wear and tear of the original buildings.

• *On the Dekert (north) side of the square is the...*

Warsaw Historical Museum (Muzeum Historyczne Warszawy)—This labyrinthine museum rambles through several reconstructed buildings fronting the Old Town Market Square. With limited descriptions in English, the museum is difficult to appreciate. You'll twist your way through room after room of historical bric-a-brac. The exhibits near the end—photos of the Old Town before and immediately after its WWII destruction—are the most interesting (6 zł, free entry but no movie on Sun, open Tue and Thu 11:00–18:00, Wed and Fri 10:00–15:30, Sat–Sun 10:30–16:30, closed Mon, last entry 45 min before closing, Rynek Starego Miasta 28/42, tel. 022-635-1625).

The museum's saving grace is its excellent 20-minute **film** in English, worth ▲▲ and the price of admission alone; unfortunately, it runs only Tuesday through Saturday at 12:00. With somber narration and black-and-white scenes from before, during, and after the wartime devastation, this film is best appreciated after you've had a chance to see some of today's Warsaw (especially along the Royal Way). The movie ends with, "They say that there are no miracles. Then what is this city on the Vistula?" Emotionally drained, you can only respond, "Amen."

• *Leave the square on Nowomiejska (at the mermaid's 2 o'clock, by the second-story niche sculpture of St. Anne). After a block, you'll reach the...*

Barbican (Barbakan)—This defensive gate of the Old Town, similar to Kraków's, protected the medieval city from invaders. Just outside the gate, you may be accosted by a pair of **village idiots,** dressed as medieval executioners. These unemployed (but undeniably creative) punks, in a sort of aggressive, costumed panhandling, will steer you to their "executioner's block" and playfully threaten to liberate your head from your body until you give them some pocket change. Actually, these guys speak English, and if you talk to them, they'll explain that at least two buildings within the Old Town actually were used for executions once upon a time.

• *Once you've crossed through the Barbican and have been granted a stay of execution, you're officially in Warsaw's...*

New Town (Nowe Miasto)—This 15th-century neighborhood is "new" in name only: It was the first part of Warsaw to spring up outside of the city walls (and therefore slightly newer than the Old Town). The New Town is a fun place to wander: Only a little less charming than the Old Town, but with a more real-life feel—like people live and work here. It also has some good Polish restaurants that are cheaper than the Old Town options (see "Eating," page 318). Its centerpiece is the **New Town Square** (Rynek Nowego Miasta), watched over by the distinctive green dome of St. Kazimierz Church.

Scientists will want to pay homage at the museum for Warsaw native **Marie Skłodowska-Curie** (at her birthplace, ulica Freta 16; overpriced at 8 zł, Mon–Sat 10:00–16:00, Sun 10:00–14:00). This Nobel Prize winner was the world's first radiologist—discovering both radium and polonium (named for her native land) with her husband, Pierre Curie. Since she lived at a time when Warsaw was controlled by oppressive Russia, she conducted her studies in France. The museum—with photos, furniture, artifacts, and a paucity of English information—is a bit of a snoozer, best left to true fans.

From the New Town to Castle Square: You can backtrack the way you came, or, to get a look at Warsaw's back streets, consider this route from the big, round Barbican gate (where the New Town meets the Old): Go back through the Barbican and over the little bridge, turn right, and walk along the houses that line the inside of the wall. You'll pass a leafy garden courtyard on the left—a reminder that people actually live in the tourist zone within the Old Town walls. Just beyond the garden on the right, look for the carpet-beating rack, used to clean rugs (these are common fixtures in people's backyards). Go left into the square called Szeroki Dunaj ("Wide Danube") and look for another mermaid (over the Thai restaurant). Continue through the square and turn right at Wąski Dunaj ("Narrow Danube"). After about 100 yards, you pass the city wall. Just to the right (outside the wall), you'll see the monument to the **Little Upriser** of 1944, an imp wearing a grown-up's helmet and too-big boots, and carrying a machine gun. Children—and especially Scouts (Harcerze)—played a key role in the resistance against the Nazis. Their job was mainly carrying messages and propaganda.

Now continue around the wall (the upper, inner part is more pleasant)—admiring more public art—back to Castle Square.

Near Nowy Świat

These sights are near Nowy Świat, within a few blocks of the Central Train Station.

Palace of Culture and Science (Pałac Kultury i Nauki, or PKiN)—This massive skyscraper, dating from the early 1950s, is Poland's tallest building (760 feet). It was a "gift" from Stalin

Near Warsaw's Central Station

1. Novotel
2. Royal Route Residence
3. Hotel Harenda
4. Hotel Gromada
5. Boutique B&B
6. Hotel Mazowiecki
7. Oki Doki Hostel
8. Szkolne Schronisko Hostel
9. Living Room Restaurant
10. Sense Restaurant
11. Sandwicz Milk Bar
12. Bar Rest. Wegetariańska Zielony Świat ("Greenland")
13. A. Blikle Bakery
14. E. Wedel Pijalnia Czekolady (Chocolate Shop)
15. Observation Deck Entrance
16. Bus #175 to Royal Way

that the people of Warsaw couldn't refuse. Varsovians call it "Stalin's Penis" (using cruder terminology than that). There were seven such "Stalin Gothic" erections in Moscow. Because it was to be "Soviet in substance, Polish in style," Soviet architects toured Poland to absorb local culture before starting the project. Since the end of communism, the younger generation doesn't mind the structure so much—and some even admit to liking it. The clock was added in 1999 as part of the millennium celebrations.

Everything about the Pałac is big. It's designed to show off the strong, grand-scale Soviet aesthetic and architectural skill. The Pałac contains various theaters (the Culture), museums of evolution and technology (the Science), a congress hall, a multiplex (showing current movies), an observation deck, and lots of office space (including UNICEF's Polish headquarters). With all of this Culture and Science under one roof, it's a shame that none of it makes for worthwhile sightseeing. While the interior is highly skippable, viewing the building from the outside is a quintessential Warsaw experience, worth ▲▲.

If you're killing time between trains, you could zip up to the observation deck (generally 10–20 zł, price varies based on special exhibitions, daily June–Sept 9:00–20:00, Oct–May 9:00–18:00, viewing terrace often open—and more expensive—until 23:45 Fri–Sat in summer, enter through main door on east side of Pałac—opposite from train station, tel. 022-656-7600, www.pkin.pl). Better yet, snap a photo from down below and save your money, since the view's a letdown. You can hardly see the Old Town, and Warsaw's most prominent big building—the Pałac itself—is missing.

▲▲**National Museum (Muzeum Narodowe)**—This museum, while short on big-name pieces, interests art-lovers and offers a fine introduction to some talented Polish artists unknown outside their home country (12 zł, more for temporary exhibits, permanent collection free on Sat, open Tue–Sun 10:00–16:00, Thu until 18:00, closed Mon, 1 block east of Nowy Świat at aleja Jerozolimskie 3, tel. 022-629-3093, www.mnw.art.pl).

On the ground floor are exhibits of ancient art (from Egyptian and Greek pieces to works by early Polish tribes), as well as room upon room of medieval altarpieces and crucifixes (including some of the most graphic I've seen). The upper floors have temporary exhibits and collections of Polish and European decorative arts and European paintings. But the reason we're here is the Gallery

Jan Matejko
(1838–1893)

Jan Matejko (yawn mah-TAY-koh) is Poland's most important painter, period. In the late 19th century, the nation of Poland had been dissolved by foreign powers, and Polish artists struggled to make sense of their people's place in the world. Rabble-rousing Romanticism seemed to have failed (inspiring many brutally suppressed uprisings), so Polish artists and writers turned their attention to educating the people about their history, with the goal of keeping the Polish traditions alive.

Matejko was at the forefront of this so-called "positivist" movement. Matejko saw what the tides of history had done to Poland, and was determined to make sure his countrymen learned from it. He painted two types of works: huge, grand-scale epics depicting monumental events in Polish history; and small, intimate portraits of prominent Poles. Polish schoolchildren study history from books with paintings of virtually every single Polish king—all painted by the incredibly prolific Matejko.

Matejko is admired not for his technical mastery (he's an unexceptional painter), but for the emotion behind—and inspired by—his works. Matejko's paintings are utilitarian, straightforward, and dramatic enough to stir the patriot in any Pole. The intense focus on history by Matejko and other positivists is one big reason why today's Poles are still so in touch with their heritage.

You'll see Matejko's works in Warsaw's National Museum and Royal Castle, as well as in Kraków's Gallery of 19th-Century Polish Art (above the Cloth Hall). You can also visit his former residence in Kraków.

of Polish Painting, one floor up. Focus on the two most important eras, at opposite ends of the building.

First, find the **Jan Matejko** room. From the lobby, take the left staircase up one level, then walk along the railing and go in the door on the left. Walk straight back (bearing right through the door) to the very back of this wing, where you'll find Matejko hiding (if you can't find him, ask the guards, "mah-TAY-koh?"). On the way, you'll pass through a whole room of Napoleon portraits. The Poles loved Napoleon, who bravely marched on Russia in an era when this part of Poland was occupied and oppressed by the Russians...sadly, not for the last time.

The Matejko room is dominated by the enormous *Battle of Grunwald*. This epic painting commemorates one of Poland's highwater marks—the dramatic victory of a Polish-Lithuanian army over the Teutonic Knights, who had been terrorizing northern Poland for decades (for more on the Teutonic Knights, see page 368). On July 15, 1410, some 40,000 Poles and Lithuanians (led by the sword-waving Lithuanian in red, Grand Duke Vytautas) faced off against 27,000 Teutonic Knights (under their Grand Master, in white) in one of the medieval world's bloodiest battles. Matejko plops us right in the thick of the battle's chaos, painting life-size figures and framing off a 32-foot-long slice of the actual two-mile battle line.

In the center of the painting, the Teutonic Grand Master is about to become a shish kebab. In red, Duke Vytautas leads the final charge. And waaaay up on a hill (in the upper right-hand corner, wearing a silver knight's suit) is Władysław Jagiełło, the first king of the Jagiellonian dynasty...ensuring his bloodline will survive another 150 years.

Matejko spent three years covering this 450-square-foot canvas in paint. The canvas was specially made in a single seamless piece. At the unveiling, this was such a popular work that there were almost as many fans as there are figures in the painting.

From Poland's high point in the *Battle of Grunwald*, turn to the canvas immediately to the left, *Stańczyk after the Loss of Smolensk*, to see how Poland's fortunes shifted drastically a century later. This smaller, more intimate portrait by Matejko depicts a popular Polish figure: the court jester Stańczyk, who's smarter than the king, but not allowed to say so. This complex character, representing the national conscience, is a favorite symbol of Matejko's. Stańczyk slumps in gloom. He's just read the news (on the table beside him) that the city of Smolensk has fallen to the Russians after a three-year siege (1512–1514). The jester had tried to warn the king to send more troops, but the king was too busy partying (behind the curtain). The painter Matejko—who may have used his own features for Stańczyk's face—also blamed the nobles of his own day for fiddling while Poland was partitioned.

Other Matejko paintings include one depicting the tragic couple of the last Jagiellonian king, Stanisław August Poniatowski, and his wife, Barbara—whom the king loved deeply, even though she couldn't bear him an heir. (In the next room, see the painful end to their sad tale: Barbara on her deathbed.)

Take a look at the **Młoda Polska** ("Young Poland") collection, featuring paintings from Poland's version of Art Nouveau (see page 231). It's in the same position on the other side of the building: From the lobby, take the right staircase up, then go in the right-hand door and work your way all the way to the back. In addition to a room of works by movement headliner Stanisław Wyspiański, you'll see the hypnotic *Strange Garden* by Józef Mehoffer, as well as several works by Jacek Malczewski. Malczewski's paintings depict the goateed, close-cropped artist in a variety of different semi-surrealistic, Polish countryside contexts. There's also a room of canvases by the only prominent female Polish painter, Olga Boznańska (past the Wyspiański room)—with a softer and more impressionistic touch than her male Młoda Polska counterparts.

▲**Chopin Museum (Muzeum Fryderyka Chopina)**—The reconstructed Ostrogski Castle houses this modest museum honoring Poland's most famous composer. Everything of interest is upstairs: manuscripts, letters, and original handwritten compositions. You'll also see Chopin's last piano, which he used for composing during the final two years of his life (1848–1849). Nearby, flip through the guest book. Chopin's music is popular in Japan, and Japanese music-lovers flock here, almost as a pilgrimage. In the next room, find Chopin's bronze death mask and admire his distinctively Polish nose, shaped like an eagle's beak (10 zł; May–Sept Mon, Wed, and Fri 10:00–17:00, Thu 12:00–18:00, Sat–Sun 10:00–14:00, closed Tue; Oct–April Mon–Wed and Fri–Sat 10:00–14:00, Thu 12:00–18:00, closed Sun; 3 blocks east of Nowy Świat at ulica Okólnik 1, tel. 022-827-5473).

The top floor has a **concert hall,** open only for special concerts. If you're in town for one, go. There's nothing like hearing Chopin's music fill this fine mansion, passionately played by a teary-eyed Pole who really feels the music (call museum to ask for concert schedule).

The **Ostrogski Castle** was destroyed down to the brick cellar in World War II. A plaque by the staircase around back notes that it was "voluntarily reconstructed" by the communists in 1970 "to celebrate the 25th anniversary of the People's Republic of Poland." In the courtyard behind is a statue of a golden duck *(złota kaczka),* a mythical creature that supposedly lived in the castle's cellar. An often-repeated but strangely anticlimactic parable explains that this duck gave a cobbler's apprentice a huge amount of money, telling him that if he frittered it away by the end of the day, he'd win great rewards. The boy gave some to a beggar, which didn't fit the duck's idea of "frittering"—but the boy found happiness anyway.

Chopin's birth house is in Żelazowa Wola, 34 miles from Warsaw. It's tourable, but not worth the trek for anyone but the most rabid Chopin fan.

South of the Center

▲**Łazienki Park (Park Łazienkowski)**—This huge, idyllic park is where Varsovians go to play. The park is sprinkled with fun Neoclassical buildings, strutting peacocks, and young Poles in love. It was built by Poland's very last king (before the final partition), Stanisław August Poniatowski, to serve as his summer residence and provide a place for his citizens to relax.

On the edge of the park (along Belwederska) is a **monument to Fryderyk Chopin**. The monument, in a rose garden, is flanked by platforms, where free summer piano concerts are given weekly (generally Sun at 12:00 and 16:00). The statue (from 1926) shows Chopin sitting under a wind-blown willow tree. While he spent his last 20 years and wrote most of his best-known music in France, his inspiration came from wind blowing through the willow trees of his native land, Poland. The Nazis melted the statue down for its metal. Today's copy was recast after World War II. Savor this spot; it's great in summer, with roses wildly in bloom, and in autumn, when the trees provide a golden backdrop for the black, romantic statue.

Venture to the center of the park, where (after a 10-min hike) you'll find King Poniatowski's striking **Palace on the Water** (Pałac na Wodzie)—literally built in the middle of a river. Nearby, you'll spot a clever amphitheater with seating on the riverbank and the stage on an island. The king was a real man of the Enlightenment, hosting weekly dinners here for artists and intellectuals. But Poland's kings are long gone, and proud peacocks now rule this roost.

Getting There: The park is just south of the city center on the Royal Way. Buses #116, #180, and #195 run from Castle Square in the Old Town along the Royal Way directly to the park (get off at the stop called Łazienki Królewskie, by Belweder Palace—you'll see Chopin squinting through the trees on your left). Maps at park entrances locate the Chopin monument, Palace on the Water, and other park attractions.

Jewish Warsaw

After centuries of living peacefully in Poland, Warsaw's Jews suffered terribly at the hands of the Nazis (see sidebar). You can visit several sights in Warsaw that commemorate those who were murdered, and those who fought back. Because the Nazis leveled the ghetto, there is literally nothing left except the street plan and the heroic spirit of its former residents.

Ghetto Walking Tour—For a quick walking tour of the former ghetto site, begin at **Ghetto Heroes Square** (plac Bohaterow Getta). To get here from the Old Town you can hop a taxi (10 zł), take a bus (to Nalewki stop, bus #180 is particularly useful), or walk (go through Barbican gate 2 blocks into New Town, turn left on Świętojerska, and walk straight 10 min—passing the new

Warsaw's Jews and the Ghetto Uprising

From the Middle Ages until World War II, Poland was a safe haven for Europe's Jews. While other kings were imprisoning and deporting Jews in the 14th century, the progressive king Kazimierz the Great welcomed Jews into Poland, even granting them special privileges (see page 228).

By the 1930s, there were more than 380,000 Jews in Warsaw—nearly a third of the population (and the largest concentration of Jews in the world). The Nazis arrived in 1939. Within a year, they had pushed all of Warsaw's Jews into one neighborhood and surrounded it with a wall, creating a miserably overcrowded ghetto (crammed full of half a million people, including many from nearby towns). Over the next year, the Nazis brought in more Jews from throughout Poland, and the number grew by a million.

By the summer of 1942, more than a quarter of the Jews in the ghetto had already died of disease, murder, or suicide. The Nazis started moving Warsaw's Jews (at the rate of 5,000 a day) into what they claimed were "resettlement camps." Most of these people were actually murdered at Treblinka or Auschwitz. After hundreds of thousands of Jews had been taken to concentration camps, the waning population—now about 60,000—began to get word from concentration camp escapees about what was actually going on there. Spurred by this knowledge, Warsaw's surviving Jews staged a dramatic uprising.

On April 19, 1943, the Jews attacked Nazi strongholds and had some initial success—but within a month, the Nazis crushed the Ghetto Uprising. The ghetto's residents and structures were "liquidated." About 300 of Warsaw's Jews survived, thanks in part to a sort of "underground railroad" of courageous Varsovians.

Warsaw's Jewish sights are moving, but even more so if you know some of their stories. You may have heard of **Władysław Szpilman,** a Jewish concert pianist who survived the war with the help of Jews, Poles, and even a Nazi officer. Szpilman's life story was turned into the highly acclaimed, Oscar-winning 2002 film *The Pianist,* which powerfully depicts events in Warsaw during World War II.

Less familiar to non-Poles—but equally affecting—is the story of Henryk Goldszmit, better known by his pen name, **Janusz Korczak.** Korczak wrote imaginative children's books that are still enormously popular among Poles. He worked at an orphanage in the Warsaw ghetto. When his orphans were sent off to concentration camps, the Nazis offered the famous author a chance at freedom. Korczak turned them down, and chose to die at Treblinka with his children.

green-glass Supreme Court building—until you reach a grassy park on Zamenhofa Street). The square is in the heart of what was the Jewish ghetto—now surrounded by bland Soviet-style apartment blocks. After the Uprising, the entire ghetto was reduced to dust by the Nazis—leaving the communists to rebuild to their own specifications. The district is called Muranów ("Rebuilt") today.

The **monument** in the middle of the square commemorates those who fought and died "for the dignity and freedom of the Jewish Nation, for a free Poland, and for the liberation of humankind." The big park across the street is the future site of the Museum of the History of Polish Jews. It's been in the works for years, with its progress slowed by controversy over exactly what form the museum will take (for the latest, see www.jewishmuseum.org.pl).

Facing the monument, head left (with the park on your left) up Zamenhofa—which, like many streets in this neighborhood, is named for a hero of the Ghetto Uprising. From the monument, you'll follow a series of three-foot-tall black stone monuments to Uprising heroes—the **Path of Remembrance.** Like Stations of the Cross, each recounts an event of the uprising. Every April 19th (the day the Uprising began), huge crowds follow this path. In a block, at the corner of Miła (partly obscured by some bushes), you'll find a **bunker** where organizers of the Uprising hid out (and where they committed suicide when the Nazis discovered them on May 8, 1943).

Continue following the black stone monuments up Zamenhofa (which becomes Dubois), then turn left at the corner and, later on that same block, cross busy Stawki street. A long block up Stawki and on the right, you'll see the **Umschlagplatz** monument—shaped like a cattle car. That's German for "transfer place," and it marks the spot where the Nazis brought Jewish families to prepare them to be loaded onto trains bound for Treblinka or Auschwitz (a harrowing scene vividly depicted in *The Pianist*). In the walls of the monument are inscribed the first names of some of the victims.

Jewish Historical Institute of Poland (Żydowski Instytut Historyczny)—For more in-depth information about Warsaw's Jewish community, including the Ghetto Uprising, visit this museum housed in the former Jewish Library building. The main floor displays well-described old photos. The 37-minute movie about life and death in the ghetto—played in English upon request—is graphic and powerful. Upstairs, you'll find more on Jewish art, culture, and temporary exhibits (10 zł, Mon–Wed and Fri 9:00–16:00, Thu 11:00–18:00, closed Sat–Sun, ulica Tłomackie

3/5, tel. 022-827-9221, www.jewishinstitute.org.pl).

The Peugeot building next door—appropriately and simply dubbed "the blue tower" by locals—was built on the former site of Warsaw's biggest synagogue, destroyed by the Nazis as a victorious final kick.

The Warsaw Uprising

While the 1944 Warsaw Uprising (see sidebar on page 314) is a recurring theme in virtually all Warsaw sightseeing, two sights in particular—one a monument, the other a museum—are worth a visit for anyone with a special interest. Neither is right on the main tourist trail; the monument is closer to the sightseeing action, while the museum is a tram or taxi ride away.

Warsaw Uprising Monument—The most central sight relating to the Warsaw Uprising is the monument at plac Krasińskich (intersection of ulica Długa and Miodowa, a few blocks northwest of the New Town). Larger-than-life soldiers and civilians race for the sewers in a desperate attempt to flee the Nazis. Just behind the monument is the rusting copper facade of Poland's Supreme Court.

▲Warsaw Uprising Museum (Muzeum Powstania Warszawskiego)—This new museum opened on August 1, 2004—the 60th anniversary of the Warsaw Uprising. Thorough, well-presented, and packed with Polish field-trip groups, the museum celebrates the heroes of the Uprising. The location is inconvenient (a 15-min tram ride west of Central Train Station), and probably not worth the trip for those with a casual interest. But for history buffs, it's Warsaw's single best museum.

The museum has several parts. The beautifully restored 1905 red-brick building, once an electrical plant, houses the permanent exhibition. The more recent gray addition behind it displays temporary exhibitions. And the park stretching around the back of the complex also has some moving sights.

The high-tech **main exhibit** occupies three floors. It chronologically tells the story of the Uprising, with a keen focus on military history. Everything is well-described in English; also look for the printed pages of English information, and collect the clever calendar pages that trace the events of the two-month Uprising day by day. The ground floor focuses on Germany's invasion and occupation of Poland. Then you'll take the elevator up to the top floor, which features exhibits on the Uprising itself. Finally you'll climb through a simulated sewer—just as many Home Army soldiers and civilians did to evade the Germans—and climb stairs down into an exhibit on the Uprising's aftermath. A chilling section at the end describes how Warsaw became a "city of graves," with burial mounds and makeshift crosses scattered everywhere.

The Warsaw Uprising

By the summer of 1944, it was becoming clear that the Nazis' days in Warsaw were numbered. The Red Army drew near, and by late July, Soviet tanks were within 25 miles of downtown Warsaw.

The Varsovians could have simply waited for the Soviets to cross the river and force the Nazis out. But they knew that Soviet "liberation" would also mean an end to Polish independence. The Polish Home Army numbered 400,000—30,000 of them in Warsaw alone—and was the biggest underground army in military history. The uprisers wanted Poland to control its own fate, and they took matters into their own hands. The resistance's symbol was an anchor made up of a P atop a W (which stands for *Polska Walcząca*, or "Poland Fighting"—you'll see this icon all around town). Over time, the Home Army had established an extensive network of underground tunnels and sewers, which allowed them to deliver messages and move around the city without drawing the Nazis' attention. These tunnels gave the Home Army the element of surprise.

On August 1, 30,000 Polish resistance fighters launched an attack on their Nazi oppressors. They poured out of the sewers and caught the Nazis off guard, initially having great success.

But the Nazis regrouped quickly, and within a few days, they had retaken several areas of the city—murdering tens of thousands of innocent civilians as they went. In one notorious incident, some 5,500 Polish soldiers and 6,000 civilians who were surrounded by Nazis in the Old Town were forced to flee through the sewers; many drowned or were shot. (This scene is depicted in the Warsaw Uprising Monument on plac Krasińskich—see page 313.)

Just two months after it had started, the Warsaw Uprising was over. The Home Army called a cease-fire. About 18,000 Polish uprisers had been killed, along with nearly 200,000 innocent civilians. An infuriated Hitler ordered that the city be destroyed—which it was, systematically, block by block, until virtually nothing remained.

Through all of this, the Soviets stood still, watched, and waited. When the smoke cleared and the Nazis left, the Red Army marched in and claimed the wasteland that was once called Warsaw. After the war, General Dwight D. Eisenhower said that the scale of destruction here was the worst he'd ever seen.

Depending on whom you talk to, the desperate uprising of Warsaw was incredibly brave, stupid, or both. As for the Poles, they remain fiercely proud of their struggle for freedom. The city of Warsaw has recently commemorated this act of bravery with the new Warsaw Uprising Museum.

The **park** features several thought-provoking sights. Around the right side, photographs along the wall show the history of the museum building. Also find the reconstructed German bunker, used by the Nazis during the occupation. Finally, along the back is the Wall of Memory, a Vietnam Wall–type monument to soldiers of the Polish Home Army who were killed in action. You'll see their rank and name, followed by their codename, in quotes. The Home Army observed a strict policy of anonymity, forbidding members from calling each other anything but their codenames. The bell in the middle is dedicated to the commander of the uprising, Antoni Chruściel (codename "Monter").

The museum also has an observation deck (in the temporary exhibits building) and a café with drinks and light snacks, decorated in prewar Warsaw style (museum entry-4 zł; Mon, Wed, and Fri 8:00–18:00, Thu 8:00–20:00, Sat–Sun 10:00–18:00, closed Tue; on the west edge of downtown at ulica Przyokopowa 28, tel. 022-626-9506, www.1944.pl). Take tram #24 from the Central Train Station or from across the street from the National Museum (near the start of Nowy Świat). Get off at the stop called Muzeum Powstania Warszawskiego, cross the tracks and the busy street, walk straight one short block up Grzybowska, and take a left on Przyokopowa. The museum is the big, red-brick building on the left.

SLEEPING

The accommodations scene in central Warsaw is difficult, with an abundance of overpriced business hotels and cheap hostel-type accommodations, but little in between. Desk clerks do their best to reinforce the communist-era stereotype of grouchy, incompetent service. Thankfully, there are a few happy exceptions—such as Boutique B&B, easily the best option in Warsaw. Since this is a convention town, prices can go up during convention times and way down on weekends. For locations, see the maps on pages 293 and 305.

$$$ Duval Apartments, named for a French woman who supposedly had an affair with the Polish king in this building, offers four beautifully appointed rooms above a restaurant a few steps off the square in the Old Town. Each one has a different theme: traditional Polish, Japanese, glass, retro. There's no reception, and the rooms aren't affiliated with the restaurant, so you'll have to arrange a meeting time when you reserve (Db-€100, lots of stairs with no elevator, Nowomiejska 10, tel. & fax 022-831-9104, mobile 0608-679-346, www.duval.net.pl, duval@duval.net.pl).

$$$ Novotel, with 734 rooms across the street from the Palace of Culture and Science, overlooks Poland's busiest intersection. Recently renovated inside and out, this is a good option for a big,

Sleep Code

(3 zł = about $1, €1 = about $1.20, country code: 48)
S = Single, **D** = Double/Twin, **T** = Triple, **Q** = Quad, **b** = bathroom,
s = shower only. Unless otherwise noted, English is spoken,
breakfast is included, and credit cards are accepted.

To help you sort easily through these listings, I've divided
the rooms into three categories, based on the price for a standard double room with bath:

$$$ Higher Priced—Most rooms 390 zł (€100) or more.
$$ Moderately Priced—Most rooms between 270–390 zł
(€70–100).
$ Lower Priced—Most rooms 270 zł (€70) or less.

downtown hotel (official rate is Sb/Db-€160, in slow times—especially weekends—you may pay €100–120, best deals are online, breakfast-€15, non-smoking rooms, elevator, ulica Nowogrodzka 24/26, tel. 022-621-0271, fax 022-625-0476, www.orbis.pl, nov .warszawa@orbis.pl).

$$ Old Town Apartments offers 28 studio, one-bedroom, and two-bedroom apartments (all with kitchen) inside Warsaw's Old Town. The prices are good and the location is excellent, but you're pretty much on your own (no real reception, no breakfast). View the apartments on their Web site, pick the one that looks best, make arrangements with them, and they'll set up a meeting to give you the keys (usually at their office, sometimes at the apartment). This is an especially good value for families and longer stays (studio-€60–80, 1-bedroom-€95, 2-bedroom-€110, some more expensive "featured" apartments also available, slightly cheaper Oct–April and last-minute, tel. 022-887-9800, fax 022-831-4956, www.warsawshotel.com, booking@warsawshotel.com). They have an office right on the Old Town Market Square that acts as a sort of reception desk (Mon–Fri 9:00–20:00, Sat–Sun 9:00–17:00, Rynek Starego Miasta 12/14 #2, same contact information as above).

$$ Royal Route Residence, run by the same folks as Old Town Apartments (above), has 15 nice apartments in a building on the happening Nowy Świat street. As with the Old Town Apartments, you're basically on your own once you check in (studio-€70, 1-bedroom-€95, 2-bedroom-€110–120, slightly cheaper Oct–April and last-minute, no breakfast, corner of Nowy Świat and Chmielna, tel. 022-820-9227, fax 022-831-4956, www.warsaw -apartments.net, booking@warsaw-apartments.net). The entrance to the office is hiding through an alley (follow signs; office open Mon–Fri 10:00–18:00, closed Sat–Sun; outside of these times, someone can meet you with the keys—be sure they know when you'll arrive).

$$ Hotel Harenda rents 43 rooms on the second and third floors of an office building right in the middle of the Royal Way, where Nowy Świat becomes Krakowskie Przedmieście. The tired, old rooms are nothing special, but the location is good, and the ground-floor pub is a popular hangout spot (March–June and Sept–Oct: Sb-295 zł, Db-315 zł; July–Aug and Nov–Feb: Sb-250 zł, Db-270 zł; breakfast-20 zł, second night is free Fri–Sun, some rowdy street noise—especially on weekends—so request a quiet room, Krakowskie Przedmieście 4/6, tel. & fax 022-826-0071, www.hotelharenda.com.pl, rezerwacja@hotelharenda.com.pl).

$$ Hotel Gromada, a 320-room conference hotel, has a dreary communist exterior, but the lobby and most rooms have been refurbished. There are three types of rooms, all of which are pretty similar: "tourist" (lightly renovated since the communist days); "standard" (a little nicer, with newer bathrooms, but still a tad scruffy); and "plus" (almost identical to standard, but in a newer building). The only thing this boring place has going for it is its location—between the Palace of Culture and Science and Nowy Świat (tourist rooms: Sb-250 zł, Db-300 zł; standard rooms: Sb-320 zł, Db-350 zł; plus rooms: Sb-420 zł, Db-450 zł; standard and plus rooms about 25 percent cheaper Fri–Sat, non-smoking rooms, elevator, plac Powstańców Warszawy 2, tel. 022-582-9900, fax 022-582-9527, www.hotele.gromada.pl, warszawahotel .centrum@gromada.pl).

$ Boutique B&B is Warsaw's best value by far. Don't let the low prices fool you: This place offers more comfort and class than a hotel twice its price, in a beautifully renovated and well-located old building. Jarek Chołodecki, who lived near Chicago for many years, returned to Warsaw and converted apartments into this wonderful bed-and-breakfast. It's a friendly, casual, stylish place, creatively decorated and impeccably maintained. You'll feel like you're staying with your Warsaw sophisticate cousin; quirky, charismatic Jarek loves to chat with his guests (standard Db-€70, junior suite-€80, big suite-€105, elevator, ulica Smolna 14, tel. 022-829-4801, fax 022-829-4882, www.bedandbreakfast.pl, office@bedandbreakfast .pl). Let Jarek know what time you're arriving. To make things easier, he can arrange for a no-stress ride in from the airport for the same price as a taxi (40 zł, request when you reserve your room).

$ Ibis Warszawa Stare Miasto, with 333 new cookie-cutter rooms, is the place for predictable comfort with zero personality. This hotel, part of the popular European chain, overlooks a WWII memorial in a nondescript, businessy-feeling neighborhood a 10-minute walk north of the Old Town (Sb/Db-259 zł, or 209 zł Fri–Sun, sometimes better deals online, breakfast-28 zł, air-con, non-smoking rooms, elevator, Muranowska 2, tel. 022-310-1000, fax 022-310-1010, www.ibishotel.com, h3714@accor.com).

$ **Hotel Mazowiecki** is a local-style place on a drab urban street between the Palace of Culture and Science and Nowy Świat. Its 56 rooms are old and basic, but well-located for the price (S-150 zł, Sb-198 zł, D-200 zł, Db-248 zł, 20 percent cheaper Fri–Sun, elevator, ulica Mazowiecka 10, tel. & fax 022-827-2365, www .mazowiecki.com.pl, recepcja.mazowiecki@hotelewam.pl).

$ **Oki Doki Hostel,** on a pleasant square a few blocks in front of the Palace of Culture and Science, is colorful, creative, and easygoing. Each of its 40 rooms was designed by a different artist with a special theme—such as van Gogh, Celtic spirals, heads of state, or Lenin. It's well-run by Ernest—a Pole whose parents loved Hemingway—and his wife Łucja, who are energetic and welcoming (S-120 zł, D-150 zł, Db-190 zł, T-190 zł; dorm bed in 4- to 5-bed room-55 zł, in 6-bed room-50 zł, in 8-bed room-45 zł, includes breakfast except for dorm-dwellers—who pay 10 zł, slightly cheaper Oct–April, free Internet access, self-service laundry-10 zł, kitchen, lots of stairs, plac Dąbrowskiego 3, tel. 022-826-5112, fax 022-826-8357, www.okidoki.pl, okidoki@okidoki.pl).

$ The IYHF **Szkolne Schronisko** hostel, with 110 beds and lots of school groups, is well-run, bright, and clean. The downside: It's on the fifth floor, with no elevator (non-members welcome, all prices per person: dorm beds-36 zł, S-65 zł, twin D-60 zł, T-55 zł, Q-45 zł, includes sheets, 3 zł for towel, cash only, no breakfast but members' kitchen, closed 10:00–16:00, curfew at 24:00, or 2:00 in the morning July–Aug; e-mail or fax ahead in summer to reserve limited S, D, and T rooms; good location across the street from National Museum at ulica Smolna 30, tel. & fax 022-827-8952, www.ssmsmolna30.pl, ssmsmolna@poczta.onet.pl).

$ **Dom Przy Rynku** is a small, friendly, charming, 40-bed hostel with two goals: housing kids from dysfunctional families, and raising money for its work by renting out beds to tourists (when it's not housing children). Located in the peaceful New Town, the cozy rooms are decorated for grade-schoolers. Beds are rented in July and August, and on Friday and Saturday nights all year (45 zł per bed in 2–5-bed rooms, rooms segregated by gender, bus #175 from station or airport to Franciszkańska stop, corner of Kościelna and Przyrynek streets at Rynek Nowego Miasta 4, tel. & fax 022-831-5033, www.cityhostel.net, info@cityhostel.net).

EATING

While the Old Town has a tourist-friendly atmosphere and traditional Polish food, Varsovians know that these days, the Nowy Świat area is where it's at—with trendy international restaurants and an enticing al fresco scene on balmy summer evenings. Most restaurants are open until the "last guest," which usually means about 23:00 (sometimes later in summer).

In or near the Old Town

Rather than wasting my money dining on the Old Town Market Square, I prefer to venture a few blocks to find a place with good food and much lower prices. For locations, see the maps on pages 293 and 305.

At **Restauracja pod Samsonem** ("Under Samson"), dine on affordable Polish-Jewish fare with well-dressed locals. The ambience is pleasant, the service is playfully opinionated, and the low prices make up for the fact that you have to pay to check your coat and use the bathroom (most main dishes 15–30 zł, enjoyable outdoor seating in summer, daily 10:00–23:00, ulica Freta 3/5, tel. 022-831-1788).

Podwale Piwna Kompania, a lively, smoky place filled with Varsovians, feels more like Prague than Warsaw. You'll enjoy the large plates of tasty food, the Pilsner Urquell beer on tap, and the Czech beer-hall or beer-garden ambience (most main dishes 20–30 zł, daily 11:00–24:00, just outside Old Town walls near the Barbican at ulica Podwale 25, tel. 022-635-6314).

Pierogarnia na Bednarskiej brags, "only our grandmothers make better pierogi." In addition to the classic Polish dumplings, the menu includes soups and a fun variety of drinks (from unusual fruit juices to *kvas*, the non-alcoholic dark beer). Order at the counter and take a seat—they'll call you when your food's ready. With mellow country decor, wooden menus, and a loyal local crowd, this is a handy spot for a quick, cheap meal along the Royal Way (12-zł plates of pierogi, 14-zł combo-plate includes soup and salad, daily 11:00–21:00, hiding on a quiet street behind the statue of Adam Mickiewicz at ulica Bednarska 28/30, tel. 022-828-0392).

Siedem Grzechów ("Seven Sins") is an old-style Warsaw restaurant serving top-notch Polish and international cuisine in a 1930s lace, velvet, and burgundy ambience. The place fills a dressy cellar with jazz and photos of prewar Warsaw (main dishes 45–65 zł, daily 11:00–23:00, live music most nights except Mon 19:30–23:00, a few blocks before the Old Town on the Royal Way at Krakowskie Przedmieście 45, tel. 022-826-4770).

On the Old Town Market Square: You'll pay triple to eat right on the Old Town Market Square, but some visitors figure it's worth the splurge (plan on 60–100 zł per main dish). If money's no object, these two places are tops: **U Fukiera,** at #27, offers traditional Polish and pan-European meals in a sophisticated setting with carefully designed prewar atmosphere. In summer, find your way back to the cozy courtyard garden (daily 12:00–23:00, tel. 022-831-1013). The pricier option is **Gessler**, at #21, with two parts: The cellar, serving countryside Polish dishes, is furnished with tables, chairs, doors, beams, and whole walls that were imported from actual country inns. Upstairs is the swanky dining room, serving very expensive (up to 140 zł), upscale Polish cuisine with live music in the evenings (both parts: daily 10:00–23:00, tel. 022-887-0344). In Gessler's lobby hang photos of famous patrons. It's the only place you'll see Hillary Rodham Clinton, George H. W. Bush, and Henry Kissinger side by side—and smiling. (A sly Fidel Castro watches over the three of them.)

On or near Nowy Świat

You'll find mostly tourists in the Old Town area. For a fun night on the town, locals flock to the Nowy Świat neighborhood (near the National Museum and Central Train Station).

On Foksal Street: Foksal—the first cross-street as you go down Nowy Świat from aleja Jerozolimskie—has a thriving assortment of about a half-dozen cafés and restaurants, most with inviting out-door seating. The cuisine is upscale international (30–60-zł main dishes), the clientele is young and sophisticated, and there's not a pierogi in sight. Find the place with the cuisine and ambience you like best. I ate well at **Living Room**, with healthy international fare and friendly service (daily 12:00–2:00 in the morning, #18, tel. 022-826-3928). **Sense,** across the street on Nowy Świat, is a well-regarded Asian fusion restaurant with a mod interior and a fun, creative menu (no outdoor seating, daily 12:00–24:00, Nowy Świat 19, tel. 022-826-6570).

Fast and Cheap: These two spots, while nothing special, will do in a pinch: **Sandwicz,** a colorful milk bar, serves up Polish grub, a self-serve salad bar, and—of course—sandwiches (7–10-zł main dishes, Mon–Fri 7:30–20:30, Sat–Sun 10:00–20:30, Nowy Świat 28). **Bar Restauracja Wegetariańska Zielony Świat** (a.k.a. "Greenland") offers a wide range of Asian-style vegetarian food, making liberal use of vegetarian "ham," "chicken," and even "fish." The decor is nothing special—contemporary Asian kitsch—but the food is good, healthy, and well-priced (most dishes 15–30 zł, daily 11:00–21:30, enter through passageway at Nowy Świat 42 to reach ulica Gałczyńskiego 5/9, tel. 022-826-4677).

Uniquely Polish Treats

These two places are on or close to the busy Nowy Świat boulevard.

A. Blikle, Poland's most famous bakery, serves a wide variety of delicious pastries. This is where locals shop for cakes when they're having someone special over for coffee. The specialty: *pączki* (2.20 zł)—the quintessential Polish doughnut, filled with rose-flavored jam. You can get your goodies "to go" in the shop (Mon–Sat 9:00–19:00, Sun 10:00–18:00), or enjoy them with coffee in the swanky, classic café (daily 10:00–22:00; both at Nowy Świat 35).

E. Wedel Pijalnia Czekolady thrills chocoholics. Emil Wedel made Poland's favorite chocolate, and today, his former residence houses this chocolate shop and café (Mon–Sat 8:00–22:00, Sun 11:00–20:00, between Palace of Culture and Science and Nowy Świat at ulica Szpitalna 1, tel. 022-827-2916). This is the spot for delicious pastries and a *real* hot chocolate, *czekolada do picia* (9 zł; that means a cup of melted chocolate, not just hot chocolate milk). The menu describes it as "true Wedel ecstasy for your mouth that will take you to a world of dreams and desires." Or, if you fancy pudding, try *pokusa*. Wedel's was *the* Christmas treat for locals under communism. Cadbury bought the company when Poland privatized after communism, but they kept the E. Wedel name, which is close to all Poles' hearts...and taste buds.

TRANSPORTATION CONNECTIONS

Virtually all trains into and out of Warsaw go through the hulking Central Train Station (see "Arrival in Warsaw," page 288.) If you're heading to Gdańsk, note that the red-brick Gothic city of Toruń and the impressive Malbork Castle are on the way (though on separate train lines, so you can't do both en route; see Gdańsk and Pomerania chapters).

From Warsaw by Train to: Kraków (hourly, 2.75 hrs), **Gdańsk** (nearly hourly, 4 hrs), **Toruń** (5/day, 3 hrs direct, more with a transfer in Kutno), **Malbork** (nearly hourly, 3.5 hrs direct), **Prague** (2/day direct including 1 night train, more with changes, 8.5–9.5 hrs), **Berlin** (3/day direct, 5.75 hrs; plus 1 direct night train, 7.75 hrs), **Budapest** (2/day direct, including 1 night train, 10.5–11.5 hrs; or 1 each per day with transfer in Győr, Hungary, or Břeclav, Czech Republic, both 10 hrs), **Vienna** (2/day direct, including 1 night train, 7.75 or 10 hrs; or 1/day with transfer in Břeclav, Czech Republic, 7.75 hrs).

GDAŃSK and the TRI-CITY

Gdańsk (guh-DANSK) is a true find on the Baltic Coast of Poland. You may associate Gdańsk with the images of dreary dock-workers you saw on the nightly news in the 1980s—but there's so much more to this city than shipyards, Solidarity, and smog. It's surprisingly easy to look past the urban sprawl to find one of northern Europe's most historic and picturesque cities.

Gdańsk is second only to Kraków as Poland's most appealing city. The gem of a Main Town boasts block after block of red-brick churches and narrow, colorful, ornately decorated Hanseatic burghers' mansions. Its history is also fascinating—from its medieval Golden Age to the headlines of our own generation, major events happen here. You might even see old Lech Wałęsa still wandering the streets.

But Gdańsk is just the beginning. From here, the "Tri-City" continues north along the coast, offering several day-trip opportunities. The faded elegance of the seaside resort Sopot beckons to tourists, while the modern burg of Gdynia sets the pace for today's Poland. Beyond the Tri-City, the sandy Hel Peninsula is a popular spot for summer sunbathing.

Planning Your Time

This region merits at least two days to make the trip here worthwhile. Gdańsk has more than enough sightseeing for a full day, but a second day allows you to see everything in town at a more relaxing pace, and take your pick from among several possible side-trips.

Gdańsk sightseeing has two major components: the "Royal Way" (historic main drag with small but good museums—described

Gdańsk

400 YARDS
400 METERS

SOLIDARITY SHIPYARD

GATE
SOLIDARITY MONUMENT
FINISH

① Great Mill
② Small Mill
③ Madison Shopping Mall
④ Żegluga Gdańska Boats
⑤ Galeon Lew to Westerplatte
⑥ ZTM "Ferry Trams" to Hel & Sopot

• • • WALKING TOUR ROUTE TO SOLIDARITY SHIPYARD

LIBRARY

OLD

TOWN

ST. BRIDGET'S

TRAIN STN.

TOWER

MKT. HALL

STRAGA

NIARSKA

CENTRAL MARITIME MUSEUM

SS SOŁDEK

TARG DRZEWNY

MAIN

ST. MARY'S

TOWN

SZEROKA

THE CRANE

ARMORY

GOLDEN GATE

LOT OFFICE

TRAM STOP

UPLAND GATE & AMBER MUS.

START

UPHAGEN HOUSE

PIWNA

TOWN HALL

DŁUGA

ARTUS COURT

MARIACKA

ARCHAEO-LOGICAL MUS.

GRANARY ISLAND

DŁUGI TARG

STAGIEWNA

GREEN GATE

NEPTUNE STATUE

OGARNA

DCH

TO NATL MUSEUM

in my self-guided walk) and the modern shipyard where Solidarity was born (with a fascinating museum, also fully described in this chapter). With just one day, do one of these activities in the morning, and the other in the afternoon. With two days, do one each day, and round your time out with other attractions: art-lovers enjoy the National Museum (with a stunning painting by Hans Memling), history buffs make the pilgrimage to Westerplatte (where World War II began), and church fans visit Oliwa Cathedral in Gdańsk's northern suburbs (on the way to Sopot).

With more time, consider the wide variety of side-trips. The most popular option is the full-day round-trip to Malbork Castle (45 min each way by train, plus at least 3 hours to tour the castle—see next chapter). Closer to Gdańsk, it only takes a few hours to get a feel for the resort town of Sopot (25 min each way by train); with more time, laze around longer on Sopot's beaches, or make a quick visit to Gdynia to round out your take on the Tri-City. If you have a full day and great weather, and you don't mind fighting the crowds for a patch of sandy beach, go to Hel.

Gdańsk gets busy in late June, when school holidays begin, and it's downright crowded in July and August—especially during St. Dominic's Fair (Jarmark Św. Dominika, 2 weeks in early Aug), with market stalls, concerts, and other celebrations. The city is dead in the winter.

ORIENTATION

(area code: 058)

Gdańsk, with 460,000 residents, is part of a larger metropolitan area called the Tri-City (Trójmiasto, total population 750,000).

But the tourist's Gdańsk is compact, welcoming, and walkable—virtually anything you'll want to see is within a 20-minute stroll of everything else.

Focus on the "Main Town" (Główne Miasto), home to most of the sights described in this chapter, including the spectacular "Royal Way" main drag, ulica Długa. The "Old Town" (Stare Miasto) has a handful of old brick buildings and faded, tall, skinny houses—but the area is mostly drab and residential, and not worth much time. Just beyond the northern end of the Old Town (about a 20-min walk from the heart of the Main Town) is the entrance to the Gdańsk Shipyard, with the excellent Solidarity museum. From here, shipyards sprawl for miles.

The second language in this part of Poland is German, not English—and German tourists flock here in droves. (This was a predominantly German city until the end of World War II.) Scandinavian shoppers come across the Baltic Sea to take advantage of the low prices.

You'll win no Polish friends calling the city by its more familiar German name, Danzig.

Tourist Information

Gdańsk's TI is in a red, high-gabled building across **ulica Długa** from the Town Hall. Pick up the free map and brochure, and browse through the other brochures and guidebooks (late June–early Sept daily 9:00–20:00; early Sept–late June Mon–Fri 9:00–17:00, Sat–Sun 9:00–14:00; ulica Długa 45, tel. 058-301-9151). There's also a small TI window in the *RUCH* kiosk in front of the **Main Train Station.**

Arrival in Gdańsk

By Train: Gdańsk's Main Train Station (Gdańsk Główny) is a pretty brick palace on the western edge of the old center. Trains to other parts of Poland (marked *PKP*) use tracks 1–3; regional trains with connections to the Tri-City (marked *SKM*) use the shorter tracks 3–5 (for more on regional SKM trains, see page 360).

In front of the station is a *RUCH* kiosk (where you can buy tram tickets) and a TI window. The pedestrian underpass by the McDonald's takes you beneath the busy road (first set of exits: tram stop; end of corridor: Old Town). To reach the heart of the Main Town, you can ride the **tram** (buy tickets—*bilety*—at *RUCH* kiosk or at any window marked *Bilety ZKM* in pedestrian underpass; access tram stop via underpass, then board tram #8, #13, or #14 going to the right with your back to the station; go just 1 stop to Brama Wyżynna, in front of the LOT airlines office). But by the time you buy your ticket and wait for the tram, you might as well **walk** the 15 minutes to the same place (go through underpass, exit to the right and follow the busy road until you reach LOT airlines office, then head left toward all the brick towers). Or even easier, take a **taxi** (shouldn't cost more than 15 zł to any of my recommended hotels).

By Plane: Gdańsk's small airport (recently named for Lech Wałęsa) is about five miles west of the city center (tel. 058-348-1163, www.airport.gdansk.pl). Bus #B connects the airport with downtown (2.50 zł, 30 min, buy ticket on board). A taxi into town will cost you about 50 zł.

Helpful Hints

Blue Monday: In the off-season, most of Gdańsk's museums are closed Monday. In the busy summertime, some of these museums are open limited hours on Monday. If museums are closed, Monday is a good day to visit churches or take a side-trip to Sopot (but not Malbork Castle, which is also closed Mon).

Last Entry: The "last entry" time for museums is 30 minutes before closing—and it's strictly enforced. Museum-goers who cut it close discover that ticket-sellers sometimes clock out a few minutes early.

Gdańsk History

Visitors to Gdańsk are surprised at how "un-Polish" the city's history is. In this cultural melting pot of German, Dutch, and Flemish merchants (with a smattering of Italians and Scots), Poles were only a small part of the picture until the city became exclusively Polish after World War II. However, in Gdańsk, cultural backgrounds traditionally took a back seat to the bottom line. Wealthy Gdańsk was always known for its economic pragmatism—no matter who was in charge, Gdańsk merchants made money.

Gdańsk is Poland's gateway to the waters of Europe—where its main river (the Vistula) meets the Baltic Sea. The town was first mentioned in the 10th century, and was seized in 1308 by the Teutonic Knights (who called it "Danzig"; for more on the Teutonic Knights, see page 368). The Knights encouraged other Germans to come settle on the Baltic coast, and gradually turned Gdańsk into a wealthy city. In 1361, Gdańsk joined the Hanseatic League, a trade federation of mostly Germanic merchant towns that provided mutual security. By the 15th century, Gdańsk was a leading member of this mighty network, which virtually dominated trade in northern Europe (and also included Toruń, Kraków, Lübeck, Hamburg, Bremen, Bruges, Bergen, Tallinn, Novgorod, and nearly a hundred other cities).

In 1454, the people of Gdańsk rose up against the Teutonic Knights, burning down their castle and forcing them out of the city. Three years later, the Polish king borrowed money from wealthy Gdańsk families to hire Czech mercenaries to take the Teutonic Knights' main castle, Malbork (see page 365). In exchange, Gdańsk merchants were granted special privileges, including exclusive export rights. Gdańsk now acted as a middleman for all trade passing through the city, but paid only a modest annual tribute to the Polish king.

The 16th and 17th centuries were Gdańsk's Golden Age. Now a part of the Polish kingdom, the city had access to an enormous hinterland of natural resources to export—yet it maintained a

Getting Around Gdańsk

If you're staying at one of my recommended hotels, everything is within easy walking distance. Public transportation is useful for residents, but not really for sightseers.

By Public Transportation: Gdańsk has a fine network of trams and buses. Buy tickets *(bilety)* at kiosks marked *RUCH* or *Bilety ZKM*. Prices depend on the time limit on the ticket (1.40 zł/10 min, 2.80 zł/30 min, 5.60 zł/1 hr, 9.10 zł/24 hrs). Tell them where you're going when you buy your ticket, and they'll sell you the right one. Stops worth knowing about: Plac Solidarności (near the shipyards), Gdańsk Główny (in front of the Main Train privileged, semi-independent status. Like Amsterdam, Gdańsk became a tolerant, progressive, and booming merchant city. Its mostly Germanic and Dutch burghers imported Dutch, Flemish, and Italian architects to give their homes an appropriately Hanseatic flourish. At a time of religious upheaval in the rest of Europe, Gdańsk became known for its tolerance—a place that opened its doors to all visitors (many Mennonites and Scottish religious refugees emigrated here). It was also a haven for great thinkers, including philosopher Arthur Schopenhauer and scientist Daniel Fahrenheit (who invented the mercury thermometer).

Gdańsk declined, along with the rest of Poland, in the late 18th century, and became a part of Prussia (today's Germany) during the partitions. But the people of Gdańsk—even those of German heritage—had taken pride in their independence, and weren't enthusiastic about being ruled from Berlin. After World War I, Gdańsk once again became an independent city-state, the Free City of Danzig (populated by 400,000 Germans and only 15,000 Poles). The city, along with the so-called Polish Corridor connecting it to Polish lands, effectively cut off Germany from its northeastern territory. On September 1, 1939, Adolf Hitler started World War II when he invaded Gdańsk to bring it back into the German fold. Nearly 80 percent of the city was destroyed in the war.

After World War II, Gdańsk officially became part of Poland, and was painstakingly reconstructed (mostly replicating its Golden Age). In 1970, and again in 1980, the shipyard of Gdańsk witnessed strikes and demonstrations that would lead to the fall of European communism. Poland's great anti-communist hero and first post-communist president—Lech Wałęsa—is Gdańsk's most famous resident, and still lives here today.

A city with a recent past that's both tragic and uplifting, Gdańsk celebrated its 1,000th birthday in 1997. This came with a wave of renovation and refurbishment, which left the gables of the atmospheric Hanseatic quarter gleaming.

Station), and Brama Wyżynna (near the heart of the tourist zone, in front of LOT airlines office). Don't confuse *ZKM* (the company that runs Gdańsk city transit) with *SKM* (the company that runs regional trains to outlying destinations).

To get beyond central Gdańsk to visit the Oliwa cathedral, see "Outer Gdańsk," (page 351). For directions to towns of Sopot and Gdynia, and the Hel Peninsula, see "Getting Around the Tri-City" (page 360).

By Taxi: They cost 5 zł to start, then 2 zł per kilometer. Find a taxi stand, or call a cab (try Super Hallo Taxi, tel. 058-9191, or City Plus Hallo Taxi, tel. 058-9686).

TOURS

Walking Tours—In peak season, the TI offers a three-hour English walking tour (80 zł, July–Aug only, departs from TI daily at 12:00, confirm details at TI).

Private Guides—Hiring a private local guide is an exceptional value. **Agnieszka Syroka** is bubbly and personable, and also does tours of Malbork Castle (300–400 zł for up to 4 hrs, more for all day, mobile 0502-554-584, asyroka@interia.pl).

SELF-GUIDED WALKS

Gdańsk's Royal Way

In the 16th and 17th centuries, Gdańsk was Poland's wealthiest city, with gorgeous architecture (much of it in the Flemish Mannerist style) rivaling that in the two historic capitals, Kraków and Warsaw. During this Golden Age, Polish kings would visit this city of well-to-do Hanseatic League merchants, and they gawked along the same route trod by tourists today. The following walk, worth ▲▲▲, introduces you to the best of historic Gdańsk. It only takes about 30 minutes, not counting multiple worthwhile sightseeing stops. This stroll turns tourists into poets. On my last visit, a traveler gasped to me, "It's like stepping into a Fabergé egg."

Begin at the west end of the Main Town, between the big, white gate and the big brick gate (near the LOT airlines office, the busy road, and the Brama Wyżynna tram stop).

City Gates: Medieval Gdańsk had an elaborate network of protection for the city, including several moats and gates—among them the white **Upland Gate** (Brama Wyżynna); the shorter, red-brick **Torture House** (Wieża Więzienna); and the taller, red-brick **Prison Tower** (Katownia). These three were all connected back then, and visitors had to pass through all of them to enter the city. These buildings, with walls up to 15 feet thick, have recently been turned into the fine Amber Museum (described on page 336). As architects excavated the site to prepare the museum, they kept discovering hidden passages, rooms, and other archaeological finds (such as spectacularly well-preserved 14th-century toilets)...so the plans were constantly delayed.

Now walk around the left side of the Torture House and Prison Tower. Look to your left to see a long brick building with four gables. This is the 16th-century **Armory** (Zbrojownia), one of the best examples of Dutch Renaissance architecture in Europe. Though this part of the building looks like four separate house facades, it's a kind of urban camouflage to hide its real purpose from potential attackers. But there's at least one clue to what it's for: Find the exploding cannonballs at the tops of the turrets.

The round, pointy-topped tower next door is the **Straw Tower.** Gunpowder was stored here, and the roof was straw—so if it exploded, it would blow its top without destroying the walls.

• *Continue around the brick buildings until you're face-to-face with the...*

Golden Gate (Złota Brama): The other gates were defensive, but this one's purely ornamental. The four women up top represent virtues that the people of Gdańsk should exhibit toward outsiders: Peace, Freedom, Prosperity, and Fame. The inscription, a psalm in medieval German, compares Gdańsk to Jerusalem: famous and important. In the middle is one of the coats of arms of Gdańsk—two crosses under a crown. You'll see this symbol many times today.

• *Now go through the gate, entering the "Long Street"...*

Ulica Długa: Look back at the gate you just came through. The women on top of this side represent virtues the people of Gdańsk should cultivate in themselves: Wisdom, Piety, Justice,

and Concord (if an arrow's broken, let's take it out of the quiver and fix it).

Begin to wander this intoxicating promenade. Gdańsk was cosmopolitan and exceptionally tolerant in the Middle Ages, attracting a wide range of people (including many who were persecuted elsewhere): Jews, Scots, Dutch, Flemish, Italians, Germans, and more. Members of each group brought with them strands of their culture, which they wove into the tapestry of this city. The eclectic homes along this street are one of the ways that cultures from throughout Europe left their mark on Gdańsk.

Today's generation is leaving its mark as well—each time I return, new cafés and restaurants have opened along this street. For example, the Rooster restaurant on the right is part of a chain that's sweeping Poland. What an innovative concept! Where these clever entrepreneurs get their creative ideas, I'll never know.

This lovely street wasn't always so lively and carefree. In fact, at the end of World War II, ulica Długa was in ruins. The city was damaged when the Germans first invaded, sparking the war. But the worst devastation came when the Soviets arrived. This was the

Gdańsk at a Gdlance

▲▲▲**Ulica Długa** Gdańsk's colorful showpiece main drag, cutting a picturesque swath through the heart of the wealthy burghers' neighborhood. **Hours:** Always open.

▲▲▲**Solidarity Sights and Gdańsk Shipyard** The shipyard that was home to the beginning of the end of European communism, housing a towering monument and an excellent museum. **Hours:** May–Sept Tue–Sun 10:00–17:00, Oct–April Tue–Sun 10:00–16:00, closed Mon year-round.

▲▲**Uphagen House** Tourable 18th-century interior, typical of the pretty houses that line ulica Długa. **Hours:** Generally open July–Aug daily 10:00–16:00 or 12:00–18:00, Sept–June similar hours, but closed Mon.

▲▲**Main Town Hall** Ornately decorated meeting rooms, exhibits of town artifacts, and climbable tower with sweeping views. **Hours:** Museum generally open July–Aug daily 10:00–16:00 or 12:00–18:00, Sept–June similar hours, but closed Mon; tower open same hours, but mid-May–mid-Oct only.

▲**Artus Court** Grand meeting hall for guilds of Golden Age Gdańsk, boasting an over-the-top tiled stove. **Hours:** Generally open July–Aug daily 10:00–16:00 or 12:00–18:00, Sept–June similar hours, but closed Mon.

---

first traditionally German city that the Red Army reached on their march toward Berlin—and the soldiers were set loose to level the place in retaliation for all of the pain the Nazis had caused. (Soviets didn't destroy nearby Gdynia—which they considered Polish, not German.) Soviet officers turned a blind eye as their soldiers raped and brutalized residents. An entire order of horrified nuns committed suicide by throwing themselves into the river. And upwards of 80 percent of this area was destroyed. It was only thanks to detailed drawings and photographs that these buildings could be so carefully reconstructed, mostly using the original brick.

During Gdańsk's Golden Age, these houses were taxed based on frontage (like the homes lining Amsterdam's canals)—so they were built skinny and deep. The widest houses belonged to the super-elite. Different as they are from the outside, each house had the same general plan inside. Each had three parts, starting with the front and moving back: First was a fancy drawing room, to show off for visitors. Then came a narrow corridor to the back

▲**St. Mary's Church** Giant red-brick church crammed full of Gdańsk history. **Hours:** Mon–Sat 9:00–17:30, Sun 13:00–17:30.

▲**Central Maritime Museum** Sprawling exhibit on all aspects of the nautical life, housed in several venues (including the landmark medieval Crane and a permanently moored steamship) connected by a ferry boat. **Hours:** July–Aug daily 10:00–18:00, Sept–June generally Tue–Sun 10:00–16:00.

Amber Museum High-tech new exhibit of valuable golden globs of petrified tree sap. **Hours:** Likely daily 10:00–20:00, until 18:00 and closed Mon off-season.

Archaeological Museum Decent collection of artifacts from this region's past. **Hours:** July–Aug Tue–Sun 10:00–17:00, closed Mon; Sept–June Tue and Thu–Fri 9:00–16:00, Wed 10:00–17:00, Sat–Sun 10:00–16:00, closed Mon.

National Museum in Gdańsk Ho-hum art collection with a single blockbuster highlight: Hans Memling's remarkable *Last Judgment* altarpiece. **Hours:** Tue–Fri 9:00–16:00, Sat–Sun 10:00–16:00, closed Mon.

Oliwa Cathedral Suburban church with long, skinny nave and playful organ. **Hours:** Church open long hours daily; frequent organ concerts in summer.

rooms—often along the side of an inner courtyard. Because the houses had only a few windows facing the outer street, this courtyard provided much-needed sunlight to the rest of the house. The residential quarters were in the back, where the people actually lived: bedroom, kitchen, office. To see the interior of one of these homes, pay a visit to the **Uphagen House** (#12, on the right, a block in front of the gate; described on page 336).

Across the street and a little farther down are some of the most striking **facades** along all of ulica Długa. The big blue house with the three giant heads is from the 19th century, when eclecticism was hot—borrowing bits and pieces from various architectural eras. This was one of the few houses on the street that survived World War II.

A bit farther up on the right is the huge, blocky **post office,** which doesn't quite fit with the skinny facades lining the rest of the street. But step inside. With doves fluttering under an airy glass atrium, the interior's a class act. (To mail postcards, take a number—category C—from the machine on the left.)

Across the street and a few doors down from the post office, notice the colorful **scenes** just overhead on the facade of the cocktail bar. These are slices of life from 17th-century Gdańsk: drinking, talking, buying, fighting, playing music. The ship is a *koga*, a typical symbol of Gdańsk.

A couple of doors down from the cocktail bar is **Neptun Cinema** (marked *KINO*). In the 1980s, this was the only movie theater in the city, and locals lined up all the way down the street to get in. Young adults remember coming here with their grandparents to see a full day of cartoons. Now, like in the United States, the rising popularity of multiplexes is threatening to close this place down.

Across the street from the theater are three houses belonging to the very influential medieval **Ferber family,** which produced many burghers, mayors, and even a bishop. On the house with the little dog over the door (#29), look for the heads in the circles. These are Caesars of Rome. At the top of the building is Mr. Ferber's answer to the constant question, "Why build such an elaborate house?"—*PRO INVIDIA*, "For the sake of envy."

Now you're just a few steps from the **Main Town Hall** (Ratusz Głównego Miasta). This building features a climbable observation tower and houses a superb museum with ornately decorated meeting rooms for the city council (see description on page 336).

• *Just beyond the Main Town Hall, ulica Długa widens and becomes...*

Długi Targ: The centerpiece of "Long Square" is one of Gdańsk's most important landmarks, the statue of **Neptune**—god of the sea. He's a fitting symbol for a city that dominates the maritime life of Poland. Behind him is another fine museum, the **Artus Court** (see page 338). This meeting hall for various Gdańsk brotherhoods is home to the most impressive stove you've ever seen.

As you continue down Długi targ, notice the **balconies** extending out into the square, with access to cellars underneath. These were far more common along ulica Długa in Gdańsk's Golden Age, but were removed in the 19th century to make way for a new tram system. You'll find more balconies like these on Mariacka street, which runs parallel to this one (2 blocks to the left).

• *At the end of Długi targ is the...*

Green Gate (Zielona Brama): This huge gate was actually built as a residence for visiting kings...who usually preferred to stay back by Neptune instead (maybe because the river, just on the other side of this gate, stunk). It might not have been good enough for kings and queens, but it's plenty fine for a former president—Lech Wałęsa's office is upstairs (see the plaque, *Biuro Lecha Wałęsy*). Other parts of the building are used for temporary exhibitions.

Notice that these bricks are much smaller than the ones we've seen earlier on this walk. That's because those were locally made, but these are Dutch. Boats would come here empty, load up with goods, and take them back to Holland. For ballast, they brought bricks on the trip from Holland—which they left here to be turned into this gate.

• *Now go through the gate, and turn left along the...*

Riverfront Embankment: The Motława River—actually a side channel of the mighty Vistula—was the source of Gdańsk's phenomenal Golden Age wealth. This embankment was jam-packed in its heyday, the 14th and 15th centuries. It was so crowded with boats that you could hardly see the water, and boats had to pay a time-based tax for tying up to a post. Instead of an actual embankment (which was built later), there was a series of wooden piers to connect the boats directly to the gates of the city. Now it's a popular place to stroll and to buy amber.

Across the river is **Granary Island** (Spichrze), where grain was stored until it could be taken away by ships. Before World War II, there were some 400 granaries here; now it's still in ruins. Three granaries have been reconstructed on the next island up, and house exhibits for the Central Maritime Museum (see page 340); another is Hotel Królewski (see "Sleeping," page 352). The local scuttlebutt is that it's only a matter of time before the rest of this prime real estate is developed into a new city-center zone of shops, restaurants, houses, and hotels.

Continue along the embankment until you see the five big, round stones on your left. These are the **five little ladies**—mysterious ancient sculptures. If you look closely, you can make out their features, especially the chubby one on the end. If you touch one, you'll come back to Gdańsk...or so the tour guides say.

The next huge red-brick fort houses the **Archaeological Museum** and a tower you can climb for a good view (see page 340). The gate in the middle leads to **Mariacka street,** a calm, atmospheric drag leading to St. Mary's Church (see page 338) and lined with old balconies, amber shops, and imaginative gargoyles (which locals call "pukers" when it rains).

• *Just up ahead on the embankment is Gdańsk's number-one symbol, and our last stop...*

The Crane (Żuraw): This monstrous 15th-century crane was used for loading ships, picking up small crafts for repairs, and uprighting masts...beginning a shipbuilding tradition that continued to the days of Lech Wałęsa. The crane mechanism was operated by several hardworking sailors scrambling around in giant hamster wheels up top (you can see the wheels if you look up). The Crane houses part of the Central Maritime Museum (described on page 340).

• *Our orientation tour is over. Now get out there and enjoy Gdańsk...do it for Lech!*

From the Main Town to the Solidarity Shipyard

This lightly guided walk links Gdańsk's two most important sightseeing areas. Along the way, you'll see some important historic landmarks, tour two of Gdańsk's more interesting red-brick churches, and wander through the city's best shopping district. The stroll takes about 20 minutes, not counting stops for sightseeing and shopping.

Begin at the top of ulica Długa, with your back to the Golden Gate. Head a few steps down the street and take a left on Tkacka. After one long block, you'll see the back of the **Armory** building (described in "Self-Guided Walks—Gdańsk's Royal Way"). This pearl of Renaissance architecture has recently been renovated, and now hosts a convenient supermarket on the ground floor.

After two more blocks, detour to the right down Świętojańska and use the side door to enter the brick **St. Nicholas Church** (Kościół Św. Mikołaja, with the ornate towers on the ends). Near the end of World War II, when the Soviet army reached Gdańsk on its march westward, they were given the order to burn all of the churches. Only this one—dedicated to Russia's patron saint—was spared. As the best-preserved church in town, today it has a more impressive interior than the others, with lavish golden Baroque altars.

Backtrack out to the main street and continue north. Immediately after the church (on the right), you'll see Gdańsk's newly renovated **Market Hall.** Look for the coat of arms of Gdańsk over each of its four doors. Inside you'll find mostly local shoppers—browsing through produce, other foods, and clothing—as well as the graves of medieval Dominican monks that were discovered when the building was renovated (in the basement).

Across the street from the Market Hall is a round red-brick **tower,** once part of the city's protective wall. This marks the end of the Main Town, and the beginning of the Old Town.

Another long block up the street is the huge **St. Catherine's Church** (Kościół Św. Katarzyny, on the right). "Katy," as locals call it, is the oldest church in Gdańsk. In a freak accident in May of 2006, the roof of this church burst into flames. Local people ran into the church and pulled everything outside, so nothing valuable was damaged. Even the carillon bells were saved. But the roof and wooden frame were totally destroyed. The people of Gdańsk are determined to rebuild this important symbol of the city, and within days of the fire, fundraising concerts were held to scrape together the money needed to raise the roof once more.

The church hiding behind Katy—named for Catherine's daughter Bridget—has important ties to Solidarity, and is worth a quick detour. To get there, walk along the side of St. Catherine's Church, past the monument to Pope John Paul II (your progress might be blocked by reconstruction on Katy, but if you're determined you can still get to the church by circling around back).

St. Bridget's Church (Kościół Św. Brygidy) was the home church of Lech Wałęsa during the tense days of the 1980s. This church and its priest, Henryk Jankowski, were particularly aggressive in supporting the ideals of Solidarity. Jankowski became a mouthpiece for the movement, and Wałęsa named his youngest daughter Brygida in gratitude for the church's support. In the back corner, find the tomb of Solidarity martyr Jerzy Popiełuszko, a famously outspoken Warsaw priest who was kidnapped, beaten, and murdered by the communist secret police. At the front of the church, check out the enormous, unfinished altar made entirely of amber. This over-the-top altar is just one example of Father Jankowski's recent missteps. Despite his fame and contributions to Solidarity, Jankowski has taken a nosedive in public opinion in the last few years—thanks to projects like this, as well as accusations of anti-Semitism and implications of pedophilia and corruption. Because of these issues, and because of his worsening health, Jankowski no longer leads this church.

Backtrack out past St. Catherine's Church to the main street. Just across from St. Catherine's is a red-brick building with lots of little windows in the roof. This is the **Great Mill** (Wielki Młyn), which has been converted into a shopping mall. As you continue north and cross the stream, you'll also see the picturesque **Small Mill** (Mały Młyn) straddling the stream on your right.

After another block, on your right, is the modern **Madison shopping mall.** Two blocks to your left (up Heweliusza) are more shopping malls and the Main Train Station. But to get to the shipyard, keep heading straight up Rajska. After another long block, jog right (between the big, green-glass skyscraper and today's Solidarity headquarters) and head for the three tall crosses.

For a self-guided tour of the shipyard and Solidarity museum, see page 343.

SIGHTS

Main Town (Główne Miasto)

The following sights are all in the Main Town, listed roughly in the order you'll see them on the self-guided walk of the Royal Way. Be warned that the three excellent museums on ulica Długa (Uphagen House, Town Hall, Artus Court) are run by the same museum, which overhauls the opening hours every six months or so. They're generally open either 10:00–16:00 or 12:00–18:00 (daily in July–Aug, otherwise closed Mon). Generally, these museums are free one day each week.

Amber Museum (Muzeum Bursztynu)—This slick, brand-new museum shows off one of Gdańsk's favorite local products. Multimedia exhibits explain the long process of how tree sap petrifies and becomes a valuable chunk of prehistory. You'll also see plenty of samples, demonstrating the full range of colors, transparency, and inclusions—items trapped in the sap (8 zł, likely open daily 10:00–20:00, until 18:00 and closed Mon off-season, in the big brick towers just outside the Golden Gate, tel. 058-767-9128). For a primer before you go, check out the "All About Amber" sidebar on page 373.

▲▲Uphagen House (Dom Uphagena)—This interesting place is your chance to get a glimpse into what's behind the colorful facades lining ulica Długa (8 zł, generally open July–Aug daily 10:00–16:00 or 12:00–18:00, Sept–June similar hours but closed Mon, sometimes an inviting café in the courtyard, ulica Długa 12, tel. 058-301-2371).

Check out the cut-away model just inside the entry to see the three parts you'll visit: dolled-up visitors' rooms in front, a corridor along the courtyard, and private rooms in the back. You'll begin upstairs, in the salon—used to show off for guests. Most of this furniture is original (saved from WWII bombs by locals who hid it in the countryside). Then you'll pass into the dining room, with knee-high paintings of hunting and celebrations. Along the passage to the back, each room has a theme: butterflies in the smoking room, then flowers, then birds in the music room. In the private rooms at the back, notice how much simpler the decor is. Back downstairs, you'll pass through the kitchen, the pantry, and a room with photos from the house before the war, which they used to reconstruct what you see today. The upper floors often house temporary exhibits.

▲▲Main Town Hall (Ratusz Głównego Miasta)—Inside this landmark building, you'll find some remarkable decorations from Gdańsk's Golden Age (8 zł, generally open July–Aug daily 10:00–16:00 or 12:00–18:00, Sept–June similar hours but closed Mon, ulica Długa 47, tel. 058-767-9100). You can also climb to the top of the **tower** for commanding views (4 zł extra, mid-May–mid-Oct only).

Buy your ticket down below (good gift shop), then head up the stairs and inside. In the entry room, examine the photo showing this building at the end of World War II (you'll see more upstairs). The ornately carved wooden **door,** which you'll pass through in a minute, also deserves a close look. Above the door are two crosses under a crown. This seal of Gdańsk is being held—as it often is—by a pair of lions. The felines are stubborn and independent, just like Gdańsk. Close the door partway to look at the carvings of crops. Around the frame of the door are mermen, reminding us that these crops, like so many other resources of Poland, are transported on the Vistula and out through Gdańsk.

Go through the door into the **Red Hall,** where the Gdańsk city council met in the summertime. (The lavish fireplace—with another pair of lions holding the coat of arms of Gdańsk—was just for show.) City council members would sit in the seats around the room, debating city policy. The shin-level paintings depict the earth; the exquisitely detailed inlaid wood just over the seats are animals; the paintings on the wall above represent the seven virtues the burghers meeting in this room should have; and the ceiling is all about theology. Examine that ceiling. You'll see 25 paintings total, with both Christian and pagan themes—meant to inspire the decision-makers in this room to make good choices. The smaller ones around the edges are scenes from mythology and the Bible. The one in the middle (from 1607) shows God's relationship to Gdańsk. In the foreground, the citizens of Gdańsk go about their daily lives. Above them, high atop the arch, God's hand reaches down (from within clouds of Hebrew characters) and grasps the city's steeple. The rainbow arching above also symbolizes God's connection to Gdańsk. Mirroring that is the Vistula River, which begins in the mountains of southern Poland (on the right), runs through the country, and exits at the sea in Gdańsk (on the left, where the rainbow ends).

Continue into the not-so-impressive Winter Hall, with another fireplace and coat of arms held by lions. Keep going through the next room, into a room with before-and-after photos of **WWII damage.** At the foot of the destroyed crucifix is a book with a bullet hole in it. The twist of wood is all that's left of the main support for the spiral staircase (today reconstructed in the room where you entered). Ponder the tragedy of war...and the inspiring ability of a city to be reborn.

Upstairs are some temporary exhibits, and several examples of **Gdańsk-style furniture.** These pieces are characterized by three big, round feet along the front, lots of ornamentation, and usually a virtually-impossible-to-find lock (sometimes hidden behind a movable decoration). You'll also see a coin collection, from the days when Gdańsk had the elite privilege of minting its own currency.

▲**Artus Court (Dwór Artusa)**—In the Middle Ages, there were many businessmen's clubs in Gdańsk. For their meetings, the city provided this elaborately decorated hall, named for King Arthur (who was a medieval symbol for prestige and power). Halls like this one were once common in Baltic Europe, but only three survive, and Gdańsk's is by far the best (8 zł, generally open July–Aug daily 10:00–16:00 or 12:00–18:00, Sept–June similar hours but closed Mon, in tall, white, triple-arched building behind Neptune statue at Długi targ 43–44, tel. 058-767-9100).

In the grand hall, you'll see various **cupboards** lining the walls. Each organization that met here had a place to keep its important documents and office supplies.

In the far back corner is the museum's highlight: a towering **stove** decorated with 520 colorful tiles featuring the faces of kings, queens, nobles, mayors, and burghers. Half of these people were Protestant, and half were Catholic, mixed together in no particular order—a reminder of the importance of religious tolerance. About 90 percent of these tiles are original, having survived WWII bombs. Of the missing tiles, three were recently discovered by a bargain-hunter wandering through a flea market in the southern part of the country—and returned to their rightful home.

Notice the huge **paintings** on the walls above, with 3-D animals emerging from flat frames. Hunting is a popular theme in local artwork. Like minting coins, hunting was a privilege usually reserved for royalty, but extended in special circumstances to special towns...like Gdańsk. If you look closely, it's obvious that these "paintings" are digitally generated reproductions of the original ones, which were damaged in World War II.

The next room—actually in the next-door building—is a typical front room of the burghers' homes lining ulica Długa. As you exit to the back, you'll see a miniature reconstruction of the whole grand room, including paintings that have yet to be re-created. As you leave, you're just down the street from St. Mary's Church; to get back to the main drag, go back around the block, to the left.

▲**St. Mary's Church (Kościół Mariacki)**—Gdańsk has so many striking red-brick churches, it's hard to keep track of them. But if you visit only one, make it St. Mary's. This is the biggest brick church in the world, accommodating up to 25,000 people (standing room only). Built over 159 years in the 14th and 15th centuries, the church is an important symbol of Gdańsk (church free for individuals to enter but donation requested, open for tourists Mon–Sat 9:00–17:30, Sun 13:00–17:30).

As you enter the church, notice all of the white, empty space—unusual in a Catholic country, where frilly Baroque churches are the norm. In the Middle Ages, Gdańsk's tolerance attracted people who were suffering religious persecution. As the Protestant population grew, they needed a place to worship. St. Mary's, like most other Gdańsk churches, eventually became Protestant—leaving these churches with the blank walls you see now. Today you'll find only one Baroque church in central Gdańsk (the domed pink-and-green chapel behind St. Mary's).

Most Gothic stone churches are built in the basilica style—with a high nave in the middle, shorter naves on the side, and flying buttresses to support the weight. (Think of Paris' Notre-Dame.) But that design doesn't work with brick. So, like all Gdańsk churches, St. Mary's is a "hall church"—with three naves the same height, and no exterior buttresses.

Also like other Gdańsk churches, St. Mary's gave refuge to the Polish people after the communist government declared martial law in 1981. If a riot broke out and violence seemed imminent, people would flood into churches for protection. The ZOMO riot police wouldn't follow them inside.

Most of the church decorations are original. A few days before World War II broke out in Gdańsk, locals hid precious items in the countryside. Take some time now to see a few of the highlights.

Head up the right nave and find the opulent family marker to the right of the main altar. Look for the falling baby. This is Constantine Ferber. As a precocious child, Constantine leaned out his window on ulica Długa to see the king's processional come through town. He slipped and fell, but landed in a salesman's barrel of fish. Constantine grew up to become the mayor of Gdańsk.

At the next post down, look for the coat of arms with the three pigs' heads. This story relates to another member of the illustrious Ferber clan. An enemy army was laying siege to the town, and tried to starve them out. A clever Ferber decided to load the cannons with pigs' heads to show the enemy that they had plenty of food—it worked, and the enemy left.

Circle around, past the front of the beautifully carved main altar. Behind it is the biggest stained-glass window in Poland, and below the window is a huge, empty glass case. The case was designed to hold Hans Memling's *Final Judgment* painting, which used to be on display here, but is currently being held hostage by the National Museum. The museum claims the church isn't a good environment for such a precious work, but the priest had this display case built to convince the museum to give it back. You can see a smaller replica up by the main door of the church (in the little chapel on the right just before you exit), but true art fans will want to venture to the National Museum to see the much larger original (described later in this chapter).

Before you head back out to the mini-Memling (and the exit), venture to the far side of the altar and check out the elaborate astronomical clock. Below is the calendar showing the saint's day, and above are zodiac signs and the time (only one hand).

If you've got the energy, climb the 408 steps up the church's 270-foot-tall **tower.** You'll be rewarded with sweeping views of the entire city (tower climb-3 zł, entrance in back-right corner).

Archaeological Museum (Muzeum Archeologiczne)—This modest museum is worth a quick peek for those interested in archaeology. The ground floor has exhibits on excavated finds from Sudan, where the museum has a branch program. Upstairs, look for the distinctive urns with cute faces, dating from the Hallstatt Period and discovered in slate graves around Gdańsk. Also upstairs are some Bronze and Iron Age tools; before-and-after photos of WWII Gdańsk; and a reconstructed 12th-century Viking-like Slavonic longboat (5 zł; July–Aug Tue–Sun 10:00–17:00, closed Mon; Sept–June Tue and Thu–Fri 9:00–16:00, Wed 10:00–17:00, Sat–Sun 10:00–16:00, closed Mon; ulica Mariacka 25–26, tel. 058-301-5031).

▲Central Maritime Museum (Centralne Muzeum Morskie)—Gdańsk's history and livelihood are tied to the sea. This collec-

tion, spread out among several buildings on either side of the river, examines all aspects of this connec-tion. While nautical types may get a thrill out of the creaky, sprawling museum, most visitors find it little more than a convenient way to pass some time and enjoy a cruise across the river.

There are four parts of the exhibit. Two of them are on the Main Town side of the river:

1. The Crane (Żuraw): The medieval Crane—Gdańsk's most important symbol—houses an exhibit on living in the city during its Golden Age (16th–17th centuries). You'll see models of Baltic buildings (including the Crane you're inside), plus traditional tools and costumes. For more on the Crane itself, see page 333.

2. Boats of the World: The building next to the Crane houses different kinds of boats from around the world, mostly from non-European cultures. A Venetian gondola greets you at the entry.

The other two parts of the museum are across the river on Ołowianka Island. You'll reach the island via the little **ferry** (*prom*,

1 zł 1-way, included in 15-zł ticket). The ferry runs about every 15 minutes in peak season (during museum hours only), but frequency declines sharply in the off-season (and it doesn't run if the river freezes). This also gives fine views back on the Crane. Once on the island, you'll visit the other two parts:

3. The Old Granaries (Spichlerze): These three rebuilt granaries make up the heart of the exhibit, tracing the history of Gdańsk—particularly as it relates to the sea—from prehistoric days to the present. Models of the town and region help put things into perspective. You'll see exhibits on underwater exploration, navigational aids, artifacts of the Polish seafaring tradition, peek-a-boo cross-sections of multi-level ships, and models of the modern-day shipyard where Solidarity was born. This place is home to more miniature ships than you ever thought you'd see, and the Nautical Gallery upstairs features endless rooms with paintings of boats.

4. The *Sołdek:* Crawl through the holds and scramble across the deck of this decommissioned steamship docked permanently across from the Crane. Below decks, you'll see where they shoveled the coal; wander through a maze of pipes, gears, valves, gauges, and ladders; and visit the rooms where the sailors lived, slept, and ate. You can even play captain in the bridge. The place would be much improved with a smarter exhibit—which is planned for the future (ship sometimes closed in winter).

Cost, Hours, Location: Each part of the museum costs 6 zł, but the 15-zł ticket gets you in everywhere and also covers the ferry across the river. It's open July–Aug daily 10:00–18:00, Sept–June generally Tue–Sun 10:00–16:00—but different branches can have slightly different hours, closed Mon (ulica Ołowianka 9–13, tel. 058-301-8611, www.cmm.pl). Throughout the museum, there's an irritating lack of English information, though some exhibits have descriptions you can borrow.

Tour: If you have a serious fascination with all matters maritime, pay the unbelievably cheap price of 20 zł to get your own private English-speaking guide (reserve ahead: tel. 058-301-8611, if they speak only Polish, they'll figure it out and find an English-speaker). The tour can last two hours or more, so if you have only a passing interest, skip the guide and see the museum at your own pace.

National Museum in Gdańsk (Muzeum Narodowe w Gdańsku)—This art collection, housed in what was a 15th-century Franciscan monastery, is worth ▲▲ to art-lovers for one reason: Hans Memling's glorious *Last Judgment* triptych altarpiece, one of the two most important pieces of art to be seen in Poland (the other is da Vinci's *Lady with an Ermine* in Kraków—see page 243). If you're not a purist, you can settle for seeing the much smaller replica in St. Mary's Church. But if medieval art is your bag, make the 10-minute walk here from the Main Town (10 zł, Tue–Fri 9:00–16:00, Sat–Sun 10:00–16:00, last entry at 15:30, closed Mon; walk 10 min due south from ulica Długa's Golden Gate, take pedestrian underpass beneath the big cross-street, then continue down the busy street until you see signs for the museum; ulica Toruńska 1, tel. 058-301-7061, www.muzeum.narodowe.gda.pl).

From the entry, the altarpiece by Hans Memling (c. 1440–1494) is at the top of the stairs. The history of the painting is as interesting as the work itself. It was commissioned in the mid-15th century by the Medicis' banker in Florence, Angelo di Jacopo Tani. The ship delivering the painting from England to Florence was hijacked by a Gdańsk pirate, who brought the altarpiece to his hometown to be displayed in St. Mary's Church. For centuries, it was admired from afar by kings, emperors, and czars, until it was finally seized by Napoleon in the early 19th century and taken to Paris, where it hung in the Louvre. Gdańsk finally got the painting back, only to have it exiled again—this time into St. Petersburg's Hermitage Museum—after World War II. On its return to Gdańsk in 1956, it was claimed by this museum—though St. Mary's wants it back.

Have a close look at Memling's well-traveled work. It's the end of the world, and Christ rides in on a rainbow to judge humankind. Angels blow reveille, waking the dead, who rise from their graves. The winged archangel Michael—dressed for battle and wielding the cross like a weapon—weighs the grace in each person, sending them either to the fires of hell (right panel) or up the sparkling-crystal stairway to heaven (left).

It takes all 70 square feet of paneling to contain this awesome scene. Jam-packed with dozens of bodies, a Bible's worth of symbolism, and executed with astonishing detail, the painting can keep even a non-art-lover occupied. Notice the serene, happy expressions of the righteous, as they're greeted by St. Peter (with his giant key) and clothed by angels. And pity the condemned, their faces filled with terror and sorrow as they're tortured by grotesque devils more horrifying than anything Hollywood can devise.

Tune into the exquisite details: the angels' robes, the devils' genetic-mutant features, the portrait of the man in the scale (a Medici banker), Michael's peacock wings. Get as close as you can to the globe at Christ's feet and Michael's shining breastplate, and you'll even make out the whole scene in mirror reflection. Then back up and take it all in—three panels connected by a necklace of bodies that curves downward through hell, across the earth, then rising up to the towers of the New Jerusalem. On the back side of the triptych, you'll see reverent portraits of the painting's patron, Angelo Tani, and his new bride, Catarina.

Beyond the Memling, the rest of the collection isn't too thrilling. The rest of the upstairs has more Flemish and Dutch art, as well as paintings from Gdańsk's Golden Age and various works by Polish artists (including canvases by Młoda Polska artists Jacek Malczewski and Olga Boznańska—explained on page 231). The ground floor features a cavernous, all-white cloister filled with Gothic altarpiece sculptures, gold- and silverware, majolica and Delft porcelain, and characteristic Gdańsk-style furniture.

Solidarity (Solidarność) and the Gdańsk Shipyard (Stocznia Gdańska)

Gdańsk's single best experience—easily worth ▲▲▲—is exploring the shipyard that witnessed the beginning of the end of communism's stranglehold on Eastern Europe. Here in the industrial wasteland that Lech Wałęsa called the "cradle of freedom," you'll learn the story of the brave Polish shipyard workers who took on—and ultimately defeated—an Evil Empire.

A visit to the Solidarity sights has two main parts: the memorial and gate out in front of the shipyard, and the excellent "Roads to Freedom" exhibit, housed in the meeting hall where the agreement to end the strike was signed. Allow 90 minutes to tour the grounds and learn the entire story.

Cost, Hours, Information: Visiting the memorial, the shipyard gate, and most of the exhibits on the shipyard grounds is free. The "Roads to Freedom" exhibit costs 6 zł (May–Sept Tue–Sun 10:00–17:00, Oct–April Tue–Sun 10:00–16:00, closed Mon year-round, ulica Doki 1, tel. 058-769-2920, www.fcs.org.pl).

Getting to the Shipyard: The Solidarity monument and shipyard are at the north end of the Old Town, about a 20-minute walk from ulica Długa. For the most interesting approach, see my self-guided walk on page 334.

◉ Self-Guided Tour: After the communists took over Eastern Europe at the end of World War II, the oppressed people throughout the Soviet Bloc rose up in different ways. The most dramatic uprisings—Hungary's 1956 Uprising (see page 432) and Czechoslovakia's 1968 "Prague Spring" (see page 53)—were both brutally crushed under the treads of Soviet tanks. The formula for freedom that finally succeeded—and was lucky enough to coincide with the *perestroika* and *glasnost* policies of the Soviet premier Mikhail Gorbachev—was a patient, decade-long series of strikes spearheaded by

Lech Wałęsa

In 1980, the world was turned on its ear by a walrus-mustachioed shipyard electrician. Within three years, this seemingly run-of-the-mill Pole had precipitated the collapse of communism, led a massive 10 million-member trade union with enormous political impact, was named *Time* magazine's Man of the Year, and won a Nobel Peace Prize.

Lech Wałęsa was born in Popowo, Poland, in 1943. After working as a car mechanic and serving two years in the army, he became an electrician at the Gdańsk Shipyard in 1967. Like many Poles, Wałęsa felt stifled by the communist government, and was infuriated that a system that was supposed to be for the workers clearly wasn't serving them.

When the shipyard massacre took place in December 1970, Wałęsa was at the forefront of the protests. He was marked as a dissident, and in 1976, he was fired. He hopped from job to job and was occasionally unemployed—a rock-bottom status reserved for only the most despicable derelicts. But Wałęsa soldiered on, fighting for the creation of a trade union and building up quite a file with the secret police.

In August 1980, Wałęsa heard news of the beginnings of the Gdańsk strike, and raced to the shipyard. In an act that has since become the stuff of legends, Wałęsa scaled the shipyard wall to get inside.

Before long, Wałęsa's dynamic personality won him the unofficial role of the workers' leader and spokesman. He negotiated with the regime to hash out the August Agreements, becoming a rock star–type hero during the so-called "16 Months of Hope"...until martial law came crashing down in December of 1981. Wałęsa was arrested and interned for 11 months in a country house. After being released, Wałęsa continued to struggle under-

Lech Wałęsa and his trade union, called Solidarność—"Solidarity." While some American politicians would like to take credit for defeating communism, Wałęsa and his fellow workers were the ones fighting on the front lines, armed with nothing more than guts. The following tour leads you through the place where the inspirational events of August 1980 took place, while explaining the story as it unfolded. Begin at the towering monument—with three anchor-adorned crosses—near the entrance gate to the shipyard.

ground, becoming a symbol of anti-communist sentiment.

Finally, the dedication of Wałęsa and Solidarity paid off, and Polish communism dissolved—with Wałęsa rising from the ashes as the country's first post-communist president. But the skills that made Wałęsa a rousing success at leading an uprising did not translate to the president's office. Wałęsa proved to be a stubborn, headstrong politician, frequently clashing with the parliament. He squabbled with his own party, declaring a "war at the top" of Solidarity and rotating higher-ups to prevent corruption and keep the party fresh. He also didn't choose his advisors well, enlisting several staffers who wound up immersed in scandal. His overconfidence was his Achilles' heel, and his governing style verged on authoritarian.

Unrefined and none too interested in scripted speeches, Wałęsa was a simple man who preferred playing ping-pong with his buddies to attending formal state functions. Though lacking a formal education, Wałęsa had unsurpassed drive and charisma... but that's not enough to lead a country—especially during an impossibly complicated, fast-changing time, when even the savviest politician would certainly have stumbled.

Wałęsa was defeated at the polls (by the Poles) in 1995, and when he ran again in 2000, he received a humiliating 1 percent of the vote. Since leaving office, Wałęsa has kept a lower profile, but still delivers speeches worldwide. Many poor Poles grumble that Lech, who started life simple like them, has forgotten the little people. But his fans point out that he gives much of his income to charity. And he still always wears a pin featuring the Black Madonna of Częstochowa—the symbol of Polish Catholicism—on his lapel.

Poles say there are at least two Lech Wałęsas: the young, working-class idealist Lech, at the forefront of the Solidarity strikes, who will always have a special place in their hearts; and the failed President Wałęsa, who got in over his head and tarnished his legacy.

Monument of the Fallen Shipyard Workers: The seeds of August 1980 were sown a decade before. Since becoming part of the Soviet Bloc, the Poles staged frequent strikes, protests, and uprisings to secure their rights, all of which were put down by the regime. But the bloodiest of these took place in December 1970—a tragic event memorialized by this monument.

The 1970 strike was prompted by price hikes. The communist government set the prices for all products. As Poland endured drastic food shortages in the 1960s and 1970s, the regime frequently announced what they called "regulation of prices"—increasing the cost of essential foodstuffs, while at the same time symbolically lowering prices of unimportant items that nobody could afford anyway (like elevators and TV sets). The regime was usually smart enough to raise prices on January 1—when the people were fat and happy after Christmas, and too hung over to complain. But on December 12, 1970, bolstered by an ego-stoking visit by West German Chancellor Willy Brandt, Polish premier Władysław Gomułka hiked up prices. The people of Poland—who cared more about the price of Christmas dinner than relations with Germany—struck back.

A wave of strikes and sit-ins spread along the heavily industrialized north coast of Poland, most notably in Gdańsk, Gdynia, and Szczecin. Thousands of angry demonstrators poured through the gate of this shipyard, marched into town, and set fire to the Communist Party Committee building. In an attempt to quell the riots, the government-run radio implored the people to go back to work. On the morning of December 17, workers showed up at shipyard gates across northern Poland—and were greeted by the army and police. Without provocation, the Polish army opened fire on the workers. While the official death toll for the massacre stands at 44, others say the true number is much higher.

This monument, with a trio of 140-foot-tall crosses, honors those lost to the regime that December. Go to the middle of the wall behind the crosses, to the monument of the worker wearing a flimsy plastic work helmet, attempting to shield himself from bullets. Behind him is a list—pockmarked with symbolic bullet holes—of workers murdered on that day. *Lat* means "years"—many teenagers were among the dead. The quote at the top of the wall was from Pope John Paul II, who was elected eight years after this tragedy. The Pope was known for his clever way with words, and this very carefully phrased quote—which served as an inspiration to the Poles during their darkest hours—skewers the regime in a way subtle enough to still be tolerated: "Let thy spirit descend, and renew the face of the earth—*this* earth" (that is, specifically, Poland). Below that is the dedication: "They gave their lives so you can live decently."

Stretching to the left of this center wall are plaques representing labor unions from around Poland—and around the world (look for the Chinese characters)—expressing solidarity with these workers. To the right is an enormous Bible verse: "May the Lord give strength to his people. May the Lord bless his people with the gift of peace" (Psalms 29:11).

More than a decade after the massacre, this monument was finally constructed. It marked the first time a communist regime ever allowed a monument built to honor its own victims. Wałęsa called it a harpoon in the heart of the communists. Inspired by the brave sacrifice of their true comrades, the shipyard workers rose up here in August of 1980, formulating the "21 Points" of a new union called Solidarity. These demands are listed in Polish on the panel at the far end of the right wall, marked *21 X TAK Solidarność* ("21 times yes Solidarity").

• *Now continue to the gate and peer through into the birthplace of Eastern European freedom.*

Gdańsk Shipyard (Stocznia Gdańska) Gate #2: When a Pole named Karol Wojtyła was elected Pope in 1978—and visited his homeland in 1979—he inspired his 40 million countrymen to believe that impossible dreams can come true. Prices continued to go up, and the workers continued to rise up. By the summer of 1980, it was clear that the dam was about to break.

In August, Anna Walentynowicz—a Gdańsk crane operator and known dissident—was fired unceremoniously just short of her retirement. This sparked a strike in the Gdańsk Shipyard (then called the Lenin Shipyard) on August 14, 1980. An electrician named Lech Wałęsa had been fired as an agitator years before, and wasn't allowed into the shipyard. But on hearing news of the strike, Wałęsa went to the shipyard and climbed over the wall to get inside. The strike had a leader.

Imagine being one of the 16,000 workers who stayed here for 18 days during the strike—hungry, cold, sleeping on sheets of Styrofoam, inspired by the new Polish pope, excited about finally standing up to the regime...and terrified that you might be gunned down at any moment, like your friends were a decade before. Because you're afraid to leave the shipyard, your only way to communicate with the outside world is through this gate—your wife or brother shows up here and asks for you, and those inside spread the word until you come talk to them. Occasionally, a truck pulls up to the gate, and Lech Wałęsa stands on its cab with a megaphone and faces the thousands of people assembled here—giving them progress reports of the negotiations, and pleading for supplies. The people of Gdańsk respond, bringing armfuls of bread and other food, keeping the workers going. This truly is Solidarity.

Two items hung on the fence. One of them (which still hangs there today) was a picture of Pope John Paul II—a reminder to believe in your dreams and have faith in God (for more on the pope and his role in Solidarity, see page 234). The other item was a makeshift list of the strikers' 21 Points—demands scrawled in red paint and black pencil on pieces of plywood. The demands included the right to strike and form unions, the freeing of political prisoners, and an increase in wages.

• *Go around the gate (to the right, past the souvenir stand) and enter the shipyard. As you walk, you'll see giant photographs from the summer of 1980.*

Path Through the Shipyard: As you walk toward the "Pathways to Freedom" exhibit, you'll pass through two huge symbolic gateways. The first resembles the rusted hull of a ship, representing the protest of the shipbuilders. Inside are two electronic strips: on the left, displaying communist slogans; on the right, the wisdom of Lech Wałęsa and Solidarity.

The next gate—a futuristic, colorful tower—is a small-scale version of a 1,000-foot-tall monument planned by the prominent Soviet constructivist architect Vladimir Tatlin. This fanciful but unfulfilled design represents the misguided, failed optimism of the communist "utopia."

After the gateways, on the left, look for the two **wall fragments.** On the right is the shipyard wall that Lech Wałęsa famously scrambled over in August of 1980 to join his comrades in the shipyard strikes. On the left, with the map of Europe, is a piece of another Wall—from Berlin—which fell less than a decade later. The message is simple: What began in this shipyard culminated in the fall of the Berlin Wall. The map showing Europe in 1980 and again in 2004 drives the point home.

At the end of the path, you see an **armored personnel carrier,** just like the ones used by the ZOMO (riot police) to terrorize Polish citizens after martial law was declared in 1981 (described below).

• *Now continue into the red-brick building. (There's talk of moving this exhibit to a building farther inside the shipyard, but the displays should remain the same.)*

"Roads to Freedom" Exhibit in BHP Conference Hall: Step inside and buy your ticket, which is designed to look like the communist ration coupons that all Poles had to carry and present before they could buy certain goods. Cashiers would stand with scissors at the ready, prepared to snip off a corner of your coupon after making the sale.

The first room shows a typical **Polish shop** (marked *spożyw,* a truncated version of *spożywczy,* or "grocery store") from the 1970s, at the worst of the food shortages. Great selection, eh? Often the only things in stock were vinegar and mustard. Milk and bread were generally available, but they were low quality—it wasn't unusual to find a cigarette butt in your loaf. The few blocks of cheese and other items in the case aren't real—they're props (marked *atrapy*—"fake"), so the shop wouldn't look completely empty. Sometimes they'd hang a few pitiful, phony salamis from the hooks—otherwise, people might think it was a tile shop. The only real meat in here was the flies on the flypaper. Shockingly, shoppers (mostly women) would sometimes have to wait in line literally all day long just to pick over these scant choices.

In the corner, the phone booth is marked *Automat Nieczynny*— "Out of Order"—as virtually all phone booths were back then. The sign in the shop window *(22 Lipca)*, draped in the Polish flag, celebrates July 22, the Soviet Liberation Day, honoring the regime. Over the cash register is a picture of Bolek and Lolek, popular cartoon characters of the era. Unlike the Polish people, these two were able to travel around the world. (They seem to be in Turkey.)

Consider picking up a Solidarity book or other souvenir at the excellent gift shop before moving into the next room.

The first part of the exhibit explains the **roots** of the shipyard strikes: the famous uprisings in Hungary and Czechoslovakia, and the December 1970 riots in Poland.

Then you move into the heart of the exhibit, **August 1980.** There are the original plywood boards featuring the 21 Points, which hung on the front gate we just saw. As you enter the next room, keep an eye out for a giant, historic pen with the image of Pope John Paul II.

The next room is **the Hall.** After 18 days of protests, it became clear to the communist government that Solidarity would not simply go away. On the afternoon of August 31, 1980, the Governmental Commission and the Inter-Factory Strike Committee (MKS) came together in this very room and signed the August Agreements, which legalized Solidarity—the first time any communist government permitted a workers' union. A video shows the giddy day. Lech Wałęsa—sitting at the big table, with his characteristic walrus moustache—signed the agreement with the big red pope pen. Other union reps, sitting at smaller tables, tape-recorded the proceedings, and played them later at their own factories to prove the unthinkable had happened. While the government didn't take the agreements very seriously, the Poles did...and before long, 10 million of them—one out of every four Poles—became members of Solidarity.

So began the **16 Months of Hope**—the theme of the next room. Newly legal, Solidarity continued to stage strikes and made its opposition known. Slick Solidarity posters and children's art convey the childlike enthusiasm with which the Poles seized their hard-won kernels of freedom. The poster with a baby in a Solidarity T-shirt—one year old, just like the union itself—captures the sense of hope. The grasp of the communist authorities on the Polish people began to slip. The rest of the Soviet Bloc looked on nervously, and the Warsaw Pact army assembled at the Polish border and glared at the uprisers. The threat of invasions hung heavy in the air.

In the next room, Solidarity's progress comes crashing down. On Sunday morning, December 13, 1981, the Polish head of state, General Wojciech Jaruzelski, appeared on national TV and announced the introduction of **martial law.** Solidarity was outlawed, and its leaders were arrested. Frightened Poles heard the announcement and looked out their windows to see Polish Army tanks rumbling through the snowy streets. Jaruzelski claimed that he imposed martial law to prevent the Soviets from invading. Today, many historians question whether martial law was really necessary—though Jaruzelski remains remorseless. Martial law was a tragic, terrifying, and bleak time for the Polish people. But Solidarity moved underground and continued the fight for freedom. Notice that their martial law–era propaganda was produced with far more primitive printing equipment than their earlier posters.

As you leave the room, look for the clandestine print shop, and for the shipbuilding equipment surrounding a Styrofoam pad on the floor. Remember, this was where those first strikers, who had no beds in the shipyard, were forced to sleep.

The next room, with sobering displays of **ZOMO riot gear,** shows a film about the ugliness of martial law. Watch the footage of General Jaruzelski—wearing his trademark dark glasses—reading the announcement of martial law. Listen to the music of the Polish Bob Dylan as he laments the evils of the regime. Chilling scenes show riots, demonstrations, and crackdowns by the ZOMO police—including one demonstrator who's run over by a truck. Another old woman is stampeded by a pack of fleeing demonstrators.

But the ZOMO couldn't crush the human spirit. The exhibit ends with two uplifting **films:** a retrospective on the entire communist era in Poland, and a general look at the fall of the Iron Curtain across Eastern Europe—right up through the 2004 "Orange Revolution" in Ukraine.

Here's your happy ending: By the time the Pope visited his homeland again in 1983, martial law was lifted, and Solidarity—still technically illegal—had gained momentum, gradually pecking away at the communists. With the moral support of the Pope and the entire Western world, the brave Poles were the first European country to throw off the shackles of communism when, in the spring of 1989, the "Round Table Talks" led to the opening up of elections. The government arrogantly called for parliamentary elections, reserving 65 percent of seats for themselves. The plan backfired, as virtually every contested seat went to Solidarity. This success inspired people all over Eastern Europe, and by that winter, the Berlin Wall had crumbled and the Czechs and Slovaks had staged their Velvet Revolution. Lech Wałęsa—the shipyard electrician who started it all by jumping over a wall—became the first president of post-communist Poland. And a year later, in Poland's first true elections since World War II, 29 different parties won seats in the *Sejm* (Parliament). This celebration of democracy was brought to the Polish people by a brave electrician and the workers of Gdańsk.

Outer Gdańsk

These two sights—worthwhile only to those with a special interest—are each within the city limits of Gdańsk, but they take several hours to see round-trip.

Oliwa Cathedral (Katedra Oliwska)—The suburb of Oliwa, at the northern edge of Gdańsk, is home to this visually striking church. The quirky, elongated facade hides a surprisingly long and skinny nave. The ornately decorated 18th-century organ over the main entrance features angels and stars that move around when the organ is played. While locals are proud of this place, it's hard to justify the effort it takes to get out here. Skip it unless you just love Polish churches or you're going to a concert.

Concerts: Concerts of the animated organ occur frequently, especially in summer (June–Aug generally at the top of each hour Mon–Fri 10:00–16:00—except at 14:00—Sat 10:00–15:00, Sun 15:00–17:00; May and Sept Mon–Sat at the top of each hour 10:00–13:00, Sun at 15:00 and 16:00; fewer off-season). Confirm the schedule before making the trip. Note that on Sundays and holidays, there are no concerts before 15:00.

Getting There: Oliwa is about six miles northwest of central Gdańsk, on the way to Sopot and Gdynia. To get to Oliwa, you have two options: Take **tram** #6 or #12 from Gdańsk's Main Train Station. These trams let you off right at the entrance to Oliwski Park. Go straight through to the back of the park; near the end, you'll see the copper roof and two skinny, pointy spires of the cathedral on your right. Exit through the back of the park, bear right, and go one block to find the entrance to the church. Your other option is to take a **commuter SKM train** from Gdańsk's Main Station 15 minutes to the "Gdańsk Oliwa" stop (see "Getting Around the Tri-City," page 360). From the Oliwa train station, it's a 15-minute walk or 10-zł taxi ride to the cathedral. Walk straight ahead out of the station and turn right when you get to the busy road. Cross the road at the light and enter the tree-filled Park Oliwski at the corner, then follow the directions above.

Westerplatte—World War II began on September 1, 1939, when Adolf Hitler sent the warship *Schleswig-Holstein* to attack this Polish munitions depot, which was guarding Gdańsk's harbor.

Though it may interest WWII history buffs, there's little to see at this site aside from a modest museum and a towering monument. As it's surrounded by shipyard sprawl, it's not a particularly pleasant trip, either.

Getting There: It's quickest to take bus #106 to the end (about 30 min). Or cruise there in 45 minutes on Żegluga Gdańska boats or the old-fashioned *Galeon Lew* (see "Transportation Connections," page 358).

SHOPPING

The big story in Gdańsk is amber *(bursztyn)*, a fossil resin available in all shades, shapes, and sizes (see "All About Amber," page 373). While you'll see amber sold all over town, the best place to browse and buy is along the atmospheric ulica Mariacka (between the Motława River and St. Mary's Church). This pretty street, with old-fashioned balconies and dozens of display cases, is fun to wander even if you're not a shopper. Other good places to buy amber are along the riverfront embankment and on ulica Długa. To avoid rip-offs—such as amber that's been melted and reshaped—always buy it from a shop, not from someone standing on the street. (But note that most shops also have a display case and salesperson out front, which are perfectly legit.) Prices everywhere are about the same, so rather than seeking out a specific place, just window-shop until you see what you want. Styles range from gaudy necklaces with huge globs of amber, to tasteful smaller pendants in a silver setting, to cheap trinkets. All shades of amber—from near-white to dark brown—cost about the same, but you'll pay more for inclusions (bugs or other objects stuck in the amber). You can get a basic amber pendant on a silver chain or a pair of small earrings for about 30 zł. If you want to pay more for bigger pieces or a more stylish setting, merchants will happily take your money.

Gdańsk also has several modern shopping malls, most of them in the Old Town or near the Main Train Station. The walk between the Main Town and the Solidarity shipyard goes past some of the best malls (see page 334).

SLEEPING

Gdańsk's accommodation scene, long miserably sparse, is steadily improving. With several new hotels cropping up in the last two years—and lots more planned for 2007 and beyond—competition should help rein in the excessively high prices. To get the best deal, it's essential to book ahead for peak season (mid-June–mid-Sept), when prices increase.

Sleep Code

(3 zł = about $1, €1 = about $1.20, country code: 48)
S = Single, **D** = Double/Twin, **T** = Triple, **Q** = Quad, **b** = bathroom,
s = shower only. Unless otherwise noted, breakfast is included,
credit cards are accepted, and English is spoken.

　　To help you sort easily through these listings, I've divided
the rooms into three categories, based on the price for a standard double room with bath:

$$$　Higher Priced—Most rooms 400 zł (€105) or more.
$$　Moderately Priced—Most rooms between 300–400
　　　　　　　zł (€80–105).
$　Lower Priced—Most rooms 300 zł (€80) or less.

Across the River

While these three places are a few minutes farther by foot from the
action, they're all well-priced and in pleasant neighborhoods.

$$ Hotel Królewski, a classy hotel in a beautifully reno-
vated red-brick granary, offers 30 stylish rooms, great rates, and a
friendly staff. It's just beyond the three granaries of the Maritime
Museum, across the river from the Crane (Sb-290–320 zł, Db-
340–370 zł, fancier suite-like Db "plus"-390–420 zł, higher prices
are for May–Sept, can be even cheaper than these rates Fri–Sun
in winter, request a view room—they cost the same as non-view
rooms, non-smoking rooms, elevator, good restaurant, ulica Oło-
wianka 1, tel. 058-326-1111, fax 058-326-1110, www.hotelkrolewski
.pl, office@hotelkrolewski.pl). You can commute to your sightsee-
ing by ferry (take the 1-zł boat trip across the river offered by the
Maritime Museum—see page 340). But the ferry runs only dur-
ing the museum's opening hours, and is sporadic off-season. If the
ferry isn't running, it's a scenic 10-minute walk along the river and
over the bridge into the Main Town.

　　$ Willa Biała Lilia ("Villa of the White Lily") is a new place
with 16 modern rooms. It's on the back side of a charmingly restored
row of colorful houses that overlook a dreary parking lot just across
the river from the main drag (Sb-210 zł, Db-245 zł, 15 zł more per
person for bigger "deluxe" rooms, extra bed-60 zł, slightly cheaper
Oct–April, parking garage-20 zł, ulica Spichrzowa 16, tel. 058-301-
7074, fax 058-320-1473, www.bialalilia.pl, bialalilia@bialalilia.pl).

　　$ Dom Muzyka, a 10-minute walk from the Main Town, rents
87 simple, new-feeling rooms. The catch: It's hiding in the back of
the big Academy of Music building (Akademia Muzyczna)—vir-
tually impossible to find in a nondescript residential neighborhood.

Gdańsk Hotels and Restaurants

**Map labels:**

SOLIDARITY SHIPYARD
GATE
SOLIDARITY MONUMENT
400 YARDS
400 METERS
LIBRARY
TO 9
OLD TOWN
ST. BRIDGET'S
ST. CATH.
KATARZYNKI
MKT. HALL
ST. NIC.
TRAIN STN.
TRAM STOP
TOWER
TARG DRZEWNY
MAIN TOWN
ARMORY
GOLDEN GATE
LOT OFFICE
TRAM STOP
UPLAND GATE & AMBER MUS.
ST. MARY'S
PIWNA
TOWN HALL
DŁUGA
POST
UPHAGEN HOUSE
BAR MLECZNY NEPTUN
NEPTUNE STATUE
OGARNA
DŁUGI TARG
ARTUS COURT
MARIACKA
ARCHAEO-LOGICAL MUS.
THE CRANE
GRANARY ISLAND
BOATS TO HEL
STAGIEWNA
GREEN GATE
TO
CENTRAL MARITIME MUSEUM
SS SOŁDEK
MOTŁAWA RIVER
STRAGANIARSKA
NIARSKA
SWIETO-JANSKA
SZEROKA
SW. DUCHA
TO NAT'L. MUSEUM
DCH

Street names: DOKI, PIAST, ŁAGIEWNIKI, WAŁOWA, WAŁY PIAST., PODWALE GRODSKIE, WAŁY JAGIELLOŃSKIE, HUCISCO, OKOPOWA, REN., HEWELIUSZA, RAJSKA, J., STOLARSKA, OLEJARNA, IGIE, PODZEN, PANSKA, KOZNA, GARN., KOW., KARM., ELM., KORZENNA, STAROMIEJSKIE, JARTACZNA, DŁUGA, WARZAWA

1. Hotel Królewski
2. Willa Biała Lilia
3. To Dom Muzyka Hotel
4. Hanza Hotel
5. Kamienica Goldwasser Hotel/Rest.
6. Hotel Wolne Miasto
7. Gotyk House B&B
8. Przy Targu Rybnym Hostel
9. To Baltic Hostel
10. Dom Harcerza Hostel
11. Bar pod Rybą Rest.
12. Bar Mleczny Neptun
13. Dom pod Łososiem Rest.
14. Pierogarnia u Dzika Rest.
15. Pi Kawa Café
16. Cukiernia Kaliszczak (Bakery)

Still, the prices are worth the hunt. Their "deluxe" rooms are bigger and overlook the quiet courtyard, while the standard rooms face a busy street. Since the deluxe rooms are mostly twins, and the standard rooms have air-conditioning and good soundproof windows, I'd go with standard (Sb-180 zł, standard Db-255 zł, deluxe Db-275 zł, apartment-380 zł, extra bed-70 zł, slightly cheaper Oct–April, elevator, ulica Łąkowa 1–2, tel. 058-326-0600, fax 058-326-0601, www.dom-muzyka.pl, biuro@dom-muzyka.pl). From the Green Gate in the Main Town, cross the two bridges, then walk a long block along the modern building and turn right just before the park (on Łąkowa, across from the big brick church). Walk to the end of this block; just before the busy road, go through the gate of the big, yellow-brick building on the right. Once inside the gate, the hotel is around the back of the yellow building, the farthest door down. If you get lost, just ask people, "Hotel?"

In the Main Town

You'll pay a premium to sleep in the Main Town itself, but many find it worth the extra expense.

$$$ Hanza Hotel offers a fun, neo-Hanseatic exterior and 60 modern, uninspired rooms. It charges—and gets—top złoty for its ideal riverfront location, little character, and disinterested staff. Prices are outrageously high in the summer, but a bit more reasonable off-season (June–Sept: Sb-665 zł, Db-695 zł; May and Oct: Sb-565 zł, Db-595 zł; Nov–April: Sb-395 zł, Db-465 zł; request riverview room for no extra charge, air-con, elevator, Tokarska 6, tel. 058-305-3427, fax 058-305-3386, www.hanza-hotel.com.pl, hotel@hanza-hotel.com.pl).

$$ Kamienica Goldwasser, renting seven rooms over a good restaurant, is perfectly located, right on the river embankment next door to the Crane. Each room is different, but all are thoughtfully decorated, with windows facing both the river and the back. Three of the rooms are smaller and cheaper—similar to the bigger rooms, but with cramped bathrooms, and an especially good value. The restaurant has a special room that guests are encouraged to use as a lounge for congregating and socializing (small Sb-250 zł, big Sb-340 zł, small Db-340 zł, big Db-430 zł, extra bed-90 zł, lots of stairs and no elevator, Długie Pobrzeże 22, tel. & fax 058-301-8878, www.goldwasser.pl, kamienica@goldwasser.pl).

$$ Hotel Wolne Miasto ("Free City") offers 43 elegant, well-priced rooms on the edge of the Main Town, just two blocks from the main drag. The catch: It's near a popular and noisy disco, so request a quieter room when you reserve (Sb-275 zł, Db-340 zł, bigger "deluxe" Db-375 zł, 15 percent cheaper Nov–April, 10 zł more per person for fancier breakfast, elevator, ulica Świętego

Ducha 2, tel. 058-305-2255, fax 058-322-2447, www.hotelwm.pl, rezerwacja@hotelwm.pl).

$ Gotyk House, Gdańsk's best deal, is run with warmth and pride by the Rybicki family. This we-try-harder B&B offers six modern, simple rooms with creative touches in what's supposedly the city's oldest house, next door to St. Mary's Church (Sb-250 zł, Db-280 zł, 30 zł less Oct–April, cash only, ulica Mariacka 1, tel. 058-301-8567, mobile 0602-844-535, www.gotykhouse.eu, reservation@gotykhouse.eu).

$ Przy Targu Rybnym, a three-minute walk from the Crane at the north end of the embankment, is Gdańsk's most central hostel. Waldemar runs this easygoing, low-key, slightly grungy place with a spirit of fun that permeates the chummy common room. Aside from dorm beds, it offers "private" rooms for two to four people with shared bathrooms down the hall (prices per person: D-70 zł, T-60 zł, Q-50 zł, bunk in dorm or crowded basement slumbermill-40 zł, private rooms 5 zł more expensive in peak season, prices include sheets and breakfast, free Internet access, 15-zł laundry service, ulica Grodzka 21, tel. 058-301-5627, www.gdanskhostel.com, gdanskhostel@hotmail.com). If they're booked up, Waldemar might send you to his **Baltic Hostel,** which is cheaper (45 zł per person in 2–4-person room, 35 zł for dorm bunk) but in a much less convenient location (away from the center, north of the train station at 3. Maya #25; tel. 058-721-9657, www.baltichostel.com, baltichostel@hotmail.com).

$ Dom Harcerza is a Polish-style budget hotel/hostel with 17 old, musty, but well-maintained rooms on the second floor of a dreary office building. It won't win any prizes for personality, and communication can be difficult, but it's nicely located in a corner of the Main Town just two blocks south of the Golden Gate (bunk in 5- to 12-bed dorm-25 zł, S-50 zł, D-100 zł, Db-210 zł, T-120 zł, Tb-260 zł, Q-140 zł, 25 percent cheaper Oct–April, includes sheets, breakfast-9 zł, cash only, fun ground-floor café, ulica Za Murami 2–10, tel. 058-301-3621, fax 058-301-2472, www.domharcerza.prv.pl, domharcerza@go2.pl).

EATING

In addition to the traditional Polish fare, Gdańsk has some fine Baltic seafood. Herring *(śledź)* is popular here, as is cod *(dorsz)*. Natives also brag that their salmon *(łosoś)* is better than Norway's. For a stiff drink, sample *Goldwasser* (better known in the US as Goldschlager). This strong liqueur, flecked with gold, was supposedly invented here in Gdańsk. The following options are all in the Main Town, within three blocks of ulica Długa.

Budget Restaurants on the Main Drag

These two places are incredibly cheap, tasty, quick, and wonderfully convenient—right on ulica Długa. They're worth considering even if you're not on a tight budget.

Bar pod Rybą ("Under the Fish") is nirvana for fans of baked potatoes *(pieczony ziemniak)*. They offer more than 20 varieties, piled high with a wide variety of toppings and sauces, from Mexican beef to herring to Polish cheeses. They also offer fish dishes with salad and potatoes, making this a cheap place to sample local seafood. The tasteful decor—walls lined with old bottles, antique wooden hangers, and paintings by the owner—is squeezed into a single cozy room packed with happy eaters. In the summer, order inside, and they'll bring your food to you at an outdoor table (potatoes and fish dishes are each about 10–15 zł, daily 11:00–19:00, until 21:00 in summer, Długi Targ 35–38, tel. 058-305-1307).

Bar Mleczny Neptun is your best milk-bar option in the Main Town. A good meal, including a drink, runs about 10 zł. This popular place has more charm than your typical institutional milk bar, including outdoor seating along the most scenic stretch of the main drag. The items on the counter are for display—rather than take what's there, point to what you want and they'll dish it up fresh (Mon–Fri 7:00–18:00, until 19:00 in summer, Sat 10:00–17:00, open Sun only in summer 11:00–17:00, ulica Długa 33–34, tel. 058-301-4988). For more on milk bars, see page 211.

Fancier Restaurants with Polish Fare

Kamienica Goldwasser, which also rents rooms (see "Sleeping"), offers good Polish and international cuisine at fair prices. This is the best choice for dining along the riverfront embankment. Choose between cozy, romantic indoor seating on several levels, or scenic outdoor seating (most main dishes 30–60 zł, daily 10:00–24:00, live piano music Thu–Sat nights 19:00–22:00, near the Crane at Długie Pobrzeże 22, tel. 058-301-8878).

Dom pod Łososiem ("House Under the Salmon"), with over-the-top formality, will make you feel like a rich burgher's family invited you over for dinner. This elegant splurge restaurant has been serving guests for more than 400 years, racking up an impressive guest list (some pictured in the lobby)—and, somewhere in there, inventing *Goldwasser* (most main dishes 50–80 zł, emphasis on fish, daily 12:00–23:00, reservations smart, ulica Szeroka 52–54, tel. 058-301-7652).

Pierogarnia u Dzika ("By the Boar") offers 16 varieties of pierogi (Polish ravioli)—plus meat and fish dishes—in a contemporary setting enhanced by all manner of stuffed and skinned boar. Locals swear by this place, as the pierogi is homemade (pierogi-12–18 zł, get the sampler "King's Plate" to try several different

varieties, main dishes-20–30 zł, daily 10:00–22:00, ulica Piwna
59–60, tel. 058-305-2676).

Coffee and Sweets

Pi Kawa (as in 3.14, pronounced "pee" in Polish) is a trendy, atmospheric café with a wide variety of coffee drinks and herbal teas,
best accompanied by the delicious *szarlotka* (Polish apple cake).
The decor is cozy Old World, and it's packed with socializing
locals (daily 10:00–22:00, ulica Piwna 5–6).

Cukiernia Kaliszczak, a bakery right on ulica Długa, is a no-
frills throwback to the communist days, with delicious cakes and
ice cream and delightfully grumpy service (daily 9:00–21:00, ulica
Długa 74).

TRANSPORTATION CONNECTIONS

By Train

Gdańsk is well-connected to the Tri-City via the commuter SKM
trains (see below). It also has frequent connections to Warsaw, and
handy night trains to Berlin and Kraków.

From Gdańsk by Train to: Hel (town on Hel Peninsula, 3/
day direct, 2.25–3.25 hrs, more with transfer in Gdynia), **Malbork**
(about 2/hr, 1 hr), **Toruń** (4/day direct, 3 hrs; more with a transfer
in Bydgoszcz or Iława, at least hourly, 3–4 hrs), **Warsaw** (nearly
hourly, 4 hrs), **Kraków** (3/day direct, 7 hrs; plus 1 night train, 10
hrs; more with transfer in Warsaw), **Berlin** (4/day, 8.25–9.25 hrs,
transfer in Szczecin, Poznań, or Frankfurt an der Oder; plus 1
direct night train, 10 hrs).

By Boat

Various boats depart from Gdańsk's embankment to nearby destinations, including **Westerplatte** (the monument marking where
World War II started), **Sopot, Gdynia,** and **Hel.** Three different
companies operate from here: the slower, more expensive Żegluga
Gdańska boats; the faster, cheaper ZTM "ferry trams"; and the
old-timey *Galeon Lew* (which only goes to Westerplatte).

Żegluga Gdańska is the biggest operation. Their boats run
from Gdańsk to Westerplatte daily April through October (29 zł
one-way, 43 zł round-trip, 40 min each way, 6/day in each direction, fewer off-season; the 17th-century replica ship *Galeon Lew*
is more atmospheric and cheaper—described below). Boats go to
Hel twice daily July–Aug (58 zł one-way, 75 zł round-trip, 2.75 hrs
each way), but the ZTM "ferry trams" are a much better deal for
that route (see below). Boats from Gdańsk to Sopot and Gdynia
run July–Aug, but schedules are sparse, and these destinations
are much more cheaply and easily reached by train (see "Getting

Around the Tri-City," page 360). All Żegluga Gdańska boats depart from the riverfront near the Green Gate, just upriver from the Crane (tel. 058-301-4926, www.zegluga.pl). In shoulder season (April–June and Sept–Oct), even though most boats stop running from Gdańsk, several routes still run between Sopot, Gdynia, and Hel. Boats don't run in winter (Nov–March).

The **ZTM "ferry trams"** offer a faster and much cheaper way to Hel. These boats zip out to Hel in two hours (16 zł one-way, 32 zł round-trip, 3/day each direction mid-June–mid-Sept, www.ztm .gda.pl/ferry). These boats depart from a 10-minute walk farther down the embankment, beyond the Crane. The same boats also connect Sopot to both Hel and Gdańsk.

For a curious mix of old and new, consider a short cruise through Gdańsk's outlying shipyards on the 17th-century replica *Galeon Lew* ("Lion Galleon"). The ship does a lazy 90-minute circuit out to the WWII monument at Westerplatte and back (if at least six people want to get off at Westerplatte and then take the bus or a different boat back, they'll stop there for you; otherwise, you're in for the full round-trip). It's not exactly pretty—you'll see more industry than scenery—but it's a fun excuse to set sail (30 zł round-trip, 20 zł one-way, departs May–Sept daily at 11:00, 13:00, 15:00, 17:00, and 19:00 from the embankment near the Crane, mobile 0501-571-383). In summer, the return trip is accompanied by live music. If you've ever wanted to hear "What Can You Do with a Drunken Sailor?" in Polish, here's your chance.

Boat schedules tend to change from year to year. Confirm your plans carefully at the TI. All boat trips are weather permitting, especially the faster hydrofoils.

Near Gdańsk: The Tri-City
(Trójmiasto)

Gdańsk is the anchor of the three cities that make up the metropolitan region known as the Tri-City (Trójmiasto). The other two parts are as different as night and day: a once-swanky resort town (Sopot) and a practical, nose-to-the-grindstone business center (Gdynia). The Tri-City as a whole is home to bustling industry and a sprawling university, with several campuses and plenty of well-dressed, English-speaking students. Beyond the Tri-City, the long, skinny Hel Peninsula—a sparsely populated strip of fishing villages and fun-loving beaches—arches dramatically into the Baltic Sea.

Sopot—boasting sandy beaches, tons of tourists, and a certain elegance—is clearly the most appealing day-trip option. Gdynia offers a glimpse into workaday Poland, but leaves most visitors

Gdańsk Day Trips

cold. Hel, which requires the better part of a day to visit, is worthwhile only if you've got perfect summer weather and a desire to lie on the beach.

Getting Around the Tri-City

Gdańsk, Sopot, and Gdynia are connected both by regional commuter trains (*kolejka*, operated by SKM) as well as trains of Poland's national railway (operated by PKP). Trains to Hel are always operated by PKP. Tickets for one system can't be used on the other. While the two different trains chug along the same tracks, they use different (but nearby) stations. For example, at Gdańsk's Main Station, national PKP trains use tracks 1–3, while regional SKM trains use tracks 3–5. And in Sopot, the SKM station is a few hundred feet before the PKP station.

Regional SKM trains are much more frequent—they go in each direction about every 10 minutes (less frequently after 19:30). In Gdańsk, buy tickets at any kiosk marked *SKM Bilety*. Figure 2.80 zł and 25 minutes to Sopot, or 5.60 zł and 40 minutes to Gdynia. Before boarding, be sure to validate your ticket by punching it in the very easy-to-miss yellow or blue slots under the boards with SKM information. Each city has multiple stops. In Gdańsk, use "Gdańsk Główny" (the end of the line); for Sopot, use the stop called simply "Sopot" (only one word); and for Gdynia, it's "Gdynia Główna" (the main station).

The bigger PKP trains are faster, but less frequent—unless you notice one happens to be leaving at a convenient time, I'd skip them and stick with the easy SKM trains.

For a more romantic—and much slower—approach, consider the boat (see Gdańsk's "Transportation Connections" earlier in this chapter).

Sopot

Sopot (SOH-poht), dubbed the "Nice of the North," was a celebrated haunt of beautiful people during the 1920s and 1930s, and remains a popular beach getaway to this day.

Sopot was created in the late 19th century by Napoleon's doctor, Jean Georges Haffner, who believed Baltic Sea water to be therapeutic. By the 1890s, it had become a fashionable seaside resort. This gambling center boasted enough high-roller casinos to garner comparisons to Monte Carlo.

The casinos are gone, but the health resorts remain, and you'll still see more well-dressed people here per capita than just about anywhere in the country. While it's not quite Cannes, Sopot features a relative feeling of high class unusual in otherwise unpretentious Poland. But even so, a childlike spirit of summer-vacation fun pervades this St-Tropez-on-the-Baltic—making it an all-around enjoyable place.

Planning Your Time

You can get the gist of Sopot in just a couple of hours. Zip in on the train, follow the main drag to the sea, wander the pier, get your feet wet at the beach, then head back to Gdańsk.

Why not come here in the late afternoon, enjoy those last few rays of sunshine, stay for dinner, then take a twilight stroll on the pier?

ORIENTATION

The main pedestrian drag, Monte Cassino Heroes street (ulica Bohaterów Monte Cassino), leads to the Molo, the longest pleasure pier in Europe. From the Molo, a broad, sandy beach stretches in each direction. Running parallel to the surf is a tree-lined, people-filled path made for strolling.

Tourist Information

Sopot's helpful TI—and the only one I've ever seen with a tip jar—is directly in front of the PKP train station (look for blue *it* sign). Pick up the free map, info booklet, and events schedule. They also offer a free room-booking service (daily June–mid-Sept 9:00–20:00, mid-Sept–May 10:00–18:00, ulica Dworcowa 4, tel. 058-550-3783, www.sopot.pl).

Arrival in Sopot

From the SKM station, exit to the left and walk down the street. After a block, you'll see the PKP train station on your left—detour here to find the TI (described above). Then continue on to the can't-miss-it main drag, ulica Bohaterów Monte Cassino (marked by the big red-brick church steeple). Follow it to the right, down to the seaside.

SIGHTS

▲**Monte Cassino Heroes Street (Ulica Bohaterów Monte Cassino)**—This in-love-with-life promenade may well be Poland's most manicured street. Especially after all the suburban and industrial dreck you passed through to get here, you'll be charmed by this pretty drag. The street is lined with happy tourists, trendy cafés, al fresco restaurants, movie theaters, and late-19th-century facades (known for their wooden balconies).

The most popular building along here (on the left, about halfway down) is the so-called **Crooked House** (Krzywy Domek), a trippy, Gaudí-inspired building that looks like it's melting. Hard-partying locals prefer to call it the "Drunken House," and say that when it looks straight...it's time to stop drinking.

At the bottom of the boulevard, just before the Molo, pay 2 zł to climb to the top of the Art Nouveau lighthouse for a waterfront panorama.

Molo (Pier)—At more than 1,600 feet long, this is Europe's longest wooden entertainment pier. While you won't find any amusement-park rides, you will be surrounded by vendors, artists, and Poles having the time of their lives. Buy a *gofry* (Belgian waffle topped with whipped cream and fruit) or an oversized cloud of *wata cukrowa* (cotton candy), grab your partner's hand, and stroll with gusto (open long hours daily; May–Sept you'll pay 2.70 zł Mon–Fri, 3.50 zł Sat–Sun; free Oct–April).

Scan the horizon for sailboats and tankers. Any pirate ships? For a jarring reality check, look over to Gdańsk. Barely visible from the Molo are two of the most important sites in 20th-century history: the towering monument at Westerplatte, where World War II started; and the cranes rising up from the Gdańsk Shipyard, where Solidarity was born and European communism began its long goodbye.

In season, the end of the Molo is sometimes home to an overpriced but fun wax museum, populated by famous Poles (Wałęsa, Copernicus, Chopin) and others (Kennedy, Beatles, Bush).

In spring and fall, the Molo is a favorite venue for pole vaulting—or is that Pole vaulting?

The Beach—Yes, Poland has beaches. Nice ones. When I heard Sopot compared to places like Nice, I'll admit that I scoffed. But when I saw those stretches of inviting sand as far as the eye can see, I wished I'd packed my swim trunks. (You could walk from Gdańsk to Gdynia on beaches like this.) The sand is finer than anything I've seen in Croatia...though the water's not exactly crystal-clear. Most of the beach is public, except for a small private stretch in front of the Hotel Grand Sopot (described below). Year-round, it's crammed with locals. At these northern latitudes, the season for bathing is brief and crowded.

Overlooking the beach next to the Molo is the **Grand Hotel Sopot.** It was renovated to top-class status just last year, but its history goes way back. They could charge admission for room #226, a multi-room suite that has hosted the likes of Adolf Hitler, Marlene Dietrich, and Fidel Castro (but not all at the same time). With all the trappings of Sopot's belle époque—dark wood, plush upholstery, antique furniture—this room had me imagining Hitler sitting at the desk, looking out to sea, and plotting the course of World War II.

Gdynia

Compared to its flashier sister cities, straightforward Gdynia (guh-DIN-yah) has retained a more working-class vibe, still in touch with its salty, fishing-village roots. Gdynia feels much less historic than Gdańsk or Sopot, as it was mostly built in the 1920s to be Poland's main harbor after Gdańsk became a free city. Although nowhere as attractive as Gdańsk or Sopot, Gdynia has an authentic feel and a fine waterfront promenade (www.gdynia.pl).

Gdynia is a major business center, and—thanks to its youthful, progressive city government—has edged ahead of the rest of Poland in transitioning from communism. It enjoys one of the highest income levels in the country. Many of the crumbling downtown buildings have been renovated, and Gdynia is becoming known for its top-tier shopping—all the big designers have boutiques here. If a local woman has been shopping on Świętojańska street in Gdynia, it means that she's got some serious złoty.

Because Gdańsk's port is relatively shallow, the biggest cruise ships must put in at Gdynia...leaving confused tourists to poke around town looking for some medieval quaintness, before coming to their senses and heading for Gdańsk. Gdynia is also home to a major military harbor, and an important NATO base.

To get a taste of Gdynia, take the SKM train to the "Gdynia Główna" station, follow signs to *wyjście do miasta,* cross the busy street, and walk 15 minutes down Starowiejska. When you come to the intersection with the broad Świętojańska street, turn right (in the direction the big statue is looking) and walk two blocks to the tree-lined park on the left. Head through the park to the Southern Pier (Molo Południowe). This concrete slab—nowhere near as charming as Sopot's wooden-boardwalk version—features a modern shopping mall and a smattering of sights, including an aquarium and a pair of permanently moored museum boats.

Hel Peninsula (Mierzeja Helska)

Out on the edge of things, this slender peninsula juts 20 miles into the ocean, providing a sunny retreat from the big cities—even as it shelters them from Baltic winds. Trees line the peninsula, and the northern edge is one long, sandy, ever-shifting beach.

On hot summer days, Hel is a great place to frolic in the sun with Poles. Sunbathing and windsurfing are practically a religion here. Small resort villages line Hel Peninsula: Władysławowo (at the base), Chałupy, Kuźnica, Jastarnia, Jurata, and—at the tip—a town also called Hel. Beaches right near the towns can be crowded in peak season, but you're never more than a short walk away from your own stretch of sand. There are few permanent residents, and the waterfront is shared by budget campgrounds and hotels hosting middle-class families, and mansions of Poland's rich and famous (former president Aleksander Kwaśniewski has a summer home here).

The easiest way to go to Hel—aside from coveting thy neighbor's wife—is by boat (see "Transportation Connections," page 358). Trains from Gdańsk also reach Hel, and from Gdynia, you can take a train, bus, or minibus. Hel is immensely popular in the summer, when it's notorious for its traffic jams.

POMERANIA

Malbork Castle and Toruń

The northwestern part of Poland—known as Pomerania (Pomorze)—has nothing to do with excitable little dogs, but it does offer plenty of attractions. Two in particular are worth singling out, both conveniently located between Gdańsk and Warsaw. Malbork, the biggest Gothic castle in Europe, also happens to be the most interesting castle in Eastern Europe. Farther south, the Gothic town of Toruń—the birthplace of Copernicus, and a favorite spot of every proud Pole—holds hundreds of red-brick buildings (and even more varieties of tasty gingerbread).

Planning Your Time

Malbork works well as a side-trip from Gdańsk (frequent one-hour trains), and it's also on the main train line from Gdańsk to Warsaw. While Toruń doesn't merit a long detour, it's worth a stroll or an overnight if you want to sample a smaller Polish city. Unfortunately, Torún is on a different train line than Malbork, making it difficult to visit both on the same day. Ideally, if traveling round-trip from Warsaw, see one of these destinations coming to Gdańsk, and visit the other on the way back. Or do Malbork as a side-trip from Gdańsk, then visit Toruń on the way to Warsaw. If choosing one or the other, do Malbork.

Malbork Castle

Malbork Castle is soaked in history. The biggest brick castle in the world, the largest castle of the Gothic period, and one of Europe's most picturesque fortresses, it sits smugly on a marshy plain at the edge of the town of Malbork, 35 miles southeast of Gdańsk. This was the headquarters of the notorious Teutonic Knights, a Germanic band of ex-Crusaders who dominated northern Poland in the Middle Ages.

When the Teutonic Knights were invited to Polish lands to convert neighboring pagans in the 13th century, they found the perfect site for their new capital here, on the bank of the Nogat River. Construction began in 1274. After the Teutonic Knights conquered Gdańsk in 1308, the order moved its official headquarters from Venice to Malbork. The Teutonic Knights remained here for nearly 150 years. They called the castle Marienburg, the "Castle of Mary," in honor of the order's patron saint.

At its peak in the early 1400s, Malbork was both the imposing home of a seemingly unstoppable army, and Europe's final bastion of chivalric ideals. Surrounded by swamplands, with only one gate in need of defense, it was a tough nut to crack. Malbork Castle was never taken by force in the Middle Ages, though it had to withstand various sieges by the Poles during the Thirteen Years' War (1454–1466)—including a campaign that lasted over three years. Finally, in 1457, the Polish king gained control of Malbork by buying off Czech mercenaries guarding the castle. Malbork became a Polish royal residence for 300 years. But when Poland was partitioned in the late 18th century, this region went back into German (Prussian) hands. The castle became a barracks, windows were sealed up, delicate vaulting was damaged, bricks were quarried for new buildings, and Malbork deteriorated.

In the late 19th century, Romantic German artists and poets rediscovered the place. An architect named Konrad Steinbrecht devoted 40 years of his life to Malbork, painstakingly restoring the palace to its medieval splendor. A half-century later, the Nazis used the castle to house POWs, and about half of it was destroyed by the Soviet army, who saw it as a symbol of longstanding German domination. If you look closely, you can still see the original and reconstructed parts.

Today Malbork has been restored once again to its Teutonic glory, and ranks among the most visit-worthy sights in Poland.

ORIENTATION

Cost, Hours, Information: Malbork has two seasons: high season (mid-April–mid-Sept) and low season (mid-Sept–mid-April). In high season, entry costs 30 zł, and the castle exhibits are open Tue–Sun 9:00–19:00 (last entry 17:30, grounds open until 20:00). In low season, it costs 25 zł, and the exhibits are open Tue–Sun 10:00–15:00 (last entry 13:00, grounds open until 16:00; sometimes open later in early April and late Sept). It's always closed on Mon and holidays. The ticket office (marked *kasa*) opens 30 minutes before the castle. You'll pay an extra 16 zł for a sticker allowing you to take photos inside. In summer, they also offer a Family Ticket for a small savings (covers 1 or 2 adults and their children: 80 zł/3 people total, 102.50 zł/4 people, 125 zł/5 people, 147.50 zł/6 people). For details, see www.zamek.malbork.pl.

Tours: You are required to enter the castle with a three-hour tour (Polish tour included in your ticket). This sounds like an intimidating commitment—but thoroughly seeing the place actually takes about that long. It's generally no problem to split away from your group—so simply enter with any tour, wander off, and explore the castle using my self-guided tour (below). Getting an **English tour** can be frustrating. In July and August, English tours run three times a day (likely at 11:00, 13:30, and 15:30; included in your ticket). But the schedule can be unpredictable, and if there's not enough demand, you may have to wait until a quorum of English-speakers gather (generally no longer than an hour). September through June, you have to pay an extra 150 zł for an English tour, but this cost can be divided by everyone in your group. Take the initiative, play "tour guide," and get together a group of frustrated English-speakers by the cashier. On my last trip, it took me only a few minutes to gather together 10 strangers (only half of us Americans) eager for some English information—bringing the per-person cost of the tour down to just 15 zł. Ideally, contact the castle a day or two ahead to see if you can join a scheduled English tour, or to reserve a guide for yourself (tel. 055-647-0978, kasa@zamek.malbork.pl); communication can be difficult, so try to get a Polish person (such as your hotelier) to help you. Agnieszka Syroka, an excellent Gdańsk-based local guide, also does tours of Malbork (see page 328).

Best Views: The views of massive Malbork are stunning—especially at sunset, when the red brick glows. Be sure to walk out across the bridge over the Nogat River. The most scenic part of the castle is probably the twin-turreted, riverside Bridge Gate, which used to be connected by a bridge to the opposite bank.

Sound-and-Light Show: Every night from May through mid-September, there's a sound-and-light show in the castle courtyard. Though the commentary is in Polish, the show gives you a different perspective on the mighty fortress (15 zł, begins after dark—which

The Teutonic Knights

The Order of the Teutonic Knights began in the Holy Land in 1191, during the Third Crusade. Officially called the "Order of the Hospital of the Blessed Virgin Mary of the German House of Jerusalem," these German monks and knights took vows of poverty, chastity, and obedience. They also built hospitals, and cared for injured knights. When the Crusades ended in the 12th century, the order found itself out of a job, and went back to Europe. They set up shop in Venice, and reorganized as a chivalric order of Christian mercenaries—pagan-killers for hire.

The Teutonic Knights were hired for a gig in northern Poland in 1226. Duke Konrad of Mazovia wanted to subdue a tribe of pagans, called the Prussians, who had been attacking his lands. (Confusingly, these were pagan Slavs—*not* the same as the later goose-stepping Prussians who lived in what would become eastern Germany.) The Teutonic Knights—claiming to be missionaries (and wearing white cloaks decorated with black crosses)—spent 60 years "saving" the pagan Prussians by turning them into serfs or brutally massacring them.

Like houseguests who didn't know when to leave, the Teutonic Knights decided they enjoyed northern Poland—and stuck around. The Knights made themselves at home, building one of Europe's biggest and most imposing fortresses: Malbork. Because they were fanatical Christians, they won the support of the pope and the Holy Roman Emperor. When the Teutonic Knights seized large parts of northern Poland in 1308, including Gdańsk—cutting off Polish access to the Baltic Sea—the Polish royals began to realize their mistake. The Teutonic Knights invited more Germans to come join them, building their numbers and tightening their grasp on the region. They grew rich from Hanseatic trade, specializing in amber, grain, and timber. The Knights conquered Estonia and Latvia, and began to threaten the Poles' pagan neighbor to the east, Lithuania. By the late 14th century, the Teutonic Knights were enjoying a Golden Age at the expense of the Prussians, Poles, and Lithuanians.

can be as late as 22:00 at these northern latitudes). Don't make a special trip (or stay late) for this show—it really only makes sense if you're spending the night (see "Sleeping," page 378).

Getting There: Malbork is on the train line between Gdańsk and Warsaw. Coming by train from Gdańsk, you'll enjoy striking views of the castle on your right as you cross the Nogat River. The Malbork train station has a handy baggage-check office (*przechowalnia bagażu*, by ticket windows, 4 zł/bag); if it's closed, be insistent, and someone should eventually help you. To get from the station to the castle, consider taking a **taxi** (shouldn't cost more

At about this time, Poland's long-lived Piast dynasty died out. Inspired by a mutual desire to fight back against the Teutonic Knights, the Poles and the Lithuanians decided to join their kingdoms. In 1386, Polish Princess Jadwiga married Lithuanian Prince Władysław Jagiełło (who converted to Christianity for the occasion), uniting Poland and Lithuania and kick-starting a grand new dynasty, the Jagiellonians.

Just as every American knows the date July 4, 1776, every Pole knows the date July 15, 1410—the Battle of Grunwald. King Władysław Jagiełło and Grand Duke Vytautas the Great led a ragtag army of some 40,000 soldiers—Lithuanians, Poles, other Slavs, and even speedy Tatar horsemen—against 27,000 Teutonic Knights. At the end of the day, some 18,000 Poles and Lithuanians were dead—but so were half of the Teutonic Knights (and the other half had been captured). Poland and Lithuania were victorious. Though the Teutonic Knights remained in Poland—extending their Germanic cultural influence on the region well into the 20th century—their political power waned, they pulled out of Lithuania, and they once again allowed free trade on the Vistula. A generation later, the Thirteen Years' War (1454–1466) finally put an end to the Teutonic Knights' domination of northern Poland. The order officially dissolved in 1575, when they converted to Protestantism... though some conspiracy theorists (and *Da Vinci Code* enthusiasts) claim the Teutonic Knights are still very much active.

The Knights' influence on Poland persists today—even beyond the striking red-brick churches and castles scattered around the northern part of the country. The Polish novelist Henryk Sienkiewicz's *The Teutonic Knights* is a cultural benchmark and a favorite work of many Poles. The 19th-century Romantics who fanned the flames of Polish patriotism turned the Teutonic Knights into a symbol of Germanic oppression. Even today, Poles—and all Slavs—think of the Teutonic Knights as murderous invaders...while the Germans see them as a mere footnote in their history.

than 10 zł, though many corrupt cabbies charge twice that—keep asking until someone agrees to 10 zł). Or you can **walk** 15 minutes to the castle: Leave the station to the right, walk straight, and go through the pedestrian underpass beneath the busy road (by the red staircase). When you emerge on the other side, follow the busy road (noticing peek-a-boo views on your right of the castle's main tower) and take your first right turn (onto Kościuszki, the main shopping street). When you reach the fork at the end of the street, jog right, and head for the big, red castle (ticket office at far end).

SELF-GUIDED TOUR

The official tour of Malbork lasts about three hours. And, while there's plenty to see, this self-guided tour allows you to see it at your own pace. (Remember, you can split off from your group at any time.) This tour also works if you're tagging along with a Polish group, since it corresponds more or less to the route most Malbork guides take. Still, every guide is a little different, exhibits tend to move around, and entrances can be unexpectedly closed. Use a map to navigate and jump around as needed. The castle complex is a bit of a maze, with various entrances and exits for each room, often behind closed (but unlocked) doors. Don't be shy about grabbing a medieval doorknob and letting yourself in.

Lower Castle and Entrance Gate

Stand in front of the gate to one of Europe's most intimidating fortresses—home to the Grand Master, monks, and knights of the Teutonic Order. Across from the gate is the Lower Castle, which was an infirmary and hospital for injured knights and retirees. The end closest to you is the Chapel of St. Lawrence; farther away, the former farm buildings have been converted into hotel rooms and restaurants (see "Sleeping," page 378).

Go through the first gate and up the wooden bridge. Above the door to the second (brick) gate is a sculpture of St. Mary with the Baby Jesus...accompanied by a shield and helmet. The two messages to visitors: This castle is protected by Mary, and the Teutonic Knights are here to convert pagans by force, if necessary (or, as it turned out, even if not necessary). Imagine the gate behind you closing. You look up to see wooden chutes where archers are preparing to rain arrows down on you. Your last thought: Maybe we should have left the Teutonic Knights alone, after all.

Before being pierced by arrows, read the castle's history into its walls: The foundation is made of huge stones, which are rare in these marshy lands—they were brought from Sweden. But most of the castle, like so many other buildings in northern Poland, was built with handmade red brick. Throughout the castle, the darker-colored, rougher brick is original, and the lighter-colored, smoother brick was used for restoration (in the 19th century, and again after World War II).

Venture through two more enclosed spaces, watching for the holes in the wall (for more guards and soldiers). The Teutonic Knights connected nearby lakes to create a system of canals, forming a moat around the castle that could be crossed only by this drawbridge. Ponder the fact that you have to go through five separate, well-defended gates to reach the...

Malbork Castle

1. Amber Collection Entrance (Downstairs)
2. Armory Exit (Upstairs)
3. "Boiler Room" (Downstairs) & Grand Refectory (Upstairs; Usually Closed)
4. Grand Master's Palace
5. Grand Master Statues
6. Well
7. Gdanisko Tower
8. St. Mary's Church

Middle Castle (Zamek Średni)

This part of Malbork, built at an uphill incline to make it even more imposing, was designed to impress. Knights and monks lived here.

Let's get oriented: To your left is the east wing, where guests would sleep. Today this houses the Amber Collection (ground floor) and the Armory (upstairs). To the right (west) as you enter the main courtyard is the Grand Refectory (closer to the entrance, closed to visitors) and the Grand Master's Palace (the taller, squarer building at the far end).

• *Before we move on, this is a good time to read up on the history of the Teutonic Knights (see sidebar). When you're ready to continue, enter the ground floor of the building on the left, and visit the...*

Amber Collection: This exhibit will make jewelry shoppers salivate. (Even as someone with zero interest in amber, I enjoyed it.) View the displays clockwise (and chronologically) from the entrance. Begin at the huge chunks of raw amber, and the illuminated display of inclusions (bugs stuck in the amber, à la *Jurassic Park*). In the next cases are ancient amber artifacts, some of them up to 3,000 years old. These were found in graves, put there by people who thought amber would help the deceased enter a better world. Along the rest of this wall are all manner of amber creations, from boxes and brooches to chess sets and pipes. Many of the finely decorated jewelry boxes and chests have ivory, silver, or shell inlays—better for contrast than gold. The portable religious shrines and altars could be used for travel, allowing people to remain reverent on the road and still pack light. At the end of the hall are two truly exquisite boxes of amber—the museum's prize possessions.

Working your way back up the other side of the room, you'll see more modern uses for amber—necklaces and other jewelry, miniature ships, wine glasses, and belts for skinny-waisted, fashion-conscious women. Look for the amber crucifix. This is a small replica of a six-foot-tall amber and silver cross presented to Pope John Paul II by the people of Gdańsk. In the display case by the door, you can see the full range of amber colors, from opaque white at the top, to transparent yellow in the middle, to virtually black at the bottom.

• *Now head upstairs to the...*

Armory: At the top of the stairs, flags commemorate the Battle of Grunwald, where the united forces of Poland (on the left) and Lithuania (on the right) defeated the Teutonic Knights (in the

All About Amber

Poland's Baltic seaside is known as the Amber Coast. You'll see amber (bursztyn) in the exhibit at Malbork, as well as in shop windows in Gdańsk (and throughout the country). This petrified pine-tree sap originated here on the north coast of Poland 40 million years ago. It comes in as many different colors as Eskimos have words for snow: 300 distinct shades, from yellowish-white to yellowish-black, from opaque to transparent. (I didn't believe it either, until I toured Malbork's collection.) Darker-colored amber is generally mixed with ash and sand—making it more fragile, and generally less desirable. Lighter amber is mixed with gasses and air bubbles.

Amber has been popular since long before there were souvenir stands. Archaeologists have found graves of Roman citizens (and their coins) who were buried with crosses made of amber. Almost 75 percent of the world's amber is mined in northern Poland, and it often simply washes up on the beaches after a winter storm. Some of the elaborate amber sculptures displayed at Malbork are created by joining pieces of amber with "amber glue"—made of melted-down amber mixed with an adhesive agent.

In addition to being good for the economy, some Poles believe amber is good for their health. A traditional cure for arthritis pain is to pour strong vodka over amber, let it set, and then rub it on sore joints.

middle). Browse your way through the staggering array of swords, armor, and other armaments (English descriptions). Look for the 700-year-old "one-and-a-half-hand swords"—too big to be held in one hand. At the end, in the display of cannons, pikes, and spears, look for the giant shield. These shields could be lined up to form a portable "wall" to protect the knights.

Head downstairs to the second room of the armory, displaying suits of armor (including for horses). Here you'll see some seven-foot-long "two-hand swords" even bigger than the ones upstairs. On the left, find the suit of armor from the Hussars—Polish knights on horseback who had wings on their armor, which created a terrifying sound when galloping.

• *Head back outside and across the main courtyard, entering the smaller courtyard through the passage next to the dark-wood-topped tower. Find the steep steps down into the...*

"Boiler Room": The Teutonic Knights had a surprisingly sophisticated method for heating this huge complex. You see a furnace for fire down below, and a sort of a holding area for super-heated rocks up above. This method allowed the rocks to send heat through the vents without also filling them with smoke. This is one of 11 such "boiler rooms" in the castle complex. As you tour the rest of the castle, keep an eye out for little saucer-sized vents in the floor where the heat came through.

• *Near the boiler room—but generally closed to the public due to ongoing renovation work—is the...*

Grand Refectory: This enormous dining hall, damaged in World War II, is still being rebuilt. With remarkable palm vaulting and grand frescoes, the Grand Refectory hosted feasts for up to 400 people to celebrate a military victory or to impress a visiting king.

• *Now we're moving on into the Grand Master's Palace. There are two entrances to the palace, either of which might be locked: one in the small courtyard near the boiler room steps, and another one a bit farther up in the main courtyard. However you get there, climb the stairs up into the...*

Grand Master's Palace: This was one of the grandest royal residences in medieval Europe, used in later times by Polish kings and German Kaisers. From the top of the stairs, you'll head down the hall to the right. The door on your right leads to the **private rooms of the Grand Master,** with show-off decor (including some 15th-century original frescoes of wine leaves and grapes). The Grand Master even had his own chapel, dedicated to St. Catherine. Though the Teutonic Order dictated that the monks sleep in dormitories, the Grand Master made an exception for himself—and you'll see his private bedroom (with rough original frescoes of four female martyrs).

• *Continue down the hall, noticing the troughs in the ground—anyone wanting an audience with the Grand Master had to wash both his hands and his feet.*

At the end of the hall, on the left, enter the elegant...

Summer Refectory: This was where the G.M. dined. With big stained-glass windows, and all of the delicate vaulting supported by a single pillar in the middle, this room was clearly not designed with defense in mind. In fact, medieval Polish armies focused their attacks on this room. On one legendary occasion, the attackers—tipped off by a spy—knew that an important meeting was going on here, and fired a cannonball into the room. It just barely missed the pillar. (You can see where the cannonball hit the wall, just above the fireplace.) The ceiling eventually did collapse during World War II.

As you continue into the **Winter Refectory,** notice fewer windows (better insulation) and the little manhole-like openings in the floor where the "central heating" came into the room.

• *Head back outside. At the top of the main courtyard, look for the four...*

Grand Master Statues: These four statues came from a 19th-century Prussian monument that was mostly destroyed when the

Soviets took Malbork at the end of World War II. Though this was a religious order, these powerful guys look more like kings than monks. From right to left, shake hands with Hermann von Salza (who was Grand Master when the Teutonic Knights came to Poland); Siegfried von Feuchtwangen (who actually moved the T.K. capital from Venice to Malbork, and who conquered Gdańsk for the Knights—oops, can't shake his hand, which was supposedly chopped off by Soviet troops); Winrich von Kniprode (who oversaw Malbork's Golden Age, and turned it into a castle fit for a king); and Markgraf Albrecht von Hohenzollern (the last Grand Master before the order dissolved and converted to Protestantism).

• *To the right of the statues, continue over the...*

Drawbridge: As you cross, notice the extensive system of fortifications and moats protecting the innermost part of the castle. Check out the cracks in the walls—an increasing threat to the ever-settling castle set on this marshy, unstable terrain. The passage is lined with holes (for surveillance), with chutes up above (to pour scalding water or pitch on unwanted visitors). It's not quite straight—so a cannon fired here would hit the side wall of the passage, rather than entering the High Castle. Which is what you're about to do now.

High Castle (Zamek Wysoki)

This is the heart of the castle, and its oldest section. As much a monastery as a fortress, the High Castle was off-limits to all but 60 monks of the Teutonic Order and their servants. (The knights stayed in the Middle Castle.) Here you'll find the monks' dormitories, chapels, church, and refectory. As this was the heart and nerve center of the Teutonic Knights—the T.K. H.Q.—it was also their last line of defense. They stored enormous amounts of food here in case of a siege.

In the middle of the High Castle courtyard is a **well.** At the top is a sculpture of a pelican. Because this noble bird is known to kill itself to feed its young (notice that it's piercing its own chest with its beak), it was often used in the Middle Ages as a symbol for the self-sacrifice of Jesus.

• *Take some time to explore the...*

Ground-Floor Exhibits: Working clockwise around the courtyard from where you entered, you'll find the following: A door leads to the prison and torture chamber (with small "solitary confinement" cells near the entrance), and a long hall behind with a single tiny window. Along the back of the cloister are WWII photos of Malbork. Beyond those, hiding in the far corner, is an exhibit on medieval stained-glass windows.

• *To the right from where you entered, you'll find the most interesting exhibit on this floor, the...*

Kitchen: This exhibit really gives you a feel for medieval monastery life. The monks who lived here ate three meals a day, along with lots of beer (made here) and wine (imported from France, Italy, and Hungary). A cellar under the kitchen was used as a primitive refrigerator—big chunks of ice were cut from the frozen river in winter, stored in the basement, and used to keep food cool in summer. Behind the long table, see the big dumbwaiter (with shelves), which connects this kitchen with the refectory upstairs. Step into the giant stove and look up the biggest chimney in the castle.

In the next room is a demonstration of how medieval money was made. The Teutonic Knights minted their own coins—and you can buy your very own freshly minted replica today.

• *Now go back out into the courtyard, and climb up the stairs near where you came in. From the top of the stairs, the first door on the left leads to the most important room of the High Castle, the...*

Chapter Room: Monks gathered here after Mass, and it was also the site for meetings of Teutonic Knights from around the countryside. If a Grand Master was killed in battle, the new one would be elected right here. Each monk had his own seal and a name over his seat. The big chair belonged to the Grand Master. Above his chair, notice the little windows, connecting this room to St. Mary's Church next door (described below). Church music would come into this room through these windows...imagine the voices of 60 monks bouncing around these acoustics.

While monks are usually thought to pursue simple lives, the elegant vaulting in this room is anything but plain. The 14th-century frescoes (restored in the 19th century) depict Grand Masters. In the floor are more vents for the central heating.

• *Leave the Chapter House and walk straight ahead, imagining the monk-filled corridors of Teutonic times. The first door on the right is the...*

Treasury: The first room has a small display of coins and amber (which helped make the Teutonic Knights rich). As you explore the rooms of the tax collector and the house administrator, notice the wide variety of safes and other lock boxes. Near the end, look for the small bed—for a small medieval person.

• *Continue around the cloister. At the end of the corridor, look for the little devil at the bottom of the vaulting (on the right, about eye level). He's pulling his beard and crossing his legs—pointing you down the long corridor to the...*

Gdanisko Tower: From the devil's grimace, you might have guessed that this tower houses the toilets. Follow his directions to the medieval WCs, in a tower set apart from the main part of the castle. The toilets dropped straight down into the moat; the bins were for cabbage leaves, used by the T.K. as T.P. This tower could also serve as a final measure of defense—it's easer to defend than the entire castle. Food was stored above, just in case.

• *Head back to the main part of the High Castle and continue around the cloister. The door halfway down on the right leads to the...*

Church Exhibition: These rooms used to be dormitories for the monks, and today they display a wide range of relics from the church (with English descriptions). The first room features an elaborate monstrance (vessel used to carry the Communion host) and a hands-less 15th-century sculpture of Jesus praying in the Garden of Gethsemane. The next room displays pictures of various eras of Malbork Castle, as well as some fragments of statues rescued from the destroyed St. Mary's Church. The huge, mangled crucifix dates from the mid-14th century. At the end of this exhibition is a replica of a Gothic altarpiece, with graphic paintings of the murder and dismemberment of Poland's patron saint, Adalbert.

• *Go back out into the hall and continue down to the end, arriving at the...*

Golden Gate: This elaborate doorway—covered in protective glass—marks the entrance to St. Mary's Church. Ringed with detailed carvings from the Old Testament, and symbolic messages about how monks of the Teutonic Order should live their lives, it's a marvelous example of late-13th-century art. On the left, find the five wise virgins who filled their lamps with oil, conserved it wisely, and are headed to heaven. On the right, the five foolish virgins who overslept and used up all their oil are damned, much to their dismay.

• *If the door's open, go ahead on into...*

St. Mary's Church: This holy site was destroyed in World War II and sat for decades with no roof. After so much neglect, it's finally being renovated...slowly. Pictures of the original church with English descriptions explain some of the fragments.

• *Go through the door on the left (as you exit St. Mary's Church) and take the narrow spiral staircase upstairs to the final set of exhibits.*

Top-Floor Exhibits: Walk through the two long hallways of temporary exhibits. At the end, go down the stairs into the monks' common room. Over the fireplace is a relief depicting the Teutonic Knights fighting the Prussians. To the left of that is the balcony where musicians could perform to entertain the monks after a meal. The next, very long room, with seven pillars, is the refectory, where the monks ate in silence. Along the right-hand wall are confessional-like, lockable storage boxes. At the end of this room, just before the door, notice the grated hole in the wall. This is where the dumbwaiter comes up from the kitchen (which we saw below).

• *Your Malbork tour ends here. A nearby door (sometimes locked) leads to the stairs up to the top of the tower. When finished, you can head back the way you came. En route, you can walk around terraces lining the inner*

Sleep Code

(3 zł = about $1, €1 = about $1.20, country code: 48)
S = Single, **D** = Double/Twin, **T** = Triple, **Q** = Quad, **b** = bathroom,
s = shower only. Unless otherwise noted, breakfast is included,
credit cards are accepted, and English is spoken.

To help you sort easily through these listings, I've divided
the rooms into two categories, based on the price for a standard double room with bath:

$$ Higher Priced—Most rooms more than 250 zł (€70).
$ Lower Priced—Most rooms 250 zł (€70) or less.

---

*moat, between the castle walls (stairs lead down off of the drawbridge).
It's hardly a must-see, but it's pleasant enough, with the Grand Master's
garden, a cemetery for monks, and the remains of the small St. Anne's
Chapel (with Grand Master tombs).*

SLEEPING

Malbork is so well-connected by rail to Gdańsk and Warsaw that
there's little sense in sleeping here. The most compelling reason to
stay in Malbork is to be here for the nighttime sound-and-light
show in the castle courtyard.

$$ Hotel Zamek is housed in Malbork's Lower Castle, a
red-brick building that was once a hospital, just across from the
main part of the fortress. The 42 rooms are overpriced, dark, old-
feeling, and a little creepy...but, hey—you're next door to one of
Europe's grandest Gothic castles (Sb-210–270 zł, Db-250–320 zł,
Tb-330–500 zł, higher prices are for mid-May–Oct, elevator, ulica
Starościńska 14, tel. & fax 055-272-3367).

TRANSPORTATION CONNECTIONS

From Malbork by Train to: Gdańsk (about 2/hr, 1 hr), **Toruń**
(about every 2 hrs, 3 hrs, transfer in Tcew or Iława), **Warsaw**
(hourly, 3.5 hrs direct).

Toruń

Toruń is a pretty, lazy Gothic town conveniently located about
halfway between Warsaw and Gdańsk. It's worth a couple of hours
to stroll the lively streets, ogle the huge red-brick buildings, and
savor the flavor of Poland's most livable city.

With about 210,000 residents and 30,000 students (at Copernicus University), Toruń is a thriving burg. Locals brag that their city is a "mini-Kraków." But that sells both cities short. Toruń lacks Kraków's over-the-top romanticism, and its sights are quickly exhausted. On

the other hand, Toruń may well be Poland's most user-friendly city: tidy streets with a sensible grid plan (and English signposts to help you find your way), wide pedestrian boulevards crammed with locals who greet each other like they're long-lost friends, and an easygoing ambience that seems to say, "Hey—relax." And, while it has its share of tourists, Toruń feels more off-the-beaten-path than the other Polish destinations in this book.

Toruń clings fiercely to its two claims to fame: It's the proud birthplace of the astronomer Copernicus (Mikołaj Kopernik), and home to a dizzying variety of gingerbread treats (*piernika;* peer-NEE-kah).

ORIENTATION

(area code: 056)

Everything in Toruń worth seeing is in the walled Old Town, climbing up a gentle hill from the Vistula River. The broad, traffic-free main drag, ulica Szeroka (called Różana at the entrance of town) bisects the Old Town, running parallel to the river.

Arrival in Toruń

Toruń's main train station (called Toruń Główny) is about a mile away—and across the river—from the Old Town. The main hall has ticket windows, an ATM, and lockers (8 zł for a large locker).

To reach the Old Town, you have two options: If you go out the door from the main hall, you'll spot **taxis** waiting to take you into town (the trip should cost no more than 10 zł). To take the **bus,** buy a 2-zł ticket from the *RUCH* kiosk overlooking the tracks near the main hall. Then follow the pedestrian underpass beneath track 4 (entrance to underpass marked with low-profile *wyjście do miasta* sign and bus icon, outside main hall and to the left). When you emerge on the other side, the bus stop for bus #22 or #27 into the center is ahead and on your right. Take the bus to Plac Rapackiego, the first stop after the long bridge. To return to the station, catch bus #22 or #27 across the busy road from where you got off.

Tourist Information

The TI is on the main square, behind the Old Town Hall. Pick up the free map, and get information about hotels in town and city tours (Tue–Fri 9:00–18:00, Mon and Sat 9:00–16:00, closed Sun except May–Aug, when it's open 9:00–13:00, Rynek Staromiejski 25, tel. 056-621-0931, www.it.torun.pl).

SELF-GUIDED WALK

Welcome to Toruń

This very lightly guided introductory stroll takes you through the heart of Toruń. With no stops, you could do it in 10 minutes.

From the Plac Rapackiego bus stop, head into the town through the passageways under the colorful buildings. Within a block, you're at the bustling **Old Town Market Square** (Rynek Staromiejski), surrounded by huge brick buildings and outdoor restaurants buzzing with lively locals. The big building in the center is the **Old Town Hall** (Ratusz Staromiejski), with a boring museum and a climbable tower. The building with the pointy spires on the right (across from the Old Town Hall) is the **Artus Court,** where the medieval town council and merchants' guilds met (sadly, unlike the similar court in Gdańsk, it's not open to the public).

The guy playing his violin in front of the Old Town Hall is a **rafter** *(retman)*—one of the medieval lumberjacks who lashed tree trunks together and floated them down the Vistula to Gdańsk. This particular rafter came to Toruń when the town was infested with frogs. He wooed them with his violin and marched them out of town. (Hmm...sounds like a certain piper in another medieval Hanseatic city, Bremen....)

The bigger statue, at the other end of the Old Town Hall, depicts **Mikołaj Kopernik,** better known as Nicholas Copernicus. This Toruń-born son of aristocrats turned the world on its ear when he suggested that the sun, not the earth, is the center of the universe (an idea called the "heliocentric theory"). Toruń is serious about this local boy done good—he's the town mascot, as well as the namesake of the local university. Among its fields of study, Copernicus U. has a healthy astronomy program. There's a planetarium in the Old Town (just past the far corner of the square) and a giant radio telescope on the town outskirts. Despite all the local fuss over Copernicus, there's some dispute about his ethnicity; he was born in Toruń, all right, but at a time when it was a predominantly German town. So is he Polish or German? (For more on Copernicus, visit his birth house—now a modest museum on the astronomer—just two blocks away, and described under "Sights").

What's that sweet smell in the air? For Poles, Toruń is

synonymous with **gingerbread** *(piernika)*. This Toruń treat can be topped with different kinds of jams or glazes, and/or dipped in chocolate. You'll see gingerbread shops all over town, mostly selling the same stuff. The shop in the Artus Court building on the Old Town Market Square is handy and atmospheric; more are around the corner on ulica Żeglarska (toward the river; the shop on the right near the end of the block has a handy bulk system—point to what looks good and get exactly the amount and types you want).

Having satisfied your ginger tooth, head back to the square and join the human stream down the appropriately named **ulica Szeroka** ("Wide Street"), an enjoyable pedestrian promenade through the heart of town. Just before the road forks at the white Empik building, look down Przedzamcze to the right to see fragments of the town wall. This marks the border between the Old Town and the New Town (chartered only about 30 years later—both in the 13th century). While these areas are both collectively known today as the unified "Old Town," they were quite different in the Middle Ages—each with its own market square, and separated by a wall. (If you're curious to see the New Town Square and Town Hall, continue up ulica Szeroka and bear left at the fork.)

To end our walk, follow the wall to the right, down Przedzamcze, to reach the **ruins** of a castle built by the Teutonic Knights who were so influential in northern Poland in the Middle Ages (see page 368). The castle was destroyed in the 15th century by the locals—who, aside from a heap of bricks, left only the tower that housed the Teutonic toilets.

Beyond the castle ruins is the **Vistula** riverbank. The road that runs along the river here is called Bulwar Filadelfijski—for Toruń's sister city in Pennsylvania.

SIGHTS

Toruń is more about strolling than it is about sightseeing—the town's museums are underwhelming. Aside from its half-dozen red-brick churches (any of which are worth dropping into), the following attractions are worth considering on a rainy day.

Gingerbread Museum (Muzeum Piernika)—This fun attraction—by far Toruń's liveliest—is an actual, working gingerbread bakery of yore. Barefoot, costumed medieval bakers greet you and walk you through the traditional process of rolling, cutting out, baking, and tasting your own batch of gingerbread cookies (30–40 min, start to finish). After aging for 12 weeks to achieve the proper consistency, the dough bakes only 12 minutes—or, according to the medieval bakers, about 50 Hail Marys (10 zł, may have to wait a few minutes for an English guide to help you, daily 9:00–18:00,

2 blocks toward the river from Old Town Market Square at Rabiańska 9, www.muzeumpiernika.pl).

Copernicus House (Dom Kopernika)—Filling a pair of beautiful, gabled brick buildings, this dull and overpriced little museum celebrates the hero of Toruń. As much about medieval Toruń as about the astronomer, and sprawling over several floors in the two buildings, the exhibits loosely explain the astronomer's life and achievements. While the displays—mostly copies of important documents and paintings, models of his instruments, and English descriptions—are pretty flat, it's mildly interesting to walk around the creaky interiors. The second part of the exhibit is a "sound-and-light show" (slideshow with recorded commentary) about medieval Toruń, with a model of the city that lights up dramatically at appropriate moments (ask for English show when you enter; museum-10 zł, slideshow-12 zł, both-18 zł, Tue–Sun 10:00–18:00, closed Mon, Kopernika 15/17). To get to the museum from the Old Town Market Square, head down Żeglarska and take the first right—on Kopernika, of course.

Ethnographic Park (Park Etnograficzny)—This open-air folk museum, while not ranking with Europe's best, is at least your most convenient opportunity to stroll through some traditional buildings from the region. It's in the middle of a pleasant park just outside the Old Town (8.50 zł; mid-April–Sept Mon, Wed, and Fri 9:00–16:00, Tue, Thu, and Sat–Sun 10:00–18:00; Oct–mid-April Tue–Fri 9:00–16:00, Sat–Sun 10:00–16:00, closed Mon; Wały Gen. Sikorskiego 19, www.met.torun.pl). To get there from the Old Town Market Square, walk up Chełmińska with the river at your back and the Old Town Hall on your left. Cross the busy road, and you're in the park. Even if you're not interested in the museum, the relaxing park surrounding it is a fine place to pass some time.

SLEEPING

Toruń's Old Town has more than its share of good-value hotels (Db-200–300 zł). The TI has a brochure listing the options, and can help you find a room for no extra charge.

$$ Hotel Karczma "Spichrz" ("Granary") is a fresh, atmospheric hotel in a renovated old granary. Its 23 rooms and public spaces are a fun blend of old and new—with huge wooden beams around every corner, and the scent of the restaurant's wood-fired grill wafting through the halls. It's comfortable, central, well-priced, and a little kitschy (Sb-190 zł, Db-250 zł, tall people may not appreciate low ceilings and beams, elevator, a block off the main drag towards the river at ulica Mostowa 1, tel. 056-657-1140, fax 056-657-1144, www.spichrz.pl, hotel@spichrz.pl). The restaurant, while pricey, is also good (grilled meat dishes-20–30 zł, daily 12:00–23:00).

$ Hotel Retman ("Rafter") has 29 older but nicely appointed rooms over a restaurant just down the street from the Gingerbread Museum (Sb-160 zł, Db-210 zł; Fri–Sun prices drop to Sb-130 zł, Db-170 zł; ulica Rabiańska 15, tel. 056-657-4460, fax 056-657-4461, www.hotelretman.pl, recepcja@hotelretman.pl).

TRANSPORTATION CONNECTIONS

Toruń is a handy stopover on the way between Warsaw and Gdańsk. It's on a different train line than Malbork—so visiting both Toruń and the mighty Teutonic castle in the same day is surprisingly time-consuming and not advisable.

From Toruń by Train to: Warsaw (5/day, 3 hrs direct, longer with a transfer in Kutno), **Gdańsk** (4/day direct, 3 hrs; at least hourly with transfer in Bydgoszcz or Ilawa, 3–4 hrs).

HUNGARY

HUNGARY

(Magyarország)

Hungary is an island of Asian-descended Magyars in a sea of Slavs. Even though the Hungarians have thoroughly integrated with their Slavic and German neighbors in the millennium since they arrived, there's still something about the place that's distinctly Magyar (MUD-jar). Visiting quirky, idiosyncratic Hungary is not quite the same as touring the rest of Eastern Europe: Everything's a little different—in terms of history, language, culture, customs, and cuisine—but it's hard to put your finger on exactly how.

Just a century ago, Hungary controlled half of one of Europe's grandest empires. Today, perhaps clinging to their former greatness, Hungarians remain old-fashioned and nostalgic. With their dusty museums and bushy moustaches, they love to remember the good old days. Buildings all over the country are marked with plaques boasting *MŰEMLÉK* ("historical monument").

Thanks to this focus on tradition, the Hungarians you'll encounter are generally polite, formal, and professional. Hungarians have class. Everything here is done with a proud flourish. You get the impression that people in the service industry wear their uniforms as a badge of honor rather than a burden. When a waiter comes to your table in a restaurant, he'll say, *"Tessék parancsolni"*—literally, "Please command, sir." The standard greeting, *"Jó napot kívánok,"* means "I wish you a good day." And when your train or bus makes a stop, you won't be alerted by a mindless, blaring beep or hoot—but instead, peppy music. (You'll be humming these contagious little ditties all day.)

Hungarians are just as orderly and tidy as Germans...in their own sometimes unexpected ways. Yes, Hungary has as much litter and graffiti—and as many crumbling buildings—as any other Eastern European country, but you'll find great reason within the chaos. My favorite town name in Hungary: Hatvan. This means "Sixty" in Hungarian...and it's exactly 60 kilometers from Budapest. You can't argue with that kind of logic.

This tradition of left-brained thinking hasn't produced many great Hungarian painters or poets. But it has made tremendous contributions to the field of science, technology, business, and industry. Hungarians of note include Edward Teller (instrumental in creating the A-bomb), John von Neumann (a pioneer of computer science), Andy Grove (who, as András Grof, immigrated to the United States and founded Intel), and George Soros (who fled to the United States under communism, became a billionaire through shrewd investment, and is loved by the Left and loathed by the Right as a major contributor to liberal causes). Perhaps the most famous Hungarian "scientist" created something you probably have in a box in your basement: Ernő Rubik, and his famous cube. Hungary's enjoyment of a good mind-bending puzzle is also evident in their fascination with chess, which you'll see played in cafés, parks, and baths.

Like their Austrian neighbors, Hungarians know how to enjoy the good life. Favorite activities include splashing and soaking in their many thermal baths (see sidebar on page 458). "Taking the waters," Hungarian-style, deserves to be your top priority while you're here. Though public baths can sound intimidating, they're a delight. I've recommended my two favorite baths in Budapest and a fine one in Eger, and given you careful instructions to help you enjoy the warm-water fun like a pro. (To allay your first fear: Yes, you can wear your swimsuit the entire time.)

Hungarians are also reviving an elegant, Vienna-style café culture that was dismantled by the communists. Classical music is revered, perhaps as nowhere else outside Austria. Aside from scientists and businessmen, the best-known Hungarians are composers: Béla Bartók, Zoltan Kodály (who popularized the famous solfege sight-singing method taught in music schools worldwide), and Franz Liszt (actually Austrian, but of Hungarian ancestry).

Hungary Almanac

Official Name: Magyar Köztársaság, or simply Magyarország.

Snapshot History: Settled by the Central Asian Magyars in A.D. 896, Hungary became Catholic in the year 1000, and went on to become Christian Europe's front line in fighting against the Ottomans (Muslims from today's Turkey) in the 16th–17th centuries. After serving as co-capital of the vast Austro-Hungarian Empire and losing World Wars I and II, Hungary became a Soviet satellite until achieving independence in 1989.

Population: Hungary's 10 million people (similar to Michigan) are 92 percent ethnic Hungarians who speak Hungarian. One in 50 is Roma (Gypsy). Half the populace is Catholic, with 20 percent Protestant and 25 percent listed as "other" or unaffiliated. Of the world's approximately 12 million ethnic Hungarians, one in six lives outside Hungary (mostly in areas of Romania, Slovakia, Serbia, and Croatia that were once part of Hungary).

Latitude and Longitude: 47°N and 20°E; similar latitude to Seattle, Paris, and Vienna.

Area: 36,000 square miles, similar to Indiana or Maine.

Geography: Hungary is situated in the Carpathian Basin, bound on the north by the Carpathian Mountains and on the south by the Dinaric Mountains. Though it's surrounded by mountains, Hungary itself is relatively flat, with some gently rolling hills. The Great Hungarian Plain—which begins on the east bank of the Danube in Budapest—stretches all the way to Asia. Hungary's two main rivers—the Danube and Tisza—run north-south through the country, neatly dividing it into three regions.

Biggest Cities: Budapest (the capital on the Danube, 1.7 million), Debrecen (in the east, 205,000), and Miskolc (in the north, 180,000).

Economy: The Gross Domestic Product is $163 billion (a third of Poland's), but the GDP per capita is $16,300 (about 20 percent more than Poland's). Thanks to its progressive "goulash communism," Hungary had a head start on many other former Soviet Bloc countries and is now thriving, privatized...and largely foreign-owned. In the 1990s, many communist-era workers lost their

As you can guess from the many grandiose structures built in Budapest in the late 1800s, Hungarians are also romantic. Over-the-top, melodramatic Latin American soap operas are popular here (dubbed into Hungarian, of course). When the European Union expanded on May 1, 2004, the biggest celebrations anywhere were here in Hungary—where people love an excuse to party.

While one in five Hungarians lives in Budapest, the country-side plays an important role in Hungary's economy—this has jobs (especially women). Today, the workforce is small (only 57 percent of eligible workers) but highly skilled. Grains, metals, and machinery are major products, and nearly a third of trade is with Germany. However, Hungary's government has run up an alarming debt over the last few years, delaying the country's adoption of the euro.

Currency: 200 forints (Ft, or HUF) = about $1.

Government: The single-house National Assembly (386 seats) is the only ruling branch directly elected by popular vote. The legislators in turn select the figurehead President (currently the right-of-center László Sólyom) and the ruling Prime Minister (the very controversial Socialist Ferenc Gyurcsány—see page 396).

Flag: Three horizontal bands, top to bottom: red (representing strength), white (faithfulness), and green (hope). It's identical to the Italian flag—only flipped 90 degrees counterclockwise. It often includes the Hungarian coat of arms: horizontal red-and-white stripes (on the left); the patriarchal, or double-barred, cross (on the right); and the Hungarian crown (on top). In the communist era, a socialistic emblem was placed in the center of the flag. A memorable symbol of dissent in those times (especially during the 1956 Uprising) was a Hungarian flag with a hole cut in the middle.

The Average Hungarian: Eats a pound of lard a week (they cook with it). One in five Hungarians uses the Internet. The average family has three members, and they spend almost three-fourths of their income on (costly) housing. According to a recent condom-company survey, the average Hungarian has sex 131 times a year (behind only France and Greece), making them Europe's third-greatest liars.

First Name Last: In Hungary, a person's family name is listed first, and the given name is last—just as in many other Eastern cultures (think of Kim Jong Il). The composer known as "Franz Liszt" in German is "Liszt Ferenc" in his homeland. To help reduce confusion, many Hungarian business cards list the surname in capital letters.

always been a highly agricultural region. You'll pass fields of wheat and corn, but the grains are secondary to Hungarians' (and tourists') true love: the wine. Hungarian winemaking standards plummeted under the communists, but many vintner families are now reclaiming their land, returning to their precise traditional methods, and making wines worth being proud of once more.

Somehow Hungary, at the crossroads of Europe, has managed to become cosmopolitan while remaining perfectly Hungarian.

In the countryside, where less mixing has occurred, Magyar culture and occasional Central Asian facial features are more evident. But in the cities, the Hungarians—like Hungary itself—are a cross-section of Central European cultures: Magyars, Germans, Czechs, Slovaks, Poles, Serbs, Jews, Ottomans, Romanians, Roma (Gypsies), and many others. Still, no matter how many generations removed they are from Magyar stock, there's something different about a Hungarian—and not just the language. Look a Hungarian in the eye, and you'll see a glimmer of the marauding Magyar, stomping in from the Central Asian plains a thousand years ago.

Practicalities

Telephones: Like many things in Hungary, the telephone system is uniquely confusing. You must dial different codes whether you're calling locally, long distance within the country, or internationally to Hungary.

To dial a number in the same city, simply dial direct, with no area code.

To dial long-distance within Hungary, you have to add the prefix 06, followed by the area code (e.g., Budapest's area code is 1, so you dial 06-1, then the rest of the number).

To make an international call to Hungary, start with the international access code (00 if calling from Europe, 011 from the United States or Canada), then Hungary's country code (36), then the area code (but not the 06) and number.

To make an international call from Hungary, dial 00, the country code of the country you're calling (see chart in appendix), the area code if applicable (may need to drop initial zero), and the local number.

Hungarian phone numbers beginning with 0680 are toll-free; those beginning with 0620, 0630, or 0670 are mobile phones; and 0681 or 0690 are expensive toll lines. To call these numbers from within Hungary, simply dial direct. To dial them from outside Hungary, you need to drop the 06 at the beginning. So to call the Hungarian mobile phone number 0620-926-0557 from the United States, you dial 011 (the US international access code), then 36 (Hungary's country code), then 20 (omitting the 06), then 926-0557.

Telephone cards, which you insert into pay phones, are sold locally at tobacco shops and newsstands. Cheap international telephone cards (which aren't insertable but can be used from virtually any phone—see page 35) are just catching on in Hungary.

Hungarian History

Hungary has a colorful and illustrious history. In terms of political influence in Eastern Europe's past, the Hungarians rank with the Germans and the Russians.

Welcome to Europe

The Magyars, led by the mighty Árpád, thundered into the Carpathian Basin in A.D. 896. They were a rough-and-tumble nomadic people from Central Asia who didn't like to settle down in one place. They'd camp out in today's Hungary in the winters, and in the summers, they'd go on raids throughout Europe—terrorizing the Continent from Constantinople (modern-day Istanbul) to the Spanish Pyrénées. For half a century, they ranked with the Vikings as the most feared people in Europe.

After decades of running roughshod over Europe, the Hungarians were finally defeated by a German and Czech army at the Battle of Augsburg in 955. If they were to survive, the nomadic Magyars had to settle down. King Géza baptized his son, István (who was Árpád's great-great-grandson), and married him to a Bavarian princess at an early age.

Magyars Tamed

On Christmas Day in the year 1000, King István (Stephen) was crowned by the pope, and Hungary became a legitimate Christian nation (see page 428). The domestication of the nomadic Magyars was difficult, but Hungary eventually emerged as a major European power. The kingdom reached its peak in the late 15th century, when the enlightened King Mátyás Corvinus fostered the arts and sparked a mini-Renaissance (see page 426).

Ottoman Invasion

Soon after the reign of good king Mátyás, the Ottomans came slicing their way through the Balkan Peninsula towards Central Europe. In 1526, they entered Hungary. By 1541, they took Buda. During the Ottoman occupation, the Magyars moved the capital of the little that remained of their land—"rump Hungary"—to Bratislava (which they called "Pozsony"). During this era, the Ottomans built many of the baths that you'll still find throughout Hungary—and spiced up the food with paprika.

Christian-centric European historians have long viewed the Ottoman rule of southeastern Europe as an oppressive regime, but some experts have recently suggested otherwise. While it was advantageous for a European subject to adopt Islam (for lower taxes and other privileges), the Ottomans did not forcibly convert anyone—unlike the arguably more oppressive Catholics who controlled other parts of Europe at the time. (Remember the Spanish Inquisition and the expulsion of the Jews from Spain in 1492?) In later years, under Catholic Hapsburg rule, the Hungarians became notorious for their frequent and fierce uprisings. But under the Ottomans, no such record exists—leading many historians to believe that Hungarians preferred Ottoman (Muslim) rule to

Who Were the Magyars?

The ancestors of today's Hungarians, the Magyars, are a mysterious lot. Of all the Asian invaders of Europe, they were arguably the most successful—integrating more or less smoothly with the Europeans, and thriving well into the 21st century. Centuries after the Huns, Tatars, and Ottomans retreated east, leaving behind only fragments of their culture, the Hungarians remain a fixture in contemporary Europe.

The history of the Magyars before they arrived in Europe in A.D. 896 is hotly contested. Because their language is related only to Finnish and Estonian, it's presumed that these three peoples were once a single group, which likely originated east of the Ural Mountains (in the steppes of present-day Asian Russia).

After the Magyars' ancestors spent some time in Siberia, climatic change pushed them south and west, eventually (likely around the fifth century A.D.) crossing the Ural Mountains and officially entering Europe. They settled near the Don River (in today's southwestern Russia) before local warfare pushed them farther and farther west. The Magyars began raiding European lands, eventually setting up camp in the Carpathian Basin—today's Hungary—in A.D. 896.

After dominating Europe for many decades, the Hungarians were routed in battle and forced to adopt Christianity—a turning point that ultimately allowed them to flourish. Over the next several centuries, the Hungarians' Asian features and customs mostly faded away as they intermarried with Germans, Slavs, and

Hapsburg (Catholic) rule.

Crippled by the Ottomans and lacking power and options, Hungary came under control of the Austrian Hapsburg Empire, which finally wrested Buda from the Ottomans in 1686. The Hapsburgs repopulated Buda and Pest with Germans, while Magyars reclaimed the countryside.

The Hapsburgs

The Hungarians resisted Hapsburg rule, and three Magyars in particular are still noted for their rebellion against Vienna: Ferenc Rákóczi, who led Hungarians in the War of Independence (1703–1711); Lajos Kossuth, who was at the forefront of the 1848 Revolution; and Kossuth's contemporary, Count István Széchenyi, who fought the Hapsburgs with money—building structures like Budapest's iconic Chain Bridge. Countless streets, squares, and buildings throughout the country are named for these three Hungarian patriots.

But centuries of alliance with the Hapsburgs eventually paid other European peoples. By the 16th century, the Hungarians became Europe's front line in fending off the invasion of another Asian group, the Ottomans. Hungarian integration with the other peoples of Europe continued over the next several centuries, and through to the present day. In fact, a recent genetic study found that Hungarians are the most ethnically diverse nationality on the planet.

But even though certain aspects of their Magyar heritage have been lost, the Hungarians have done a remarkable job of clinging on to their Asian roots. They still do things their own way, making Hungary subtly but unmistakably different from its neighboring countries. And people of German-Hungarian, Slavic-Hungarian, and Jewish-Hungarian descent still speak a language that's not too far removed from the Asian tongue spoken by those original Magyars.

Were the Hungarians (Magyars) descended from the Huns, a similarly violent nomadic tribe that lived in the same area centuries earlier? Until recently, legends and historians speculated a tie between these two groups. In fact, the word "Hungarian" is at least partly derived from "Hun." But, even though it's a popular romantic notion to link these two mysterious tribes, recent historians strongly doubt that the two ever had anything to do with each other. Even so, many Hungarians still take pride in the legendary link to the Huns...and "Attila" remains a popular name even today.

off. After the 1848 Revolution in Hungary and an important military loss to the Prussians, Austria realized that it couldn't control its rebellious Slavic holdings all by itself. With the Compromise of 1867, Austria granted Budapest the authority over the eastern half of their lands, creating the so-called Dual Monarchy of the Austro-Hungarian Empire.

Hungary enjoyed a Golden Age and Budapest prospered, governing large parts of today's Slovakia, Croatia, and Transylvania (northwest Romania). Composers Franz Liszt (more Germanic than Magyar) and Béla Bartók incorporated the folk and Roma (Gypsy) songs of the Hungarian and Transylvanian countryside into their music.

The Crisis of Trianon

Hungary, allied with Austria and Germany, came up on the losing end of World War I. As retribution, the 1920 Treaty of Trianon (named for the palace on the grounds of Versailles where it was signed) reassigned two-thirds of Hungary's former territory and half of its population to Romania, Czechoslovakia, Slovenia, Croatia, and Serbia. Not unlike Berlin with the overnight construction of the Berlin Wall, towns along the new Hungarian borders were suddenly divided down the middle. Many Hungarians found themselves unable to visit relatives or commute to jobs that were in the same country the day before. This sent hundreds of thousands of Hungarian refugees—now "foreigners" in their own towns—into Budapest, sparking an enormous boom in the capital.

To this day, the Treaty of Trianon is regarded as one of the greatest tragedies of Hungarian history. More than two million ethnic Hungarians live outside Hungary (mostly in Romania)—and many Hungarians claim that these lands still belong to the Magyars. The sizeable Magyar minorities in neighboring countries have often been mistreated—particularly in Romania (under Ceauşescu), Yugoslavia (under Milošević), and Slovakia (under Mečiar). You'll see maps, posters, and bumper stickers with the distinctive shape of a much larger, pre-WWI Hungary...patriotically displayed by Magyars who feel as strongly about Trianon as if it happened yesterday. When the European Union expanded in 2004, some Hungarians saw it as a happy ending in the big-picture sense—they were once again united with Slovakia, part of the territory they had lost.

After World War I, the newly shrunken Kingdom of Hungary had to reinvent itself. The WWI hero Admiral Miklós Horthy had won many battles with the Austro-Hungarian navy. Though the new Hungary had no sea and no navy, Horthy retained his rank and ruled the country as a regent. A popular joke points out that during this time, Hungary was a "kingdom without a king" and a landlocked country ruled by a sea admiral. This sense of compounded deficiency pretty much sums up the morose attitude Hungarians have about those gloomy post-Trianon days.

World War II and the Arrow Cross

As Hitler rose to power, some countries that had felt unfairly treated in the aftermath of World War I—including Hungary and Croatia—saw Nazi Germany as a vehicle to greater independence. Admiral Horthy ceded power to the Nazis with the hope that they might help Hungary regain the crippling territorial losses of Trianon. Being an ally to the Nazis, rather than an occupied state, also allowed Hungary a certain degree of self-determination through the war—saving its sizeable Jewish population from immediate deportation to concentration camps. Winning back chunks of Slovakia, Transylvania, and Croatia in the early days of World War II also bolstered the Nazis' popularity in Hungary.

As Nazism took hold in Germany, the Hungarian fascist movement—spearheaded by the Arrow Cross Party (Nyilaskeresztes

Top 10 Dates That Changed Hungary

A.D. 896—The nomadic Magyars (a tribe from Central Asia) arrive in the Carpathian Basin and begin to terrorize Europe.

1000—The pope crowns King István (Stephen), marking the domestication of the Magyars.

1541—Invading Ottomans take Buda and Pest...and cook with paprika.

1686—The Austrian Hapsburgs drive out the Ottomans, making Hungary part of their extensive empire (despite occasional rebellions from nationalistic Hungarians).

1848—A Golden Age begins, as Hungary gains semi-autonomy from Austria, rebuilds Budapest, rules surrounding territories, and inspires great artists.

1920—Losers in World War I, Hungary is stripped of two-thirds its territory and half its population in the Treaty of Trianon... and they're still angry about it.

1945—After World War II, the Soviet Union "liberates" the country and establishes a communist state.

1956—Hungarians bravely revolt. A massive invasion of Soviet tanks and soldiers brutally suppresses the rebellion, killing 25,000.

1989—Hungary is the first Soviet satellite to open its borders to the West, sparking similar reforms throughout Eastern Europe.

2004—Hungary joins the European Union.

Párt)—gained popularity within Hungary. As Germany increased its demands for Hungarian soldiers and food, Admiral Horthy resisted...until Hitler's patience wore thin. In March of 1944, the Nazis invaded and installed the Arrow Cross in power. The Arrow Cross made up for lost time, immediately beginning a savage campaign of executing Hungary's Jews—not only sending them to concentration camps, but butchering them in the streets. Almost 600,000 Hungarian Jews were murdered. For more on this dark era of Hungarian history, see the "House of Terror" museum listing on page 445 of the Budapest chapter.

The Soviet Army eventually liberated Hungary—but at the expense of Budapest, where a months-long siege reduced the proud city to rubble.

Communism...with a Pinch of Paprika

After World War II, the Soviets installed Mátyás Rákosi as head of state. In 1956, the Hungarians staged an uprising, led by

Communist Party reformer Imre Nagy (see page 432). Moscow sent in troops, 25,000 Hungarians were killed, and 250,000 fled to the West. (If you know any Hungarians in the US, their families more than likely fled there in 1956.) János Kádár was installed to run a harder-line government, and though he cooperated with Moscow, he gradually allowed the people of Hungary more freedom than citizens of neighboring countries had.

Life here became better and livelier than elsewhere in the Soviet bloc—a system dubbed "goulash communism." With little fanfare, the Hungarian parliament—always skeptical of the Soviets—peacefully voted to end the communist regime in February of 1989. Later that year, Hungary was the first Eastern Bloc nation to open its borders to the West, a major advance in the fall of communist regimes across Eastern Europe. Hungary's first post-communist president, Árpád Göncz, was a protestor from the 1950s who was famous for translating *The Lord of the Rings* into Hungarian while he was in prison.

Gyurcsány's Gaffe and Hungary Today

In 2004, Hungary eagerly joined the EU, excited about its future in a united Europe. But as they've adjusted to life after communism, Hungary's leaders have struggled with how to afford the generous social-welfare network its people have come to expect. The Hungarian Socialist Party, which took control of parliament in 2002, impressed citizens by maintaining and even extending some social programs, but experts began to worry the mounting public debt would bankrupt the country.

Hungary made international headlines in the fall of 2006, when Prime Minister Ferenc Gyurcsány, a Socialist, was involved in an embarrassing gaffe that almost led to a minor revolution. After the Hungarian Socialist Party won re-election in April 2006, Gyurcsány gave a secret speech to his party. The intent of his shockingly frank remarks was to give his colleagues a wake-up call. But Gyurcsány's method—ranting on and on about how badly they'd fouled things up (and using very colorful language)—was ill-advised. Someone in the meeting recorded the whole thing, waited a few months, then turned the audio tape over to the press.

On September 17, 2006, Hungarians turned on their TVs to hear their Prime Minister detailing the ways he and his party had driven their country to the brink of ruin, and then shamelessly lied about it to stay in power: "We have screwed up. Not a little but a lot. No country in Europe has screwed up as much as we have... We have obviously lied throughout the past 18 to 24 months. It was perfectly clear that what we were saying was not true...We did not actually do anything for four years. Nothing. You cannot mention any significant government measures that we can be proud of—nothing. If we have to give an account to the country of what we have done in four years, what are we going to say?... I almost perished because I had to pretend for 18 months that we were governing. Instead, we lied morning, noon, and night."

The Hungarians take their young democracy very seriously. So the following night, demonstrators (many of them members of fringe political groups—and even, according to local scuttlebutt, known gangs of soccer hooligans) showed up at two strategic squares in downtown Budapest, demanding Gyurcsány's resignation. The worst damage occurred when they broke into the state TV headquarters. Riot police were sent in to subdue the looters with water cannons and tear gas.

The violence was quickly put down, but the unrest continued to simmer. Then, on October 23, the nation celebrated the 50th anniversary of the 1956 Uprising. Protestors seeking Gyurcsány's resignation used the occasion as an opportunity to riot, and isolated violence again swept through the streets of Budapest. It remains to be seen how Gyurcsány's goof will affect his own future, and that of his party. But most observers see the recent unrest as a healthy sign of a country dealing with the growing pains of a transition to capitalism. And, regardless of the sensationalistic coverage of the events on international news networks, Hungary remains an enjoyable, welcoming, and safe place to travel.

Hungarian Food

Hungary is known in Eastern Europe for its spicy food. Hungarian cuisine is as rich and complex as Polish and Czech food are simple. Everything is heavily seasoned: with paprika, tomatoes, and peppers of every shape, color, size, and flavor.

Hungarians dine at a *vendéglő* or *étterem* (restaurant). They gather with friends at a *kávéház* (café, literally, "coffeehouse"), which sometimes has light food, too. And for dessert, it's a *cukrászda* (pastry shop—*cukr* means "sugar").

Many American visitors to Hungary can't wait to taste goulash in its homeland—only to be disappointed that it isn't quite what they expected. The word "goulash" comes from the Hungarian *gulyás leves,* or "shepherd's soup." Here in its homeland, it's a clear, spicy broth with chunks of meat, potatoes, and other vegetables. Only outside of Hungary is the word used to describe a thick stew.

Aside from the obligatory *gulyás,* make a point of trying another unusual Hungarian specialty: cold fruit soup *(hideg gyümölcs leves).* This cream-based treat—generally eaten before the meal, even though it tastes more like a dessert—is usually made with *meggy* (sour cherries), but you'll also see versions with *alma* (apples) or *körte* (pears). Other Hungarian soups *(levesek)* include

Paprika Primer

The quintessential ingredient in Hungarian cuisine is paprika. In Hungarian, the word *paprika* can mean both peppers (red or green) and the spice that's made with them. Peppers can be stewed, stuffed, sautéed, baked, grilled, or pickled. For seasoning, red shakers of dried paprika join the salt and pepper on tables.

There are more than 40 varieties of paprika spice, with two main types: hot (*csípős* or *erős*) and sweet (*édesnemes* or simply *édes*, often comes in a white can). A can of paprika is a handy and tasty souvenir of your trip (see "Shopping" in the Budapest chapter, page 465). On menus, anything cooked *paprikás* (PAH-pree-kash) will be a little spicy.

In the fall of 2004, Hungary endured a paprika crisis. The spice was banned because some warehouse supplies were contaminated with aflatoxin, a poisonous substance caused by fungus. Because aflatoxin doesn't grow in the Hungarian climate, imported paprika from the tropics was blamed. After this scare, you can rest assured that today's Hungarian paprika is top-quality.

bableves (bean soup), *zöldségleves* (vegetable soup), *gombaleves* (mushroom soup), and *halászlé* (fish broth with paprika).

Hungarians adore all kinds of meat *(hús)*. *Csirke* is chicken, *borjú* is veal, *kacsa* is duck, *liba* is goose, *libamáj* is goose liver (which shows up more often than you'd think), *sertés* is pork, *sonka* is ham, *kolbász* is sausage, *szelet* is schnitzel (*Bécsi szelet* means Wiener schnitzel)—and the list goes on. Lard is used quite a bit in cooking, making Hungarian cuisine very rich and filling. Meat goes well with *káposzta* (cabbage), which may be *töltött* (stuffed) with the meat.

Vegetarians have a tricky time in Hungary, with many restaurants offering only a plate of deep-fried vegetables. They haven't quite figured out how to do a good, healthy, leafy salad; a traditional restaurant will generally offer only marinated cucumbers (listed on menus as "cucumber salad"), a plate of sliced-up pickles ("pickled cucumbers"), marinated spicy peppers, or something with cabbage—using lettuce only as a garnish.

In Hungary, you sometimes pay for *köretek* (starches) separately from the meat course. You'll be asked to choose between *galuska* (noodles), *burgonya* (potatoes), *krumpli* (French fries), *krokett* (like Tater Tots), or *rizs* (rice). *Kenyér* (bread) often comes with the meal.

A popular snack, especially in Budapest, is *lángos*—a savory deep-fried doughnut spread with cheese, garlic, and sour cream. In restaurants, a fancier version (often with meat) can be served as an entrée.

Pastries are a big deal here. Hungary's streets are lined with *cukrászda* (pastry shops). You have many options; simply point to what you want, and chow down. Try the *Dobos torta* (a layered chocolate-and-caramel cream cake), *somlói galuska* (a dumpling with vanilla, nuts, and chocolate), anything with *gesztenye* (chestnuts), and *rétes* (strudel with various fillings, including *túrós*, curds). On dessert menus at restaurants, you'll also see *palacsinta* (pancakes), usually served *diós* (with walnuts), *mákos* (with poppy seeds), or *gündel* (with nuts, chocolate, cream, and raisins). And many *cukrászda* also serve *fagylalt* (ice cream, *fagyi* for short), sold by the *gomboc* (ball).

To drink: *Sör* means "beer," and *bor* means "wine" (*vörös* is red and *fehér* is white). For more on Hungarian wines, see page 503 in the Eger chapter. *Kávé* and *tea* (pronounced TEY-ah) are coffee and tea, and *víz* (water) comes as *szódavíz* (soda water, sometimes just carbonated tap water) or *ásványvíz* (spring water, more expensive).

Unicum is a unique and beloved Hungarian liqueur made of 40 different herbs and aged in oak casks. The flavor is powerfully unforgettable—like Jägermeister, but harsher. A swig of Unicum is often gulped before the meal, but it's also used as a cure for an upset stomach (especially if you've eaten too much rich food—not an uncommon problem in Hungary). The liqueur has a history as unique and complicated as its flavor. Invented by a Doctor Zwack in the late 18th century, the drink impressed Hapsburg emperor Josef II, who supposedly declared: *"Das ist ein Unikum!"* ("This is a specialty!"). The Zwack company went on to thrive during Budapest's late-19th-century Golden Age (when Unicum was the subject of many whimsical Guinness-type ads). But when the communists took over after World War II, the Zwacks fled to America—taking their secret recipe for Unicum with them. The communists continued to market the drink with their own formula, which left Hungarians (literally and figuratively) with a bad taste in their mouths. In a landmark case, the Zwacks sued the communists for infringing on their copyright...and won. In 1991, Péter Zwack—who had been living in exile in Italy—triumphantly returned to Hungary and resurrected the original family recipe. To get your own taste of this family saga, look for the round bottle with the red cross on the label (www.zwack.hu).

If you're drinking with some new Magyar friends, impress them with the standard toast: *Egészségedre* (EH-gehs-sheh-geh-dreh; "to your health"). But don't clink your beer glasses with theirs. They still remember the 1848 Revolution against the Hapsburgs, which ended with the Hapsburg execution of 13 great Hungarian leaders. The Hapsburgs clinked their beer mugs to the victory. To this very day, clinking beer mugs is, for many Hungarians, just bad style. (Clinking wine glasses is perfectly fine, but always make meaningful eye contact as you clink.)

When your waiter brings your food, he'll probably say, *"Jó étvágyat!"* (Bon appétit!). When you're ready for the bill, you can simply say, *"Fizetek"* (FEE-zeh-tehk—"I'll pay").

Hungarian Language

Hungarians have an endearing habit of using the English word "hello" for both "hi" and "bye," just like the Italians use *"ciao."* You'll often overhear a Hungarian end a telephone conversation with a cheery "Hello!" While the language is overwhelming for tourists, one easy word is *"Szia"* (SEE-yah), which actually does mean hello or goodbye.

Even though Hungary is surrounded by Slavs, Hungarian is not at all related to Slavic languages. In fact, Hungarian isn't related to *any* European language (except for very distant relatives Finnish and Estonian). It isn't even an Indo-European language—which means that English is more closely related to Hindi, Russian, and French than it is to Hungarian.

Hungarian is agglutinative, which means that you start with a simple root word and then start tacking on suffixes to create meaning—sometimes resulting in a pileup of extra sounds at the end of a very long word. The emphasis always goes on the first syllable, and the following syllables are droned downhill in a kind of a monotone—giving the language a distinctive cadence that Hungary's Slavic neighbors love to tease about.

Hungarian pronunciation is straightforward, once you remember a few key rules. The trickiest: *s* alone is pronounced "sh," while *sz* is pronounced simply "s." This explains why you'll hear in-the-know travelers pronouncing Budapest as "BOO-dah-pesht." You might catch the *busz* up to Castle Hill—pronounced "boose." And "Franz Liszt" is easier to pronounce than it looks: It sounds just like "list."

The letter *c* and the combination *cz* are both pronounced "ts" (as in "cats"). The combination *zs* is pronounced "zh" (like "measure"). The letters *j* and *ly* are interchangeable, and both are pronounced as "y."

Hungarian has a set of unusual palatal sounds that don't quite have a counterpart in English. To make these sounds, gently press the thick part of your tongue to the roof or your mouth (instead of using the tip of your tongue behind your teeth, as we do in English): *gy* sounds more or less like "dg" in "ledger"; *ny* sounds kind of like the "ny" in "canyon"; and *cs* sounds like "ch."

As for vowels: The letter *a* almost sounds like o (aw); but with

Key Hungarian Phrases

English	Hungarian	Pronounced
Hello. (formal)	*Jó napot kívánok.*	yoh NAH-pot KEE-vah-nohk
Hi. / Bye. (informal)	*Szia.*	SEE-yah
Do you speak English?	*Beszél angolul?*	BEH-sehl AHN-goh-lool
Yes. / No.	*Igen. / Nem.*	EE-gehn / nehm
Please.	*Kérem.*	KAY-rehm
You're welcome.	*Szívesen.*	SEE-veh-shehn
Can I help you?	*Tessék.*	TEHSH-shehk
Thank you.	*Köszönöm.*	KUR-sur-nurm
I'm sorry. / Excuse me.	*Bocsánat.*	BOH-chah-nawt
Good.	*Jól.*	yohl
Goodbye.	*Viszontlátásra.*	VEE-sohnt-lah-tahsh-rah
one / two	*egy / kettő*	edj / KEH-tur
three / four	*három / négy*	HAH-rohm / nedj
five / six	*öt / hat*	urt / hawt
seven / eight	*hét / nyolc*	heht / NEE-ohlts
nine / ten	*kilenc / tíz*	KEE-lehnts / teez
hundred	*száz*	sahz
thousand	*ezer*	EH-zehr
How much?	*Mennyi?*	MEHN-yee
local currency	*forint (Ft)*	FOH-reent
Where is...?	*Hol van...?*	hohl vawn
...the toilet	*...a toalet*	aw TOH-ah-leht
men	*férfi*	FEHR-fee
women	*női*	NUR-ee
water / coffee	*víz / kávé*	veez / KAH-veh
beer / wine	*sör / bor*	shewr / bohr
Cheers!	*Egészségedre!*	EH-gehs-sheh-geh-dreh
the bill (literally, "I'll pay")	*fizetek*	FEE-zeh-tehk

an accent *(á)*, it brightens up to the more standard "ah." As with Czech, an accent *(á, é, í, ó, ú)* indicates that you linger on that vowel (but not necessarily that you stress that syllable). Like German, Hungarian has umlauts *(ö, ü)*, meaning you purse your lips when you say that vowel. A long umlaut *(ő, ű)* is the same sound, but you hold it a little longer.

Okay, maybe it's not *so* simple. But you'll get the hang of it.

As you're tracking down addresses, these definitions will help: *tér* (square), *utca* (road), *út* (boulevard), *körút* (ring road), *fürdő* (bath), and *híd* (bridge). Words ending in *k* are often plural.

BUDAPEST

Budapest is the capital of Eastern Europe. It's a city of nuance and paradox—cosmopolitan, complicated, and challenging for the first-timer to get a handle on. Novices are sometimes overwhelmed by Budapest—but seasoned travelers enjoy this grand city more with each return visit. Though Prague and Kraków have more romance (and crowds), travelers in the know find Budapest (BOO-dah-pehst) to be Eastern Europe's most fascinating and rewarding destination.

Budapest is hot—literally. The city sits on a thin layer of earth above thermal springs, which power its many baths. Even the word *Pest* comes from a Slavic word for "oven." Two thousand years ago, the Romans had a settlement (called Aquincum) on the north edge of today's Budapest. Several centuries later, in A.D. 896, the Magyars arrived from the steppes of Central Asia and took over the Carpathian Basin (roughly today's Hungary). In the 16th century, the Ottomans invaded—occupying the region for 145 years. When the Ottomans were forced out, Buda and Pest were in ruins. The Hapsburgs repopulated them, giving the cities a more Austrian style.

The Great Compromise of 1867 granted Hungary an equal stake in the Austro-Hungarian Empire. Six years later, the cities of Buda, Pest, and Óbuda united to form the capital city of Budapest, which governed a huge chunk of Eastern Europe. For the next few decades, Hungarian culture enjoyed a Golden Age, and Budapest was a boomtown. The expansion reached its peak with a flurry of construction surrounding the year 1896—Hungary's 1,000th birthday (see page 413).

During the Soviet era, Hungary's milder "goulash communism"

meant that Budapest, though still oppressed, was a place where other Eastern Europeans felt they could let loose. Twenty years ago, a stroll down Váci utca was the closest Czechs and Poles could get to a day pass to the West—including a chance to taste a Big Mac at the first McDonald's behind the Iron Curtain.

Budapest was built as the head of a much larger empire than it currently governs. Like Vienna, the city today feels a bit too grandiose for the capital of a small country. But Budapest remains the heart and soul of Eastern Europe. It's a rich cultural stew made up of Hungarians, Germans, Slavs, and Jews, with a dash of Turkish paprika—simmered for centuries in a thermal bath. Each group has left its mark, but through it all, something has remained that is distinctly…Budapest.

Planning Your Time

Budapest demands at least three nights and two full days. The city has oodles of good museums, but none of them is strictly must-see; which ones you visit depends entirely on your interests. Skim my listings and figure out which sights sound good to you. I've suggested where you might fit them in below.

I like this efficient but ambitious two-day plan:

Day 1: Begin at the square called Vörösmarty tér, consider coffee at Gerbeaud, and stroll down Váci utca (see page 434). At the end of the street, explore the Great Market Hall.

From the Great Market Hall, you're a quick walk or tram ride (#47 or #49) from the Great Synagogue and the National Museum. If you'd prefer to tour the Parliament—farther to the north—do it this morning (tram #2 or #2A zips you right there from the Great Market Hall).

After lunch in Pest, stroll over the Chain Bridge and ride the funicular up to Castle Hill. Following my self-guided walk (page 436), visit Matthias Church, Fishermen's Bastion, and the Castle Hill museums of your choice.

After dinner, take a twilight sightseeing cruise, go to a concert (folk music nightly at 20:00) or the opera, or stroll the Danube embankments and bridges.

Day 2: Start at St. István's Basilica, then work your way up the lively boulevard called Andrássy út. Depending on your interests, you can stop at (in this order): the Commerce and Catering Museum, the Postal Museum, the Opera House (duck in to see the lobby, or return later for a full-blown tour at 15:00 or 16:00), Franz Liszt Square (lots of cafés and restaurants), busy Oktogon square, and the House of Terror museum. To skip ahead (or backtrack quickly), hop on the M1 Metro line, which runs beneath Andrássy út from start to finish. At the end of Andrássy út, explore Heroes' Square and the City Park.

Budapest Overview

Reward yourself with a nice, long soak in the Széchenyi Baths (secure lockers, rental suits, open until 22:00, get there by 20:00 to have enough time). The ritzy Gundel Restaurant is across from the baths, and other, less-fancy dining options are nearby. For the evening, consider the same options as for Day 1.

To speed things up and fit in Statue Park, squeeze in the statues in the morning of Day 2 (bus departs Deák tér at 11:00), then do an accelerated ramble down Andrássy boulevard.

You'll have no trouble filling a third day—it gives you more time to fit in Statue Park, more museums, and outlying areas (such as Óbuda and Szentendre). After many years, I still discover new joys each time I return.

Eger is the best day trip (2.25 hrs by train each way, even better if you spend the night—see Eger chapter). Szentendre, on the Danube Bend, is closer but very touristy (doable in a half-day or even just in the late afternoon/evening). With a car (or a hired

Budapest Essentials

English	Hungarian	Pronounced
Square	Tér	tehr (said pulling cheeks back)
Street	Utca	OOT-zah
Boulevard	Út	oot
Bridge	Híd	heed
Ring Road	Körút	KUR-root
Funicular	Sikló	SHEE-kloh
Bath	Fürdő	FEWR-dur
Pest's Main Pedestrian Street	Váci utca	VAH-tsee OOT-zah
Pest's Main Square	Vörösmarty tér	VOO-roosh-mar-tee tehr
Pest's Grand Boulevard	Andrássy út	AHN-drah-shee oot
City Park	Városliget	VAH-rohsh-lee-geht
(Buda) Castle	(Budai) Vár	BOO-die vahr
Castle Hill	Várhegy	VAHR-hayj
Chain Bridge	Széchenyi lánchíd	SAY-chehn-yee LAHNTS-heed
Liberty Bridge (green, a.k.a. Franz Josef Bridge)	Szabadság híd	SAW-bawd-shahg heed
Elisabeth Bridge (white, modern)	Erzsébet híd	EHR-zheh-bayt heed
Margaret Bridge (crosses Margaret Island)	Margit híd	MAWR-geet heed
Danube River	Duna	DOO-naw
Eastern Train Station	Keleti pályaudvar	KEH-leh-tee PAH-yuh-uhd-vahr
Western Train Station	Nyugati pályaudvar	NYOO-gaw-tee PAH-yuh-uhd-vahr
Southern Train Station	Déli pályaudvar	DAY-lee PAH-yuh-uhd-vahr
Suburban Train System	HÉV	hayv

driver—see "Drivers," page 414), you could spend a day seeing the entire Danube Bend—Szentendre, Visegrád, and Esztergom—ideally on the way to Vienna or Bratislava (see Danube Bend chapter).

ORIENTATION

(area code: 1)
Budapest is huge—with nearly two million people, it's much larger than Prague. The city is split down the center by the Danube River. On the west side of the Danube is hilly **Buda,** dominated by Castle Hill (packed with tourists by day, dead at night). The pleasant Víziváros ("Water Town"; VEE-zee-vah-rohsh) neighborhood is between the castle and the river.

On the east is flat **Pest** (pronounced "pesht"), the commercial heart of the city, which bustles day and night. The red-domed, riverside Parliament, visible from any point along the Danube, marks the northern edge of the tourists' Pest. A few blocks to the south, the Váci utca pedestrian drag runs parallel to the Danube, ending at the steps of the Great Market Hall. From Deák Square in the center of Pest, Andrássy út (and the yellow M1 Metro line beneath it) runs out past the Opera House to the Oktogon, House of Terror museum, Heroes' Square, City Park, and Széchenyi Baths.

Buda and Pest are connected by a series of characteristic **bridges.** From north to south, there's the low-profile Margaret Bridge (Margit híd, crosses Margaret Island), the famous Chain Bridge (Széchenyi lánchíd), the white and modern Elisabeth Bridge (Erzsébet híd), and the green Liberty Bridge (Szabadság híd). The bridges are fun to cross by foot, but it's faster to go under the river (on the M2 Metro line), or to cross over it by tram (#47 and #49 over the Liberty Bridge) or by bus (#16 over the Chain Bridge and #8 across the Elisabeth Bridge are both handy).

Pest is surrounded by a series of **ring roads** *(körút).* The innermost ring road—called the Kiskörút, or "Small Boulevard"—surrounds central Pest. The outer ring road—Nagykörút, or "Great Boulevard"—is about halfway between the river and City Park. The ring roads change names every few blocks, but they are always called *körút.* Arterial **boulevards** called *út* (such as Andrássy út) stretch from central Pest into the suburbs, like spokes on a wheel. Almost everything a tourist wants to see in Pest is either inside the innermost ring—in the **Belváros** ("Inner City")—or along one of these main boulevards (and therefore well-covered by public transit). Buda is also surrounded by a ring road, and the busy Hegyalja út rumbles through the middle of the tourists' Buda (between Castle and Gellért hills).

Budapest uses a **district** system (like Paris and Vienna), and addresses often start with the district number (as a Roman numeral). Districts are called *kerület*. Castle Hill is district I. Notice that the district number does not necessarily indicate how central a location is: Districts II and III are to the north of Buda, where few tourists go, while the heart of Pest is district V.

Tourist Information

Budapest has six TIs (www.budapestinfo.hu, tel. 1/438-8080): **Franz Liszt Square,** a block south of the Oktogon on Andrássy út (mid-June–Oct daily 9:00–19:00; Nov–mid-June Mon–Fri 10:00–18:00, Sat 10:00–16:00, closed Sun; Liszt Ferenc tér 11, tel. 1/322-4098); **Deák tér** (daily 8:00–20:00, Sütő utca 2); **Castle Hill,** across from Matthias Church (May–Oct daily 9:00–20:00; Nov–April Mon–Fri 10:00–19:00, Sat–Sun 10:00–16:00; Szentháromság tér, tel. 1/488-0475); **Nyugati Train Station** (May–Oct daily 9:00–19:00; Nov–April Mon–Fri 9:00–18:00, Sat–Sun 9:00–15:00; tel. 1/302-8580); and in both Terminals 1 and 2B at the **airport** (daily 8:00–23:00).

At all of the TIs, you can collect a pile of free brochures (on sights, bus tours, and more). Most important: the free, good city map; the *Budapest Panorama* events guide; and the information-packed *Budapest City Guide* booklet. TIs are handy places to buy your Budapest Card.

Budapest Card: Even though this sightseeing card has shot up in price in recent years, it can still sometimes be a good value for busy sightseers. You get free travel on public transportation and entry to virtually all of Budapest's museums, plus minor discounts on other worthwhile attractions (including boat tours and thermal baths). With the Budapest Card, you have the freedom to hop the Metro for one stop to save 10 minutes of walking, or drop into semi-interesting sights for a peek. This is especially useful since Budapest has lots of "quickie" museums that don't really merit a long visit. The card costs 6,450 Ft for 48 hours, or 7,950 Ft for 72 hours (includes handy 108-page booklet with maps, updated hours, and brief museum descriptions). You can buy the card all over Budapest—at TIs, travel agencies, major Metro stations, sights, and many hotels. Be sure to sign and date your card before you use it.

Note that all state-run museums (including Budapest History Museum, Museum of Military History, Museum of Ethnography, Hungarian National Museum, Museum of Fine Arts, and Museum of Hungarian Agriculture) are free, but charge for special exhibitions. The Budapest Card gets you a 20 percent discount on the entrance fee to these special exhibitions.

Alternative Tourist Information Offices: Ben Frieday, an American in love with Budapest (and one of its women), runs

Sightseeing Modules

Budapest is a sprawling city, with sights scattered over a huge area. But if you organize your sightseeing efficiently and dive into the easy-to-master public transportation system, Budapest gets small. Break the city into manageable chunks, and digest them one at a time:

Buda
- **Castle Hill** (Royal Palace, Matthias Church, and various museums)
- **Gellért Hill** (Gellért Baths, Citadella, and Cave Church)

Pest
- **Central Pest, a.k.a. Belváros** (north to south: Parliament, Vörösmarty Square, Váci utca pedestrian drag, Danube embankment and cruises, Great Synagogue, National Museum, and Great Market Hall)
- **Andrássy út** (from center to outskirts: St. István's Basilica, Commerce and Catering Museum, Opera House, Franz Liszt Square, Oktogon, House of Terror, Heroes' Square, City Park, and Széchenyi Baths)

Outer Budapest
- **Óbuda** (Vasarely Museum, Imre Varga Collection, and Aquincum Roman ruins)
- **Statue Park**
- **Danube Bend** (begins just north of Óbuda: Szentendre, Visegrád, and Esztergom; see Danube Bend chapter)

Discover Hungary. This alternative to the TIs specializes in answering questions Americans (especially backpackers) have about Budapest. They have two locations in central Budapest: at Deák tér (Sütő utca 2, in the courtyard between the McDonald's and TI, marked "Yellow Zebra") and near Andrássy út (behind the Opera House at Lázár utca 16). At either branch, you can use the Internet (100 Ft/15 min), rent a bike, and find out more about Budapest (both offices open May–Oct daily 9:30–19:30, shorter hours off-season, tel. 1/266-8777, www.discoverhungary.com). The Andrássy út office has a fun exhibit of communist relics in the basement (500 Ft). Ben also runs Yellow Zebra bike tours, Absolute Walking Tours, and Segway Tours (see page 420).

Arrival in Budapest

Budapest has three major train stations (*pályaudvar*, abbreviated *pu.*): Keleti (Eastern) Station, Nyugati (Western) Station, and Déli (Southern) Station. A century ago, the name of the station indicated which part of Europe it served. But these days, there's no connection: Trains going to the east might leave from the Western Station, and vice-versa. Even more confusing, the station used by a particular train can change from year to year—so it's essential to carefully confirm which station your train departs from.

The Keleti (Eastern) Station and Nyugati (Western) Station— both cavernous, late-19th-century Erector-set masterpieces in Pest—are the ones you're most likely to use. Déli (Southern) Station, behind Castle Hill in Buda, is less useful for most tourists.

The taxi stands in front of each train station are notorious for ripping off tourists—it's better to call for a taxi (see "Getting Around Budapest—By Taxi," page 417).

By Train at the Keleti (Eastern) Station: The Keleti Station (Keleti pu.) is just south of City Park, east of central Pest. On arrival, go to the front of long tracks 6–9 to reach the exits and services. Several travel agencies with "Tourist Information" signs cluster near the head of the tracks. None is official, but all have a few helpful fliers, and most can sell you a Budapest Card. Along track 6, you'll find a baggage-check desk, an ATM (at K&H Bank), money-exchange booths (avoid Interchange, which has bad rates), and international information and ticket windows (hiding down a hallway, look for *nemzetközi pénztár;* lockers nearby).

The big staircase at the head of the tracks leads down to domestic ticket windows, WCs, telephones, more ATMs, and (a few minutes' walk straight ahead) a passageway to the Metro station entrance (M2 line; see "Getting Around Budapest—by Metro," page 416). If you go out the front door, you'll stumble over a cluster of suspicious-looking, unmarked taxis. You can try to negotiate with these goons—the fair rate to downtown is about 1,500 Ft—but it's far more reliable and less hassle to phone for a taxi (buy phone card at newsstand, go to the phone bank downstairs, call 1/266-6666 or 1/211-111, tell the English-speaking dispatcher where you are, and go out front to meet your taxi).

By Train at the Nyugati (Western) Station: The Nyugati Station (Nyugati pu.) is the most central of Budapest's stations, on the northeast edge of downtown Pest. Most international arrivals use tracks 1–9, which are set back from the main entrance. From the head of these tracks, exit straight ahead into a parking lot with taxis and buses, or use the stairs just inside the doors to reach an underpass and the Metro (M3 line, see "Getting Around Budapest—by Metro," page 416). If you're homesick, leave through this door and go immediately to the right to discover the huge, American-style **WestEnd City Center mall** (complete with a T.G.I. Friday's, daily 8:00–23:00).

To reach an official TI and ticket windows, follow tracks 10–13 to the station's main entrance. The TI is by the head of track

10 (May–Oct daily 9:00–19:00; Nov–April Mon–Fri 9:00–18:00, Sat–Sun 9:00–15:00; tel. 1/302-8580). The TI can call an honest taxi for you, allowing you to avoid the crooked cabbies parked out front. Ticket windows are through an easy-to-miss door, across the tracks by platform 13 (marked *cassa* and *információ;* once you enter the ticket hall, international windows are in a second room at the far end—look for *nemzetközi*).

From the head of tracks 10–13, exit straight ahead and you'll be on Teréz körút, the very busy Great Boulevard ring road. (Váci utca, at the center of Pest, is dead ahead, about 20 min away by foot). In front of the building is another taxi stand and access to handy trams #4 and #6 (zipping all the way around Pest's great ring); to the right you'll find stairs leading to an underpass (use it to avoid crossing this busy intersection, or to reach the Metro's M3 line); and to the left you'll see the classiest Art Nouveau McDonald's on the planet. (Seriously. Take a look inside.)

By Train at the Déli (Southern) Station: The smaller, more modern Déli Station (Déli pu.) is at the end of the line for the M2 Metro line, which connects you easily to several key points in town: Batthyány tér (on the Buda embankment, at the north end of the Víziváros neighborhood), Deák tér (the heart of Pest, with connections to other Metro lines), and the Keleti train station.

By Car: A car is unnecessary at best and a headache at worst. Unless you're heading to an out-of-town sight (such as Statue Park), park the car at your hotel and take public transportation. Public parking costs 120–400 Ft per hour (pay in advance at machine and put ticket on dashboard—watch locals and imitate; free parking Mon–Fri after 18:00, Sat after 12:00, and all day Sun—but you'll have to pay all the time in touristy zones). Be careful to park within the lines—otherwise, your car is likely to get booted (I've seen more than one confused tourist puzzling over the giant red brace on their wheel). A guarded parking lot is safer, but more expensive (figure 3,000–4,000 Ft/day, ask your hotel or look for the blue *P*s on maps).

By Plane: Budapest Ferihegy Airport is 10 miles southeast of the center (airport code: BUD, tel. 1/296-7000, www.bud.hu). The airport has two terminals, connected by an airport bus. Terminal 1 is used by the low-cost airlines. Terminal 2 has two adjacent parts: 2A is for Malev, the Hungarian national airline, while all other carriers use 2B. (If you're flying out of Budapest, confirm which terminal your flight leaves from.) Both terminals have similar services, including ATMs and TI desks (at Terminals 1 and 2B).

The options for getting into town are the same from either terminal. The airport-shuttle **minibus** is easiest (2,300 Ft/person to any hotel in the city center, 15 percent discount with Budapest Card—buy the card at the minibus desk when you buy your ticket, tel. 1/296-8555; if arranging a minibus transfer *to* the airport, call 24 hours before). Because they prefer to take several people at once, you may have to wait a while for a quorum to show up (about 15 minutes in busy times, up to an hour when it's slow—they can give you an estimate). Alternatively, you can take a **taxi** (fixed off-meter price is generally 5,000–6,000 Ft to downtown depending on your hotel—the best deal for three or more people). Finally, the cheapest but most complicated option is to take the **public bus** to the Kőbánya-Kispest M3 Metro station, and then take the Metro into town (allow about an hour total for the trip to the center).

Helpful Hints

Rip-Offs: Budapest feels—and is—safe, especially for a city of its size. There's little risk of violent crime here. And, while people routinely try to rip me off in Prague, I've never had a problem in Budapest. Still, many of my readers report falling victim to scams and con artists in Budapest. As in any big city, it's especially important to beware of pickpockets in crowded and touristy places, particularly on the Metro and in trams. Wear a money belt and watch your valuables closely. Keep your wits about you and refuse to be bullied or distracted. Any deal that seems too good to be true...probably is.

Budapest restaurants—especially on the Váci utca shopping street—are notorious for overcharging tourists. Don't eat at a restaurant that doesn't list prices on the menu, and always check your bill carefully. It's best to steer clear of those overpriced Váci utca eateries entirely—even if they charge you what's listed, it's still a rip-off.

If you're a male in a touristy area and a gorgeous local girl (nicknamed a *konzumlany,* or "consumption girl") takes a liking to you, avoid her. The foreplay going on here will climax in your grand rip-off. Another common scam involves a man stopping you on the street to "change money." A policeman arrests him—and you—and needs to see your wallet to find out if he's a con artist. They are a team and you are being robbed.

Budapest's biggest crooks? Unscrupulous cabbies (see "Getting Around Budapest—By Taxi," page 417). I've said it before, I'll say it again: Locals *always* call for a cab, rather than hail one on the street or at a taxi stand. If you're not comfortable making the call yourself, ask your hotel or restaurant to call for you.

Blue Monday: Virtually all of Budapest's museums are closed on Mondays. But never fear—you can still take advantage of these sights and activities: both major baths, Statue Park, Great Synagogue, Matthias Church and Budapest History

Tonight We're Gonna Party Like It's 1896

Visitors to Budapest need only remember one date: 1896. For the millennial celebration of their ancestors' arrival in Europe, Hungarians threw a huge blowout party. In the thousand years between 896 and 1896, the Magyars had gone from being a nomadic Central Asian tribe that terrorized the Continent to sharing the throne of one of the most successful empires Europe had ever seen.

Much as the year 2000 saw a fit of new construction worldwide, Budapest used its millennial celebration as an excuse to build monuments and buildings appropriate for the co-capital of a huge empire, including:

- **Heroes' Square** and the **Millennium Monument**
- **Vajdahunyad Castle** (in City Park)
- The riverside **Parliament** building (96 meters tall, with 96 steps at the main entry)
- **St. István's Basilica** (also 96 meters tall)
- The M1 (yellow) Metro line, a.k.a. *Földalatti* ("Underground")—the first subway on the Continent
- The **Great Market Hall** (and four other market halls)
- **Andrássy út** and most of the fine buildings lining it
- The **Opera House**
- A complete rebuilding of **Matthias Church** (on Castle Hill)
- The **Fishermen's Bastion** decorative terrace (by Matthias Church)
- The green **Liberty Bridge** (then called Franz Josef Bridge, in honor of the ruling Hapsburg emperor)

Ninety-six is the key number in Hungary—even the national anthem (when sung in the proper tempo) takes 96 seconds. But after all this fuss, it's too bad that the date was wrong: A commission—convened to establish the exact year of the Magyars' debut—determined it happened in 895. But city leaders knew they'd never make an 1895 deadline, and requested the finding be changed to 896.

Museum on Castle Hill, St. István's Basilica, Parliament tour, Opera House tour, City Park (and Zoo), Great Market Hall, Danube cruises, concerts, and bus, walking, and bike tours.

Internet Access: Internet cafés are everywhere—just look for signs or ask your hotel. In Pest, I like **Discover Hungary/Yellow Zebra,** with fast access and good prices (100 Ft/15 min; for locations, hours, and contact information, see "Discover Hungary" listing on page 409). In Buda's Víziváros neighborhood, try the **Soho Coffee Company** (on Fő utca—see page 480).

Post Offices: These are marked with a smart green *posta* logo (usually open Mon–Fri 8:00–18:00, Sat 8:00–12:00, closed Sun).

Laundry: Options are scarce, and there's not yet a coin-op, self-serve launderette in town. The easiest solution is simply to have your hotel do it for you, though there are two places where you can drop off your laundry and pick it up later.

In Pest, try the cheap and central **Patyolat Gyorstisztító** (they say it's "self-service," but usually you can just drop off your clothes with the monolingual laundry ladies in the morning and pick them up in the afternoon; borrow the English information sheet, allow 2,500 Ft to wash and dry a load, Mon–Fri 7:00–19:00, closed Sat–Sun, just up from Váci utca at the corner of Vármegye utca and Városház utca).

In Buda's Víziváros neighborhood, on Batthyány tér, go upstairs in the big market hall to find **Topclean** (allow 1,200 Ft/kilogram, Mon–Fri 9:00–19:00, Sat 9:00–14:00, closed Sun; drop off before 10:00 and pick up that afternoon, or drop off after 10:00 and pick up the next day; above the Spar supermarket, tel. 1/487-0639).

English Newspapers: Newsstands sell two weekly English newspapers: the *Budapest Sun* (399 Ft, often free at hotels or TIs) and the *Budapest Times* (580 Ft, more business-oriented).

Local Guidebook: András Török's fun, idiosyncratic *Budapest: A Critical Guide* is the best book by a local writer. Its quirky walking tours do a nice job capturing the city's spirit (available in English at most souvenir stands).

English Bookstores: Pendragon, the recently expanded bookstore of Central European University, sells guidebooks and popular American magazines and paperbacks, and offers the best selection anywhere of scholarly books about this region (all in English; Mon–Fri 10:00–18:00, closed Sat–Sun, enter Central European University building at Nádor utca 9 and look left, tel. 1/327-3096). This university—offering graduate study for Americans and students from all over Eastern Europe—is predominantly funded by George Soros, a Hungarian who emigrated to the US and became a billionaire and high-profile donor to left-wing causes. **Red Bus Bookstore** has shelves of used books in English—and they buy books, too (Mon–Fri 11:00–18:00, Sat 10:00–14:00, closed Sun, Semmelweis utca 14, tel. 1/337-7453).

Bike Rental: Rent a bike at **Yellow Zebra,** part of Discover Hungary (500 Ft/hr, 2,000 Ft/half-day, 3,000 Ft/full day; for locations, hours, and contact information, see "Discover Hungary" listing on page 409).

Drivers: Friendly, English-speaking **Gábor Balázs** can drive you around the city or into the surrounding countryside (3,500

Ft/hr, 3-hr minimum in city, 4-hr minimum in countryside—
good for a Danube Bend excursion, mobile 0620-936-4317,
from the US call 011-36-20-936-4317, balazs.gabor@chello
.hu). **József Király** runs a 10-car company, Artoli, with good,
generally English-speaking drivers (€17/hr, more for larger
cars and vans, tel. 1/240-4050, mobile 0620-369-8890, from
the US call 011-36-20-369-8890, artoli@t-online.hu). Note
that these are drivers, not tour guides.

Best Views: Budapest is a city of marvelous vistas. Some of the best
are from the Citadella (high on Gellért Hill), the promenade
in front of Buda Castle, the embankments or many bridges
spanning the Danube (especially the Chain Bridge), and tour
boats on the Danube—lovely at night.

Getting Around Budapest

Budapest is huge. Connecting your sightseeing by foot is tedious
and unnecessary; use the excellent public transportation system
instead. The same tickets work for the Metro, trams, and buses.
Buy them at kiosks, Metro ticket windows, or machines. The new
machines are slick and easy, but the old orange ones are tricky: Put
in the appropriate amount of money, then wait for your ticket or
press the button. As it can be frustrating to find a ticket machine
(especially when you see your tram or bus approaching), I generally invest in a multi-day ticket or Budapest Card so I have the
freedom of hopping on at will.

Your options are:

• Single ticket (*vonaljegy,* for a ride of up to an hour with no
transfers)—185 Ft;

• Short single Metro ride (*metroszakaszjegy,* 3 stops or fewer
on the Metro)—130 Ft;

• Transfer ticket (*átszállójegy*—allowing up to 90 minutes,
including 1 transfer)—320 Ft; or

• Unlimited multi-day tickets (1,150 Ft/1 day, 2,500 Ft/3 days,
3,400 Ft/7 days)—but if you're here more than a day and plan to do
lots of sightseeing, consider a Budapest Card instead (see "Tourist
Information," page 408).

Always validate your ticket as you enter the bus, tram, or
Metro station (stick it in the elbow-high box). On older buses and
trams that have little red validation boxes, stick your ticket in the
black slot, then pull the slot towards you to punch holes in your
ticket. A transfer ticket must be validated a second time when you
transfer. The stern-looking guys with blue-and-green armbands
waiting as you exit the Metro want to see your validated ticket or
signed and dated Budapest Card. Cheaters are fined 2,500 Ft on
the spot, and you'll be surprised how often you're checked (inspectors are widely believed to target tourists, and are most commonly

seen at train stations and along the touristy M1 line). All public transit runs from 4:30 in the morning until 23:10. A useful route-planning Web site is www.bkv.hu.

By Metro: Riding Budapest's Metro, you really feel like you're down in the efficient guts of the city. It's every bit as convenient and slick as Vienna's or Berlin's—but it has more character than those stodgy systems.

There are three lines:

• **M1 (yellow)**—The first Metro line on the Continent, this shallow line runs under Andrássy út from the center to City Park (see "The Millennium Underground of 1896," page 441).

• **M2 (red)**—Built during the communist days, it's 115 feet deep, doubles as a bomb shelter, and comes with a tornado ventilation system—notice the gale. The only line going under the Danube to Buda, M2 connects the Déli train station, Moszkva tér (where you catch the *várbusz* to the top of Castle Hill), Batthyány tér (where you catch the HÉV train to Óbuda or Szentendre), and the Keleti train station.

• **M3 (blue)**—This line makes a broad, boomerang-shaped swoop north to south. Key stops include the Nyugati train station and Kálvin tér (near the Great Market Hall and many recommended hotels).

The three lines cross only once: at the **Deák tér** stop (sometimes signed as *Deák Ferenc tér*) in the heart of Pest, where Andrássy út begins. Most M2 and M3 Metro stations are at intersections of ring roads and other major arterials. You'll usually exit the Metro into a confusing underpass packed with kiosks, fast-food stands, and makeshift markets. Orange directional signs help you find the right exit.

The Metro stops themselves are usually very well-marked, with a list of upcoming stops on the wall behind the tracks. The red digital clocks tell you how long it's been since the last train left; you'll rarely wait more than five minutes for the next.

You'll ride very long, steep, fast-moving escalators to access the M2 and M3 lines. Hang on tight, enjoy the breeze as trains below shoot through the tunnels...and don't make yourself dizzy by trying to read the Burger King ads.

Note that Budapest is renovating its Metro stations. If a particular stretch of Metro line is closed, buses run the same route instead. This can extend the length of your trip—allow plenty of time. For the latest on which stations are closed, ask your hotel or the TI, or check www.bkv.hu.

By Tram: Budapest's trams are handy and frequent, taking you virtually anywhere the Metro doesn't. Here are some trams you might use:

Trams #2 and #2A: Run along Pest's Danube embankment

parallel to Váci utca, between the Parliament and the Great Market Hall.

Trams #19 and #41: Run along Buda's Danube embankment, stopping at Gellért Hotel, the bottom of the Castle Hill funicular (Adam Clark tér), several recommended Víziváros hotels, and Batthyány tér (end of the line, M2 Metro station, and HÉV trains to Óbuda and Szentendre).

Trams #4 and #6: Zip around Pest's Great Boulevard ring road (Nagykörút), connecting the Nyugati train station and Oktogon with the tip of Margaret Island and Buda's Moszkva tér (M2 Metro station).

Trams #47 and #49: Connect the Gellért Baths in Buda with Pest's Small Boulevard ring road (Kiskörút), with stops at the Great Market Hall, the National Museum, the Great Synagogue (Astoria stop), and Deák tér (end of the line).

By Bus: The tram and Metro network can get you nearly anywhere, so you're less likely to take a bus. One exception is getting to the top of Castle Hill: Take the *várbusz* ("castle bus," from Moszkva tér) or handy bus #16 (Deák tér, Roosevelt tér, crosses Chain Bridge, Adam Clark tér, and up to Dísz tér atop Castle Hill near the Royal Palace).

By Taxi: Budapest's public transportation is good enough that you probably won't need to take many taxis. If you do, you're likely to run into a dishonest driver. Locals always call a cab from a reputable company. Try **Taxi 6x6** (tel. 1/266-6666) or **City Taxi** (tel. 1/211-111).

Cabbies are not allowed to charge more than a drop rate of 300 Ft, and then 240 Ft per kilometer (more expensive 22:00–6:00)—though the more reputable companies charge less. Prices are per ride, not per passenger. A 10 percent tip is expected. A typical ride within central Budapest shouldn't run more than 2,000 Ft. Despite what some slimy cabbies may tell you, there's no legitimate extra charge for crossing the river.

Many cabs you'd hail on the streets are there only to prey on rich, green tourists. Avoid unmarked taxis and cabs waiting at tourist spots and train stations. If you do wave down a cab on the street, choose one that's marked with a company logo and telephone number. Ask for a rough estimate before you get in—if it doesn't sound reasonable, walk away. If you wind up being dramatically overcharged for a ride, simply pay what you think is fair and go inside. If the driver follows you (unlikely), your hotel receptionist will defend you.

On my last trip to Budapest, I arrived late at night at the Keleti train station. The lone, unmarked taxi out front wanted 4,000 Ft for the ride to my hotel. Following my own advice, I called a legitimate company and ordered a taxi from the English-speaking

Budapest at a Glance

In Buda

▲▲Matthias Church Landmark Neo-Gothic church with gilded history-book interior and revered 16th-century statue of Mary and Jesus. **Hours:** Mon–Sat 9:00–17:00, Sun 13:00–17:00, sometimes closed Sat after 13:00 for weddings.

▲▲Gellért Baths Touristy baths in elegant hotel. **Hours:** May–Sept daily 6:00–19:00; Oct–April Mon–Fri 6:00–19:00, Sat–Sun 6:00–17:00.

▲▲Statue Park Larger-than-life communist big shots all collected in one park, on the outskirts of town. **Hours:** Daily 10:00–sunset.

▲Imre Varga Collection Evocative sculpture collection capturing communist times, in Óbuda. **Hours:** Tue–Sun 10:00–18:00, closed Mon, artist visits at 10:00 Sat.

Royal Palace Reconstructed fortress on Castle Hill housing a pair of decent museums (Budapest History Museum and National Gallery). **Hours:** History Museum—mid-May–mid-Sept daily 10:00–18:00; March–mid-May and mid-Sept–Oct Wed–Mon 10:00–18:00, closed Tue; Nov–Feb Wed–Mon 10:00–16:00, closed Tue. National Gallery—Tue–Sun 10:00–18:00, closed Mon.

Cave Church House of worship carved into the cliff face of Gellért Hill. **Hours:** Open long hours daily, but closed to sightseers during frequent services.

In Pest

▲▲▲Széchenyi Baths Budapest's steamy soaking scene in the City Park—the city's single best attraction. **Hours:** Daily 6:00–22:00, possibly until 19:00 or 17:00 in winter.

▲▲Great Market Hall Colorful Old World mall with produce, cheap eateries, souvenirs, and great people-watching. **Hours:** Mon 6:00–17:00, Tue–Fri 6:00–18:00, Sat 6:00–14:00, closed Sun.

▲▲House of Terror Harrowing remembrance of Nazis and communist secret police in former headquarters/torture site. **Hours:** Tue–Fri 10:00–18:00, Sat–Sun 10:00–19:30, closed Mon.

▲▲Heroes' Square Mammoth tribute to Hungary's historic figures, fringed by a couple of art museums. **Hours:** Square always open; Museum of Fine Arts—Tue–Sun 10:00–17:30, closed Mon;

Palace of Art—Tue–Wed and Fri–Sun 10:00–18:00, Thu 12:00–20:00, closed Mon.

▲▲City Park Budapest's backyard, with Art Nouveau zoo, Transylvanian castle replica, amusement park, and Széchenyi Baths. **Hours:** Park always open.

▲Váci utca Hopping pedestrian boulevard and tourist magnet, featuring Eastern Europe's first McDonald's. **Hours:** Always open.

▲Hungarian Parliament Vast, riverside Neo-Gothic government center. **Hours:** English tours usually daily at 10:00, 12:00, and 14:00.

▲Postal Museum Funky tribute to old postal service objects in elegant old Andrássy út mansion. **Hours:** Tue–Sun 10:00–18:00, closed Mon.

▲Hungarian State Opera House Neo-Renaissance splendor and affordable opera. **Hours:** Lobby/box office open Mon–Sat from 11:00 until show time—generally 19:30; Sun open three hours before performance—generally 16:00–19:00, or 10:00–13:00 if there's a matinee; English tours nearly daily at 15:00 and 16:00.

▲Vajdahunyad Castle Disney World–type complex in the City Park with replicas of historic Hungarian architecture, anchored by a massive Transylvanian castle. **Hours:** Grounds always open.

▲Great Synagogue The world's second-largest after New York's, with museum and garden memorial. **Hours:** April–Oct Mon–Thu 10:00–17:00, Fri and Sun 10:00–14:00; Nov–March Mon–Thu 10:00–15:00, Fri and Sun 10:00–14:00; always closed Sat and Jewish holidays.

▲Holocaust Memorial Center Excellent memorial and museum honoring Hungarian victims of the Holocaust. **Hours:** Tue–Sun 10:00–18:00, closed Mon.

Hungarian National Museum Extensive collection of fragments from Hungary's history. **Hours:** Tue–Sun 10:00–18:00, closed Mon.

Commerce and Catering Museum Intriguing time-tunnel look at 19th-century businesses. **Hours:** Wed–Fri 10:00–17:00, Sat–Sun 10:00–18:00, closed Mon–Tue.

dispatcher. A few minutes later, an honest cabbie picked me up and took me to my hotel...for 1,500 Ft.

TOURS

Walking Tours—A youthful, backpacker-oriented company, **Absolute Walking Tours,** is run by Oregonian Ben Frieday. These tours are loose and informal, but informative. You can choose from a number of different itineraries, which include the following: The Absolute Walk gives you a good overview of Budapest (4,000 Ft, mid-May–Sept daily at 9:30 and 13:30, Oct–mid-May daily at 10:30, 3.5 hrs). The Hammer and Sickle Tour includes a guided visit to Statue Park with no commentary en route—you're on the regular city bus to Statue Park with other passengers—then a quick visit to a mini-museum of communist artifacts (5,500 Ft, 4/week, 3 hrs). Absolute Hungro Gastro, focused on Hungarian cuisine, gives you information on traditional recipes and ingredients, and a chance to taste several specialties and wines at a local restaurant (7,000 Ft, 3/week, 1/week in winter, 3 hrs). In the evening, consider the Absolute Night Stroll (4,000 Ft, mid-May–Sept only, 3/week, 2.5 hrs) or the rowdier Pub Crawl, which sometimes continues late into the night (5,500 Ft, departs 20:00, 3/week, at least 3 hrs). Historians can ask about their 1956 Uprising Tour, which runs through the end of 2007.

All tours depart from Deák tér (tel. 1/266-8777, www .absolutetours.com). Travelers with this book get a 500-Ft discount on any tour in 2007, as does anyone with a student card.

Private Guides—Budapest has plenty of enthusiastic, hardworking young guides who speak fine English and enjoy showing off their exciting city. Given the reasonable fees and efficient use of your time, hiring your own personal expert is an excellent value. I have two favorites: **Péter Pölczman** charges €70 for a four- or five-hour tour and €100 for a full-day tour (mobile 0620-926-0557, from the US call 011-36-20-926-0557, polczman@freestart.hu or peter.polczman@guideclub.net). **Andrea Makkay** leads four-hour tours (23,000 Ft) and seven-hour tours (39,000 Ft; mobile 0620-962-9363, from the US call 011-36-20-962-9363, www .privateguidebudapest.com, amakkay@t-online.hu—arrange details by e-mail), and can also take you outside Budapest by car or minivan—ask.

Danube Boat Tours—Cruising the Danube, while touristy, is fun and convenient. The most established company, **Legenda,** runs boats day and night. By day, the one-hour cruise costs 3,800 Ft (2,750 Ft with Budapest Card or this book in 2007); most departures include an optional one-hour walking tour around Margaret Island, Budapest's playground (8/day May–Aug, 7/day April and

Sept, 3/day March and Oct, 1/day Nov–Feb).

By night, the one-hour cruise (with no Margaret Island option) costs 4,700 Ft (3,250 Ft with Budapest Card or this book in 2007, 3/day March–Oct, 1/day Nov–Feb).

Both cruises include two drinks and headphone commentary. By night, TV monitors show the interior of the great buildings as you float by. The Legenda dock is in front of the Marriott on the Pest embankment (find pedestrian access under tram tracks just downriver from Vigadó tér, tel. 1/317-2203, www.legenda.hu).

Bike Tours—A sister company of Absolute Walking Tours, **Yellow Zebra,** wheels by Budapest's major sights on a 3.5-hour tour (5,500 Ft, April–Oct daily at 11:00, also at 16:00 July–Aug, no tours Nov–March, meet at Deák tér, tel. 1/266-8777, www .yellowzebrabikes.com).

Segway Tours—In addition to walking and bike tours, Ben Frieday's Discover Hungary also offers tours of Budapest by Segway (stand-up electric scooter). While expensive, it's a unique way to see the city while trying out a Segway (12,500 Ft, daily at 10:00, also daily at 18:30 April–Oct, 2.5–3 hrs with 30–45-min training beforehand, 6 people per group, must reserve and pre-pay at www.citysegwaytours.com or call the office when in Budapest— tel. 1/269-3843).

Bus Tours—Several companies run bus tours that glide past all the big sights. A basic three-hour bus tour will run you 6,000–6,500 Ft per person, and the different companies are essentially the same. **Budatours** runs a shorter, cheaper two-hour version (4,300 Ft). A new hop-on, hop-off bus tour by **City Circle Sightseeing** makes five stops as it cruises around town (4,500 Ft for the 2-hour tour, or 7,000 Ft for an all-day ticket). Most companies also offer a wide variety of other tours, including dinner boat cruises and trips to the Danube Bend. Pick up fliers about all these tours at the TI or in your hotel lobby.

SIGHTS

Buda

Castle Hill (Várhegy)

Buda's main sights are all on Castle Hill. While many visitors expect this high-profile district to be time-consuming, for most it's enough to simply stroll through in a couple of hours. The major landmarks are the huge, green-domed Royal Palace at the south end of the hill (housing a pair of ho-hum museums) and the frilly-spired Matthias Church near the north end. In between are tourist-filled pedestrian streets and historic buildings. A few other interesting but non-essential museums are scattered around the hill. I've listed the sights in order from south to north, and linked

Buda Center Sights

TO MOSZKVA SQUARE & Ⓜ

100 YARDS
100 METERS

VIENNA GATE

VÁRFOK
OSTROM
HATTYU
BATTHYANY
CSALOCANYUTCA

⑫
⑪
ORSZAG.
FORTUNA
TANCSICS
SZABO
TOLDY
DONATI
SKOLDI

BATTHYÁNY SQUARE

MKT. HALL
HÉV TRAIN STN.
Ⓜ

URI
HESS SQ.
⑩
⑨
⑧
St. ANNE'S

MATTHIAS CHURCH

FISHERMEN'S BASTION

VÍZI-VÁROS

CALVINIST CHURCH

TÁRNOK
⑦
Post
⑥
VÁR. BUS STOP
DÍSZ SQ.

HUNYADI JÁNOS
SONS
PONTY
FO UTCA
HALASZ
RAKPART

TRAM #19 & #41

Ⓜ

ATTILA
PALOTA
LOGODI
LOVAS
ALAGUT UT

⑤
SZINHAZ
SN
GYORGY
④
③

DANUBE RIVER

CHAIN BRIDGE

TO PEST →

ROYAL PALACE→
②
①

FUNICULAR "SIKLÓ"

Ⓜ - METRO STOP
↗ - VIEW

KRISZTINA
ATTILA
VARALJA
LANCHID
BEM
DCH

TABÁN

① Budapest History Museum

② Hungarian National Gallery

③ *Turul* Bird Statue

④ Sándor Palace

⑤ Former Ministry of War

⑥ Crafts Market

⑦ Entrance to Labyrinth of Buda Castle

⑧ Fishermen's Bastion

⑨ Matthias Church —

⑩ Hilton Hotel

⑪ Remains of St. Mary Magdalene Church

⑫ Museum of Military History

them together on a self-guided tour.

When to Visit: Castle Hill is packed with tour groups in the morning, but it's much less crowded in the afternoon. Since restaurants up here are expensive and low quality, Castle Hill is an ideal after-lunch activity.

Getting to Castle Hill: The Metro and trams won't take you to the top of Castle Hill. You can hike, taxi, ride the funicular, or catch **bus #16** from either side of the Chain Bridge (departs from Deák, Roosevelt, and Adam Clark squares). A special **castle bus** *(várbusz)* does a loop from Moszkva tér (Moscow Square) north of the castle (M2: Moszkva tér, bus stops just uphill from Metro station, look for small bus with the words *vár* or *Dísz tér* and a little picture of a castle). Castle Hill buses are specially designed to be light, as the hill is honeycombed with limestone caves. The handiest stop for either of these buses is at Dísz tér, right in the middle of the hill (across from old Ministry of War building). If you arrive at Dísz tér, you can backtrack to the Royal Palace and *turul* bird statue, or skip ahead to the Dísz tér listing in the walking tour (all of this is described below).

The **funicular** *(sikló, SHEE-kloh)*, lifting visitors from the Chain Bridge to the top of Castle Hill, is a Budapest landmark. Built in 1870 to provide cheap transportation to Castle Hill workers, today it's a pricey little tourist trip. Read the fun first-person history you'll see in glass cases at the top station (700 Ft one-way, 1,300 Ft round-trip, not covered by Budapest Card, daily 7:30–22:00, departs every 5 min, closed for maintenance every other Mon).

• *From the top of the funicular, enjoy the views of the Danube and go a few yards to the big bird at the top of the stairs. You can survey the immense palace and Danube panorama from here, or wander to the equestrian statue and circle through and around the huge building.*

The *Turul*—This mythical bird of Magyar folk tales watches over the palace. The *turul* supposedly led the Hungarian migrations in the ninth century. He dropped his sword in the Carpathian Basin, indicating that this was to be the permanent home of the Magyar people. During a surge of nationalism in the 1920s, a movement named after this bird helped revive traditional Hungarian culture. *Turul* birds also top the towers of the green Liberty Bridge, just downriver.

Royal Palace (Királyi Palota)—The imposing palace on Castle Hill is a dull contemporary construction, barely hinting at the colorful story of this hill since the day that the legendary *turul* dropped his sword.

Originally, the main city of Hungary wasn't Buda or Pest, but Esztergom (just up the river, described in Danube Bend chapter). In the 13th century, Tatars swept through Eastern Europe, destroying much of Hungary. King Béla IV decided to rebuild a walled Buda here, a more protected location in the interior of the country. The city has dominated the region ever since, gradually becoming the Hungarian capital. Over the years, the original Romanesque fortress here was rebuilt and accentuated with a textbook's worth of architectural styles: Gothic, Renaissance, and Baroque. It was one of Europe's biggest palaces by the early 15th century, when King Mátyás Corvinus made the palace even more extravagant, putting Buda—and Hungary—on the map.

Just a few decades later, the invading Ottomans occupied Buda and turned the palace into a military garrison. When the Hapsburgs laid siege to the hill for 77 days in 1686, gunpowder stored in the cellar exploded, destroying the palace. The Hapsburgs took the hill, but Buda was deserted and in ruins. The town was resettled by Austrians, who built a new Baroque palace, hoping that the Hapsburg monarch would move in—but none ever did. The useless palace became a garrison, then a university, and later the viceroy's residence. It was damaged again during the 1848 Revolution, but was repaired and continued to grow right along with Budapest's prominence (for more on the 1848 Revolution, see page 432).

As World War II drew to a close, Buda became the front line between the Nazis and the approaching Soviets, who laid siege to the hill for about 100 days. The palace was again destroyed.

While grand and impressive from afar, the current version of the palace—a historically inaccurate, post-WWII reconstruction—feels dull and soulless, like a tuxedo on a mannequin. It's a loose rebuilding of previous versions, lacking the style and sense of history that this important site deserves. The most prominent feature of today's palace—the green dome—didn't even exist in earlier versions.

• *Before heading on to Matthias Church (Castle Hill self-guided tour continues below), consider visiting the...*

Castle Museums—The palace houses two worthwhile (but not must-see) museums. The history museum is decent, but the art museum ranks pretty low on a European scale.

• *To get to the museums, take this scenic detour: Go down the stairs by the* turul *bird statue, then along the panorama terrace to the equestrian statue (depicting Jan Sobieski, a Polish general who had great success fighting the Hungarians' hated enemies, the Ottomans). The main entrance to the National Gallery is just behind this statue. To reach the History Museum, go in the small passageway to the right of the National Gallery entrance. You'll pass an ornate statue of Mátyás Corvinus, then hook left into the palace courtyard (under the dome). The entrance is at the far end of the courtyard.*

The **Budapest History Museum** (Budapesti Történeti Múzeum), a good but stodgy museum begging for a makeover, celebrates the earlier grandeur of Castle Hill. If Budapest really intrigues you, this is a fine place to explore its history. You'll start at the top floor and work down. Along the way, you'll see artifacts of Budapest's prehistoric residents and a good collection of 14th-century sculptures, many of them with strong Magyar features—notice that they look Central Asian, like Mongolians. The highlight is the "Budapest in the Modern Times" exhibit, tracing the last two rocky centuries of the city, with a focus on the gradual movement towards merging Buda and Pest. The cellar illustrates just how much this hill has changed over the centuries—and how dull today's version is in comparison. You'll wander through a maze of old palace parts, including the remains of an original Gothic chapel, a knights' hall, and marble remnants (reliefs and fountains) of Mátyás Corvinus' lavish Renaissance palace (800 Ft, covered by Budapest Card, good English descriptions posted, other descriptions are borrowable, mid-May–mid-Sept daily 10:00–18:00; March–mid-May and mid-Sept–Oct Wed–Mon 10:00–18:00, closed Tue; Nov–Feb Wed–Mon 10:00–16:00, closed Tue; tel. 1/487-8800).

The huge **Hungarian National Gallery** (Magyar Nemzeti Galéria) has an excellent collection of 15th-century winged altars, plus halls and halls of paintings and sculptures by Hungarian artists you've never heard of—for good reason (free, charge for special exhibitions, Tue–Sun 10:00–18:00, closed Mon, tel. 1/201-9082).

• *Ready to move on? The following walk connects the dots between the palace and Matthias Church.*

From the Funicular and Royal Palace to Matthias Church: From the *turul* bird and the top of the funicular (with your back to the Royal Palace), walk along the non-river side of the big white building, **Sándor Palace.** This mansion underwent a very costly renovation under the previous Hungarian prime minister, who hoped to make it his residence. But in 2002, the same year it was finished, he lost his bid for reelection. The spunky new PM refused to move in. By way of compromise, now the president's office is here.

As you continue along the side of Sándor Palace, you'll notice the remains of a medieval monastery and church in the field to your left. Beyond that, past the flagpoles, is the ongoing excavation of the medieval Jewish quarter—more reminders that most of what you see on today's Castle Hill has been destroyed and rebuilt many times over.

After Sándor Palace, you'll pass the yellow National Dance Theater, where Beethoven once performed. The hulking, war-damaged building beyond that (on the left) used to house the **Ministry of War.** Most of the bullet holes are from World War

Mátyás Corvinus: The Last Hungarian King

The Árpád dynasty—descendants of the original Magyar tribes—died out in 1301. For more than 600 years, Hungary would be ruled by foreigners...with one exception.

In the middle of the 15th century, Hungary had bad luck hanging on to its foreign kings: Two of them died unexpectedly within seven years. Meanwhile, homegrown military general János Hunyadi was enjoying great success on the battlefield against the Ottomans. When the five-year-old Ladislas V was elected king, Hunyadi was appointed regent and essentially ruled the country.

Hunyadi defeated the Ottomans in the crucial 1456 Battle of Belgrade, which kept them out of Hungary (at least for another 70 years) and made him an even greater hero to the Hungarian people. During this time, Hunyadi was briefly imprisoned by the Ottomans, and his family feared him dead. According to legend, a raven appeared in the window of his cell, and Hunyadi gave the bird his ring. The raven flew it to Hunyadi's family to reassure them that he lived on. The raven (often with a ring in its beak) became part of the family crest, as well as the family name: Corvinus (Latin for "raven").

Tragically, soon after his escape from prison and great victory over the Ottomans, Hunyadi died of the plague. When King Ladislas also died (at the tender age of 16), the nobles looked for a new hero...and found one in Hunyadi's son, Mátyás (Matthias) Corvinus. He became the first Hungarian-descended king in more than 150 years.

II, while others were left by the Soviets who occupied this hill in response to the 1956 Uprising (see page 432). The building is a political hot potato—prime real estate, but nobody can decide what to do with it.

Just after the Ministry of War, at the cross street, you reach **Dísz tér** (Parade Square), which has a convenient bus stop for connecting to other parts of Budapest (the castle bus to Moszkva tér, or bus #16 to the Pest side of the Chain Bridge).

Across the street from the Ministry of War (on the right) is the entrance to a courtyard with an open-air Hungarian **crafts market.** While it's fun to browse, prices here are high (haggle away). The Great Market Hall has a better selection and generally lower prices (see page 437).

Continue uphill on **Tárnok utca.** This area often disappoints visitors. After being destroyed by Ottomans, it was rebuilt in sensible Baroque, lacking the romantic time-capsule charm of a medieval old town (like perfectly preserved Prague or Kraków). But if

Progressive and well-educated, Mátyás Corvinus (r. 1458–1490) was the quintessential Renaissance king—a benefactor of the poor and a true humanist. He patronized the arts and built palaces legendary for their beauty. He dressed up as a commoner and ventured into the streets to see firsthand how the nobles of his realm treated his people.

Mátyás was a strong, savvy leader. He created Central Europe's first standing army—30,000 mercenaries known as the Black Army. No longer reliant on the nobility for military support, Good King Mátyás was able to drain power from the nobles and make taxation of his subjects more equitable—earning him the nickname the "people's king."

King Mátyás was also a shrewd military tactician. Realizing that squabbling with the Ottomans would squander his resources, he made peace with the Ottoman sultan to stabilize Hungary's southern border. Then he swept north, invading Moravia, Bohemia, and even Austria. By 1485, Mátyás moved into his new palace in Vienna, and Hungary was enjoying a Golden Age.

Five years later, Mátyás died mysteriously at the age of 47, and his empire disintegrated. It is said that when Mátyás died, justice died with him. To this day, Hungarians consider him the greatest of all kings, and they sing of his siege of Vienna in their national anthem. They're proud that for a few decades in the middle of half a millennium of foreign oppression, they had a truly Hungarian king—and a great one at that.

you poke your head into some courtyards, you'll almost always see some original Gothic arches and other medieval features.

• *A block to the left, you'll find the entrance to a highly optional attraction...*

Labyrinth of Buda Castle (Budavári Labirintus)—There are miles of caves burrowed under Castle Hill, carved out by water, expanded by the Ottomans, and used by locals during the siege of Buda at the end of World War II. Armchair spelunkers can explore these caverns and see a conceptual exhibit that traces human history (1,400 Ft, 25 percent discount with Budapest Card, daily 9:30–19:30, last entry 19:00, entrance between Royal Palace and Matthias Church at Úri utca 9, Budapest I, tel. 1/212-0207, www.labirintus.com). After 18:00, they turn the lights out and give everyone gas lanterns. The exhibit loses something in the dark, but it's nicely spooky and a fun chance to startle amorous Hungarian teens—or be startled by mischievous ones.

• *Back on Tárnok utca, continue up to the little park with the TI (on your right; pick up their handy* Castlewalk *map). Just beyond the park, a warty plague column marks the main square of old Buda (though column may be missing for restoration). Across the square is the...*

Fishermen's Bastion (Halászbástya)—This Neo-Romanesque fantasy rampart offers beautiful views over the Danube to Pest. In the Middle Ages, the fish market was just below here (in today's Víziváros, or Water Town), so this part of the rampart actually was guarded by fishermen. The current structure, though, is completely artificial—an example of Budapest sprucing itself up for 1896 (see page 413). Its seven towers represent the seven Magyar tribes. The cone-headed arcades are reminiscent of tents the nomadic Magyars called home before they moved west to Europe.

Survey Pest across the Danube from this viewpoint. The two domes are the Parliament and St. István's Basilica—both 96 meters high, built in...you guessed it...1896. The Chain Bridge cuts Pest in two: The left half is administrative, with government ministries, embassies, banks, and so on; the right half (stretching to the modern, white Elisabeth Bridge) is the commercial center of Pest, with the best riverside promenade.

Paying to climb up the bastion makes little sense (330 Ft, 10 percent discount with Budapest Card, buy ticket at kiosk near TI in park, daily mid-March–mid-Oct 9:00–23:00; after closing time and off-season, no tickets are sold, but bastion is open and free to enter). Enjoy virtually the same view through the windows (left of café) for free. The café offers a scenic break if you don't mind the tour groups.

• *Between the bastion and the big church stands a...*

Statue of St. István (Stephen)—Hungary's first Christian king tamed the nomadic, pagan Magyars and established strict laws and the concept of private property. István's father, King Géza, lost a major battle against the forces of Christian Europe—and realized that he must raise his son as a Catholic and convert his people, or they would ultimately be forcefully driven out of Europe. The reliefs on this statue show the Pope crowning St. István (EESHT-vahn) in the year 1000, bringing Hungary into Christendom. This meant the rest of Europe was now inclined to help Hungary against the Ottomans and to bully Slavs. Without this pivotal event, locals believe that the Magyar nation would have been lost. A passionate evangelist—more for the survival of his Magyar nation than for the salvation of his people—István beheaded those who wouldn't convert. To make his point perfectly clear, he quartered his reluctant uncle and sent him on four separate, simultaneous tours of the country to show Hungarians that Christianity was a smart choice. Gruesome as he was, István was sainted within 30 years of his death.

• *Next to St. István is the can't-miss-it...*

▲▲**Matthias Church (Mátyás-Templom)**—Budapest's best church has been destroyed and rebuilt several times in the 800 years since it was founded by King Béla IV. Today's version—renovated at great expense in the late 19th century, and restored after World War II—is an ornately decorated lesson in Hungarian history. While it's officially named the "Church of Our Lady," everyone calls it the Matthias Church, for the popular Renaissance king who got married here...twice.

Cost and Hours: 600 Ft, includes Museum of Ecclesiastical Art, covered by Budapest Card, 12-stop audioguide-300 Ft, Mon–Sat 9:00–17:00, Sun 13:00–17:00, may close Sat after 13:00 for weddings, Szentháromság tér 2, tel. 1/488-7716, www.matyas-templom.hu.

● **Self-Guided Tour:** Examine the **exterior**. While the nucleus of the church is Gothic, most of what you see outside—including the frilly, flamboyant steeple—was added for the 1896 celebrations. At the top of the spire facing the river, notice the raven—the ever-present symbol of King Mátyás Corvinus.

The sumptuous **interior** is wallpapered with gilded pages from a Hungarian history textbook. Different eras are represented by symbolic motifs. For example, the wall immediately to the left of the entry represents the Renaissance, with a giant coat of arms of the beloved King Mátyás Corvinus. (The tough guys in armor on either side are members of his mercenary Black Army, the source of his power.) Notice another raven, with a ring in its beak. Meanwhile, the wall across from the entry—with Oriental motifs—commemorates the Ottoman reign of Buda.

Work your way clockwise around the church from the entry. The first chapel (in the back corner, by the entry)—the **Loreto Chapel**—holds the church's prize possession. Peer through the black iron grill to see the 1515 statue of Mary and Jesus. Anticipating Ottoman plundering, locals walled over this precious statue. The occupying Ottomans used the church as their primary mosque—oblivious to the statue plastered over in the niche. Then, a century and a half later, during the siege of Buda in 1686, gunpowder stored in the castle up the street detonated, and the wall crumbled. Mary's triumphant face showed through, terrifying the Ottomans. Supposedly this was the only part of town taken from the Ottomans without a fight.

Continue circling around the church. As you look down the **nave,** notice the 500-year-old Hungarian battalion banners, left here after the Mass that celebrated János Hunyadi's victory over the Ottomans at the Battle of Belgrade in 1456. The stained glass is 160 years old; during World War II, it was removed and hidden to avoid destruction.

On the left side of the church (toward the altar from the gift shop) is the tomb of St. Imre, the son of the great King (and later Saint) István. This heir to the Hungarian throne was mysteriously killed by a boar while hunting when he was only 19 years old. Though he didn't live long enough to do anything important, he rode his father's coattails to sainthood. The next chapel is the tomb of Béla III, utterly insignificant except that this is one of only two tombs of Hungarian kings that still exist in the country. The rest—including all of the biggies—were defiled by the Ottomans. Up next to the main altar is the chapel of László—St. István's nephew, who stepped in as king of Hungary when the rightful heir, St. Imre, was killed.

By the main altar is the entrance to the upstairs gallery, which holds the **Museum of Ecclesiastical Art** (Egyházművészeti Gyűjteménye, same ticket and hours as church). The original Hungarian crown is under the Parliament's dome, and a hassle to visit (see page 439)—but a replica is up here, and worth a peek. The church also hosts concerts (about 2/month, signs posted outside, ticket desk inside).

• *To continue your exploration of Buda, take a stroll along...*

North Castle Hill: The following walk takes you through Buda north of Matthias Church. As this was the site of a Nazi military headquarters, it was heavily bombed toward the end of World War II. (During a 100-day siege, 80 percent of the city's buildings were damaged or destroyed.)

Leave the courtyard beside the church and turn right—passing the 1713 Holy Trinity plague column on your left—so that you're walking along the front of the glassy, modern **Hilton Hotel.** To minimize the controversy of building upon so much history, architects thoughtfully incorporated the medieval ruins into its modern design. Built in 1976, the Hilton was the first plush Western hotel in town. Before 1989, it was a gleaming center of capitalism, offering a cushy refuge for Western travelers and a stark contrast to what was, at the time, a very gloomy city. Halfway down the hotel's facade, you'll see fragments of a 13th-century wall, with a monument to King Mátyás Corvinus.

After the wall, continue along the second half of the Hilton Hotel facade. Turn right into the gift-shop entry, and then go right again inside the second glass door. Stairs on the left lead down to a reconstructed 13th-century Dominican cloister; at the far end of the cloister are more stairs, to the Faust Wine Cellar (daily 16:00–23:00), a friendly place with fine wine by the glass. For an even better look at what was here back then, go back up the stairs and turn left. As you enter the lounge, look out the back windows to see fragments of the 13th-century Dominican church incorporated into the structure of the hotel. If you stood here eight centuries ago, you'd be looking straight down the church's nave. You can even see tomb markers in the floor.

Back out on the street, cross the little park and duck into the entryway of the **Fortuna Passage.** Along the passageway to the courtyard, you can see the original Gothic arches of the house that once stood here. In the Middle Ages, every homeowner had the right to sell wine without paying taxes—but only in the passage of his own home. He'd set up a table here, and his neighbors would come by to taste the latest vintage. These passageways evolved into very social places, like the corner pub.

Leaving the passage, turn left down Fortuna utca and walk to the end of the street, where you'll see the **Vienna Gate.** If you go through it and walk for about 10 days, you'll get to Vienna. (For now, settle for climbing up to the top for a view of some Buda residential neighborhoods.)

• *Now walk along the hulking, mosaic-roofed National Archive building (with your back to the Danube) until you reach the...*

Remains of St. Mary Magdalene Church—This was once known as the Kapisztrán Templom, named after a hero of the Battle of Belgrade in 1456, an early success in the struggle to keep the Ottomans out of Europe. (King Mátyás' father, János Hunyadi, led the Hungarians in that battle.) The Pope was so tickled by the victory that he decreed that all church bells should toll at noon in memory of the battle—and, technically, they still do. Californians will recognize the Kapisztrán's Spanish name: San Juan de Capistrano. This church was destroyed by bombs in World War II, though no worse than Matthias Church. But, since this part of town was depopulated after the war, there was no longer a need for a second church. The remains of the church were torn down, the steeple was rebuilt as a memorial, and a carillon was added—so that every day at noon, the bells can still toll.

• *Across the square from the church is a monument to San Juan de Capistrano. Walking around the big building, you come to a viewpoint overlooking modern Buda, and on the green hill beyond that, you find the Beverly Hills of Budapest—where the local rich and famous live. To the right, near the flagpole, is the entry to the...*

Museum of Military History (Hadtörténeti Múzeum)—This fine museum explains various Hungarian military actions through history in painstaking detail. Watch military uniforms and weaponry evolve from the time of Árpád to today. With enough old uniforms and flags to keep an army-surplus store in stock for a decade, this place might interest military and history buffs (free, charge

Hungarian Revolutions

Foreign powers who have oppressed the Hungarians have found them difficult to suppress. In each case, the Hungarians initially encountered bloodshed and more oppression, but ultimately brought about positive change. The dates these revolutions began remain national holidays.

Lajos Kossuth and the 1848 Revolution

Of the many Hungarian uprisings against Hapsburg rule (1526–1918), the 1848 Revolution was the most dramatic. In 1848, a wave of nationalism spread across Europe. The spirit of change caught on in Hungary, where lawyer and parliamentarian Lajos Kossuth led an uprising sparked on March 15. Though the Austrians were initially overwhelmed by the revolt, they eventually brought in Russian troops to regain control. For a few years, the Hapsburgs cracked down on their Hungarian subjects—but within 20 years, they ceded half the authority of their empire to Budapest, creating the Dual Monarchy.

Imre Nagy and the 1956 Uprising

The Hungarian politician Imre Nagy (EEM-ray nodge, 1896–1958) was a lifelong communist. In the 1930s, he allegedly worked for the Soviet secret police. In the late 1940s, he quickly moved up the hierarchy of Hungary's communist government, becoming prime minister in 1953. But in the Moscow shuffle following Stalin's death, Nagy was quickly demoted.

When violence broke out in Budapest on October 23, 1956, Nagy reemerged as the leader of the reform movement. For a few short days, it seemed as though Hungary's communism would moderate—until Soviet tanks rumbled into Budapest, brutally put down the uprising, and occupied the city. By the time the Red Army left, 25,000 protesters were dead, and 250,000 Hungarians had fled to Austria. Nagy was arrested, given a sham trial, and executed in 1958. He was buried disgracefully, face-down in an unmarked grave, and his name was taboo in Hungary for 30 years.

Though the uprising met a tragic end, within a few years Hungary's harshness did soften, and the milder, so-called "goulash communism" emerged. As the Eastern Bloc thawed in 1989, Nagy became a martyr and a hero. His body was discovered and given a proper reburial in July of that exciting year—heralding the quickly approaching end of the communist era.

for special exhibitions, April–Sept Tue–Sun 10:00–18:00, closed
Mon; Oct–March Tue–Sun 10:00–16:00, closed Mon; closed mid-
Dec–mid-Jan, Tóth Árpád sétány 40, Budapest I, tel. 1/356-9522).
• *Your tour is over. From here, you can backtrack to enjoy more time
on Castle Hill. Or consider going back to the Vienna Gate and head-
ing downhill. You'll run into bustling Moszkva tér, which has a handy
Metro stop (M2 line) and a huge, modern, popular shopping complex
(Mammut, or "Mammoth"; Mon–Sat 10:00–21:00, Sun 10:00–18:00,
Lövőház utca 2–6).*

Gellért Hill (Gellérthegy)

The hill rising from the Danube banks just downriver from the
castle is Gellért Hill. When King István converted Hungary to
Christianity in the year 1000, he brought in Bishop Gellért, a
monk from Venice, to tutor his son. But some rebellious Magyars
had other ideas. They put the bishop in a barrel, drove long nails in
from the outside, and rolled him down this hill…tenderizing him
to death. Gellért became the patron saint of Budapest and gave his
name to the hill that killed him.

Gellért Hill's only real attraction is the **baths** at Gellért Hotel
(see page 461 of "Budapest's Baths"). The hill is a fine place to commune with nature on a hike or jog.

Monument Hike—The north slope of Gellért Hill is good for a
low-impact hike. You'll see many interesting monuments, most
notably the memorial to Bishop Gellért himself (you can't miss it
as you cross the Elisabeth Bridge on Hegyalja út). A bit farther up,
seek out a newer monument to the world's great philosophers—
Eastern, Western, and in between—from Gandhi to Plato to Jesus.
Nearby is a scenic overlook with a king and a queen holding hands
on either side of the Danube.

Citadella—This strategic, hill-capping fortress was built by the
Hapsburgs after the 1848 Revolution to keep an eye on their
Hungarian subjects. There's not much to do up here (no museum
or exhibits, just a hotel), but it's a good destination for an uphill
hike, and provides excellent views over all of Budapest.

The hill is crowned by the **Liberation Monument,** featuring
a woman holding aloft a palm branch. The locals call it "the lady
with the big fish" or "the great bottle opener." The heroic Soviet
soldier—who once inspired the workers with a huge red star from
the base of the monument—is now in Statue Park (see page 453).

Cave Church (Sziklatemplom)—Hidden in the hillside on the
south end of the hill (across the street from Gellért Hotel) is
Budapest's atmospheric cave church—literally burrowed into the
rock face. The communists bricked up this church when they came
to power, but now it's open for visitors once again (free entry, but
closed to sightseers during frequent services).

Pest

Central Pest (Belváros), Along Váci utca

▲**Vörösmarty tér**—The prominent square called Vörösmarty tér (VOO-roosh-mar-tee tehr), at the north end of the Váci utca pedestrian boulevard, is named for a 19th-century Romantic poet (see his statue in the center) who stirred nationalistic spirit with his writing.

Find the landmark **Gerbeaud** pastry shop at the north end of the square. Between the World Wars, the well-to-do ladies of Budapest would meet here after shopping their way up Váci utca. Today it's still *the* meeting point in Budapest (described under "Cafés and Pastry Shops," page 479).

As you face Gerbeaud, the street to your left leads to the Danube embankment (ideal for a scenic stroll), and the street to your right leads past Erzsébet tér (once Pest's market square) to Andrássy út, lined with sights, restaurants, and hotels (see "Andrássy út and City Park," page 441). If you jog left around the Gerbeaud and then go straight, you'll reach the Parliament in about 10 minutes (see "More Sights in Central Pest," page 438).

The yellow M1 Metro stop in the middle of the square is the entrance to the shallow *Földalatti*, or "underground"—the first subway on the Continent (built for the millennial celebration in 1896). Today, it still carries passengers to Andrássy út sights (it runs under that street all the way to City Park).

Three hundred years ago, Vörösmarty tér was a rough-and-tumble, often flooded quarter just outside the Pest city walls. People came here to enjoy brutal, staged fights between blood-hounds and bears (like cockfights, only bigger and angrier, with more fur and teeth). The Ottoman invaders had finally been forced out of Pest, and the city was nearly deserted. After a series of battles for Hungarian independence, the Hapsburgs moved into ruined Pest in the 1710s. They populated the city with Austrians. (While there was a small Hungarian minority, most Magyars lived in the countryside.) The Austrians of Pest began rebuilding the city, virtually from scratch—most of the buildings you'll see are no older than 300 years.

For more of the story, stroll down the street across the square from Gerbeaud: Váci utca.

▲**Váci utca**—This pedestrian boulevard—Budapest's shopping and tourism artery—was dreamland for Eastern Europeans back in the 1980s. It was here that they fantasized about what it might be like to be free, while drooling over Nikes, Reeboks, and Big Macs before any of these Western evils were introduced elsewhere in the Warsaw Pact region.

Ironically, this street—once prized by Hungarians and other Eastern Europeans because it felt so Western—is what many

Pest Center Sights

TO
NYUGATI
TRAIN STN.

TRAM LINE
W/ STOPS

M – METRO STOP

PARLIAMENT   MUSEUM
OF
ETHNOGRAPHY

TO
CITY PARK

ALKOTMANY

A   BATHORY UT.

OKTOGON

OPERA   ANDRASSY

ST. ISTVÁN'S

POSTAL MUSEUM

CHAIN

BRIDGE

JÓZSEF ATTILA UT.

GREAT
SYNAGOGUE

DANUBE

LEGENDA
BOAT DOCK

TO
KELETI
TRAIN STN.

B
U
D
A

SERBIAN
CHURCH

NATIONAL
MUSEUM

GELLÉRT
HILL

GREAT
MARKET
HALL

100 YARDS
100 METERS

GELLÉRT HOTEL   DCH

❶ Attila József Statue
❷ Imre Nagy Statue
❸ Holocaust Monument
❹ Kossuth Lajos Square
❺ Szabadság Square
❻ Roosevelt Square
❼ Vigadó Square
❽ Vörösmarty Square
❾ Erzsébet Square
❿ Deák Square
⓫ Commerce &
  Catering Museum
⓬ Liszt Ferenc Square
⓭ Pendragon Bookstore
⓮ Párisi Udvar
  Shopping Gallery
⓯ Red Bus Bookstore
⓰ Danube Palace
  (Duna Palota
  Concert Tickets)

Western tourists today mistakenly think is the "real Budapest." You could have a fun and fulfilling trip to this city without setting foot on Váci utca (VAH-tsee OOT-zah). But many visitors are mesmerized by this people-friendly stretch of souvenir stands, Internet cafés, and upscale boutiques—and a ramble along Váci utca does have stories to tell. The following commentary will help you uncover artifacts of authentic Pest between the postcard racks.

◒ Self-Guided Walk: "Váci utca" means "street to Vác"—a town 25 miles to the north. This has long been the street where the elite of Pest would go shopping, then strut their stuff for their neighbors on an evening promenade (*korzó* in Hungarian). Today, the tourists do the strutting here—and the Hungarians go to suburban shopping malls.

As you walk, be sure to look up. Along this street and throughout Pest, spectacular facades begin on the second floor, above a plain entryway (in the 1970s, ground-floor shop windows were made uniformly dull by the communist government). Pan up to see some of Pest's best architecture. These were the townhouses of the aristocracy whose mansions dotted the countryside.

At the end of the first block, next to the Tatuum store on the right, a **plaque** notes that Pest's medieval town wall was torn down in 1789. The no-longer-needed wall had been gradually crumbling for centuries, and as residents rebuilt from the Ottoman occupation, it was just getting in the way.

On the next block, find the quirky **Modernist facade** at #8 on the left (over the Clinique shop). Compare this one to the building marked *Douglas* (#11A, across the street a few doors up). The first is more traditional Modernism, but the second is a great example of the **Secession** style. Modernist architecture was rebellious: It rejected what came before—which is why it still looks weird to us today. But the Secession did one better and rejected Modernism.

At the end of the block, the unassuming **McDonald's** (on the right, down Régi Posta utca) was a landmark in Eastern Europe— the first McDonald's behind the Iron Curtain. Budapest has always been a little more rebellious, independent, and cosmopolitan than its Eastern European neighbors, who flocked here during the communist era. Since you had to wait in a long line—stretching around the block—to get a burger, it wasn't "fast food"—but at least it was "West food."

Continuing your stroll, you'll notice that some of the **facades** are plain (like the one above the tobacco shop on the right, just after the street leading to McDonald's). Many of these used to be more ornate, like the others, but they were destroyed by WWII bombs and rebuilt in a stripped-down style.

At the halfway point on your Váci utca stroll (midway between the square and Great Market Hall), an underpass takes you below the busy street called Szabad Sajtó út. While you're down there, enjoy photos of Budapest (with English descriptions) from the turn of the 20th century, when the city was booming.

The last stretch of Váci utca dead-ends at the huge market hall. This used to be a strongly Serbian neighborhood. (Around the next corner to the left, on Szerb utca, there's still a **Serbian Orthodox church**—heavy with incense and packed with icons.) Traditionally, Hungary's territory included most of Slovakia and large parts of Romania, Croatia, and Serbia—and people from all of those places (along with Jews and Gypsies) flocked to Buda and Pest. And yet, most of the residents of this cosmopolitan city still speak Hungarian. Through centuries of foreign invasions and visitors, Budapest remains Magyar. (Remember that after the Ottomans left, Budapest was mostly Austrian. The Austrians didn't go anywhere...they "became" Hungarian, assimilated into the local culture.)

At the end of Váci utca, you'll come to the...

▲▲**Great Market Hall (Nagyvásárcsarnok)**—This market hall (along with four others) was built—you know it—around the

year 1896. The cavernous interior features three levels. The ground floor has produce stands, bakeries, butcher stalls, heaps of paprika, goose liver, and sausages. Upstairs are fun, super-cheap, stand-up, Hungarian-style fast-food joints and six-stool pubs, along with a great selection of souvenirs both traditional (paprika) and not-so-traditional (commie kitsch T-shirts; for all the details, see "Shopping" on page 465). Along the upstairs back wall are historic photos of the market hall (and WCs). The basement is pungent with tanks of still-swimming carp, catfish, and perch, and piles of pickles.

The market was kept open during communism. Margaret Thatcher came to visit in 1989. She expected atrocious conditions compared to English markets, but was pleasantly surprised to find this place up to snuff. This was, after all, "goulash communism" (Hungary's pragmatic mix, which allowed a little private enterprise to keep people going). On the steps of this building, she delivered a historic speech about open society, heralding the impending arrival of the market economy.

The market hall is ideal for lunch, picnic shopping, and people-watching (Mon 6:00–17:00, Tue–Fri 6:00–18:00, Sat 6:00–14:00, closed Sun, Fővám körút 1–3, Budapest IX, M3: Kálvin tér). See "Eating," page 475, for ideas.

From the market, walk to the river. You'll pass (on the left) the **University of Economics,** which was called Karl Marx University 15 years ago. The bridge leads straight to Gellért Hotel, with its famous hot-springs bath, at the foot of Gellért Hill (see "Gellért Baths," page 461). Trams #2 and #2A run from here along the Danube directly back to central Pest, the Chain Bridge, and the Parliament.

More Sights in Central Pest
Hungarian National Museum (Magyar Nemzeti Múzeum)—
One of Budapest's biggest museums features all manner of Hungarian historic bric-a-brac, from the Paleolithic age to a more recent infestation of dinosaurs (the communists). The first floor focuses on the Carpathian Basin in the pre-Magyar days, with ancient artifacts and Roman remains. The basement features a lapidarium, with medieval tombstones and more Roman ruins. On the second floor, 20 rooms take you on a very fast overview trip from the arrival of the Magyars in 896 up to the 1989 revolution. Unless you've got a pretty good handle on Hungarian history, the exhibits are difficult to appreciate (with only a few big-picture English explanations). The most interesting part comes at the very end, with an exhibit on the communist era, featuring both pro- and anti-Party propaganda. The exhibit ends with video footage of the 1989 end of communism—demonstrations, monumental parliament votes, and a final farewell to the last Soviet troops leaving Hungarian soil. Another uprising—the 1848 Revolution against Hapsburg rule—was declared from the steps of this impressive Neoclassical building (free, charge for special exhibitions, Tue–Sun 10:00–18:00, closed Mon, last entry 30 min before closing, near Great Market Hall at Múzeum körút 14–16, Budapest VIII, tel. 1/338-2122, www.hnm.hu).

▲**Courtyards and Galleries**—If you only experience what's on the street in Budapest, you'll miss a big part of the story. Pest is filled with once-grand, now-crumbling facades, and behind most of them, you'll find cozy courtyards where residents carry out much of their lives. These courtyards, shared among neighbors and ringed by a common balcony, stay cool through the summer. Poking into some of these courtyards (which are generally open to the public, offering a handy shortcut through city blocks) is an essential Back Door experience for understanding the inner life of the city.

Pest's streets also hide some impressive galleries, once used for elegant shopping, now faded and ignored. The most spectacular—with delicate woodwork and a breathtaking stained-glass dome—is the **Párisi Udvar.** It's dead-center in Pest, along the busy Lajos Kossuth út, a few blocks up from the big, white Elisabeth

Bridge (enter at Lajos Kossuth út 11; can also enter the other end, around the corner at Petőfi Sándor utca 2). If you're passing by (it's near the recommended local-style Jégbüfé café and the Leo Panzió hotel—see "Eating" and "Sleeping"), it's certainly worth a look. While many of the storefronts inside are abandoned, a few are still alive and kicking (including a bookstore with English guidebooks).

▲Hungarian Parliament (Országház)—The Parliament building, like so much of Budapest, was built for the city's millennial celebration in 1896. Its elegant Neo-Gothic design and riverside location were inspired by its counterpart in London. Architecture snobs shake their heads and wonder why this frilly Gothic monstrosity is topped with a Renaissance dome. (To make matters worse, there used to be a huge red communist star on top of the tallest spire.) But I think it's beautiful.

The best views of the building are from across the Danube—especially in the late afternoon sunlight.

This enormous building—with literally miles of stairs—was appropriate for a time when Budapest ruled much of Eastern Europe. But today it's just plain too big—the legislature only occupies an eighth of the building. Like Britain's Parliament, this building used to be home to a House of Lords and a House of Commons. The Lords are long gone, and their vacated territory is what visitors tour. Guided tours of the Parliament's opulent interior include the elegant main entryway, a legislative chamber, and the Hungarian crown, under the ornate dome (2,300 Ft, not covered by Budapest Card, English tours usually daily at 10:00, 12:00, 14:00, and 18:00—but schedule can change so confirm in advance; follow signs around back to entry *X*, find the line marked *for buying tickets*, wait for the guard to let you enter the door marked *X*, pay cashier, and return to the mob to wait for your tour; Kossuth tér 1–3, Budapest V, M2: Kossuth tér, tel. 1/441-4904, www.mkogy.hu).

Kossuth (Lajos) Tér—The square behind the Parliament building, named for the hero of the 1848 Revolution against the Hapsburgs (described on page 432), is sprinkled with several interesting monuments. Just behind the Parliament is a grassy park with statues of various important Hungarians. A newer monument features a Hungarian flag with a hole cut out of the middle. This commemorates the 1956 Uprising, when protesters removed the socialist-style seal the Soviets had added to their flag. In the early days of that uprising, communist police (ÁVH) on the rooftops above opened fire on demonstrators gathered in this square—massacring many and leaving no doubt that Moscow would not tolerate any form of dissent.

Now imagine this square in the fall of 2006, when it became the site of demonstrations—initially impromptu, then carefully choreographed—against Hungary's prime minister, Ferenc Gyurcsány. Using particularly colorful language in a speech intended only for his own party members, Gyurcsány admitted to lies, deceit, and deception in the way he'd run the government and the recent election. When the tape was leaked to the media, Hungarians showed up here to (unsuccessfully) demand Gyurcsány's resignation. While a few of the demonstrations turned violent, most remained peaceful...and lucrative (concessions stands appeared just a few days into the weeks-long demonstration). For more information on these recent events, see page 396.

Near the Parliament are three other interesting monuments. Just beyond the southeast corner of Kossuth tér, on Vértanúk tere, a contemplative statue of **Imre Nagy,** hero of the 1956 Uprising, stands on a bridge (see page 432). Down closer to the river, by the tram tracks on the end of the Parliament facing the Chain Bridge, look for a statue of the pensive **Attila József,** a popular modern poet who committed suicide at age 32. He's looking over the Danube, a common motif in his works. From this statue, look along the river's edge toward the Chain Bridge. In the distance, lining the embankment, you'll see a new **Holocaust Monument** consisting of 50 pairs of bronze shoes. This commemorates the Jews who were killed when the Nazis' puppet government, the Arrow Cross, came to power in Hungary in 1944. While many Jews were sent to concentration camps, the Arrow Cross simply massacred some of them right here, shooting them and letting their bodies fall into the Danube. You can't get to the shoes directly from here (there's no safe crosswalk over the embankment road); for a closer look, you'll have to access the embankment from near the Chain Bridge, then walk back up this way along the water.

At the top end of Kossuth tér is the...

Museum of Ethnography (Néprajzi Múzeum)—This museum, housed in one of Budapest's grandest venues (the former supreme court building), feels deserted. Its fine exhibit on Hungarian folk culture (mostly from the late 19th century) takes up only a small corner of the cavernous building. This permanent exhibit, with surprisingly good English explanations, shows off costumes, tools, wagons, boats, beehives, furniture, and ceramics of the many peoples who lived in pre-WWI Hungary (which also included much of today's Slovakia and Romania). The museum also has a collection of artifacts from other European and world cultures, which it cleverly assembles into good temporary exhibits (free, charge for

The Millennium Underground of 1896

Built to get the masses of visitors conveniently out to Heroes' Square, this fun and extremely handy little Metro line follows Andrássy út from Vörösmarty Square (Pest's main square) to City Park. Just 20 steps below street level, it's so shallow that you must follow the signs on the street (listing end points) to gauge the right direction, because there's no underpass for switching platforms. The first underground on the Continent (London's is older), it originally had horse-drawn cars. Trains depart every couple of minutes. Recently renovated, the M1 line retains its 1896 atmosphere, along with fun black-and-white photos of the age.

special exhibitions, Tue–Sun 10:00–18:00, closed Mon, Kossuth tér 12, Budapest V, M2: Kossuth tér, tel. 1/473-2442).

Andrássy út and City Park

Connecting central Pest to City Park, Andrássy út is Budapest's main boulevard, lined with shops, theaters, cafés, and locals living well. Budapesters claim it's like the Champs-Elysées and Broadway rolled into one. While that's a stretch, it is a good place to stroll and get a feel for today's urban Pest. The best part to wander is between the boulevard's beginning at Deák tér and the Oktogon.

The following sights are listed in order, from Deák tér (in central Pest) to City Park. The M1 line runs every couple of minutes just under the street—so if you get tired of walking, it's easy to skip several blocks ahead (stops marked by yellow *Földalatti* signs; see "Millennium Underground" sidebar, above).

St. István's Basilica (Szent István Bazilika)—Step into Budapest's largest Catholic church and you'll see not Jesus, but St. István (Stephen), Hungary's first Christian king, glowing above the high altar. (See the "Statue of St. István" listing on page 428 for more on this important Hungarian.) The church is only about 100 years old—like most Budapest landmarks, it was built around 1896. Recently renovated, the interior sparkles proudly. But even though it looks like a major landmark and it's packed with tour groups, the church isn't that compelling (free, Mon–Fri 9:00–17:00, Sat 9:00–13:00—but often closed on summer Saturdays for weddings, Sun

Andrássy út

1 K+K Hotel Opera
2 Hotel Medosz
3 Cotton House
4 Hotel Délibáb
5 Menza Rest.
6 Duran Szendvics & Rest. Művészinas
7 Bohémtanya Pub
8 Gundel Restaurant
9 Robinson Rest.
10 Bagolyvár Rest.
11 Művész Kávéház
12 Discover Hungary/ Yellow Zebra Bike & Inernet Access (2)

Count Andrássy and Sisi

You'll see the names Andrássy and Sisi (or Elisabeth) a lot in Budapest. A key player in the 1848 Revolution, **Count Julius Andrássy** ultimately helped forge the Dual Monarchy of the Austro-Hungarian Empire. He served as the Hungarian prime minister and Austro-Hungarian foreign minister (1871–1879), eventually being forced to step down after his unpopular campaign to appropriate Bosnia and Herzegovina (and consequently boost the Slav population).

Sisi was **Empress Elisabeth,** the Princess Diana of the early 20th-century Hapsburgs (see page 750). Her pet project was advancing the cause of Hungarian autonomy within the empire. While she was married to Emperor Franz Josef, she spent seven years in Budapest—enjoying horseback riding, the local cuisine, and the company of the charming and good-looking Count Andrássy. Her third daughter—believed to be the count's—was known as the Little Hungarian Princess.

13:00–17:00, Szent István tér, Budapest V, M1: Bajcsy-Zsilinszky út or M3: Arany János utca).

The church's primary claim to fame is the **"holy right hand" of St. István.** The sacred fist—a somewhat grotesque, 1,000-year-old withered stump—is in a jeweled box in the chapel to the left of the main altar (follow signs for *Szent Jobb Kápolna*, chapel often closed). Pop in a coin for two minutes of light.

The church also has a measly treasury (300 Ft) and panoramic **observation deck,** with a decent view that gives a sense of the sprawl of Pest (500 Ft, 20 percent discount with Budapest Card, elevator to midlevel, then 137 stairs or smaller elevator, plus a few stairs to top of tower, daily April–May 10:00–16:30, June–Aug 9:30–18:00, Sept–Oct 10:00–17:30, closed Nov–March).

Commerce and Catering Museum (Magyar Kereskedelmi és Vendéglátóipari Múzeum)—Far more interesting than it sounds, this museum takes a nostalgic look at workaday 19th-century Pest commerce. Since it just recently moved into this new location, the museum's full collection likely won't be up and running until late 2007 (or later). Until then, you might see fun old-fashioned posters, as well as other artifacts offering a peek into the fancy hotels, restaurants, and coffeehouses of the day. Past highlights have included a section on the 1896 festivities (with kitschy souvenirs) and an exhibit of old toys. The attendants are enthusiastic grannies who seem old enough to remember all this history firsthand. If you're lucky, one of them will speak English well enough to take you by the hand and explain it all to you (price and hours not finalized, but likely 500 Ft, covered by Budapest Card, Wed–Fri 10:00–17:00, Sat–Sun 10:00–18:00, closed Mon–Tue; hiding around the back of St. Isván's Basilica—to the left as you face the church—at Szent István tér 15; Budapest V, tel. 1/375-6249).

▲**Postal Museum (Postamúzeum)**—This quirky museum, in a fine old apartment from Budapest's Golden Age, features a delightful collection of postal artifacts. You'll see post office coats of arms, 100-year-old postal furniture, antique telephone boxes, historic mailman uniforms, and all manner of postal paraphernalia that was cutting-edge a century ago. It's displayed in an elegant old merchant's mansion with big Murano crystal chandeliers, all the original ornate woodwork, and creaky parquet floors. The apartment—decorated as it was when built in the 1880s—is as interesting as the museum's collection. English-speaking Nora, who's usually around, loves to explain the place and demonstrate the old telephone-operator switchboard (200 Ft, covered by Budapest Card, Tue–Sun 10:00–18:00, closed Mon, loaner English information in each room—or buy the 500-Ft guidebook, just up the street from St. István's Basilica at Andrássy út 3, look for easy-to-miss sign and dial 10 to get upstairs, Budapest VI, M1: Bajcsy-Zsilinszky út, tel. 1/269-6838, www.postamuzeum.hu).

▲**Hungarian State Opera House (Magyar Állami Operaház)**— The Neo-Renaissance home of the Hungarian State Opera features performances almost daily (except July–Aug, during outdoor music season). Designed by Miklós Ybl, the building was constructed in the 1890s using almost entirely Hungarian materials. After being damaged in World War II, it was painstakingly restored in the early 1980s. Today, with lavish marble-and-frescoes decor, a gorgeous gilded interior, and high-quality performances at bargain prices, this is one of Europe's finest opera houses. To take in an opera here, see "Budapest Music Scene," page 464.

Even if you don't see a performance, you can slip in the front door and check out the sumptuous entryway when the box office is open (Mon–Sat from 11:00 until show time—generally 19:00; Sun open 3 hours before the performance—generally 16:00–19:00, or 10:00–13:00 if there's a matinee; Andrássy út 22, Budapest VI, M1: Opera). Better yet, take one of the excellent 45-minute **tours** in English (nearly daily at 15:00 and 16:00, reservations not necessary, but it's smart to call ahead and confirm schedule; 2,500 Ft, 10 percent discount with Budapest Card, buy ticket in opera shop—enter the main lobby and go left, shop open Mon–Fri 10:30–12:45 & 13:30–17:00, Sat–Sun 13:30–17:00, open later during performances, tel. 1/332-8197).

Franz Liszt Square (Liszt Ferenc tér)—This leafy, trendy square on the right (south) side of Andrássy út is surrounded by hip, expensive cafés and restaurants. (The best is the kitschy communist themed restaurant Menza—see page 476.) This is *the* scene for Budapest's yuppies. At the far end of the square is the Music Academy also named for Liszt—a German composer with a Hungarian name, who loved his family's Magyar heritage (though he didn't speak Hungarian) and spent his last five years in Budapest.

The happening Liszt Square scene continues along two streets near the Opera House, **Hajós utca** and **Nagymező utca**—each with its own chic cluster of restaurants and bars. Loosely referred to as the "Broadway Quarter," this zone also has several theaters, and is an enjoyable place to stroll on a summer evening.

Oktogon—During the communist era, this square—at the intersection of Andrássy út and the Great Ring Road (Nagykörút)—was called "November 7 tér" in honor of the Bolshevik Revolution. (Andrássy út was renamed "Sztálin út"; later, after Stalin fell out of fashion, it was simply "People's Republic Boulevard.") Today kids have nicknamed it "American tér" for the fast-food joints littering the square and streets nearby. From this square, Andrássy út gradually becomes the dull diplomatic quarter—less colorful, with tame, embassy-lined streets and stately mansions. From the center of Andrássy út, you can see the column of Heroes' Square at the end of the boulevard.

▲▲House of Terror (Terror Háza)—The former headquarters of the darkest sides of two different regimes—the Arrow Cross (Nazi-occupied Hungary's version of the Gestapo) and the ÁVO/ÁVH (communist Hungary's secret police)—is now, fittingly, an excellent museum of that time of terror.

Hungary initially allied with Hitler to retain a degree of self-determination, and to try to regain their huge territorial losses after World War I. But in March 1944, the country was taken over by the Nazi-affiliated Arrow Cross. The Arrow Cross immediately set to work exterminating Budapest's Jews (most of whom had survived until then). By May, trains were already heading for Auschwitz. As the end of the war neared, Arrow Cross members resorted to more desperate measures, lining Jews up along the Danube and shooting them into the river (now commemorated by a monument near the Parliament—see page 440). To save bullets, they'd sometimes tie several victims together, shoot one of them, and throw him into the freezing Danube—dragging the others in with him. They executed hundreds in the basement of this building. When the communists moved into Hungary, they took over the same building as headquarters for their secret police (the ÁVO, later renamed ÁVH). To keep dissent to a minimum, the secret police terrorized, tried, deported, or executed anyone suspected of being an enemy of the state.

An overhang casts the shadow of the word "TERROR" onto the building. The museum's atrium features a Soviet tank and a huge wall covered with portraits of the victims of this building. The modern, stylish, high-tech exhibit (starting on the top floor and spiraling down) is designed for Hungarians, but the English audioguide (1,300 Ft extra) and free handouts help visitors appreciate the experience.

The museum has many memorable exhibits, including rooms featuring gulag life, Social Realist art and propaganda, a labyrinth of pork-fat bricks reminding old-timers of the harsh conditions of the 1950s (lard on bread for dinner), and religion (joining the Church was a way to express rebellion). This is a powerful experience, particularly for elderly Hungarians who knew many of the victims and perpetrators and have personal memories of the terrors that came with Hungary's "double occupation."

The last section begins with a three-minute video of a guard explaining the execution process, which plays as you descend by elevator into the prison basement. In the early 1950s, this basement was the scene of torture; in 1956, it became a clubhouse of sorts for the local communist youth. It has now been reconstructed circa 1955. During the 1956 Uprising, 250,000 fled to Austria and the West during the two weeks of chaos before the USSR pulled a Tiananmen Square–style crackdown (see page 432). The Hall of Tears remembers 25,000 who died in '56. The last two rooms—with the only color video clips—show the festive and exhilarating days in 1991 when the Soviets departed, making way for freedom. Scenes include the reburial of the Hungarian hero, Imre Nagy; the Pope's visit; and walls of "victimizers"—members and supporters of the Arrow Cross and ÁVO, many of whom are still living, and who were never brought to justice.

Cost, Hours, Location: 1,500 Ft, 20 percent discount with Budapest Card, more for special exhibitions, Tue–Fri 10:00–18:00, Sat–Sun 10:00–19:30, closed Mon, café, bookshop, Andrássy út 60, Budapest VI, M1: Vörösmarty utca—*not* the Vörösmarty tér stop, tel. 1/374-2600, www.terrorhaza.hu.

Audioguide: The 1,300-Ft English audioguide is good but almost too thorough, and can be difficult to hear over the din of the Hungarian soundtracks in each room. You can't fast-forward through the very dense and sometimes long-winded commentary. As an alternative, each room is stocked with good, free English fliers.

▲▲**Heroes' Square (Hősök tere)**—Like much of Budapest, this Who's Who of Hungarian history at the end of Andrássy út was built to celebrate the city's 1,000th birthday in 1896 (M1: Hősök tere). More than just the hottest place in town for skateboarding, this is the site of several museums and the gateway to City Park (filled with diversions for sightseers).

Step right up to the **Millennium Monument** to meet the world's most historic Hungarians (who look to me like their language sounds). The grand-daddy of all Magyars, Árpád, stands proudly at the bottom of the pillar, peering down Andrássy út. The 118-foot-tall pillar supports the archangel Gabriel as he offers the crown to St. István (he accepted it and Christianized the Magyars). In front of the pillar is the Hungarian War Memorial (fenced in now to keep skateboarders from enjoying its perfect slope). Behind the pillar, colonnades feature Hungarian VIPs. Look for names you recognize: István, Béla IV, Mátyás Corvinus. But hey...where are the Hapsburgs? At the time of the monument's construction, Budapest was part of the Austrian Empire, and Hapsburgs stood in the right-hand colonnade. When Hungary regained its independence in World War I, the people tore down the sculpture of the unpopular Franz Josef. (A statue of the less-hated Maria Theresa was left alone...but was ultimately destroyed by a WWII bomb.) After World War II, the Hapsburgs were replaced by Hungarians. In fact, the last two heroes—Ferenc Rákóczi and Lajos Kossuth—were revolutionaries who fought against Austria. The sculptures on the top corners of the two colonnades represent, in order from left to right: Work and Welfare, War, Peace, and the Importance of Packing Light.

As you face Árpád, the **Museum of Fine Arts** (Szépművészeti Múzeum), which has an especially good Spanish collection, is to your left (free, charge for special exhibitions, Tue–Sun 10:00–17:30, closed Mon, tel. 1/469-7100). The **Palace of Art** (Műcsarnok), used for temporary contemporary art exhibits, is to your right (700 Ft, covered by Budapest Card, Tue–Wed and Fri–Sun 10:00–18:00, Thu 12:00–20:00, closed Mon, tel. 1/460-7000).

If you leave Heroes' Square between the two colonnades behind the main pillar, you'll cross a bridge into...

▲▲**City Park (Városliget)**—This is the city's not-so-central Central Park. The park was the site of the overblown 1896 Millennium Exhibition, celebrating Hungary's 1,000th birthday...

and it's still packed with huge party decorations: a zoo with quirky Art Nouveau buildings, a replica of a Transylvanian castle, a massive bath/swimming complex, walking paths, and an amusement park. The park is also filled with unwinding locals. If the sightseeing grind gets you down, spend the afternoon taking a mini-vacation from your busy vacation the way Budapesters do—stroll in the park and soak in the baths.

Orient yourself from the bridge behind Heroes' Square: The huge Vajdahunyad Castle is on your right (go straight and look for bridge to enter complex). Straight into the park and on the left are the big copper domes of the fun, relaxing Széchenyi Baths (see "Budapest's Baths" page 457). And the zoo is past the lake on the left. Three recommended restaurants are at the end of the lake near the zoo (see "Eating," page 474).

▲**Vajdahunyad Castle (Vajdahunyad Vára)**—The huge complex is a replica of a famous castle in Transylvania (part of Hungary for centuries), surrounded by other styles of traditionally Hungarian architecture (textbook Romanesque, Gothic, Renaissance, and Baroque). Some find it artificial in a Walt Disney World sort of way; others think it's pretty cool. You can enter the castle complex for free to poke around the grounds. (After crossing the bridge behind Heroes' Square, turn right.)

As you enter the complex through the castle facade, you'll see a replica of a 13th-century **Benedictine chapel** on the left—Budapest's most popular spot for weekend weddings in the summer. Farther ahead on the right, you'll see a big Baroque mansion—which houses, of all things, the **Museum of Hungarian Agriculture** (Magyar Mezőgazdasági Múzeum). The museum brags that it's Europe's biggest agriculture museum, but the lavish interior is more interesting than the exhibits (free, charge for special exhibitions; April–Oct Tue–Sun 10:00–17:00, closed Mon; Nov–March Tue–Fri 10:00–16:00, Sat–Sun 10:00–17:00, closed Mon; last entry 30 min before closing, tel. 1/363-2711).

Across the street from the museum entry, you'll see a monument to **Anonymous**—specifically, the Anonymous who penned the first Hungarian history in the Middle Ages.

Zoo (Állatkert)—Aside from animals, the zoo also has redeeming sightseeing value: Many of its structures are playful bits of turn-of-the-20th-century Art Nouveau. To reach the beautiful Art Nouveau elephant house, turn right inside the main entry, then right again at the fork, and look for the white-and-turquoise tower. The zoo is a perfect example of a sight that's not really worth the price of entry, but makes for a fun 15-minute walk-through with the Budapest Card (1,400 Ft, covered by Budapest Card; May–Aug Mon–Thu 9:00–17:30, Fri–Sun 9:00–18:00; April and Sept Mon–Thu 9:00–16:30, Fri–Sun 9:00–17:00; Oct–March Mon–Thu

9:00–16:00, Fri–Sun 9:00–16:30; Állatkerti körút 6–12, Budapest XIV, tel. 1/364-0109, www.zoobudapest.com).

Jewish Budapest

As the former co-capital of an empire that included millions of Jews, Budapest always had a high concentration of Jewish residents. Before World War II, 5 percent of Hungary's population and 25 percent of Budapest's was Jewish (the city was dubbed "Judapest" by its snide Viennese neighbors up the river). Hungary lost nearly 600,000 Jews to the Holocaust, at the hands of the brutal Nazi puppet government called the Arrow Cross. (For more about the Holocaust in Hungary, see the "House of Terror" listing on page 445.) Today, only half of one percent of Hungarians are Jewish—and most of them are in Budapest. In recent years, since the thawing of communism, Hungarian Jews have been taking a renewed interest in their heritage.

The first sight listed here is very central, close to Pest's Deák tér; the other is just outside central Pest, a Metro ride plus a five-minute walk away.

▲**Great Synagogue (Zsinagóga)**—This impressively restored synagogue is the second biggest in the world, after one in New York

City. Your synagogue ticket also includes the **Jewish Museum** (Zsidó Múzeum, in the same building).

While several traditional synagogues are nearby (this is Pest's Jewish quarter), the Great Synagogue is reformed, and—with its nave, pulpit, and pipe organ flanking the high altar—it looks like a church with the symbols switched. It was built in the 1850s, when Jews wanted to feel more integrated into the community. The balconies were originally for women, but today men and women sit together anywhere.

The Moorish-flavored decor is a reminder of how Jewish culture flourished in Iberia. After World War II, the synagogue was refurbished with financial support from Tony Curtis, an American actor of Hungarian-Jewish origin (he and his daughter Jamie Lee continue to support these causes today).

Behind the synagogue, the *Tree of Life* sculpture was built on the site of mass graves of those killed by the Nazis. The willow makes an upside-down menorah, each individual leaf lists the name of a victim, and pebbles represent prayers. You can visit the *Tree* even if you don't buy a ticket for the synagogue (enter through synagogue security gate and go straight ahead through doors and under arcade to the park behind the synagogue; if synagogue is closed, go around left side to view monument through a fence).

Cost and Hours: 1,200 Ft includes Great Synagogue and Jewish Museum, 20 percent discount with Budapest Card; April–Oct Mon–Thu 10:00–17:00, Fri 10:00–15:00, Sun 10:00–18:00; Nov–March Mon–Thu 10:00–15:00, Fri and Sun 10:00–14:00; always closed Sat and Jewish holidays, often closed mid-Dec–mid-Jan, last entry 30 minutes before closing, Dohány utca 2, Budapest VII, M2: Astoria, tel. 01/344-5131, www.aviv.hu.

Tours: Aviv Travel leads tours—ranging in length from 35 to 90 minutes—of the synagogue, museum, and Jewish quarter. The 60-minute version, which combines the Great Synagogue, the museum, and the *Tree of Life*, offers the best overview (1,900 Ft). The longer version covers the above, plus another synagogue nearby (2,300 Ft, 90 min). The quickie version includes only the Great Synagogue and *Tree of Life* (1,600 Ft, 35 min). Tours include admission (Mon–Thu and Sun hourly on the half-hour 10:30–15:30; Fri at 10:30, 11:30, and 12:30 only; quickie version also goes hourly on the hour; no Sat tours). Tickets are sold, and tours depart, from the kiosk next to the Great Synagogue entry.

▲Holocaust Memorial Center (Holokauszt Emlékközpont)— This new center is making great strides in honoring the nearly 600,000 Hungarian victims of the Nazis (one in every 10 Holocaust victims was Hungarian). Located a short Metro ride outside of central Pest, the impressive modern complex (with a beautifully restored 1920s synagogue as its centerpiece) is intended to serve as a museum of the Hungarian Holocaust, a monument to its victims, a space for excellent temporary exhibits, and a research and documentation center of Nazi atrocities. A black marble wall in the courtyard is etched with the names of victims, and an information center downstairs helps teary-eyed Hungarians locate the names of their relatives.

The permanent exhibit, called "From Deprivation of Rights to Genocide," traces in English the gradual process of marginalization, then dehumanization, that befell Hungary's Jews as World War II wore on. The one-way route uses high-tech exhibits, including interactive touch screens and movies, to tell the story. By showing there was pervasive anti-Semitism long before World War II, the pointed commentary casts doubt on the widely held belief that Hungary allied itself with the Nazis partly to protect its Jews. While the exhibit occasionally acknowledges Roma (Gypsy) victims, its primary focus is on the fate of the Hungarian Jews. Occasionally the exhibit zooms in to tell the story of an individual or single family, following their personal story through those horrific years. The finale is the interior of the synagogue, now a touching memorial filled with glass seats, each one displaying the image of a Jewish worshipper who once filled it (1,000 Ft, 500-Ft

English audioguide repeats posted English information, Tue–Sun 10:00–18:00, closed Mon, Páva utca 39, Budapest IX, M3: Ferenc körút, tel. 1/455-3333, www.hdke.hu). To reach the complex, take the M3 Metro line to Ferenc körút. Use the exit marked *Üllői út 45–51* and take the left fork at the exit. Walk straight ahead two long blocks, then turn right down Páva utca.

The Danube (Duna)

The mighty river coursing through the heart of the city defines Budapest. For many visitors, a highlight is taking a touristy but beautiful boat cruise up and down the Danube—especially at night (see "Tours," page 420). Here are some other river-related activities to consider.

▲**Danube Embankment (Dunakorzó)**—Pest's breezy riverfront promenade (from Elisabeth Bridge to the Chain Bridge) is a fine place for a stroll. Start on Vigadó tér, two blocks towards the river from Vörösmarty tér, and head south. Along the way, keep an eye out for the *Little Princess* statue leaning on the railing—one of Budapest's symbols, even though it's just over a decade old. When Prince Charles visited Budapest, he liked this statue so much that he had a replica made for himself. You'll pass a few souvenir stalls and big, fancy hotels (including Hyatt and InterContinental), and enjoy sweeping views of Buda, some of the international river-cruise ships, and the city's many bridges. While dining values aren't good here, Spoon—on the boat moored in front of the InterContinental Hotel—is fun (see "Eating," page 474).

▲**Chain Bridge (Széchenyi Lánchíd)**—One of the world's great bridges connects Pest's Roosevelt tér and Buda's Adam Clark

tér. This historic, iconic bridge, guarded by lions (symbolizing power), is Budapest's most enjoyable and convenient bridge to cross on foot. (This is especially handy for commuting to the top of Castle Hill, since both bus #16 and the funicular to the top depart from the Buda end of the bridge.)

Until the mid-19th century, only pontoon barges spanned the Danube between Buda and Pest. In the winter, the pontoons had to be pulled in, leaving locals to rely on ferries (in good weather) or a frozen river. People often walked across the frozen Danube, only to get stuck on the other side during a thaw, with nothing to do but wait for another cold snap.

Count István Széchenyi was stranded for a week trying to get to his father's funeral. After missing it, Széchenyi commissioned

Budapest's first permanent bridge. The Chain Bridge was built by Scotsman Adam Clark between 1842 and 1849, and it immediately became an important symbol of Budapest. Széchenyi—a man of the Enlightenment—charged both commoners and nobles a toll for crossing his bridge, making it an emblem of equality in those tense times. Like all of the city's bridges, the Chain Bridge was destroyed by the Nazis at the end of World War II, but was quickly rebuilt.

Margaret Island (Margitsziget)—Budapesters come to play in this huge, leafy park, a wonderful spot for strolling, jogging, biking, and people-watching (accessible from Margaret Bridge— trams #4 and #6 stop at the gateway to the island). The island is also home to some of Budapest's many baths.

Outer Budapest

The following sights, while technically in Budapest, take a little more time to reach.

Óbuda

Budapest was originally three cities: Buda, Pest, and Óbuda. Óbuda (or "Old Buda") is the oldest of the three—the first known residents of the region (Celts) settled here, and today it's still lit- tered with ruins from the next occupants (Romans). Despite all the history, the district is disappointing, worth a look only for those interested in Roman ruins or 20th-century Hungarian painting and sculpture. To reach the first three sights listed here, go to Batthyány tér in Buda (M2 Metro line) and catch the HÉV suburban train north to the Árpád híd stop. The Vasarely Museum is 50 yards from the station. The town square is 100 yards beyond that, and 200 yards later (turn left at the ladies with the umbrellas), you'll find the Imre Varga Collection. Aquincum is three stops farther north on the HÉV line.

Vasarely Museum—This museum features two floors of eye-pop- ping, colorful paintings by the founder of Op Art, Victor Vasarely. The exhibition follows his artistic evolution from his youth as a graphic designer to the playful optical illusions he was most famous for. (If this art gets you pondering Rubik's Cube, it may come as no surprise that Ernő Rubik was a professor of mathemat- ics right here in Budapest.) Vasarely, and the movement he pio- neered—which was heavy on optical illusions—helped to inspire the trippy styles of the 1960s (600 Ft, covered by Budapest Card, Tue–Sun 10:00–17:30, closed Mon, Szentlélek tér 6, Budapest III, tel. 1/388-7551). This museum is immediately on the right as you leave the Árpád híd HÉV station.

Óbuda Main Square (Fő Tér)—If you keep going past the Vasarely Museum and turn right, you enter Óbuda's cute Main Square. The big, yellow building was the Óbuda Town Hall when this was its own city. Today it's still the office of the district mayor. To the right of the Town Hall, you'll see a whimsical, much-photographed statue of women with umbrellas. Replicas of this sculpture, by local artist Imre Varga, decorate the gardens of wealthy summer homes on Lake Balaton. Varga created many of Budapest's distinctive monuments. His museum is just down the street (turn left at the umbrella ladies).

▲**Imre Varga Collection (Varga Imre Kiállítóház)**—Imre Varga worked from the 1950s through the 1990s. His statues, while occasionally religious, mostly commented on life during communist times, when there were three types of artists: banned, tolerated, and supported. Varga was tolerated. His themes included forced marches and mass graves. One headless statue comes with medallions nailed into his chest. (These medallions were Varga's own, from his pre-communist military service. Anyone with such medallions was persecuted by communists in the 1950s...so Varga disposed of his this way.) Varga actually drops by each Saturday morning at 10:00 to chat with visitors. He speaks English, and, while now in his 80s, he enjoys explaining his art. Don't miss the garden, where you'll see three prostitutes illustrating "the passing of time" (500 Ft, covered by Budapest Card, Tue–Sun 10:00–18:00, closed Mon, Laktanya utca 7, Budapest III, tel. 1/250-0274).

Aquincum Museum—Long before Magyars laid eyes on the Danube, Óbuda was the Roman city of Aquincum. Here you can explore the remains of the 2,000-year-old Roman town and amphitheater. The museum is proud of its centerpiece, a water organ (700 Ft, covered by Budapest Card, May–Sept Tue–Sun 9:00–18:00, closed Mon; Oct and late April Tue–Sun 9:00–17:00, closed Mon; closed Nov–mid-April, Szentendrei út 139, Budapest III, HÉV north to Aquincum stop, tel. 1/250-1650). From the HÉV stop, cross the busy road and turn to the right. Go through the railway underpass, and you'll see the ruins ahead and on the left as you emerge.

Statue Park (Szoborpark)

When regimes fall, so do their monuments. Just think of all those statues of Stalin and Lenin—or Saddam Hussein—crashing to the ground. Throughout Eastern Europe, people couldn't wait to get rid of these reminders of their oppressors. But some clever entrepreneur hoarded Budapest's, and has collected them in a park just southwest of the city—where tourists flock to get a taste of the communist era. Though it can be time-consuming to visit, this collection is worth ▲▲ (or ▲▲▲ for those fascinated by the Red old days).

Under the communists, creativity was discouraged. Art was

acceptable only if it furthered the goals of the state. The only sanctioned art in communist Europe was **Social Realism.** Aside from a few important figureheads, individuals didn't matter. Everyone was a cog in the machine—strong, stoic, doing their job well and proudly for the good of the people. Individual characteristics and distinguishing features were unimportant; people are represented as automatons serving their nation. Artistic merit was virtually ignored. Most figures are trapped in stiff, unnatural poses that ignore the 3,000 years of artistic evolution since the Egyptians.

Cost, Hours, Location: 600 Ft, covered by Budapest Card, daily 10:00–sunset, six miles southwest of city center at the corner of Balatoni út and Szabadka út, Budapest XXII, tel. 1/424-7500, www.szoborpark.hu.

Getting There: The park runs a direct bus from Deák tér in downtown Budapest (where all three Metro lines converge, bus stop marked with Statue Park logo, year-round daily at 11:00, July–Aug also at 15:00; round-trip takes 1.75 hours total, including a 40-min visit to the park, 2,450 Ft round-trip, 1,950 Ft with Budapest Card, price includes park entry). The trip by public transportation is too complicated—skip the park unless you can catch this bus.

● Self-Guided Tour: As you approach the park, you're greeted by an imposing red-brick **entry facade** featuring three of the Communist All-Stars—Lenin, Marx, and Engels. (They couldn't save the biggest "star" of all, Stalin—he was destroyed in the 1956 Uprising.) Like the rest of the park, this gate is highly conceptual in its design: It looks impressive and monumental...but, like the rotted-out pomp of communism, there's nothing behind it. It's a glossy stage-set with no substance. If you try to go through the main, central part of the gate, you'll run into an always-locked door. Instead, as with the communist system, you have to find another way around (in this case, the smaller gate to the left).

Once inside and past the ticket-window building, notice that the main road takes you confidently toward...a dead end (the brick wall). Once again, as with life under the communists, you'll have to deviate from this main axis to actually accomplish anything. Even so, notice that the six cul-de-sacs branching off the main road all bring you right back to where you started—the futility of communism.

Work your way counterclockwise around the park. Dominating the first cluster of statues (to your right as you enter) is a **giant solder** holding the Soviet flag. This statue once stood at the base of the Liberation Monument that still overlooks the Danube from Gellért Hill—in honor of the Red Army that saved Budapest from the Nazis. Typical of Social Realist art, this soldier has a clenched fist (symbolizing strength) and a face that shows no emotion. After the fall of communism, some critics wanted the entire monument torn down. As a compromise, they covered it with a sheet for a while to exorcise the communist mojo, then re-unveiled it. To the left of this soldier, see the **two comrades** stiffly shaking hands: the Hungarian worker thrilled to meet the Soviet soldier. Beyond them is a **long wall,** with a triumphant worker breaking through the left end—too busy doing his job to be very excited. (The three big blocks protruding from the wall are for hanging commemorative wreaths.)

In the next set of statues, you'll see a bust of the Bulgarian communist leader **Gregori Dimitrov**—one of communist Hungary's many Soviet Bloc comrades. After the 1956 Uprising, protestors put a noose around this bust's neck, and hanged it from a tree. Next is a full-size statue of Dimitrov, a gift from "the working people of Sofia." (Talk about a white elephant.) At the back of this loop are three blocky portraits. The middle figure is an important symbol of Hungarian communism: **Béla Kun** fought for the Austro-Hungarian Empire in World War I. He was captured by the Red Army, taken to the Soviet Union, and became mysteriously smitten with communism. After proving himself too far left even for Lenin, Kun returned to Hungary in 1918 and formed a Hungarian Communist Party at a time when communism was most definitely not in vogue. We'll see more of Kun later in the

park. To the left is one of the park's best-loved, most-photographed, and most artistic statues: **Vladimir Lenin,** in his famous "hailing a cab" pose.

In the final circle of statues on this side, you'll see a rusty pair of **workers' hands** holding a sphere (which was once adorned with a red star). The sphere represents the hard-won ideals of communism, carefully protected by the hands—but also held out for others to appreciate. The **monument to Hungarian soldiers** honors those who fought against Francisco Franco in the Spanish Civil War. Dominating this group is a **communist worker** charging into the future, clutching the Soviet flag. (Budapesters of the time had a different interpretation: a thermal bath attendant running after a customer who'd forgotten his towel.) To the left is a monument to the communist version of the Boy Scouts: the elementary school-age **Little Drummers,** and the older **Pioneers.** While these organizations existed before the communists, they were slowly infiltrated and turned into propaganda machines by the regime. These kids—with their jaunty red and blue neckerchiefs—were sent to camp to be properly raised as good little communists; today, many of them have forgotten the brainwashing, but still have fond memories of the socializing.

Where the main path dead-ends at the wall, it's flanked by statues of two **Soviet officers** who negotiated with the Nazis to end the WWII siege of Budapest. One was killed by a Nazi land mine, while the other was shot under mysterious circumstances as he returned from a successful summit. Both became heroes for the communist cause. Were they killed by wayward Nazi soldiers, as the Soviets explained—or by their own Red Army, to create a pair of convenient martyrs?

Continuing counterclockwise to the back-left circle, you'll see a plundered monument (missing its figures and red star), then a **fallen hero** with arm outstretched, about to fall to the ground—mortally wounded, yet victorious. This monument to "the Martyrs of the Counter-Revolution" commemorates those who died attempting to put down the 1956 Uprising. The long, **white wall** at the back of this section tells quite a story (from left to right): The bullet holes lead up to a jumbled, frightful clutter (reminiscent of Pablo Picasso's *Guernica*) representing World War II. Then comes the bright light of the Soviet system, and by the end everyone's looking boldly to the future (and enjoying a bountiful crop, to boot).

The next group—which includes a statue of an interior minister made a foot shorter at the bottom when the Iron Curtain fell—is dominated by a dramatic, unusually emotive sculpture by an actual artist, **Imre Varga** (described on page 453). Designed to commemorate the 100th anniversary of Béla Kun's birth, this clever statue accomplishes seemingly contradictory feats. On the one hand, it reinforces the communist message: Under the able leadership of Béla Kun (safely overlooking the fray from above), the crusty, bourgeois old regime of the Hapsburg Empire (on the left, with the umbrellas and fancy clothes) was converted into the workers' fighting force of the Red Army (on the right, with the bayonets). And yet, those silvery civilians in back seem more appealing than the lunging soldiers in front. And notice the lamppost next to Kun: In Hungarian literature, a lamppost is a metaphor for the gallows—reminding viewers that Kun was ultimately executed by the very communist system he espoused, during Stalin's purges of the late 1930s.

The final group of statues, up near the front, all commemorate the key communist holiday of **April 4, 1945,** when the Soviets forced the final Nazi soldier out of Hungary. At the back of the loop, the Hungarian worker and Soviet soldier (who appear to be doing calisthenics) are absurdly rigid even though they're trying to be dynamic. (Even the statues couldn't muster genuine enthusiasm for communist ideals.) The woman holding the palm leaf is reminiscent of the Liberation Monument back on the Danube—who, after all, celebrates the same glorious day. The tall panel nearest the entrance shows a Hungarian woman and a Soviet woman setting free the doves of peace. According to the inscription, "Our freedom and peace is based on the enduring Hungarian-Soviet friendship." (With friends like these....)

As you exit, peruse the gift shop's fun parade of communist kitsch; consider picking up the good English guidebook, the CD of *Communism's Greatest Hits,* and maybe a model of a Trabant (the classic two-stroke commie-mobile). A real Trabant is often parked just inside the gate.

EXPERIENCES

Perhaps more than anything else, Budapest is about enjoying the good life. Two experiences in particular are "must-dos" while in Budapest: soaking in a thermal bath and taking in a fine musical performance.

Budapest's Baths

Splashing and relaxing in Budapest's thermal baths is the city's only ▲▲▲ activity. Though it might sound daunting, bathing with the Magyars is far more accessible than you'd think. Before you go—or if you need more convincing—read the "Taking the Waters" sidebar. The short version: These baths are basically like your hometown swimming pool—except the water is 100 degrees, there are plenty of jets and bubbles to massage away your stress, and you're surrounded by Hungarians in bikinis and Speedos. Overcome your jitters, follow my instructions, and dive in...or miss out on *the* quintessential Budapest experience.

Budapest's two-dozen baths *(fürdő)* were taken over by the communist government, and they're all still owned by the city. The two baths listed here are the best known, most representative, and most convenient for first-timers: Széchenyi Baths are more casual and popular with locals, while the Gellért Baths are elegant and touristy. To me, Széchenyi is second to none, but some travelers prefer the famous, swankier Gellért experience. For more information, see www.spasbudapest.com.

Széchenyi Baths (Széchenyi Fürdő)

To soak with the locals, head for this bath complex—the big, yellow, copper-domed building in the middle of City Park. Worth ▲▲▲, Széchenyi (SAY-chehn-yee) is the best of Budapest's many

Taking the Waters

American tourists often feel squeamish at the thought of bathing with Speedo-clad, pot-bellied Hungarians. Relax! If you choose the right bath (such as the ones I've recommended), "taking the waters" is no more challenging than a trip to a water park. I was nervous on my first visit, too. But now I feel like a trip to Hungary just isn't complete without a splish-splash in the bath.

All this fun goes way back. Hungary's Carpathian Basin is a thin crust on top of a lot of hot water. The Romans named their settlement at present-day Budapest "Aquincum"—meaning "abundant waters"—and took advantage of those waters by building many baths. Centuries later, the occupying Ottomans revived the custom. Locals brag that if you poke a hole in the ground anywhere in Hungary, you'll find a hot-water spring. Judging from Budapest, they may be right: The city has 123 natural springs and some two-dozen thermal baths *(fürdő)*. While these spas have traditionally served a medicinal purpose, today Hungary is trying a new angle on its hot water: entertainment. Adventure water parks are springing up all over the country.

While Hungary has several mostly nude, segregated Turkish baths, the places I list are less intimidating: Men and women are usually together, and you can keep your swimsuit on the entire time. (Even at mixed baths, there generally are a few clothing-optional, gender-segregated areas, where locals are likely to be nude—or wearing a *kötény*, or loose-fitting loincloth.)

The baths I recommend have various types of pools. Big pools with cooler water are for serious swimming, while the smaller, hotter thermal baths *(gyógyfürdő, or simply göz)* are for relaxing, enjoying the jets and current pools, and playing chess. Most pools are marked with the water temperature in Celsius (cooler pools are about 30°C/86°F; warmer pools are closer to 36°C/97°F or 38°C/100°F, about like the hot tub back home; and the hottest are 40°C/104°F...yowtch!). You'll also usually find a steam room, as well as sunbathing areas (which may be segregated and clothing-optional).

The most difficult part of visiting a Hungarian bath is the inevitably complicated entrance procedure. This is one of today's best time-travel experiences to communist Eastern Europe. Expect monolingual staff, a complex payment and locker-rental scheme, and lengthy menus of massages and other treatments. I've explained the specifics for each bath, but be forewarned that they can change from year to year, or even from day to day. Keep track of any receipt or slip of paper you're given, as you may be asked to show it later (for a refund or to get your deposit back). Hang in there, go where people direct you, and enjoy this unique cultural experience. Remember, they're used to tourists—so don't be afraid to act like one. If you can make it through those first few confusing minutes, you'll soon be relaxing like a pro.

While enjoying the baths, you can leave your clothing and other belongings in your locked cabin or locker. While I've found these to be safe, and bath employees assure me that thefts are rare, it's at your own risk. Another option is to leave valuables in a safe (generally costs 500 Ft, ask when you buy ticket). People have been known to steal rental towels from around the pools to collect the deposit—keep an eye on your towels and any other belongings you bring to the poolside. Many locals bring plastic shopping bags to hold their essentials: towels, leisure reading, and sunscreen.

Note that the jets, bubbles, waves, waterfalls, and whirlpools sometimes take turns running. For example, a current pool runs for 10 minutes, then a series of jets starts up and the current pool stops for 10 minutes, then the current pool starts up again, and so on. If a particularly fun feature of the pool doesn't seem to be working, just give it a few minutes.

If you stay less than a designated time (usually three hours), you will usually get a refund when you leave—if you get a receipt, take it to the ticket window and see if they'll give you anything back.

Here are some useful phrases:

English	Hungarian	Pronounced
Bath	*Fürdő*	FEWR-dur
Men	*Férfi*	FEHR-fee
Women	*Női*	NUR-ee
Changing Cabin	*Kabin*	KAH-been
Locker	*Szekrénye*	SEHK-rayn
Ticket Office	*Pénztár*	PAYNZ-tar
Thermal Bath	*Gyógyfürdő,*	JODGE-fewr-dur,
	Göz	gorz

Please trust me, and take the plunge. If you go into it with an easygoing attitude and a sense of humor, I promise you'll have a blast.

bath experiences—and, thanks to a recent renovation, it feels even classier than the famous Gellért Baths. Relax and enjoy some Hungarian good living. Magyars of all shapes and sizes stuff themselves into tiny swimsuits and strut their stuff. Housewives float blissfully in the warm water. Intellectuals and Speedo-clad elder statesmen stand in chest-high water around chessboards and ponder their next moves. This is Budapest at its best.

Cost: 2,600 Ft for personal changing cabin, 2,200 Ft for locker in gender-segregated locker room, 100-Ft discount with Budapest Card, cheaper if you arrive within three hours of closing time, price includes thermal baths, swimming pool, and sauna. Couples can share a changing cabin: One person pays the cabin rate, the other pays the locker rate, but both use the same cabin. There's also a wide array of massages and other special treatments—find the English menu in the lobby (make an appointment as you enter). Once inside the complex, you can rent a swimsuit or towel (about 700 Ft each with a 1,000-Ft deposit).

Hours: Swimming pool entrance generally open daily 6:00–22:00, thermal bath entrance daily 6:00–19:00, last entry one hour before closing. The bath hours have changed frequently the last few years, and may unexpectedly revert to shorter hours—until 19:00 or 17:00—in winter.

Location and Entrances: Állatkerti körút 11, Budapest XIV, M1: Széchenyi fürdő. The huge bath complex has three entrances. The busiest one—technically the **"thermal bath entrance"**—is the grand main entry, facing south (roughly towards Vajdahunyad Castle). I avoid this entrance—there's often a line during peak times, and it's a bit more confusing to find your way once inside. Instead, I prefer the **"swimming pool entrance,"** facing the zoo on the other side of the complex—it's faster, has shorter lines, and is open later. A smaller third entrance, to the right as you face the Zoo entry (near the Metro stops), provides access to either the thermal bath changing rooms or the swimming pool changing rooms, but can also have long lines.

Entry Procedure: Pay the cashier, and you'll be given a receipt (keep this for later) and a plastic card (red for a changing cabin, blue for a locker). Wave your plastic card over the turnstile to enter the complex. Once inside, rent a towel or swimsuit if needed (do this before you change, as you'll need money). To find the towel/suit rental desk from the swimming pool entrance, take the first staircase down on your right as you enter the hallway to the cabins.

Once you've got your towel/suit, show your plastic card to one of the attendants (who wear white smocks and occasionally speak a few words of English). They'll either direct you to a locker room (remember, men are *férfi* and women are *női*) or show you to a changing cabin (again, couples can share a cabin). After changing, find your attendant and have them lock your cabin for you. They'll tell you to remember your cabin number, and give you a little metal disc to put around your wrist to claim your cabin later.

Phew. Now let's have some fun.

Taking the Waters: The bath complex has two parts. Inside is the thermal bath section, a series of mixed-gender indoor pools. The water here is quite hot—most about 40 degrees Celsius, or 104 Fahrenheit—and some of the pools have very green water, supposedly caused by the many healthy minerals. Outside is the swimming pool area, with three pools. Orient yourself with your back to the main building: The pool to the right is for fun (cooler water—30 degrees Celsius, or 86 Fahrenheit, warmer in winter, lots of jets and bubbles, lively and often crowded, includes fun current pool); the pool on the left is for relaxation (warmer water—38 degrees Celsius, or 100 Fahrenheit, mellow atmosphere, a few massage jets, chess); and the main pool in the center is all business (the coolest water, doing laps, swimming cap required). Stairs to saunas are below the doors to the inside pools. You get extra credit for joining the gang in a chess match.

Exit Procedure: If you rented a towel or swimsuit, return it to the desk where you got it, and present your receipt to get your deposit back. Then, as you exit the complex, insert your card into the turnstile and a receipt will print out. If you stayed less than three hours, the receipt will indicate the amount of your refund *(Visszatérités: Jár* [amount] *Ft)*. Present this and your original receipt at the cashier as you exit to claim your "time-proportional repayment." (If you arrived within three hours of closing time, you already got a discount and won't get a refund.) Then continue your sightseeing...soggy, but relaxed.

Gellért Baths (Gellért Fürdő)

Budapest's classic bath experience—worth ▲▲—is at Gellért Hotel. You'll pay more and won't run into nearly as many locals—this is definitely a more upscale, touristy, spa-like scene. Because most of the hottest pools are in gender-segregated areas, it's not ideal for opposite-sex couples or families who want to spend time together. But if you want a soothing, luxurious bath experience in an elegant setting, this is the place. And if it's fun you're looking for, the Gellért Baths have something Széchenyi doesn't: a huge, deliriously enjoyable wave pool that'll toss you around like a queasy surfer (summer only).

Note that this bath complex has long been planning (and delaying) a renovation, which might affect open areas and the entry procedure (for example, certain days may be men- or women-only).

Cost: 3,000 Ft for personal changing cabin, 2,500 Ft for locker in gender-segregated locker room, cheaper after 16:00, 10 percent discount with Budapest Card. When you buy your ticket, tell them if you want to buy a massage or rent a towel (600 Ft with a 4,000-Ft deposit) or a swimsuit (600 Ft, plus 2,500-Ft deposit for men or 2,800-Ft deposit for women). The 700-Ft visitor ticket to see—but not use—the baths is pointless, as you'll see virtually nothing more than what's visible from the ticket window.

Hours and Location: May–Sept daily 6:00–19:00; Oct–April Mon–Fri 6:00–19:00, Sat–Sun 6:00–17:00; last entry 1 hour before closing. It's on the Buda side of the green Liberty Bridge (trams #47 and #49 from Deák tér in Pest, or tram #19 along the Buda embankment from Víziváros below the castle). The entrance to the baths is under the white dome opposite the bridge (Kelenhegyi út 4–6, Budapest XI, tel. 1/466-6166, ext. 165).

Entry Procedure: As you enter, a generally English-speaking information desk is dead ahead, with cashiers on either side. Beyond the cashier on the left is a window where you can deposit valuables in the safe (500 Ft).

Confusingly, in the summer they sell two different tickets based on which changing area you'll use. With a **thermal bath ticket,** you'll change in a large, gender-segregated area that connects directly to the also-segregated thermal baths (so some people walk nude directly from their cabins to the bath); this means that opposite-sex couples can't share a changing cabin. With a **swimming pool ticket,** you'll go to a mixed area where opposite-sex couples can share a cabin (this area also has gender-segregated locker rooms). Both tickets allow you to move freely between the thermal baths and swimming pool areas once you're inside.

Be warned that you may not be sold precisely the ticket you ask for. The ticket-seller sometimes decides which ticket fits you best. For example, on my last visit I asked for a swimming pool ticket with a cabin and a towel. She sold me a thermal bath ticket with no towel. Her logic was that the thermal bath ticket includes a big sheet—so the towel was an unnecessary expense. (Though I was confused at first, she was right, and saved me 600 Ft.)

Your entry ticket consists of two parts: a receipt-like slip of paper (which you'll surrender to get into the changing area); and a plastic card used to keep track of how long you're inside (which you'll insert in the turnstile to exit). Keep track of both of these items until you're asked for them.

A dizzying array of **massages** and **treatment options** are also sold at the ticket window. Most are available only with a doctor's note, but anyone can get a "medical massage" (with oil, 2,400 Ft/15 min, 3,300 Ft/30 min) or a "refreshing massage" (with cold soapy water, 2,000 Ft/15 min, 3,000 Ft/30 min). In a different area of the complex, you can also get a "Thai massage"—but you have to arrange that separately.

Pay for everything you want (including massages or towel rentals), enter, and glide through the swanky lobby. Look for the indoor swimming pool on your right, about halfway down the main hall. Just under the window into the pool are stairs leading down to a maze of corridors that take you to the changing rooms (for swimming pool tickets). If you have a thermal bath ticket, the entrances are to the right (women/*női*, closer to the entrance) and the left (men/*férfi*, at the end of the hall) of the swimming pool entrance. If you paid to rent a towel or swimsuit, pick it up from the attendant on your way.

Taking the Waters: Once you've changed, you can spend your time either indoors or out. Outside are several sunbathing areas and a warm thermal pool (up the stairs). But the main attraction out here is the big, unheated wave pool in the center (closed Oct–April). Not for the squeamish, this pool thrashes fun-loving swimmers around like driftwood. The swells in the deeper area are fun and easy to float on, but the crashing waves at the shallow end are vigorous, if not dangerous. If there are no waves, just wait around a while (you'll hear a garbled message on the loudspeaker five minutes before the tide comes in).

Inside, the central, genteel-feeling hall is home to a cool-water swimming pool (swimming cap required—free loaners available) and a crowded hot-water pool. Off of that pool are doors to the gender-segregated, clothing-optional massage rooms and thermal baths, with nude or loinclothed bathers stewing in pools at 36 and 38 degrees Celsius (97 and 100 degrees Fahrenheit), as well as cold plunge pools and eucalyptus-scented steam rooms. If you paid for a massage, report to the massage room in this section when you're ready (no appointments—first-come, first-served; you may wait 30 min or more).

Exit Procedure: When you're finished, return your towel and swimsuit to get the slip to reclaim your deposit money (at cashier as you leave). If you were at the bath for less than four hours, you'll also get money back when you leave (if the change isn't automatically dispensed when you go through the exit turnstile, take your plastic card to the cashier).

Budapest Music Scene

Budapest is a great place to catch a good—and inexpensive—concert. In fact, Viennese music lovers often make the three-hour trip here just to take in a fine, cheap opera in a luxurious setting. Options range from a performance at one of the world's great opera houses to light, touristy "Gypsy" folk concerts (with musicians and routines suspiciously similar to tomorrow's "Hungarian folk music" concerts). The tourist concerts are the simplest option—you'll see the fliers everywhere—but you owe it to yourself to do a little homework and find something more authentic. The monthly *Budapest Panorama* brochure makes it easy (free, available at the TI)—listing performances with dates, venues, performers, and contact information for getting tickets. Or check schedules online (try www.wherebudapest.hu).

A Night at the Opera—Consider taking in an opera by one of the best companies in Europe, in one of Europe's loveliest opera houses, for bargain prices. The Hungarian State Opera performs almost nightly, both at the main Opera House (Andrássy út 22, Budapest VI, M1: Opera, see page 444) and in the Erkel Színház theater (not nearly as impressive, near the Keleti train station at Köztársaság tér 30, Budapest VIII, tel. 1/333-0540). Be careful to get a performance in the Opera House—not the Erkel Színház. Ticket prices range from 800 to 11,000 Ft, but the best music deal in Europe may be the 400-Ft, obstructed-view tickets (easy to get, as they rarely run

out). If you chose to buy one of these opera-tickets-for-two-bucks, you'll get a seat at the back of one of the boxes along the side of the theater. You can either sit comfortably, and see nothing; or stand and crane your neck to see about half the stage. If the seats in front of you don't fill up, scooting up to an empty seat when the show starts is less than a capital offense. Either way, you'll hear every note along with the big spenders. If a full evening of opera is too much for you, you can leave early or come late (but buy ticket ahead of time, as box office closes when performance starts). Note that there are no performances in July and August, when Budapest's outdoor music season is in full swing. To get tickets, call, fax, or visit the box office at the main Opera House, or order online (box office open and phone answered Mon–Sat from 11:00 until show time—generally 19:00; Sun open 3 hours before the performance—generally 16:00–19:00, or 10:00–13:00 if there's a matinee; box office tel. 1/353-0170, fax 1/311-9017, www.opera .hu). If you reserve by phone, you can pick up your ticket up to

30 minutes before the performance. There are often a few tickets available at the door (even if it's supposedly "sold out").

Tourist Concerts—A company called Duna Palota offers a wide range of made-for-tourist concerts. The most popular options are Hungarian folk music and dancing by various interchangeable troupes (3,300–5,600 Ft, May–Oct almost daily at 20:00) and classical "greatest hits" by the Danube Symphony Orchestra (the best group, 6,400–8,100 Ft, 12–15 percent discount with Budapest Card for this concert only, May–Oct Sat at 20:00). These concerts take place in one of three historic venues: the Budai Vigadó ("Buda Concert Hall"—on Corvin tér in Víziváros, between Castle Hill and the Danube); the Bábszinház ("Puppet Theater"—near the House of Terror at Andrássy út #69, M1: Vörösmarty utca); or a former casino called the Duna Palota ("Danube Palace"—3 long blocks north of Vörösmarty tér in Pest, behind Roosevelt tér and the Chain Bridge at Zrínyi utca 5). You can also take in an organ concert in the Baroque St. Anne's Church (3,600 Ft, June–Sept Fri and Sun at 20:00, May only Fri at 20:00, on Batthyány tér at the north end of Víziváros).

While highbrow classical music buffs will want a more serious concert, these shows are real crowd-pleasers. Your hotel can book for you (and take a commission), or you can book directly with Duna Palota (main office in Danube Palace at Zrínyi utca 5, call or visit for tickets, daily April–Dec 8:00–20:00, Jan–March 8:00–18:00, open later during concerts, tel. 1/317-2754, http://ticket .info.hu).

SHOPPING

Budapest's single best shopping venue is the Great Market Hall (see page 437). Aside from all the colorful produce downstairs, the upstairs gallery is full of fiercely competitive souvenir vendors (bargaining is the norm). There's also a folk-art market on Castle Hill (near the bus stop at Dísz tér), but it's generally more touristy and a little more expensive. And, while Váci utca has been Budapest's main shopping thoroughfare for generations, today it features the city's highest prices and worst values. At any outdoor markets, you're welcome to haggle, but not inside shops.

The most popular souvenir is the quintessential Hungarian spice: **paprika.** Sold in metal cans, linen bags, or porcelain vases— and often accompanied by a tiny wooden scoop—it's a nice way to spice up your cooking with memories of your trip. (But remember that only sealed containers will make it through Customs on your way back home.) For more on paprika, see page 398.

Another popular local item is a hand-embroidered **linen tablecloth.** The colors are often red and green—the national colors of Hungary, of course—but white-on-white designs are also available (and classy). If the stitching is too regular and perfect, it's done by machine, and therefore less valuable.

You'll see **crystal** sold in some shops; it's mostly of Czech origin, but cut in Hungary. Other handicrafts to look for include **chess sets** (most from Transylvania) and **nesting dolls.** While these dolls have more to do with Russia than with Hungary, you'll see just about every modern combination available: from *South Park* characters, to Russian heads of state, to infamous terrorists, to American Presidents. Tacky...but fun. Fans of communist kitsch can look for cool **T-shirts** that poke fun at that bygone era (but the very best selection is at the Statue Park gift shop—see page 453).

If you're looking for a modern, American-style shopping mall, look no further than **WestEnd City Center** (daily 8:00–23:00, next door to Nyugati train station at Váci út 1–3, M3: Nyugati pu., www.westend.hu) or **Mammut** ("Mammoth"; Mon–Sat 10:00–21:00, Sun 10:00–18:00, next to Moszkva Square at Lővőház utca 2–6, M2: Moszkva tér, www.mammut.hu).

SLEEPING

The hotel scene in Budapest is decent, but not ideal. Over the last few years, supply has not kept up with demand—so prices have gone up without a corresponding improvement in quality. Still, I've unearthed a few gems. Book as far ahead as possible to get the best deal. Most rates drop 10–25 percent in the off-season (generally Nov–March). The Formula 1 races (Aug 5 in 2007) send rates through the roof; the rest of August is also tight and expensive. If

Sleep Code

(€1 = $1.20, 200 Ft = about $1, country code: 36, area code: 1)
S = Single, **D** = Double/Twin, **T** = Triple, **Q** = Quad, **b** = bathroom, **s** = shower only. Unless otherwise noted, breakfast is included and credit cards are accepted. Everyone speaks English, and prices are quoted in euros.

To help you sort easily through these listings, I've divided the rooms into three categories, based on the price for a standard double room with bath:

$$$ **Higher Priced**—Most rooms €100 (24,000 Ft) or more.
$$ **Moderately Priced**—Most rooms between €70–100 (16,800–24,000 Ft).
$ **Lower Priced**—Most rooms €70 (16,800 Ft) or less.

you're arriving on an international train, you may be approached by room-hawkers on board, offering accommodations in private homes and hotels. These places get mixed reviews; you're better off using my listings.

Pest

Staying in Pest is more convenient, but a little less romantic, than sleeping in Buda. Most sights worth seeing are in Pest, and this half of the city also has a much higher concentration of Metro and tram stops, making it a snap to get around. Pest also feels more lively and local than stodgy, touristy Buda. I've arranged my listings by neighborhood, clustered around the most important sightseeing sectors.

Central Pest (Belváros), near Váci utca

Sleeping on the very central and convenient Váci utca comes with overly inflated prices. But these less expensive options—just a block or two off Váci utca—offer some of the best values in Budapest.

$$$ Peregrinus Hotel, a bit overpriced despite its good location, has 25 high-ceilinged, spacious, outdated rooms. Because it's run by the big ELTE university, many of its guests are visiting professors and lecturers (Sb-€70, Db-€100, extra bed-€27, 20 percent cheaper Nov–March, elevator, just off Váci utca at Szerb utca 3, Budapest V; 5-min walk to M3: Kálvin tér, or tram #47 or #49 to Fövám tér; tel. 1/266-4911, fax 1/266-4913, www.peregrinushotel .hu, peregrinushotel@elte.hu).

$$ Leo Panzió is a peaceful oasis with 14 modern rooms in a hulking building that's seen better days. The location is central, the antique elevator is wonderfully rickety, the staff is polite and professional, and the double-paned windows keep out most of the noise from the busy street below (Sb-€73, Db-€89, Tb-€118 extra bed-€29, 15 percent cheaper Nov–March, all rooms have a strange but well-marked little step down in the middle of the room, entirely non-smoking, air-con, Kossuth Lajos utca 2A, Budapest V, M3: Ferenciek tere, tel. 1/266-9041, tel. & fax 1/266-9042, www.leopanzio.hu, leo@leopanzio.hu).

$$ Kálvin-Ház, a long block up from the Great Market Hall, offers 37 big rooms with old-fashioned furnishings and squeaky parquet floors. The new top-floor rooms have a bit less classic character, but are air-conditioned and tidier than the older rooms (all rooms cost the same: Sb-€70, Db-€95, apartment-€115, extra bed-€20, 20 percent cheaper Nov–March, non-smoking rooms, elevator, Internet access, Gönczy Pál utca 6, Budapest IX, M3: Kálvin tér, tel. 1/216-4365, fax 1/216-4161, www.kalvinhouse.hu, info@kalvinhouse.hu).

Pest Hotels and Restaurants

- ❶ Peregrinus Hotel
- ❷ Leo Panzió Hotel
- ❸ Kálvin-Ház Hotel
- ❹ Ibis Hotel Centrum & Ráday Utca "Restaurant Row"
- ❺ Mellow Mood Central Hostel
- ❻ Marco Polo Hostel
- ❼ Domino Hostel
- ❽ Hotel Queen Mary
- ❾ Spoon Restaurant
- ❿ Shalimar Restaurant
- ⓫ Gerbeaud Café
- ⓬ Centrál Kávéház
- ⓭ Jégbüfé Snack Bar
- ⓮ Historic McDonald's
- ⓯ Patyolat G. Laundry
- ⓰ Discover Hungary/ Yellow Zebra Bike & Internet Access (2)

$$ Ibis Hotel Budapest Centrum, with 126 rooms, is part of the no-frills chain that's sweeping Europe. Like all other Ibis branches, this place has spongy carpets, cookie-cutter predictability, and utterly no charm. But it's cheap, well-equipped for the price, and beautifully located at the start of the happening Ráday utca restaurant scene, just up the street from the Great Market Hall and Váci utca (Sb/Db-€88 April–Oct, Sb/Db-€74 Nov–March, Sb/Db-up to €105 during conventions and special events, does not include 3 percent tax, breakfast-€8/person, air-con, elevator, Ráday utca 6, M3: Kálvin tér, tel. 1/456-4100, fax 1/456-4116, www.ibis -centrum.hu, h2078@accor.com).

$ Mellow Mood Central Hostel is Budapest's biggest, best-run, best-located, and most expensive hostel. With 176 beds in 33 bright, cheery, clean rooms (including four twins), it's a winner (prices per person: twin Db-€22–30, T-€17–26, Q-€16–23, bunk in 6-bed dorm-€14–21, in 8-bed dorm-€13–20, price depends on season, cash only, includes sheets, towel-500 Ft, breakfast-450 ft, pay laundry, Internet access, a block north of Váci utca at Bécsi utca 2, tel. 1/411-1310, fax 1/411-1494, www.mellowmoodhostel .com, sales@mellowmoodhostel.com). This place has two sister hostels: **$ Marco Polo,** with dorm beds, 36 more twin rooms, and similar rates in a less convenient location (Nyár utca 6, M2: Blaha Lujza tér, tel. 1/413-2555, fax 1/413-6058, www.marcopolohostel .com, sales@marcopolohostel.com); and the brand-new **$ Domino,** with 146 beds near the Great Market Hall (slightly lower rates than Mellow Mood, Váci utca 77, enter at Havas utca 6, tel. 1/266-4111, www.dominohostel.com, info@dominohostel.com).

Near Andrássy út

Andrássy boulevard is handy, local-feeling, and endlessly entertaining. It's lined with appealing cafés, restaurants, theaters, and bars—and the living is good. The frequent Metro stations make getting around the city easy from here. None of these hotels is on Andrássy út, but they're all within a two-block walk away. For locations, see the map on page 442.

$$$ K+K Hotel Opera is wonderfully located beside the opera in the fun "Broadway Quarter." It's a regal splurge, where wicker and bamboo seem classy. It has helpful, professional service and 205 rooms. The published rates are sky-high (Sb-€181, Db-€225), but most of the time you can get a better deal (often Sb-€120–130 and Db-€130–140 in summer, Sb/Db-€110 in winter, non-smoking floors, air-con, elevator, Internet access, parking garage-€15/ day, Révay utca 24, Budapest VI, M1: Opera, tel. 1/269-0222, fax 1/269-0230, www.kkhotels.com, kk.hotel.opera@kkhotels.hu).

$ Hotel Medosz is cheap and dumpy, overlooking a seedy square. But the prices are low and the location is wonderfully central, around the corner from the Oktogon and across busy Andrássy út from the trendy Franz Liszt Square. Beyond the chilling concrete communist facade and gloomy lobby are 67 rooms—old and uninspired but perfectly adequate, comrade (Sb-€55, Db-€65, 15 percent cheaper Nov–March, elevator, nearby nightclubs can be noisy—ask for a quieter courtyard room, Jókai tér 9, Budapest VI, M1: Oktogon, tel. 1/374-3000, fax 1/332-4316, www.medoszhotel.hu, info@medoszhotel.hu).

Elsewhere in Pest

These fine values are scattered around central Pest.

$$$ Cotton House is a fun, blast-from-the-past theme hotel. Its 20 retro rooms are fresh and comfy, with 1930s themes; each room is devoted to a different mobster (Al Capone) or old-time performer (Ella Fitzgerald, Elvis Presley, Frank Sinatra). The stylish furnishings are a clever mix of actual old and neo-old (Sb/Db-€100 with shower, €110 with bathtub, €120 with Jacuzzi, 20 percent less Jan–March, air-con, close to the Nyugati Station and a few blocks from the Oktogon at Jókai utca 26, Budapest V, M3: Nyugati pu., tel. 1/354-2600, fax 1/354-1341, www.cottonhouse.hu, info@cottonhouse.hu). In the basement is an elaborate jazz club, with a restaurant, cigar room (with a wall of rentable humidor lockers), and oodles of atmosphere. Live ragtime music fills the lower floors almost nightly until 23:00—request a quieter upstairs room if you turn in early.

$$ Hotel Queen Mary (named not for the British monarch, but for the owner's wife) is simple and affordable, with 26 tight, unimaginative, but new-feeling rooms. The neighborhood—a block south of the Great Boulevard ring road and two blocks beyond the end of Franz Liszt Square—is central and safe, but not very pretty (Sb-€75, Db-€85, Tb-€105, 30 percent cheaper Nov–March, air-con, elevator, Kertész utca 34, between M1: Oktogon and M2: Blaha Lujza tér, tel. 1/413-3510, fax 1/413-3511, www.hotelqueenmary.hu, info@hotelqueenmary.hu). Request a quieter back room, overlooking the garden.

$$ Hotel Délibáb is spartan but a decent value, located across the street from Heroes' Square. The 34 rooms are a bit old and worn, with thin walls, but they're comfy enough. Most face a busy street and come with some noise (Sb-€68, Db-€79, Tb-€95, 15 percent cheaper Nov–March, free Internet access, parking-€10/day, Délibáb utca 35, Budapest VII, M1: Hősök tere, tel. 1/342-9301, fax 1/342-8153, www.hoteldelibab.hu, info@hoteldelibab.hu).

$ Mária and István, your chatty Hungarian aunt and uncle, are saving a room for you in their Old World apartment. For warmth and hospitality at youth-hostel prices, consider bunking in one of their two rooms, which share a bathroom (S-€20–24,

D-€30–36, T-€42–48, price depends on size of room and length of stay—longer is cheaper, no breakfast but guests' kitchen, cash only, elevator, Ferenc körút 39, Budapest IX, M3: Ferenc körút, tel. & fax 1/216-0768, www.mariaistvan.hu, mariaistvan@t-online.hu). Mária and István also rent two apartments farther from the center (Db-€50–56, Tb-€60–66, Qb-€68–80, family apartment, both near M3: Nagyvarad tér).

Buda

Víziváros

The Víziváros neighborhood—"Water Town"—is the lively part of Buda, squeezed between Castle Hill and the Danube, where fishermen and tanners used to live. Across the river from the Parliament building, it comes with fine views. Víziváros is the most pleasant central area to stay on the Buda side of the Danube. It's expensive and a little less convenient than Pest, but also less urban-feeling.

The following hotels (except the last one) are between the Chain Bridge and Buda's busy Margit körút ring road. Trams #19 and #41 zip along the embankment in either direction. Batthyány tér, a few minutes' walk away, is a handy center with lots of restaurants (see "Eating," page 474), a place to drop off your laundry (Topclean—see "Laundry," page 414), and a Metro stop (M2 line). For a good hangout with Internet access near these hotels, try Soho Coffee Company (see page 480). Each of these places comes with professional, helpful staff.

$$$ Hotel Victoria, with 27 business-class rooms—each with a grand river view—is a fine value. This tall, narrow place (three rooms on each of nine floors) is run with pride and attention to detail. It's a winner (Sb-€112, Db-€118, extra bed-€46, 30 percent less Nov–March, elevator, free sauna, Internet access, parking garage-€12/day or park free on street, Bem rakpart 11, Budapest I, tel. 1/457-8080, fax 1/457-8088, www.victoria.hu, victoria@victoria.hu).

$$$ art'otel impresses New York City sophisticates. Every detail of the 165-room art'otel—from the breakfast dishes to the carpets to the good-luck blackbird perched in each room—was designed by American artist Donald Sultan. This big, stylish hotel is a fun, classy splurge (rack rates: Sb-€198, Db-€218, Danube view-€20 more, bigger "executive" rooms-€50 more, deluxe "art suites"-€100 more, rates drop as low as Sb-€148/Db-€168 during slow times, even lower rates—often Db-€150—if you book online, non-smoking rooms, elevator, Internet access in business lounge, free sauna and mini-exercise room, Bem rakpart 16–19, Budapest I, tel. 1/487-9487, fax 1/487-9488, www.artotel.hu, budapest@artotel.hu).

$$$ Hotel Astra is quiet, old-fashioned, and well-maintained. Its 12 rooms—surrounding a peaceful courtyard—are woody, elegant, and spacious (Sb-€93, Db-€108, sumptuous Sb or Db suite-€135, extra bed-€20, 10 percent less Nov–March, cash only, Vám utca 6, Budapest I, tel. 1/214-1906, fax 1/214-1907, www .hotelastra.hu, hotelastra@euroweb.hu).

$$$ Carlton Hotel, with 95 small rooms, is all business and no personality. But the location—where the Castle Hill funicular meets the Chain Bridge—is handy for getting to both Buda and Pest (Sb-€90, Db-€105, extra bed-€21, prices 15 percent lower Nov–March, non-smoking rooms, elevator, Internet access, parking garage-€12/day, Apor Péter utca 3, Budapest I, tel. 1/224-0999, fax 1/224-0990, www.carltonhotel.hu, carltonhotel@t-online.hu).

$ Hotel Papillon is farther north, in a forgettable residential area a 10-minute walk past Moszkva tér. It's a cheery little place with 30 homey, pastel rooms, a garden with a tiny pool, and great prices (Sb-€43, Db-€54, 25 percent less Nov–March, 10 percent more for air-con, tram #4 or #6 from Moszkva tér to Mechwart stop, Rózsahegy utca 3B, tel. 1/212-4750, fax 1/212-4003, www .hotelpapillon.hu, rozsahegy@t-online.hu).

Castle Hill
Romantics often like calling Castle Hill home. The next three hotels share Holy Trinity Square (Szentháromság tér) with Matthias Church. They couldn't be closer to the Castle Hill sights, but they're in a tourist zone—dead at night—and less convenient to Pest than other listings.

$$$ Burg Hotel, with 26 rooms, is simply efficient: concrete, spacious, and comfy, with a professional staff. You'll find more conveniently located hotels for less money elsewhere, but if you simply *must* stay in a modern hotel across the street from Matthias Church, this is it (Sb-€105, Db-€115, Db apartment-€134, extra bed-€39, 10 percent discount with this book in 2007 unless they're very busy, 30 percent cheaper for 3-night stays, prices 15 percent less Nov–March, no elevator, entirely non-smoking, top-floor rooms are extremely long, Szentháromság tér 7–8, Budapest I, tel. 1/212-0269, fax 1/212-3970, www.burghotelbudapest.com, hotel .burg@mail.datanet.hu).

$$$ Budapest Hilton is a 322-room landmark—the first big Western hotel in town, back in the gloomy days of communism. Today it remains the top of the top, offering a complete escape from Hungary and a chance to be surrounded by rich tourists mostly from Japan, Germany, and the United States (rack rates: Sb/Db-€220, you'll usually pay closer to Db-€120 in slower times, check for deals online—best rates are for 3-week advance booking with full pre-payment, €30 more for Danube-view rooms, breakfast-€25, elevator, Hess András tér 1–3 on Castle Hill next to Matthias Church, tel. 1/889-6000, fax 1/889-6644, www.budapest.hilton.com,

Buda Hotels and Restaurants

1. Hotel Victoria
2. art'otel
3. Hotel Astra
4. Carlton Hotel
5. To Hotel Papillon
6. Burg Hotel
7. Budapest Hilton
8. Hotel Kulturinnov
9. Tabáni Terasz Restaurant
10. Horgásztanya Restaurant
11. Café Alexandre Dumas
12. Batthyány Tér Eateries & Topclean Laundry
13. Soho Coffee Co. & Internet

reservations.budapest@hilton.com).

$$ Hotel Kulturinnov, run by the Hungarian Culture Foundation and sweetly managed by Judit, is tucked away in the upper floor of a big building that feels more like a museum than a hotel. The 16 rooms are basic, with old, frumpy furnishings. But it's still a great value for the location—or for anywhere in central Budapest (Sb-€64, Db-€80, Tb-€100, extra bed-€20, 25 percent less Nov–March, elevator, through the lobby and upstairs at Szentháromság tér 6, Budapest I, tel. 1/224-8102, fax 1/375-1886, www.mka.hu, hotel@mka.hu).

EATING

Dining in Budapest is surprisingly expensive (by Eastern European standards). With the recent influx of tourists, and the resulting increase in prices, most Budapesters can't afford to eat out in the areas where you'll be spending your time. If you really want to eat local-style, head for the big shopping malls (like the WestEnd City Center near Nyugati Station, or Mammut near Moszkva tér). There, you can truly dine with the Budapesters...at T.G.I. Friday's and McDonald's, just like back home.

In lieu of actual "local" restaurants, I've sniffed out a few good options with an at least partly local clientele—as well as a few memorable, decidedly touristy places that are just plain fun. I've focused on eateries serving traditional Hungarian fare (see page 397), but also included a few international and ethnic alternatives.

Pest

I've listed these options by neighborhood, for easy reference with your sightseeing.

Central Pest (Belváros), near Váci utca

When you ask natives about good places to eat on Váci utca, they just roll their eyes. Budapesters know that only rich tourists who don't know better would throw their money away on the relatively bad food and service along this high-profile pedestrian drag. But wander a few blocks off the tourist route, and you'll discover alternatives with fair prices and better food.

Centrál Kávéház, while famous as a grand, old-fashioned café, is also one of Budapest's best spots for a central, characteristic meal. Since it's across the street from the university library, it's popular with students and professors. Choose between the lively, vast downstairs, or the more refined upstairs dining room—both featuring elegant, early-1900s ambience (small but filling 1,200–1,400-Ft "Zóna" plates, larger 2,000–3,000-Ft main dishes, read the fun history in the menu, daily 8:00–24:00, Károlyi Mihály utca 9, Budapest V, tel. 1/266-2110).

Great Market Hall: At the far south end of Váci utca, you can eat a quick lunch on the upper floor of the Great Market Hall (Nagyvásárcsarnok). The stalls along the right side of the building offer the lowest prices, lots of choices, a sense of adventure, and the most local atmosphere. Grab a bar stool or you'll stand while you munch. Produce and butcher stands line the main floor, and it's easy to miss the big, modern grocery store in the basement (the end nearest Váci utca). For an actual (but expensive) restaurant in the market, **Fakanál Étterem** ("Wooden Spoon Cafeteria")—a glassed-in, sit-down cafeteria above the main entrance—is good, with real tables and English on the blackboard. It's frequented mostly by tourists (and priced accordingly), but it's a convenient spot for heavy, traditional Hungarian food (most main dishes 2,000–3,000 Ft, Mon–Fri 10:00–17:00, Sat 10:00–14:00, closed Sun, Fővám körút 1–3, Budapest IX, M3: Kálvin tér).

Ráday Utca: Ráday utca is Budapest's "restaurant row." While tourists foolishly blow their budgets a few blocks away on Váci utca, Budapesters dine on good food at decent prices in trendy, inventive eateries and pubs. This is one of the hottest bits of central Budapest, and while the similar scene at Franz Liszt Square is becoming more touristy, locals still outnumber visitors on Ráday utca. It's worth going out of your way to come here and simply wander, choosing the place that looks best. Just take the M3 Metro line to Kálvin tér Metro stop—a three-minute walk from the Great Market Hall—and stroll south.

Danube Promenade: The riverbank facing the castle is lined with hotel restaurants and permanently moored restaurant boats. You'll find bad service, mediocre food, mostly tourists, and sky-high prices...but the atmosphere and people-watching are marvelous. **Spoon,** a boat in front of the InterContinental Hotel next to the Chain Bridge, is your best Danube dining option. This hip, upscale place offers pricey, elaborately prepared European and Asian cuisine (2,500–5,000-Ft main dishes). Choose between a dressy candlelit dining room or outdoor tables above decks. The bathrooms—Budapest's most scenic—are a must, even if you don't have to go. If you're going to pay too much to eat along the river, you might as well do it here (daily 12:00–24:00, often booked for special events—call ahead to be sure it's open and to reserve a riverside table, Vigadó tér, dock #3, tel. 1/411-0933, www.spooncafe.hu).

On or near Andrássy Út

Franz Liszt Square (Liszt Ferenc Tér): Franz Liszt Square, on the most interesting stretch of Andrássy út, has sprouted a stylish cluster of yuppie restaurants, many with outdoor seating (lively on a balmy summer evening). This is *the* place for Budapesters to see and be seen...but only for the ones who can afford it (most main dishes hover around 2,500–3,000 Ft). Take the Metro to Oktogon and follow your nose (more good options on Hajós utca and Nagymező utca near the Opera House). My favorite Liszt Square eatery, **Menza** (the old communist word for "School Cafeteria"), wins the "Best Design" award. Recycling 1970s furniture and an orange-and-brown color scheme, it's a postmodern parody of an old communist café. Half kitschy-retro, half brand-new-feeling, it's got more personality than all the other Franz Liszt Square eateries combined. When locals come in here, they can only chuckle and say, "Yep. This is how it was." With tasty and well-priced updated Hungarian cuisine, embroidered leather-bound menus, breezy jazz on the soundtrack, and indoor or outdoor seating, it's a memorable spot (1,400–2,900-Ft main dishes, daily 10:00–24:00, halfway up Andrássy út at Liszt Ferenc tér 2, tel. 1/413-1482, www .menza.co.hu).

Indian: **Shalimar** hides in a musty cellar in a dreary neighborhood two blocks beyond the end of Franz Liszt Square. Everything about this place is unexceptional...except the food. The restaurant—packed with young locals who know they're on to something good—is my number-one place in Eastern Europe for a curry-and-naan fix (1,700–2,500-Ft main dishes, daily 12:00–16:00 & 18:00–24:00, reservations smart for dinner, Dob utca 50, tel. 1/352-0297).

~~*Cheap Sandwiches:*~~ **Duran Szendvics,** a cheery little eatery, is reminiscent of Scandinavian open-faced sandwich shops, where a dozen or so tempting little treats are displayed. Two sandwiches and a drink make a quick and healthy meal for about $3 (they'll also box things to go for a classy picnic). Look at the window outside before ordering. This is your chance to try caviar cheaply (120–150 Ft per sandwich, Mon–Fri 8:00–18:00, Sat 9:00–13:00, Sun 8:00–12:00; near Basilica, Postal Museum, and Deák tér Metro stop at the start of Andrássy út; Bajcsy-Zsilinszky utca 7, tel. 1/267-9624). Similar places are popping up all over the city.

Restaurant Művészinas is expensive, fancy, and central, serving traditional Hungarian and international cuisine. Its 1920s and 1930s atmosphere is plush yet homey—like the candlelit living room of an artist who happens to be playing his favorite jazz on the phonograph (2,000–4,200-Ft main dishes, daily 12:00–24:00, always several good vegetarian options, reservations wise, 100 yards from Deák tér Metro stop, Bajcsy-Zsilinszky út 9, Budapest VI, tel. 1/268-1439).

Bohémtanya ("Bohemian Pub") serves inexpensive, hearty Hungarian food in a humble restaurant actually frequented by some locals, huddled around their beers in a smoke-filled room (and neatly segregated from the tourists in the non-smoking room). The service can be stand-offish, the chef seems to have a thing for pigs' brains, and the food's pretty basic...but that's the point (1,300–2,000-Ft main dishes, daily 12:00–23:00, just up the street next to Duran Szendvics and Művészinas at Paulai Ede utca 6, Budapest VI, tel. 1/267-3504).

Near City Park

These three touristy eateries cluster around the end of the lake behind the Millennium Monument in City Park. All are open for both lunch and dinner. The first one is Budapest's best-known, fanciest splurge; the other two are more reasonable and casual, but still pretty pricey.

Gundel Restaurant has been the dining spot for VIPs and celebrities since 1894. The place is an institution—President Bill Clinton ate here. Pope John Paul II didn't, but when his people called out for dinner, they called Gundel. The elegant main room is decorated with fine 19th-century Hungarian paintings and an Art Deco flair, while the more casual outdoor garden terrace is leafy and delightful. The Hungarian cuisine flirts with sophisticated international influences (4,000–10,000-Ft main courses, 17,000–36,000-Ft fixed-price meals). At lunch, choose from the same pricey à la carte items, or opt for a more affordable fixed-price meal (3,300–4,300 Ft). Sunday brunch is popular here (5,400 Ft, served 11:30–14:30). Reserve ahead for dinner, and request near or far from the live "Gypsy" music (open daily 12:00–15:00 & 18:30–24:00, music nightly, Állatkerti út 2, tel. 1/468-4040, www.gundel.hu). The dress code is formal: Jackets are required for dinner in the dining room, but not for lunch, for Sunday brunch, or if you sit outside. (You can borrow a free jacket at the door if you travel like me. Ties and dresses are not required.)

Robinson, stranded on an island in City Park's lake, is a hip, playful, mellow theme restaurant. With island-castaway ambience and more outdoor seating than indoor, it's made to order for lazing away a sunny afternoon at the park. The upstairs terrace café has a long menu of ice-cream treats, coffee drinks, and light 1,500–2,000-Ft salads and sandwiches (daily in summer 11:00–23:00). The downstairs terrace and elegant, glassed-in dining room feature pricey Mediterranean and Hungarian cuisine (2,500–6,000-Ft main dishes, daily 12:00–16:00 & 18:00–24:00, reserve ahead and ask for lakefront seating, Városligeti tó, tel. 1/422-0222, www.robinsonrestaurant.hu).

Bagolyvár ("Owl's Castle") is managed and staffed entirely by women. Owned by the Gundel people, it has lower prices and a strict focus on traditional Hungarian cuisine. Riding Gundel's coattails, this restaurant's quality has gone a bit downhill lately, but it's still a reasonable choice for Hungarian dishes near the park

(1,800–4,000-Ft main dishes, 2,500–3,500-Ft fixed-price meals, daily 12:00–22:30, reservations smart, around the corner from Gundel at Állatkerti út 2, tel. 1/468-3110, www.bagolyvar.com).

Buda

Eateries on Castle Hill are generally overpriced and touristy—as with Váci utca, locals never eat here. Instead, they head down the hill into the Víziváros (Water Town) neighborhood.

Víziváros

My first listing is just beyond the southern tip of Castle Hill, near the Elisabeth Bridge. The rest are in the heart of Víziváros, right between Castle Hill and the river. For specific locations, see the map on page 473.

Tabáni Terasz offers delicious, well-priced food between the castle and the big, white Elisabeth Bridge. The historic 250-year-old building has several seating options: in a cozy, classy drawing-room interior; on a terrace out front; or in the inner courtyard (1,800–3,100-Ft main dishes, daily 12:00–24:00, by the single-spired yellow church at Arpód utca 10, tel. 1/201-1086).

Horgásztanya ("Fishermen's Pub"), with a confused fisherman suspended from the ceiling, is cheaper and more local than most of my listings. Natives go here for reliable, unpretentious Hungarian food (1,000–2,000-Ft main dishes, daily 12:00–23:00, lots of fish on the menu, a block up from Danube at corner of Halász utca and Fő utca, Fő utca 27, Budapest I, tel. 1/212-3780).

Café Alexandre Dumas—an airy, modern, glassy eatery on the ground floor of the French Institute—is a good option for Internet access and 500–1,000-Ft salads and sandwiches. Ideal for a quick and inexpensive meal in Víziváros, this place is filled with students...and their cigarette smoke. Escape to the outdoor terrace, with fine river views (Mon–Fri 8:00–21:00, Sat 9:00–13:00, closed Sun, Fő utca 17).

Batthyány Tér: This bustling square—the transportation hub for Víziváros—is overlooked by a recently renovated, late-19th-century market hall (today housing a supermarket downstairs and a handy laundry upstairs—see page 414). Several worthwhile, affordable eateries cluster around this square (all open long hours daily). Survey your options before settling in. **Nagyi Palacsintázója** (roughly, "Granny's Pancakes")—just to the right of the market hall entrance—serves up cheap and tasty crêpes *(palacsinta)* to a local crowd (200–300-Ft savory crêpes, 100–200-Ft sweet crêpes, convenient 800–1,000-Ft combo-meals, ask for English menu, Batthyány tér 5). As you face the market hall, go up the street that runs along its left side (Markovits Iván utca) to reach a few more good eateries: About a block ahead on the left is **Coyote**

Farkasodú, with heavy self-serve dishes, including hamburgers and deep-fried Hungarian specialties (point to what you want). Across the street, and a culinary world away, is **Éden Vegetarian Restaurant,** another self-service, point-and-shoot place—this one more like a salad bar. And around the back side of the market hall is **Bratwursthäusle/Kolbászda,** a fun little beer hall/beer garden with specialties and blue-and-white checkerboard decor from Bavaria.

Cafés and Pastry Shops (Kávéház and Cukrászda)

Budapest once had a thriving café culture, like Vienna's. But realizing that these neighborhood living rooms were breeding grounds for dissidents, the communists closed the cafés or converted them into *esszpresszós* (with uncomfortable stools instead of easy chairs) or *bisztros* (stand-up fast-food joints with no chairs at all). Today Budapest's café scene is slowly coming back to life. Unless otherwise noted, these places serve only coffee and cakes—not light meals.

On Vörösmarty Square: **Gerbeaud** (zhehr-BOH) isn't just a café—it's a landmark, the most famous restaurant in Budapest. Aside from coffee and pastries, you can also get a sandwich, salad, or other light meals. It's touristy, but central, historic, and great for people-watching (650–750-Ft coffee drinks, 600–900-Ft cakes, 1,300–3,000-Ft salads and sandwiches, daily 9:00–21:00, on Vörösmarty tér, tel. 1/429-9000). *not main entrace. side .*

Two Blocks up from Váci utca: **Centrál Kávéház** is the Budapest café that best recaptures the early-1900s ambience, with elegant cakes and coffees, loaner newspapers, and a management that encourages loitering (daily 8:00–24:00, Károlyi Mihály utca 9, Budapest V, tel. 1/266-2110). This is also a great spot for a meal (see page 474).

Near Ferenciek tere: **Jégbüfé** is where Pest urbanites get their quick, cheap, stand-at-a-counter fix of coffee and cakes. And for those feeling nostalgic for the communist days, little has changed here. First, choose what you want at the counter. Then try to explain it to the cashier across the aisle. Finally, take your receipt back to the appropriate part of the counter (figure out the four different zones: coffee, soft drinks, ice cream, cakes), trade your receipt for your goodie, go to the bar, and enjoy it standing up (Mon–Sat 7:00–21:30, Wed until 20:30, Sun 8:00–21:30, Ferenciek tere 10). Now...back to work.

Across from the Opera House: **Müvész Kávéház** is a classic coffeehouse with 19th-century elegance, indoor or outdoor seating, a wide variety of tasty cakes, and a convenient location (daily 9:00–23:45, Andrássy út 29, tel. 1/352-1337).

In Buda's Víziváros Neighborhood: **Soho Coffee Company** is a taste of Seattle with a Hungarian accent, combining good American-style lattes, cozy stay-awhile atmosphere, Internet access (500 Ft/hr), and a jazz soundtrack (Mon–Fri 8:00–21:00, Sat–Sun 9:00–21:00, Fő utca 25).

TRANSPORTATION CONNECTIONS

Budapest has three main stations (*pályaudvar*, or *pu.* for short): Keleti (Eastern), Nyugati (Western), and Déli (Southern). There's no telling which station each train will use, especially since it can change from year to year—always confirm carefully which station your train leaves from. For general rail information in Hungary, call 1/461-5400; for information about international trains, call 1/461-5500.

From Budapest by Train to: Vienna (that's *Bécs* in Hungarian, 6/day direct, 3 hrs), **Bratislava** (that's *Pozsony* in Hungarian, 4/day direct, more with transfers, 2.25–4 hrs), **Prague** (every 2 hours, 7–8.5 hrs, 1 direct night train, 9 hrs), **Kraków** (1 direct night train/day with early arrival in Kraków, 11 hrs; otherwise transfer in Katowice, Poland, or Břeclav, Czech Republic; 9–10 hrs), **Ljubljana** (2/day direct, 7.75–8.5 hrs, no convenient night train), **Munich** (1/day direct, 7.5 hrs; plus 1 direct night train/day, 10 hrs; otherwise transfer in Regensburg, Germany, or Vienna), **Berlin** (3/day direct, 13 hrs; plus 1 direct night train/day, 14 hrs), **Zagreb** (2/day direct, 5 or 7 hrs), **Eger** (5/day direct, 2 hrs, more with transfer in Füzesabony), **Szentendre** (4–7/hr, 40 min on suburban HÉV train, leaves from Batthyány tér), **Visegrád** (trains arrive at Nagymaros-Visegrád station, across the river—take shuttle boat to Visegrád; hourly, 1 hr), and **Esztergom** (hourly, 1.5 hrs). Note that Nagymaros (the Visegrád station) and Esztergom are on opposite sides of the river—and on different train lines.

By Boat: In the summer, Mahart runs daily high-speed hydrofoils up the Danube to Vienna. While this is not particularly scenic, and slower than the train, it's a fun alternative for nautical types. The boat leaves Budapest May–Oct daily at 9:00 and arrives in Vienna at 15:20 (Vienna to Budapest: 9:00–14:30). The trip costs €79 one-way. On any of these boats, you can also stop in the Slovak capital, Bratislava. To confirm times and prices, and to buy tickets, contact Mahart (Budapest tel. 1/484-4010, www.mahartpassnave.hu).

THE DANUBE BEND

(Dunakanyar)

The Danube, which begins as a trickle in Germany's Black Forest, becomes the Mississippi River of Central Europe as it flows east through Vienna, then makes a sweeping right turn—called the Danube Bend—south towards Budapest, Belgrade, and the Black Sea. Three river towns, north of Budapest on the Danube Bend, offer a convenient day-trip getaway for urbanites who want to commune with nature.

Hungarians sunbathe and swim along the banks of the Danube, or hike in the rugged hills that rise up from the river. This is also one of Hungary's most historic stretches—for centuries, Hungarian kings ruled not from Buda or Pest, but from Visegrád and Esztergom.

Closest to Budapest is Szentendre, whose colorful, storybook-cute Baroque center is packed with tourists. The ruins of a mighty castle high on a hill watch over the town of Visegrád. Esztergom, birthplace of Hungary's first Christian king, has the country's biggest and most important church. All of this is within a one-hour drive of the capital, and also reachable (up to a point) by public transportation.

Planning Your Time

Szentendre is the easiest Danube Bend destination—just a quick suburban-train (HÉV) ride away, it can be done in a half-day. Visegrád and Esztergom are more difficult to reach by public transportation; both require a substantial walk from the train or bus stop to the town's major sight.

Don't try to see all three towns in one day by public transportation—focus on one or two. Take a tour, rent a car, or hire a driver

The Danube Bend

to see all three (for recommended drivers, see "Drivers" on page 414 of the Budapest chapter). With a car, do the Danube Bend this way: 9:00–Leave Budapest; 9:30–Arrive at Szentendre and see the town; 12:00–Leave Szentendre; 12:30–Lunch in Visegrád; 13:30–Tour Visegrád Royal Palace and Citadel; 15:30–Leave Visegrád, 16:00–Visit Esztergom Basilica, 17:00–Head back to Budapest. With extra time, or if you enjoy folk architecture, add a visit to the Hungarian Open-Air Folk Museum ("Skanzen") near Szentendre.

If you're driving between Budapest and Vienna (or Bratislava), the Danube Bend towns are a fine way to break up the journey, but seeing all three en route makes for a very long day. Again, choose one or two.

Getting Around the Danube Bend

Going north from Budapest, the three towns line up along the same road on the west side of the Danube—Szentendre, Visegrád, Esztergom—each spaced about 15 miles apart.

By Car: It couldn't be easier. Get on road #11 going north out of Buda, and it'll take you through each of the three towns—the road bends with the Danube. As you approach Szentendre, watch for signs for *Centrum Szentendre* to branch off to the right, toward the old center and the river promenade.

Returning from Esztergom to Budapest, consider "cutting the bend." Road #10 is most direct, but can have heavy traffic on weekdays. The smaller road farther north (by way of Pilisszentkereszt) is slower and windier, but more scenic and less crowded.

By Boat: From early April to late October, Budapest-based Mahart runs boats and hydrofoils up the Danube Bend. Various options connect Budapest and the three towns, ranging from slow excursion ships (1.5 hrs to Szentendre, 2.5–3.5 hrs to Visegrád, 5.5 hrs to Esztergom) to speedy hydrofoils (summer weekends only, 1 hr to Visegrád, 2 hrs to Esztergom). Boats generally don't run in winter (Nov–March). Check schedules and buy tickets at Mahart in Budapest (dock near Vigadó tér in Pest, tel. 1/484-4010, www.mahartpassnave.hu).

By Train: The three towns are on three separate train lines. Szentendre is truly handy by train, while Esztergom and Visegrád are less convenient.

Getting to **Szentendre** is a breeze by train—the HÉV, Budapest's suburban rail, zips you right there (catch train at Batthyány tér Metro station, 4–7/hr, 40 min each way, last train returns from Szentendre around 23:00).

The nearest train station to **Visegrád** is actually across the river in Nagymaros (this station is called "Nagymaros-Visegrád"; don't get off at the station called simply "Nagymaros"). From the station, you'll walk five minutes to the river and take a ferry across to Visegrád (see "Arrival in Visegrád," page 487). Trains run hourly between Nagymaros-Visegrád and Nyugati Station in Budapest (1 hr).

To **Esztergom,** trains run hourly from Budapest's Nyugati Station (1.5 hrs), but the Esztergom train station is a 45-minute walk from the basilica.

By Bus: Buses are the best way to hop between the three towns. They're as quick as the train if you're coming from Budapest, but can be standing-room only. All buses to the Danube Bend leave from Budapest's Árpád híd bus station (by the M3 Metro station of the same name). There are two main routes. The river route (roughly hourly, more frequent during weekday rush hours) runs from Budapest along the Danube through Szentendre (30 min) and

Visegrád (80 min), then past Esztergom Basilica to the Esztergom bus station (2 hrs). The inland route goes over the hills and through the town of Piliscsaba on the way to the Esztergom bus station (every 15–30 min, 80 min, last bus back leaves Esztergom 22:00). Buses make many stops en route, so you'll need to pay attention for your stop (ask driver or other passengers for help).

By Tour from Budapest: If you want to see all three towns in one day, don't have a car, and don't want to shell out for a private driver, a bus tour is the most convenient way to go. All of the companies are about the same (all three towns in 9–10 hrs, including lunch and shopping stops, plus return by boat, for around 18,000 Ft); look for fliers at the TI or in your hotel's lobby.

Szentendre

The old town of Szentendre (SEHN-tehn-dreh, "St. Andrew" in English, pop. 23,000) rises gently from the Danube, a postcard-pretty village with a twisty Mediterranean street plan filled with Austrian Baroque houses. Szentendre's old center rivals Budapest's Castle Hill as the most touristy spot in Hungary. It promises a taste of Hungarian village life without having to stray far from Budapest...but it sometimes feels like too many people had the same idea.

In addition to attracting tourists, Szentendre is also where Budapesters bring their wives or girlfriends for that special weekend lunch. The town has a long tradition as an artists' colony, and it still has more than its share of museums and galleries. Venture off the souvenir-choked, tourist-clogged main streets and you'll soon have quiet back lanes under colorful Baroque steeples all to yourself.

Tourist Information
The TI is along the tourist route between the station and the main square (Dumtsa Jenő utca 22, just by the stream, tel. 26/317-965, www.szentendre.hu).

Arrival in Szentendre
The combined **train/HÉV and bus station** is at the southern edge of town. To reach the town center from the station, go through the pedestrian underpass at the head of the train tracks. This funnels you onto the small Kossuth Lajos utca, which leads in 10 minutes to the main square. (A handy map of town is posted by the head of the tracks.) Some **boats** arrive right near the main square (including a convenient summer express boat from Budapest), but most come to a pier about a 15-minute walk north of the center. After

you get off the boat, take the first path to your left; stay on this, and it'll lead you straight ahead into town.

SIGHTS

▲**Main Square (Fő Tér)**—Szentendre's top sight is the town itself. Start at the main square, Fő tér. Take a close look at the cross, erected in 1763 to give thanks for surviving the plague. Notice the Cyrillic lettering. After the Ottomans were forced out of Hungary, this town was rebuilt primarily by Serbs who had fled those same Ottomans down south. Look at the very narrow alleyways around the square. Mediterranean towns often have walls close together to create shade in the hot sun. Even though Hungary has a milder climate, old habits die hard: The Serbs built the town in that style anyway. Various minor sights and museums line the lanes that branch off this square.

Just up Alkotmány utca from the square, the tallest of Szentendre's church spires belongs to the red-painted **Serbian Orthodox cathedral,** with a fine iconostasis (partition with icons) inside, and an icon collection in the attached museum (500 Ft, Tue–Sun 10:00–18:00, closed Mon).

Leave the square on Görög utca and take your first right to find the **Margaret Kovács Museum** (Kovács Margit Múzeum), dedicated to a local artist (1902–1977) famous for whimsical, wide-eyed pottery sculptures based on Hungarian folktales and biblical themes (700 Ft, Tue–Sun 9:00–17:00, closed Mon, Vastagh György utca 1).

Between the square and the TI, you'll find the **Marzipan Museum**—a candy and ice-cream store whose upper floor displays marzipan models of the Hungarian Parliament, the *turul* bird, the Muppets, Michael Jackson, and much more. It's fun for kids, but skippable for adults (shop free, upper floor 400 Ft, daily May–Sept 9:00–19:00, Oct–April 10:00–18:00, Dumtsa Jenő utca 12, tel. 26/311-931).

Enjoy a stroll through town. Head off to the back streets (try the hill behind the square) and you'll be surprised at how quickly you find yourself alone with Szentendre.

▲**Hungarian Open-Air Folk Museum (Szabadtéri Néprajzi Múzeum, a.k.a. Skanzen)**—Three miles northwest of Szentendre is an open-air museum featuring examples of traditional Hungarian architecture from all over the country. As with similar museums throughout Europe, these aren't replicas—each building was taken apart at its original location, transported piece by piece, and reassembled here. The museum is huge and spread out, so a thorough visit could take several hours. The admission price includes a map in English, and the museum shop sells a more comprehensive

English guidebook (650–800 Ft depending on special exhibits, April–Oct Tue–Sun 9:00–17:00, closed Mon and Nov–March, last entry 30 min before closing, Sztaravodai út, tel. 26/502-500, www .skanzen.hu).

Buses from the Szentendre station leave for Skanzen every 60–90 minutes (100 Ft, departs from platform 7, 12-min trip, no buses 12:00–14:00 on weekends). A **taxi** to the museum should cost no more than 2,000 Ft; the TI can call one for you.

SLEEPING

(€1 = $1.20, 200 Ft = about $1, country code: 36, area code: 26)

In recent years, the delightful little burg of Szentendre has become a bedroom community for nearby Budapest. I don't advise staying here if Budapest is your main interest—it takes too long to get into the city. But if you must stay here, these two places rent acceptable second-story rooms along the Danube embankment just north of the center.

Corner Panzió has six cozy, woody rooms. Prices rise in the summer, when they turn on the air-conditioning (June–Sept: Sb/Db-€40, breakfast-€4; Oct–May: Sb/Db-€30, breakfast-€2; cash only, Dunakorzó 4, tel. & fax 26/301-524, www.radoczy.hu, nikov@freemail.hu).

Centrum Panzió has eight pleasant-enough rooms with a dark red color scheme (Db-€49, includes breakfast, cash only, air-con, Bogdányi utca 15, at corner of Dunakorzó, tel. & fax 26/302-500, hotel.centrum@t-online.hu).

Visegrád

Visegrád (VEE-sheh-grahd, Slavic for "High Castle," pop. 1,600) is a small village next to the remains of two major-league castles: a hilltop citadel and a royal riverside palace.

At this strategic site overlooking the river, there has been—since Roman times—a citadel atop the steep hill. When Károly Róbert (Charles Robert), from the French Anjou dynasty, became Hungary's first non-Magyar king in 1323, he was so unpopular with the nobles in Buda that he had to set up court in Visegrád, where he built a new residential palace down closer to the Danube. Later, King Mátyás Corvinus—notorious for his penchant for Renaissance excess—ruled from Buda but made Visegrád his summer home, and turned the riverside palace into what some called a "paradise on earth." Mátyás knew how to party; during his time here, red marble fountains flowed with wine.

In memory of these grand times, **Hotel Visegrád** today runs a Renaissance-themed restaurant, with period cookware, food, costumed waitstaff, and live lute music—just the spot for Danube Bend tour groups (can't miss it, by the palace).

Today, both citadel and palace are but a shadow of their former splendor. The citadel was left to crumble after the Hapsburg reoccupation of Hungary in 1686, while the palace was covered by a mudslide during the Ottoman occupation, and is still being excavated. The citadel is more interesting, but difficult to reach by public transport. Non-drivers who don't want to make the steep hike to the citadel, and are in too much of a hurry to sort through the taxi and bus options, should skip this town.

ORIENTATION

The town of Visegrád is basically a wide spot in the riverside road, squeezed between the hills and the riverbank. At Visegrád's main intersection (coming from Szentendre/Budapest), the cross road leads to the left through the heart of the village, then hairpins up the hills to the citadel. To the right is the dock for the ferry to Nagymaros (home to the closest train station, called Nagymaros-Visegrád—see "Arrival in Visegrád").

The town has two sights. The less interesting riverside Royal Palace is a 15-minute walk downriver (towards Szentendre/Budapest) from the village center. The hilltop citadel, high above the village, is the focal point of a larger recreational area best explored by car.

Tourist Information

The **Visegrád Tours** travel agency at the village crossroads is not an official TI, but does have transport schedules posted in the window, sells maps, and hands out a few free leaflets (daily April–Oct 8:00–17:30, Nov–March 10:00–16:00, Rév utca 15, tel. 26/398-160).

Arrival in Visegrád

Train travelers arrive across the river at the Nagymaros-Visegrád station (don't get off at the station called simply "Nagymaros"). Walk five minutes to the river and catch the ferry to Visegrád, which lands near the village's main crossroads (300 Ft, hourly, usually in sync with the train, last ferry 20:45). Visegrád's most convenient **bus stop** is at the main crossroads, but there's also a stop a little downstream, by the river boat dock. This **dock,** near the Royal Palace and Hotel Visegrád, is where boats from Budapest stop. To reach the village center from the dock, follow the paved riverside footpath 15 minutes upriver (towards Esztergom).

SIGHTS

▲**Visegrád Citadel (Fellegvár)**—The remains of Visegrád's hilltop citadel are fun to explore. Scramble across the ramparts,

try your hand with a bow and arrow, or pose with a bird of prey perched on your arm. See fun wax sculptures enjoying a medieval feast—and demonstrating the collection of torture devices. Only a few exhibits have English labels, but you can borrow the English audioguide. You can also some-times find a small English book about the citadel. At the top, you have commanding views over the Danube Bend—which, of course, is exactly why they built it here (900 Ft, mid-March–mid-Oct daily 10:00–18:00; mid-Oct–mid-March Sat–Sun 10:00–16:00 in good weather only, usually closed Mon–Fri; last entry 30 min before closing, tel. 26/398-101, www .visegrad.hu).

Around the citadel is a **recreational area** that includes three restaurants, a picnic area, a luge and toboggan run, a network of hiking paths, a Waldorf school, and a children's nature education center and campground. By the luge run and walkable from the citadel, the **Nagy-Villám restaurant** is elegant, with breathtaking views from the best tables (April–Oct daily 12:00–22:00, closed Nov–March, tel. 26/398-070). A bit farther away, the simpler **Mogyoróhegy restaurant** is in an early building by Organic archi-tecture pioneer Imre Makovecz, who also designed the striking school gymnasium in Visegrád village—white and brown, with a row of 12 spikes on the roof (restaurant open mid-April–Sept daily 9:00–20:00, closed Oct–mid-April, tel. 26/398-237). For more on Makovecz, see page 503. Only drivers can reach the **picnic area** (called Telgárthy-rét), in a shady valley with paths and waterfalls.

Getting to Visegrád Citadel: To **drive** to the citadel, simply follow *Fellegvár* signs down the village's main street and up into the hills. To get to the citadel from the town center without a car, you have three options:

1. **Hike.** Buy a map at the Visegrád Tours office and figure on 40 steep minutes from the village center.

2. Take the **taxi service** called "City Bus." The minivan trip up and back costs 2,000 Ft total, no matter how many people ride along (ask at Visegrád Tours or call 26/397-372).

3. Take the **public bus** (200 Ft, April–Sept only, 2/day, catch from bus stop on Danube side of main road at the cross-roads, generally departs around 12:28 and 15:28 or 1 min earlier at

Royal Palace, reconfirm schedules in advance; this bus comes from Szentendre, where it departs about 45 min earlier).

Royal Palace (Király Palota)—Under King Mátyás Corvinus, this riverside ruin was one of Europe's most elaborate Renaissance palaces. During the Ottoman occupation, it was deserted and eventually buried by a mudslide. For generations, the palace's existence faded into legend, so its rediscovery in 1934 was a surprise. Today, the partially excavated remains are tourable; unfortunately, there's no English-language guidebook. Keep your eye out for the red marble fountain, which spouted wine for parties (500 Ft; mid-April–mid-Oct Tue–Sun 9:00–18:00, closed Mon; mid-Oct–mid-April Tue–Sun 9:00–16:00, closed Mon; tel. 26/398-026, www .visegradmuzeum.hu).

 # Esztergom

Esztergom (EHS-tehr-gohm, pop. 29,000) is an unassuming town with a big Suzuki factory. You'd never guess it was the first capital of Hungary—until you see the towering 19th-century Esztergom Basilica, built on the site where István (Stephen) I, Hungary's first Christian king, was crowned in A.D. 1000.

Arrival in Esztergom

Esztergom's **boat dock** is more convenient to the basilica than the bus or train stations are (can't miss the basilica as you disembark—hike on up). If arriving by **bus** from Visegrád, get off by the basilica, not at the bus station. (Buses taking the inland route from Budapest via Piliscsaba do not pass the basilica.) To reach the basilica on foot from the **train station,** allow at least 45 minutes. Continue in the same direction as the train tracks, and when the street forks, go straight along the residential Ady Endre utca. After a few minutes, you'll pass the bus station, from which it's 30 minutes farther to the basilica. Local buses run between the train station and the basilica roughly hourly. On Wednesdays and Fridays, an open-air market livens up the street between the bus station and the center.

If you happen to be on your way to Bratislava, there is also a handy train station across the river in **Štúrovo, Slovakia** (cross the border on foot as you cross the bridge).

SIGHTS

Esztergom Basilica

The basilica commemorates Hungary's entry into the fold of Western Christendom. It tops a hill a steep hike up from the center

Cardinal József Mindszenty
(1892–1975)

Mindszenty was a Catholic Church leader who spoke out aggressively against the communist government. In 1948, the communists arrested him and tortured him for 39 days. He was imprisoned in Budapest until the 1956 Uprising, when he was freed and took refuge in the US Embassy. There he stayed for 15 years, unable to leave for fear of being captured. (Many Catholic Americans remember praying for Cardinal Mindszenty every day when they were kids.) In 1971, he agreed to step down from his position, then fled to Austria.

On his deathbed in 1975, Mindszenty said that he did not want his body returned to Hungary as long as there was a single Russian soldier still stationed there. As the Iron Curtain was falling in 1989, Mindszenty emerged as an important hero to post-communist Hungarians, who wanted to bring his remains back to his homeland. But Mindszenty's secretary, in accordance with the Cardinal's final wishes, literally locked himself to the coffin—refusing to let the body be transported as long as any Soviet soldier remained in Hungary. In May 1991, when only a few Russians were still in Hungary, Mindszenty's remains were finally brought to the crypt in the Esztergom Basilica.

of town and the boat dock. The hill was once strongly fortified, and some ruins of its castle survive (housing a mediocre museum). The Neoclassical basilica, completed in 1869, was built on top of these remains. With a 330-foot-tall dome, this is the biggest church in Hungary. St. István was born in Esztergom, and on Christmas Day in the year 1000—shortly after marrying the daughter of the king of Bavaria and accepting Christianity—he was crowned here by the Pope (for more on St. István, see page 428).

Enter through the side door, which is on the left as you face the front of the basilica (free, daily 6:00–18:00). In the foyer, the stairway leading down to the right takes you to the crypt housing the remains of Cardinal József Mindszenty, revered for standing up to the communist government (200 Ft, daily 9:00–16:30, last entry 15 min before closing). The stairway leading up goes to the church tower (400 Ft).

Enter the cavernous **nave.** There are plenty of fancy tour-guide stats about this church—for example, the altarpiece supposedly has the biggest single-canvas painting in the world. But mostly, the sheer size of the church is what impresses visitors.

As you face the altar, find the chapel on the left before the transept. This Renaissance **Bakócz Chapel** actually predates the basilica by 350 years. When the basilica was built, they disassembled the chapel into 1,600 pieces and rebuilt it inside the new structure. The heads around the chapel's altar were defaced by Ottomans, who believed that only God—not sculptors—can create man.

The **treasury** is to the right of the main altar (500 Ft, daily 9:00–16:30). Though the collection is standard ecclesiastical stuff, there are some interesting models inside the entry: a big one showing off the even more ambitious original plans for the basilica complex; smaller ones of the frames of the basilica's wooden nave and metal dome; and yet another showing what Esztergom looked like in the early 16th century (notice the more modest church that stood where this basilica is today).

When you're finished in the basilica, head around to the back for a thrilling **Danube overview.** That's Štúrovo, Slovakia, across the river. The bridge connecting them was destroyed in World War II and rebuilt only recently. Before its reconstruction, no bridges spanned the Danube between Budapest and Bratislava.

Eating: A huge restaurant catering to tour groups is built into the fortifications underneath the basilica (enter from bus parking lot). On Batthyány Lajos utca, a block into the residential neighborhood across the street, are two smaller restaurants with garden seating: the Szent Tamás-hegyi Kisvendeglő and the more expensive Csülök Csárda.

EGER

You've probably never heard of the enchanting Back Door town of Eger (EH-gehr). It's a mid-sized city (pop. 70,000) in northern Hungary, the seat of a bishop and home to a small teacher-training college. Hungarians think proudly of Eger as the town that, against all odds, successfully held off the Ottoman advance into Europe in 1552. This stirring history makes Eger the mecca of Hungarian school field trips. If the town is known internationally for anything, it's for the surrounding wine region (its best-known red wine is Bull's Blood, or Egri Bikavér).

But don't let its lack of fame keep you away—in fact, that's part of Eger's charm. Rather than growing jaded from floods of American tourists, Egerites go about their daily routines amidst lovely Baroque buildings, watched over by one of Hungary's most important castles. Everything in Eger is painted with vibrant colors, and even the communist apartment blocks seem quaint. It all comes together to make Eger an ideal introduction to small-town Hungary.

Planning Your Time

Mellow Eger is just the spot to catch your breath in the middle of an intense itinerary. The town is worth a relaxing day on a trip between Kraków and Budapest, or as a side-trip from Budapest (possible in a day, but better as an overnight). The sights are few but fun, the ambience is great, and strolling is a must.

A perfect day in Eger begins with a browse through the colorful market and a low-key ramble on the castle ramparts. Then head to the college building called the Lyceum to visit the library

Eger

1. Panoráma Hotel
2. Imola Udvarház Rooms
3. Offi Ház Hotel & Rest.
4. Szent János Hotel
5. Senator Ház Hotel & Rest.
6. Dobó Vendégház Rooms
7. HBH Bajor Sörház Rest.
8. Elefanto Pizza
9. Palacsintavár Rest.
10. Szantofer Vendéglő Rest.
11. Rádi Bisztró
12. Dobós Cukrászda Pastries
13. Sárvári Cukrászda Pastries
14. Népműveszét Shop
15. Castle Entrance
16. Hist. Exhibition of Weapons
17. Palóc Folklore Museum

and astronomy museum, and climb up to the thrillingly low-tech camera obscura. Take in the 11:30 organ concert in the cathedral across the street from the Lyceum. In the afternoon, unwind on the square or, better yet, at the thermal bath. If you need more to do, consider a drive into the countryside (including visits to local vintners—get details at TI). Round out your day with a visit to Eger's touristy wine caves in the Sirens' Valley.

ORIENTATION

(area code: 36)
Eger Castle sits at the top of the town, hovering over Dobó Square (Dobó István tér). This main square is divided in half by the Eger Creek, which bisects the town. Two blocks west of Dobó Square is the main pedestrian drag, Széchenyi utca, where you'll find the Lyceum and the cathedral. A few blocks due south from the castle (follow Eger Creek) are Eger's various spas and baths.

Tourist Information

Eger's on-the-ball, eager-to-please TI (TourInform) is the most efficient place to get any Eger question answered. They give out a free brochure and town map, as well as piles of other brochures about the city and region. They can't book rooms, but they can help you find one—or anything else you're looking for (mid-June–mid-Sept Mon–Fri 9:00–18:00, Sat–Sun 9:00–13:00; mid-Sept–mid-June Mon–Fri 9:00–17:00, Sat 9:00–13:00, closed Sun; Bajcsy-Zsilinszky utca 9, tel. 36/517-715).

Arrival in Eger

By Train: Eger's tiny train station is a 20-minute walk south of the center. You can check your bag at the information desk (go through door marked *Information*). The closest ATM is at the Spar grocery store just up the street (turn left out of station, walk about 2 blocks, and look for red-and-white supermarket on your right; ATM is around front).

A **taxi** into the center will cost you about 1,000 Ft. To catch the **bus** toward the center, go straight out of the station, and when the road you're on veers right, cross it to get to the bus stop on the busier road above it. Bus #11, #12, or #14 cut about 10 minutes off the walk into town (180 Ft, buy ticket from driver; or 120 Ft if you buy it inside train station—ask for *helyijárat buszjegy*). Get off the bus when you see the big, yellow cathedral. To **walk** all the way, leave the station straight ahead, turn right with the road, and then continue straight ahead (on Deák Ferenc utca) until you run into

---

Eger Essentials

English	Hungarian	Pronounced
Main Square ("Dobó Square")	Dobó István tér	DOH-boh EESHT-vahn tehr
(Eger) Castle	(Egri) Vár	(EHG-ree) vahr
Market Hall	Csarnok	CHAWR-nohk
Bull's Blood (local blend of red wines)	Egri Bikavér	EH-gree BEE-kah-vehr

---

the cathedral. With your back to the cathedral entry, the main square is two blocks in front of you and to the left.

By Car: In this small town, most hotels will provide parking or help you find a lot. For a short visit, the most central lot is behind the department store on Dobó Square.

Getting Around Eger

Everything of interest in Eger is within walking distance, except maybe the Sirens' Valley wine caves—for these, catch a cab (starts at 220 Ft, then around 250 Ft/km; try City Taxi, tel. 36/555-555).

Helpful Hints

Language Barrier: Having fewer American visitors means that Egerites are not as likely to speak English as in more mainstream Eastern European destinations. (Consider it part of the adventure.) Eger does get lots of German tourists, so if you speak any German, it may come in handy. The TI is happy to act as a go-between with a Hungarian-only sight or business.

Tours: A hokey little **tourist train** leaves the main square at the top of each hour. It does a circuit around town, then heads out to the Sirens' Valley wine caves (500 Ft, 50-min trip). There are no organized town walking tours, but the TI can put you in touch with a **local guide** (figure 3,000 Ft/hr).

Internet Access: Internet cafés open and close all the time in Eger. Ask your hotelier for the latest option.

Shopping: For folk art, try the **Népműveszét** shop (Mon–Fri 9:00–17:00, Sat 9:00–13:00, closed Sun, Bajcsy-Zsilinszky utca 8, at intersection with Jókai utca).

Organ Concert: Daily from mid-May to mid-October, Hungary's second-biggest organ booms out a glorious 30-minute concert in the cathedral (500 Ft, Mon–Sat at 11:30, Sun at 12:45).

SIGHTS

▲▲Dobó Square (Dobó István tér)—Dobó Square is the heart of Eger. In most towns this striking, the main square is packed with postcard stalls and other tourist traps. Refreshingly, Eger's square seems mostly packed with Egerites. Ringed by breathtaking Baroque buildings, decorated with vivid sculptures depicting the city's noble past, and watched over by Eger's historic castle, this square is one of the most pleasant spots in Hungary.

The statue in the middle is **István Dobó,** the square's namesake and Eger's greatest hero, who defended the city—and all of Hungary—from an Ottoman invasion in 1552 (see his story in the sidebar). Next to Dobó is his co-commander, István Mekcsey. And right at their side is one of the brave women of Eger—depicted here throwing a pot down onto the attackers.

Use the square to orient yourself to the town. Behind the statue of Dobó is a bridge over the stream that bisects the city, and on the other side of the bridge is the charming **Little Dobó Square,** home to the town's best hotels (see "Sleeping," page 505). As you cross the bridge toward Little Dobó Square, look to the left and you'll see the northernmost Ottoman minaret in Europe—once part of a mosque (see page 501). Hovering above Little Dobó Square is Eger Castle.

Now face in the opposite direction, with Dobó's statue at your back. On your right is a handy department store. On your left,

dominating the square, is the picturesque pink Minorite Church; next to that is the town hall. The **monument** in front of you and on the left also commemorates the 1552 defense of Eger: one Egerite against two Ottoman soldiers, reminding us of the townspeople's bravery despite the odds. Straight ahead, two blocks beyond the end of the square, runs Széchenyi utca, Eger's main pedestrian drag. At the left end of Széchenyi utca are the cathedral and the Lyceum. To reach the TI, jog left at the end of this square, then right onto Bajcsy-Zsilinszky utca (TI one block ahead on right). To visit the Market Hall, leave Dobó Square to the right (on Zalár József utca, with department store on your right-hand side; you'll

István Dobó and the Siege of Eger

In the 16th century, Ottoman invaders swept into Hungary. They easily defeated a Hungarian army—in just two hours—at the notorious Battle of Mohács in 1526. When Buda and Pest fell to the Ottomans in 1541, all of Europe looked to Eger as the last line of defense. István Dobó and his second-in-command, István Mekcsey, were put in charge of Eger's forces. They prepared the castle (which still overlooks the square) for a siege and waited.

On September 11, 1552—after a summer spent conquering more than 30 other Hungarian fortresses on their march northward—40,000 Ottomans arrived in Eger. Only about 2,000 Egerites (soldiers, their wives, and their children) remained to protect their town. The Ottomans expected an easy victory, but the siege dragged on for 39 days. Eger's soldiers fought valiantly, and the women of Eger also joined the fray, pouring hot tar down on the Ottomans...everyone pitched in. A Hungarian officer named Gergely Bornemissza, sent to reinforce the people of Eger, startled the Ottomans with all manner of clever and deadly explosives. Finally, the Ottomans left in shame, Eger was saved, and Dobó was a national hero.

The unfortunate epilogue: The Ottomans came back in 1596 and, this time, succeeded in conquering an Eger Castle guarded by unmotivated mercenaries. The Ottomans sacked the town and controlled the region for close to a century.

In 1897, a castle archaeologist named Géza Gárdonyi moved from Budapest to Eger, and tales of the siege captured his imagination. Gárdonyi wrote a book about István Dobó and the 1552 Siege of Eger called *Egri Csillagok* ("Stars of Eger," translated into English as *Eclipse of the Crescent Moon,* available at local bookstores and souvenir stands). The book—a favorite of many Hungarians—is taught in schools, keeping the legend of Eger's heroes alive today.

see the Market Hall on the left).

▲**Eger Castle (Egri Vár)**—This castle is Hungary's Alamo, where István Dobó defended Eger from the Ottomans in 1552. These days, it's usually crawling with school-age kids on field trips from all over the country.

The great St. István—Hungary's first Christian king—built a church on this hill a thousand years ago. The church was destroyed by Tatars in the 13th century, and this fortress was built to repel another attack.

The castle grounds feature several small museums, including a history museum, picture gallery, dungeon, underground casements (tunnels through the castle walls), Heroes' Hall (with the grave of István Dobó), and temporary exhibits. For those of us who didn't grow up hearing the legend of István Dobó, the whole complex is hard to appreciate. Most visitors find that the most rewarding plan is to stroll up, wander around the grounds, enjoy the view overlooking the town (find the minaret and other landmarks), maybe pay a visit to the waxworks (see "Other Castle Sights"), and then head back down past a gaggle of colorful shops.

Cost and Hours: A 400-Ft ticket gets you into the castle grounds only (free Nov–March). To go inside all the museums (except the privately run "Other Castle Sights," described in next paragraph), buy the 1,000-Ft ticket. The underground casements and Heroes' Hall are only accessible by one-hour tour (600 Ft extra, call ahead to ask if English tour is scheduled, tel. 36/312-744, ext. 111; tours likely July–Aug, otherwise depends on guides' schedules). The castle grounds are open April–Aug daily 8:00–20:00, Sept until 19:00, March and Oct until 18:00, Nov–Feb until 17:00. The castle museums are open March–Oct Tue–Sun 9:00–17:00, Nov–Feb Tue–Sun 10:00–16:00 (last entry 40 min before closing). On Monday, all of the official castle museums are closed except the casements, which—as usual—you can visit only with a guided tour (800 Ft, plus 600 Ft extra if you go with English tour; some of the "Other Castle Sights" are open Mon). General castle info: tel. 36/312-744, www.div.iif.hu.

Other Castle Sights: In addition to the official castle museums, there are four privately run exhibits, each with its own sporadic hours and prices: an **armory** stocked with a millennium's worth of weapons (500 Ft); an **archery** exhibit (200–300 Ft per arrow to use old-fashioned bows and crossbows); the **mint** (200 Ft); and the **waxworks,** or "Panoptikum" (350 Ft, daily April–Oct 9:00–18:00, Nov–March 9:00–16:00). Of these, the waxworks is by far the best—in fact, it's the most enjoyable part of the whole castle complex. You'll see a handful of eerily realistic heroes and villains from the siege of Eger (including István Dobó himself and the leader of the Ottomans sitting in his colorful tent). Notice the exaggerated Central Asian features of the Egerites—a reminder that the Magyars were more Asian than European. Sound effects add to the fun...think of it as a very low-tech, walk-through *Ottomans of the Caribbean*. You'll also have the chance to scramble through a segment of the casements that run inside the castle walls.

Getting to Eger Castle: To reach the castle from Dobó Square, cross the bridge toward Senator Ház Hotel, then jog right around the hotel, turning right on Dobó István utca. Take this street a few blocks until it swings down to the right; the ramp up to the castle is to your left.

▲▲**Lyceum (Líceum)**—In the mid-18th century, Bishop Károly Eszterházy wanted a university in Eger, but Hapsburg Emperor Josef II refused to allow it. So instead, Eszterházy built the most impressive teacher-training college on the planet, and stocked it with the best books and astronomical equipment money could buy. The Lyceum still trains local teachers (enrollment: about 2,000). Since Eger is expensive by Hungarian

standards, many families live in the surrounding countryside. The kids all come into Eger for school—and lots of teachers are needed. But the halls of the Lyceum are also roamed by tourists who have come to visit its classic old library (500 Ft), and its astronomy museum, with a fascinating camera obscura (covered by a separate 600-Ft ticket; both parts open April–Sept Tue–Sun 9:30–15:30, closed Mon; Oct–March Sat–Sun only 9:30–13:30, closed Mon–Fri; last entry 30 min before closing, Eszterházy tér 1, at south end of Széchenyi utca at intersection with Kossuth utca, enter through main door across from cathedral and buy tickets just inside and to the left).

First, visit the old-fashioned **library** (from main entry hall, go around the right wing of the courtyard, then climb the stairs partway down the hall on your right-hand side; at top of first flight of stairs, turn right into the hall and look for the library halfway down on the right; watch for easy-to-miss signs). The library houses 50,000 books (here and in the two adjoining rooms, with several stacked two deep; plus another 100,000 elsewhere in the building). Dr. Imre Surányi and his staff have spent the last decade cataloging these books. This is no easy task, since they're in over 100 languages—from Thai to Tagalog—and are shelved according to size, rather than topic. You'll likely meet Dr. Surányi's assistant, Dénes Szabó (if he's not away for a choral contest), or the resident tour guide, Katalin Bódi. Either of them will happily show you a copy of the library's pride and joy: a letter from Mozart. The shelves are adorned with golden seals depicting great minds of science, philosophy, and religion. Take some time to marvel at the gorgeous ceiling fresco, dating from 1778. If you want to thank the patron of this museum, say *köszönöm* to the guy in the second row up, to the right of the podium (second from left, not wearing a hat)—that's Bishop Károly Eszterházy. While the Lyceum now belongs to Eger, his library is still the property of the archbishop.

A few flights above (leave library to the right, go to end of hall to reach stairs) is the **Astronomical Tower,** with some dusty old stargazing instruments, as well as a meridian line in the floor (the dot of sunlight hits the line every day exactly at noon).

Yet a few more flights up is the Lyceum's treasured **camera obscura.** You'll enter a dark room around a big, bowl-like canvas, and the guide will fly you around the streets of Eger. Fun as it is today, this camera must have seemed like a miracle when it was built in 1776—well before anyone had seen "moving pictures." It's a bit of a huff to get up here (nine flights of stairs, 302 steps all together)—but the camera obscura and the view of Eger from the outdoor terrace are worth it. If a Hungarian school group is waiting to see the camera obscura, let them go first, then try to get a viewing session all to yourself.

▲▲**Eger Cathedral**—Eger's 19th-century bishops peppered the city with beautiful buildings—including the second biggest church in Hungary (after Esztergom's—see Danube Bend chapter). With a quirky, sumptuous, Baroque-feeling interior, Eger's cathedral is well worth a visit (free entry, cathedral is the big, can't-miss-it yellow building at Pyrker János tér 1, just off Széchenyi utca).

Eger Cathedral was built in the 1830s by an Austrian archbishop who had previously served in Venice and thought Eger could use a little more class. The colonnaded Neoclassical facade, painted a pretty Hapsburg yellow, boasts some fine Italian sculpture. As you walk up the main stairs, you'll pass saints István and László—Hungary's first two Christian kings—and then the apostles Peter and Paul.

Enter the cathedral and walk to the first collection box, partway down the nave. Then, facing the door, look up at the ornate **ceiling fresco:** On the left, it shows Hungarians in traditional dress, and on the right, the country's most important historical figures. At the bottom, you see this cathedral, celestially connected with St. Peter's in Rome (at the top). This symbol of devotion to the Vatican was a brave statement when it was painted in 1950. The communists were closing churches in other small Hungarian towns, but the Eger archbishop had enough clout to keep this one open.

Continue to the **transept.** A few years ago, the windows at either end were donated to the cathedral by a rich Austrian couple to commemorate the 1,000th anniversary of Hungary's conversion to Christianity—notice the dates 1000 (when King István was crowned by the Pope) and 2000.

As you leave, notice the enormous **organ**—Hungary's second-largest—above the door. In the summer, try to catch one of the cathedral's daily half-hour organ concerts (500 Ft, mid-May–mid-Oct Mon–Sat at 11:30, Sun at 12:45, no concerts off-season).

If you walk up Széchenyi utca from here, you'll see the fancy Archbishop's Palace on your left—still home to Eger's archbishop.

▲**Market Hall (Csarnok)**—Wandering Eger's big indoor market will give you a taste of local life—and maybe some local food, too. It's packed with Egerites choosing the very best of the fresh produce. Tomatoes plus peppers of all colors and sizes are abundant—magic ingredients that give Hungarian food its kick (and that won't grow in colder Poland or the Czech Republic, with tamer cuisine). To reach the market, leave Dobó Square with the castle to your back; turn right on Zalár József utca, and you'll see the market on your left in two blocks, at the intersection with Dr. Sándor utca (mid-April–mid-Oct Mon–Fri 6:00–18:00, Sat–Sun 6:00–10:00; mid-Oct–mid-April Mon–Fri 6:00–17:00, Sat 6:00–13:00, closed Sun).

Minaret—Once part of a mosque, this slender, 130-foot-tall minaret represents the century of Ottoman rule that left its mark on Eger and all of Hungary. The little cross at the top symbolizes the eventual Christian victory over Hungary's Ottoman invaders. You can climb the minaret's 97 steps for fine views of Eger, but it's not for those scared of heights or tight spaces (200 Ft, April–Oct daily 10:00–18:00, closed Nov–March; if it's locked, ask for the key at nearby Hotel Minaret).

Minorite Church—The church that stands over Dobó Square is often said to be the most beautiful Baroque church in Hungary—even if it could use some touch-up work. It's exquisitely photogenic outside, but the shabby interior is less interesting, aside from the hand-carved pews, each of which is a little different.

Other Museums—Two small museums lie between Little Dobó Square and the entrance to the castle; neither is worth a visit, unless you have a special interest in the subject matter. The **Palóc Folklore Museum** is a measly little place with a handful of traditional tools, textiles, ceramics, costumes, and pieces of furniture (140 Ft, no English whatsoever, April–Oct Tue–Sun 9:00–17:00, closed Mon and Nov–March, Dobó utca 12). The **Historical Exhibition of Weapons** (Történeti Tárház) is just that, featuring centuries of Eger armaments: clubs, rifles, and everything in between (300 Ft, Tue–Sun 10:00–18:00, closed Mon, 450-Ft booklet labels weapons in English, 1,600-Ft English book gives more info, Dobó utca 9, actually just down Fazola Henrik utca).

EXPERIENCES

Aqua Eger

Swimming and water sports are as important to Egerites as good wine. They're proud that many of Hungary's Olympic medalists in aquatic events have come from this county.

To test the waters of this part of Eger, you can join the locals lounging and laughing around in the city bath (see "Taking the Waters" on page 458). Or you can take a more serious approach—

doing laps (and appreciating the unique architecture) at the city swimming pool.

▲Thermal Bath Complex (Eger Thermálfürdő)—For a refreshing break from the sightseeing grind, consider a splash in the spa. This is a fine opportunity to try a Hungarian bath: modern enough to feel accessible (men and women are clothed and together most of the time), but frequented mostly by locals. While Budapest has many great baths (see page 458), you may want to take a dip in low-key Eger and save your Budapest time for big-city sights.

You'll enter and be given a little barcode to swipe across the turnstile scanner. Trade this in for a key to a locker (1,000-Ft deposit per key, which will be refunded when you return the key). Change (private changing cabins available in the locker room for no extra charge), stow your stuff in a locker, put the key around your wrist, then join the fun. The heart of the complex is the new, green-domed, indoor-outdoor "adventure bath." Its cascades, jets, bubbles, geysers, and powerful current pool will make you feel like a kid again. For some warmer water, follow your nose to the old-fashioned sulfur pool—where Egerites sit peacefully, ignore the slight stink, and (supposedly) feel their arthritis ebb away. There's also a big outdoor lap pool (closed off-season).

Note that you can't rent a swimsuit or a towel; bring both with you, along with shower sandals for the locker room (if you've got them).

Cost, Hours, Location: 950 Ft, adventure bath included Oct–April but 600 Ft extra May–Sept. Open May–Sept Mon–Fri 6:00–19:30, Sat–Sun 8:00–19:00; Oct–April daily 9:00–18:30. It's at Petőfi tér 2 (tel. 36/314-142, www.egertermal.hu). From Dobó Square, follow the stream four blocks south (signs for *Strand*), past the big, unusual Bitskey Aladár swimming pool building. Continue following the stream into the park; you'll see the main entrance to the bath on your left over a bridge.

Turkish Bath (Török Fürdő)—This very traditional place is open to the public only on weekends (700 Ft, Sat 14:00–18:00, Sun 8:00–18:00, Fürdő utca 1–3, tel. 36/413-356).

Bitskey Aladár Pool—This striking new swimming pool was designed by Imre Makovecz, the father of Hungary's trendy Organic style of architecture. Some Eger taxpayers resented the pool's big price tag, but it left the city with a truly distinctive building. You don't need to be an architecture student to know that the pool is special. It's worth the five-minute walk from Dobó

Hungary's Organic Architecture

In recent years, a uniquely Hungarian style of architecture has caught on: Organic, developed and championed by Imre Makovecz. After being blackballed by the communists for his nationalistic politics, Makovecz was denied access to building materials, so he taught himself to make impressive structures with nothing more than sticks and rocks.

Now that the regime is dead and Makovecz is Hungary's premier architect, he still keeps things simple. He believes that a building should be a product of its environment, rather than a cookie-cutter copy. Organic buildings use indigenous materials (especially wood) and take on untraditional forms—often inspired by animals or plants—that blend in with the landscape. Organic buildings look like they're rising up out of the ground, rather than plopped down on top of it. You generally won't find this back-to-nature style in big cities like Budapest; Makovecz prefers to work in small communities such as Eger (see photo on page 502), instead of working for corporations.

Organic architecture has caught on throughout Hungary, becoming *the* post-communist style. Even big supermarket chains are now imitating Makovecz. If you see a building with white walls and a big, overhanging roof (resembling a big mushroom)...that's Organic.

Square just to take a look. Oh, and you can swim in it, too (750 Ft; Mon–Fri 6:00–20:00, until 21:00 on Mon, Wed, and Fri, Sat 8:00–20:00, Sun 8:00–18:00; follow Eger Creek south from Dobó Square to Frank Tivadar utca, tel. 36/511-810). Like the thermal bath complex, this place does not rent out swimsuits—B.Y.O.S.S.

Eger Wine

Eger is at the heart of one of Hungary's best-known wine regions, internationally famous for its **Bull's Blood** (Egri Bikavér). You'll likely hear various stories as to how Bull's Blood got its name during the Ottoman siege of Eger. My favorite version: The Ottomans were amazed at the ferocity displayed by the Egerites, and wondered what they were drinking that boiled their blood and stained their beards so red...it must be potent stuff. Local merchants, knowing that the Ottomans were Muslim and couldn't drink alcohol, told them it was bull's blood. The merchants made a buck, and the name stuck.

Creative as these stories are, they're all bunk—the term dates only from 1851. Egri Bikavér is a blend—everyone has their own recipe—so you generally won't find it at small producers. Cabernet

Sauvignon, Merlot, Kékfránkos, and Kékoportó are the most commonly used grapes.

Try Egri Bikavér, but then move quickly on to the more special and characteristic Hungarian wines, such as Leányka ("Little Girl"), Kékfránkos ("Blue Frankish"), Furmint, Hárslevélű, and Kéknyelű. You also might have heard of Tokaji Aszú wine (a sweet white made from a grape of Hungarian origin, also grown in the Alsace region of France—where it's known as *tokay*). Tokaj is a town (not too far from Eger), and Aszú is a "noble rot" grape. These grapes are harvested immediately after the first frost, when they burst and wither on the vine like raisins.

Sirens' Valley (Szépasszony-völgy)—When the Ottoman invaders first occupied Eger, residents moved into the valley next door, living in caves dug into the hillside. Eventually the Ottomans were driven out, the Egerites moved back to town, and the caves became wine cellars. (Most Eger families who can afford it have at least a modest vineyard in the countryside.) There are more than 300 such caves in the valley to the southwest of Eger, several of which are open for visitors.

The best selection of these caves (about 50) is in the Sirens' Valley (sometimes also translated as "Valley of the Beautiful Women," or, on local directional signs, the less poetic "Nice Woman Valley"). It's a fun scene—locals showing off their latest vintage, with picnic tables and tipsy tourists spilling out into the street. Most caves offer something to eat with the wine, and you'll also see lots of non-cave, full-service restaurants. Some of the caves are fancy and finished, staffed by multilingual waiters in period costume. Others feel like a dank basement, with grandpa leaning on his moped out front. (The really local places—where the decor is cement, bottles don't have labels, and food consists of potato chips and buttered Wonder Bread—can be the most fun.) Hopping from cave to musky cave can make for an enjoyable evening, but be sure to wander around a bit to see the options before you dive in. Caves #43, #34, and the one called "Kiss" have a particularly good reputation (cellars generally open 10:00–22:00 in summer, best June–Aug after 19:00; it's much quieter off-season, when only a handful of cellars remain open, with shorter hours).

Getting to the Sirens' Valley: The valley is a 25-minute walk southwest of Eger. Figure about 1,400 Ft for a **taxi** between your hotel and the caves. During the summer, you can catch the 500-Ft **tourist train** from Eger's main square to the caves (see "Helpful Hints," page 495), then take a later train back. To **walk,** leave the pedestrian zone on the street next to the cathedral (Törvényház utca), with the cathedral on your right-hand side. Take the first left just after the back end of the cathedral (onto Trinitárius utca), go one long block, then take the first right (onto Király utca). At the fork, bear to the left. You'll stay straight on this road—crossing busy Koháry István utca—for several blocks, through some nondescript residential areas (on Szépasszony-völgy utca). When you crest the hill and emerge from the houses, you'll see the caves (and tour buses) below you on the left—go left (downhill) at the fork to get there. First you'll come to a stretch of touristy non-cave restaurants; keep going past these, and eventually you'll see a big loop of caves on your left.

SLEEPING

Eger is a good overnight stop, and a couple of quaint, well-located hotels in particular—Senator Ház and Offi Ház—are well worth booking in advance. The TI can help you find a room; if you're stumped, the area behind the castle has a sprinkling of guesthouses *(vendégház)*. A tax of 300 Ft per person will be added to your bill (not included in the prices listed here).

$$$ Panoráma Hotel is a good big-hotel option, still close to Dobó Square. You'll miss the quaintness of some of the other listings—its 38 rooms are all business—but you get free access to its "Unicornis Thermarium" spa facility (Sb-18,000 Ft, Db-21,500 Ft, Tb-26,000 Ft, 10 percent cheaper Nov–March, apartments also available, non-smoking rooms, elevator, free parking, Dr. Hibay K. utca 2, tel. 36/412-886, fax 36/410-136, www.panoramahotels .hu, hoteleger@panoramahotels.hu).

$$$ Imola Udvarház rents six spacious apartments—with kitchen, living room, bedroom, and bathroom—all decorated in modern Scandinavian style (read: Ikea). They're pricey, but roomy and well-maintained, with a great location near the castle entrance

---

Sleep Code

(€1 = about $1.20, 200 Ft = about $1, country code: 36, area code: 36)

S = Single, **D** = Double/Twin, **T** = Triple, **Q** = Quad, **b** = bathroom, **s** = shower only. Unless otherwise noted, English is spoken, breakfast is included, and credit cards are accepted.

To help you sort easily through these listings, I've divided the rooms into three categories, based on the price for a standard double room with bath:

$$$ **Higher Priced**—Most rooms 18,000 Ft (€75) or more.
$$ **Moderately Priced**—Most rooms between 10,000–18,000 Ft (€42–75).
$ **Lower Priced**—Most rooms 10,000 Ft (€42) or less.

(July–Aug: Sb-19,000 Ft, Db-22,000 Ft, Tb-24,000 Ft, Qb-26,000 Ft; each room 2,000 Ft less April–June and Sept–Oct and 4,000 Ft less Nov–March; enter through restaurant courtyard at Dózsa György tér 4, tel. & fax 36/516-180, udvarhaz@imolanet.hu).

$$ Senator Ház Hotel is one of my favorite small, family-run hotels in all of Eastern Europe. Though the 11 rooms are a bit worn, this place is cozy and well-run by András Cseh, with oodles of character and a picture-perfect location just under the castle on Little Dobó Square (Sb-13,600 Ft, Db-19,800 Ft, extra bed-5,400 Ft, 15–30 percent cheaper mid-Oct–May, Internet access for guests-300 Ft/30 min, Dobó István tér 11, tel. & fax 36/411-711, www.senatorhaz.hu, senator@enternet.hu). The Cseh family also runs **Pátria Vendégház**—two doubles (19,800 Ft) and four apartments (22,000 Ft) with new, luxurious decor around a courtyard in a nearby building (same contact info as Senator Ház Hotel).

$$ Offi Ház Hotel shares Little Dobó Square with Senator Ház. Its five rooms are classy and romantic (Sb-13,500 Ft, Db-15,500 Ft, Db suite-18,500 Ft, Tb suite-23,000 Ft, extra bed-4,500 Ft, 15 percent cheaper Nov–March, non-smoking, Dobó István tér 5, tel. & fax 36/518-210, www.offihaz.hu, offihaz@t-online.hu).

$$ Szent János Hotel, less charming and more businesslike than the Senator Ház and Offi Ház, offers a good but less atmospheric location, 11 straitlaced rooms, and a slightly better value (Sb-€58, Db-€71, extra bed-€21, 15 percent cheaper Nov–April, non-smoking rooms, air-con, McDonald's walk-up window across the street can be noisy at night—especially weekends—so request a quiet back room, a long block off Dobó Square at Szent János utca 3, tel. 36/510-350, fax 36/517-101, www.hotelszentjanos.hu, hotelszentjanos@hotelszentjanos.hu).

$ Dobó Vendégház, run by friendly Mariann Kleszo, has seven basic but colorful rooms just off Dobó Square. Mariann speaks nothing but Hungarian, but gets simple reservation e-mails and faxes translated by a friend (Sb-€30, Db-€40, Tb-€50, Qb-€60, cash only, Dobó utca 19, tel. 36/421-407, fax 36/515-715, www.hotels.hu/dobo_vendeghaz, dobovh@t-online.hu).

EATING

Bajor Sörház (known to locals as "HBH" for the brand of beer on tap) is favored by tourists and locals alike for its excellent Hungarian cuisine. Everything's good here. You could make a meal of their spicy *gulyás leves* soup (that's real Hungarian goulash, described on page 397)—but it's fun to supplement it with some other well-prepared Hungarian dishes. They also feature some Bavarian specialties...but with a Hungarian accent (most main dishes 1,000–2,000 Ft, daily 11:30–22:00, right at the bottom of Dobó Square at Bajcsy-Zsilinszky utca 19, tel. 36/515-516). If you're lucky, you may get to meet animated István "Call Me Steve Miller" Molnár, one of my favorite Hungarians.

The recommended hotels **Senator Ház** and **Offi Ház** both have restaurants at the top end of Dobó Square that are open long hours daily (both are listed under "Sleeping"). These places have fine Hungarian and international food (most main dishes 1,500–2,200 Ft) and postcard-perfect outdoor seating that shares Little Dobó Square with a gazebo featuring cheesy live music in summer. This is *the* place to see and be seen in Eger.

Elefanto, above the Market Hall, offers good, inexpensive pizzas (600–1,100 Ft) and international dishes (1,300–2,000 Ft) in a pleasant treehouse ambience. In warm weather, enjoy the covered terrace seating (daily 12:00–23:00, Katona István tér 2, tel. 36/412-452).

Palacsintavár ("Pancake Castle"), near the ramp leading up to the castle, isn't your hometown IHOP. This cellar bar serves up inventive, artfully presented crêpe-wrapped main courses to a mostly-students clientele. It's decorated with old cigarette boxes, and cutting-edge rock music plays on the soundtrack (most main dishes 1,300–1,500 Ft, daily 12:00–22:30, Dobó utca 9).

Szantofer Vendéglő serves mostly traditional Hungarian food at local prices to both Egerites and tourists. The decent, fill-the-tank food is presented with an artistic flourish—some plates fly miniature Hungarian flags. Steer clear of the few non-Hungarian offerings (like chicken tikka), and you'll do fine (most main dishes 900–1,400 Ft, daily 11:30–22:00, Bródy Sándor utca 3, tel. 36/517-298).

Rádi Bisztró is a popular student hangout and a convenient spot for pastries and inexpensive, pre-made sandwiches (less than 400 Ft, Mon–Fri 7:00–18:00, Sat 7:00–14:00, closed Sun, just down the street from the Lyceum at Széchenyi utca 2).

Dessert: Cukrászda (pastry shops) line the streets of Eger. For deluxe, super-decadent pastries of every kind imaginable—most for less than 400 Ft—drop by **Dobós Cukrászda** (daily 9:30–21:00, point to what you want inside and they'll bring it out to your table, Széchenyi utca 6, tel. 36/413-335). For a more local scene, find the tiny **Sárvári Cukrászda,** behind the Lyceum. Their pastries are good, but Egerites line up here after a big Sunday lunch for their homemade gelato (120 Ft/scoop, Mon–Fri 7:00–19:00, Sat–Sun 10:00–18:00, Kossuth utca 1, between Jókai utca and Fellner utca).

TRANSPORTATION CONNECTIONS

From Eger by Train: The only major destination you'll get to directly from Eger's train station is **Budapest** (5/day direct to Budapest's Keleti Station, 2 hrs; more with a transfer in

Füzesabony). For most other destinations, you'll connect through Budapest.

For destinations to the north—such as Kraków—you'll save time by transferring in **Füzesabony** (FOO-zesh-ah-boyn, 13/day, 17 min), a nearby smaller village that happens to be on the Budapest–Kraków line. The very rustic Füzesabony station does not have lockers, but—oddly enough—does have a modest museum of local artifacts. There is no ATM at the station—exit straight from the station and walk about two blocks, and you'll find ATMs on either side of the street.

Night Train Between Eger and Kraków

In either direction, this train transfers at Füzesabony.

From Kraków to Eger: Note that your train actually continues on to Budapest—so you'll have to be on your toes to get off at Füzesabony (at 7:39 in 2006; confirm specific time before you travel). When you board the night train, make sure the conductor knows when you're getting off; he should wake you up 20 minutes before reaching Füzesabony, and he'll have to unlock the door to let you off the train. Once in Füzesabony, you'll have about 35 minutes before the next Eger-bound train leaves. That's plenty of time to get some local cash, buy your ticket to Eger (about 200 Ft), and hop on the train.

From Eger to Kraków: First you'll have to transfer in Füzesabony. You can either take the 20-minute train trip from Eger to Füzesabony (about 200 Ft), or—if you've got more money than time—skip the walk to the station and take a 20-minute taxi ride (about 7,000 Ft) directly to Füzesabony to catch the train on to Kraków.

SLOVENIA

SLOVENIA

(Slovenija)

 Tiny, overlooked Slovenia is one of Europe's most unexpectedly charming destinations. At the intersection of the Slavic, German, and Italian worlds, Slovenia is an exciting mix of the best of each culture. Though it's just a quick trip away from the tourist throngs in Venice, Munich, Salzburg, and Vienna, Slovenia has stayed off the tourist track—a handy detour for in-the-know Back Door travelers.

Today, it seems strange to think that Slovenia was ever part of Yugoslavia. Both in the personality of its people and in its landscape, Slovenia feels more like Austria. Slovenes are more industrious, organized, and punctual than their fellow former Yugoslavs... yet still friendly, relaxed, and Mediterranean. Locals like the balance. Visitors expecting minefields and rusting Yugo factories are pleasantly surprised to find Slovenia's rolling countryside dotted instead with quaint alpine villages and the spires of miniature Baroque churches, with breathtaking, snowcapped peaks in the distance.

Only half as big as Switzerland, but remarkably diverse for its size, Slovenia can be easily appreciated on a brief visit. Travelers can hike on alpine trails in the morning and explore some of the world's best caves in the afternoon, before relaxing with a seafood dinner on the Adriatic.

Slovenia enjoys a powerhouse economy—the healthiest in Eastern Europe. Of the 10 new nations that joined the European Union in 2004, Slovenia was the only one rich enough to be a net donor (with a higher per-capita income than the average), and the only one already qualified to join the euro currency zone (it adopted the euro in January of 2007). Thanks to its long-standing ties to the West and can-do spirit, Slovenia already feels more Western than any other destination in this book.

The country has a funny way of making people fall in love with it. Slovenes are laid-back, easygoing, and fun. They won't win any world wars (they're too well-adjusted to even try)...but they're exactly the type of people you'd love to chat with over a cup of coffee. Many of today's American visitors are soldiers who participated in the conflict in nearby Bosnia and have good memories of their vacations here. Now they're bringing their families back with them. They're not the only ones. One of your co-authors has decided that Slovenia is his hands-down favorite European country.

The Slovene language is as mellow as the people. While Slovenes use Serb and German curses in abundance, the worst they can say in their native tongue is, "May you be kicked by a horse." For "Darn it!" they say, "Three hundred hairy bears!"

Coming from such a small country, locals are proud of the few things that are distinctly Slovenian, such as the roofed hayrack.

Foreigners think that Slovenes' fascination with these hayracks is strange...until they visit, and see them absolutely everywhere (especially in the northwest part of the country). Because of the frequent rainfall, the hayracks are covered by a roof that allows the hay to dry thoroughly. The most traditional kind is the *toplar*, consisting of two hayracks connected by one big roof. It looks like a skinny barn with open, fenced sides. Hay hangs on the sides to dry; firewood, carts, tractors, and other farm implements sit on the ground inside; and dried hay is stored in the loft up above. But these wooden *toplarji* are firetraps, and a stray bolt of lighting can burn one down in a flash. So in recent years, more farmers are moving to single hayracks *(enojni)*; these are still roofed, but have posts made of concrete, rather than wood.

Slovenia Almanac

Official Name: Republika Slovenija, or simply Slovenija.

Snapshot History: After being dominated by Germans for centuries, Slovenian culture proudly emerged in the 19th century. After World War I, Slovenia merged with its neighbors to become Yugoslavia, then broke away and achieved independence for the first time ever in 1991.

Population: Slovenia's two million people (similar to Nevada) are 83 percent ethnic Slovenes who speak Slovene, plus a smattering of Serbs, Croats, and Muslim Bosniaks. The majority of the country is Catholic.

Latitude and Longitude: 46°N and 14°E (latitude similar to Lyon, France; Quebec, Canada; or Bismarck, North Dakota).

Area: At 7,800 square miles, it's about the size of New Jersey, but with a fourth the population.

Geography: Tiny Slovenia has three extremely different terrains and climates: the warm Mediterranean coastline (just 29 miles long—about one inch per inhabitant); the snow-capped, forested alpine mountains in the northwest (including 9,400-foot Mount Triglav); and the moderate-climate, central limestone plateau that includes Ljubljana and the cave-filled Karst region. If you look at a map of Slovenia and kind of squint, it really begins to look like a chicken running toward the east.

Biggest Cities: Nearly one in five Slovenes lives in the two biggest cities: Ljubljana (the capital, pop. 265,000) and Maribor (in the east, pop. 115,000). Half the country lives in rural villages.

Economy: With a Gross Domestic Product of $43 billion and a GDP per capita of nearly $21,500, Slovenia's economy is much stronger than the average Eastern European country. Slovenia's wealth comes largely from manufactured metal products (trucks, machinery) traded with a diverse group of partners.

Currency: Slovenia adopted the euro currency in January of 2007. €1 = about $1.20. For more, see "Euro Conversion" under "Practicalities" on page 514.

Government: The country is headed by Prime Minister Janez Janša, who heads up the leading vote-getting party in legislative elections. He governs along with the figurehead president, Janez Drnovšek. For health reasons, Drnovšek has adopted a vegan diet and lives in the countryside outside of Ljubljana, and has announced he will not run for re-election when his term is up in December 2007. (Drnovšek's predecessor, Milan Kučan, took a brave stand for independence as Yugoslavia was disintegrating.

Slovenia's relatively peaceful succession is credited largely to Kučan, who remains a popular figure.) The National Assembly of about 90 elected legislators (along with a second house of parliament, which has much less power) is not currently dominated by any single party. Despite the country's small size, it is divided into some 200 municipalities.

Flag: Three horizontal bands of white (top), blue, and red. A shield in the upper left shows Mount Triglav, with a wavy-line sea below and three stars above.

The Average Slovene: The average Slovene skis, in this largely alpine country, and is an avid fan of the oddly popular sport of team handball. He or she lives in a 250-square-foot apartment, earns $1,400 a month, watches 16 hours of TV a week (much of it in English with Slovene subtitles), and enjoys a drink-and-a-half of alcohol every day.

Notable Slovenes: A pair of prominent Ohio politicians—presidential candidate Dennis Kucinich and Senator George Voinovich, both from the Cleveland area—are each half-Slovene. Classical musicians might know composers Giuseppe Tartini and Hugo Wolf. Even if you haven't heard of architect Jože Plečnik yet, you'll hear his name a hundred times while you're in Slovenia—especially in Ljubljana (see page 541). Most famous of all is the illustrious Melania Knauss—a *GQ* cover girl who's also Mrs. Donald Trump.

If you follow alpine sports or team handball, you'll surely know some world-class athletes from Slovenia. NBA fans might recognize basketball players Primož Brezec and Bostjan Nachbar, as well as some lesser players. The athletic Slovenes—perhaps trying to compensate for the miniscule size of their country—have accomplished astonishing feats: Davo Karničar has skied down from the summits of some of the world's tallest mountains (including Everest, Kilimanjaro, and McKinley; www.davokarnicar.com). Benka Pulko became the first person ever to drive a motorcycle around the world (that is, all seven continents, including Antarctica; total trip: 118,000 miles in 2,000 days—also the longest solo motorcycle journey by a woman; www.benkapulko.com). Dušan Mravlje ran across all the continents (www.dusanmravlje.si). And ultra-marathon swimmer Martin Strel has swam the entire length of several major rivers, including the Danube (1,775 miles), the Mississippi (2,415 miles), and the Yangtze (3,915 miles). Next up: The Amazon (3,393 miles—follow along at www.martinstrel.com).

You'll find postcards and miniature wooden models of both kinds of hayracks (a fun souvenir).

Another good (and uniquely Slovenian) memento is a creatively decorated front panel from a beehive *(panjske končnice)*. Slovenia has a strong beekeeping tradition, and beekeepers once believed that painting the fronts of the hives made it easier for bees to find their way home. Replicas of these panels are available at gift shops all over the country. (For more on the panels and Slovenia's beekeeping heritage, see page 578.)

To really stretch your euros, try one of Slovenia's more than 200 farmhouse B&Bs, called "tourist farms" *(turistične kmetije)*. Use the B&B as a home base to explore the entire country—remember, the farthest reaches of Slovenia are only a day trip away. You can get a comfortable, hotelesque double with a private bathroom—plus a traditional Slovenian dinner and a hearty breakfast—for as little as $40. Request a listing from the Slovenian Tourist Board (see page 9), or visit www.slovenia-tourism.si/touristfarms.

Slovenia is poised to become one of Eastern Europe's top destinations in the next few years. Now is the time to visit, while the locals are still friendly, the prices are still reasonable, and the lanes and trails are yours alone.

Practicalities

Euro Conversion: Slovenia has been using the euro currency only since January of 2007. This means that Slovenes are still getting used to the transition, and many still think in terms of the previous currency, the *tolar*. There were about 190 tolars in one dollar, and about 240 tolars in one euro. The prices in this book were researched before the euro was introduced, so you may find some variation from the actual prices. (Many Slovenes spent the months leading up to the euro introduction fretting that it would dramatically increase the price of everything. Whether this is true remains to be seen.)

Sunday Closures: In a typically mellow step to counteract Europe's race into the future, Slovenia recently passed a law mandating that virtually all retail shops in the country must be closed on Sunday. This means that buying a phone card or a sweater can become an ordeal on Sunday, even in Ljubljana—plan ahead. Fortunately, restaurants remain open, plus a select few grocery stores.

Telephones: Insertable phone cards, sold at newsstands and kiosks everywhere, get you access to the modern public phones.

When calling locally, dial the seven-digit number. To make a long-distance call within the country, start with the area code (which begins with 0). To call a Slovenian number from abroad, dial the international access number (00 if calling from Europe,

011 from the United States or Canada) followed by 386 (Slovenia's country code), then the area code (without the initial 0) and the seven-digit number. To call out of Slovenia, dial 00, the country code of the country you're calling (see chart in appendix), the area code if applicable (may need to drop initial zero), and the local number.

Slovenian phone numbers beginning with 080 are toll-free; 090 and 089 denote expensive toll lines. Mobile phone numbers usually begin with 031, 041, 051, 040, or 070.

Slovenian History

Slovenia has a long and not very interesting history as part of various larger empires. Charlemagne's Franks conquered the tiny land in the eighth century, and, ever since, Slovenia has been a backwater of the Germanic world—first as a holding of the Holy Roman Empire, and later, the Hapsburg Empire. Slovenia often seems as much German as Slavic. But even as the capital, Ljubljana, was populated by Austrians (and called Laibach by its German-speaking residents), the Slovenian language and cultural traditions survived in the countryside.

Ljubljana rose to international prominence for half a decade (1809–1813) when Napoleon named it the capital of his "Illyrian Provinces," stretching from Austria's Tirol to Croatia's Dalmatian Coast. During this time, the long-suppressed Slovene language was used for the first time in schools and the government. Inspired by the patriotic poetry of France Prešeren, national pride surged.

The most interesting chapter in Slovenian history happened in the last century. Some of World War I's fiercest fighting occurred at the Soča (Isonzo) Front in northwest Slovenia—witnessed by young Ernest Hemingway, who drove an ambulance. After the war, from 1918 to 1991, Slovenia was Yugoslavia's smallest, northernmost, and most affluent republic. Concerned about Serbian strongman Slobodan Milošević's politics, Slovenia seceded in 1991. Because more than 90 percent of the people here were ethnic Slovenes, the break with Yugoslavia was simple and virtually uncontested. Its war for independence lasted just 10 days and claimed only a few dozen lives. (For more details, see the Understanding Yugoslavia chapter, page 808.)

After centuries of looking to the West, Slovenia became the first of the former Yugoslav republics to join the European Union in May 2004. The Slovenes are practical about this move, real-izing it's essential for their survival as a tiny nation in a modern world. But there are trade-offs, and "Euroskeptics" are down on EU bureaucracy. As borders disappear, Slovenes are experiencing more crime. Local farming is threatened by EU standards. There are no more cheap bananas (because brown ones must be trashed),

Slo-what?-ia

"The only thing I know about Slovakia is what I learned firsthand from your foreign minister, who came to Texas."

—George W. Bush, to a Slovak journalist
(Bush had actually met with Dr. Janez Drnovšek,
who was then Slovenia's prime minister)

Maybe it's understandable that many Americans confuse Slovenia with Slovakia. Both are small, mountainous countries that not too long ago were parts of bigger, better known, now defunct nations. But anyone who has visited Slovenia and Slovakia will set you straight—they feel worlds apart.

Slovenia, wedged between the Alps and the Adriatic, is a tidy, prosperous country with a strong economy. Until 1991, Slovenia was one of the six republics that made up Yugoslavia. Historically, Slovenia has had very strong ties with Germanic culture—so it feels German.

Slovakia—two countries away, to the northeast—is slightly bigger. Much of its territory is covered by the Carpathian Mountains, most notably the dramatic, jagged peaks of the High Tatras. In 1993, the Czechs and Slovaks peacefully chose to go their separate ways, so the nation of Czechoslovakia dissolved into the Czech Republic and the Slovak Republic (a.k.a. Slovakia). Slovakia was hit hard by the communists, and still suffers from a weak economy and high poverty levels. Slovakia was part of Hungary until the end of World War I, and feels Hungarian (especially the southern half of the country, where many Hungarians still live).

To make things even more confusing, there's also **Slavonia.** This is the thick, inland "panhandle" that makes up the northeast half of Croatia, along Slovenia's southeast border. Much of the warfare in Croatia's 1991–1995 war took place in Slavonia (including Vukovar; see Understanding Yugoslavia chapter).

I won't tell on you if you mix them up. But if you want to feel smarter than the president, do a little homework and get it right.

and "you can't sell a cucumber with more than a three-degree curve." Slovenian businesses are having difficulty competing with big German and Western firms. Before EU membership, only Slovenes could own Slovenian land. But now wealthy foreigners are buying property, driving up the cost of real estate.

As Slovenia became the first post-communist country to adopt the euro currency in January of 2007, locals worried about a potential increase in prices...even as they felt proud of their economic achievements. It seems that throughout all of the changes in the last two decades, Slovenes have maintained their sense of humor and easygoing attitude.

Slovenian Food

Slovenian cuisine has enjoyed influence from a wide variety of sources. Slovenes brag that their cuisine melds the best of Italian and German cooking—but they also embrace other international influences, especially French. Like Croatian food, Slovenian cuisine also features some pan-Balkan elements. The eggplant-and-red-bell-pepper condiment *ajvar* is popular here. For fast food, you'll find *burek, čevapčiči,* and *ražnjiči* (see "Balkan Flavors," page 616). Slovenia enjoys Italian-style fare, with a pizza or pasta restaurant on seemingly every corner. Hungarian food simmers in the northeast corner of the country (where many Magyars reside). But most of all, Slovenian food has a distinctly German vibe—including the "four S's": sausages, schnitzels, strudels, and sauerkraut.

Traditional Slovenian dishes are prepared with groats—kind of a grainy mush made with buckwheat, barley, or corn. Buckwheat, which thrives in this climate, often appears on Slovenian menus. You'll also see plenty of *štruklji* (dumplings), which can be stuffed with cheese, meat, or vegetables. *Repa* is turnip prepared like sauerkraut. Among the hearty soups in Slovenia is *jota*—a staple for Karst peasants, made from *repa,* beans, and vegetables.

The cuisine of Slovenia's Karst region (the arid limestone plain south of Ljubljana) is notable. The small farms and wineries of this region have been inspired by Italy's "Slow Food" movement, and believe that cuisine is meant to be gradually appreciated, not rushed—making the Karst a destination for gourmet tours. Karstic cuisine is similar to France's nouvelle cuisine—several courses in small portions, with a focus on unusual combinations and preparations—but with an Italian flair. The Karst's tasty air-dried ham *(pršut),* available throughout the country, is worth seeking out (see sidebar). Istria (the peninsula just to the south of the Karst, in southern Slovenia and Croatia) produces truffles that, locals boast, are as good as those from Italy's Piedmont, but much cheaper.

Voda is water, and *kava* is coffee. Radenska, in the bottle with the three little hearts, is Slovenia's best-known brand of mineral water—good enough that the word *Radenska* is synonymous with bottled water all over Slovenia and throughout the former Yugoslavia.

Adventurous teetotalers should forego the Coke and sample Cockta, a Slovenian cola with an unusual flavor (which supposedly comes from berry, lemon, orange, and 11 herbs). Originally called "Cockta-Cockta," the drink was introduced during the communist

---

Pršut

In Slovenia and Croatia, *pršut* (purr-SHOOT) is one of the essential food groups. This air-cured ham (like Italian prosciutto) is soaked in salt and sometimes also smoked. Then it hangs in open-ended barns for up to a year and a half, to be dried and seasoned by the howling Bora wind. Each region produces a slightly different *pršut*. In Dalmatia, a layer of fat keeps the ham moist; in Istria, the fat is trimmed, and the *pršut* is dryer.

Since Slovenia joined the European Union, strict new standards have swept the land. Separate rooms must be used for the slaughter, preparation, and curing of the ham. While this seems fair enough for large producers, small family farms that want to produce just enough *pršut* for their own use— and maybe sell one or two ham hocks to neighbors—find they have to invest thousands of euros to be compliant.

---

period, as an alternative to the difficult-to-get Coke. This local variation developed a loyal following...until the Iron Curtain fell, and the real Coke became readily available. Cockta sales plummeted. But in recent years—prodded by the slogan "The Taste of Your Youth"— nostalgic Slovenes are drinking Cockta once more. Aside from having happy childhood memories of sipping Cockta, Slovenes figure they can be proud that their little country produced a soft drink that rivals Coca-Cola.

To toast, say, *"Na ZDRAHV-yeh!"*—if you can't remember it, think of "Nice driving!" The premier Slovenian brand of *pivo* (beer) is Union (OO-nee-ohn), but you'll also see a lot of Laško, whose mascot is the Zlatorog (or "Golden Horn," a mythical goat-like animal).

Slovenia produces some fine *vino* (wine). The Celts first grew wine in Slovenia; the Romans improved the process and spread it throughout the country. Slovenia has three primary wine regions. Podravje, in the northeast, is dominated by Laški and Renski Riesling and other top-quality wines. Posavje, in the southeast, produces both white and red wines, but is famous for the light, russet-colored Cviček wine. Primorska, in the southwest, has a Mediterranean climate and produces mostly reds, including Teran, made from *refošk* grapes.

Key Slovene Phrases

English	Slovene	Pronounced
Hello. (formal)	*Dober dan.*	DOH-behr dahn
Hi. / Bye. (informal)	*Živjo.*	ZHEEV-yoh
Do you speak English?	*Ali govorite angleško?*	AH-lee goh-voh-REE-teh ahng-LEHSH-koh
yes / no	*ja / ne*	yah / neh
Please. / You're welcome.	*Prosim.*	PROH-seem
Can I help you?	*Izvolite?*	eez-VOH-lee-teh
Thank you.	*Hvala.*	HVAH-lah
I'm sorry. / Excuse me.	*Oprostite.*	oh-proh-STEE-teh
Good.	*Dobro.*	DOH-broh
Goodbye.	*Nasvidenje.*	nahs-VEE-dehn-yeh
one / two	*ena / dve*	EH-nah / dveh
three / four	*tri / štiri*	tree / SHTEE-ree
five / six	*pet / šest*	peht / shehst
seven / eight	*sedem / osem*	SEH-dehm / OH-sehm
nine / ten	*devet / deset*	deh-VEHT / deh-SEHT
hundred	*sto*	stoh
thousand	*tisoč*	TEE-sohch
How much?	*Koliko?*	KOH-lee-koh
local currency	*tolar (SIT)*	TOH-lar
Where is...?	*Kje je...?*	kyeh yeh
...the toilet	*...vece*	VEHT-seh
men	*moški*	MOHSH-kee
women	*ženski*	ZHEHN-skee
water / coffee	*voda / kava*	VOH-dah / KAH-vah
beer / wine	*pivo / vino*	PEE-voh / VEE-noh
Cheers!	*Na zdravje!*	nah ZDRAHV-yeh
the bill	*račun*	rah-CHOON

Slovenia's national dessert is *potica,* a rolled pastry with walnuts and sometimes also raisins. For more tasty treats, see the "Bled Desserts" sidebar on page 576. Locals claim that Ljubljana has the finest gelato outside of Italy—which, after all, is just an hour down the road.

Slovenian Language

Slovene is surprisingly different from languages spoken in the other former Yugoslav republics. While Serbian and Croatian are mutually intelligible, Slovene is gibberish to Serbs and Croats. Most Slovenes, on the other hand, know Serbo-Croatian—because, a generation ago, everybody in Yugoslavia had to learn it.

The tiny country of Slovenia borders Italy and Austria, with important historical and linguistic ties to both. For self-preservation, the Slovene population has always been forced to function in many different languages. All of these factors make Slovenes excellent linguists. Most young Slovenes speak effortless, flawless English—then admit that they've never set foot in the United States or Britain, but love watching American movies and TV shows (which are always subtitled, never dubbed).

Slovene is perhaps the easiest Eastern European language to pronounce. As with most Slavic languages, *c* is pronounced "ts" (like "cats"). The letter *j* is pronounced as "y"—making "Ljubljana" easier to say than it looks (lyoob-lyee-AH-nah). In contrast to other Eastern European languages—which tend to have a wide array of confusing little doohickeys over the letters—Slovene only has one diacritical mark: the *strešica,* or "little roof." This makes *č* sound like "ch," *š* sound like "sh," and *ž* sound like "zh" (as in "measure").

The only trick: As in English, which syllable gets the emphasis is unpredictable. Slovenes use many of the same words as Croatians, but put the stress on an entirely different place.

As you're tracking down addresses, these definitions will help: *trg* (square), *ulica* (street), *cesta* (avenue), and *most* (bridge).

LJUBLJANA

Slovenia's capital, Ljubljana (lyoob-lyee-AH-nah), with a lazy Old Town clustered around a castle-topped mountain, is often likened to Salzburg. It's an apt comparison—but only if you inject a healthy dose of breezy Adriatic culture, add a Slavic accent, and replace Mozart with local architect Jože Plečnik.

Ljubljana feels much smaller than its population of 265,000. While big-league museums are in short supply, the town itself is an idyllic place that sometimes feels too good to be true. Festivals fill the summer, and people enjoy a Sunday stroll any day of the week. Fashion boutiques and cafés jockey for control of the Old Town, while the leafy riverside promenade crawls with stylishly dressed students sipping *kava* and polishing their near-perfect English. Laid-back Ljubljana is the kind of place where graffiti and crumbling buildings seem elegantly atmospheric instead of shoddy.

Batted around by history, Ljubljana has seen cultural influences from all sides—most notably Prague, Vienna, and Venice. This has left the city a happy hodgepodge of cultures. Being the midpoint between the Slavic, Germanic, and Italian worlds gives Ljubljana a special spice.

People often ask me: What's the "next Prague"? I have to answer Kraków. But Ljubljana is the *next* "next Prague."

Planning Your Time

Ljubljana deserves a full day. While there are few must-see sights, the city's biggest attraction is its ambience. You'll spend much of your time strolling the pleasant town center, exploring the many interesting squares and architectural gems, shopping the boutiques, and sipping coffee at sidewalk cafés along the river.

Here's the best plan for a low-impact sightseeing day: Begin on Prešeren Square, the heart of the city. Cross the Triple Bridge and wander through the riverside produce market before joining the town walking tour at 10:00 (daily May–Sept; less frequent off-season). After the tour, enjoy a lunch and some leisurely people-watching in the center before hiking or riding the tourist train up to the castle. After descending, wander along the Ljubljanica River to Jože Plečnik's National and University Library, French Revolution Square, and on to my favorite Ljubljana museum, the Jože Plečnik House (note this sight's limited hours, and plan accordingly: Tue–Thu 10:00–18:00, Sat 10:00–15:00, closed Sun–Mon and Fri). With more time, or if the Plečnik House is closed, stroll from Prešeren Square up Čopova street to Tivoli Park, where you can visit the Contemporary History Museum (daily until 18:00).

There are plenty of good day trips close to Ljubljana. With a second day, visit one of the two impressive caves (Škocjan or Postojna) and nearby sights in the Karst region south of the city (see The Karst chapter, page 553).

Ljubljana is dead and disappointing on Sundays (virtually all shops are closed and the produce market is quiet, but museums are generally open, a modest flea market stretches along the riverfront, and the TI's walking tour still runs). The city is also relatively quiet in August, when the students are on break and many locals head to beach resorts. They say that in August, even homeless people go to the coast.

ORIENTATION

(area code: 01)

Ljubljana—with narrow lanes, architecture that mingles the Old World and contemporary Europe, and cobbles upon cobbles of wonderful distractions—can be disorienting for a first-timer. But the charming central zone is compact, and with a little wandering, you'll quickly get the hang of it.

The Ljubljanica River—lined with cafés, restaurants, and a buzzing outdoor market—bisects the city, making a 90-degree turn around the base of a castle-topped mountain. Most sights are either on or just a short walk from the river. Visitors enjoy the distinctive bridges that span the Ljubljanica, including the landmark Triple Bridge (Tromostovje) and pillared Cobblers' Bridge (Čevljarski Most)—both designed by Jože Plečnik. Between them is a very plain wooden bridge dubbed "the Ugly Duckling." The center of Ljubljana is Prešeren Square, watched over by a big statue of Slovenia's national poet, France Prešeren.

The Story of Ljubljana

In ancient times, Ljubljana was on the trade route connecting the Mediterranean (just 60 miles away) to the Black Sea (toss a bottle off the bridge here, and it can float to the Danube and, eventually, all the way to Russia). Legend has it that Jason and his Argonauts founded Ljubljana when they stopped here for the winter on their way home with the Golden Fleece. The town was Romanized (and called Emona) before being over-run by Huns, only to be resettled later by Slavs.

In 1335, Ljubljana fell under the jurisdiction of the Hapsburg Emperors (who called it Laibach). After six centuries of Hapsburg rule, Ljubljana still feels Austrian—especially the abundant Austrian Baroque and Viennese Art Nouveau archi-tecture—but with a Mediterranean flair.

Napoleon put Ljubljana on the map when he made it the capital of his Illyrian Provinces, a realm that stretched from the Danube to Dubrovnik, from Austria to Albania (for only four years, 1809–1813). For the first time, the Slovene lan-guage was taught in schools, awakening a newfound pride in Slovenian cultural heritage. People still look back fondly on this very brief era, which was the first (and probably only) time when Ljubljana rose to prominence on the world stage. After more than 600 years of being part of the Hapsburg Empire, Ljubljana has no "Hapsburg Square"...but they do have a "French Revolution Square."

In the mid-19th century, the railway connecting Vienna to the Adriatic (Trieste) was built through town—and Ljubljana boomed. But much of the city was destroyed by an earthquake in 1895. It was rebuilt in the Art Nouveau style so popular in Vienna, its capital at the time. A generation later, architect Jože Plečnik bathed the city in his distinctive, artsy-but-sensible, classical-meets-modern style.

In 1991, Ljubljana became the capital of one of Europe's youngest nations. Today the city is filled with university stu-dents, making it a very youthful-feeling town. Ljubljana has always felt free to be creative, and recent years—with unprece-dented freedoms—have been no exception. This city is on the cutting edge when it comes to architecture, public art, and trendy pubs. But the scintillating avant-garde culture has soft edges—hip, but also non-threatening and user-friendly.

Ljubljana

1. Grand Hotel Union
2. To Union Hotel Garni
3. Hotel Emonec
4. Pri Mraku Guesthouse
5. To Hotel Park & Hostel Celica
6. Alibi Hostel
7. Sokol Restaurant
8. Gostilna As Rest. & Lounge
9. Ribca Restaurant
10. Zlata Ribica Rest.
11. Emonska Klet
12. Pizzeria Foculus
13. Ljubljanski Dvor Pizzeria
14. Paninoteka Sandwiches
15. To Nobel Burek & Olympia Burek
16. Restaurant Chez Eric & Bar Minimal
17. Čajna Hiša Teahouse
18. Zvezda Kavarna (Desserts)
19. To Krakovo Eateries
20. Kod & Kam Map Store
21. Dom Trgovina Souvenir Shops (2)
22. Funicular

Ljubljana's Two Big Ps

Mind your Ps, and your visit to Ljubljana becomes more meaningful:

Jože Plečnik (YOH-zheh PLAYCH-neek, 1872–1957) is the architect who shaped Ljubljana, designing virtually all of the city's most important landmarks. For more information, see page 541.

France Prešeren (FRAHN-tseh preh-SHAY-rehn, 1800–1849) is Slovenia's greatest poet and the namesake of Ljubljana's main square. Some civic-minded candy shops—trying to imitate the success of Austria's "Mozart Ball" chocolates—have started marketing chocolate "Prešeren Balls."

I've organized the sights in this chapter based on which side of the river they're on: the east (castle) side of the river, where Ljubljana began, with more medieval charm; and the west (Prešeren Square) side of the river, which has a more Baroque/Art Nouveau feel and most of the urban sprawl. At the northern edge of the tourist's Ljubljana is the train station; at the southern edge is the garden district of Krakovo and the Jože Plečnik House.

Tourist Information

Ljubljana's helpful TI has an office at the **Triple Bridge** (across from Prešeren Square; daily June–Sept 8:00–21:00, Oct–May 8:00–19:00, Stritarjeva ulica, tel. 01/306-1215, www.ljubljana -tourism.si). Another TI branch is at the **train station** (daily June–Sept 8:00–22:00, Oct–May 10:00–19:00, Trg O.F. 6, tel. 01/433-9475). A third TI, at the upper, far end of the **market** at Krekov trg 10, also offers information about the rest of Slovenia and has several Internet terminals (daily June–Sept 8:00–21:00, Oct–May 8:00–19:00, tel. 01/306-4575).

At any TI, pick up a pile of free resources: the big city map, the Tourist Guide, the *Ljubljana A to Z* directory, the monthly *Where to?* events guide, *Ljubljana Life* magazine (with restaurant reviews), and a wide range of informative brochures. Skip the **Ljubljana City Card,** which includes access to public transportation and free entry or discounts at several city museums (€13/72 hrs).

Arrival in Ljubljana

By Train: Ljubljana's modern, user-friendly train station (Železniška Postaja) is on the north edge of the city center. Emerging from the passage up to track 1a, turn right to find the Tir Bar (**bike rental**—see "Getting Around Ljubljana," page 528) and the yellow arrivals hall, which has a **TI** (see above), an **ATM,**

Ljubljana Essentials

English	Slovene	Pronounced
Ljubljana Castle	Ljubljanski Grad	lyoob-lyee-AHN-skee grahd
Prešeren Square	Prešernov trg	preh-SHEHR-nohv turg
Congress Square	Kongresni Trg	kohn-GREHS-nee turg
French Revolution Square	Trg Francoske Revolucije	turg frant-SOH-skeh reh-voh-LOOT-see-yeh
Square of the Republic	Trg Republike	turg reh-POOB-lee-keh
Triple Bridge	Tromostovje	troh-moh-STOHV-yeh
Cobblers' Bridge	Čevljarski Most	chehv-LAR-skee mohst
Dragon Bridge	Zmajski Most	ZMAY-skee mohst
Jože Plečnik, the architect	Jože Plečnik	YOH-zheh PLAYCH-neek
France Prešeren, the poet	France Prešeren	FRAHN-tseh preh-SHAY-rehn

and helpful English signs (arrivals hall open daily 5:00–22:00). Arrivals are *prihodi*, departures are *odhodi*, and track is *tir*.

The main square—and all of my recommended hotels—are within easy **walking** distance. It's a 10-minute stroll to get to the city center: Leave the arrivals hall to the right and walk a long block along the busy Trg Osvobodilne Fronte (or "Trg O.F." for short). At the post office (yellow *pošta* sign), cross Trg O.F., head straight down Miklošičeva, and you'll reach Prešeren Square.

Taxis, usually with unscrupulous cabbies, wait for you in front of the station. These mafia-type thugs are accustomed to charging you whatever they want without using the meter. The most likely scenario is that you'll pay a euro or two too much for the convenience of taking a taxi to your hotel—but *never* pay more than €5 total to any of my recommended hotels. For more on taxis—and how to avoid rip-off cabbies—see "Getting Around Ljubljana—By Taxi," below.

By Bus: Ljubljana's bus station (Autobusna Postaja) is a low-profile building (with ticket windows, Internet access, a bakery, and newsstands) in the middle of Trg O.F., right in front of the train station. To get into the center, see "By Train," above.

By Car: As you approach Ljubljana on the expressway, the toll road ends. Once you're on the ring road, you can take any exit, then follow bull's-eye signs for *Center*. Once you get into the city center, you'll begin to see directional signs to individual hotels. Ask your hotel about parking—most have some available, usually for a price. If you need to gas up your rental car before returning it, you'll find a huge gas station on Tivolska Cesta (just west of the train station). Otherwise, your options in the center are limited—it's better to look for a gas station on the expressway as you approach the city.

By Plane: See "Transportation Connections," page 550.

Helpful Hints

Pedestrian Safety: Ljubljana residents prefer to commute by bike. As a pedestrian, I've had many close calls with bikes that go whizzing by. Keep your eyes open and stay out of the designated bike lanes on the sidewalks (often marked in red).

Closed Days: Most Ljubljana museums (except the castle) are closed on Mondays. Remember that the highly recommended Jože Plečnik House is closed Sundays, Mondays, and Fridays—time your visit here carefully to coincide with a scheduled English tour.

Markets: In addition to the regular **market** that sprawls along the riverfront (described under "Sights," page 533), a colorful **flea market** hops along the castle side of the Ljubljanica River (south of the TI) every Sunday 8:00–13:00.

Money: Most banks are open Mon–Fri 9:00–12:00 & 14:00–17:00, Sat 9:00–12:00, closed Sun.

Internet Access: Most hotel lobbies have Internet access for guests. The TI at the upper end of the market has several terminals (see "Tourist Information," above). **Cyber Café Xplorer** is more expensive but has longer hours (Mon–Fri 10:00–22:00, Sat–Sun 14:00–22:00, across the river from the market at Petkovškovo nabrežje 23). The other TIs have free terminals allowing you to check your e-mail (but only Hotmail and Yahoo).

Post Office: The main post office *(pošta)* is in a beautiful yellow Art Nouveau building a block up Čopova from Prešeren Square, at the intersection with the busy Slovenska cesta (Mon–Fri 7:00–20:00, Sat 7:00–13:00, closed Sun).

Map Store: Kod & Kam has a huge selection of maps, English guidebooks, and other books about Slovenia (Mon–Fri 9:00–19:00, until 20:00 May–Aug, Sat 8:00–13:00, closed Sun, hiding at the bottom of French Revolution Square by the City Museum at Trg Francoske Revolucije 7, tel. 01/200-2732).

Architecture Guidebook: Ljubljana turns on architecture buffs. If you want to learn more about this city's quirky buildings, consider the excellent but expensive €30 *Architectural Guide to Ljubljana* (sold at TIs and many bookstores).

Laundry: Most hotels can do your laundry, but it's pricey. **Hostel Celica** serves as the town's self-serve launderette (€5/load, not very central at Metelkova 8, see page 546).

Car Rental: Figure about €50 per day (includes tax and insurance, no extra charge for drop-off elsewhere in Slovenia). **Europcar** (Mon–Fri 8:00–18:00, Sat 8:00–13:00 & 18:00–20:00, Sun 8:00–13:00, in City Hotel at Dalmatinova 15, tel. 01/234-9170, www.europcar.si) is slightly cheaper than **Avis** (Mon–Fri 7:00–19:00, Sat 7:00–13:00, Sun 8:00–12:00, Čufarjeva 2, tel. 01/430-8010, www.avis.si).

Best Views: Now that The Skyscraper is closed (see page 539), the best view in Ljubljana is from the castle tower. On sunny, blue-sky days, the colorful architecture on and near Prešeren Square pops, and you'll take photos like crazy along the river promenade.

Upcoming Events: Ljubljana will get lots of Europe-wide press in the coming years—in April of 2007, the city hosts the World Championship for ice hockey, and a year later, a Slovene will be elected to the European Union's rotating six-month presidency.

Getting Around Ljubljana

By Bus: Virtually all of Ljubljana's sights are easily accessible by foot, so public transportation probably isn't necessary. But just in case: A token, or *žeton,* for a bus trip costs €0.80 (buy at kiosk, bus station, or TI). If you pay on board, it's €1.25 and you need exact change. An all-day ticket costs €3.75 (sold only at bus station, TI, or LPP transit office).

By Taxi: There are several companies with different rates, but taxis usually start at about €1, and then charge €1 per kilometer. Additional "surcharges" (such as for luggage) are bogus—and are often tacked on as a surprise after you reach your destination. Crooked cabbies are a huge problem in Ljubljana (especially those hanging out at the train station and tourist attractions). A ride within the city center (such as from the station to a hotel) shouldn't cost more than €5. Your best strategy is to ask for an estimate up front. The cabbie will probably want to just take you for a flat price without using the meter. This is the easiest solution, but realize you'll probably wind up paying 10–20 percent more than you would if he used the meter. (If you're feeling stingy and feisty, try insisting on the meter.) Another common trick is to charge you the "Sunday and holidays" *(nedelja in počitnice)* rate even on weekdays.

Ljubljana at a Glance

▲▲▲Jože Plečnik House Final digs of the famed hometown architect who shaped so much of Ljubljana, explained by an enthusiastic guide. **Hours:** English tours begin at the top of each hour Tue–Thu 10:00–18:00, Sat 10:00–15:00, last tour departs 1 hour before closing, closed Sun–Mon and Fri.

▲▲Riverside Market Lively market area in the Old Town with produce, clothing, souvenirs—even wild boar salami. **Hours:** Best in the morning, especially Sat; market hall open Mon–Sat 7:00–14:00, Thu–Fri until 16:00, closed Sun.

▲▲Ljubljana Castle Tower with good views and so-so 3-D film. **Hours:** Grounds open daily May–Sept 9:00–22:00, Oct–April 10:00–21:00; castle open daily May–Sept 9:00–21:00, Oct–April 10:00–18:00, film plays all day on the half-hour.

▲▲National and University Library Plečnik's pièce de résistance, with an intriguing facade, piles of books, and a bright reading room. **Hours:** Main stairwell open Mon–Fri 9:00–20:00, Sat 9:00–14:00, closed Sun; student reading room open to the public mid-July–mid-Aug Mon–Fri 14:00–20:00.

▲Dragon Bridge Distinctive Art Nouveau bridge adorned with the city's mascot. **Hours:** Always roaring.

▲Contemporary History Museum Baroque mansion in Tivoli Park, with exhibit highlighting Slovenia's last 100 years. **Hours:** Daily 10:00–18:00.

▲Architectural Museum of Ljubljana Castle with Plečnik exhibit on the edge of town. **Hours:** Mon–Fri 9:00–15:00, Sat 11:00–18:00, Sun 11:00–14:00.

If you're suspicious, ask your cabbie to explain why he's chosen the tariff. You'll likely (but not definitely) avoid crooked cabbies if you call for a taxi. While this might sound intimidating, dispatchers generally speak a little English. Your hotel, restaurant, or maybe the TI (if they're not too busy) can call a cab for you. **Yellow Taxi** is more reputable than the norm (mobile 041-731-831); **Metro Taxi** is known for being inexpensive (mobile 041-240-200).

By Bike: Ljubljana is a cyclist's delight, with lots of well-marked bike lanes. Cheap bikes are rented all over the city, including at the market square TI, next to the big, pink Franciscan Church on Prešeren Square, and at the train station's Tir Bar (€1/2 hrs, €4.50/day, low prices subsidized by private companies that put ads on bikes).

TOURS

Most of Ljubljana's museums are disappointing; the town's ambience, architecture, and public art are its best attraction. To help you appreciate it all, taking a walking tour—either through the TI or by hiring your own local guide—is worth ▲▲.

Walking Tour—The TI organizes excellent two-hour guided town walks of Ljubljana in English, led by knowledgeable guides. From April through September, there are two tours daily: at 10:00 (a walking tour of the Old Town) and at 18:00 (a quick walking tour of the Old Town, followed by a trip by tourist train up to the castle). From October through March, the walking tour (no castle) goes only on Fridays, Saturdays, and Sundays at 11:00 (€7.50 for any of these tours, meet at Town Hall around corner from Triple Bridge TI).

Local Guide—Having an expert show you around his hometown for two hours for $45 has to be the best value in town. Ljubljana's hardworking guides lead tours on a wide variety of topics and can tailor their tour to your interests (figure €35/2 hrs, 50 percent more for same-day booking, contact TI for details, arrange at least 24 hours before). **Marijan Kriškovič,** who leads tours for me throughout Europe, is an outstanding guide (€35/2 hrs, mobile 040-222-739, kriskovic@yahoo.com).

Boat Cruise—Consider seeing the town from the Ljubljanica River. Various boat-cruise options (some guided, others with no guide or commentary) leave a block from the Triple Bridge TI (away from the market). Ask the TI about cruise times (€7.50 with a guide or €4 with no guide, sometimes combined with a short walking tour, weather permitting, few or no cruises Nov–March).

Bike Tour—The TI offers a bike tour of the city by request (€13, 2 hrs, 3-person minimum, arrange at least 24 hours ahead, get details at TI).

SELF-GUIDED SPIN-TOUR

Prešeren Square

The heart of Ljubljana is lively Prešeren Square (Prešernov trg). The city's meeting point is the large **statue of France Prešeren,** Slovenia's greatest poet, whose works include the lyrics to the Slovenian national anthem (and whose silhouette adorns Slovenia's €2 coin). The statue shows Prešeren, an important catalyst of 19th-century Slovenian nationalism, being inspired from overhead by the Muse. This statue provoked a scandal and outraged the bishop when it went up a hundred years ago—a naked woman sharing the square with a church! To ensure that nobody could be confused about the woman's intentions, she's conspicuously depicted with typical muse accessories: a laurel branch and a cloak.

Stand at the base of the statue to get oriented. Notice the bridge crossing the Ljubljanica River. This is one of Ljubljana's most important landmarks, Jože Plečnik's **Triple Bridge** (Tromostovje). The middle (widest) part of this bridge already existed, but Plečnik added the two side spans to more efficiently funnel the six streets of traffic on this side of the bridge to the one street on the other side. The bridge's Venetian vibe is intentional: Plečnik recognized that Ljubljana, located midway between Venice and then-capital Vienna, is itself a bridge between the Italian and Germanic worlds. Across the bridge is the TI, WCs, ATMs, market and cathedral (to the left), and the Town Hall (straight ahead).

Now turn 90 degrees to the right, and look down the first street after the riverbank. Find the pale woman in the picture frame on the second floor of the yellow house. This is **Julija,** the love of Prešeren's life. Tour guides spin romantic tales about how the couple met. But the truth is far less exciting: He was a teacher in her father's house when he was in his 30s and she was four. Later in life, she inspired him from afar—as she does now, from across the square—but they never got together. She may have been his muse, but when it came to marriage, she opted for wealth and status.

Ljubljana—especially the streets around this square—is an architecture-lover's paradise, starting with the **Hauptmann House,** to the right of Julija. This was the only building in town that survived the devastating 1895 earthquake. A few years later, the owner renovated it anyway in the then-trendy Viennese Art Nouveau style you see today. All that remains of the original is the Baroque balcony above the entrance.

Just to the right of the Hauptmann House is a car-sized **model** of the city center—helpful for orientation. The street next to it (with the McDonald's) is **Čopova,** once the route of Ljubljana's Sunday promenade. A century ago, locals would put on their Sunday best and stroll from here to Tivoli Park, listening to musicians and dropping into cafés along the way. Plečnik called it the "lifeline of the city," connecting the green lungs of the park to this urban center. Today, busy Slovenska avenue and railroad tracks cross the route, making the promenade less inviting. But in the last decade, Ljubljana has been trying to recapture its golden age, and some downtown streets are pedestrian-only on weekends once again. The new evening *paseo* thrives along the river between the Triple Bridge and Cobblers' Bridge.

Continue looking to the right, past the big, pink landmark Franciscan Church of St. Mary. To the right of the church, the street called **Miklošičeva cesta** connects Prešeren Square to the train station. When Ljubljana was rebuilding after the 1895 earthquake, town architects and designers envisioned this street as a showcase of its new, Vienna-inspired Art Nouveau image. Down the street and on the left is the prominent **Grand Hotel Union,** with a stately domed spire on the corner. When these buildings were designed, Prague was the cultural capital of the Slavic world. The new look of Ljubljana paid homage to "the golden city of a hundred spires" (and copied Prague's romantic image). There was actually a law for several years that corner buildings had to have these spires. Even the trees you'll see around town were part of the vision. When the architect Plečnik designed the Ljubljanica River embankments a generation later, he planted tall, pointy poplar trees and squat, rounded willows—imitating the spires and domes of Prague.

Across from the Grand Hotel Union (not visible from here, but worth a wander up the street) is a Secessionist building with classic red, blue, and white colors (for the Slovenian flag) next to the noisy, pink, zigzagged **Cooperative Bank.** The bank was designed by Ivan Vurnik, an ambitious Slovenian architect who wanted to invent a distinctive national style after World War I, when the Hapsburg Empire broke up and Eastern Europe's nations were proudly emerging for the first time.

On the near corner of Miklošičeva cesta, look for the characteristic glass awning of **Centromerkur**—the first big post-quake department store, today government-protected. At the top of the building is Mercury, god of commerce, watching over the square that has been Ljubljana's commercial heart since the city began. Since this was across the river from medieval Ljubljana (beyond the town's limits...and the long arm of its tax collector), this area was the best place to sell and buy goods. Today it's the heart of Ljubljana's boutique culture. Step into the Centromerkur store to admire the interior, which is exactly the same as when it was built. The old-fashioned layout isn't convenient for modern shoppers—no elevator, tight aisles—but no matter how much anyone complains, the management isn't allowed to change a thing.

Prešeren Square is the perfect springboard to explore the rest of Ljubljana. Now that you're oriented, visit some of the areas listed below.

SIGHTS

East of the River, Under the Castle

The castle side of the river is the city's most colorful and historic quarter, packed with Old World ambience.

▲▲**Riverside Market**—In Ljubljana's thriving Old Town market, big-city Slovenes enjoy buying directly from the producer. The market, worth an amble anytime, is best on Saturday mornings, when the townspeople take their time wandering the stalls. In this tiny capital of a tiny country, you may even see the president searching for the perfect melon.

Begin your walk through the market at the Triple Bridge (and TI). The riverside **colonnade** was designed by (who else?) Jože Plečnik. This first stretch—nearest the Triple Bridge—is good for souvenirs: woodcarvings, miniature painted frontboards from beehives, and lots of colorful candles (bubbly Marta will gladly paint a special message on your candle for no extra charge).

Farther in, the market is almost all local, and the colonnade is populated by butchers, bakers, fishermen, and lazy cafés. Peek down at the actual river and see how the architect wanted the town and river to connect. The lower arcade is a people zone, with easy access from the bridge, public WCs, inviting cafés, and a stinky fish market offering a wide variety. The restaurant just below, **Ribca,** serves fun fishy plates, beer, and coffee with great riverside seating (open Mon–Sat only until 16:00; see "Eating," page 547).

Walk along the colonnade with the river on your left. When you come to the first small market square on your right, notice the 10-foot-tall concrete **cone.** Plečnik wanted to make Ljubljana the "Athens of the North," and imagined a huge hilltop cone as the center of a national acropolis—a complex for government, museums, and culture. This ambitious plan never panned out, but part of Plečnik's Greek idea did: this marketplace, based on an ancient Greek *agora.* But the Slovenes haven't given up on Plečnik's vision: His never-completed giant cone adorns Slovenia's €0.10 coin (probably the only nonexistent building ever to grace a piece of currency).

At the top of this square, you'll find the 18th-century **cathedral** *(stolnica)* standing on the site of a 13th-century Romanesque church. The cathedral is dedicated to St. Nicholas, patron saint of the fishermen and boatmen who have long come to sell their catch at the market. Take a close look at the intricately decorated side door under the passageway. This remarkable door was created for Pope John Paul II's visit here in 1996. Buried deeply in the fecund soil of their ancient and pagan history, the nation's linden tree of life sprouts with the story of the Slovenes. Crusaders and Ottomans battle at the bottom. At the top is Pope John Paul II, the Pole who oversaw the fall of communism, and—below him—the man who will become Slovenia's first saint. Around back is a similar door, carved with images of the six 20th-century bishops of Ljubljana. The interior is stunning Italian Baroque.

The building at the end of this first market square is the seminary palace. In the basement is a **market hall,** with vendors selling cheeses, meats, dried fruits, and other goodies (Mon–Sat 7:00–14:00, Thu–Fri until 16:00, closed Sun). This place is worth a graze. Most merchants are happy to give you a free sample (point to what you want, and say *probat, prosim*—"a taste, please").

When you leave the market hall, continue downstream into the big **main market square,** packed with produce and clothing stands. (The colorful flower market hides behind the seminary palace/market hall.) These producers go out of their way to be old-fashioned—many of them still follow the tradition of pushing their veggies on wooden carts (called *cizas*) to the market from their garden patches in the suburbs. Once at their stalls, they handle their produce wearing special gloves—it's considered rude for customers to touch the fruits and vegetables before they're bought. Over time, shoppers develop friendships with their favorite producers. On busy days, you'll see a long line at one stand, while the other merchants stand bored. Your choice is simple: Get in line, or eat sub-par produce.

Look for the little **scales** in the wooden kiosks marked *Kontrola Tehtnica*—allowing buyers to immediately check whether the producer cheated them (not a common problem, but just in case). The Hapsburg days left locals with the old German saying, "Trust is good; control is better."

At the corner of this market square (toward Prešeren Square), you'll notice a big gap along the riverfront colonnade. This was to be the site of a huge, roofed **Butchers' Bridge** designed by Jože Plečnik, but the plans never materialized. Aware of Plečnik's newfound touristic currency, some town politicians have recently dusted off the old plans and proposed building the bridge after all these years. (If you look across the river, you'll see that the cornerstone was already put in place by an overzealous politician.) It's a controversial project, and anytime a new mayor is elected, the decision is reversed.

If you want a unique taste as you finish exploring the market, enter the colonnade near the very end and find the **Divjač'na Hubert** stand at #22, specializing in game. Ask charming Minka (it's her shop) for a *probat* (taste) of *div. prašič salama*—wild boar salami.

Just beyond the end of the market colonnade is the...

▲**Dragon Bridge (Zmajski Most)**—The dragon has been the symbol of Ljubljana for centuries, ever since Jason (of Argonauts and Golden Fleece fame) supposedly slew one in a nearby swamp. While the dragon is the star of this very photogenic Art Nouveau bridge, it was officially dedicated to Hapsburg Emperor Franz Josef. (Tapping into the emp's vanity got new projects funded—vital as the city rebuilt after its devastating earthquake of 1895.) But the Franz Josef name never stuck; those dragons are just too darn memorable.

▲▲Town Square (Mestni Trg)—This square—just across the Triple Bridge and up the street from Prešeren Square—is home to the **Town Hall** (Rotovž), highlighted by its clock tower and pillared loggia. Step inside the Renaissance courtyard to see artifacts and a map of late-17th-century Ljubljana. Studying this map, notice how the river, hill, and wall worked together to fortify the town. Courtyards like this (but humbler) are hidden through the city. As rent in these old places is cheap, many such courtyards host funky and characteristic little businesses. Be sure to get off the main drag and poke into Ljubljana's nooks and crannies.

In the square is the **Fountain of Three Carolinian Rivers,** inspired in style and theme by Rome's many fountains. The figures with vases represent this region's three main rivers: Ljubljanica, Sava, and Krka. Over the centuries, the wild fluctuations in temperature that come with Ljubljana winters took its toll on this fountain—so recently, it's been undergoing a years-long restoration project (if it's missing, that's why).

In the early 19th century, Ljubljana consisted mainly of this single street, running along the base of Castle Hill (plus a small "New Town" across the river). Stretching south from here are two other "squares"—Stari trg (Old Square) and Gornji trg (Upper Square)—that have long since grown together into one big, atmospheric promenade lined with quaint shops and cafés (perfect for a stroll). Virtually every house along this drag has a story to tell, of a famous resident or infamous incident. As you walk, keep your eyes open for Ljubljana's mascot dragon—it's everywhere. At the end of the pedestrian zone (at Gornji trg), look uphill and notice the village charms of the oldest buildings in town (four medieval houses with rooflines slanted at the ends, different from the others on this street).

▲▲Ljubljana Castle (Ljubljanski Grad)—The castle above town offers enjoyable views of Ljubljana and the surrounding countryside. There has probably been a settlement on this site since prehistoric times, though the first castle here was Roman. The

12th-century version was gradually added on to over the centuries,
until it fell into disrepair in the 17th
century. Today's castle was rebuilt
in the 1940s, renovated in the 1970s,
and is still technically unfinished
(subject to ongoing additions). The
castle houses a restaurant, a gift
shop, temporary exhibition halls,
and a Gothic chapel with Baroque
paintings of the coat of arms of St.
George (Ljubljana's patron saint,

the dragon-slayer). Above the restaurant are two wedding halls—
Ljubljana's most popular places to get married. While the castle
and its attractions are ho-hum, the views are worth the climb.

It's free to enter the castle grounds (daily May–Sept 9:00–
22:00, Oct–April 10:00–21:00, tel. 01/232-9994). Inside are two
optional activities you have to pay for (€3.50 covers both, daily
May–Sept 9:00–21:00, Oct–April 10:00–18:00): the **castle tower,**
with 92 steps leading to one of the best views in town; and a 20-
minute **3-D film** about the history of Ljubljana (touted as a "virtual museum," but barely worth your time; plays all day on the
half-hour).

Tours of the castle in Slovene and English leave from the
entry bridge daily June through mid–September at 10:00 and 16:00
(€5, tour lasts 60–90 min). The castle is also home to the Ljubljana
Summer Festival, with **concerts** throughout the summer (tel.
01/426-4340, www.festival-lj.si).

Getting to the Castle: A brand-new **funicular** whisks visitors to the top in a jiff (€2, daily 10:00–21:00, catch it at Krekov
trg, across the busy street from the market square TI). Another
sweat-free route to the top is via the **tourist train** that leaves at
the top of each hour (or more frequently, with demand) from
Prešeren Square (€2.50, daily in summer 9:00–21:00, shorter hours
off-season, doesn't run in snow or other bad weather). There are
also two handy **trails** to the castle. The steeper-but-faster route
begins near the Dragon Bridge (find Studentovska lane, just past
the statue of Vodnik in the market). Slower but easier is Reber, just
off Stari trg (Old Square), a few blocks south of the Town Hall
(once on the trail, always bear left, then go right when you're just
under the castle—follow signs).

West of the River, Beyond Prešeren Square

The Prešeren Square (west) side of the river is the heart of modern
Ljubljana, and home to several prominent squares and fine museums. These sights are listed roughly in order from Prešeren Square,

and can be linked to make an interesting walk.

• *Leave Prešeren Square in the direction the poet is looking, bear to your left (up Wolfova, by the picture of Julija), and walk a block to...*

Congress Square (Kongresni Trg)—This grassy, tree-lined square is ringed by some of Ljubljana's most important buildings: the University headquarters, the Baroque Ursuline Church of the Holy Trinity, a classical mansion called the Kažina, and the Philharmonic Hall. At the top end of the square, by the entry to a pedestrian underpass, a Roman sarcophagus sits under a gilded statue of a **Roman citizen**—a replica of an artifact from 1,700 years ago, when this town was called Emona. The busy street above you has been the main trading route through town since ancient Roman times. This square hosts the big town events. Locals remember how, when President Clinton visited, tens of thousands packed the square. (When President George W. Bush came, almost nobody showed up.)

• *Take the underpass beneath busy Slovenska avenue (the town's main traffic thoroughfare) to the...*

▲Square of the Republic (Trg Republike)—This unusual square is essentially a parking lot ringed by an odd collection of buildings. While hardly quaint, the Square of the Republic gives you a good taste of a modern corner of Ljubljana. And it's historic—this is where Slovenia declared its independence in 1991.

The **twin office towers** (with the world's biggest digital watch, flashing the date, time, and temperature) were designed by Plečnik's protégé, Edvard Ravnikar. As harrowing as these seem, imagine if they had followed the original plans—twice as tall as they are now, and connected by a bridge, representing the gateway to Ljubljana. These buildings were originally designed as the Slovenian parliament—but the ambitious plans were scaled back when Tito didn't approve (since it would have made Slovenia's parliament bigger than the Yugoslav parliament in Belgrade). Instead, the **Slovenian Parliament** is across the square, in the strangely low-profile office building with the sculpted entryway. The carvings are in the Social Realist style, celebrating the noble Slovenian people conforming to communist ideals for the good of the entire society. Completing the square are a huge conference center (Cankarjev Dom, the white building behind the skyscrapers), a shopping mall, and some public art.

• *Just a block north (on Trg Narodni Herojev), you'll find the...*

Slovenian National Museum (Narodni Muzej Slovenije) and Slovenian Museum of Natural History (Prirodoslovni Muzej Slovenije)—These two museums share a single historic building facing a park behind the Parliament. While neither collection is particularly good, they're both worth considering if you have a special interest or if it's a rainy day (€3 for each museum, or €4.60

for both, some English descriptions, daily 10:00–18:00, Thu until 20:00, Muzejska 1, tel. 01/241-0940, www2.pms-lj.si).

The **National Museum** occupies the ground floor, featuring a lapidarium with carved-stone Roman monuments and exhibits on Egyptian mummies. (Temporary exhibits are also on this level.) Upstairs and to the right are more exhibits of the National Museum, loosely tracing Slovenian history with artifacts ranging from old armor and pottery to the museum's pride and joy, a fragment of a 45,000-year-old Neanderthal flute.

Upstairs and to the left is the **Natural History** exhibit, featuring the flora and fauna of Slovenia. You'll see partial skeletons of a mammoth and a cave bear, plenty of stuffed reptiles, fish, and birds, and an exhibit on "human fish" (*Proteus anguinus*—long, skinny, pale-pink salamanders).

Behind the museum is a pretty yellow chalet housing the **US Embassy**—my vote for quaintest embassy building in the world.

• *Just up the street are two decent but skippable art museums:*

National Gallery (Narodna Galerija)—This museum has three parts: European artists, Slovenian artists, and temporary exhibits. Find the work of Ivana Kobilca, a late-19th-century Slovenian Impressionist. Art-lovers enjoy her self-portrait in *Summer*. If you're going to Bled, you can get a sneak preview with Marko Pernhart's huge panorama of the Julian Alps (€4.25, free on Sat after 14:00, open Tue–Sun 10:00–18:00, closed Mon, enter through big glass box between two older buildings at Prešernova 24, tel. 01/241-5435, www.ng-slo.si).

Museum of Modern Art (Moderna Galerija Ljubljana)—This has a ho-hum permanent collection of modern and contemporary Slovenian artists, as well as temporary exhibits by both Slovenes and international artists (€4.25; July–Aug Tue–Sat 12:00–20:00, closed Mon; Sept–June Tue–Sat 10:00–18:00, closed Mon; Tomšičeva 14, tel. 01/241-6800, www.mg-lj.si).

• *Near the art museums, look for the...*

Serbian Orthodox Church—The church was built in 1936, soon after the Slovenes joined a political union with the Serbs. Wealthy Slovenia attracted its poorer neighbors from the south—so it built this church for that community. Since 1991, the Serb population continues to rise—people from the poorer parts of the former Yugoslavia, such as Serbia, are flocking to prosperous Slovenia. The church is decorated without a hint of the 20th century, mirroring a very conservative religion. You'll see Cyrillic script in this building, which feels closer to Moscow than to Rome.

• *On the other side of the busy street is...*

Tivoli Park (Park Tivoli)—This huge park, just west of the center, is where Slovenes relax on summer weekends. The easiest access is by underpass from Cankarjeva cesta (between the National Gallery and the Museum of Modern Art). As you emerge, the Neoclassical pillars leading down the promenade clue you in that this part of the park was designed by Jože Plečnik.

• *Aside from taking a leisurely stroll, the best thing to do in the park is visit the...*

▲**Contemporary History Museum (Muzej Novejše Zgodovine)**—In a Baroque mansion (Cekinov Grad) in Tivoli Park, a well-done exhibit called "Slovenians in the 20th Century" traces the last hundred years of Slovenian history. Downstairs are temporary exhibits, and upstairs are several rooms using models, dioramas, and light-and-sound effects to creatively tell the story of one of Europe's youngest nations. It's a little difficult to fully appreciate, even with the English descriptions. But the creativity and the spunky spirit of the place are truly enjoyable. The most moving room has artifacts from the Slovenes' brave declaration of independence from a hostile Yugoslavia in 1991. The well-organized Slovenes had only to weather a 10-day skirmish to gain their autonomy. (It's chilling to think that bombers were en route to leveling this gorgeous city. The planes were called back at the last minute, because diplomatic negotiations were improving.) The free English brochure explains everything (€3.50, permanent exhibit free first Sun of the month, open daily 10:00–18:00, in Tivoli Park at Celovška cesta 23, tel. 01/300-9610, www.muzej-nz.si).

Getting There: The museum is a 20-minute walk from the center, best combined with a wander through Tivoli Park. The fastest approach: As you emerge from the Cankarjeva cesta underpass into the park, turn right and go straight ahead for five minutes, continue straight up the ramp, then turn left after the tennis courts and look for the big pink mansion.

• *On your way back to the center, consider stopping by...*

The Skyscraper (Nebotičnik)—This 1933 Art Deco building was the first skyscraper in Slovenia, for a time the tallest building in Central Europe, and one of the earliest European buildings that was clearly influenced by American architecture.

The Skyscraper has weathered an often-unlucky history. At the time it was constructed, Jože Plečnik was calling the shots when it came to Ljubljana architecture, so this building's designer had to get Plečnik's approval before he could build. Plečnik agreed, but didn't like the plan for 12 stories—so he asked to make it nine instead. After agreeing, the building's architect went ahead and built the last three stories anyway.

Ever since, say the locals, The Skyscraper has been cursed. The 12th-story observation deck—with Ljubljana's best view—had to close a few years back because it had become the most popular spot in the country for suicide attempts. Now it has been (ineffectively) retrofitted to try to prevent people from diving off. Two different restaurants on the top floor have come and gone over the last five years, and plans for a new one are constantly on-again, off-again (2 blocks from Prešeren Square at Štefanova ulica 1).

• *A few blocks south, near several Jože Plečnik sights (see below) at the river end of French Revolution Square, you'll find the...*

City Museum of Ljubljana (Mestni Muzej Ljubljana)—This highly conceptual museum, in the recently restored Auersperg Palace, offers a high-tech, in-depth look at the history of Ljubljana. The cellar features Roman ruins and medieval artifacts, while the second floor hosts a permanent exhibition about the culture, politics, and economy of Ljubljana. Rounding out the museum's collection is a wide range of special exhibitions, and a relaxing movie theater showing films about the city (free but will likely begin charging entry fee for permanent exhibit in 2007, well-described in English, Tue–Sun 10:00–18:00, closed Mon, Gosposka 15, tel. 01/241-2500, www.mm-lj.si).

Jože Plečnik's Architecture

Jože Plečnik is to Ljubljana what Antoni Gaudí is to Barcelona: a homegrown and amazingly prolific genius who shaped his town with a uniquely beautiful vision. And, as in Barcelona, Ljubljana has a way of turning people who couldn't care less about architecture into huge Plečnik fans. There's plenty to see. In addition to the top sights listed below, Plečnik designed the embankments along the Ljubljanica and Gradaščica Rivers in the Trnovo neighborhood; the rebuilt Roman wall along Mirje street, south of the center; the Church of St. Francis, with its classicist bell tower; St. Michael's Church on the Marsh; Orel Stadium; Žale Cemetery; and many more buildings throughout Slovenia.

▲▲▲**Jože Plečnik House (Plečnikova Zbirka)**—Ljubljana's favorite son lived here from 1921 until his death in 1957. He added on to an existing house, building a circular bedroom for himself and filling the place with clever furniture and other gizmos he designed, as well as artifacts, photos, and gifts from around the world that inspired him as he shaped Ljubljana.

Today the house is decorated exactly as it was the day Plečnik died, containing much of his equipment, models, and plans. There are very few barriers, so you are in direct contact with the world of the architect. Perhaps no other museum in Europe gives such an intimate portrait of an artist; you'll feel like Plečnik invited you over for dinner. It's still furnished with unique, Plečnik-designed furniture and ingenious, one-of-a-kind inventions. Whether or not you care about Plečnik, architecture, or design, you can't help but be tickled by this man's sheer creativity, and by the world he forged for himself to live in.

The house can be toured only with a guide, whose enthusiasm

Jože Plečnik
(1872–1957)

There is probably no single architect who has shaped one city as Jože Plečnik (YOH-zheh PLAYCH-neek) shaped Ljubljana.

Everywhere you go, you can see where he left his mark. While he may not yet register very high on the international Richter scale of important architects, the Slovenes' pride in this man's work is understandable.

Plečnik was born in Ljubljana and studied in Vienna under the Secessionist architect Otto Wagner (see page 774). His first commissions, done around the turn of the 20th century in Vienna, were pretty standard Art Nouveau stuff. Then Tomáš Masaryk, president of the new nation of Czechoslovakia, decided that the dull Hapsburg design of Prague Castle could use a new look to go with its new independence. In 1921, Masaryk chose Jože Plečnik, who sprinkled the castle grounds with his distinctive touches. By now, Plečnik had perfected his simple, eye-pleasing style, which mixes modern and classical influences with lots of columns and pyramids—simultaneously austere and playful.

By the time Plečnik finished in Prague, he had made a name for himself. His prime years were spent creating for the Kingdom of Yugoslavia (before the ideology-driven era of Tito). Plečnik returned home to Ljubljana and set to work redesigning the city, both as an architect and as an urban planner. He lived in a simple house behind the Trnovo Church (now a tourable museum—see page 540), and on his walk to work every day, he pondered ways to make the city even more livable. Wandering through town, notice how thoughtfully he incorporated people, nature, the Slovenian heritage, town vistas, and symbolism into his works—it's feng shui on a grand urban scale. Many of his ideas became reality; even more did not. (It's fun to imagine what this city would look like if Plečnik had always gotten his way.)

After his death in 1957, Plečnik was virtually forgotten by Slovenes and scholars alike. But in 1986, an exposition about Plečnik at Paris' Pompidou Center jump-started interest in the architect. Within a few years Plečnik was back in vogue. Today, scholars hail him as a genius who was ahead of his time, while locals and tourists simply enjoy the beauty of his brilliant works. In 2007, Ljubljana celebrates the "Year of Plečnik," commemorating the 50th anniversary of the architect's death.

brings the place to life. Thirty-minute English tours begin at the top of each hour (€5, €2.50 guidebook, Tue–Thu 10:00–18:00, Sat 10:00–15:00, last tour departs 1 hour before closing, closed Fri and Sun–Mon, Karunova ulica 4, tel. 01/280-1600, www.aml.si, pz @aml.si, well-run by Ana and Natalija).

Getting There: The 15-minute stroll from the center is nearly as enjoyable as the house itself. First find your way to French Revolution Square, surrounded by other Plečnik works (described below). From the square's obelisk, walk down Emonska for about 10 minutes toward the twin-spired church. You'll pass (on the left) the delightful Krakovo district—a patch of green countryside in downtown Ljubljana. Many of the veggies you see in the riverside market come from these carefully tended gardens. (This mellow residential zone also has a pair of good restaurants—see "Eating.") When you reach the Gradaščica stream, head over the bridge (also designed by Plečnik) and go around the left side of the church to find the house.

▲▲**National and University Library (Narodna in Univerzitetna Knjižnica, or NUK)**—Just a block up from the river at Novi trg is Plečnik's masterpiece. The theme of the building is overcoming obstacles to attain knowledge. The facade has blocks of odd sizes and shapes, representing a complex numerological pattern that suggests barriers on the path to enlightenment. The sculpture on the river side is Moses—known for leading his people through 40 years of hardship to the Promised Land. On the right side of the building, find the horse-head doorknobs—representing the winged horse Pegasus (grab hold, and he'll whisk you away to new levels of enlightenment). Step inside. The main staircase is dark and gloomy—modeled after an Egyptian tomb. But at the top, through the door marked *Velika Čitalnica*, is the bright, airy main reading room: the ultimate goal, a place of learning.

Aside from being a great work of architecture, the building also houses the most important library in Slovenia, with more than two million books (about one per Slovene). The library is supposed to receive a copy of each new book printed in the country. In a freaky bit of bad luck, this was the only building in town damaged in World War II, when a plane crashed into it. But the people didn't want to see their books go up in flames—so hundreds of locals formed a human chain, risking life and limb to get the books out of the burning building.

You can easily duck into the main stairwell (free, Mon–Fri 9:00–20:00, Sat 9:00–14:00, closed Sun). The quiet student reading room is officially open for visitors during very limited hours, when it's technically closed to students (mid-July–mid-Aug Mon–Fri 14:00–20:00). If you're not here during that one-month span, and you're really determined to see the room, you can stick close to a student going inside. To get out, follow another student—or push gently on the door (it usually opens easily).

The library is at the corner of Turjaška and Gosposka streets. To get here from Prešeren Square, simply follow the river south and turn right up Novi trg (the parking-lot square just after Cobblers' Bridge).

▲French Revolution Square (Trg Francoske Revolucije)— Many of Plečnik's finest works are on or near this square, just around the corner from the National and University Library (described earlier).

Plečnik designed the **obelisk** in the middle of the square to commemorate Napoleon's short-lived decision to make Ljubljana the capital of his Illyrian Provinces. It's rare to find anything honoring Napoleon outside of Paris, but he was good to Ljubljana. Under his rule, Slovenian culture flourished, schools were established, and roads and infrastructure were improved. The monument contains ashes of the unknown French soldiers who died in 1813, when the region went from French to Austrian control.

The Teutonic Knights of the Cross established the nearby **monastery** (Križanke, ivy-capped wall and gate, free entry) in 1230. The adaptation of these monastery buildings into the Ljubljana Summer Theatre was Plečnik's last major work (1950–1956).

▲Architectural Museum of Ljubljana (Arhitekturni Muzej Ljubljana)—If your visit to Ljubljana has infected you with Plečnik fever, you can trek out to this interesting museum, located in Fužine Castle on the outskirts of Ljubljana. The permanent exhibit features parts of the 1986 Paris exhibition that made Plečnik famous all over again. Downstairs is a display of plans and photos from Plečnik's earlier works in Vienna and Prague, and upstairs, you'll find an exhibit on his works in Slovenia, including some detailed plans and models for ambitious projects he never completed (like the huge, cone-shaped parliament atop Castle Hill). It's worthwhile, but a bit of a hassle to reach—only true enthusiasts should pay a visit (€2.50, Mon–Fri 9:00–15:00, Sat 11:00–18:00, Sun 11:00–14:00, last entry 30 min before closing, Pot na Fužine 2, tel. 01/540-9798, www.aml.si). Take bus #20 from Congress Square (direction: Fužine) to the end of the line (about 20 min).

SHOPPING

Ljubljana, with its easygoing ambience and countless boutiques, is made to order for whiling away an afternoon shopping. It's also a fun place to stock up on souvenirs and gifts for the folks back home. Popular items include wood carvings (especially of the characteristic hayracks that dot the countryside), different flavors of schnapps (the kind with a whole pear inside—cultivated to actually grow right into the bottle—is the classiest), honey mead brandy (*medica*—sweet and smooth), and those adorable painted frontboard panels from beehives (see page 578).

The most atmospheric trinket-shopping is in the first stretch of the **market colonnade,** along the riverfront next to the Triple Bridge (see page 531). The best souvenir shop in town is **Dom Trgovina,** just a block across the Triple Bridge from Prešeren Square and facing the Town Hall (Mon–Fri 9:00–19:00, Sat 9:00–13:00, closed Sun, Mestni trg 24, tel. 01/241-8300). Another location is across from the TI on the main market square (Mon–Fri 8:00–19:00, Sat 8:00–13:00, closed Sun, Ciril-Metodov trg 5).

Another item you'll see sold all over the country are **Peko shoes.** Made in a town north of Ljubljana called Tržič, Pekos are similar to high-fashion Italian models, but much cheaper. The name is an abbreviation of its founder's name: Peter Kozina (www.peko.si).

SLEEPING

Ljubljana's accommodations scene, once abysmal, is steadily improving. Still, it's challenging. Only a handful of places are within convenient walking distance of the center, and most are overpriced. For the best value, stick with the Pri Mraku or the Emonec (though even these "good" options come with caveats). The most expensive hotels raise their prices even more during conventions (often Sept–Oct, and sometimes also June). To locate hotels and restaurants, see the map on page 524. The TI can give you a list of cheap private rooms *(sobe)*.

$$$ Grand Hotel Union is as much an Art Nouveau landmark as a hotel. You'll pay dearly for its Old World elegance, hundred years of history, professional staff, big pool, and perfect location (right on Prešeren Square). The 194 plush "Executive" rooms are in the main building (Sb-€149–159, Db-€177, extra bed-€27, prices 20 percent higher during conventions, can be 20 percent cheaper during slow times—including most weekends and mid-July–mid-Aug, non-smoking floors, elevator, Internet access, parking-€12.50/day, Miklošičeva cesta 1, tel. 01/308-1270, fax 01/308-1015, www.gh-union.si, hotel.union@gh-union.si). Its 133 "Business" rooms

> # Sleep Code
>
> **(€1 = about $1.20, country code: 386, area code: 01)**
> **S** = Single, **D** = Double/Twin, **T** = Triple, **Q** = Quad, **b** = bathroom,
> **s** = shower only. Unless otherwise noted, credit cards are
> accepted, breakfast is included, and the modest tourist tax (€1
> per person, per night) is not. Everyone speaks English.
>
> To help you easily sort through these listings, I've divided
> the rooms into three categories based on the price for a stan-
> dard double room with bath:
>
> $$$ **Higher Priced**—Most rooms €110 or more.
> $$ **Moderately Priced**—Most rooms between €55–110.
> $ **Lower Priced**—Most rooms €55 or less.

next door are a lesser value: less luxurious and almost as expensive (Sb-€129–140, Db-€164, same price increases and deals as
"Executive" prices, non-smoking floors, elevator, parking and
Internet access at main hotel, Miklošičeva cesta 3, tel. 01/308-1170,
fax 01/308-1914, www.gh-union.si, hotel.business@gh-union.si).

$$$ Union Hotel Garni, technically part of the Grand Hotel
Union up the street, has been threatening to change its name for
years. Whatever it's called, the hotel has 74 modern, business-class
rooms with less panache than the main Hotel Union, but it's nicely
situated between Prešeren Square and the train station (Sb-€107–
117, Db-€140, 20 percent less weekends and mid-July–mid-Aug,
extra bed-€27, non-smoking rooms, elevator, parking garage-€11/
day, Miklošičeva cesta 9, tel. 01/308-4300, fax 01/230-1181, www
.astralhotel.net, hotel.garni@gh-union.si).

$$ Hotel Emonec, a great value with some of the best-located
rooms in Ljubljana, hides between Prešeren and Congress squares.
Its 26 rooms—in two buildings across a courtyard from each
other—are simple and institutional, but the price is right, and you
can't be more central. If you're a light sleeper, be warned that the
hotel shares its courtyard with a disco that can be noisy into the
wee hours—request a quiet room (Sb-€57, small Db-€64, bigger
"standard" Db-€74, Tb-€89, Qb-€104, Internet access, free loaner
bikes for guests, Wolfova 12, tel. 01/200-1520, fax 01/200-1521,
www.hotel-emonec.com, hotelemonec@siol.net).

$$ Pri Mraku Guesthouse has 36 comfortable, slightly worn
rooms in a very pleasant neighborhood near French Revolution
Square. Despite its quirks (a so-so breakfast, lots of stairs with no
elevator, occasionally frustrating staff), it's my sentimental favorite
in Ljubljana (Sb-€65–75, Db-€100, extra bed-€20, ground-floor
and top-floor rooms have air-con and cost about €10 more, prices

about 20 percent cheaper July–Aug, non-smoking floor, beautiful new breakfast room and restaurant, Rimska 4, tel. 01/421-9600, fax 01/421-9655, www.daj-dam.si, mrak@daj-dam.si).

$$ Hotel Park is housed in a soulless, 12-story communist apartment block in a dull neighborhood a 10-minute walk from Prešeren Square. Its 145 inexpensive rooms come in two types: "two-star" rooms, nicer than you'd expect from the exterior; and "one-star" rooms, with no TV, old linoleum, and worn furniture, but reasonably well-maintained. The staff is often aggravating, but the elevator, which seems possessed, always manages to top them. I'd consider this one a last resort (one-star rooms with toilet but no shower: S-€38, D-€46, 10 percent discount for hostel members for these rooms only; one-star rooms with full bathrooms: Sb-€50, Db-€64; two-star rooms: Sb-€55, Db-€71; possessed elevator, Tabor 9, tel. 01/300-2500, fax 01/433-0546, www.hotelpark.si, hotel.park@siol.net).

$ Hostel Celica rents the cheapest beds in town in an unforgettable setting. This innovative hostel is funded by the city and run by a nonprofit student arts organization. Once an old military prison, this remarkable place has 20 cells *(celica)* converted into hostel rooms—each one unique, decorated by a different designer (tours of the hostel daily at 14:00, usually led by the architect on Tue and Wed). The top floor features more typical hostel rooms (each with its own bathroom, for 3–14 people). The building also houses an art gallery, tourist information, Internet access, self-serve laundry, restaurant, and shoes-off "Oriental" café. The surrounding neighborhood—a bit run-down and remote, but safe—is gradually emerging as a happening nightlife zone; in fact, a nearby disco can make things noisy on weekends (all prices listed are per person—cell rooms: S-€45, D-€25, T-€20; top-floor rooms with bathrooms: 3–5-bed room-€23, 6–7-bed dorm-€20, 14-bed dorm-€18; includes breakfast and sheets, no curfew, non-smoking, Metelkova 8, a dull 15-min walk to Prešeren Square, 10 min to the train station, tel. 01/230-9700, fax 01/230-9712, www.souhostel .si, info@souhostel.si).

$ Alibi Hostel, loosely run by Gorazd, offers 110 beds and a funkier, more laid-back scene than Celica. The rooms are colorful and scruffy, and it's ideally located right on Ljubljana's main riverfront-café drag. The imaginative graffiti murals—featuring a stripper with memorable piercings, and a certain cowboy president—are guaranteed to offend just about anyone over 30 (dorm bed-€20, D-€60, includes sheets and tax, breakfast-€2, €20 key deposit, free Internet access, Cankarjevo nabrežje 27, tel. 01/251-1244, www.alibi.si).

EATING

Though heavy, meat-and-starch Slovenian food is available, Ljubljana also offers an abundance of pizza and other Italian fare—not to mention plenty of other international options (French, Indian, Chinese, even Mexican). The main drag through the Old Town is lined with inviting eateries, their tables spilling out into the cobbled pedestrian street. Prešeren Square thrives in the evenings, often with live bands leading a celebration of life and youth. To locate these restaurants, see the map on page 524.

Mid-Range, Local-Style Cuisine

Very few places serve strictly Slovenian food; at this crossroads of cultures (and cuisines), Italian and French flavors are just as "local" as anything else. But the following eateries are as close to "real Slovenian cuisine" as you'll get.

Sokol, with brisk, traditionally clad waiters serving truly typical Slovenian food, is a reliable option (soup in a bread bowl is a favorite starter). The sprawling Slovenian-village interior is fun and woody, jaunty polka plays on the soundtrack, and the location is very central. All of this means it's deluged by tourists, so don't expect top quality or a good value (€6–18 main dishes, salads, veggie options, Mon–Sat 7:00–23:00, Sun 10:00–23:00, on castle side of Triple Bridge at Ciril-Metodov trg 18, tel. 01/439-6855).

Gostilna As Lounge, a cheaper side-restaurant of the fancy As (described under "Upscale International" on page 549), features drinks, €5–7 salads and sandwiches, €6–8 pastas, and €8–13 main dishes. Dine in the cellar, or head outside to the lively, leafy courtyard (daily 12:00–24:00, Čopova ulica 5A, or enter courtyard with *As* sign near image of Julija, tel. 01/425-8822). The courtyard also has several other fun eateries—and, in the summer only, live music and a much-loved gelato stand.

Ribca ("Fish"), under the first stretch of market colonnade near the Triple Bridge, is your best bet for a relatively quick and cheap riverside lunch. Choose between the two menus: grilled and fried. There's a long list of straightforward fish dishes (€3–7.50 dishes, fish and chips for €6)—and, with the fragrant fish market right next door, you know it's fresh. If you just want to enjoy sitting along the river below the bustling market, this is also a fine spot for a coffee or beer (open Mon–Sat 7:00–16:00, closed Sun).

Zlata Ribica ("Golden Fish")—not to be confused with plain old Ribca, above—is along the castle side of the embankment, with the best riverfront view in town. But the food lives up to the location: modern Slovenian cuisine (with an emphasis on fish, of course) and delicious pastas, especially gnocchi (€5–8 pastas, €10–18 main dishes, daily 8:00–24:00, between the Triple and Cobblers' Bridges at Cankarjevo nabrežje 5–7, tel. 01/241-2680).

Emonska Klet, a student favorite, is in a monastery cellar. With energetic music, Ljubljana's longest bar, and good food under a cavernous medieval vault, it's a fun dining experience. Their €5 lunch deals are a cheap way to fill the tank (€5–10 main dishes, good €5 pizzas, so-so salad bar, Mon–Sat 8:00–2:00 in the morning, Sun 12:00–24:00, go through underpass at the top of Congress Square—it's on your left as you emerge on the other side, Plečnikov trg 1, tel. 01/421-9300).

Pizzerias

Ljubljana has lots of great sit-down pizza places. Expect to pay €5–10 for an average-sized pie (wide variety of toppings).

Pizzeria Foculus, tucked in a boring alleyway a few blocks up from the river, has a loyal local following, a happening atmosphere, an innovative, leafy interior, Ljubljana's best pizza (over 50 types), and a good salad bar (Mon–Fri 10:00–24:00, Sat–Sun 12:00–24:00, just off French Revolution Square across the street from Plečnik's National and University Library at Gregorčičeva 3, tel. 01/251-5643).

Ljubljanski Dvor enjoys the most convenient location and most scenic setting...even if the pizza isn't quite as good. On a sunny summer day, the outdoor riverside terrace is unbeatable. Inside is a simple pizza parlor downstairs, with a more refined dining room upstairs (selling the same pizzas, plus €10–15 Italian main dishes; daily 12:00–23:00, upstairs restaurant closed Sun, just 50 yards from Cobblers' Bridge at Dvorni trg 1, tel. 01/251-6555). For cheap take-away, go around back to the walk-up window on Congress Square (€1.50 slices to go, along with other light food, picnic in the park or down on the river—plenty of welcoming benches, Mon–Sat 9:00–24:00, closed Sun).

Fast and Cheap

Paninoteka serves €2–4 grilled sandwiches just over the Cobblers' Bridge from the castle (order at the display case or sit at a table to be waited on, Mon–Sat 8:00–1:00 in the morning, Sun 9:00–23:00, fine outdoor seating, Jurčičev trg 3, tel. 01/425-0055).

Burek, the typical Balkan snack (see "Balkan Flavors" sidebar on page 616), can be picked up at street stands around town. Most are open 24 hours and charge about €2 for a hearty portion. Try **Nobel Burek,** next to Miklošičeva cesta 30, or **Olympia Burek,** around the corner on Pražakova ulica (across the street from #1).

Upscale International

These fine restaurants—serving mostly French cuisine, with Slovenian and other influences—are good for a splurge. At either place, it's important to make a dinner reservation.

Gostilna As ("Ace"), tucked into a courtyard just off Prešeren Square, offers fish-lovers the best splurge in town. It's dressy, pricey, and pretentious (waiters recommend what's fresh, rather than what's on the menu). Everything is specially prepared each day and beautifully presented. Servings are small, so you're expected to take your time and order two or three courses (mostly fish and Italian, €8–15 starters, €15–25 main dishes, daily 12:00–24:00, enter courtyard with *As* sign near image of Julija at Čopova ulica 5A, tel. 01/425-8822). For cheaper food from the same kitchen, eat at their attached Gostilna As Lounge (see "Mid-Range, Local-Style Cuisine").

Restaurant Chez Eric is *the* place for French cuisine in town, with white-tablecloth-and-shiny-crystal formality. The dining rooms—some under medieval brick vaults, all under fancy chandeliers—are simply elegant, and the outdoor seating is on Ljubljana's most historic square (€15–20 main dishes, €25–30 fixed-price dinners, summer Mon–Sat 12:00–22:30, winter Mon–Sat 12:00–16:00 & 19:00–22:30, always closed Sun, a few doors down from Town Hall at Mestni trg 3, tel. 01/251-2839). Their three-course, fixed-price business lunch is a great deal (€9, served Mon–Fri).

In Krakovo

The Krakovo district—just south of the city center, where garden patches nearly outnumber simple homes—is a pleasant area to wander. It's also home to a pair of tasty restaurants. Consider combining a meal here with your trip to the Jože Plečnik House (which is just beyond Krakovo).

Harambaša is the closest thing to a ticket to Sarajevo. Serving Balkan grilled meats, this popular-with-students eatery has Turkish-flavored decor, old pictures, and cuisine reminiscent of the Bosnian capital. For a refresher on the meat dishes, see "Balkan Flavors" on page 616. The menu is limited, which makes ordering easy. Their handy €4.50 *pola-pola* combo-plate—with lotsa meat combined with chopped onions, *kajmak* (a buttery spread), and *lepinja* (bread)—makes for a simple but filling lunch. Vegetarians need not apply (€3–5 main dishes, Mon–Fri 10:00–22:00, Sat 12:00–22:00, Sun 12:00–18:00, Vrtna ulica 8).

Pri Škofu ("By the Bishop") is a laid-back, informal place with a focus on freshness and traditional Slovenian cuisine. There's no menu—the waiter tells you what's good today...and it is (€7 lunches, €20–25 dinners, Mon–Fri 8:00–24:00, Sat–Sun 12:00–24:00, reserve ahead, Rečna 8, tel. 01/426-4508).

Coffee, Tea, and Treats

Riverfront Cafés: Enjoying a coffee, beer, or ice-cream cone along the Ljubljanica River embankment (between the Triple and Cobblers' bridges) is Ljubljana's single best experience. Tables spill out into the street, and some of the best-dressed, best-looking students on the planet happily fill them day and night. (A common question from first-time visitors to Ljubljana: "Doesn't anybody here have a job?") This is simply some of the top people-watching in Europe. Rather than recommend a particular place (they're all about the same), I'll leave you to explore and find the spot with the breezy ambience you like best. When ordering, the easiest choice is a *bela kava*—"white coffee," basically a latte.

Tea House: If coffee's not your cup of tea, go a block inland to the teahouse **Čajna Hiša**. They have a shop (called "Cha") with over 100 varieties of tea, plus porcelain teapots and cups from all over (Mon–Fri 9:00–20:00, Sat 9:00–13:30, closed Sun). The café serves about 50 different types of tea, light food, and desserts (€1.50–3 sandwiches, €4–6 salads, Mon–Fri 9:00–23:00, Sat 9:00–15:00 & 18:00–23:00, closed Sun, on castle side of the river a few steps from Cobblers' Bridge at Stari trg 3, tel. 01/252-7010).

Treats: **Zvezda Kavarna,** a trendy, central place at the bottom of Congress Square, is a local favorite for cakes, pastries, and ice cream (Mon–Sat 7:00–23:00, Sun 10:00–20:00, a block up from Prešeren Square at Wolfova 14, tel. 01/421-9090).

Trendy Pub: **Bar Minimal** is my favorite of Ljubljana's many theme cafés and pubs. Stripped down to bare basics, this totally black-and-white place is as simple as it gets. While the cubical chairs aren't the most comfortable, the clever design here turns on architecture students (coffee and cocktails, €2–3 sandwiches, daily 8:00–1:00 in the morning, next to Town Hall at Mestni trg 4, tel. 01/426-0138).

Ice Cream: Ljubljana is known for its Italian gelato–style ice cream. You'll see fine options all along the Ljubljanica River embankment. Favorites include the courtyard garden at **Gostilna As** (summer only) and **Zvezda Kavarna** (both described above).

TRANSPORTATION CONNECTIONS

Note that in Slovene, Vienna is "Dunaj."

Getting to the Dalmatian Coast: If connecting directly to Croatia's Dalmatian Coast, you have three options: Train to

Zagreb (2.5 hrs), where you'll catch a cheap Croatia Air flight or a bus; take the long, once-daily train connection from Ljubljana to Split (8 hrs, requires a change in Zagreb); or, much slower, take the train to Rijeka, then cruise on a boat down the coast from there. (For specifics on flights, buses, and boats, see "Getting to the Dalmatian Coast," page 606.)

From Ljubljana by Train to: Lesce-Bled (roughly hourly, 1 hr—but bus is better), **Divača** (close to Škocjan caves and Lipica, hourly, 1.75 hrs), **Postojna** (roughly hourly, 1 hr), **Maribor** (roughly hourly, 1.75–3 hrs), **Ptuj** (3/day, 2.5 hrs—1 direct, the others transfer in Pragersko), **Zagreb** (8/day, 2.5 hrs), **Rijeka** (2–3/day direct, 2.5 hrs), **Split** (1/day, 8 hrs, transfer in Zagreb), **Vienna** (that's *Dunaj* in Slovene, 1/day direct, 6 hrs; otherwise 6/day, 7 hrs with transfer in Villach, Maribor, or Graz), **Venice** (2/day direct, 4 hrs), **Munich** (3/day direct, 7 hrs, including 1 night train; otherwise transfer in Salzburg), **Salzburg** (5/day direct, 5 hrs), **Budapest** (2/day direct, 7.75–8.5 hrs, no convenient night train). Train info: tel. 01/291-3332, www.slo-zeleznice.si.

By Bus to: Bled (Mon–Fri 11/day, Sat–Sun 8/day, 1.25 hrs, €6.25), **Divača** (close to Škocjan caves and Lipica, every 2 hrs, 1.5 hrs, €7.50), **Postojna** (at least hourly, 1 hr, €5.50), **Piran** (6/day, 2.5 hrs, €11.25), **Rovinj** (1/day in season). Bus info: tel. 090/4230 (toll number—about €0.75/min), www.ap-ljubljana.si. If you pick up the blue phone in the bus station, you'll be connected to a free information line.

Ljubljana's Airports

Slovenia's only airport, **Aerodrom Ljubljana** (airport code: LJU), is at Brnik, 14 miles north of the city—conveniently located about halfway between Ljubljana and Bled. Almost every flight is operated by Adria Airways (www.adria-airways.com), but recently, easyJet (www.easyjet.com), Wizz Air (www.wizzair.com), and Czech Airlines (www.csa.cz) have also entered the fray. Since Slovenia joined the EU, it's recommended you arrive two hours before your flight (tel. 04/206-1000, www.lju-airport.si). An airport bus connects Brnik with Ljubljana's bus station (€3.50 for 45-min ride, €4.25 for express 30-min bus, buses run hourly, some gaps in the schedule Sat–Sun—confirm in advance). There's also a private shuttle that does the same trip (€4.25, every 2 hrs, get details at TI or your hotel). Figure about €25 for a taxi to the airport.

Since Ljubljana's airport is the only one in the country and thus charges extremely high taxes and airport fees, many Slovenes prefer to fly out of Austria. The airport in **Klagenfurt** (airport code: KLU, also known as "Alpe-Adria Airport"), just over the Austrian border to the north, is subsidized by the local government to keep prices low and compete with Ljubljana's airport.

Especially if you're connecting to Bled, it's somewhat handy to reach (from Ljubljana or Bled, take the train to Villach, then to Klagenfurt's Annabichl station, which is a 5-min walk from the airport; total trip 3 hrs from Ljubljana, or 2 hrs from Bled; www .klagenfurt-airport.com). A taxi transfer to Bled runs a hefty €120 and takes about an hour (see "Helpful Hints" in the Lake Bled chapter). Austrian Airlines (www.aua.com) flies from Klagenfurt, as do low-cost carriers such as Ryanair (www.ryanair.com) and Hapag-Lloyd Express (www.hlx.com).

All this competition is keeping Slovenia's national airline, Adria, on its toes. While it's generally pretty pricey to fly Adria, the airline often posts a few heavily discounted fares for each flight on its Web site (such as €110 one-way from Ljubljana to London or Paris; first come, first served, www.adria-airways.com).

THE KARST

Caves, Castles, and Horses

In Slovenia's Karst region, about an hour on the A-1 expressway south of Ljubljana, you'll find some of the most impressive cave systems on the planet, a chance to see the famous Lipizzaner stallions for a fraction of what you'd pay in Vienna, and one of Europe's most dramatically situated castles—built into the face of a mountain.

The term "karst" is used worldwide to refer to an arid limestone plateau, but Slovenia's is the original. It comes from the Slovenian word "Kras"—a specific region near the Italian border. Since this limestone terrain is easily dissolved by water, karstic regions are punctuated by remarkable networks of caves and underground rivers.

Your top Karst priority is a cave visit. Choose between Slovenia's two best caves, Škocjan or Postojna—each with a handy side-trip nearby (to help you pick, see the sidebar on page 556).

In the neighborhood of Škocjan is Lipica, where the Lipizzaner stallions strut their stuff. Just up the road from Postojna is Predjama Castle, picturesquely nestled into the side of a cliff.

Sleeping: To sleep in the heart of the Karst—a short drive from all these sights—consider **Tourist Farm Hudičevec,** halfway between Škocjan and Postojna. It's as comfortable and private as a hotel. A roomy, spick-and-span double with a private bathroom—including a Slovenian dinner and farm-fresh eggs for breakfast—costs only €56 for two people (Db without dinner-€40, Razdrto 1, tel. 05/703-0300, fax 05/703-0320, www.hudicevec .com, hudicevec@siol.net, Simčič family). Idyllic and remote as this place sounds, it's actually close to the expressway—and large tour groups frequently show up for dinner.

Škocjan Caves and the Lipica Stud Farm

Škocjan Caves (Škocjanske Jame)

Škocjan (SHKOHTS-yahn) offers good formations and a vast canyon with a raging underground river. You'll end up walking around two miles, going up and down more than 400 steps. While anyone in good shape can enjoy Škocjan, those who have trouble walking or tire easily are better off touring Postojna (see "Postojna Caves and Predjama Castle," page 557).

Upon arrival, get a ticket for the next tour (they rarely fill up). You'll pass waiting time at a covered terrace with a tiny gift kiosk and a bar serving light meals and drinks. At tour time, your guide (toting an industrial-strength flashlight) calls everyone together, and you march silently for 10 minutes to the cave entrance. There you split into language groups and enter the cave.

The first half of the experience is the "dry caves," with wondrous formations and what seem like large caverns. Then you get to the truly colossal "finale" cavern, with a mighty river crashing through the bottom. You feel like a bit player in a sci-fi thriller. It's a world where a thousand evil *Wizard of Oz* monkeys could comfortably fly in formation. You hike high above the river for about a mile, crossing a breathtaking (but stable-feeling) footbridge 150 feet above the torrent. Far below, the scant remains of century-old trails from the early days of tourism are evocative. The cave finally widens, sunlight pours in, and you emerge—like lost creatures seeking daylight—into a lush canyon. A steep, somewhat strenuous hike leads to a small funicular, which lifts you back to the ticket booth/café/shop.

Cost and Hours: The guided tour is mandatory and takes about two hours (€11, June–Sept tours daily at the top of each hour 10:00–17:00, Oct–May tours daily at 10:00 and 13:00 and sometimes also at 15:00 or 15:30, call or pick up current brochure—which you'll find everywhere in Slovenia—to confirm schedule before making the trip, tel. 05/763-2840, www.park-skocjanske-jame.si).

Getting to Škocjan: By car, take the A-1 expressway south from Ljubljana about 90 minutes and get off at the Divača exit (also marked with brown signs for Lipica and Škocjanske jame) and follow signs for Škocjanske jame. (Before or after Škocjan, drivers can easily visit the Lipica Stud Farm.) The caves have free and easy parking.

By public transportation, it's trickier. Take the train or bus to Divača (see Ljubljana's "Transportation Connections," page 550),

The Karst Region

which is about three miles from the caves. Either hike in or take a taxi from the Divača station (tel. 05/734-5428). A better but less predictable option is to take one of the buses from Ljubljana to Piran that goes along the older road (not all of them do; ask for details at bus station). This bus can drop you off closer to the caves (one mile away—ask for "Škocjanske jame," SHKOHTS-yahn-skeh YAH-meh).

Lipica Stud Farm (Kobilarna Lipica)

The Lipica (LEE-peet-suh) Stud Farm, a 10-minute drive from the Škocjan Caves, was founded in 1580 to provide horses for the Hapsburg court in Vienna. Horse-loving Hapsburg Archduke Charles wanted to create the perfect animal: He imported Andalusian horses from his homeland of Spain, then mixed them with a local line to come up with an extremely intelligent and easily trainable breed. Charles' creation, the Lipizzaner stallions—known for their noble gait and Baroque shape—were made famous by Vienna's Spanish Riding School. Italian and Arabian bloodlines were later added to tweak various characteristics. These regal horses have changed shape with the tenor of the times: They were bred strong and stout during wars, frilly and slender in more

Postojna vs. Škocjan: Which Caves to Visit?

To Postojna or to Škocjan?—that is the question. Each cave system is massive, cut into the limestone by rivers for more than two million years. Stalagmites and stalactites—in a slow-motion love story—silently work their way towards each other until that last drip never drops. Minerals picked up by the water as it seeped through various rocks create the different colors (iron makes red, limestone makes white, and so on). Both caves were excavated and explored in the mid-19th century.

Slovenes debate long and hard about which cave system is better. The formations at Postojna are slightly more abundant, varied, and colorful, with stalagmites and stalactites as tall as 100 feet. Postojna is easier to reach by public transportation, and far less strenuous to visit than Škocjan—of the three-mile route, you'll walk only about a mile (the rest of the time, you're on a Disney World–type people-mover). But Postojna is also more expensive and much more touristy—you'll wade through tour buses and tacky souvenir stands on your way to the entrance. Most importantly, Postojna lacks Škocjan's spectacular, massive-cavern finale. Škocjan also comes with a fairly strenuous hike, leaving you feeling like you really did something adventurous. Finally, the choice of likely side-trip might help you decide: Near Postojna is the cliff-hanging Predjama Castle, while Škocjan is closer to the Lipica Stud Farm.

No matter which cave you visit, you'll find it chilly, but not really cold (a light sweater is fine). Both caves forbid photography (a laughable rule that nobody takes seriously).

cultured eras. But they're always born black, fade to gray, and turn a distinctive white in adulthood. Until World War I, Lipica bred horses for Austria's needs. Now Austria breeds its own line, and these horses prance for Slovenia—a treasured part of its cultural heritage (and featured on Slovenia's €0.20 coin).

Today you can tour the Lipizzaner stables to visit the magnificent animals, whose stalls are labeled with purebred bloodlines. Unlike in Vienna, tickets to see the horses perform here are cheap and easy to get. Visitors thrill to the Lipizzaners' clever routine—stutter-stepping sideways to the classical beat. This excursion—offering an up-close horse encounter—is less polished (and cheaper) than the Lipizzaner experience in Vienna (see page 756). It's worth a visit only if you're a horse enthusiast, or if you have a car and it fits your schedule (for example, drivers visiting the Škocjan Caves are only a few minutes away).

By the way, the hills less than a mile away are in Italy. Aside from the horses, Lipica's big draw is its casino. Italians across the border are legally forbidden from gambling in their own town's casinos—for fear of addiction—so they flock here to Slovenia to try their luck. Farther north, the Slovenian border town of Nova Gorica has Europe's biggest casino, packed with gamblers from the Italian side of town.

Visiting the Stud Farm: There are three activities at Lipica: **Touring** the farm for a look at the horses; watching a **performance** of the prancing stallions; and, on days when there's no performance, watching a **training session.** If you're coming all the way to Lipica, you might as well time it so that you can do both the tour and a performance (or a training session). Call ahead to confirm performance and tour times before you make the trip (tel. 05/739-1580, www.lipica.org).

Cost: Stud farm tour only-€7, tour plus performance-€14, tour plus training session-€9.

Tours: July–Aug daily on the hour 9:00–18:00 except 12:00; April–June and Sept–Oct daily on the hour 10:00–17:00 except 12:00 (also at 9:00 and 18:00 Sat–Sun); off-season daily at 11:00, 13:00, 14:00, and 15:00 (plus 10:00 and 16:00 Sat–Sun in March). Note that on days when there's a 15:00 performance, you can tour the farm before (14:00) or after (15:40) the show; likewise, if you attend a 12:00 training session, you can do the tour before (11:00) or after (13:00).

Performances: April–Oct Tue, Wed, Fri, and Sun at 15:00, none Nov–March.

Training Sessions: April–Oct Thu at 12:00, none Nov–March.

Getting to Lipica: The Lipica Stud Farm is in Slovenia's southwest corner (a stone's throw from Trieste, Italy). By car, exit the A-1 expressway at Divača and follow brown *Lipica* signs. (As you drive into the farm, you'll go through pastures where the stallions often roam.) It's a major hassle by public transportation. You can take the train or bus from Ljubljana to Divača (see "Getting to Škocjan," earlier in this chapter)—but that's still about five miles from Lipica, with no bus connections. You could take a taxi (about €15 one-way from Divača station, tel. 05/734-5428) or try hitching a ride on a friendly tour bus. Note that there's also no bus connection between Škocjan and Lipica.

Postojna Caves and Predjama Castle

Postojna Caves (Postojnska Jama)

Postojna (poh-STOY-nah) is the most accessible—and touristy—cave experience in the region. It's the biggest cave system in Slovenia (and, before borders shifted a few generations ago, it was the biggest in Italy...a fact that envious Italians still haven't forgotten).

Whether you arrive by car, tour bus, or on foot, you'll walk past a paved outdoor mall of shops, eateries, and handicraft vendors to the gaping hole in the mountain. Buy your ticket and board a train, which slings you deep into the mountain, whizzing past wonderful formations. (The ride alone is exhilarating.) Then you get out, assemble into language groups, and follow a guide on a well-lit, circular, paved path through more formations. You'll see 100-foot-tall stalagmites and stalactites, as well as translucent "curtains" of rock and ceilings dripping with skinny "spaghetti stalactites." You'll wind up peering at the strange "human fish" (a.k.a. olm or *Proteus anguinus*)—sort of a long, skinny, pale-pink salamander with fingers and toes. The world's biggest cave-dwelling animal, these amphibians can survive up to seven years without eating (the live specimens you see here are never fed during the four months they're on display). Then you'll load back onto the train and return to the bright daylight.

Cost and Hours: Your visit, which is by tour only, costs €18 and lasts 90 minutes. Tours leave May–Sept daily at the top of each hour 9:00–18:00 (off-season daily at 10:00, 12:00, and 14:00; April and Oct and Nov–March Sat–Sun also at 16:00; call to confirm schedule or pick up brochure at any TI). From mid-May through August, try to show up 30 minutes early for the morning tours (popular with tour buses); otherwise, aim for 15 minutes ahead. Information: tel. 05/700-0100, www.postojna-cave.com.

"Proteus Vivarium": This exhibit gives you the chance to learn more about karstic caves and about speleobiology—the study of cave-dwelling animal life. While troglodytes, science nuts, and those who just can't get enough of those human fish may get a charge out of this exhibit, it's basically just an attempt to wring a little more cash out of gullible tourists (€6; May–Sept daily 8:30–18:30; April and Oct daily 9:30–16:30; Nov–March Mon–Fri 10:30–14:30, Sat–Sun 9:30–16:00).

Getting to Postojna: The caves are just outside the town of Postojna, about an hour south of Ljubljana on the A-1 expressway (Jamska cesta 30). By car, take the expressway south from Ljubljana and get off at the Postojna exit. Turn right after the tollbooth and follow the *jama/grotte/cave* signs through town until you see the tour buses. Drivers pay €3 to park 200 yards from the cave entry. The train from Ljubljana to Postojna arrives at a station 20 minutes by foot from the caves. The bus drops you just five minutes from the caves. (For details, see Ljubljana's "Transportation Connections," page 550.)

Predjama Castle (Predjamski Grad)

Burrowed into the side of a mountain close to Postojna is dramatic Predjama Castle (prehd-YAH-mah), one of Europe's most scenic castles. Predjama is a hit with tourists for its striking setting, exciting exterior, and romantic legend.

What a wonderful site for a castle. Notice as you approach that you don't even see Predjama—crouching magnificently in its cave—until the last moment. The first castle here was actually a tiny ninth-century fortress embedded deep in the cave behind the present castle. Over the centuries, different castles were built here, and they gradually moved out to the mouth of the cave. While the original was called "the castle in the cave," the current one is *pred jama*—"in front of the cave."

While enjoying the view, ponder this legend: In the 15th century, a nobleman named Erasmus killed the emperor's cousin in a duel. He was imprisoned under Ljubljana Castle, and spent years nursing a grudge. When he was finally released, he used his castle—buried deep inside the cave above this current version—as a home base for a series of Robin Hood–style raids on the local nobility and merchants. (Actually, Erasmus stole from the rich and kept for himself—but that was good enough to make him a hero to the peasants, who hated the nobles.)

Soldiers from Trieste were brought in to put an end to Erasmus' raids, laying siege to the castle for over a year. Back then, the only way into the castle was through the cave in the valley below—then up, through an extensive labyrinth of caves, to the top. While the soldiers down below froze and starved, Erasmus' men sneaked out through the caves to bring in supplies. (They liked to drop their leftovers on the soldiers below to taunt them, letting them know that the siege wasn't working.)

Eventually, the soldiers came up with a plan. They waited for Erasmus to visit the latrine—which, by design, had to be on the thin-walled outer edge of the castle—and then, on seeing a signal by a secret agent, blew Erasmus off his throne with a cannonball. Today, Erasmus is supposedly buried under the huge linden tree in the parking lot.

As the legend of Erasmus faded, the function of the castle changed. By the 16th century, Predjama had become a castle for hunting more than for defense—explaining its current picturesque-but-impractical design.

After driving all the way here, it seems a shame not to visit the interior—but it's truly skippable. The management (which also runs the nearby Postojna Caves) is very strict about keeping the interior 16th-century in style, so there's virtually nothing inside except 20th-century fakes of 16th-century furniture, plus a few forgettable paintings and cheesy folk displays. English descriptions are sparse, and the free English history flier is not much help. But for most, the views of the place alone are worth the drive.

Cost and Hours: €7, daily May–Sept 9:00–19:00, April and Oct 10:00–18:00, Nov–March 10:00–16:00. Information: tel. 05/751-6015.

Cave Tours: If you're already visiting the caves at Postojna or Škocjan, a visit to the caves under this castle is unnecessary (€7, 45 min, May–Sept daily at 11:00, 13:00, 15:00, and 17:00, no tours Oct–April).

Getting to Predjama: Predjama Castle is on a twisty rural road 5.5 miles beyond Postojna Caves. By car, just continue on the winding road past Postojna, following signs for *Predjama* and *Predjamski Grad* (coming back, follow signs to *Postojna*). By public transportation, it's difficult. There is one bus per day from Postojna to Predjama, and another to Bukovje (about a half-mile from Predjama)—but you'll be stranded at Predjama, with no return bus. Consider hitching a ride at Postojna on a friendly Predjama-bound tour bus or tourist's car, as most visitors do both sights.

LAKE BLED

Lake Bled—Slovenia's leading mountain resort—comes complete with a sweeping alpine panorama, a fairy-tale island, a cliff-hanging medieval castle, a lazy lakeside promenade, and the country's most sought-after desserts. While Bled has all the modern resort-town amenities, its most endearing qualities are its stunning setting, its natural romanticism, and its fun-loving wedding parties.

Since the Hapsburg days, Lake Bled (pronounced like it looks) has been *the* place where Slovenes have wowed visiting diplomats. Tito had one of his vacation homes here (today's Hotel Vila Bled), and more recent visitors have included Prince Charles, Madeleine Albright, and Laura Bush.

The lake's main town, also called Bled, has plenty of ways to while away an afternoon. While the town itself is more functional than quaint, it offers postcard views of the lake and handy access to the region. Hike up to Bled Castle for intoxicating vistas. Make a wish and ring the bell at the island church. Wander the dreamy path around the lake. Then relax with some of Bled's famous desserts while you take in the view of Triglav, Slovenia's favorite mountain (see "Mount Triglav" sidebar on page 588). Bled quiets down at night—no nightlife beyond a handful of pubs—giving hikers and other holiday-makers a chance to recharge. Bled is also a great jumping-off point for a car trip through the Julian Alps (see next chapter).

Planning Your Time

Bled and its neighboring mountains deserve two days. With one day, spend it in and around Bled (or, to rush things, spend the

Bled Town

1 Hotel Lovec & Okarina Etno Rest.
2 Grand Hotel Toplice
3 Mayer Penzion, Hotel Berc & Penzion Berc
4 To Alp Penzion
5 Hotel Jadran
6 Hotel Trst
7 Penzion Bledec
8 To Vila Bled
9 Oštarija Peglez'n Rest. & Bled Pub
10 Gostilna Pri Planincu Rest. & Pub
11 Pizzeria Rustika
12 Mercator Grocery & Kompas Bled Travel Agency
13 Šimon Slaščičarna Pastry Shop
14 Irish Pub
15 Art Café

morning in Bled and the afternoon day-tripping). With a second day and a car, drive through the Julian Alps using the self-guided tour in the next chapter. The circular route takes you up and over the stunning Vršič Pass, then down the scenic and historic Soča River Valley. Without a car, skip the second day, or spend it doing nearby day trips: Bus to Radovljica to see the bee museum, hike to Vintgar Gorge, or visit the more rustic Lake Bohinj (all described under "Near Lake Bled," at the end of this chapter).

ORIENTATION

(area code: 04)
The town of Bled is on the east end of 1.5-mile-long Lake Bled. The lakefront is lined with cafés and resort hotels. A 3.5-mile path meanders around the lake. Lake Bled is particularly peaceful, as no motorized boats are allowed.

The tourists' center of Bled is a cluster of big resort hotels, dominated by the giant, red Hotel Park (dubbed the "red can"). The busy street called **Ljubljanska cesta** leads out of Bled town towards Ljubljana and most other destinations. Just up from the lakefront, across Ljubljanska cesta from Hotel Park, is the modern **commercial center** (Trgovski Center Bled), with a travel agency, grocery store, ATM, shops, a smattering of lively cafés, and (on Thursday evenings) a traditional polka dance. Nicknamed "Gadhafi" by the people of Bled, the commercial center was designed for a Libyan city, but the deal fell through—so the frugal Slovenes built it here instead. Just up the road from the commercial center, you'll find the post office and library (with Internet access).

Bled's less-touristy old town is under the castle, surrounding the pointy spire of St. Martin's Church. There you'll find the bus station, several good restaurants, a few hotels, and more locals than tourists.

The mountains poking above the ridge at the far end of the lake are the Julian Alps, crowned by the three peaks of Mount Triglav. The big mountain behind the town of Bled is Stol ("Chair"), part of the Karavanke range that defines the Austrian border.

Tourist Information

Bled's helpful TI is in the long, lakefront building across from the big, red Hotel Park (as you face the lake, the TI is hiding around front at the far left end, by the casino). Pick up the map with updated prices and schedules and the free Bled guide booklet (if they have it in stock). Get advice on hikes and day trips. If you're doing any hiking, spring for a good regional map. The TI can't find you a room, but can give you a list of accommodations (open unpredictable hours, but usually July–Aug Mon–Sat 8:00–21:00,

Bled and the Julian Alps Essentials

English	Slovene	Pronounced
Slovenia's Biggest Mountain	Triglav	TREE-glahv
Lake Bled	Blejsko Jezero	BLAY-skoh YAY-zay-roh
The Island	Otok	OH-tohk
Bled Castle	Blejski Grad	BLAY-skee grahd
Town near Bled with Train Station	Lesce	lest-SEH
Town with Bee Museum	Radovljica	rah-DOH-vleet-suh
Gorge near Bled	Vintgar	VEENT-gar
Rustic Lake near Bled	Bohinj	BOH-heen
Scenic High-Mountain Pass	Vršič	vur-SHEECH
Historic River Valley	Soča	SOH-chah

Sun 8:00–18:00; May–June and Sept Mon–Sat 8:00–19:00, Sun 11:00–17:00; Oct–April Mon–Sat 9:00–18:00, Sun 12:00–16:00; Cesta Svobode 10, tel. 04/574-1122, www.bled.si).

Arrival in Bled

By Train: Two train stations have the name "Bled." The **Bled Jezero** ("Bled Lake") station is across the lake from Bled town, and is used only by slow, tourist-oriented trains into the mountains. You're much more likely to use the **Lesce-Bled** station in the nearby village of Lesce. The Lesce-Bled station is on the main line and has much better connections to Ljubljana and international destinations. So if you're buying a train ticket or checking schedules, request "Lesce-Bled" rather than just "Bled." (This is so important, I'll remind you again later.)

The small **Lesce-Bled station** is in the village of Lesce, about 2.5 miles from Bled. As you leave the station, the nearest ATM is upstairs in the shopping center across the street. A taxi to Bled should run about €10, or you can take the bus (at least hourly, 10 min, €1.50). If taking the train out of Lesce-Bled, you can buy tickets at the station—nobody in Bled town sells tickets.

By Bus: Bled's bus station is just up from the lake in the old town. To reach the lake, walk straight downhill on Cesta Svobode. To get from the bus station to the commercial center, jog uphill and turn right on Prešernova cesta, which runs into Ljubljanska cesta just above the commercial center.

By Car: Coming from Ljubljana, you'll wind your way into Bled on Ljubljanska cesta, which rumbles through the middle of town before swinging left at the lake. Ask your hotel about parking. Also see "Route Tips for Drivers," on page 577.

Helpful Hints

Money: Bled town's handiest ATMs are **SKB Banka** (upstairs in round building at commercial center) and **Gorenjska Banka** (at far end of Hotel Park).

Internet Access: Most of the bigger hotels have access for guests in the lobby. The public library has fast access (free up to 1 hour per day, Mon 8:00–19:00, Tue–Fri 14:00–19:00, Sat 8:00–12:00, closed Sun, next to the post office on Ljubljanska cesta).

Post Office: If you're coming up from the lake on Ljubljanska cesta, it's just past the commercial center and library (Mon–Fri 7:00–19:00, Sat until 12:00, closed Sun, slightly longer hours July–Aug, tel. 04/575-0200).

Laundry: Most hotels can do laundry for you, but it's expensive. The only self-service option is at the campground at the far end of the lake (April–Oct only, call first to confirm they're open, tel. 04/575-2000).

Car Rental: The Julian Alps are ideal by car. Several big chains rent cars in Bled—figure €50–60 per day, including tax, insurance, and unlimited mileage (no extra charge for drop-off elsewhere in Slovenia). **Europcar** (in Hotel Krim, tel. 04/574-1155) usually has better rates than **Avis** (in the commercial center, tel. 04/576-8700).

Travel Agency: Kompas Bled Travel Agency, in the commercial center, exchanges money, rents bikes, sells books and maps, offers a room-booking service (including many cheap rooms in private homes—though most are away from the lake), and sells various tours around the region (Mon–Sat 8:00–19:00, Sun 8:00–12:00 & 16:00–19:00, June–Sept until 20:00, Ljubljanska cesta 4, tel. 04/572-7500, www.kompas-bled.si, kompas.bled@siol.net).

Getting Around Lake Bled (Literally)

By Bike: You can rent a mountain bike at Kompas Bled Travel Agency (above)—great for biking around the lake (€3/hr, €6.50/3 hrs, €8/half-day, €11/day). For a longer pedal, a brand-new bike path to the nearby village of Radovljica (and its bee museum) should be open in 2007 (about 4 miles each way, get details at Kompas or the TI).

By Horse and Buggy: Buggies called *fijakers* are the romantic, expensive, and easy way to get around the lake. You'll see them along the lakefront between Hotel Park and the castle (around the lake-€25, one-way up to castle-€25, round-trip to castle with 30-min wait time-€35, mobile 041-710-970).

By Tourist Train: A touristy little train makes a circuit around the lake every 40 minutes in summer (€3, daily 9:00–18:00, shorter hours off-season, weather-dependent, tel. 041-608-689).

By Tourist Bus: A handy shuttle bus passes through Bled once daily in summer. It leaves the bus station at 10:00, stops at a few hotels (including Grand Hotel Toplice), then goes up to the castle and on to the Vintgar Gorge entrance (€2.50, mid-June–Sept only, confirm schedule at TI or bus station).

By Taxi: Bled Tours, run by friendly, English-speaking Sandi Demšar, can take you to various destinations near Bled (€10 to Lesce-Bled train station, €11 to Radovljica, €45 to Ljubljana airport, €120 to Klagenfurt airport, mobile 031-205-611, info @bledtours.si). Your hotel can also call a taxi for you.

By Boat: For information on boat rental, see "Boating," page 570. For details on the characteristic *pletna* boats, see "Getting to the Island," page 568.

By Plane: If you have perfect weather and deep pockets, there's no more thrilling way to experience Slovenia's high-mountain scenery than from a little propeller plane soaring over the peaks. Flights depart from a grass airstrip near the village of Lesce, a 10-minute drive or taxi ride from Bled. Expensive...but unforgettable (€70 for 15-min hop over Lake Bled only, €120 for 30-min flight that also buzzes Lake Bohinj, €170 for deluxe 45-min version around the summit of Triglav, arrange at least a day in advance, tel. 04/532-0100, www.alc-lesce.si, info@alc-lesce.si).

TOURS

Local Guides—**Tina Hiti** and **Sašo Golub** are fine guides who enjoy sharing the town and region they love with American visitors. Hiring one of them can add immeasurably to your enjoyment and understanding of Bled (€30/2 hrs, arrange several days in advance; Tina: mobile 040-166-554, tinahiti@gmail.com; Sašo: mobile 040-524-774, sasogolub@gmail.com). Either one can drive you in their car on a long day tour into the Julian Alps—or anywhere in Slovenia—for €120. (This price is for two people; it's more expensive for three or more people, since they have to rent a van.) I've spent great days with both Tina and Sašo, and was thankful they were behind the wheel.

Excursions—To hit several far-flung day-trip destinations in one go, you could take a package tour from Bled. Destinations range from Ljubljana and the Karst region to the Austrian or Italian Alps to Venice (yes, Venice—it's doable as a long day trip from here).

An all-day Julian Alps trip to the Vršič Pass and Soča Valley runs about €35 (sold by various agencies, including Kompas Bled—see above). This tour is handy, but two people can rent a car for the day for less and do it at their own pace using the self-guided driving tour in the next chapter. There's also a scenic "Old-Timer Train" tour connecting some of the alpine sights, but it runs infrequently (ask at Kompas Bled for details).

SIGHTS AND ACTIVITIES

Lake Bled

Bled doesn't have many "sights" (except the dull castle museum, described below). But there are plenty of rewarding and pleasant activities.

▲▲**The Island (Otok)**—Bled's little island—capped by a super-cute church—nudges the lake's quaintness level over the top.

Locals call it simply "The Island" *(Otok)*. While it's pretty to look at from afar, it's also fun to visit.

The island has long been a sacred site with a romantic twist. On summer Saturdays, a steady procession of brides and grooms cheered on by their entourages head for the island. Ninety-eight steps lead from the island's dock up to the Church of the Assumption on top. It's tradition for the groom to carry—or try to carry—his bride up these steps. About four out of five are successful (proving themselves "fit for marriage"). During the communist era, the church was closed, and weddings were outlawed here. But the tradition reemerged—illegally—even before the regime ended, with a clandestine ceremony in 1989.

An eighth-century Slavic pagan temple dedicated to the goddess of love and fertility once stood here; the current Baroque version (with Venetian flair—the bell tower separate from the main church) is the fifth to occupy this spot. As you enter the church (€3), look straight ahead to the painting of Mary on the wall. She doesn't quite look like other Madonnas, because she has the face of Maria Theresa—the Hapsburg empress who controlled Slovenia at the time (see page 760). The Madonna at the altar in front of the church is similarly pudgy...er, imperial.

Find the rope for the church bell, hanging in the middle of the aisle just before the altar. A local superstition claims that if you ring this bell three times, your dreams will come true. Worth a try.

Pletna Boats

The *pletna* is an important symbol of Lake Bled. These boats provide a pleasant way to reach the island and carry on an important tradition dating back for generations. In the 17th century, Hapsburg Empress Maria Theresa granted the villagers from Mlino—the little town along the lakefront just beyond Bled—special permission to ferry visitors to the island. (Since Mlino had very limited access to farmland, they needed another source of income.) Mlino residents built their *pletnas* by hand, using a special design passed down from father to son for centuries—like the equally iconic gondolas of Venice. Eventually, this imperial decree and family tradition evolved into a modern union of *pletna* oarsmen, which continues to this day.

Today *pletna* boats are still hand-built according to that same centuries-old design. There's no keel, so the skilled oarsmen work hard to steer the flat-bottomed boat with each stroke—boats piloted by an inexperienced oarsman can slide around a bit on very windy days. There are 21 official *pletnas* on Lake Bled, all belonging to the same union. The gondoliers dump all of their earnings into one fund, give a cut to the tourist board, and divide the rest evenly among themselves. Occasionally a new family tries to break into the cartel, underselling his competitors with a "black market" boat that looks the same as the official ones. While some see this as a violation of a centuries-old tradition, others view it as good old capitalism. Either way, competition is fierce.

If you're waiting for a herd of tourists to ring out their wishes, pass the time looking around the front of the church. When the church was being renovated in the 1970s, workers dug up several medieval graves (you can see one through the glass under the bell rope). They also discovered Gothic frescoes on either side of the altar, including, above the door on the right, an unusual ecclesiastical theme: the *bris* (Jewish circumcision ritual) of Christ.

A café (with a WC) and souvenir shop (with an exhibit of nativity scenes) are near the church at the top of the steps.

To descend by a different route, walk down the trail behind the church, then follow the path around the island's perimeter back to where your *pletna* boat awaits.

Getting to the Island: The most romantic route to the island is to cruise on one of the distinctive *pletna* boats (€10 per person round-trip, includes 30-min wait time at the island; catch one at several spots around the lake—most convenient from in front of Grand Hotel Toplice or just below Hotel Park; generally run from dawn until around 20:00 in summer, stop earlier off-season, replaced by enclosed electric boats in winter—unless the lake freezes, mobile 031-316-575). For more on these characteristic little vessels, see the *"Pletna* Boats" sidebar. You can also **rent your own boat** to row to the island (see "Boating"). It's even possible to **swim** to the island, especially from the end of the lake nearest the island (see "Swimming")—but you're not allowed into the church in your swimsuit.

▲▲**Walk Around the Lake**—Strolling the 3.5 miles around the lake is enjoyable, peaceful, and scenic. At a leisurely pace, it takes about an hour and a half...not counting stops to snap photos of the ever-changing view. On the way, you'll pass some great villas, mostly from the beginning of the 19th century. The most significant one was a former residence of Marshal Tito—today the Hotel Vila Bled, a great place to stop for a coffee and pretend Tito invited you over for a visit (see "Tito's Vila Bled"). For the more adventurous, hiking paths lead up into the hills surrounding the lake (ask TI for details and maps; or hike to Vintgar Gorge, described under "Near Lake Bled").

Tito's Vila Bled—Before World War II, this villa on Lake Bled was the summer residence for the Yugoslav royal family. When Tito ran Yugoslavia, he entertained international guests here (big shots from the communist and non-aligned world, from Indira Gandhi to Khrushchev to Kim Il Sung). Since 1984, it's been a classy hotel and restaurant, offering guests grand Lake Bled views and James Bond ambience. For some, this is a nostalgic opportunity to send e-mail from Tito's desk, sip tea in his lounge, and gawk at his Social Realist wall murals.

The villa is a 20-minute lakeside walk from the town of Bled at Cesta Svobode 26 (it's the big, white villa with the long staircase at the southern end of lake, near the village of Mlino). You can also ask your *pletna* gondolier to drop you off here after visiting the island. Those hiking around the lake will pass the gate leading through Tito's garden to the restaurant, where they are welcome to drop in for a meal, the salad bar, or just a cup of coffee. Tito fans might want to splurge for an overnight here (basic Db-€190, tel. 04/579-1500, www.vila-bled.com).

▲**Bled Castle (Blejski Grad)**—Bled's cliff-hanging castle, dating in one form or another from a thousand years ago, was the seat of the Austrian Bishops of Brixen, who controlled Bled in the Middle Ages. Your castle admission includes a modest castle museum (with a couple of interesting videos, creaky rooms, and good English descriptions), a small theater continuously showing a fun 20-minute movie about Bled (under the restaurant), and a rampart walk with an "herbal gallery" (gift shop of traditional-meets-modern herbal brandies, cosmetics, and perfumes). These attractions are less than thrilling, but the sweeping views over Lake Bled and the surrounding mountainscapes justify the trip (€6, daily May–Oct 8:00–20:00, Nov–April 9:00–17:00, tel. 04/578-0525).

In addition, the castle is home to a pair of interesting, old-fashioned shops: You can visit a working replica of a **printing press** from Gutenberg's time, and press your own custom-made souvenir certificate for €5 (in the castle's oldest tower—from the 11th century). Or, at the **wine cellar** *(grajska klet de Adami),* bottle and cork your own bottle of wine (€5–17). These attractions are manned by a pair of gregarious guys—one dressed as a medieval printer and the other as a monk. Both men happen to be named Andrej (they switch costumes sometimes for a change of pace). Both shops are generally open daily 10:00–18:00 (until 16:00 Dec–Feb; if one of the shops is closed, the other should be open).

Eating at the Castle: The **restaurant** at the castle is fairly expensive, but your restaurant reservation gets you into the castle grounds for free (international cuisine and some local specialties, €8–20 main dishes, tel. 04/579-4424). Better yet, there's a scenic little **picnic spot** in the castle courtyard, with fine tables and views (buy sandwiches at the Mercator grocery store in the commercial center before you ascend—see listing under "Eating").

Getting to the Castle: Most people **hike** up the steep hill (20 min). The handiest trails are behind big St. Martin's Church: Walk past the front door of the church with the lake at your back, and look left after the first set of houses for the *Grad* signs marking the steepest route up (on this trail, bear uphill—or right—at the benches); or, for a longer but less steep route, continue past the church on the same street about five minutes, bearing uphill (left) at the fork, and find the *Grad* sign just after the Pension Bledec hostel on the left. Once you're on this second trail, don't take the sharp-left uphill turn at the fork (instead, continue straight up, around the back of the hill). Instead of hiking, you can take the 10:00 **tourist bus** (see "Getting Around Lake Bled," page 565), your **rental car,** a **taxi** (around €6), or—if you're wealthy and romantic—a **horse and buggy** (€25, €10 extra to wait 30 min and bring you back down, see "Getting Around Lake Bled").

Boating—Bled is the rowing center of Slovenia. Town officials even lengthened the lake a bit so it would perfectly fit the standard two-kilometer laps, with 100 meters more for the turn. Three world championships have been held here. The town has produced many Olympic medalists, winning gold in Sydney and silver in Athens. You'll notice that local crew team members are characters—with a tradition of wild and colorful haircuts. You'll likely see them running or rowing. This dedication to rowing adds to Bled's tranquility, since no motorized boats are allowed on the lake.

If you want to get into the action, you'll find **rental rowboats** at the swimming pool under the castle (small 3-person boat: first hour-€10.50, additional hours-€6.50 each; bigger 5-person boat: first hour-€12.50, then €7.50/hr) or at the campground on the far side of the lake (4-person boat-€8.50/hr, closed in bad weather and off-season).

Swimming—Lake Bled has several suitable spots for a swim. The swimming pools under the castle are filled with lake water and routinely earn the "blue flag," meaning the water is top-quality (swim all day-€5, less for afternoon only, June–Sept daily 8:00–19:00, closed Oct–May, tel. 04/578-0528). Bled's two beaches are at the far end of the lake. Both are free; the one at the campground (southwest corner) has lots of tourists, while locals prefer the one at the rowing center (northwest corner). If you swim to the island, remember that you can't get into the church in your swimsuit.

Luge Ride (Polento Sankanje)—Bled's new "summer toboggan" luge ride allows you to scream down a steep, curvy metal rail track on a little plastic sled. A chairlift takes you to the top of the track, where you'll sit on your sled, take a deep breath, and remind yourself: Pull back on the stick to slow down, push forward on the stick to go faster. You'll drop 480 feet in altitude on the 570-yard-long track, speeding up to about 25 miles per hour as you race toward the lake. You'll see the track on the hillside just south of town, beyond the Grand Hotel Toplice (€4.50/ride, cheaper for multiple rides, chairlift only-€2, weather-dependent—if it rains, you can't go; mid-June–mid-Sept daily 9:00–12:00 & 16:00–20:00; May–mid-June Sat–Sun only 10:00–19:00, closed Mon–Fri; mid-Sept–Oct Sat–Sun only 10:00–18:00, closed Mon–Fri; closed Nov–April).

Day Trips—For details on some easy and enjoyable nearby side-trips—including a quirky bee museum, a scenic gorge hike, and a more remote lake experience—see "Near Lake Bled" at the end of this chapter.

NIGHTLIFE

Bled is quiet after hours. If you're not a drinker or a dancer, you're down to mini golf...open late in summer across from the commercial center.

Pub Crawl—Bled has several fun bars that are lively with a young crowd (all open nightly until 2:00 in the morning). Since many young people in Bled are students at the local tourism school, they're likely to speak English...and eager to practice with a native speaker. Try a "Smile," a Corona-type Slovenian lager. *Šnops* (schnapps) is a local specialty—popular flavors are plum *(slivovka)*, honey *(medica)*, blueberry *(borovničevec)*, and pear *(hruškovec)*.

Kick things off with the fun-loving local gang at **Gostilna Pri Planincu** near the bus station (described under "Eating"). Then head down Cesta Svobode toward the lake; just below Hotel Jelovica, you'll find the rollicking **Irish Pub** (a.k.a. "The Pub"), with Guinness and indoor or outdoor seating. For a more genteel atmosphere, duck across the street and wander a few more steps down toward the lake to find the **Art Café**, with a mellow ambience reminiscent of a van Gogh painting. Around the lake near the commercial center, **Bled Pub** (a.k.a. "The Cocktail Bar" or "Troha"—for the family that owns it) is a trendy late-night spot where bartenders sling a dizzying array of mixed drinks to an appreciative crowd (between the commercial center and the lake, above the recommended Oštarija Peglez'n restaurant). If you're still standing, several other, more low-key bars and cafés populate the commercial center.

Polka—Slovenia is the land of polka. Slovenes claim it was invented here, and singer/accordionist Slavko Avsenik—from the nearby village of Begunje—cranks out popular oompah songs that make him bigger than the Beatles (and therefore, presumably, Jesus) in Germany. The easiest way to hear accordion music and yodeling in Bled is to attend a free polka evening with a local band at the commercial center (outside on the lower terrace; every Thu from around 20:00, mid-June–mid-Sept only). While the audience is mostly local, tourists are more than welcome. (You can spot the tourists—they're the ones who can't polka.) There's also a Slovenian folk evening once a week at a Bled hotel (ask at TI).

SLEEPING

Bled is packed with gradually decaying, communist-era convention hotels. A few have been nicely renovated, but most are stale, outmoded, and overpriced. It's a strange, incestuous little circle—the vast majority of the town's big hotels and restaurants are owned by the same company. Only a handful of Bled accommodations are modern and a good value, and I've listed them here—along with a few older places that work in a pinch. Quaint little family-run pensions are rare, and they book up fast with Germans and Brits; reserve these places as far ahead as possible. I've listed the high-season prices (May–Oct). Off-season, the big hotels lower prices 10–15 percent. For cheaper beds, consider one of the many *sobe* (rooms in private homes) scattered around the lake (about €25 per person in peak season, often with a hefty 30 percent surcharge for stays shorter than three nights). Several agencies in town can help

Sleep Code

(€1 = about $1.20, country code: 386, area code: 04)
S = Single, **D** = Double/Twin, **T** = Triple, **Q** = Quad, **b** = bathroom.
Unless otherwise noted, credit cards are accepted. Everyone speaks English, and all of these accommodations include breakfast. Bled levies a €1 tourist tax per person, per night (not included in below prices unless noted).

To help you sort easily through these listings, I've divided the rooms into three categories based on the price for a standard double room with bath:

$$$ Higher Priced—Most rooms €100 or more.
$$ Moderately Priced—Most rooms between €50–100.
$ Lower Priced—Most rooms €50 or less.

you find a *soba* (including Kompas Bled—see page 565). But be sure the location is convenient before you accept.

$$$ Hotel Lovec, a Best Western, sits in a convenient (but non-lakefront) location just above the commercial center. Gorgeously renovated inside and out, and run by a helpful and friendly staff, it's a welcoming, cheery, well-run alternative to Bled's many old, dreary communist hotels. Its 60 plush rooms come with all the comforts (Sb-€122, Db-€144, €15 more for a lake-view balcony, €50 more for "deluxe" room with balcony and Jacuzzi, €24 less per room Nov–April, family and "executive" suites available, delicious breakfast, elevator, Internet access, indoor pool, parking garage-€8.50/day, Ljubljanska Cesta 6, tel. 04/576-8615, fax 04/576-8625, www.lovechotel.com, sales@lovechotel.com).

$$$ Grand Hotel Toplice is the grande dame of Bled, with 87 rooms, an elegant view lounge, posh decor, all the amenities, and a long list of high-profile guests—from Madeleine Albright to Jordan's King Hussein. Rooms in the back are cheaper, but have no lake views and overlook a noisy street—try to get one as high up as possible (non-view: Sb-€120, Db-€150; lake view: Sb-€170, Db-€210; suites mostly with lake views-€260; 15–20 percent less Nov–April, elevator, Cesta Svobode 12, tel. 04/579-1000, fax 04/574-1841, www.hotel-toplice.com, info@hotel-toplice.com). The hotel's name—*toplice*—means "spa"; guests are free to use the hotel's natural-spring-fed indoor swimming pool (a chilly 72 degrees Fahrenheit).

$$ Mayer Penzion, perched on a bluff above Grand Hotel Toplice, is a steep five-minute uphill walk from lake. Wonderfully run by the Trseglav family, this place comes with 13 great-value rooms, a friendly and professional staff, an excellent restaurant, and an atmospheric wine-tasting cellar. They book up fast in summer with return clients, so reserve early (Sb-€45, Db-€65–75 depending on size and balcony, extra bed-€20, elevator, Želeška cesta 7, tel. 04/576-5740, fax 04/576-5741, www.mayer-sp.si, penzion@mayer-sp.si). They also rent a cute little two-story Slovenian farm cottage next door (Db-€70, Tb-€80, Qb-€90).

$$ Hotel Berc and **Penzion Berc,** run by the Berc brothers, are next door to Mayer Penzion. The new hotel building has 15 rooms with pleasantly woody decor (Sb-€40, Db-€65–70, all rooms have balconies, Pod Stražo 13, tel. 04/576-5658, fax 04/576-5659, hotel@berc-sp.si, run by Luka). The older, adjacent *penzion* offers 11 cheaper, almost-as-nice rooms (Sb-€30–35, Db-€50–60, most rooms have balconies, Želeška cesta 15, tel. & fax 04/574-1838, penzion@berc-sp.si, run by Miha). Both have cozy public spaces and are worth reserving ahead (for both: cash only, 10 percent more for 1-night stays, 10 percent less off-season, prices include tax, free Internet access, free loaner bikes, www.berc-sp.si).

$$ Alp Penzion, sitting in cornfields a 15-minute walk from the lake and just out of town, is the most tranquil and only farm-feeling option. Its 11 rooms are small and faded, but comfortable. The place is enthusiastically run by the Sršen family, who offer lots of fun activities: tennis court, summer barbecue grill, wine-tasting, and a sauna (Sb-€40, Db-€55–60, Tb-€80, 10 percent more for 1-night stays, cheaper Nov–March, family rooms, free Internet access, free loaner bikes, Cankarjeva cesta 20A, tel. 04/574-1614, fax 04/574-4590, www.alp-penzion.com, bled@alp-penzion.com).

Grand Hotel Toplice (listed earlier) runs two nearby annexes with much lower prices: **$$ Hotel Jadran,** on a hill behind the Toplice, has 45 tired, old rooms (reception tel. 04/579-1365). **$$ Hotel Trst** is less homey, but its 31 rooms are a little bigger and have been lightly renovated (reception and breakfast at the Toplice, often closed in winter). Both have the same prices and can be reserved through Grand Hotel Toplice (non-view: Sb-€56, Db-€72; lake view: Sb-€81, Db-€96; extra bed-€21, all rooms €10 less Nov–April, Cesta Svobode 12, tel. 04/579-1000, fax 04/574-1841, www.hotel-toplice.com, info@hotel-toplice.com). At either place, ask for a room on the higher floors to avoid road noise (both have elevators).

$ Penzion Bledec is just below the castle at the top of the old town. While technically an IYHF hostel, each of the 13 rooms has its own bathroom, and some can be rented as doubles (though "doubles" are actually underutilized triples and quads, with separate beds pushed together—so they're not reservable July–Aug). The friendly staff is justifiably proud of the bargain they offer (bed in 4–7-bed dorm-€19, Db-€50, Tb-€63, cheaper Nov–April, members pay 10 percent less, includes sheets and breakfast, entirely non-smoking, great family rooms, Internet access, full-service laundry for guests–€9/load, Grajska 17, tel. 04/574-5250, fax 04/574-5251, www.mlino.si, bledec@mlino.si).

EATING

Okarina Etno, run by charming, well-traveled Leo Ličof, serves a diverse array of cuisines, all of them well-executed: international fare, traditional Slovenian specialties, and Indian (Himalayan) dishes. Leo has a respect for salads and vegetables and a passion for fish. Creative cooking, fine presentation, friendly service, and an atmosphere as tastefully eclectic as the food make this place a winner (€7–12 pastas, €9–20 main dishes, handy €10 fixed-price lunch deal includes a drink; April–Oct Mon–Fri 12:00–15:00 & 18:00–24:00, Sat–Sun 12:00–24:00; Nov–March daily 12:00–15:00 & 18:00–24:00; next to Hotel Lovec at Ljubljanska cesta 8, tel. 04/574-1458). Skim the guest-book to find the page with Paul McCartney's visit from May 2005.

Oštarija Peglez'n ("The Old Iron"), conveniently located on the main road between the commercial center and the lake, cooks up tasty meals with an emphasis on fish. Choose between the delightful Slovenian cottage interior or the shady streetside terrace (€5–7 salads, €6–7 pastas, €10–20 main dishes, daily 10:00–24:00, fun family-style shareable plates, Cesta Svobode 7A, tel. 04/574-4218).

Mayer Penzion, just up the hill from the lakefront, has a dressy restaurant with good traditional cooking that's worth the short hike. This is where a Babel of international tourists come to swap hiking tips and day-trip tales (main dishes €8–20, Tue–Fri 17:00–24:00, Sat–Sun 12:00–24:00, closed Mon, indoor or outdoor seating, above Hotel Jadran at Želeška cesta 7, tel. 04/576-5740).

Gostilna Pri Planincu ("By the Mountaineers") is a homey, informal bar coated with license plates and packed with fun-loving and sometimes rowdy natives. Behind the small, local-feeling pub sprawls a large dining area. The big menu features good-enough Slovenian pub grub and Balkan grilled-meat specialties (€6–10 main dishes, fish splurges up to €15, daily 9:00–23:00, huge portions, traditional daily specials, Grajska cesta 8, tel. & fax 04/574-1613).

Pizzeria Rustika, in the old town, offers good wood-fired pizzas, pastas, and salads (Tue–Sun 12:00–23:00, Mon 15:00–23:00, marked only with low-profile *pizzeria* sign at Riklijeva cesta 13, tel. 04/576-8900). Its upstairs roof terrace is relaxing on a balmy evening.

Bled Desserts

While you're in Bled, be sure to enjoy the town's specialty, a cream cake called **kremna rezina** (KRAYM-nah ray-ZEE-nah; often referred to by its German name, **kremšnita,** KRAYM-shnee-tah). It's a layer of cream and a thick layer of vanilla custard artfully sandwiched between sheets of delicate, crispy crust. Heavenly. Slovenes travel from all over the country to sample this famous dessert.

Slightly less renowned—but just as tasty—is **grmada** (gur-MAH-dah, "bonfire"). This dessert was developed by Hotel Jelovica as a way to get rid of their day-old leftovers. They take yesterday's cake, add rum, milk, custard, and raisins, and top it off with whipped cream and chocolate syrup.

Finally, there's *prekmurska gibanica*—or just **gibanica** (gee-bah-NEET-seh) for short. Originating in the Hungarian corner of the country, *gibanica* is an earthy pastry filled with poppy seeds, walnuts, apple, and cheese, and drizzled with rum.

These desserts are typically enjoyed with a lake-and-mountains view—the best spots are the Panorama restaurant by Grand Hotel Toplice and the terrace across from the Hotel Park (figure around €5 for cake and coffee at any of these places). For a more local (but non-lake view) setting, consider Šmon Slaščičarna (only slightly cheaper; see "Dessert," below).

The **Mercator** grocery store, in the commercial center, has the makings for a bang-up picnic. They sell €2–3 pre-made sandwiches, or will make you one to order (point to what you want). This is a great option for hikers and budget travelers (Mon–Sat 7:00–19:00, Sun 8:00–12:00).

Dessert: While tourists generally gulp down their cream cakes on a hotel restaurant's lakefront terrace, local residents know the best desserts are at **Šmon Slaščičarna** (a.k.a. the "Brown Bear," for the bear on the sign). It's nicely untouristy, but lacks the atmosphere of the lakeside spots (daily 7:30–22:00, near bus station at Grajska cesta 3, tel. 04/574-1616).

TRANSPORTATION CONNECTIONS

The most convenient train connections to Bled leave from the Lesce-Bled station, about 2.5 miles away (see details under "Arrival in Bled" on page 564). Remember, when buying a train ticket to Lake Bled, make it clear that you want to go to the Lesce-Bled station (not the Bled Jezero station, which is poorly connected to the main line). No one in the town of Bled sells train tickets; buy them at the station just before your train departs. If the ticket window there is closed, buy your ticket on board from the conductor (who will likely waive the €2.50 additional fee).

Note that if you're going to **Ljubljana,** the bus (which leaves from Bled town itself) is better than the train (which leaves from the Lesce-Bled train station).

From Lesce-Bled by Train to: Ljubljana (roughly hourly, 1 hr—but bus is better), **Salzburg** (5/day, 4 hrs), **Munich** (3/day, 6 hrs), **Vienna** (that's *Dunaj* in Slovene, 5/day, 6 hrs, transfer in Villach, Austria), **Venice** (3/day with transfer in Ljubljana or Villach, 6 hrs), **Zagreb** (5/day, 3.5 hrs).

By Bus to: Ljubljana (Mon–Fri 11/day, Sat–Sun 8/day, 1.25 hrs, €6.25), **Radovljica** (Mon–Fri at least 2/hr, Sat hourly, Sun almost hourly, 15 min, €2), **Lesce-Bled train station** (at least hourly, 10 min, €1.50), **Lake Bohinj** (hourly, 30 min to Bohinj Jezero stop, 35 min to Bohinj Vogel stop, 40 min to Bohinj Zlatorog stop, €3.50–4 depending on stop), **Podhom** (20-min hike away from Vintgar Gorge, Mon–Fri 9/day, none Sat, 1/day Sun, 15 min, €1.25), **Spodnje Gorje** (also near Vintgar Gorge, take bus in direction of Krnica, hourly, 15 min, €1.25). Confirm times at the Bled bus station.

By Plane: The Ljubljana-Brnik Airport is between Lake Bled and Ljubljana, about a 45-minute drive from Bled. Connecting by taxi costs around €45 (set price up front—since it's outside of town, they don't use the meter). The bus connection from Bled to the airport is cheap (total cost: about €5), but complicated and time-consuming: First, go to Kranj (Mon–Fri 12/day, Sat–Sun 8/day, 35 min), then transfer to a Brnik-bound bus (at least hourly, 20 min). Many Bled residents prefer to fly from Klagenfurt, Austria. For details on both the Ljubljana and the Klagenfurt airports, see page 551.

Route Tips for Drivers: Bled is less than an hour north of Ljubljana. From Ljubljana, take the A-2 expressway north until it ends, diverting you onto a smaller two-lane road. (You'll notice construction on the new expressway that will connect this stretch directly to the Karavanke tunnel to Austria—due to be completed in 2008. North of Bled, the expressway is already finished.) Watch for signs to *Bled*. This road will take you directly to the lake (where it's called Ljubljanska cesta).

To reach Radovljica (bee museum) or Lesce (train station), drive out of Bled on Ljubljanska cesta toward the expressway. Watch for the turnoff to those two towns on the right (they're on the same road).

Near Lake Bled

The countryside around Bled offers several day trips that can be done easily without a car (bus connections to each one described below). The three listed here are the best (one village/museum experience, two hiking/back-to-nature options). They're more convenient than can't-miss, but each one is worthwhile on a longer visit, and all give a good taste of the Julian Alps. For a self-guided driving tour through farther-flung (and even more striking) parts of the Julian Alps, see the next chapter.

Radovljica

The village of Radovljica (rah-DOH-vleet-suh) is larger than Bled, perched on a plateau above the Sava River. The town itself is nothing exciting, though its old center pedestrian zone, Linhartov trg, makes for a pleasant stroll. But the town is home to a fascinating and offbeat beekeeping museum—which, with only a few rooms, still ranks as one of Europe's biggest on the topic.

Radovljica's **Apicultural Museum** (Čebelarski Muzej)—worth ▲—celebrates Slovenia's long beekeeping heritage. Since the days before Europeans had sugar, Slovenia has been a big honey producer. Slovenian farmer Anton Janša is considered the father of modern beekeeping; he was Europe's first official teacher of beekeeping (in Hapsburg Vienna).

The first two rooms of the museum trace the history of beekeeping, from the time when bees were kept in hollowed-out trees to the present day. Notice the old-fashioned tools in the first room. When a new queen bee is born, the old queen takes half the hive's bees to a new location. Experienced beekeepers used the long, skinny instrument (a beehive stethoscope) to figure out when the swarm would fly the coop. Then, once the bees had moved to a nearby tree, the beekeeper used the big spoons to retrieve the queen—surrounded by an angry ball of her subjects—from her new home before she could get settled in. The beekeeper transported the furious gang into a manmade hive designed for easier, more sanitary collection of the honey. You can also see the tools beekeepers used to create smoke, which makes bees less aggressive. Even today, some of Slovenia's old-fashioned beekeepers simply light up a cigarette and blow smoke on any bees that get ornery.

The third room features the museum's highlight: whimsically painted beehive frontboards (called *panjske končnice*). Nineteenth-century farmers, believing these paintings would help the bees find their way home, developed a tradition of decorating their hives with religious, historical, and satirical folk themes (look for the devil sharpening a woman's tongue). The depiction of a hunter's

Near Lake Bled

funeral shows all the animals happy...except his dog. There's everything from portraits of Hapsburg emperors, to a "true crime" sequence of a man murdering his family as they sleep, to proto-"Lockhorns" cartoons of marital strife, to 18th-century erotica (one with a woman showing some leg, and another with a flip-up, peek-a-boo panel).

The life-size wooden statues were used to "guard" the beehives—and designed to look like fearsome Ottoman and Napoleonic soldiers.

You'll also find an interactive multimedia exhibit, a good video in English, temporary exhibitions, and—in the summer only—an actual, functioning beehive (try to find the queen). The gift shop is a good place for souvenirs, with hand-painted replicas of front-boards, honey brandy, candles, ornaments, and other bee products (museum entry-€2.50, good English descriptions, free sheet of English info, €2 English guidebook is a nice souvenir; May–Oct Tue–Sun 10:00–13:00 & 15:00–18:00, closed Mon; March–April and Nov–Dec Wed and Sat–Sun 10:00–12:00 & 15:00–17:00, closed Mon–Tue and Thu–Fri; closed Jan–Feb; Linhartov trg 1, tel. 04/532-0520, www.muzeji-radovljica.si).

Eating in Radovljica: Several Radovljica restaurants near the bee museum have view terraces overlooking the surrounding mountains and valleys. **Lectar** offers hearty Slovenian fare in a rural-feeling setting with a user-friendly, super-traditional menu. The restaurant is known for its heart-shaped cookies, decorated with messages of love (€12 plates, Wed–Mon 12:00–23:00, closed Tue, family-friendly, Linhartov trg 2, tel. 04/537-4800). **Grajska Gostilnica** dishes up good, basic pub grub closer to the bus station (salads, pizza, pastas, open long hours daily, inside Hotel Grajski Dvor at Kranjska 2, tel. 04/531-5585).

Getting to Radovljica: When planning your day, note that the Bee Museum closes for two hours after lunch. **Buses** to Radovljica generally leave Bled every half-hour (fewer on weekends, check schedules at hotel or station, €2, buy ticket from driver, trip takes about 15 min). To reach the old town square and the bee museum, leave the station going straight ahead, cross the bus parking lot and the next street, then turn left down the far street (following brown sign for *Staro Mesto*). In five minutes, you'll get to the pedestrianized Linhartov trg (TI on right just before you enter pedestrian zone). At the end of this square, just before the church, you'll see the bee museum, which shares an old Baroque mansion with a music school (bee museum upstairs). Coming back to Bled, there are fewer buses; check the schedule when you arrive (usually about 2/hr, but fewer Sat–Sun). **Drivers** leave Bled on Ljubljanska cesta, then turn right at the sign for *Radovljica* and go through the village of Lesce; the road dead-ends at Radovljica's pedestrian zone, a short walk from the bee museum. A brand-new **bike** path, scenically and peacefully connecting Bled with Radovljica (about 4 miles), should open in 2007 (get details at TI).

Vintgar Gorge

Just north of Bled, the river Radovna has carved this mile-long, picturesque gorge into the mountainside. Boardwalks and bridges put you right in the middle of the action of this "poor man's Plitvice." A hike here is worth ▲. You'll cross over several waterfalls and marvel at the clarity of the water. The easy hike is on a boardwalk trail with handrails (sometimes narrow and a bit slippery). At the end of the gorge, you'll find a restaurant, WCs, and a bridge with a gorgeous view. Go back the way you came, or take a prettier return to Bled (see "Scenic Hike Back to Bled"). The gorge is easily reachable from Bled by bus or foot, and is the best option for those who are itching for a hike but don't have a car (€3, daily May–late Oct 8:00–19:00 or until dusk, June–Aug until 20:00, closed late Oct–April, tel. 04/572-5266).

Getting to Vintgar Gorge: The gorge is 2.5 miles north of Bled. You can walk (1 hour) or bus (15-min ride plus 15-min walk, or 30-min ride on summer tourist bus) to the gorge entrance. **Walkers** leave Bled on the road between the castle and St. Martin's Church and take the uphill (left) road at the fork. Soon after you pass the Pension Bledec hostel, turn right at the stop sign, then turn left at the bend in the road (following signs for *Podhom* and *Vintgar;* ignore the other *Vintgar* sign pointing back toward the way you came). At the fork just after the little bridge, go left for Podhom, then simply follow signs for *Vintgar.* In summer, the easy **tourist bus** takes you right to the gorge entrance in 30 minutes (see "Getting Around Lake Bled," page 565). Otherwise, take a **local bus** to one of two stops: Podhom (15 min, 9/day Mon-Fri, none Sat, 1/day Sun) or Spodnje Gorje (15 min, take bus in direction of Krnica, hourly). From either the Podhom or the Spodnje Gorje bus stop, it's a 15-minute walk to the gorge (follow signs for *Vintgar*). **Drivers** follow signs to *Podhom,* then *Vintgar* (see walking instructions, above).

Scenic Hike Back to Bled: If you still have energy once you reach the end of the gorge, consider this longer hike back with panoramic views. Behind the restaurant, find the trail marked *Katarina Bled.* You'll go uphill for 25 strenuous minutes (following the red-and-white circles and arrows) before cresting the hill and enjoying beautiful views over Bled town and the region. Continue straight down the road 15 minutes to the typical, narrow, old village of Zasip, then walk (about 30 min) or take the bus back to Bled.

Lake Bohinj

The pristine alpine Lake Bohinj (BOH-heen), 16 miles south-west of Bled, enjoys a quieter scene and (in clear weather) even

better vistas of Triglav and the surrounding mountains. This is a real back-to-nature experience, with just a smattering of hotels and campgrounds, rather than the well-oiled resort machine of Bled. Some people adore Bohinj; others are bored by it. If you think Bled is too touristy to allow you to really enjoy the nature, go to Bohinj.

Getting to Lake Bohinj: From Bled, hourly **buses** head for Bohinj, stopping at three different destinations: Bohinj Jezero (the village of Ribčev Laz, 30 min, €3.50), then Bohinj Vogel (a 10-minute walk from the base of the Vogel Mountain cable car, 35 min, €3.75), and finally Bohinj Zlatorog (Hotel Zlatorog and the one-hour hike to the Savica waterfall trailhead, 40 min, €4). Off-season, there are fewer buses—confirm times before you depart. **Drivers** leave Bled going south along the lakefront road, Cesta

Svobode; once you reach the village of Mlino, you'll peel off from the lake and follow signs to *Boh. Bistrica* (a midsize town near Lake Bohinj). Once in the town of Bohinjska Bistrica, turn right, following *Bohinj Jezero* signs. The road takes you to the village of Ribčev Laz and along the lakefront road with all the attractions.

Sights and Activities: A visit to Bohinj has three parts: a village, a cable car (and nearby cemetery), and a waterfall hike.

Coming from Bled, your first views of Bohinj will be from the little village at the southeast corner of the lake called **Ribčev Laz** (loosely translated as "Good Fishin' Hole"). Here you'll find a TI, a handful of hotels and ice-cream stands, and the Bohinj Jezero bus stop.

The town's trademark is its church, St. John the Baptist (to your right as you face the lake, past the distinctive stone bridge). One of the area's oldest churches, St. John's features a rustic exterior and a fresco-packed interior (if it's locked, borrow key from TI). In the other direction, a five-minute stroll down the lakefront road, is a dock where you can catch an electric tourist boat to make a silent circuit around the lake (€8 round-trip, €6.50 one-way, daily 10:00–18:00, 2/hr, less off-season). The boat stops at the far end of the lake, at Camp Zlatorog—a 10-min walk from the Vogel cable car (see below). Across from the Ribčev Laz dock is a fun concrete 3-D model of Triglav (compare to the real thing, hovering across the lake). Finally, a few more steps down the road, just beyond a boat rental dock, you'll see a statue of Zlatorog, the "Golden Horn"—a mythical chamois-like creature native to the Julian Alps.

The remaining sights are along this same road, which follows the lake to its end.

For a mountain perch without the sweat, take the cable car up to **Vogel Mountain,** offering impressive panoramic views of Mount Triglav and the Julian Alps (€10 round-trip, runs every 30 min, daily 7:00–19:00 in summer, 8:00–18:00 in winter, shorter hours and less frequent departures in spring and fall—confirm schedule before you make the trip, closed Nov, www.vogel.si). The top is a ski-in-winter, hike-in-summer area with fine views and a chairlift experience. The alpine hut Merjasec ("Wild Boar") offers tasty strudel and a wide variety of local brandies (including the notorious "Boar's Blood"—a concoction of several different flavors guaranteed to get you snorting). To reach the cable-car station, drivers follow signs to *Vogel* (to the left off the main lakefront road); by bus, get off at the Bohinj Vogel stop (request this stop from driver) and hike about 10 minutes up the steep road on the left (away from the lake).

Just beyond the cable-car station and Bohinj Vogel bus stop, look for the metal gate on the left marking a **World War I cemetery**—the final resting place for Soča Front soldiers (see sidebar on page 596). While no fighting occurred here (it was mostly on the other side of these mountains), injured soldiers were brought to a nearby hospital. Those who didn't recover ended up here. Notice that many of the names are not Slovene, but Hungarian, Polish, Czech, and so on—a reminder that the entire multiethnic Austro-Hungarian Empire was involved in the fighting. If you're walking down from the cable-car station, the cemetery makes for a poignant detour on your way to the main road (look for it through the trees).

Up the valley beyond the end of the lake is Bohinj's final treat, a waterfall called **Slap Savica** (sah-VEET-seh). Hardy hikers enjoy following the moderate-to-strenuous uphill trail (including 553 stairs) to see the cascade, which dumps into a remarkably pure pool of aquamarine snowmelt (€2, daily in summer from 8:00 until dusk, allow about 90 min for the round-trip hike). Drivers follow the lakefront road to where it ends, right at the trailhead. Without a car, getting to the trailhead is a hassle. If you take the public bus from Bled, or the boats on the lake, they'll get you only as far as the Bohinj Zlatorog stop—the end of the line, and still a one-hour hike from the trailhead (from the bus stop, follow signs to *Slap Savica*). In summer, a sporadic shuttle bus takes you right to the trailhead. But frankly, it's not worth it if you don't have a car.

Sleeping near Lake Bohinj: Like most people who live in these parts, **$ Bojan and Ksenija Kočar** (BOH-yawn and kuh-SAYN-yah KOH-char) have spent years building their alpine home. In addition to housing the Kočars and their two teenagers, this delightful chalet also has several affordable rooms for tourists, as well as a beautifully hand-carved lounge/breakfast room. If you have a car and want to really get away from it all, consider sleeping here, in the countryside less than a mile from Lake Bohinj (about a 30-min drive from Lake Bled). Friendly, English-speaking Bojan—who's a bus driver—is often out of town, but Ksenija (who speaks less English) will take good care of you (Db-€34, or €44 for 1-night stays, includes breakfast, closed Jan–March, tel. 04/574-6660—best to call after 21:00, mobile 041-478-490, kocar .bojan@siol.net). Driving from Lake Bled, you'll go through the town of Bohinjska Bistrica, then the village of Polje; they're just beyond Polje, but before Lake Bohinj itself (the first farmhouse on the left after Polje, #49, look for *Rooms* sign).

THE JULIAN ALPS

The countryside around Lake Bled has its own distinctive beauty. But to get the full Slovenian mountain experience, head for the hills. The northwestern corner of Slovenia—within yodeling distance of Austria and Italy—is crowned by the Julian Alps (named for Julius Caesar). Here, mountain culture has a Slavic flavor.

The Slovenian mountainsides are laced with hiking paths, blanketed in a deep forest, and speckled with ski resorts and vacation chalets. Beyond every ridge is a peaceful alpine village nestled around a quaint Baroque steeple. And in the center of it all is Mount Triglav—ol' "Three Heads"—Slovenia's symbol and tallest mountain (see page 588).

The single best day in the Julian Alps is spent driving up and over the 50 hairpin turns of the breathtaking Vršič Pass (vur-SHEECH, open May–Oct), and back down via the Soča (SOH-chah) River Valley, lined with offbeat nooks and Hemingway-haunted crannies. As you curl on twisty roads between the cut-glass peaks, you'll enjoy stunning high-mountain scenery, whitewater rivers with superb fishing, rustic rest stops, thought-provoking World War I sights, and charming hamlets.

A pair of Soča Valley towns holds watch over the region. Bovec is all about good times (it's the whitewater adventure-sports hub), while Kobarid attends to more serious matters (WWI history). While neither is a destination in itself, both Bovec and Kobarid are pleasant, functional, and convenient home bases for exploring this gloriously beautiful region.

Getting Around the Julian Alps

The Julian Alps are best by **car**. Even if you're doing the rest of your trip by train, consider renting a car here for maximum mountain day-trip flexibility. I've included a self-guided driving tour incorporating the best of the Julian Alps (Vršič Pass and Soča Valley).

It's difficult to do the Vršič Pass and Soča Valley without your own wheels. Hiring a **local guide** with a car can be a great value, making your time not only fun, but also informative. Cheaper but less personal, you could join a day-trip **excursion** from Bled. (Both options are explained in the "Tours" section of the previous chapter, page 566.) Or stay closer to Bled, and get a taste of the Julian Alps by taking advantage of easy and frequent **bus** connections to more convenient day-trip destinations (Radovljica, the Vintgar Gorge, and Lake Bohinj—all described under "Near Lake Bled" in the previous chapter).

Julian Alps Self-Guided Driving Tour

This all-day, ▲▲▲ self-guided driving tour takes you over the highest mountain pass in Slovenia, with stunning scenery and a few quirky sights along the way. From waterfalls to hiking trails, World War I history to queasy suspension bridges, this trip has it all.

ORIENTATION

Most of the Julian Alps are encompassed by the Triglav National Park (Triglavski Narodni Park). (Some sights near Lake Bled—such as Lake Bohinj and the Vintgar Gorge—are also part of this park, but are covered in the previous chapter.) This drive is divided into two parts: the Vršič Pass and the Soča River Valley. While not for stick-shift novices, all but the most timid drivers will agree the scenery is worth the many hairpin turns. Frequent pull-outs offer plenty of opportunity to relax, stretch your legs, and enjoy the vistas.

Planning Your Time: While this drive can be done in a day, consider spending the night along the way for a more leisurely pace. You can start and end in Bled or Ljubljana. For efficient sightseeing, I prefer to begin in Bled (after appreciating the mountains from afar for a day or two) and end in the capital.

Length of This Tour: These rough estimates do not include stops: Bled to the top of Vršič Pass—1 hour; Vršič Pass to Trenta (start of Soča Valley)—30 min; Trenta to Bovec—30 min; Bovec to Kobarid—30 min; Kobarid to Ljubljana or Bled—2 hours (remember, it's an hour between Ljubljana and Bled). In other words, if you started and ended in Bled and drove the entire route without stopping, you'd make it home in less than five hours...but you'd miss so much. It takes at least a full day to really do the region justice.

Tourist Information: The best sources of information are the Bled TI (see page 563), the Triglav National Park Information Center in Trenta (page 590), and the TIs in Bovec and Kobarid (pages 592 and 595).

Maps: Pick up a good map before you begin (available at local TIs, travel agencies, and gas stations). The all-Slovenia *Autokarta Slovenija* includes all the essential roads, but several more detailed options are also available. The 1:50,000 Kod & Kam *Posoče* map covers the entire Vršič Pass and Soča Valley (but doesn't include the parts of the drive near Bled and Ljubljana).

OK...let's ride.

Part 1: Vršič Pass

From Bled or Ljubljana, take the A-2 expressway north, enjoying views of **Mount Triglav** on the left as you drive. About 10 minutes past Bled, you'll approach the industrial city of **Jesenice,** whose iron-and steelworks are now mostly closed. The nearby village of **Kurja Vas** ("Chicken Village") is famous for producing hockey players (18 of the 20 players on the 1971 Yugoslav hockey team—which went to the World Championships—were from this tiny hamlet).

As you zip past Jesenice, keep your eye out for the Hrušica exit (also marked for Jesenice, Kranjska Gora, and the Italian border; it's after the gas station, just before the tunnel to Austria). When you exit, turn left towards Kranjska Gora (yellow sign) and the Italian border.

Slovenes brag that their country—"with 56 percent of the land covered in forest"—is one of Europe's greenest. As you drive towards Kranjska Gora, take in all this greenery...and the characteristic Slovenian hayracks (recognized as part of the national heritage and now preserved; see page 511). The Vrata Valley (on the left) is a popular starting point for climbing Mount Triglav. On the right, watch for the statue of Jakob Aljaž, who actually bought Triglav back when such a thing was possible (he's pointing at his purchase). Ten minutes later, you'll cross a bridge and enjoy a great head-on view of Špik Mountain.

Entering Kranjska Gora, you'll see a turnoff to the left marked

Northwest Slovenia

for *Vršič*. But winter sports fanatics may want to take a 15-minute detour to see the biggest ski jump in the world, a few miles ahead (stay straight through Kranjska Gora, then turn left at signs for **Planica,** the last stop before the Italian border). Every year, tens of thousands of sports fans flock here to watch the ski-flying world championships. This is where a local boy was the first human to fly more than 100 meters (328 feet) on skis. Today's competitors routinely set new world records (currently 784 feet—that's 17 seconds in the air). From the ski jump, you're a few minutes' walk from Italy or Austria. This region—spanning three nations—lobbied unsuccessfully under the name Senza Confini (Italian for "without borders") to host the 2006 Winter Olympics. Despite the failed Olympic bid, this philosophy is in tune with the European Union's vision for a Europe of regions, rather than nations.

Back in Kranjska Gora, follow the signs for Vršič. Before long, you'll officially enter **Triglav National Park** and come to the first of this road's 50 hairpin turns—each one numbered and labeled with the altitude in meters. Notice that they're cobbled to provide better traction. If the drive seems daunting, remember that 50-seat

Mount Triglav

Mount Triglav ("Three Heads") stands watch over the Julian Alps and all of Slovenia. Slovenes say that its three peaks are the guardians of the water, air, and earth. This mountain defines Slovenes, even adorning the nation's flag: Look for the national seal, with three peaks. The two squiggly lines under it represent the Adriatic. Or take a look at one of Slovenia's €0.50 coins.

From the town of Bled, you'll see Triglav peeking up over the ridge on a clear day. (You'll get an even better view from nearby Lake Bohinj.)

It's said that you're not a true Slovene until you've climbed Triglav. One native took these words very seriously, and climbed the mountain 853 times...in one year. Climbing to the summit—at 9,396 feet—is an attainable goal for any hiker in decent shape. If you're here for a while and want to become an honorary Slovene, befriend a local and ask if he or she will take you to the top.

If mountain climbing isn't your style, relax at an outdoor café with a piece of cream cake and a view of Triglav. It won't make you a Slovene...but it's close enough on a quick visit.

tour buses routinely conquer this pass...if they can do it, so can you.

After switchback #8, with the cute waterfall, park your car on the right and hike up the stairs to the little **Russian chapel** (recently renovated, so it looks shiny and new). This road was built during World War I by 10,000 Russian POWs of the Austro-Hungarian Empire to supply the front lines of the Soča Front. The POWs lived and worked in terrible conditions, and several hundred died of illness and exposure. On March 8, 1916, an avalanche thundered down the mountains, killing hundreds more workers. This chapel was built where the final casualty was found. Take a minute to pay your respects to the men who built the road you're enjoying today.

After #22, at the pullout for Erjavčeva Koča restaurant, you may see tour-bus groups making a fuss about the mountain vista. They're looking for a ghostly face in the cliff wall, supposedly belonging to the mythical figure **Ajda.** This village girl was cursed by the townspeople after correctly predicting the death of the Zlatorog (Golden Horn), a magical, beloved, chamois-like animal. Her tiny image (with a Picasso nose) is just above the tree line, a little to the right—try to get someone to point her out to you (you can see her best if you stand at the signpost near the road).

After #24, you reach the **summit** (5,285 feet). On the right, a long gravel chute gives hikers a thrilling glissade down. (From the pullout just beyond #26, it's easy to view hikers "skiing" down.) As you begin the descent, keep an eye out for old WWI debris. A lonely guard tunnel stands after #28, followed by a tunnel marked *1916* (on the left) that was part of the road's original path. Then you'll see abandoned checkpoints from when this was the border between Italy and the Austro-Hungarian Empire. At #48 is a statue of **Julius Kugy,** an Italian botanist who wrote books about alpine flora.

At #49, the road to the right (marked *Izvir Soče*) leads to the **source of the Soča River.** If you feel like stretching your legs after all that shifting, drive about five minutes down this road to a restaurant parking lot. From here, you can take a 20-minute uphill hike to the Soča source. This is also the starting point for a new, well-explained Soča Trail (Soška Pot) that leads all the way to the town of Bovec, mostly following the road we're driving on today. With plenty of time and a hankering to hike rather than drive, consider taking this trail (about 12 miles one-way).

Nearing the end of the switchbacks, follow signs for Bovec. Crossing the Soča River, you begin the second half of this trip.

Part 2: Soča River Valley

During World War I, the terrain between here and the Adriatic made up the Soča (Isonzo) Front. As you follow the Soča River south, down what's nicknamed the "Valley of the Cemeteries," the scenic mountainsides around you tell the tale of this terrible warfare. Imagine a young Ernest Hemingway driving his ambulance through these same hills.

But it's not all so gruesome. There are plenty of other diversions—interesting villages and churches, waterfalls and suspension bridges, and lots more.

The last Vršič switchback (#50) sends you into the village of **Trenta.** You'll pass a church and a botanical garden of alpine plants (Alpinum Juliana), then go over a bridge. Immediately after the bridge on the right is the parking lot for the Mlinarica Gorge. While the gorge is interesting, the bridge leading to it was damaged in a severe storm and hasn't yet been rebuilt—so it's best left to hardy hikers.

As you get to the cluster of buildings in Trenta's downtown, look on the left for the **Triglav National Park Information Center,** which also serves as a regional TI (May–Oct daily 10:00–18:00, closed Nov–April, tel. 05/388-9330, www.tnp.si). The humble €4 museum here provides a look (with English explanations) at the park's flora, fauna, traditional culture, and mountaineering history. A poetic 15-minute slideshow explains the wonders and fragility of the park (included in museum entry, ask for English version as you enter).

About five miles after Trenta, in the town of Soča, visit the **Church of St. Joseph** (with red onion dome, hiding behind the big tree on the right). The church was damaged in the earthquakes of 1998 and 2004, so the interior will likely be covered with scaffolding. But if it's not covered, you'll see some fascinating art. During World War II, an artist hiding out in the mountains filled this church with patriotic symbolism. The interior is bathed in Yugoslav red, white, and blue—a brave statement made when such nationalistic sentiments were dangerous. On the ceiling is St. Michael (clad in Yugoslav colors) with Yugoslavia's three WWII enemies at his feet: the eagle (Germany), the wolf (Italy), and the serpent (Japan). The tops of the walls along the nave are lined with saints—but these are Slavic, not Catholic. Finally, look carefully at the Stations of the Cross and find the faces of hated Yugoslav enemies: Hitler (fourth from altar on left) and Mussolini (first from altar on right). Behind the church is a typical cemetery, with civilian and (on the hillside) military sections.

For a good example of how the Soča River cuts like God's bandsaw into the land, stop about two minutes past the church at **Velika Korita Soče,** where you can venture out onto a suspension bridge over a gorge. Bounce if you dare. Just beyond this bridge is the turnoff (on the left) to the Lepena Valley, home of the recommended Pristava Lepena pension—and their Lipizzaner horses (see page 555).

Roughly five miles after the town of Soča, you exit the National Park and come to a fork. The main route leads to the left, through Bovec. But first, take a two-mile detour to the right (marked *Predel*), where the WWI **Kluže Fort** keeps a close watch over the narrowest part of a valley leading to Italy (€2, daily 10:00–19:00). In the 15th century, the Italians had a fort here to defend against the Ottomans. Half a millennium later, during World War I, it was used by Austrians to keep Italians out of their territory. Notice the ladder rungs fixed to the cliff face across the road from the fort—allowing soldiers to quickly get up to the mountaintop.

Back on the main road, continue to **Bovec.** This town, which saw some of the most vicious fighting of the Soča Front, was hit hard by a 2004 earthquake. Today, it's being rebuilt and remains the adventure-sports capital of the Soča River Valley, famous for its whitewater activities. For a good lunch stop in Bovec, see my suggestions on page 594. But if you're not eating or spending the night here, feel free to skip it (continue along the main road to bypass the town center).

Heading south along the river—with water somehow both perfectly clear and spectacularly turquoise—watch for happy kayakers. When you pass the intersection at Žaga, you're just four miles from Italy. Along the way, you'll also pass a pair of waterfalls: The well-known Boka ("Slovenia's second-longest waterfall," just before Žaga) and the hidden gem Veliki Kozjak (unmarked, on the left just before Kobarid). For either, you'll have to park your car and hike uphill to see the falls.

Signs lead to the town of **Kobarid,** home to a bustling square and some fascinating WWI sights. Even if you don't think you're interested in the Soča Front, consider dropping in the Kobarid Museum (page 578). Driving up to the Italian Mausoleum hovering over the town is a must (page 580).

Leaving Kobarid, continue south along the Soča to **Tolmin.** Before you reach Tolmin, decide on your route back to civilization.

Finishing the Drive

To Ljubljana: From Tolmin, you have two possible driving routes to the capital. Either option brings you back to the A-1 expressway south of Ljubljana, and will get you to the city in about two hours (though the second route has fewer miles).

The option you'll encounter first (turnoff to the right before Tolmin) is the smoother, longer route southwest to **Nova Gorica** (a city divided in half by the Italian border, and packed with casinos catering to Italian gamblers). From Nova Gorica, you can hop on the expressway—but the entire route between there and Ljubljana isn't finished yet, so you'll have to transfer to a secondary road for a while. (Once this entire expressway is finished, this will be hands-down the faster route.)

I prefer the more rural second option: Continue through Tolmin, then head southeast through the hills back towards Ljubljana. Along the way, you could stop for a bite and some sightseeing at the town of **Idrija** (EE-dree-yah), known to all Slovenes for three things: its tourable mercury mine, fine delicate lace, and tasty *žlikrofi* (like ravioli). Back at the expressway (at Logatec), head north to Ljubljana or on to Bled.

To Bled: The fastest option is to load your car onto a **"Car Train"** (Autovlak) that cuts directly through the mountains. The train departs at 18:05 from Most na Soči (just south of Tolmin, along the Idrija route described above) and arrives at Bohinjska Bistrica, near Lake Bohinj, at 18:50 (about €10 for the car; confirm schedule at the Bled TI before making the trip). From Bohinjska Bistrica, it's just a half-hour drive back to Bled. No reservations are necessary, but arrive at the train station about 30 minutes before the scheduled departure to allow time to load the car.

To **drive** all the way back, the fastest route (about 2 hours) is partially on a twisty, rough, very poor-quality road (go through Tolmin, turn off at Bača pri Modreju to Podbrdo, then from Petrovo Brdo take a very curvy road through the mountains into Bohinjska Bistrica and on to Bled). For more timid drivers, it's more sane and not too much longer to start out on the Idrija route toward Ljubljana (described above), but turn off in Želin (before Idrija) towards Skofja Loka and Kranj, then on to Bled. Or take one of the two routes described above for Ljubljana, then continue on the expressway past Ljubljana and back up to Bled (allow 3 hours).

Bovec

The biggest town in the area, Bovec has a happening main square and all the tourist amenities. It's best known as a hub for whitewater adventure sports. While not exactly quaint, Bovec is charming enough to qualify as a good lunch stop or overnight home base. If nothing else, it's a nice jolt of civilization wedged between the alpine cliffs.

ORIENTATION

(area code: 05)

Tourist Information
The helpful TI on the main square offers fliers on mountain biking and water sports (summer Mon–Fri 9:00–20:00, Sat–Sun 9:30–13:00; winter Mon–Fri 9:00–17:00, closed Sat–Sun; Trg Golobarskih Žrtev 8, tel. 05/389-6444, www.bovec.si).

Arrival in Bovec
The main road skirts Bovec (BOH-vets), but you can turn off (watch for signs on the right) to take the road that goes through the heart of town, then re-joins the main road farther along. As

you approach the city center, you can't miss the main square, Trg Golobarskih Žrtev, with the TI and a pair of good restaurants (described in "Eating").

SLEEPING

In Bovec

$$$ Dobra Vila is a gorgeous new hotel with classy traditional-meets-contemporary decor that feels out of place in little, remote Bovec. Not that I'm complaining. Its 12 rooms are swanky, and the public spaces (including a sitting room/library, breakfast room/restaurant, wine cellar, small "movie theater," winter garden porch, and terrace with cozy mountain-view chairs) are welcoming. Enthusiastically run by Andrea and Sebastian Kovačič, it's a winner (Sb-€93, Db-€110, 20 percent more for 1-night stays, same prices year-round, fun old-fashioned elevator, on the left just as you enter town on the main road from the Vršič Pass at Mala Vas 112, tel. 05/389-6400, fax 05/389-6404, www.dobra-vila-bovec .com, welcome@dobra-vila-bovec.com).

$$ Martinov Hram has 12 nondescript modern rooms over a popular restaurant a few steps from Bovec's main square. While the rooms are an afterthought to the busy restaurant (reception at the bar), they're comfortable (mid-July–Aug: Sb-€36, Db-€60; a few euros less off-season, no extra charge for 1-night stays, Trg Golobarskih Žrtev 27, tel. 05/388-6214).

Near Bovec

$$$ Pristava Lepena is a relaxing oasis hiding out in the Lepena Valley just north of Bovec. Well-run by Milan and Silvia Dolenc,

---

Sleep Code

(€1 = about $1.20, country code: 386, area code: 05)
S = Single, **D** = Double/Twin, **T** = Triple, **Q** = Quad, **b** = bathroom. Unless otherwise noted, breakfast is included and credit cards are accepted. Everyone speaks English and all of these accommodations include breakfast. These prices don't include the €1 tourist tax per person, per night.

To help you sort easily through these listings, I've divided the rooms into three categories based on the price for a standard double room with bath:

  $$$ Higher Priced—Most rooms €100 or more.
  $$ Moderately Priced—Most rooms between €50–100.
  $ Lower Priced—Most rooms €50 or less.

this place is its own little village: a series of rustic-looking cabins, a restaurant, and a sauna/outdoor swimming pool. Hiding behind the humble split-wood shingle exteriors is surprising comfort: 13 cozy apartments (with wood-burning stoves, TV, telephone, and all the amenities) that make you feel like relaxing. This place whispers "second honeymoon" (Db rates: July–Aug-€116, May–June and Sept-€100, early Oct and late April-€84, closed in winter, multi-night stays preferred, 1-night stays may be possible for 20 percent extra, dinner-€16, lunch and dinner-€27, nonrefundable 30 percent advance payment when you reserve; just before Bovec, turn left off the main road toward Lepena, and follow the white horses to Lepena 2; tel. 05/388-9900, fax 05/388-9901, www.pristava-lepena.com, pristava.lepena@siol.net). The Dolences also have four Welsh ponies and four purebred Lipizzaner horses (two mares, two geldings) that guests can ride (in riding ring-€12/hr, on trail-€15/hr, riding lesson-€18; non-guests may be able to ride for a few euros more—call ahead and ask).

$ **Tourist Farm Pri Plajerju,** on a picturesque plateau at the edge of Trenta (the first town at the bottom of the Vršič Pass road), is your budget option. Run by the Pretner family, this organic farm raises sheep and goats, and rents four apartments and one room in three buildings separate from the main house. While not quite as tidy as other tourist farms I recommend, it's the best one I found in the Soča Valley (July–Aug: Db-€30–42; March–June and Sept–Dec: Db-€26–34; price depends on size of room or apartment, closed Jan–Feb, breakfast-€4.50, dinner-€6.50, watch for signs to the left after passing through the village of Trenta, Trenta 16a, tel. & fax 05/388-9209, www.eko-plajer.com, farma_plajer@hotmail.com).

EATING

In Bovec

Letni Vrt Pizzeria, dominating the main square, is the busiest place in town—with pizzas, pastas, salads, and more (closed Tue, Trg Golobarskih Žrtev 12, tel. 05/388-6335).

Martinov Hram, run by the Berginc family, is also good. The nicely traditional decor goes well with Slovenian specialties focused on sheep (good homemade bread, closed Thu, on the main road through Bovec, just before the main square on the right at Trg Golobarskih Žrtev 27, tel. 05/388-6214).

Kobarid

Kobarid feels older, and therefore a bit more appealing, than its big brother Bovec. This humble settlement was immortalized by a literary giant. Ernest Hemingway, who drove an ambulance on the Soča Front in World War I, described Kobarid—which he called by its Italian name, Caporetto—as "a little white town with a campanile in a valley. It was a clean little town and there was a fine fountain in the square." Sounds about right. Aside from its brush with literary greatness, Kobarid is known as a hub of Soča Front information (with an excellent WWI museum, a hilltop Italian mausoleum, and walks that connect the nearby sights), and for its surprisingly good restaurants.

ORIENTATION

The main road cuts right through the heart of little Kobarid, bisecting its main square (Trg Svobode). The Kobarid Museum is along this road, on the left before the square. To reach the museum from the main square, simply walk five minutes back toward Bovec.

Tourist Information

The TI is across the street from the Kobarid Museum (summer daily 9:00–19:00, even later in peak season; winter Mon–Fri 9:00–16:00, Sat 9:00–13:00, closed Sun; Gregorčičeva 8, tel. 05/380-0490, www.lto-sotocje.si and www.kobarid.si).

SIGHTS

▲▲▲**Kobarid Museum (Kobariški Muzej)**—This modest but world-class museum offers a haunting look at the tragedy of the Soča Front. This proud little place, with fine English descriptions, was voted Europe's best museum in 1993. The entry is lined with hastily made cement and barbed-wire gravestones, pictures of soldiers, and flags of all of the nationalities involved in the fighting. Maps show how Europe changed from 1914 to 1918. The rotating ground-floor exhibit features a different country each year.

Upon arrival, ask to watch the English version of the 19-minute film on the history of the Soča Front (plays on top floor). Upstairs are exhibits on the way these soldiers lived, the tragedies they encountered (with some horrific images of war injuries), the devastating effects of the war on civilians, the strategies involved in the various battles (including a huge model of the successful Austrian-German *Blitzkrieg* attack), and the history of this region before and after World War I. Naturally, the exhibit focuses on

The Soča (Isonzo) Front

The northwest corner of Slovenia—called Soča in Slovene, and Isonzo in Italian—saw some of World War I's fiercest fighting. While the Western Front gets more press, this eastern border between the Central Powers and the Allies was just as significant. In a series of 13 battles involving 16 different nationalities, 300,000 soldiers died, 700,000 were wounded, and 100,000 were declared MIA. In addition, tens of thousands of civilians died. Among the injured soldiers was a young Ernest Hemingway, who drove an ambulance for the Italian army. (Later in life, he would write the novel *A Farewell to Arms* about his experiences here.)

On April 26, 1915, Italy joined the Allies. A month later, they declared war on the Austro-Hungarian Empire (which included Slovenia). Italy invaded the Soča Valley, quickly taking the tiny town of Kobarid, which they planned to use as a home base for attacks deeper into Austrian territory. For the next 29 months, Italy launched 10 more offensives, all of them unsuccessful. This was difficult warfare—Italy had to attack uphill, waging war high in the mountains, in the harshest of conditions.

In October 1917, the Central Powers of Austria-Hungary and Germany retook Kobarid, launching a downhill attack of 600,000 soldiers. For the first time ever, the Austrian-German army used a new surprise-attack technique called *Blitzkrieg*, carried out by a German general named Erwin Rommel against orders from a superior. (He was demoted for his insolence despite its success, but climbed the ranks again to become famous as Hitler's "Desert Fox" in North Africa.) The Central Powers caught the Italian forces off-guard, quickly breaking through three lines of defense. Within three days, the Italians were forced to retreat. The Austrians called it the "Miracle at Kobarid," but Italy felt differently—to this day, when an Italian finds himself in a mess, he says he had a *Caporetto* (the Italian name for Kobarid).

A year later, Italy came back—this time with the aid of British, French, and US forces. The Allies were successful, and on November 4, 1918, Austria-Hungary conceded defeat. After more than a million casualties, the fighting at Soča was finally over.

the crucial 12th battle of the Soča Front—the Battle of Kobarid (€4, good €3 museum guide, €10 *Soča Front* book; April–Sept Mon–Fri 9:00–18:00, Sat–Sun 9:00–19:00; Oct–March Mon–Fri 10:00–17:00, Sat–Sun 9:00–18:00; Gregorčičeva 10, tel. 05/389-0000, www.kobariski-muzej.si).

At the museum (and local TIs), you can pick up a free brochure outlining the **"Kobarid Historical Walk"** tracing WWI sites in town and the surrounding countryside (3 miles, mostly uphill, allow 3–5 hours). History buffs can also call ahead to arrange a private guide (€15/hr, tel. 05/389-0000).

In 2007, the museum—and all of Kobarid—commemorates the 90th anniversary of the end of the Soča Front warfare, culminating in a town-wide festival in October.

▲▲**Italian Mausoleum (Kostnica)**—The 55 miles between here and the Adriatic are dotted with more than a hundred cemeteries, reminders of the countless casualties of the Soča Front. One of the most dramatic is this mausoleum, overlooking Kobarid. The access road, across Kobarid's main square from the side of the church, is marked by stone gate towers (with the word *Kostnica*). One of these towers used to be topped with a star, and the other with a cross—but now the star (representing Yugoslav communism) has gone missing. Hmm.

Take the road up Gradič Hill—passing Stations of the Cross—to the mausoleum. Built in 1938 (when this was still part of Italy) around the existing Church of St. Anthony, this fascist-style octagonal pyramid holds the remains of 7,014 Italian soldiers. Names are listed alphabetically, along with mass graves for more than 1,700 unknown soldiers *(militi ignoti)*. Walk behind the church and find the WWI battlements high on the mountain's rock face (with your back to church, they're at 10 o'clock). Incredibly, the fighting was done on these treacherous ridges; civilians in the valleys only heard the distant battles. If the church is open, go inside and look above the door to see a brave soldier standing over the body of a fallen comrade, fending off enemies with nothing but rocks. When Mussolini came to dedicate the mausoleum, local revolutionaries plotted an assassination attempt that couldn't fail. But at the last minute, the triggerman had a change of heart, Mussolini had an uneventful trip, and fascism continued to thrive in Italy.

SLEEPING AND EATING

$$$ Hotel Hvala, right on the main square, is your best bet. Run by the Hvala family, its 31 simple, contemporary rooms feel a few years out of date—but they're comfortable, and the location can't be beat (late July and Aug: Sb-€65, Db-€100; April–late July and Sept–Oct: Sb-€59, Db-€88; off-season: Sb-€54, Db-€78; 20 percent more for 1-night stays, hotel closed Feb and weekdays in Nov, Trg Svobode 1, tel. 05/389-9300, fax 05/388-5322, www.hotel-hvala.si, topli.val@siol.net).

The Hotel Hvala's restaurant, **Topli Val** ("Heat Wave"), is highly regarded for its fish dishes (€8–10 pastas, €10–20 main dishes, lengthy list of Slovenian wines, daily 12:00–16:00 & 18:00–24:00, Trg Svobode 1, tel. 05/389-9300).

For other options, you won't need to look far—pizzerias, pubs, and cafés are scattered around the main square. **Kotlar Restaurant,** across the square from Hotel Hvala, is well-regarded, and also has rooms for rent if you're in a pinch.

Split

1. Hotel/Rest. Adriana
2. Villa Ana & Villa Diana
3. Šperun Restaurant & Modrulj Launderette
4. Konoba Varoš Restaurant
5. Buffet Fife
6. Ristorante Pizzeria Galija
7. Backpacker Internet Café
8. Kuća Sladoleda Karmen Ice Cream
9. Hajduk Ice Cream

boats in Split. But the city is the perfect real-life contrast to the lazy, prettified Dalmatian beach resorts—it deserves a full day. Begin by strolling the remains of Diocletian's Palace, then have lunch or a coffee break along the Riva promenade. After lunch, browse the shops or visit a couple of Split's museums (the Meštrović Gallery, which is a long walk or short bus ride from the Old Town, is tops). Promenading along the Riva with the natives is *the* evening activity.

ORIENTATION

(area code: 021)

Split sprawls, but almost everything of interest to travelers is around the City Harbor (Gradska Luka). At the top of this harbor is the Old Town (Stari Grad). Between the Old Town and the sea is the Riva, a waterfront pedestrian promenade lined with cafés and shaded by palm trees. The main ferry terminal (Trajektni Terminal) juts out into the harbor from the east side. Along the harborfront embankment between the ferry terminal and the Old Town are the long-distance bus station (Autobusni Kolodvor) and the forlorn little train station (Željeznička Stanica). West of the Old Town, poking into the Adriatic, is the lush and hilly Marjan peninsula.

Split's domino-shaped Old Town is made up of two square sections. The east half was once Diocletian's Palace, and the west half is the medieval town that sprang up next door. The shell of Diocletian's ruined palace provides a checkerboard street plan, with a gate at each end. At the center of the former palace is the Peristyle square (Peristil), where you'll find the TI, cathedral, and highest concentration of Roman ruins.

Tourist Information

Split's disinterested TI is on the Peristyle square, in the very center of Diocletian's Palace (Mon–Fri 8:00–20:00, Sat–Sun 8:00–13:00, tel. 021/345-606, www.visitsplit.com). Pick up the free town map, monthly events guide, and other materials. The TI also sells books, maps, and the Splitcard (museum discount card—not worth considering for most visits).

Arrival in Split

For all the details on getting to Split, and getting around the Dalmatian Coast, read "Dalmatian Coast Practicalities" on page 606.

Split Essentials

English	Croatian	Pronounced
Old Town	Stari Grad	STAH-ree grahd
City Harbor	Gradska Luka	GRAHD-skah LOO-kah
Harborfront Promenade	Riva	REE-vah
Peristyle (old Roman square)	Peristil	PEH-ree-steel
Soccer Team	Hajduk	HIGH-dook
Local Sculptor	Ivan Meštrović	EE-vahn MESH-troh-veech
Adriatic Sea	Jadran	YAH-drahn

By Boat, Bus, or Train: Passenger boats (like the speedy *Krilo* catamaran to Hvar and Korčula) put in at the Obala Lazareta embankment right in front of the Old Town. Bigger **car ferries** use the main terminal (Trajektni Terminal) at the far end of the harbor. If you arrive at this ferry terminal, wade through the *sobe* hawkers to the main terminal building, where you'll find ATMs, WCs, a grocery store, and offices for all of the main ferry companies, including Jadrolinija (open long hours daily).

Split's **car ferry** terminal, **bus station** (Autobusni Kolodvor), and **train station** (Željeznička Stanica) all share a busy and very practical strip of land called Obala Kneza Domagoja, on the east side of the City Harbor. From any of them, you can see the Old Town and Riva; just walk around the harbor toward the big bell ιι··· ⌐about a 10-min walk). Along the way, you'll pass travel agencι₋ ₋₋gage-check offices, locals trying to rent rooms, a post office, ana ⌐ternet cafés. Arriving or leaving from this central location, you never need to deal with the concrete, exhaust-stained sprawl of outer Split.

By Plane: Split's airport (Zračna Luka Split-Kaštela) is across the big bay (Kaštelanski Zaljev), 15 miles northwest of the center, near the town of Trogir. A bus leaves Split 90 minutes before each Croatia Airlines flight (and some other companies' flights) from the small Air Terminal near the southeast corner of Diocletian's Palace, and meets each arriving flight at the airport (30 kn, 40 min). Figure on paying a hefty 300 kn for a taxi to the center. Airport info: tel. 021/203-506, www.split-airport.hr.

By Car: Drivers are treated to the ugly side of Split as they approach (don't worry—it gets better). Coming into town, begin by following *Centar* signs. The road forks while you're still outside of downtown: One way is simply marked *Centar* (west end of Old

Town), while the other directs you to the bus and train stations and the ferry terminal (east end of Old Town). Ask your hotel which is more convenient (many hotels are individually signposted at the fork). If you follow the signs for the ferry terminal, you'll pop out right at the southeast corner of Diocletian's Palace (by the Green Market). For handy (but expensive) parking, continue straight when the road swings left to the ferry terminal, and you'll drive right into a handy parking lot just outside the palace walls (10 kn/hr).

Driving around the city center can be tricky—Split is split by its Old Town, which is welded to the harbor by the pedestrian-only Riva promenade. This means drivers needing to get 300 yards from one side of the Old Town to the other must drive about 15 minutes entirely around the center, which can be miserably clogged with traffic. A semicircular ring road makes this better than it might be. To get to the west end, you'll go through a tunnel under the Marjan peninsula. To reach the ferry terminal (east side), follow *Trajektni* signs (look for the tiny ferry icon).

Helpful Hints

Internet Access: Internet cafés are plentiful in the Old Town; look for signs, especially around the Peristyle square. Closer to the stations and ferry terminal is **Backpacker C@fé,** run by Australian Steve Potter. This place has Internet access, coffee and drinks with outdoor eating, and used guidebooks and paperbacks for sale (daily July–Aug 6:00–24:00, shoulder season 8:00–21:00, even shorter hours off-season, near the beginning of Obala Kneza Domagoja, tel. 021/338-548). Modrulj Launderette (below) also has Internet access.

Post Office: A modern little post office is next to the bus station (Mon–Sat 7:00–21:00, closed Sun, on Obala Kneza Domagoja).

Laundry: Modrulj Launderette, a rare coin-operated launderette, is well-run by an Australian couple, Shane and Julie (50 kn/load self-service, 75 kn/load full-service, air-con, Internet access, left-luggage service; April–Oct daily 8:00–20:00; Nov–March Mon–Sat 9:00–17:00, closed Sun; Šperun 1, tel. 021/315-888). It's conveniently located just off the harbor at the west end of the Old Town, near the recommended Šperun and Konoba Varoš restaurants—handy if multitasking is your style.

Travel Agency: Turistički Biro, between the two halves of the Old Town on the Riva, books *sobe* and hotels, sells guidebooks and maps, and sells tickets for excursions (mid-June–Sept Mon–Fri 8:00–21:00, Sat 8:00–20:00, open Sun 8:00–13:00 mid-July–Aug only; Oct–mid-June Mon–Fri 8:00–20:00, Sat

8:00–13:00, closed Sun; Riva 12, tel. & fax 021/347-100, turist -biro-split@st.t-com.hr).

Baggage Check: The train and bus stations both have safe and efficient baggage-check services *(garderoba)*. If one is very crowded, the other may be empty—check both before waiting in a long line. At the opposite (west) end of the Old Town, Modrulj Launderette also has a left-luggage service (see above).

Wine Shop: At **Vinoteka Bouquet,** at the west end of the Riva (near the restaurants and launderette on Šperun street), knowledgeable Denis can help you pick out a bottle of Croatian wine to suit your tastes (Mon–Fri 8:30–12:30 & 17:00–20:30, Sat 9:00–13:30, closed Sun, Obala Hrvatskog Narodnog Preporoda 3, tel. 021/348-031). For a wine primer before you visit, see page 617.

Getting Around Split

Most of what you'll want to see is within walking distance, but some sights (such as the Meštrović Gallery) are more easily reached by bus or taxi.

By Bus: Local buses, run by Promet, cost 9 kn per ride (or 8 kn if you buy ticket from a kiosk; ask for a *putna karta;* zone 1 is fine for any ride within Split). Validate your ticket as you board the bus. Suburban buses to towns near Split (such as Salona or Trogir) generally use the Suburban Bus Station (Prigradski Autobusni Kolodvor), a 15-minute walk due north of the Old Town on Domovinskog rata. Bus information: www.promet-split.hr.

By Taxi: Taxis start at 18 kn, then cost around 8 kn per kilometer. Figure 50–60 kn for most rides within the city (for example, from the ferry terminal to most hotels)—but if going from one end of the Old Town to the other, it can be faster to walk. To call for a taxi, try Radio Taxi (tel. 021/970).

TOURS

Of Split

The only regularly scheduled **walking tours** of Split are run by Lifejacket Adventures, based at Modrulj Launderette (90 kn, April–Nov nearly nightly at 20:00—call ahead to confirm; tours depart from in front of launderette, last about 2 hours, and include a drink at the end; mobile 098-931-6400).

To hire your own **private guide,** contact the guide association, with an office on the Old Town's Peristyle square (330 kn for 2 people on a 2-hour tour, about 50 kn per person after that; June–Aug Mon–Fri 9:00–13:00 & 15:00–19:00, Sat 9:00–14:00, closed Sun; May and Sept Mon–Fri 9:00–17:00, Sat 9:00–15:00, closed Sun; even shorter hours Oct–April; tel. 021/360-058, tel. & fax 021/346-267, mobile 098-361-936).

From Split

Lifejacket Adventures, run by Australian couple Shane and Julie, works hard to come up with culturally meaningful excursions that connect travelers to the Croatia they came to see. You can choose among various full-day and multi-day trips to nearby islands. To get out on the open sea, consider their day trip to Brač Island on an authentic, old-fashioned *falkuša* fishing boat (730 kn, departs daily in summer at 8:30, includes a visit to the 16th-century Blaca Monastery and a traditional lunch with wine before return-ing to Split at 20:30). Once a week, the *falkuša* takes romantics out on a sunset tour, including traditional snacks and a swim on Čiovo Island (150 kn, 15 kn for drinks). They also arrange cus-tom excursions, with a focus on kayaking, hiking, wine, history, archaeological sites, and rock climbing. Reserve ahead for any of these trips (call mobile 098-931-6400 or stop by Split's launder-ette, which Shane and Julie also run—see "Helpful Hints"; www .lifejacketadventures.com).

Elite Travel and **Atlas Travel** offer a variety of excursions from Split (mostly full-day, about €45–65). Itineraries include a tour of Split and Trogir, whitewater rafting on the nearby Cetina River, the island of Brač, the island of Hvar, Brač and Hvar together, the island of Korčula, Dubrovnik, and Plitvice Lakes National Park. This can be a quick, convenient way to get to places that are time-consuming to reach by public transportation. Get information and tickets at any travel agency, such as the Turistički Biro on the Riva (see "Tourist Information").

SELF-GUIDED WALK

Diocletian's Palace (Dioklecijanova Palača)

Split's only ▲▲▲ sight is the remains of Roman Emperor Diocletian's enormous retirement palace, sitting on the harbor in the heart of the city. Since the ruins themselves are now integrated into the city's street plan, exploring them is free (though you'll pay to enter a few parts—such as the cellars and the cathedral/mauso-leum). As fragments of the palace are poorly marked, and there are not yet any good guidebooks or audioguides for tracking down the remains, Split is a good place to take a walking tour or hire a local guide (see "Tours"). This self-guided tour explains the basics. To begin the tour, stand in front of the palace (at the east end of the Riva, at the corner with the map of Split and palace illustration) to get oriented.

Background: Diocletian grew up just inland from Split,

Diocletian's Palace

>‐=View

1 Palace Facade View
2 Cellar Entrance (Below)
3 Passage to Peristyle (Below) & Ethnographic Museum (Above)
4 Peristyle Square
5 Entry Vestibule
6 Cathedral of St. Dominus
7 Jupiter's Temple/ St. John's Baptistery
8 View up Cardo Street
9 Bishop Gregory of Nin Statue

10 Split City Museum
11 Peristil Hotel
12 Hotel Vestibul Palace
13 Hotel Slavija
14 Hotel Kaštel
15 Sobe "Base"
16 Hostel Split
17 Zlagogajnica None Pizza
18 Zlatna Vrata Pizza & Pasta
19 Gradska Kavana Café
20 Turistički Biro Travel Agency
21 Croata Tie Shop
22 Air Terminal Bus Stop

in the town of Salona (Solin in Croatian)—which was then the capital of Dalmatia. He worked his way up the Roman hierarchy and became emperor (A.D. 284–305). Despite all of his achievements, Diocletian is best remembered for two questionable legacies: dividing the huge empire among four emperors (which helped administer it more efficiently, but began a splintering effect that arguably led to the empire's decline); and torturing and executing Christians, including thousands right here on the Dalmatian Coast.

As Diocletian grew older, he decided to return to his homeland for retirement. (Since he was in poor health, the medicinal sulfur spring here was another plus.) His massive palace took only 11 years to build—and this fast pace required a big push (more than 2,000 slaves died during construction). Huge sections of his palace still exist, modified by medieval and modern developers alike. To get a sense of the original palace, check out the big illustration posted across from the palace entry.

Palace Facade: The "front" of today's Split—facing the harbor—was actually the back door of Diocletian's Palace. There was no embankment in front of the palace back then, so the water came right up to this door—sort of an emergency exit by boat.

Visually trace the outline of the gigantic palace, which was more than 600 feet long on each side. On the corner to the right stands a big, rectangular guard tower (one of the original 16). To the left, the tower is gone and the corner is harder to pick out (look for the beginning of the newer-looking buildings). Erase in your mind the ramshackle two-story buildings added 200 years ago, which obscure the grandness of the palace wall.

Halfway up the facade, notice the row of 42 arched window frames (mostly filled in today). Diocletian and his family lived in the seaside half of the palace. Imagine him strolling back and forth along this fine arcade, enjoying the views of his Adriatic homeland. The inland, non-view half of the palace was home to 700 servants, bodyguards, and soldiers.

• *Now go through the door in the middle of the palace (known as the "Brass Gate"; under the* Substructure of Diocletian's Palace *banner). Just inside the door is the entrance to...*

Diocletian's Cellars (Podromi): Since the palace was built on land that sloped down to the sea, these chambers were built to level out the main floor (like a modern "daylight basement"). The cellars weren't used for storage; they were filled with water from three different sources: a freshwater spring, a sulfur spring, and the sea. Later, medieval residents used them as a dump. Rediscovered only in the last century, the cellars enabled archaeologists to derive the floor plan of some of the palace's long-gone sections. Today, these underground chambers are used for art exhibits and a little strip of souvenir stands. But before you go shopping, explore the cellars at this end (15 kn, skimpy 10-kn guidebook; hours sporadic, but generally opens daily at 9:00 and closes June–Aug at 21:00, Sept at 20:00, May and Oct at 18:00, April at 17:00; Nov–March Mon–Sat 9:00–14:00, closed Sun).

Wander through the labyrinthine area beyond the ticket desk (on the left, or west, side of the palace). When those first villagers took refuge in the abandoned palace from the rampaging Slavs in 641, the elite lived upstairs, grabbing what was once the emperor's wing. They carved the rough holes you see in the ceiling to dump their garbage and sewage. Over the generations, the basement (where you're standing) filled up with waste and solidified, ultimately becoming a once-stinky, then-precious bonanza for 20th-century archaeologists. Today, the huge, vaulted main hall is used for everything from flower and book shows to fashion catwalks. As you poke around, notice the unexcavated wings—a compost pile of ancient lifestyles, awaiting the tiny shovels and toothbrushes of future archaeologists. The headless black granite sphinx is one of 13 that Diocletian brought home from Egypt. The two beams on display once supported floorboards overhead (see the holes on either side of the vaults).

You can also explore the cellars on the east side (same ticket). Among other things, you'll see a semicircular marble table used by the Romans, who—as shown in Hollywood movies—ate lying down (three would lounge and feast, while servants dished things up from the straight side).

• *When you're finished, head back to the main gallery, where you can shop your way down the passage and up the stairs into the...*

Peristyle (Peristil): This square was the centerpiece of Diocletian's Palace. As you walk up the stairs, the entry vestibule into the residence is above your head, Diocletian's mausoleum

(today's Cathedral of St. Dominus) is to your right, and the street to Jupiter's Temple is on your left. The little chapel straight ahead houses the TI, and beyond that is the narrow street to the former main entrance to the palace, the Golden Gate.

Go to the middle of the square and take it all in. The red

granite pillars—which you'll see all over Diocletian's Palace—are from Egypt, where Diocletian spent many of his pre-retirement years. Imagine the pillars defining fine arcades—now obscured by medieval houses. (As the Peristyle is undergoing a lengthy restoration, you may notice some of the ruins are lighter-colored than others.) The black sphinx is the only one of Diocletian's collection of 13 that's still (mostly) intact. Here or elsewhere in the Old Town, you're likely to run into a roving band of CD-selling *klapa* singers, performing traditional a cappella harmonies.

• *Climb the stairs (above where you came in) into the domed, open-ceilinged...*

Entry Vestibule: Impressed? That's the idea. This was the grand entry to Diocletian's living quarters, meant to wow visitors. Emperors were believed to be gods. Diocletian called himself "Jovius"—the son of Jupiter, the most powerful of all gods. Four times a year (at the change of the seasons), Diocletian would stand here and overlook the Peristyle. His subjects would lie on the ground in worship, praising his name. Notice the four big niches at floor level, which once held statues of the four tetrarchs who ruled the unwieldy empire after Diocletian retired. The empty hole in the ceiling was once capped by a dome (long since collapsed), and the ceiling itself was covered with frescoes and mosaics. Wander out back to the harbor side through medieval buildings (some with seventh-century foundations), which evoke the way local villagers came in and took over the once-spacious and elegant palace. Back in this area, you'll find the beautifully restored new home of the Ethnographic Museum (described under "Sights and Activities" later in this chapter).

• *Now go back into the Peristyle square and turn right, climbing the steps to the...*

Cathedral of St. Dominus (Katedrala Sv. Duje): The original octagonal structure was Diocletian's elaborate mausoleum, built in the fourth century. But after the fall of Rome, it was converted into the town's cathedral. Construction on the bell tower began in the 13th century and took 300 years to complete. Before you go inside, notice the sarcophagi ringing the cathedral. In the late Middle Ages, this was prime post-mortem real estate, since being buried closer to a cathedral improved your chances of getting to heaven.

Step inside the oldest building used as a cathedral anywhere in Christendom (5 kn, get the 10-kn combo-ticket that includes Jupiter's Temple—see below, daily 7:00–19:00, may be closed for midday siesta, Kraj Sv. Duje 5, tel. 021/344-121). Imagine the place in pre-Christian times, with Diocletian's tomb in the center. The only surviving decor from those days are the granite columns and the relief circling the base of the dome (about 50 feet up)—a ring of carvings heralding the greatness of the emperor. The small, multi-colored marble pillars around the top of the pulpit (near the entry) were scavenged from Diocletian's sarcophagus. These pillars are all that remains of Diocletian's remains.

Diocletian brutally persecuted his Christian subjects, sometimes in the crypt of this very building. To kick off his retirement upon his arrival on the Dalmatian Coast, he had Bishop Dominus of Salona killed, along with several thousand Christians. When Diocletian died, there were riots of happiness. In the seventh century, his mausoleum became a cathedral dedicated to the martyred bishop. The extension behind the altar was added in the ninth century, and the doors are 12th-century walnut originals. The sarcophagus of St. Dominus (to the right of the altar, with early-Christian carvings) was once the cathedral's high altar. To the left of today's main altar is the altar of St. Anastasius—lying on a millstone, which is tied to his neck. On Diocletian's orders, this Christian martyr was drowned in the Adriatic. Posthumous poetic justice: Now Christian saints are entombed in Diocletian's mausoleum...and Diocletian is nowhere to be found.

For another 5 kn, you can climb steep steps to the top of the **bell tower.** You'll be rewarded with sweeping views of Split, but it's not for claustrophobes or those scared of heights. The building's **crypt** was also recently opened to the public (5 kn, yet another separate ticket).

Jupiter's Temple/St. John's Baptistery: Remember that Diocletian believed himself to be Jovius (that's Jupiter, Jr.). On exiting the mausoleum of Jovius, worshippers would look straight ahead to the temple of Jupiter. (Back then, of course, all of these medieval buildings weren't cluttering up the view.) Make your way through the narrow alley, past another headless, pawless sphinx, to explore the small temple (using the 10-kn combo-ticket you bought at the cathedral, same hours as cathedral; if it's locked, go ask the guy at the cathedral to let you in).

The temple has long since been converted into a baptistery—with a big 12th-century baptismal font and a statue of St. John by the great Croatian sculptor Ivan Meštrović (EE-vahn MESH-troh-veech, see page 670). The half-barrel vaulted ceiling is considered the best preserved of its kind anywhere. Every face and each patterned box is different.

• Back at the Peristyle square, stand in front of the TI with your back to the entry vestibule (and harbor). The little street just beyond the TI (going left to right) connects the east and west gates. If you've had enough

Roman history, head right (east) to go through the "Silver Gate" and find Split's busy, open-air Green Market. Or, head to the left (west), which takes you to the "Iron Gate" and People's Square (see below), and, beyond that, the fresh-and-smelly fish market. But if you want to see one last bit of Roman history, continue straight ahead up the...

Cardo: This street—which translates as "Hot Street"—was the most important in Diocletian's Palace, connecting the main entry with the heart of the complex. As you walk, you'll pass a bank with modern computer gear all around its exposed Roman ruins (first building on the right, look through window), a Venetian merchant's palace (a reminder that Split was dominated by Venice from the 15th century on—step into his courtyard, first gate on left), an alley to the City Museum (on the right—see "Sights and Activities"), and a fan shop for Hajduk Split, the city's extremely popular soccer team (on left, with *Umbro* sign).

• *Before long, you'll pass through the...*

Golden Gate (Zlatna Vrata): This great gate was the main entry of Diocletian's Palace. Its name came from the golden statues of Diocletian and other Roman VIPs that once adorned it. Standing inside the gate itself, you can appreciate the double-door design that kept the palace safe. Also notice how this ancient building is now being used in very different ways from its original purpose. Up above on the outer wall, you can see the bricked-in windows that contain part of a Dominican convent. At the top of the inner wall, notice somebody's garden terrace.

Go outside the gate, where you'll get a much clearer feel for the way the palace looked before so many other buildings were grafted on. Straight ahead from here is Salona (Solin), which was a major city of 60,000 (and Diocletian's hometown) before there was a Split. The big statue by Ivan Meštrović is **Bishop Gregory of Nin,** a 10th-century Croatian priest who tried to convince the Vatican to allow sermons during Mass to be said in Croatian, rather than Latin. People rub his toe for good luck (though only non-material wishes are given serious consideration).

• *Your tour is finished. Now enjoy the rest of Split.*

SIGHTS AND ACTIVITIES

In or near the Old Town

▲▲**Strolling the Riva (Obala Hrvatskog Narodnog Preporoda)**—The official name for this seaside pedestrian drag is the "Croatian National Revival Embankment," but locals just call it "Riva" (Italian for "harbor"). This is the town's promenade, an integral part of Mediterranean culture. After dinner, Split residents collect their families and friends for a stroll on the Riva. It offers some of the best people-watching in Croatia; make it a point to be here for an hour or two after dinner. At the west end of the Riva, the people-parade of Croatian culture turns right and heads away from the water, up Marmontova. The stinky smell that sometimes accompanies the stroll isn't a sewer. It's sulfur—a reminder that the town's medicinal sulfur spas have attracted people here since the days of Diocletian.

▲**People's Square (Narodni Trg)**—The lively square at the center of the Old Town is called by locals simply *Pjaca*, pronounced the same as the Italian *piazza*. Stand in the center and enjoy the bustle. Look around for a quick lesson in Dalmatian history. When Diocletian lived in his palace, a Roman village popped up here, just outside the wall. Face the former wall of Diocletian's Palace (behind and to the right of the 24-hour clock tower). This was the western gate, or so-called "Iron Gate." By the 14th century, the medieval town had developed, making this the main square of Split. The city's grand old café, Gradska Kavana, has been the Old Town's venerable meeting point for generations (drinks and cakes but no meals, daily 7:00–24:00). Across the square, the white building jutting out into the square was once the City Hall, and now houses temporary exhibitions. The loggia is all that remains of the original Gothic building. Directly to your left as you face the loggia is the Nakić House, built in the early-20th-century Viennese Secession style—a reminder that Dalmatia was part of the Hapsburg Empire, ruled by Vienna, from Napoleon's downfall through World War I. The lane on the right side of this building leads to Split's fish market (Ribarnica).

Ethnographic Museum (Etnografski Muzej)—This museum uses temporary exhibits to show off the culture, costumes, and customs of Dalmatia. The collection was recently transplanted to this gorgeously renovated early-medieval palace, hiding on the upper level of the Old Town behind Diocletian's entry vestibule. Check out the artsy "golden fleece" entry door. On the ground floor, you'll find the remains of a seventh-century church. The upstairs exhibit often includes a look at traditional folk dress (10 kn, some English explanations; June–mid-Sept Mon–Fri 9:00–21:00, Sat 9:00–13:00, closed Sun; mid-Sept–May Mon–Fri 9:00–14:00, Sat 9:00–13:00, closed Sun; Severova 7, tel. 021/344-164).

Split City Museum (Muzej Grada Splita)—This museum traces how the city grew over the centuries. It's a bit dull, but it can help you appreciate a little better the layers of history you're seeing in the streets. The ground floor displays Roman fragments (including coins from the days of Diocletian) and temporary exhibits. The upstairs focuses on the Middle Ages (find the terrace, displaying carved stone monuments), and the top floor goes from the 16th century to the present (10 kn, some English descriptions, 75-kn guidebook is overkill; May–Sept Tue–Fri 9:00–21:00, Sat–Sun

9:00–16:00, closed Mon; Oct–April Tue–Fri 9:00–16:00, Sat–Sun 10:00–13:00, closed Mon; Papalićeva 1, tel. 021/344-917, www .mgst.net).

The 15th-century Papalić Palace, which houses the City Museum, is a sight all its own. At the end of the palace, near Cardo street, look up to see several typical Venetian-style Gothic-Renaissance windows. The stone posts sticking out of the wall next to them were used to hang curtains.

Radić Brothers Square (Trg Braće Radića)—A Venetian citadel watches over this square, just off the Riva between the two halves of the Old Town. After Split became part of the Venetian Republic, there was a serious danger of attack by the Ottomans, so octagonal towers like this were built all along the coast. But this imposing tower had a second purpose: to encourage citizens of Split to forget about any plans of rebellion. In the middle of the square is a studious sculpture by Ivan Meštrović of the poet Marko Marulić, who is considered the father of the Croatian language. Marulić was the first to write literature in the Croatian vernacular, which before then had generally been considered a backward peasants' tongue.

On the downhill (harbor) side of the square is **Croata,** a necktie boutique that loves to explain how Croatian soldiers who fought with the French in the Thirty Years' War (1618–1648) had a distinctive way of tying their scarves. The French found it stylish, adopted it, and called it *à la Croate*—or eventually, *cravate*—thus creating the modern tie that many people wear to work every day throughout the world. Croata's selection includes ties with traditional Croatian motifs, such as the checkerboard pattern from the flag or writing in the ninth-century Glagolitic alphabet. Though pricey, these ties are good souvenirs (cheaper ties-149 kn, top-quality ties-399 kn, Mon–Fri 8:00–20:00, Sat 8:00–14:00, closed Sun).

Green Market—This lively open-air market bustles at the east end of Diocletian's Palace. Locals shop for produce and clothes here, and there's plenty of tourist souvenirs as well. Browse the wide selection of T-shirts, and ignore the creepy black-market tobacco salesmen who mutter at you: *"Cigaretta?"*

Split's Outskirts

▲▲**Meštrović Gallery (Galerija Meštrović)**—Split's best art museum is dedicated to the sculptor Ivan Meštrović (1883–1962), the most important and most famous of all Croatian artists. Many of Meštrović's finest works are housed in this palace, designed by the sculptor himself. If you have time, it's worth the 20-minute walk or short bus or taxi ride from the Old Town.

Meštrović grew up in a family of poor, nomadic farm workers

just inland from Split. At an early age, his drawings and wooden carvings showed promise, and a rich family took him in and made sure he was properly trained. He eventually went off to school in Vienna, where he fell in with the Secession movement and found fame and fortune. Later in life—like Diocletian before him—Meštrović returned to Split and built a huge seaside mansion (today's Meštrović Gallery). During World War II, Meštrović moved abroad to escape the Nazi puppet government and lectured at Notre Dame (in Indiana, not France) and Syracuse (in New York, not Italy).

You'll see Meštrović's works all over Split and throughout Croatia. Most are cast bronze, depicting biblical, mythological, political, and everyday themes. Whether whimsical or emotional, Meštrović's expressive, elongated faces—often with a strong-profile nose—connect with the viewer. In this collection, don't miss *Job*, howling with an agony verging on insanity—carved by the artist in exile, as his country was turned upside-down by World War II. A moving contrast is the quietly poignant *Roman Pietà*, with mournful faces at painful angles pondering the dead body of Christ (20 kn, in summer Tue–Sat 9:00–21:00, Sun 12:00–21:00, closed Mon, shorter hours off-season—call to confirm it's open before making the trip, Šetalište Ivana Meštrovića 46, tel. 021/340-800, www.mdc.hr/mestrovic).

If you enjoy the gallery, continue walking five more minutes down Šetalište Ivana Meštrovića to **Kaštelet Chapel** ("Chapel of the Holy Cross"), a 16th-century fortified palace Meštrović bought to display his wooden carvings of Jesus' life. The centerpiece is a powerful wooden crucifix (included in ticket for gallery, but open shorter hours: in summer Tue–Sat 9:30–16:00, Sun 12:00–17:00, closed Mon; even shorter hours off-season).

Marjan Peninsula—This long, hilly peninsula extends west from the center of Split. This is where Split goes to relax, with out-of-the-way beaches and lots of hiking trails (great views and a zoo on top).

Hit the Beach—Since it's more of a big city than a resort, Split's beaches aren't as scenic (and the water not as clear) as small towns elsewhere along the coast. The beach that's most popular—and crowded—is Bačvice, in a sandy cove just east of the main ferry terminal. You'll find less crowded beaches just to the east of Bačvice. Locals like to hike around Marjan, the peninsular city park (see above), ringed with several sunbathing beaches.

NIGHTLIFE

The Riva—Every night in Split, the sea of Croatian humanity laps at the walls of Diocletian's Palace along the town's pedestrian promenade. Choose a bench and watch life go by, or enjoy a drink at one of the many outdoor cafés.

Old Town Pubs—Wander the labyrinthine lanes of the Old Town to find the pub of your choice. Several cluster along Majstora Jurja (just inside Golden Gate and—facing outside—to the left about a block) and near Radić Brothers Square (Trg Braće Radića; from the square's statue of Marulić, enter the Old Town and bear right, following the beat).

Bačvice Beach—This family-friendly beach by day becomes a throbbing party zone for young locals late at night. Since all Old Town bars have to close by 1:00 in the morning, night owls hike on over to the Bačvice crescent of clubs. The three-floor club complex is a cacophony of music, with the beat of each club melting into the next—all with breezy terraces overlooking the harbor.

SLEEPING

Several new hotels have cropped up in Split over the last few years, but there still aren't enough beds in peak season—so hoteliers are shameless about gouging their customers.

Many of my recommended hotels are conveniently located in the Old Town. Unfortunately, this is also a happening nightlife zone, so you're likely to encounter some noise (especially on weekends). Bring earplugs and request a quiet room, if one is available. Old Town bars are required to close by 1:00 in the morning, so at least things will quiet down before the birds start chirping. To locate these accommodations, see the maps on pages 657 and 663.

$$$ Peristil Hotel is my favorite Old Town splurge, with 12 classy rooms over a restaurant just steps from the couldn't-be-more-central square of the same name. Well-run by the Caktaš family, it's homey and convenient, if a bit pricey (July–Aug: Sb-850 kn, Db-1,000 kn; May–June and Sept–Oct: Sb-750 kn, Db-900 kn; Nov–April: Sb-650 kn, Db-800 kn; air-con, stairs with no elevator, just behind TI and inside Silver Gate at Poljana Kraljice Jelene 5, tel. 021/329-070, fax 021/329-088, www.hotelperistil.com, hotel.peristil@email.t-com.hr).

$$$ Hotel Vestibul Palace is the swankiest splurge in Split. Tucked in a corner just behind the entry vestibule on the upper level of Diocletian's Palace, this plush new place offers seven rooms with maximum comfort and style for maximum prices (July–Sept: Sb-980–1,150 kn, Db-1,650 kn; Oct–June: Sb-820–960 kn, Db-1,400 kn; prices depend on size and amenities of room, pricier

---

Sleep Code

(€1 = about $1.20, 6 kn = about $1, country code: 385, area code: 021)

S = Single, **D** = Double/Twin, **T** = Triple, **Q** = Quad, **b** = bathroom. The modest tourist tax (7 kn or €1 per person, per night, lower off-season) is not included in these rates. Hotels generally accept credit cards and include breakfast in their rates, while most *sobe* accept only cash and don't offer breakfast. All my recommended accommodations speak English.

To help you sort easily through these listings, I've divided the rooms into three categories based on the price for a standard double room with bath in peak season:

$$$ **Higher Priced**—Most rooms 800 kn (€110) or more.

$$ **Moderately Priced**—Most rooms between 500–800 kn (€70–110).

$ **Lower Priced**—Most rooms 500 kn (€70) or less.

---

suites also available, air-con, Iza Vestibula 4, tel. 021/329-329, fax 021/329-333, www.vestibulpalace.com, info@vestibulpalace.com).

$$$ Hotel Adriana has 15 nice, new-feeling rooms perched right above the people-packed Riva. Choose between harborview front rooms or quieter back rooms. Unfortunately, the place suffers from absentee management and iffy service, and the rooms are an afterthought to the busy restaurant (Sb-650 kn, Db-850 kn, 100 kn less off-season, pricier apartments also available, air-con, elevator, Riva 8, tel. 021/340-000, fax 021/340-008, www.hotel-adriana.hr, info@hotel-adriana.hr).

$$ Villa Ana may just be the best small hotel on the Dalmatian Coast, with five modern, comfortable rooms in a smart little house a five-minute walk from the Old Town. This delightful, free-standing stone home is well-run by Danijel Bilobrk and his family. Though it's in a boring urban neighborhood, it's pristine and welcoming inside (Sb-600 kn, Db-750 kn, Tb-850 kn, roughly 150 kn less Nov–March, air-con, reception open 7:00–24:00, may be closed Dec–Feb, street parking or a tight little parking spot, 2 long blocks east of Old Town up busy Kralja Zvonimira, follow the driveway-like lane opposite Koteks skyscraper to Vrh Lučac 16, tel. 021/482-715, fax 021/482-721, www.villaana-split.hr, info @villaana-split.hr).

$$ Villa Diana, a new place right next door to Villa Ana (see above), has six similar but smaller rooms over a lively cocktail bar. It's a lesser value than the Ana, but still plenty nice and comfortable (April–Oct: Sb-610 kn, Db-750 kn; Nov–March: Sb-550 kn,

Db-690 kn; pricier apartments also available, air-con, Kuzmanića 3, follow walking directions for Villa Ana, tel. & fax 021/482-451, www.villadiana.hr, info@villadiana.hr).

$$ Hotel Slavija shares a tiny square with some very popular late-night discos and cafés, so it can be noisy—especially on weekends (new windows attempt, with only some success, to keep out the throbbing dance beat; try requesting a quieter back room). Each of its 25 starkly modern rooms is a little different, some with balconies for no extra charge. Ongoing improvements are planned, so rates may increase in the near future (Sb-550 kn, Db-790 kn, Tb-900, suites, huge family rooms, air-con, a block from Radić Brothers Square at Buvinina 2—look for the low-profile sign at the top of a white staircase, tel. 021/323-840, fax 021/323-868, www.hotelslavija.com, info@hotelslavija.com).

$ Hotel Kaštel, run by the quirky Čaleta family, has seven rooms and five apartments at the end of a forgotten alley just inside the wall of Diocletian's Palace. The rooms (some with views overlooking the Riva) are basic but newish, making this a decent budget choice. It's in a slightly quieter area than some Old Town hotels, and most of the rooms have double-paned windows, but a little noise can sneak in (complicated pricing structure, figure Db-€60–65 July–Aug, €50–55 June and Sept, cheaper off-season, 10 percent less for Sb, Mihovilova širina 5, mobile 091-120-0348, www.kastelsplit.com, info@kastelsplit.com).

$ Sobe "Base" has three of the nicest rooms in the Old Town, each with most of the big hotel amenities (including Internet terminals). You can't be more central: All of the rooms—over an artsy gallery—overlook the front steps of the cute little Jupiter's Temple (Sb/Db-450 kn, no extra charge for 1- or 2-night stays, cash only, air-con, Kraj Svetog Ivana 3, tel. 021/317-375, mobile 098-361-387, www.base-rooms.com, mail@base-rooms.com). Because a bustling nightlife zone is just around the corner, expect some nighttime noise (even though the double-paned windows do their darnedest to provide silence).

$ Other *Sobe*: Though there are very few *sobe* inside Split's Old Town, there are plenty within a 10-minute walk. As in any coastal town, you can simply show up at the boat dock or bus station, be met by locals trying to persuade you into their rooms, and check out the best offer (about 250 kn for a double). Or you can try the **Turistički Biro,** a booking agency. You can generally make a reservation in advance, then drop by their office, pay, pick up your welcome packet, and head off to your awaiting landlady. Or you can just drop in—they can always find you something (mid-July–mid-Aug: S-240 kn, Sb-280 kn, D-350 kn, Db-400 kn; June–mid-July and mid-Aug–Sept: S-190 kn, Sb-220 kn, D-300 kn, Db-340 kn;

Oct–May: S-170 kn, Sb-190 kn, D-250 kn, Db-290 kn; plus 7 kn per person, per night for tourist tax, no breakfast, 30 percent less for stays of 4 nights or more; office open mid-June–Sept Mon–Fri 8:00–21:00, Sat 8:00–20:00, open Sun 8:00–13:00 mid-July–mid-Sept only, otherwise closed Sun; Oct–mid-June Mon–Fri 8:00–20:00, Sat 8:00–13:00, closed Sun; Riva 12, tel. & fax 021/347-100, turist-biro-split@st.t-com.hr).

$ Hostel Split is a brand-new place just off of Narodni Trg in the very heart of town. Run by a pair of Aussie women with the simple slogan "booze & snooze," it's Split's most central hostel option (€17 per person in 6–8-bed rooms, €3 cheaper off-season, 8 Narodni Trg, tel. 021/342-787, www.splithostel.com, info@splithostel.com).

EATING

Split's Old Town has oodles of atmosphere, but if you venture just a couple of blocks west of the Old Town, you'll discover my three favorite places (Šperun, Konoba Varoš, and Buffet Fife). To locate most of these eateries, see the map on page 657; for Nona, Zlatna Vrata, and Adriana, see the map on page 663.

Šperun Restaurant has a classy, cozy Old World ambience and a passion for good Dalmatian food. Zdravko Banović and his son Damir serve a mix of Croatian and "eclectic Mediterranean," specializing in seafood. A "buffet" table in the lower dining room shows you what you're getting, so you can select your ideal meal (not self-service—order from the waiter). This place distinguishes itself by offering a warm welcome and high-quality food for reasonable prices (35–50-kn pastas, 40–80-kn meat and seafood, air-con interior, a few sidewalk tables, reservations wise June–Aug, daily 9:00–23:00, Šperun 3, tel. 021/346-999).

Konoba Varoš, though pricier than Šperun and a bit impersonal, is beloved by natives and tourists alike for its great food. Serious, vest-wearing waiters serve a wide range of Croatian cooking (including pastas, seafood, and meat dishes) under droopy fishnets. Their 60-kn carpaccio starter—thinly sliced strips of raw meat or fish sprinkled with lemon and olive oil and served with lettuce and cheese—will get you in an Adriatic-seaside mood (55–95-kn main dishes, lots of groups, reservations smart—busiest 20:00–22:00, daily 9:00–24:00, Ban Mladenova 7, tel. 021/396-138).

Buffet Fife is your cheap, dream-come-true fish joint, where a colorful local crowd shares rough wood tables, and the waitstaff seem brusque until you crack them up. Zvonko (the charming-as-a-cartoon waiter) ignores the menu, declaring, *"Ja sum meni!"* (*"I am the menu!"*) to the chuckles of his regulars. You can eat in the tiny, mostly locals bar in the main building; out front, on the tourist-laden terrace; or across the alley, in their little annex (35–45-kn main dishes, 10-kn sides, daily 7:00–24:00, walk 200 yards along the waterfront west of Old Town to Trumbičeva obala 11, poorly marked—look for salty locals standing out front, tel. 021/345-223).

Fast and Cheap: **Zlagogajnica None** ("Grandma's") is a stand-up or take-away pizza joint handy for a quick bite in the Old Town. In addition to pizzas, sandwiches, and bruschettas with various toppings, they serve up a pair of traditional pizza-like specialties (with crust on bottom and top, like a filled pizza): *viška pogača,* with tomatoes, onion, and anchovy; and *soparnik,* with a thin layer of spinach, onion, and olive oil (8–18 kn, Sun–Fri 7:00–23:00, closed Sat except in summer, just outside Diocletian's Palace on the skinny street that runs along the wall at Bosanska 4, tel. 021/347-252).

Pizzerias: **Zlatna Vrata** ("Golden Gate"), right in the Old Town, offers wood-fired pizzas and pasta dishes. The food and interior are nothing special, but there's wonderful outdoor seating in a tingle-worthy Gothic courtyard with pointy arches and lots of pillars (30–50 kn, Mon–Sat 7:00–24:00, closed Sun except maybe in summer, just inside the Golden Gate and—as you face outside—up the skinny alley to the left, on Majstora Jurja, tel. 021/345-015). **Ristorante Pizzeria Galija,** at the west end of the Old Town, has a local following and good wood-fired pizza, pasta, and salads (25–50-kn pizzas and pasta dishes, air-con, Mon–Sat 9:00–24:00, Sun 12:00–24:00, just a block off of the pedestrian drag Marmontova at Tončićeva 12, tel. 021/347-932).

On the Riva: **Restaurant Adriana** is your only choice for dining (not just drinks and desserts) on the harborfront promenade. It's packed with tourists, so you'll get crank-'em-out food and service for top prices. But with entertaining people-watching, it's not a bad place for a slow meal or scenic drink (55–90-kn main dishes, 45–50-kn pizzas, daily 7:00–24:00, Riva 8, tel. 021/340-000).

Gelato: Split has several spots for delicious Italian gelato-style ice cream *(sladoled).* Locals swarm to a pair of ice-cream parlors near Trg Gaje Bulata (the modern shopping square—with a McDonald's, big Prima mall, and modern-looking church—at the end of the Marmontova pedestrian drag just beyond the northwest corner of the Old Town): **Kuća Sladoleda Karmen** (daily 8:00–24:00, hides behind the building in the middle of the square, facing the modern church on Kačićeva) and **Hajduk** (daily 8:00–24:00, a block west from the top of Marmontova and around the corner from Galija pizzeria at Matošićeva 4). To my taste buds, these two spots are much better than the other options in town.

TRANSPORTATION CONNECTIONS

Split Boat Connections

As the transport hub for the Dalmatian Coast, Split has good boat connections to most anywhere you want to go. Big car ferries use the main ferry terminal at the end of the harbor, while passenger boats (including fast catamarans) depart from the handy Obala Lazareta embankment just in front of the Old Town. Be warned that the following boat information, based on the 2006 schedules, is highly subject to change—always confirm before you make your plans. Split's Jadrolinija boat ticket office is in the main ferry terminal (see "Arrival in Split," page 658), with several smaller branch offices between there and the Old Town (tel. 021/338-333).

Big Jadrolinija Car Ferries: These hulking boats generally leave Split early in the morning (at 6:30 or 7:00) and head south, stopping at **Stari Grad** on Hvar Island (20-min bus ride from Hvar town; 5/week July–mid-Sept, 2/week mid-Sept–June, 1.75 hrs; the catamarans described below are faster and take you right to Hvar town), **Korčula town** (5/week July–mid-Sept, 3/week June, 2/week mid-Sept–May, 3.5–6 hrs), and **Dubrovnik** (2/week year-round, 8.25–9.25 hrs, more with transfer in Korčula). You can also sleep on the boat as it heads north to **Rijeka** (2/week, 11 hrs overnight).

Other Boats to Hvar Island: Ideally, catch a boat heading to Hvar town, the most interesting part of the island. Speedy **Jadrolinija catamarans** run from Split to Hvar town twice a day June through September (departing Split at 11:30 and 15:00, 50 min to Hvar town, occasionally stops at Milna on Brač Island). A different company runs the similar *Krilo* catamaran directly from Split to Hvar town (June–Sept: departs Split daily at 17:00; Oct–May: departs Split 4/week at 16:00; 1.25 hrs to Hvar town). Six days a week in the summer, a much **slower car ferry** putters from Split to Hvar town (late June–early Sept only, departs Split at 10:00, arrives Hvar at 12:00; even though this is a car ferry, only foot passengers can get on and off at Hvar). Finally, if you're desperate, you can also reach Hvar Island on the **frequent slow car ferries** from Split to the town of Stari Grad, across the island from Hvar town (at least 3/day, more in summer; from Stari Grad, it's an easy 20-minute bus trip into Hvar town).

Other Boats to Korčula Island: Many of the same boats that go to Hvar town (described above) continue on to Korčula Island. The most convenient is the *Krilo* **catamaran,** which takes you right to Korčula town (June–Sept: departs Split daily at 17:00; Oct–May: departs Split 4/week at 16:00, 2.75 hrs to Korčula). The other boats leave you at Vela Luka, at the far end of Korčula Island from Korčula town (buses meet arriving boats to take passengers on the one-hour trip into Korčula town). The 15:00 **Jadrolinija catamaran** goes from Split to Hvar town, then to Vela Luka (June–Sept, 1.75 hrs to Vela Luka, occasionally stops at Mlina on Brač Island). Slower **car ferries** also go from Split to Vela Luka (2/day late June–early Sept, 1/day late Sept–early June, 2.75 hrs).

Split Overland Connections

By Bus to: Zagreb (at least hourly, 5–8 hrs, depending on route, about 140 kn), **Dubrovnik** (almost hourly, less off-season, 5 hrs, about 100 kn), **Korčula** (1 night bus leaves 24:45 and arrives 6:00, 90–125 kn), **Trogir** (at least hourly, 30 min, about 20 kn), **Zadar** (at least hourly, 3 hrs, about 70 kn), **Rijeka** (nearly hourly, 8.5 hrs). Zagreb-bound buses sometimes also stop at **Plitvice** (confirm with driver and ask him to stop; about 8/day, 4–6 hrs, 70–80 kn). Each of these routes is served by multiple companies, which charge slightly different rates, so the prices listed here are rough estimates. Reservations for buses are generally not necessary, but always ask about the fastest option—which can save hours of bus time. Bus info: www.ak-split.hr, tel. 021/338-483 or toll tel. 060-327-777.

By Train to: Zagreb (3/day, 5.5 hrs, plus 1 direct night train, 8 hrs). Train info: tel. 021/338-525 or toll tel. 060-333-444.

KORČULA

While not yet matching the fame of Dubrovnik or Split, the little island town of Korčula (KOHR-choo-lah) offers one of the most pleasant stopovers on the Dalmatian Coast. Conveniently located midway between Dubrovnik and Split, Korčula boasts an atmospheric Old Town, some surprisingly engaging museums, and a dramatic, fjord-like mountain backdrop.

Korčula was founded by ancient Greeks. It became part of the Roman Empire, and was eventually a key southern outpost of the Venetian Republic. Four centuries of Venetian rule left Korčula with a quirky Gothic-Renaissance mix and a strong siesta tradition. Korčulans take great pride in the fact that Marco Polo was born here in 1254—the explorer remains the town's poster boy. Korčula is also known for its traditional *Moreška* sword dance.

You'll discover that there are two Korčulas: the tacky seaside resort and the historic Old Town. Savvy visitors ignore the tourist sprawl and focus on Korčula's medieval quarter, a mini-Dubrovnik poking out into the sea on a picture-perfect peninsula. Tiny lanes branch off the humble main drag like ribs on a fishbone. This street plan is designed to catch both the breeze and the shade. All in all, this laid-back island village is an ideal place to take a vacation from your busy vacation.

Planning Your Time

Korčula offers little to do besides taking it easy. Wander the medieval Old Town, explore the handful of tiny museums, kick back at a café or restaurant, or bask on the beach. If you're here on a Thursday, be sure to catch the performance of the *Moreška* dance (also Mon July–Aug). One day is more than enough for Korčula—

but because of sometimes-sparse ferry schedules, you may end up stranded here for longer. With the extra time, consider a one-day package excursion to Mljet Island and its national park.

ORIENTATION

(area code: 020)

The long, skinny island of Korčula runs alongside the even longer, skinnier Pelješac Peninsula (famous for its wine—see page 617).

The main town and best destination on the island—just across a narrow strait from Pelješac—is also called Korčula.

Korčula is centered on its compact **Old Town** (Stari Grad) peninsula, which is connected to the mainland at a big staircase leading to the Great Land Gate. In the area in front of this staircase, you'll find ATMs, travel agencies, the Jadrolinija ferry office, several Internet cafés, the Konzum supermarket, a colorful outdoor produce market, and other handy tourist services.

Stretching to the south and east of the Old Town is **"Shell Bay,"** surrounded by a strip of tacky tourist shops and resort hotels. This seamier side of Korčula—best avoided—caters mostly to Europeans here to worship the sun for a week or two.

To the west of Old Town is the serene waterfront street **Put Sv. Nikola,** where you'll find several *sobe* (including Rezi Depolo's—see page 688), great views back on the Old Town, and more locals than tourists.

Tourist Information

Korčula's we-try-harder TI, run by Stanka Kraljević, is next to Hotel Korčula on the west side of the Old Town waterfront (mid-June–Sept Mon–Sat 8:00–15:00 & 16:00–22:00, Sun 9:00–14:00; Oct–mid-June Mon–Sat 8:00–15:00, closed Sun, may be open Sun in shoulder season; tel. 020/715-701, www.korcula.net). Pick up the free cartoon map (marked with "rambling paths") and *Korčula* magazine (with maps, pictures, hotel information, and other town information).

Arrival in Korčula

For all the details on getting to Korčula, and getting around the Dalmatian Coast, read "Dalmatian Coast Practicalities" on page 606.

Korčula

100 YARDS

100 METERS

OLD TOWN WALLS

WESTERN FERRY DOCK

MARCO POLO'S HOUSE

ROZAN · ROKA · KORC. BRAT. · POM · SV. PETRA

ŠPANICEVA · LUKE · V. FORETICA · SV. · L. TOLENT. · DEPOLO · DON PAVLA · KAZA · VELIKA

TUDMANA

TOWN MUSEUM

MIROŠEVICA

ISMAELLI

GIUNIO

TEATRA

ŽITNICA

OBALA DR FRANJO

St MARK'S CATHEDRAL

BISK.

MARK AND

CHURCH MUSEUM

BANIC

IVE MATIJACE

KAPOROVA

ST. MICHAEL · DOBRO.

RAMPADA

ICON MUSEUM

ALL SAINTS' CHURCH

TOWN HALL

FOSA

POST →

PUT SV. NIK.

TO ❷ ❶

PLOKATA 19 TRAVNJA 1921

GREAT LAND GATE

DCH

★ = ST. MARK'S SQUARE

JADROLINIJA OFFICE

TO BUS STN. & ❻

EASTERN FERRY DOCK

❶ Royal Apartments
❷ To Depolo Rooms
❸ Modrinić Rooms
❹ Vitaić Family Rooms
❺ Hotel Korčula
❻ To Hotels Liburna, Park, Marko Polo, & Bon Repos
❼ Korčula Backpacker Hostel
❽ Konoba Morski Konjic Rest.
❾ Adio Mare Restaurant
❿ Riblji Restoran Kanavelić

⓫ Konoba Marinero Rest.
⓬ Pizzeria Amfora
⓭ Fresh Eatery
⓮ Konzum Supermarket
⓯ Buffet "Massimo"
⓰ Marko Polo Tours
⓱ Atlas Travel
⓲ *Moreška* Dance Exhibit
⓳ Marco Polo Gift Shop

By Boat: The big Jadrolinija ferries can arrive on either side of the Old Town peninsula, depending on the wind. (The Orebić passenger ferry and the fast catamarans generally dock at the west side of town.) From either side of the peninsula, it's just a two-minute walk to where it meets the mainland and all of the services described in "Orientation," earlier in this chapter.

A few boats (car ferries from Orebić and Drvenik) use the Dominče dock two peninsulas east of Korčula (near Hotel Bon Repos). Regular buses connect this dock with Korčula.

Some boats from Split and Hvar town arrive at Vela Luka, at the far end of Korčula Island. Each boat arriving at Vela Luka is met by a bus waiting to bring arriving travelers to Korčula town (about 1 hour).

By Bus: The bus station is at the southeast corner of Korčula's Shell Bay. If you leave the station with the bay on your right, you'll reach the Old Town. If you leave with the bay on your left, you'll get to hotels Liburna, Park, and Marko Polo.

By Car: See "Route Tips for Drivers" at the end of this chapter. Once in Korčula town, there's plenty of free parking at the bus station along the marina.

Helpful Hints

Jadrolinija Office: This office, essential for sorting through and confirming boat schedules, is located where the Old Town meets the mainland (peak season Mon–Fri 8:00–20:00, Sat 8:00–13:00 & 18:00–22:00, Sun 6:00–13:30, much shorter hours off-season—depends on boat schedules, tel. 020/715-410, www.jadrolinija.hr). But note that they don't sell tickets on the convenient *Krilo* catamaran to Hvar town and Split (buy *Krilo* tickets at Marko Polo Tours—see below). For a run-down of the confusing boat options to and from Korčula, see the end of this chapter.

Travel Agencies: Korčula has two major travel agencies. At either one, you can book an excursion, browse shelves of books and souvenirs, and get information about car rental and other activities: **Marko Polo Tours** (also sells tickets for *Krilo* catamaran; located just outside the Old Town gate at Biline 5, tel. 020/715-400, fax 020/715-800) and **Atlas Travel** (Trg 19. Travnja, tel. 020/711-231, fax 020/715-580). Both agencies are open similar hours (long hours daily in summer, closed for mid-afternoon break in shoulder season, open Mon–Sat mornings and closed Sun in winter).

Festivals: Korčula has a couple of fun annual festivals. The Marco Polo Festival is in late June and early July, with lots of exhibitions, concerts, dances, and a parade with a costumed Marco Polo returning to his native Korčula after his long visit to

China. For 10 days at the beginning of September, Korčula remembers the great 1298 naval battle that took place just off-shore, when the Genoese captured Marco Polo. The festivities culminate in a 14-ship reenactment, complete with smoke and sound effects.

SIGHTS

Korčula's few sights cluster within a few yards of each other in the Old Town. I've listed them roughly in order from the Great Land Gate (the Old Town's main entry) to the tip of the Old Town peninsula. All museums are officially "closed" November through April, but most will usually open by request (ask the TI to call for you...or just try knocking on the door).

▲▲*Moreška* **Dance**—Lazy Korčula snaps to life when locals perform a medieval folk dance called the *Moreška* (moh-REHSH-kah). The plot helps Korčulans remember their hard-fought past: A bad king takes the good king's bride, the dancing forces of good and evil battle, and there's always a happy ending (80 kn, June–mid-Oct every Thu at 21:00, July–Aug also Mon at 21:00, in Gradska Vijećnica outdoor theater next to Great Land Gate, or in a nearby congress center if bad weather; buy tickets from travel agency, at your hotel, or at the door).

▲**Great Land Gate (Veliki Revelin)**—A noble staircase leads up to the main entrance to the Old Town. Like all of the town's towers,

it's adorned with the Venetian winged lion and the coats of arms of the doge of Venice (left) and the rector of Korčula (right; the offset coat of arms below was the rector who later renovated the gate). You can climb the tower to visit a small exhibit on the *Moreška* dance and enjoy panoramic town views (10 kn, generally May–Oct daily 9:30–21:30, may be closed for midday break in shoulder season, likely closed Nov–April, English descriptions).

Just inside the gate is **Franjo Tuđman Square,** renamed in 2001 for the controversial first president of an independent Croatia (see page 612). During the war, Tuđman was considered a hero. In later years, it was revealed that he had held secret negotiations with the Serbian leader Slobodan Milošević. As the key figure of a recent-but-bygone era that combined both joy and terror, Tuđman remains controversial in today's Croatia. But members of his party are still in power and hold local offices throughout the country, and sometimes adorn a square or street with his name.

On the left inside the gate is the 16th-century **Town Hall and Rector's Palace.** The seal of Korčula (over the center arch) symbolizes the town's importance as the southernmost bastion of the Venetian Republic: St. Mark standing below three defensive towers. The little church on the other side of the square is dedicated to **St. Michael** (Crkva Sv. Mihovila). Throughout Croatia, you'll often find churches to St. Michael just inside the town gates, as he is believed to offer saintly protection from enemies. Notice that a passageway connects the church to the building across the street—home to the Brotherhood of St. Michael, one of Korčula's many religious fraternal organizations (see "Icon Museum," page 686).

• *Now begin walking up the...*

Street of the Korčulan Statute of 1214 (Ulica Korčulanskog Statuta 1214)—This street is Korčula's backbone—in more ways than one (remember that the street plan is designed as a fish skeleton). While most medieval towns slowly evolved with twisty, mazelike lanes, Korčula was carefully planned. The streets to the west (left) of this one are straight, to allow the refreshing northwesterly Maestral winds into town. To the east (right), they're curved (notice you can't see the sea) to keep out the bad-vibe southeasterly Jugo winds.

The street's complicated name honors a 1214 statute—the oldest known written law in Central Europe—with regulations about everyday life and instructions on maintaining the walls, protecting nature, keeping animals, building a house, and so on. As you head up the street, look up to notice some interesting decorations on the houses' upper floors.

• *If you continue up the street, you'll reach St. Mark's Square (Trg Sv. Marka). From here, you're a few steps from the next four sights.*

▲**St. Mark's Cathedral (Katedrala Sv. Marka)**—Korčula became a bishopric in the 14th century. In the 19th century—36 bishops later—the Hapsburgs decided to centralize ecclesiastical power in their empire, and removed Korčula's bishop. The town still has this beautiful "cathedral"—but no bishop. On the ornately decorated tympanum above the main door, you'll see another Venetian statue of St. Mark (flanked by Adam and Eve). Inside, above the main altar, is an original Tintoretto painting (recently restored in Zagreb). As you leave, notice the weapons on the back wall, used in some of the pivotal battles that have taken place near strategically situated Korčula (free, May–Oct daily 9:00–14:00 & 17:00–19:00, may be open all day long in peak season, closed during church services, generally closed Nov–April but may be open Mon–Fri 9:00–12:00 after Easter).

▲**Church Museum (Opatska Riznica)**—This small museum has an unusual and fascinating collection. Try to find the following items: a ceremonial necklace from Mother Teresa (who came from Macedonia, not far from here—she gave this necklace to a friend from Korčula), some old 12th-century hymnals, two tiny drawings by Leonardo da Vinci, a coin collection (including a 2,400-year-old Greek coin minted here in Korčula), some Croatian modern paintings, and two framed reliquaries with dozens of miniscule relics (15 kn, May–Oct Mon–Sat 9:00–19:00, closed Sun except sometimes in the morning, may be open later in peak season and have shorter hours in shoulder season, generally closed Nov–April but may be open Mon–Fri 9:00–12:00 after Easter).

▲**Town Museum (Gradski Muzej)**—Housed in an old mansion, this museum does a fine job of bringing together Korčula's eclectic claims to fame. It's arranged like a traditional Dalmatian home: shop on the ground floor, living quarters in the middle floors, kitchen on top. Notice that some of the walls near the entry have holes in them. Archaeologists are continually doing actual "digs" into these walls to learn how medieval houses here were built.

On the ground floor is a lapidarium, featuring fragments of Korčula's stone past (see the first-century Roman jugs). Upstairs is a display on Korčula's long-standing shipbuilding industry, including models of two modern steel ships built here (the town still builds ship parts today). There's also a furnished living room and, in the attic, a kitchen. This was a smart place for the kitchen—if it caught fire, it was less likely to destroy the whole building. Notice the little WC in the corner. A network of pipes took kitchen and other waste through town and out to sea (10 kn, limited posted English information—pick up the free English guide brochure at entry; mid-June–Aug Mon–Sat 9:30–21:00, closed Sun; Sept–mid-June Mon–Fri 8:00–15:00—if it's locked, try knocking, closed Sat–Sun).

Marco Polo's House (Kuća Marka Pola)—Korčula's favorite son is the great 13th-century explorer Marco Polo. Though Polo sailed under the auspices of the Venetian Republic, and technically was a Venetian (since the Republic controlled this region), Korčulans proudly claim him as their own. Marco Polo was the first Westerner to sail to China, bringing back amazing stories and exotic goods (like silk) that Europeans had never seen before. After his trip, Marco Polo fought in an important naval battle against the Genoese near Korčula. He was captured, taken to Genoa, and imprisoned. He told his story to a cellmate, who wrote it down, published it, and made the explorer a world-class and much-in-demand celebrity. To this day, kids in swimming pools around the world try to find him with their eyes closed.

Today, Korčula is the proud home to "Marco Polo's House"— actually a more recent building on the site of what may or may not have been his family's property. The house is in poor repair, but most of the property has been purchased by the city to open to visitors. Currently you can just climb the tower and wander the gardens, but in the coming years the town hopes to turn the complex into a world-class museum about the explorer (10 kn, likely open May–Oct only; just north of cathedral on—where else?— ulica Depolo).

Across the street from the house's entrance, you'll find a clever **Marco Polo gift shop** selling various relatively classy items relating to the explorer—herbs, brandies, honey, and so on. Each one comes with a little tag telling a tale of M.P.—for example, how he invented the word "million" (because no existing word was superlative enough for his discoveries). There's even a life-size Marco Polo and Kublai Khan you can pose with (daily in summer 9:00–21:00, shorter hours off-season, closed in winter, ulica Depolo 1A).

▲**Icon Museum (Zbirka Ikona)**—Korčula is known for its many brotherhoods—centuries-old fraternal organizations that have sprung up around churches. The Brotherhood of All Saints has been meeting every Sunday after Mass since the 14th century, and they run a small but interesting museum of icons. These golden religious images were brought back from Greece in the 17th century by Korčulans who had been fighting the Ottomans on a Venetian warship (10 kn, hours depend on demand, but generally May–Oct daily 10:00–13:00 & 17:00–20:00, may be open all day long in peak season, closed Nov–April—but try ringing the bell, on Kaprova ulica at the Old Town's southeast tip).

Brotherhoods' meeting halls are often connected to their church by a second-story walkway. Use this one to step in to the Venetian-style **All Saints' Church** (Crkva Svih Svetih). Under the loft in the back of the church, notice the models of boats and tools—donated by Korčula's shipbuilders. Look closely at the painting to the right of the altar. See the guys in the white robes kneeling under Jesus? That's the Brotherhood, who commissioned this painting.

▲**Old Town Walls**—For several centuries, Korčula held a crucial strategic position: This was one of the most important southern outposts of the Venetian Republic (the Republic of Dubrovnik started at the Pelješac Peninsula, just across the channel). The original town walls around Korčula date from at least the 13th century, but the fortifications were extended (and new towers built) over several centuries to defend against various foes of Venice—mostly Ottomans and pirates.

The most recent tower dates from the 16th century, when the Ottomans attacked Korčula. The rector and other VIPs fled to the mainland, but a brave priest remained on the island and came up with a plan. All of the women of Korčula dressed up as men, and then everybody in town peeked over the wall—making the Ottomans think they were up against a huge army. The priest prayed for help, and the strong northerly Bora wind blew. Not wanting to take their chances with the many defenders and the weather, the Ottomans sailed away, and Korčula was saved.

By the late 19th century, Korčula was an unimportant Hapsburg beach town, and the walls had no strategic value. The town decided to quarry the top half of its old walls to build new homes (and to improve air circulation inside the city). While today's walls are half as high as they used to be, the town has restored many of the towers, giving Korčula its fortified feel today. Each one has a winged lion—a symbol of Venice—and the seal of the rector of Korčula when the tower was built.

ACTIVITIES

Excursions—Various companies offer day-long excursions to nearby destinations (generally available June–Oct, each itinerary offered 2–3 times per week). The most popular options are Dubrovnik (420 kn) and the national park on Mljet Island (310 kn, includes park entry fee). Korčula's two big travel agencies—Marko Polo and Atlas—sell tickets for different companies. If one isn't running a tour to the destination you want, the other might be (both agencies are listed under "Helpful Hints" earlier in this chapter). Several new, more active tour companies have popped up recently, offering canoe trips, snorkeling, kayaking, and other "adventures"—look for flyers around town (Sokol is well-regarded, www.korcula-adventures.com).

Swimming—The water around Korčula is clean and popular for swimming. You'll find pebbly beaches strewn with holiday-goers all along Put Sv. Nikola, the street that runs west from the Old Town. Another popular swimming spot is at the very end of the Old Town peninsula.

SLEEPING

Korčula's accommodations options are extremely limited. There are five hotels in town—all decaying, overpriced, resort-style hotels, and all owned by the same company (which is, in turn, government-run). The lack of competition keeps quality low and prices ridiculously high—which makes *sobe* a particularly good alternative.

Sleep Code

(€1 = about $1.20, 6 kn = about $1, country code: 385, area code: 020)

S = Single, **D** = Double/Twin, **T** = Triple, **Q** = Quad, **b** = bathroom. The modest tourist tax (7 kn or €1 per person, per night, lower off-season) is not included in these rates. The hotels accept credit cards and include breakfast in their rates, while most *sobe* accept only cash and don't offer breakfast. Everyone listed here speaks at least enough English to make a reservation (or knows someone nearby who can translate).

To help you sort easily through these listings, I've divided the rooms into three categories based on the price for a standard double room with bath in peak season:

$$$ Higher Priced—Most rooms 700 kn (€97) or more.
$$ Moderately Priced—Most rooms between 400–700 kn (€55–97).
$ Lower Priced—Most rooms 400 kn (€55) or less.

Sobe

My favorite *sobe* in Korčula offer similar comfort to the hotels at far lower prices—some of them with TVs and air-conditioning, to boot.

$$ Royal Apartments are some of the most hotelesque (and most expensive) rooms in town. The five apartments are classy and new, making the place feel more like a small hotel with no real reception desk—arrange your arrival time carefully (July–Aug: small apartment-€80, big apartment-€90; June and Sept: small apartment-€70, big apartment-€80; closed Oct–May, no extra charge for 1- or 2-night stays, no breakfast, cash only, air-con, well-marked with green awning just west of Old Town at Trg Petra Šegedina 4, mobile 098-184-0444, royalapt@ica.net, Jelavić family).

$ Rezi and Andro Depolo, probably distant relatives of Marco, rent four comfy rooms on the bay west of the Old Town. Three of the rooms offer beautiful views to the Old Town, and the five-minute stroll into town is pleasant and scenic. English-speaking Rezi is very friendly and works to make her guests feel welcome (Db-200 kn, or 240 kn July–Aug, room with kitchen-40 kn more, 30 percent more for 1- or 2-night stays, continental breakfast-25 kn, big breakfast-35 kn, cash only, air-con, Put Sv. Nikola 43; walk along waterfront from Old Town with bay on your right, look for *sobe* sign at the yellow house set back from the street, just before the 2 monasteries; tel. 020/711-621, viladepolo@hotmail.com).

$ Lenni and Periša Modrinić, both of whom are outgoing and speak good English, rent three tight, modern, comfortable rooms and two apartments right in the heart of the Old Town (Db-€45, or €50 July–Aug; apartment-€55, or €60 July–Aug; €5 less off-season, 10 percent more for 1- or 2-night stay, no breakfast, cash only, air-con, near Konoba Marko Polo restaurant at Jakova Baničevića 13, tel. 020/711-400, www.ikorcula.net/lenni, perisa .modrinic@du.t-com.hr).

$ The **Vitaić family** is a father-and-sons operation renting three rooms in the Old Town (July–Aug: Db-400 kn; May–June and Sept–Oct: Db-250 kn; closed Nov–April, no extra charge for 1- or 2-night stays, no breakfast, cash only, Dinko Mirošević 8, tel. 020/715-312, mobile 098-932-7670, avitaic@net.hr).

$ **Booking** *Sobe* **Through an Agency:** While you can walk along Put Sv. Nikola and generally find a fine deal on a private room, you can also book one through one of Korčula's travel agencies for an additional 20 percent (figure Db-€35–50 in high season, €20–35 off-season, 30 percent more for 1- or 2-night stays). For information on the two main agencies—Marko Polo Tours and Atlas Travel—see "Helpful Hints," earlier in this chapter.

Hotels

All five of Korčula's hotels are owned by HTP Korčula. If you don't want to stay in a *soba*, these are the only game in town. You can reserve rooms at any of them through the main office (tel. 020/726-336, fax 020/711-746, www.korcula-hotels.com, marketing@htp-korcula.hr; at all hotels, credit cards are accepted, there is no air-con, and there are no non-smoking rooms). I've listed peak-season prices with breakfast only; rates are progressively lower the farther off-season you get. You can pay 10 percent more per person for half-board (dinner at the hotel). It's much cheaper to stay a week or longer. There's a long-term plan to renovate all of these hotels, but so far the Marko Polo is the only one that's seen any progress.

$$$ Hotel Korčula has by far the best location, right on the waterfront alongside the Old Town. It has a fine seaside terrace restaurant and friendly staff, even if the 20 rooms are outmoded and waaay overpriced. The rooms are on two floors: The more expensive "first-floor" rooms (actually on the third floor) have big windows and sea views; the cheaper "second-floor" rooms (actually on the fourth floor) have tiny windows and no views (July–Aug: Sb-720–900 kn, Db-960–1,200 kn; June and Sept: Sb-546–683 kn, Db-780–976 kn; cheaper Oct–May, reception tel. 020/711-078).

$$$ *Other Hotels:* Three more hotels cluster a 15-minute walk away, around the far side of Shell Bay. All are poorly maintained, overpriced (similar rates to Hotel Korčula), and relatively inconvenient to the Old Town, but they share a nice beach. **Hotel Marko Polo** has 94 crisp, newly renovated rooms and an elevator; they plan to renovate the lobby and pool area in 2007 (reception tel. 020/726-004). **Hotel Liburna,** with a clever split-level design that reflects the skyline of the Old Town, has 109 rooms, some of them accessible by elevator; half the rooms face the sea and cost an additional 10 percent (reception tel. 020/726-006). Dreary **Hotel Park** has 153 rooms (reception tel. 020/726-100). The fifth hotel, **Hotel Bon Repos**—another 15 minutes by foot from the Old Town—is, in every sense, the last resort.

Hostel

$ Korčula Backpacker, well-run by a South African–born Croat named Zlatko, is a youthful, fun-loving, easygoing place nicknamed the "Happy House." The 10-minute time limit on the shared bathrooms is strictly enforced (no locks on the doors). The ground-floor bar spills out into a nearby square, becoming a popular hangout on summer evenings (4- and 6-bed dorms, plus a 15-bed attic slumbermill dubbed the "fun club"; prices per bed: 120 kn mid-July–Aug, 100 kn mid-June–mid-July, 90 kn May–mid-June and Sept, closed Oct–April, no breakfast, cash only, Internet access, boat and bike rental, right where the Old Town meets the mainland on Trg Petra at Šegedina Hrvatske Bratske Zajednice 6, tel. 020/716-755, mobile 098-997-6353, www.korculabackpacker.com, bookings@korculabackpacker.com).

EATING

Korčula has plenty of interchangeable seafood restaurants. These are all good options, but (with the exception of Fresh) everything in town is pretty similar—make your decision based on atmosphere and what looks best to you.

Konoba Morski Konjic ("Moorish Seahorse") has tables spilling along the seawall, offering *al fresco* dining with salty views and jaded service. If you want romantic harborside dining, this is your best option (60–100-kn main dishes, daily 8:00–24:00).

Adio Mare, with fine seafood, may have the best decor in town: a cavernous stone dining room, or a tiny little upstairs nook (50–100-kn main dishes, daily 17:30–24:00, sometimes also 12:00–14:00 in peak season, near Marco Polo's House, tel. 020/711-253).

Riblji Restoran Kanavelić, near the far end of the Old Town peninsula, serves good seafood. Choose between the big outdoor terrace or the formal-feeling dining room (non-seafood dishes from 30 kn, 60-120 kn for seafood, daily 18:00–23:00, tel. 020/711-800).

Konoba Marinero has pleasantly nautical decor and a simple menu of Dalmatian specialties (50–100-kn main dishes, Easter–Oct daily 11:00–24:00, closed Nov–Easter, Marka Andrijića 13, tel. 020/711-170).

Pizzas and Pasta: **Pizzeria Amfora,** along the route of the people-parade up Korčula's main drag in the Old Town, features good, inexpensive, quick pizzas and pastas. Squeeze into the small dining room, or enjoy the sidewalk tables (35–50 kn, long hours daily, tel. 020/711-739).

Quick and Tasty: **Fresh,** an innovative new spot run by a Canadian-Croatian couple, offers 25-kn wraps and 20-kn smoothies. If you want a break from grilled seafood and pizza, this is the place (July–Aug daily 9:00–2:00 in the morning, until 19:00 in shoulder season, closed in winter, along Shell Bay behind the sunken-ship playground on the way to the bus station).

Picnics: Just outside the main gate, you'll find a lively produce market and a big, modern, air-conditioned Konzum supermarket (next to Marko Polo Tours). A short stroll from there, down Put Sv. Nikola, takes you to beach perches with the best Korčula views. Otherwise, there are plenty of picnic spots along the Old Town embankment.

A Scenic Drink: The best setting for drinks is at **Buffet "Massimo,"** a youthful-feeling cocktail bar in a city-wall tower at the very tip of the Old Town peninsula. You can have a drink on one of three levels: the downstairs bar, the main-floor lounge, or climb the ladder (at your own risk) to the tower-top terrace (terrace is only for cocktail-sippers—no beer or wine). If you're up top, notice the dumbwaiter for hauling up drinks (daily in summer 18:00–2:00 in the morning, shoulder season 17:30–1:00 in the morning, closed Nov–April, tel. 020/715-073).

TRANSPORTATION CONNECTIONS

Korčula is reasonably well-connected to the rest of the Dalmatian Coast by boat, but service becomes sparse in the off-season. If you're here during a lull in the sailing schedule, buses are your ticket out of town. No matter when you travel, it's smart to carefully study current boat schedules when planning your itinerary, as they are always subject to change (the following information is based on the 2006 schedules).

Korčula Boat Connections

Boats big and small depart from the embankment surrounding Korčula's Old Town peninsula. Which side of the peninsula a boat uses can depend on the weather—be flexible and inquire locally about where to meet your boat. Some boats leave from other parts of the island, most notably the town of Vela Luka (at the opposite tip of the island, a 1-hour bus ride from Korčula town—described below). Other boats, including the car ferry to Orebić (described under "Route Tips for Drivers" at the end of this chapter), leave from the Dominče dock, about a five-minute drive east of Korčula town.

Big Jadrolinija Car Ferries: These huge, handy vessels go north, to **Stari Grad** on Hvar Island (20-min bus ride from Hvar town; 4/week July–mid-Sept, 2/week mid-Sept–June, 3.5 hrs; the catamaran described below is faster and takes you right to Hvar town) and **Split** (5/week July–mid-Sept, 3/week June, 2/week mid-Sept–May, 3.5–6 hrs); or south, to **Sobra** on Mljet Island (1.25-hr bus ride from the national park, 3/week July–Sept, 2/week June, none Oct–May, 2 hrs; for details, see below) and **Dubrovnik** (5/week July–Sept, 4/week June, 2/week Oct–May, 3–4 hrs).

Speedy *Krilo* Catamaran from Korčula Town to Hvar Town and Split: A speedy catamaran called *Krilo* leaves Korčula town at 6:00 and zips to Hvar town and Split (daily June–Sept, 4/week Oct–May, 1.75 hrs to Hvar, 2.75 hrs to Split, some summer boats stop at Prigradica on Korčula Island—in which case these times are longer). In Korčula, tickets for the *Krilo* boat are sold at Marko Polo Tours—not the Jadrolinija office (35 kn one-way to Hvar, 55 kn to Split). Since it returns from Split and Hvar the same afternoon, this extremely handy catamaran allows you to effortlessly day-trip to either place (see "Transportation Connections" for each town).

From Vela Luka to Hvar Town and Split: There are additional boats to points north, but they usually require a very early bus from Korčula town (departing at 4:10) to the port at Vela Luka, an hour away at the other end of the island. A Jadrolinija **fast catamaran** goes daily from Vela Luka to both Hvar town and Split (Mon–Sat departs at 5:30, Sun at 8:00, 45 min to Hvar, 2 hrs to Split). A much slower **car ferry** also travels daily from Vela Luka to Split (departs Mon–Sat at 6:30, Sun at 14:45, 2.75 hrs, does not stop at Hvar town). From late June through early September, a second car ferry leaves Vela Luka for Split every afternoon, stopping at Hvar town en route (1.5 hours to Hvar town, 3.75 hrs to Split, does not stop at Hvar on Sat). Since reaching Vela Luka from Korčula town is a hassle, carefully confirm these boat schedules and understand all your options (at the Korčula TI or Jadrolinija office) before you get up early to make the trip.

Korčula Bus Connections

All buses from Korčula town (except those to Vela Luka) first drive to Dominče, where they meet the car ferry to cross over to Orebić, on the Pelješac Peninsula. Don't be surprised if you have to get off the bus, walk onto the ferry, and meet a different bus across the channel. It takes close to two hours to drive the length of the Pelješac Peninsula and meet the main coastal road.

From Korčula Town by Bus to: **Dubrovnik** (peak season: 2/day, 3–4 hrs; off-season: Mon–Sat 1/day with an early departure, Sun 2/day), **Zagreb** (1/day, 9–13.5 hrs depending on route), **Split** (1/day, 5 hrs, same bus goes to Zagreb), **Vela Luka** (at far end of island, Mon–Fri 7/day, Sat 6/day, Sun 4/day, 1 hr, first bus at 4:10 gets you to the early-morning ferries—see above).

Route Tips for Drivers: Between Korčula and the Mainland

The island of Korčula is connected to the mainland by a small car ferry that runs between Dominče—about a mile east of Korčula town—and Orebić, across the channel on the Pelješac Peninsula (50 kn/car, 12 kn/passenger, 15-min crossing, departs Dominče at the top of most but not all hours—check carefully in Korčula, departs Orebić at :30 past most hours).

If you're driving via the mainland, you'll first cross on this car ferry to Orebić on the Pelješac Peninsula, which is known for its wines. The Pelješac Peninsula is extremely long and narrow, and the roads are very rough, so it can take longer than you'd expect to reach the main coastal road (figure 1.5–2 hours). Where the peninsula meets the mainland, you'll see the cute little "Great Wall of Croatia" town of Ston.

If you're heading south to **Dubrovnik,** the coastal road zips you right there (about an hour from Ston). If you're heading north to **Split,** soon after joining the coastal road you'll actually pass through Bosnia-Herzegovina for a few miles (around the town of Neum—just flash your passport as you enter and exit the country).

Because of the ferry crossing and the long drive along the Pelješac Peninsula, driving from Split to Korčula is time-consuming and tiring. (Notice on the map that the whole time you're driving down the coast parallel to the Pelješac Peninsula, you're actually going in the opposite direction from Korčula—then you have to backtrack as you head up the peninsula itself.) Instead, I prefer to take the longer car ferry the whole way from Split to Vela Luka, at the far end of Korčula Island (described above; allow 1 hour for the drive from Korčula town to Vela Luka, about 315 kn per car). The scenic and relaxing 2.75-hour boat ride saves you more than that much driving time.

ZAGREB

While Zagreb doesn't have the urban bustle of Budapest or the stay-awhile charm of Ljubljana, the Croatian capital offers historic neighborhoods, worthwhile museums, a thriving café culture, and an illuminating contrast to the beaches. As a tourist destination, Zagreb pales in comparison to the sparkling coastal towns. But you can't get a complete picture of modern Croatia without a visit here—away from the touristy resorts, in the lively and livable city that is home to one out of every six Croatians (pop. 780,000).

Zagreb began as two walled medieval towns, Gradec and Kaptol, separated by a river. As Croatia fell under the control of various foreign powers—Budapest, Vienna, Berlin, and Belgrade—the two hill towns that would become Zagreb gradually took on more religious and civic importance. Kaptol became a bishopric in 1094, and it's still home to Croatia's most important church. In the 16th century, the *Ban* (Croatia's governor) and the *Sabor* (parliament) called Gradec home. The two towns officially merged in 1850, and soon after, the railroad connecting Budapest with the Adriatic port city of Rijeka was built through the city. Zagreb prospered.

After centuries of being the de facto religious, cultural, and political center of Croatia, Zagreb officially became a European capital when the country declared its independence in 1991. In the ensuing war with Serbia, Zagreb was hardly damaged—Serbian bombs hit only a few strategic targets (the bloodiest fighting was to the east and south of here).

Today, just over a decade later, Zagreb has long since repaired

Zagreb

City Map Legend:

1. Hotel Dubrovnik
2. Hotel Astoria
3. Hotel Jadran
4. Hotel Central
5. Hostel Fulir
6. Tkalčićeva St. Eateries
7. Nokturno Rest.
8. Sandwich Bar Pingvin
9. Mimice Restaurant
10. Vinodol Restaurant
11. Restaurant Jägerhorn
12. Millennium Ice Cream
13. Marko Polo Travel Agency
14. Plitvice Lakes Office

★ = Jelačić Square

the minimal damage, and the capital feels safe, modern, and accessible.

Planning Your Time

Most American visitors just pass through Zagreb, but the city is worth a look. Check your bag at the station and zip into the center for a quick visit—or consider spending the night.

You can get a decent sense of Zagreb in just a few hours. With whatever time you have, make a beeline for Jelačić Square to visit the TI and get oriented. Take the funicular up to Gradec, visit the excellent Museum of Naive Art, and stroll St. Mark's Square. Then wander down through the Stone Chapel to the lively Tkalčićeva scene (good for a drink or meal), through the market (closes at 14:00), and on to Kaptol and the cathedral.

With more time, visit some of Zagreb's museums or wander the series of parks called the "Green Horseshoe."

If you're moving on from Zagreb to Plitvice Lakes National Park (see next chapter), be warned that there are generally no buses between 17:30 and 22:00 (or sometimes later). Confirm your bus departure carefully to ensure that you don't get stranded in Zagreb.

ORIENTATION

(area code: 01)
Zagreb, just 30 minutes from the Slovenian border, stretches from the foothills of Medvednica ("Bear Mountain") to the Sava River. In the middle of the sprawl, you'll find the modern **Lower Town** (Donji Grad, centered on **Jelačić Square**) and the historic **Upper Town** (Gornji Grad, comprising the original hill towns of **Gradec** and **Kaptol**). To the south is a U-shaped belt of parks, squares, and museums that make up "Lenuci's Green Horseshoe." The east side of the U is a series of three parks, with the train station at the bottom (south) and Jelačić Square at the top (north).

Zagrebians have devised a brilliant scheme for confusing tourists: Street names can be depicted several different ways. For example, the street that is signed as ulica Kralja Držislava ("King Držislav Street") is often called by locals simply Držislavova ("Držislav's"). So if you're looking for a street, don't search for an exact match—be willing to settle for something that just has a lot of the same letters.

Tourist Information
Zagreb has two TIs. The bigger, better one is at **Jelačić Square** (Mon–Fri 8:30–20:00, Sat 9:00–17:00, Sun 10:00–14:00, sometimes longer hours in summer, Trg bana Jelačića 11, tel. 01/481-4052, www.zagreb-touristinfo.hr); the other is just a few blocks south, between Jelačić Square and the train station along the west side of **Zrinjevac Park** (Mon–Fri 9:00–17:00, closed Sat–Sun, Trg Nikole Šubića Zrinskoga 14, tel. 01/492-1645). Zagreb's TIs offer piles of free, well-produced tourist brochures that desperately try to convince visitors to do more than just pass through. Pick up the one-page city map (with handy transit map and regional map on back), the *Zagreb Info A–Z* booklet (including accommodations and restaurant listings), the monthly events guide, the great

Zagreb Essentials

English	Croatian	Pronounced
Jelačić Square	Trg bana Jelačića	turg BAH-nah YEH-lah-chee-chah
Gradec (original civic hill town)	Gradec	GRAH-dehts
Kaptol (original religious hill town)	Kaptol	KAHP-tohl
Café street between Gradec and Kaptol	Tkalčićeva (or "Tkalči" for short)	tuh-KAHL-chee-chay-vah (tuh-KAHL-chee)
Main Train Station	Glavni Kolodvor	GLAHV-nee KOH-loh-dvor
Bus Station	Autobusni Kolodvor	OW-toh-boos-nee KOH-loh-dvor

City Walks brochure (with a couple of mildly diverting self-guided walking tours), the museum guide, the booklet about the surrounding region, and more.

The **Zagreb Card** gives you free transportation and discounts on Zagreb sights for 72 hours (90 kn, sold at TI). This usually doesn't make sense for folks who are day-tripping here, but it can be a good deal if you're taking the city tour (below) and doing some sightseeing.

To get oriented, consider the fun daily **city tours** (2-hour walking tour: 95 kn, usually Mon–Thu; 3-hr bus-plus-walking tour: 150 kn, usually Fri–Sun; 25 percent discount on either tour with Zagreb Card). For the weekday walking tour, just show up at the TI; for the weekend bus-plus-walk, call the TI the day before by 14:00 to confirm the schedule, reserve a space, and request an English guide. The same company runs theme tours and excursions into the surrounding countryside (about 2/month, tel. 01/481-4052, www.event.hr).

Arrival in Zagreb

By Train: Zagreb's Main Train Station (Glavni Kolodvor) is conveniently located a few blocks south of Jelačić Square on the Green Horseshoe. The straightforward arrivals hall has a train information desk, ticket windows, ATMs, WCs, and newsstands. The left-luggage office is at the left end of the station, with your back to the tracks (look for low-profile *garderoba* sign, open daily 24 hours). To reach the city center, go straight out the front door. You'll run into a taxi stand, and then the tracks for tram #6 (buy 6.50-kn ticket from kiosk, then hop on: direction Črnomerec zips you to Jelačić Square; direction Sopot takes you to the bus station—the third stop, just after you turn right and go under the big overpass). If you walk straight ahead through the long, lush park, you'll wind up at the bottom of Jelačić Square in 10 minutes.

By Bus: The user-friendly bus station (Autobusni Kolodvor) is a few long blocks southeast of the Main Train Station. The station has all the essentials—ATMs, post office, mini-grocery store, left-luggage counter...everything from a smut store to a chapel. Upstairs, you'll find ticket windows and access to the buses (follow signs to *perone;* wave ticket in front of turnstile to open gate). Tram #6 (in direction Črnomerec) takes you to the Main Train Station, then on to Jelačić Square.

By Plane: Zagreb's airport is 10 miles south of the center (tel. 01/626-5222, www.zagreb-airport.hr). The Croatia Air bus connects the airport to Zagreb's bus station (30 kn, every 30 min, 25-min trip). Figure around 200 kn for a taxi from the airport to the center.

Getting Around Zagreb

The main mode of public transportation is the **tram,** operated by ZET (Zagreb Electrical Transport, www.zet.hr). A single ticket (good for 90 min in one direction, including transfers) costs 8 kn if you buy it from the driver (6.50 kn at kiosk, ask for *ZET karta*—zeht KAR-tah). A day ticket *(dnevna karta)* costs 18 kn. The most useful tram for tourists is #6, connecting Jelačić Square with the train and bus stations.

Taxis start at 19 kn, then run 7 kn per kilometer (20 percent more Sun and at night, 3 kn extra for each piece of baggage; beware of corrupt cabbies—ask for an estimate up front, or call Radio Taxi, tel. 01/970 or 01/661-0200).

Helpful Hints

Important Days: Virtually all Zagreb museums are closed on Sunday afternoon and all day Monday. On Sunday morning, the city is thriving—but by afternoon, it's extremely quiet.

Ferry Tickets: If you're heading for the Dalmatian Coast, note that there isn't a Jadrolinija ferry office in the center. But you can reserve and buy tickets at the **Marko Polo** travel agency (Mon–Fri 9:00–17:00, Sat 9:00–13:00, closed Sun, Masarykova 24, tel. 01/481-5216).

Plitvice Lakes Office: If you're going to Plitvice Lakes National Park, you can get a preview and ask any questions at their helpful information office in Zagreb (Mon–Fri 8:00–16:00, closed Sat–Sun, a block in front of Main Train Station at Trg Kralja Tomislava 19, tel. 01/461-3586).

SELF-GUIDED WALK

Zagreb's Upper Town

The following one-way circular orientation walk, worth ▲▲, begins at Jelačić Square. The entire route takes about an hour at

a leisurely pace (not counting museum stops).

Jelačić Square (Trg bana Jelačića): The "Times Square" of Zagreb bustles with life. It's lined with cafés, shops, trams, Baroque buildings, and the TI. When Zagreb consisted of the two hill towns of Gradec and Kaptol, this Donji Grad ("lower town") held the townspeople's farm fields. Today, it features a prominent equestrian statue of national hero **Josip Jelačić** (YOH-seep YEH-lah-cheech, 1801–1859), a 19th-century governor who extended citizens' rights and did much to unite the Croats within the Hapsburg Empire. In Jelačić's time, the Hungarians were exerting extensive control over Croatia, even trying to make Hungarian the official language. Meanwhile, Budapesters revolted against Hapsburg rule in 1848. Jelačić, ever mindful of the need to protect Croatian cultural autonomy, knew that he'd have a better shot at getting his way from Austria than from Hungary. Jelačić chose the lesser of two evils, and fought alongside the Hapsburgs to put down the Hungarian uprising. In the Yugoslav era, Jelačić was considered dangerously nationalistic, and this statue was taken down. But when Croatia broke away in 1991, Croatian patriotism was in the air, and Jelačić returned. Though Jelačić originally faced his Hungarian foes to the north, today he's staring down the Serbs to the south.

Get oriented. If you face Jelačić's statue, a long block to your left is a funicular that takes you up to one of Zagreb's original villages, Gradec. To the right, look for the TI. If you leave the square ahead and to the right, you'll reach the other original village, Kaptol, and the cathedral (you can't miss its huge, pointy, Neo-Gothic spires—visible from virtually everywhere in Zagreb). If you leave the square ahead and to the left, you'll come to the market (Dolac) and the lively café street, Tkalčićeva.

For now, we'll head up to Gradec. Go a long block down the busy Ilica. On the way, consider ducking inside the big shopping gallery on the left (at #5; look for the tie shop from the chain called Croata—for the story, see page 670). Then continue up Ilica and turn right on Tomičeva, where you'll see a small **funicular** (ZET Uspinjača) crawling up the hill. Dating from the late 19th century, this funicular is looked upon fondly by Zagrebians—both as a bit of nostalgia and as a way to avoid some steps. You can walk up if you want, but the ride is more fun and takes only 55 seconds (3 kn, validate ticket in orange machine before you board, leaves every 10 min daily 6:30–21:00).

Gradec: From the top of the funicular, you'll enjoy a fine panorama over Zagreb. The tall tower you face as you exit is one of Gradec's original watchtowers, the **Burglars' Tower** (Kula Lotršćak). After the Tatars ransacked Central Europe in the early 13th century, King Béla IV decreed that towns be fortified—so Gradec built a wall and guard towers (just like Kraków and Buda did). Look for the little cannon in the top-floor window. Every day at noon, this cannon fires a shot, supposedly to commemorate a 15th-century victory over the besieging Ottomans. Zagrebians hold on to other traditions, too—the lamps on this hill are still gas-powered, lit by a city employee every evening.

Head up the street next to the tower. Little remains of medieval Gradec. When the Ottomans overran Europe, they never managed to take Zagreb—but the threat was enough to scare the nobility into the countryside. When the Ottomans left, the nobles came back, and replaced the medieval buildings here with Baroque mansions. At the first square, to the right, you'll see the Jesuit **Church of St. Catherine.** It's not much to look at from the outside, but the interior is intricately decorated. The same applies to several mansions on Gradec. This simple-outside, ornate-inside style is known as "Zagreb Baroque."

As you continue up the street, on the left you'll see the **Croatian Museum of Naive Art**—Zagreb's best museum, and well worth a visit (see listing under "Sights"). In the next block, on the left, look for the monument to Nikola Tesla (1856–1943), a prominent Croatian scientist who championed alternating current as an alternative to Thomas Edison's direct current.

At the end of the block, you'll come to the low-key **St. Mark's Square** (Markov trg), centered on the **Church of St. Mark.** The original church here was from the 12th century, but only a few fragments remain. The colorful tile roof, from 1880, depicts two coats of arms. On the left, the red-and-white checkerboard symbolizes north-central Croatia, the three lions' heads stand for the Dalmatian Coast, and the marten (*kuna*, like the money) running between the two rivers (Sava and Drava) represent Slavonia—Croatia's northern, inland panhandle. On the right is the seal of

Zagreb: a walled city with wide-open doors (strong, but still welcoming to visitors...like you). The interior is a bit stark, livened up by a few sculptures by Ivan Meštrović, whose former home is about a block straight ahead (go down the street behind the church on the left-hand side, and you'll see the museum on the right; see listing under "Sights").

As you face the church, to the right is the *Sabor*, or parliament. From the 12th century, Croatian noblemen would gather to make important decisions regarding their territories. This gradually evolved into today's modern parliament. (If you walk along the front of the *Sabor* and continue straight ahead 2 blocks, you'll run into the Zagreb City Museum, described under "Sights".)

Across the square from the *Sabor* (to your left as you face the church) is the **Ban's Palace** (Banski Dvori), today the offices for the president and prime minister. This was one of the few buildings in central Zagreb destroyed in the recent war. In October of 1991, the Serbs shelled it from afar, knowing that Croatian President Franjo Tuđman was inside...but Tuđman survived.

Walk from Gradec to Kaptol: For an interesting stroll from St. Mark's Square to the cathedral, head down the street (Kamenita ulica) to the right of the parliament building. Near the end of the street, you'll see the oldest **pharmacy** in town—recently restored and gleaming (c. 1355, on the right, marked *gradska ljekarna*).

Just beyond, you'll reach Gradec's oldest surviving gate, the **Stone Gate** (Kamenita Vrata). Inside is an evocative chapel. The focal point is a painting of Mary that miraculously survived a major fire in 1731. When this medieval gate was reconstructed in the Baroque style, they decided to turn it into a makeshift chapel. The candles (purchased in the little shop and lit in the big metal box) represent Zagrebians' prayers, and the stone plaques on the wall give thanks *(Hvala)* for prayers that were answered. You may notice people doing the sign of the cross as they walk through here, and often a crowd of worshippers gathers, staring intently at the painting. Mary was made the official patron saint of Zagreb in 1990.

As you leave the Stone Gate and come to Radićeva, turn right. Take the next left, onto the street called **Krvavi Most**—"Blood Bridge." At the end of Krvavi Most, you'll come to **Tkalčićeva.** This lively café-and-restaurant street used to be a river—the natural boundary between Gradec and Kaptol. The two towns did not always get along, and sometimes fought against each other. Blood was spilled, and the bridge that once stood here between them became known as Blood Bridge. By the late 19th century, the towns had united, and the river began to stink—so they covered it over with this street.

As you cross Tkalčićeva, you enter the old town of Kaptol. You'll come to the **market** *(dolac)*, packed with colorful stalls selling produce of all kinds (Mon–Sat 7:00–14:00, Sun 7:00–13:00). At the back-left corner is the fragrant fish market *(ribarnica)*, and under your feet is an indoor part of the market *(tržnica)*, where farmers sell farm-fresh eggs and dairy products (same hours as outdoor market, entrance down below in the direction of Jelačić Square).

Your walk is over. On the other side of the market, visit the cathedral (see description in "Sights").

SIGHTS

Museums in Gradec

▲▲**Croatian Museum of Naive Art (Hrvatski Muzej Naivne Umjetnosti)**—This remarkable spot is one of the most enjoyable little museums in Eastern Europe. It features expressionistic paintings by untrained peasant artists of the mid-20th century. These stirring images—fantasy worlds rich with detail—are well worth a look. The exhibit kicks off with works by the movement's star, Ivan Generalić, then moves on to his followers. Mijo Kovačić's paintings are particularly striking, with hauntingly detailed layers of twisted tree branches (10 kn, pick up the English explanations as you enter, Tue–Fri 10:00–18:00, Sat–Sun 10:00–13:00, closed Mon, ulica Sv. Čirila i Metoda 3, tel. 01/485-1911, www.hmnu.org).

▲**Ivan Meštrović Atelier**—Ivan Meštrović, the only Croatian artist worth remembering, lived in this house from 1922 until 1942 (before he fled to the US during World War II). The house has been converted into a delightful gallery of the artist's works, displayed in two parts: residence and studio. Split's Meštrović Gallery is the definitive museum of the 20th-century Croatian sculptor, but if you're not going there, Zagreb's gallery is a convenient place to gain an appreciation for the prolific, thoughtful artist (20 kn, 20-kn English catalog, Tue–Fri 10:00–18:00, Sat–Sun 10:00–14:00, closed Mon, behind St. Mark's Square at Mletačka 8, tel. 01/485-1123). For more on Meštrović, see page 670.

Zagreb City Museum (Muzej Grada Zagreba)—This collection, with a modern, engaging exhibit that sprawls over two floors of an old convent, traces the history of the city through town models, paintings, furniture, clothing, and other artifacts. After buying your ticket, head through the door and turn left, then work your way up through the ages. But save your time and energy for the most interesting section: the early days of independence from

Yugoslavia (including an exhibit on damage sustained during the warfare) and a hall of illuminating propaganda posters (20 kn, English descriptions, Tue–Fri 10:00–18:00, Sat–Sun 10:00–13:00, closed Mon, at north end of Gradec at Opatička 20, tel. 01/485-1361, www.mdc.hr/mgz).

Cathedral (Katedrala)

By definition, Croats are Catholics. Before the recent war, relatively few people practiced their faith. But as the Croats fought with their Orthodox and Muslim neighbors, Catholicism took on a greater importance. Today, more and more Croats are attending Mass. This is Croatia's single most important church, worth ▲.

In 1094, when a diocese was established at Kaptol, this church quickly became a major center of high-ranking church officials. In the mid-13th century, the original cathedral was destroyed by invading Tatars, who actually used it as a stable. It was rebuilt, only to be destroyed again by an earthquake in 1880. The current version—undergoing yet another renovation for the last several years—is Neo-Gothic. Surrounding the church are walls with pointy-topped towers (part of a larger archbishop's palace) that were built for protection against the Ottomans. The full name is the Cathedral of the Assumption of the Blessed Virgin Mary and the Saintly Kings Stephen and Ladislav (whew!)—but most locals just call it "the cathedral."

Step inside (free, Mon–Sat 10:00–17:00, Sun 13:00–17:00). Look closely at the silver relief on the first **altar:** a scene of the Holy Family doing chores around the house (Mary sewing, Joseph and Jesus building a fence...and angels helping out).

In the front-left corner, find the tombstone of **Alojzije Stepinac.** He was the Archbishop of Zagreb in World War II, when he shortsightedly supported the Nazis—thinking, like many Croatians, that this was the ticket to greater independence from Serbia. When Tito came to power, he put Stepinac on trial and sent him to jail for five years. But Stepinac never lost his faith, and remains to many the most important inspirational figure of Croatian Catholicism.

As you leave the church, look to the back of the left apse. This strange script is the **Glagolitic alphabet** *(glagoljca),* invented by Byzantine missionaries Cyril and Methodius in the ninth century to translate the Bible into Slavic languages. Though these mi~~~ aries worked mostly in Moravia (today's eastern C their alphabet caught on only here, in Croatia. (adapted in Bulgaria to become the Cyrillic alp Serbia, Russia, and other parts east.) In 1991, wl its own country and nationalism surged, the c the idea of making this the official alphabet.

The Green Horseshoe

With extra time, stroll around the Green Horseshoe (the U-shaped belt of parks and museums in the city center). The museums here aren't nearly as interesting as those on Gradec, but may be worth a peek on a rainy day.

Mimara Museum (Muzej Mimara)—This grand, empty-feeling building displays the eclectic collection of a wealthy Dalmatian, ranging from ancient artifacts to paintings by European masters. While the names are major—Rubens, Rembrandt, Velázquez, Renoir, Manet—the paintings themselves are minors. Still, art buffs may find something to get excited about (20 kn, 90-kn English guidebook, otherwise virtually no English, Tue–Sat 10:00–17:00, Thu until 19:00, Sun 10:00–14:00, closed Mon, Rooseveltov trg 5, tel. 01/482-8100).

Arts and Crafts Museum (Muzej za Umjetnost i Obrt)—This decorative arts collection, mostly furniture, ceramics, and clothes, is well-displayed. From the entry, go upstairs, then work your way clockwise and up to the top floor—passing through each artistic style, from Gothic to the present. It's mostly furniture, with a few paintings and other items thrown in (20 kn, some rooms have laminated English descriptions to borrow, otherwise very limited English, Tue–Sat 10:00–19:00, Sun 10:00–14:00, closed Mon, Trg Maršala Tita 10, tel. 01/488-2111, www.muo.hr).

Botanical Garden (Botanički Vrt)—For a back-to-nature change of pace from the urban cityscape, wander through this relaxing garden, run by the University of Zagreb (free, Mon–Tue 9:00–14:30, Wed–Sun 9:00–18:00, Wed–Sun until 19:00 in summer, at southwest corner of the Green 'Shoe).

SLEEPING

Hotels in central Zagreb are very expensive—you won't get much for your money. I prefer sleeping in Ljubljana or at Plitvice Lakes National Park, both of which offer better values. But if you must stay in Zagreb, these are the best deals right in the main tourist zone.

$$$ Hotel Dubrovnik has an ideal location (at the bottom of Jelačić Square) and 268 business-class rooms (small Sb-780 kn, bigger Sb-880–950 kn, Db with 1 big bed-1,050 kn, twin Db-1,200 kn, suite-1,400–1,600 kn, extra bed-250 kn, rooms overlooking the square don't cost extra—try to request one, often cheaper on week-nds, prices soft, non-smoking floors, elevator, Gajeva 1, tel. 01/486-, fax 01/486-3506, www.hotel-dubrovnik.hr, reservations -dubrovnik.hr).

Sleep Code

(€1 = about $1.20, 6 kuna = about $1, country code: 385, area code: 01)

S = Single, **D** = Double/Twin, **T** = Triple, **Q** = Quad, **b** = bathroom, **s** = shower only. English is spoken at each place. Unless otherwise noted, credit cards are accepted, breakfast is included, and the modest tourist tax (7 kn per person, per night) is not.

To help you sort easily through these listings, I've divided the rooms into three categories based on the price for a standard double room with bath:

$$$ Higher Priced—Most rooms 800 kn or more.
$$ Moderately Priced—Most rooms between 500–800 kn.
$ Lower Priced—Most rooms 500 kn or less.

$$$ Hotel Astoria, a Best Western, was recently renovated from top to bottom. Now it offers 102 smallish but plush rooms and a high-class lobby. It's on a grimy street near the train station, so I wouldn't splurge here unless I were in town on a weekend, when rates drop by a third (Sb-850–970 kn, Db-1,100 kn; Fri–Sun: Sb-570 kn, Db-735 kn; prices can also be soft on some weekdays, fancier suites also available, elevator, Petrinjska 71, tel. 01/480-8900, fax 01/480-8908, www.bestwestern.com, info@hotelastoria.hr).

$$ Hotel Jadran has 49 decent rooms near the cathedral, a few blocks east of Jelačić Square (Sb-510 kn, Db-717 kn, Tb-894 kn, some street noise—request quiet room, elevator, Vlaška 50, tel. 01/455-3777, fax 01/461-2151, www.hup-zagreb.hr, jadran@hup-zagreb.hr).

$$ Hotel Central's 76 overly perfumed rooms are comfortable and modern, and the price is right. This place seems to get a little better every year, and the location—right across from the Main Train Station—is convenient for rail travelers (Sb-550–600 kn, Db with one big bed-720 kn, twin Db-780 kn, bigger Db-830 kn, extra bed-160 kn, elevator, Branimirova 3, tel. 01/484-1122, fax 01/484-1304, www.hotel-central.hr, info@hotel-central.hr).

$ Hostel Fulir, named for a legendary Zagrebian bon vivant, is energetically run by Davor and Leo, a pair of can-do Croats who lived in Ohio. It's new, colorful, and friendly, with a big 10-bunk dorm and a smaller four-bed room sharing two bathrooms. Just a few steps from Jelačić Square, this hostel puts you in the heart of Zagreb (€19.50 per bunk, includes sheets, no breakfast, free lockers, Internet access, upstairs at the end of the courtyard at Radićeva 3a, tel. 01/483-0882, mobile 098-193-0552, www.fulir-hostel.com).

EATING

For the perfect place to sip a lazy cup of coffee, look no further than Jelačić Square—Zagreb's heart and soul. To venture a little farther, try these places. The last five eateries are on or near the main street (called Ilica to the west, Jurišićeva to the east) that runs along the bottom of Jelačić Square.

On Tkalčićeva: This is Zagreb's main café street, "restaurant row," and urban promenade rolled into one. It's a parade of fashionable locals, and *the* place to see and be seen. Wander here and choose your favorite spot (starts a block behind Jelačić Square, next to the market). For good pizza and pasta, wander a few feet up Skalinska (near the Jelačić Square end of the street) to find **Nokturno,** with a lively interior and fun outdoor seating (18–30-kn pizzas, pastas, and salads, 25–45-kn meat and fish dishes, daily 9:00–1:00 in the morning, Skalinska 4, tel. 01/481-3394).

At the Market (Dolac): Zagreb's lively market offers plenty of options (Mon–Sat 7:00–14:00, Sun 7:00–13:00). Buy a fresh picnic direct from the producers. Or, for something already prepared, duck into one of the many cheap restaurants and cafés on the streets around the market. The middle level of the market, facing Jelačić Square, is home to a line of places with cheap food and indoor or outdoor seating.

Sandwich Bar Pingvin is a favorite for quick, cheap, tasty sandwiches. The photo menu—featuring sandwiches with chicken, turkey, steak, fish, even salmon—makes ordering easy. They'll wrap it all in a piece of grilled bread and top it with your choice of veggies and sauces (16–24 kn, open long hours daily, Teslina 7).

Mimice, a local institution and an old-habits-die-hard favorite of the older generation, serves up simple fish dishes (20–30 kn, order starches and sauces separately). Choose what you want from the limited menu, pay, and take your receipt to the next counter to claim your food. Then eat it standing or sitting on high stools (closed Sun, Jurišićeva 21). As Zagreb is a Catholic town, you'll have to wait in line if you're here on a Friday.

Vinodol is your white-tablecloth classy dinner spot, with a peaceful covered terrace and a smartly appointed dining room under an impressive vaulted ceiling (55–90-kn main dishes, daily 10:00–24:00, Teslina 10, tel. 01/481-1427).

Restaurant Jägerhorn shares a delightful garden courtyard with a serene waterfall. The menu includes game (60–90 kn) or simpler grilled dishes (45–90 kn; daily 10:00–22:30, at the end of a courtyard a block from Jelačić Square at Ilica 14, tel. 01/483-3877). They also rent 13 small, musty, overpriced rooms.

Ice Cream!: Zagreb's favorite *sladoled* (Italian gelato-style ice cream) is at **Millennium,** just a block from Jelačić Square. With giant mounds of the widest variety of flavors I've seen in Croatia, this is the city's best dessert stop (Mon–Sat 8:00–23:00, Sun 9:00–23:00, Bogovićeva 7, tel. 01/481-0850).

TRANSPORTATION CONNECTIONS

From Zagreb by Train to: Rijeka (3/day, 4 hrs), **Split** (3/day, 5.5 hrs, plus 1 direct night train, 8 hrs), **Ljubljana** (8/day, 2.5 hrs), **Vienna** (2/day, 6.5 hrs), **Budapest** (2/day, 5 or 7 hrs), **Lake Bled** (via Lesce-Bled, 5/day, 3.5 hrs).

By Bus to: Plitvice Lakes National Park (about hourly until 17:30, 2–2.5 hrs; then none until about 22:00), **Split** (about 2/hr, 5–9 hrs), **Dubrovnik** (2 in the early morning, sometimes 1–2 midday, then 4–6 overnight, 11–12.5 hrs), **Korčula** (1/night, 13.5 hrs).

Bus schedules can be sporadic (e.g., several departures clustered around the same time, then nothing for hours)—confirm carefully locally in person (schedules also online at www.akz.hr). Popular buses, such as the afternoon express to Split, can fill up quickly in peak season. Unfortunately, it's impossible to buy bus tickets anywhere in the center, so to guarantee a seat, you'd have to get to the station early (locals suggest even two hours in advance). Better yet, call the central number for the bus station to check schedules and reserve the bus you want: tel. 060-313-333 (from abroad, dial +385-1-611-2789). If you can't get an English speaker on the line, and the TI isn't too busy, they might be able to call for you.

PLITVICE LAKES NATIONAL PARK

(Nacionalni Park Plitvička Jezera)

Plitvice (PLEET-veet-seh) is one of Europe's most spectacular natural wonders. Imagine Niagara Falls diced and sprinkled over a heavily forested Grand Canyon. There's nothing like this lush valley of 16 terraced lakes, laced together by waterfalls and miles of pleasant plank walks. Countless cascades and water that's both strangely clear and full of vibrant colors make this park a misty natural wonderland. Years ago, after eight or nine visits, I thought I really knew Europe. Then I discovered Plitvice, and realized you can never exhaust Europe's surprises.

Planning Your Time

Plitvice deserves at least a few good hours. Since it takes some time to get here (two hours by car or bus from Zagreb), the most sensible plan is to spend the night in one of the park's hotels (no character, but comfortable and convenient) or a nearby private home (cheaper, but practical only if you're driving). If you're coming from the north (e.g., Ljubljana), head to Zagreb in the morning, spend a few hours seeing the Croatian capital, then take the bus (no buses 17:30–22:00) or drive to Plitvice in the late afternoon to spend the night at the park. Get up early and hit the trails (ideally by 8:30 or 9:00); by early afternoon, you'll be ready to move on (perhaps by bus to the coast, or back to Zagreb). Two nights and a full day at Plitvice is probably overkill for all but the most avid hikers.

Getting to Plitvice

Plitvice Lakes National Park, a few miles from the Bosnian border, is two hours by car south of Zagreb on National Road #1 (a.k.a. D-1).

By **car** from Zagreb, you'll take the expressway south for about an hour, exiting at Karlovac (marked for *1* and *Plitvice*). From here, D-1 takes you directly south about another hour to the park.

Buses leave from Zagreb's main bus station in the direction of Plitvice. Various bus companies handle the route; just go to the ticket window and ask for the next departure (about 70 kn, trip takes 2–2.5 hours). Buses run from Zagreb about hourly until 17:30, and then there are generally no departures until 22:00 (or sometimes later). With the opening of the new freeway connecting Zagreb and Split, some buses now bypass the park altogether, so confirm that your bus will actually stop at Plitvice. (The driver may be willing to take you to your specific hotel, or, worst-case scenario, he'll drop you at the official Plitvice bus stop, which is a 10-min walk beyond the hotels.) Confirm the schedule online (www.akz.hr) or at the Plitvice office in Zagreb (Mon–Fri 8:00–16:00, closed Sat–Sun, Trg Kralja Tomislava 19, tel. 01/461-3586).

By car or bus, you'll see some thought-provoking terrain between Zagreb and Plitvice. As you leave Karlovac, you'll pass through the village of **Turanj,** part of the war zone just a decade ago. The destroyed, derelict houses belonged to Serbs who have not come back to reclaim and repair them. Farther along, about 25 miles before Plitvice, you'll pass through the striking village of **Slunj,** picturesquely perched on travertine formations (like Plitvice's) and surrounded by sparkling streams and waterfalls. If you're in a car, this is worth a photo stop. This town, too, looks very different than it did before the war—when it was 30 percent Serb. As in countless other villages in the Croatian interior, the Orthodox church has been destroyed...and locals still seethe when they describe how occupying Serbs "defiled" the town's delicate beauty.

ORIENTATION

(area code: 053)

Plitvice's 16 lakes are divided into the Upper Lakes (Gornja Jezera) and the Lower Lakes (Donja Jezera). The park officially has two entrances *(ulaz),* each with ticket windows and snack and gift shops. Entrance 1 is at the bottom of the Lower Lakes, across the busy D-1 road from the park's best restaurant, Lička Kuća (see "Eating," page 717). Entrance 2 is about 1.5 miles south, at the cluster of Plitvice's three hotels (Jezero, Plitvice, and Bellevue; see "Sleeping," page 715). There is no town at Plitvice. The nearest

village, Mukinje, is a residential community mostly for park workers (boring for tourists, but has some good private room options).

Cost and Hours: The price to enter the park during peak
season (April–Oct) is a hefty 110 kn (70 kn Nov–March, ticket
good for entire stay, including park entry, boat, shuttle bus, and
parking). Park hours vary (generally from 7:00 in summer, 8:00
in spring and fall, and 9:00 in winter; closes at dusk). Night owls
should note that the park never "closes"; these hours are for the
ticket booths and the boat and shuttle bus system. You can just
stroll right into the park at any time, provided that you aren't using
the boat or bus. For fewer tour-group crowds, visit early or late in
the day.

Tourist Information

A handy map of the trails is on the back of your ticket, and big
maps are posted all over the park. The big 20-kn map is a good
investment; the various English-language guidebooks are generally poorly translated and not very helpful (both sold at entrances,
hotels, and shops throughout the park). The park has a good Web
site: www.np-plitvicka-jezera.hr.

Getting Around Plitvice

Of course, Plitvice is designed for hikers. But the park has a few
ways (included in entry cost) to help you connect the best parts.

By Shuttle Bus: Buses connect the hotels at Entrance 2 (stop
ST2, below Hotel Jezero) with the top of the Upper Lakes (stop
ST4) and roughly the bottom of the Lower Lakes (stop ST1, a
10-min walk from Entrance 1). Between Entrance 2 and the top
of the Upper Lakes is an intermediate stop (ST3, at Galovac
lake)—designed for tour groups, available to anyone, and offering
a convenient way to skip the less interesting top half of the Upper
Lakes. Buses start running early and continue until late afternoon
(frequency depends on demand—generally 3–4/hr; buses run from
March until the first snow—often Dec). Note that the park refers
to its buses as "trains," which confuses some visitors. Also note that
no local buses take you along the major road (D-1) that connects
the entrances. The only way to get between them without a car is
by shuttle bus (inside the park) or by foot (about a 40-min walk).

By Boat: Low-impact electric boats ply the waters of the
biggest lake, Kozjak, with three stops: below Hotel Jezero (stop
P1), the bottom of the Upper Lakes (P2), and at the far end of
Kozjak, at the top of the Lower Lakes (P3). From Hotel Jezero
to the Upper Lakes is a quick five-minute ride; the boat goes
back and forth continuously. From the Upper Lakes to the Lower
Lakes takes closer to 20 minutes, and the boat goes about twice
per hour—often at the top and bottom of every hour. (With up to

Plitvice Lakes National Park

N

UPPER LAKES

LOWER LAKES

CIGINOVAC
OKRUGLJAK
KOZJAK
GRADINSKO
GALOVAC
MILANOVAC
GAVANOVAC
KORANA RIVER
BIG WATERFALL
ŠUPLJARA CAVE
KALUĐEROVAC

ENTRY 1
TO ZAGREB

ENTRY 2
DRY ROAD

ST-1
ST-2
ST-3
ST-4

P-1
P-2
P-3

"GALOVAC" INTERMEDIATE STOP ST-3

Post

TO RIJEKA, SPLIT, MUKINJE & ④

DCH

½ MILE
1 KM

······ BOAT
━━━━ SHUTTLE BUS
─ ─ ─ MAIN TRAILS
╌╌╌╌ MINOR TRAILS

P-1, P-2, P-3 — BOAT STOPS

ST-1, ST-2, — TRAM STOPS
ST-3 & ST-4

① Hotel Jezero
② Hotel Plitvice
③ Hotel Bellevue & Restaurant Poljana
④ To Knežević Guest House
⑤ Lička Kuća Restaurant
⑥ Supermarket

The Science of Plitvice

Virtually every visitor to Plitvice eventually asks the same question: How did it happen? A geologist once explained to me that Plitvice is a "perfect storm" of unique geological, climatic, and biological features you'll rarely find elsewhere on earth.

Plitvice's magic ingredient is calcium carbonate ($CaCO_3$), a mineral deposit from the limestone. Calcium is the same thing that makes "hard water" hard. If you have hard water, you may get calcium deposits on your cold-water faucet. But these deposits build up only at the faucet, not inside the pipes. That's because when hard water is motionless (as it usually is in the pipes), it holds on to the calcium. But at the point where the water is subjected to pressure and movement—as it pours out of the faucet—it releases the calcium.

Plitvice works the same way. As water flows over the park's limestone formations, it dissolves the rock, and the water becomes supersaturated with calcium carbonate. When the water is still, it holds on to the mineral—which causes the beautiful deep-blue color of the pools. But when the water speeds up and spills over the edge of the lakes, it releases carbon dioxide gas. Without the support of the carbon dioxide, the water can't hold on to the calcium carbonate, so it gets deposited on the lake bed and at the edges of the lakes. Eventually, these deposits build up to form a rock called travertine (the same composition as the original limestone, but formed in a different way). The travertine coating becomes thicker, and barriers—and eventually dams and new waterfalls—are formed. The ongoing process means that Plitvice's landscape is always changing.

And why is the water so clear? For one thing, it comes directly from high-mountain runoff, giving it little opportunity to become polluted or muddy. Also, the calcium carbonate in the water both gives it more color and makes it highly basic, which prevents the growth of plant life (such as certain algae) that could cloud the water.

Wildlife found in the park includes deer, wolves, wildcats, lynx, wild boar, voles, otters, and more than 160 species of birds (including eagles, herons, owls, grouse, and storks). The lakes (and local menus) are full of trout. Perhaps most importantly, Plitvice is home to about 50 brown bears—a species now extremely endangered in Europe. You'll see bears, the park's mascot, plastered all over the tourist literature (and in the form of a scary representative in the lobby of Hotel Jezero).

10,000 people a day visiting the park, you might have to wait for a seat on this boat.) Unless the lake freezes (about every five years), the boat also runs in the off-season—though frequency drops to hourly, and it stops running earlier.

SIGHTS AND ACTIVITIES

Plitvice is a refreshing playground of 16 terraced lakes, separated by natural travertine dams and connected by countless waterfalls.

Over time, the water has simultaneously carved out, and, with the help of mineral deposits, built up this fluid landscape.

Plitvice became Croatia's first national park in 1949. On Easter Sunday in 1991, the first shots of Croatia's war with Yugoslavia were fired right here—in fact, the war's first casualty was a park policeman, Josip Jović. The Serbs occupied Plitvice until 1995, and most of the Croatians you'll meet here were evacuated and lived near the coastline as refugees. Today, the war is a fading memory, and the park is again a popular tourist destination, with 750,000 visitors each year (relatively few from the US).

Hiking the Lakes

Plitvice's system of trails and boardwalks makes it possible for visitors to get immersed in the park's beauty. (In some places, the path leads literally right up the middle of a waterfall.) The official park map and signage recommend a variety of hikes, but there's no need to adhere strictly to these suggestions; invest in the big 20-kn map and create your own route.

I like hiking uphill from the Lower Lakes to the Upper Lakes, which offers slightly better head-on views of the best scenery. (Even though this route has a gradual uphill slope, remember that if you go the other way—downhill—there's a steep climb back up at the end.) I've described a one-way hiking route (going uphill), divided between Upper and Lower. Walking briskly and with a few photo stops, figure on an hour for the Lower Lakes, an hour for the Upper Lakes, and a half-hour to connect them by boat. It's essential to get an early start (9:00 or even 8:30) to get in front of the hordes of international tour groups that descend on the trails each morning.

Start at the...

Lower Lakes (Donja Jezera)—The lower half of Plitvice's lakes are accessible from Entrance 1. If you start here, the route marked

G2 (intended for groups, but doable for anyone) leads you along the boardwalks to Kozjak, the big lake that connects the Lower and the Upper Lakes (see below).

From the entrance, you'll descend down a steep path with lots of switchbacks, as well as thrilling views over the canyon of the Lower Lakes. As you reach the lakes and begin to follow the boardwalks, you'll have great up-close views of the travertine formations that make up Plitvice's many waterfalls. See any trout? If you're tempted to throw in a line, don't. Fishing is strictly forbidden. (Besides, they're happy.)

Near the beginning of the Lower Lakes trails, an optional 10-minute detour (to the right) takes you down to the **Big Waterfall** (Veliki Slap). It's the biggest of Plitvice's waterfalls, where the Plitvica River plunges 250 feet over a cliff into the valley below. Depending on recent rainfall, the force of the Big Waterfall varies from a light mist to a thundering deluge.

After seeing the Big Waterfall, continue on the boardwalks. On the left, a smaller trail branches off towards **Šupljara Cave.** You can actually climb through this slippery cave all the way up to the trail overlooking the Lower Lakes (though it's not recommended). This unassuming cavern is a surprisingly big draw. In the 1960s, several German and Italian "Spaghetti Westerns" were filmed at Plitvice and in other parts of Croatia (which, to European eyes, has terrain similar to the American West). The most famous, *Der Schatz im Silbersee (The Treasure in Silver Lake)*, was filmed here at Plitvice, and the treasure was hidden in this cave. The movie— complete with *Deutsch*-speaking "Native Americans"—is still a favorite in Germany, and popular theme tours bring German tourists to movie locations here in Croatia. If you drive the roads near Plitvice, keep an eye out for strange, Native American–sounding names (like Winnetou)—fictional characters from these beloved stories of the Old West, by the German writer Karl May.

After Šupljara Cave, you'll stick to the east side of the lakes, then cross over one more time to the west, where you'll cut though a comparatively dull forest. You'll emerge at a pit-stop-perfect clearing with WCs, picnic tables, a souvenir shop, and a self-service restaurant. Here you can catch the shuttle boat across Lake Kozjak to the bottom of the Upper Lakes (see "Getting Around Plitvice," earlier in this chapter). While you're waiting for the next boat (usually every 30 min), visit the friendly old ladies in the kiosks selling wheels of cheese and a variety of strudel (10 kn per piece).

Lake Kozjak (Jezero Kozjak)—The park's biggest lake, Kozjak, connects the Lower and Upper Lakes. The 20-minute boat ride between Plitvice's two halves offers a great chance for a breather. You can hike between the lakes along the west side of Kozjak, but the scenery's not nearly as good as in the rest of the park.

Upper Lakes (Gornja Jezera)—Focus on the lower half of the Upper Lakes, where nearly all the exotic beauty is. From the boat dock, signs for *C* and *G2* direct you up to Gradinsko Lake through the most striking scenery in the whole park. Enjoy the stroll, take your time, and be thankful if you have an extra-large memory card for your digital camera.

After Gradinsko Lake, when you reach the top of Galovac Lake, you'll have three options:

1. Make your hike a loop by continuing around the lake (following *H* and *G1* signs back to the P2 boat dock), then take the boat back over to the hotels (P1 stop).

2. Hike a few steps up to the ST3 bus stop to catch the shuttle bus back to the hotel (more efficient, but doesn't give you a second look at the lakes).

3. Continue hiking up to the top of the Upper Lakes; you'll get away from the crowds and feel like you've covered the park thoroughly. From here on up, the scenery is less stunning, and the waterfalls are fewer and farther between. At the top, you'll finish at shuttle bus stop ST4 (with food stalls and a WC), where the bus zips you back to Entrance 2.

Nice work!

SLEEPING

At the Park

The most convenient way to sleep at Plitvice is to stay at the park's lodges. Book any of these hotels through the same office (reservation tel. 053/751-015, fax 053/751-013, www.np-plitvicka-jezera .hr, info@np-plitvicka-jezera.hr; reception numbers for each hotel listed below). Because of high volume in peak season, the hotels often don't return e-mails; it's better to call or fax for a reservation—they speak English.

$$$ Hotel Jezero is big and modern, with all the comfort—and charm—of a Holiday Inn. It's well-located right at the park entrance, and offers 200 rooms that feel newish, but generally have at least one thing that's broken. Rooms facing the park have big glass doors and balconies (July–Aug: Sb-€83, Db-€118; May–June and Sept–Oct: Sb-€76, Db-€108; Nov–April: Sb-€61, Db-€86, elevator, reception tel. 053/751-500).

$$ Hotel Plitvice, a better value than Jezero, offers 50 rooms and mod, wide-open public spaces on two floors with no elevators. For rooms, choose from economy (fine, older-feeling; July–Aug: Sb-€72, Db-€96; May–June and Sept–Oct: Sb-€65, Db-€82; Nov–April: Sb-€50, Db-€70), standard (just a teeny bit bigger; July–Aug: Sb-€77, Db-€106; May–June and Sept–Oct: Sb-€70, Db-€96; Nov–April: Sb-€55, Db-€74), or superior (bigger still,

Sleep Code

(€1 = about $1.20, country code: 385, area code: 053)
English is spoken, credit cards are accepted, and breakfast is included at each place. The tourist tax (€1 per person, per day) is not included in these prices.

To help you sort easily through these listings, I've divided the rooms into three categories based on the price for a standard double room with bath in peak season:

$$$ Higher Priced—Most rooms €100 or more.
  $$ Moderately Priced—Most rooms between €50–100.
    $ Lower Priced—Most rooms €50 or less.

with a sitting area; July–Aug: Sb-€82, Db-€116; May–June and Sept–Oct: Sb-€75, Db-€106; Nov–April: Sb-€60, Db-€84, reception tel. 053/751-100).

$$ Hotel Bellevue is simple and bare-bones (no TVs or elevator). It has an older feel to it, but the price is right and the 80 rooms are perfectly acceptable (July–Aug: Sb-€55, Db-€74; May–June and Sept–Oct: Sb-€50, Db-€68; Nov–April: Sb-€40, Db-€54, reception tel. 053/751-700).

Near the Park

While the park's lodges are the easiest choice for non-drivers, those with a car should consider these cheaper alternatives.

$ Kneževic Guest House, with 11 bright, modern rooms, is a new family-run hotel a five-minute drive south of the park in the nondescript workers' town of Mukinje. The street is modern and dull, but the yard is peaceful, with an inviting hammock (Db-€35, breakfast-€5, family rooms; driving south from the park, take first right turn into Mukinje and you'll see #57; tel. 053/774-081, mobile 098-168-7576, www.knezevic.hr, guest_house@vodatel.net, daughter Kristina speaks English).

$ Sobe: Drivers looking for character and preferring to spend €40, rather than €80, should simply find a room in a private home, advertised with *sobe* signs for miles on either side of the park. For details, see "Dalmatian Accommodation," page 608.

EATING

The park runs all of the restaurants at Plitvice. These places are handy, and the food is tasty and affordable. If you're staying at the hotels, you have the option of paying for half-board with your room (lunch or dinner, €12 each). This option is designed for the restaurants inside hotels Jezero and Plitvice, but you can also use the voucher at other park eateries (you'll pay the difference if the bill is more). The half-board option is worth doing if you're here for dinner, but don't lock yourself in for lunch—you'll want more flexibility as you explore Plitvice (excellent picnic spots and decent food stands abound inside the park).

Hotel Jezero and **Hotel Plitvice** both have big restaurants with good food and friendly, professional service (half-board for dinner, described above, is a good deal; or order à la carte: fish and meat dishes 60–100 kn; both open daily until 23:00).

Lička Kuća, across the pedestrian overpass from Entrance 1, has a wonderfully dark and smoky atmosphere around a huge open-air wood-fired grill (grilled trout-50 kn, more elaborate dishes up to 100 kn, daily 11:00–24:00, tel. 053/751-024).

Restaurant Poljana, behind Hotel Bellevue, has the same boring, park-lodge atmosphere in both of its sections: cheap, self-service cafeteria (25–40 kn) and sit-down restaurant with open wood-fired grill (same choices and prices as the better-atmosphere Lička Kuća, above; both parts open daily but closed in winter, tel. 053/751-092).

For **picnic** fixings, there's a small supermarket at Entrance 2, and another one with a larger selection across road D-1 (use the pedestrian overpass). The boat docks come with a few eating options. At the P3 boat dock, locals sell homemade goodies, and at the P1 boat dock, you can buy grilled meat and drinks.

TRANSPORTATION CONNECTIONS

To reach the park, see "Getting to Plitvice," earlier in this chapter. Moving on from Plitvice is trickier. Buses pass by the park in each direction—northbound (to **Zagreb,** 2–2.5 hrs) and southbound (to coastal destinations such as **Split,** 4–6 hrs, and **Dubrovnik,** 9–10 hrs).

There is no bus station—just a low-profile *Plitvice Centar* bus stop shelter. To reach it from the park, go out to the main road from either Hotel Jezero or Hotel Plitvice, then turn right; the bus stops are just after the pedestrian overpass. The one on the hotel side of the road is for buses headed for the coast; the stop on the opposite side is for Zagreb. But here's the catch: Many buses that pass through Plitvice don't stop (either because they're full, or because they don't have anyone to drop off there). You can stand at the bus stop and try to flag one down, but it's safer to get help from the park's hotel staff. They can help you figure out which bus suits your schedule, then they'll call ahead to be sure the bus stops for you. If you don't want to make the 10-minute walk out to the bus stop, someone at the hotel can usually drive you out for a modest fee.

AUSTRIA

AUSTRIA

(Österreich)

Most people wouldn't consider Austria "Eastern Europe." The country barely slipped out of communism's clutches in 1955, when it became an independent country with the Soviet Union's blessing...provided it remained neutral (it never joined NATO).

Cold War blinders have forced us to separate the communist East from the capitalist West. But consider this part of Europe in the days before Hitler. A hundred years ago, Austria was the head of an enormous empire that encompassed virtually every destination in this book. In the big picture, no other city had more of a cultural and political impact in Eastern Europe than Vienna. In fact, the German name for Austria—Österreich—literally means "the Kingdom of the East."

From a practical standpoint, Vienna serves as a prime "gateway" city. The location is central and convenient for most major Eastern European destinations. Actually farther east than Prague, Ljubljana, and Zagreb, and just upstream on the Danube from Budapest and Bratislava, Vienna is an ideal launchpad for a journey into the East.

In its 18th- and 19th-century glory days, the Austrian Empire (a.k.a. the Austro-Hungarian Empire, a.k.a. the Hapsburg Empire)

Key German Phrases

English	German	Pronounced*
Hello.	*Guten Tag.*	GOO-tehn tahg
Do you speak English?	*Sprechen Sie Englisch?*	SHPREHKH-ehn zee ENG-lish
yes / no	*ja / nein*	yah / nīn
Please. / You're welcome. / Can I help you?	*Bitte.*	BIT-teh
Thank you.	*Danke.*	DAHNG-keh
I'm sorry.	*Es tut mir leid.*	ehs toot meer līd
Excuse me. (to pass or to get attention)	*Entschuldigung.*	ehnt-SHOOL-dig-oong
Good.	*Gut.*	goot
Goodbye.	*Auf Wiedersehen.*	owf VEE-der-zayn
one / two	*eins / zwei*	īns / tsvī
three / four	*drei / vier*	drī / feer
five / six	*fünf / sechs*	fewnf / zehks
seven / eight	*sieben / acht*	ZEE-behn / ahkht
nine / ten	*neun / zehn*	noyn / tsayn
hundred	*hundert*	HOON-dert
thousand	*tausend*	TOW-sehnd
How much?	*Wie viel?*	vee feel
local currency	*euro (€)*	OY-roh
Where is...?	*Wo ist...?*	voh ist
...the toilet	*...die Toilette*	dee toy-LEH-teh
men	*Herren*	HEHR-ehn
women	*Damen*	DAH-mehn
water / coffee	*Wasser / Kaffee*	VAH-ser / kah-FAY
beer / wine	*Bier / Wein*	beer / vīn
Cheers!	*Prost!*	prohst
the bill	*die Rechnung*	dee REHKH-noong

*When using the phonetics, pronounce ī as the long i sound in "light."

was arguably the most powerful European entity since Rome. The Hapsburg family built this giant kingdom of more than 60 million people by making love, not war—having lots of children and marrying them into the other royal houses of Europe.

Today, this small, landlocked country (with just 8 million people) does more to cling to its elegant past than any other nation in Europe. The waltz is still the rage. Austrians are very sociable; it's important to greet people in the breakfast room and those you pass on the streets or meet in shops. The Austrian version of "Hi" is a cheerful *"Grüss Gott"* ("May God greet you"). You'll get the correct pronunciation after the first volley—listen and copy.

While they speak German and talked about unity with Germany long before Hitler ever said *Anschluss,* the Austrians cherish their distinct cultural and historical traditions. They are not Germans. Austria is mellow and relaxed compared to Deutschland—but stiff and formal compared to most Eastern Europeans (except maybe the Hungarians). *Gemütlichkeit* is the local word for this special Austrian cozy-and-easy approach to life. It's good living—whether engulfed in mountain beauty or bathed in lavish high culture. The people stroll as if every day were Sunday, topping things off with a cheerful visit to a coffee or pastry shop.

It must be nice to be past your prime—no longer troubled by being powerful, able to kick back and celebrate life in the clean, untroubled mountain air. While the Austrians make more money than their Eastern European neighbors, they enjoy a short workweek and a long life span. And compared to much of Eastern Europe, which only recently joined the European Union, Austria is a long-established EU member that adopted the euro as its currency years ago.

Austrians eat on about the same schedule we do. Treats include Wiener schnitzel (breaded veal cutlet), *Knödel* (dumplings), *Apfelstrudel,* and fancy desserts like the *Sachertorte,* Vienna's famous chocolate cake.

In Austria, all cars must have a **Vignette** toll sticker stuck to the inside of their windshield to legally drive on the freeways. These are sold at all border crossings (24 hours a day), big gas stations near borders, and car-rental agencies. Stickers cost €8 for 10 days (€22 for 2 months). Not having one earns you a stiff fine.

VIENNA

(Wien)

Vienna is a head without a body. For 640 years the capital of the once-grand Hapsburg Empire, she started and lost World War I, and with it her far-flung holdings. Today, you'll find a grand and elegant capital of 1.6 million people (one-fifth of Austria's population) ruling a small, relatively insignificant country. Culturally, historically, and from a sightseeing point of view, this city is the sum of its illustrious past. The city of Freud, Brahms, Maria Theresa's many children, a gaggle of Strausses, and a dynasty of Holy Roman Emperors ranks right up there with Paris, London, and Rome.

Vienna has always been the easternmost city of the West. In Roman times, it was Vindobona, on the Danube facing the Germanic barbarians. In the Middle Ages, Vienna was Europe's bastion against the Ottomans—a Christian breakwater against the riding tide of Islam (hordes of up to 200,000 Ottomans were repelled in 1529 and 1683). During this period, as the Ottomans dreamed of conquering what they called "the big apple" for their sultan, Vienna lived with a constant fear of invasion (and the Hapsburg court ruled from safer Prague). You'll notice none of Vienna's great palaces were built until after 1683, when the Ottoman threat was finally over.

While Vienna's old walls held out the Ottomans, World War II bombs destroyed nearly a quarter of the city's buildings. In modern times, neutral Austria took a big bite out of the USSR's Warsaw Pact buffer zone. And today, Vienna is a springboard for newly popular destinations in Eastern Europe.

The truly Viennese person is not Austrian, but a second-generation Hapsburg cocktail, with grandparents from the distant

Greater Vienna

corners of the old empire—Hungary, the Czech Republic, Slovakia, Poland, Slovenia, Croatia, Bosnia-Herzegovina, Serbia, Romania, and Italy. Vienna is the melting-pot capital of a now-collapsed empire that, in its heyday, consisted of 60 million people—only eight million of whom were Austrian.

In 1900, Vienna's 2.2 million inhabitants made it the world's fifth-largest city (after New York, London, Paris, and Berlin). But these days—with dogs being the preferred "child" and the average Viennese mother having only 1.3 children—the population is down to around 1.6 million.

The Hapsburgs, who ruled the enormous Austrian Empire from 1273 to 1918, shaped Vienna. Some ad agency has convinced Vienna to make Elisabeth, wife of Emperor Franz Josef—with her narcissism and struggles with royal life—the darling of the local tourist scene. You'll see "Sisi" (SEE-see) all over town. But stay focused on the Hapsburgs who mattered: Maria Theresa (r. 1740–1780, see page 760) and Franz Josef (r. 1848–1916, see page 751).

After Napoleon's defeat and the Congress of Vienna in 1815 (which shaped 19th-century Europe), Vienna enjoyed its violin-filled belle époque, which shaped our romantic image of the city: fine wine, chocolates, cafés, and waltzes.

Planning Your Time

For a big city, Vienna is pleasant and laid-back. Packed with sights, it's worth two days and two nights on the speediest trip. To be grand-tour efficient, you could sleep in and sleep out on the train (Berlin, Kraków, Venice, Rome, the Swiss Alps, Paris, and the Rhine Valley are each handy night trains away). With two days in Vienna, spend them this way:

Day 1: 9:00–Circle the Ring by tram, following my self-guided tour (page 731); 10:00–Drop by the TI for any planning and ticket needs, then see the sights in Vienna's old center (using my self-guided commentary)—Monument Against War and Fascism, Kaisergruft crypt, Kärntner Strasse, St. Stephen's Cathedral, and Graben; 12:00–Finger sandwiches for lunch at Buffet Trzesniewski; 13:00–Tour the Hofburg and treasury; 16:00–Hit one more museum, or shop, browse, and people-watch; 19:30–Choose classical music (concert or opera), Haus der Musik, or *Heuriger* wine garden.

Day 2: Morning—choose between Schönbrunn Palace (redundant if you saw the Hofburg on Day 1; arrive at 9:00, return to central Vienna by noon) or the Lipizzaner stallions' morning practice (Tue–Sat 10:00–12:00, no practice Sun–Mon); 12:00–Have lunch at Naschmarkt; 13:00–Tour the Opera (check red sign on door for today's schedule); 14:00–Kunsthistorisches Museum; 16:00–Your choice of the many sights left to see in Vienna; Evening–See Day 1 evening options.

Sightseeing After Dark: Several of Vienna's sights are open late one or more evenings a week: Kunsthistorisches Museum (Thu until 21:00), Haus der Musik (nightly until 22:00), Albertina Museum (Wed until 21:00), Secession (Thu until 20:00), Museum of Applied Art (MAK, Tue until 24:00), and Mozart Haus Museum (nightly until 20:00).

Picking a Palace: The Hofburg and Schönbrunn are both world-class palaces, but seeing both is redundant—with limited time or money, I'd choose just one. The Hofburg comes with the popular new Sisi Museum and is right in the town center, making for an easy visit. With more time, a visit to Schönbrunn, set outside town amid a grand and regal garden, is also a great experience. For efficient sightseeing, drivers should note that Schönbrunn Palace is conveniently on the way out of town toward Salzburg.

ORIENTATION

(area code: 01)
Vienna—Wien in German (pronounced "veen")—sits between the Vienna Woods (Wienerwald) and the Danube (Donau). To the southeast is industrial sprawl. The Alps, which arc across Europe from Marseille, end at Vienna's wooded hills, providing a popular playground for walking and sipping new wine. This greenery's momentum carries on into the city. More than half of Vienna is parkland, filled with ponds, gardens, trees, and statue-maker memories of Austria's glory days.

Think of the city map as a target. The bull's-eye is St. Stephen's Cathedral, the first circle is the Ringstrasse, and the second is the Gürtel outerbelt. The old town—snuggling around towering cathedral south of the Danube—is bound tightly by the Ringstrasse, marking what used to be the city wall. The Gürtel, a broader ring road, contains the rest of downtown.

Addresses start with the district, or *Bezirk,* followed by street and building number. The Ring circles the first *Bezirk.* Any address higher than the ninth *Bezirk* is beyond the Gürtel, far from the center. The middle two digits of Vienna's postal codes show the *Bezirk.* The address "7, Lindengasse 4" is in the seventh district, #4 on Linden street. Its postal code would be 1070.

Nearly all your sightseeing will be done in the core first district or along the Ringstrasse. As a tourist, concern yourself only with this compact old center. When you do, sprawling Vienna suddenly becomes manageable.

Tourist Information

Vienna's one real tourist office is a block behind the Opera at Albertinaplatz (daily 9:00–19:00, tel. 01/24555, press 2 for English info, www.vienna.info). Confirm your sightseeing plans and pick up the free and essential city map with a list of museums and hours (also available at most hotels), the monthly program of concerts (called *Wien-Programm*—details below), the biannual city guide *(Vienna Journal)*, and the youth guide *(Vienna Hype)*. The TI also books rooms for a €2.90 fee. While hotel and ticket-booking agencies at the train stations and airport can answer questions and give out maps and brochures, I'd rely on the official TI if possible.

The ***Wien-Programm*** monthly entertainment guide is particularly important in Europe's music capital. It includes a daily calendar and information on the contemporary cultural scene, including live music, jazz, walks, expositions, and evening museum options.

First you see the month's events, then guided walks offered (*E* means in English), then the opera schedule, followed by other theaters and concert halls (with phone numbers to call direct to check seat availability, and to save the 20 percent booking fees you'll pay for buying tickets through an agency). Last is the calendar section (with codes for venues that are all listed, with their phone numbers, on the first page of the section).

Consider the TI's handy €3.60 *Vienna from A to Z* booklet. Every important building sports a numbered flag banner that keys into this guidebook. *A to Z* numbers are keyed into the TI's city map. When lost, find one of the "famous-building flags" and match its number to your map. If you're at a famous building, check the map to see what other key numbers are nearby, then check the *A to Z* book description to see if you want to go in. This system is especially helpful for those just wandering aimlessly among Vienna's historic charms.

The much-promoted €17 **Vienna Card** might save the busy sightseer a few euros. It gives you a 72-hour transit pass (worth €12) and discounts of 10 to 50 percent at the city's museums. For most, this is not worth the mental overhead. (Seniors and students will do better with their own discounts.)

Arrival in Vienna

By Train at the South Station (Südbahnhof): Those arriving from most of Eastern Europe (including the Czech Republic, Poland, Slovenia, Croatia, and some Budapest trains) will most likely land here. The Südbahnhof has all the services, including left luggage and a TI (daily 9:00–19:00). To reach Vienna's center, tram D goes to the Ring (departs every 5 minutes, stops right at the Opera). Bus #13A goes to Mariahilfer Strasse. (You can also take the S- or U-Bahn, but the tram or bus is much easier.)

By Train at the West Station (Westbahnhof): Trains arriving from Western Europe (such as Munich and Salzburg), and some trains from Budapest, land at the Westbahnhof. The *Reisebüro am Bahnhof* books hotels (for a €5 fee), has maps, answers questions, and has a train info desk (daily 7:30–21:00). The Westbahnhof also has a grocery store (daily 5:30–23:00), ATMs, Internet access (including a modern Speednet at the Starbucks-like coffee shop), change offices, and storage facilities. Airport buses and taxis wait in front of the station.

To get to the city center (and most likely, your hotel), take the U-Bahn on the U-3 line (buy your ticket or transit pass—described under "Getting Around Vienna"—from a *Tabak* shop in the station or from a machine). *U-3* signs lead down to the tracks (direction Simmering for Mariahilfer Strasse hotels or the center). If your hotel is along Mariahilfer Strasse, your stop is on this line (see page

795). If you're sleeping in the center or just sightseeing, ride five stops to Stephansplatz, escalate in the exit direction Stephansplatz, and you'll hit the cathedral. From the cathedral, the TI is a five-minute stroll down the busy Kärntner Strasse pedestrian street.

By Plane: Vienna International Airport is 12 miles from the center (airport code: VIE, tel. 01/700-722-233, www.viennaairport.com). It's connected to the very central Wien-Mitte station by S-Bahn (S-7 yellow, €3, 2/hr, 24 min) and the newer City Airport Train (CAT, follow green signs, €9, 2/hr, usually departs at :05 and :35, 16 min, www.cityairporttrain.com). Express airport buses (parked immediately in front of the arrival hall, €6, 2/hr, 30 min, buy ticket from driver, note time to destination on curbside TV monitors) go conveniently to Schwedenplatz (for city-center hotels), Westbahnhof (for Mariahilfer Strasse hotels), and Südbahnhof, where it's easy to continue by taxi or public transportation (see above). Taxis into town cost about €35 (including the €11 airport surcharge); taxis also wait at the downtown terminus of each airport transit service. Hotels arrange for fixed-rate car service to the airport (€30, 30-min ride).

Some budget carriers—especially SkyEurope—fly into nearby **Bratislava Airport.** For details, see page 179.

Helpful Hints

Money: ATMs are everywhere. Banks are open weekdays roughly from 8:00 to 15:00 (until 17:30 on Thu). After hours, you can change money at train stations, the airport, post offices, or the American Express office (Mon–Fri 9:00–17:30, Sat 9:00–12:00, closed Sun, Kärntner Strasse 21-23, tel. 01/5124-0040).

Internet Access: The TI has a list of Internet cafés. **BigNet** is the dominant outfit (www.bignet.at), with lots of stations at Kärntner Strasse 61 (daily 10:00–24:00) and Hoher Markt 8–9 (daily 10:00–24:00). **Surfland Internet Café** is near the Opera (daily 10:00–23:00, Krugerstrasse 10, tel. 01/512-7701).

Post Offices: Choose from the main post office (Postgasse in center, daily 8:00–20:00, handy metered phones), Westbahnhof (Mon–Fri 7:00–22:00, Sat–Sun 9:00–20:00), Südbahnhof (daily 7:00–22:00), near the Opera (Mon–Fri 7:00–19:00, closed Sat–Sun, Krugerstrasse 13), and many other locations scattered around town.

English Bookstores: Consider the **British Bookshop** (Mon–Fri 9:30–19:30, Sat 9:30–18:00, closed Sun, at corner of Weihburggasse and Seilerstätte, tel. 01/512-1945; same hours at branch at Mariahilfer Strasse 4, tel. 01/522-6730) or **Shakespeare & Co.** (Mon–Sat 9:00–19:00, closed Sun, north of Hoher Markt square, Sterngasse 2, tel. 01/535-5053).

Keeping Up with the News: Don't buy newspapers. Read them for free in Vienna's marvelous coffeehouses. It's much classier.

Travel Agency: Intropa is convenient, with good service for flights and train tickets (Mon–Fri 9:00–18:00, Sat 10:00–13:00, closed Sun, couples pay only one booking fee with this book in 2007, Neuer Markt 8, tel. 01/513-4000). Train tickets come with a €7 service charge when purchased from an agency rather than at the station—but, for many, the convenience is worth it.

Getting Around Vienna

By Public Transportation: Take full advantage of Vienna's simple, cheap, and super-efficient transit system, which includes trams, buses, subway (U-Bahn), and faster suburban trains (S-Bahn). I use the tram mostly to zip around the Ring (tram #1 or #2) and take the U-Bahn to outlying sights or hotels. Numbered lines (such as #38) are trams, and numbers followed by an *A* (such as #38A) are buses. The smooth, modern trams are Porsche-designed, with "backpack technology" locating the engines and mechanical hardware on the roofs for a lower ride and easier entry. Lines that begin with U (e.g., U-3) are U-Bahn lines (directions are designated by the end-of-the-line stops). Blue lines are the speedier S-Bahns. Take a moment to study the eye-friendly city-center map on station walls to internalize how the transit system can help you. The free tourist map has essentially all the lines marked, making the too-big €1.50 transit map unnecessary (information tel. 01/790-9105).

Trams, buses, the U-Bahn, and the S-Bahn all use the same tickets. Buy your tickets from *Tabak* shops, station machines, *Vorverkauf* offices in the station, or on board (just on trams, single tickets only, more expensive). You have lots of choices:

- Single tickets (€1.50, €2 if bought on tram, good for one journey with necessary transfers);
- 24-hour transit pass (€5);
- 72-hour transit pass (€12);
- 7-day transit pass (*Wochenkarte,* €12.50, pass always starts on Mon); or
- 8-day card *(Acht Tage Karte)*, covering eight full days of free transportation for €24 (can be shared—for example, 4 people for 2 days each). With a per-person cost of €3/day (compared to €5/day for a 24-hour pass), this can be a real saver for groups. Kids under 15 travel free on Sundays and holidays.

Stamp a time on your ticket as you enter the Metro system, tram, or bus (stamp it only the first time for a multiple-use pass). Cheaters pay a stiff €50 fine if caught—and then they make you buy a ticket. Rookies miss stops because they fail to open the door. Push buttons, pull latches—do whatever it takes. Study the excellent wall-mounted street map before you exit the U-Bahn station. Choosing the right exit—signposted from the moment you step off the train—saves lots of walking.

Cute little electric buses wind through the tangled old center (bus #1A is best for a joy ride—hop on and see where it takes you).

By Taxi: Vienna's comfortable, civilized, and easy-to-flag-down taxis start at €2.50. You'll pay about €8 to go from the Opera to the Westbahnhof. Pay only what's on the meter—any surcharges (other than the €2 fee added to fares when you telephone them, or €10 for the airport) are just crude cabbie rip-offs.

By Car with Driver: Consider the luxury of having your own car and driver. Johann (a.k.a. John) Lichtl is a kind, honest, English-speaking cabbie who can take up to four passengers in his car (€25/1 hr, €20/hr for 2 or more hours, mobile 0676-670-6750). Consider hiring gentle Johann for a day trip to the Wachau Valley (up the Danube from Vienna, €110, up to 8 hrs), or to drive you to Salzburg with Wachau sightseeing en route (€300, up to 14 hrs; other trips by negotiation). These special prices are valid with this book in 2007.

By Bike: Vienna is a great city for biking—*if* you own a bike. The bike path along the Ring is wonderfully entertaining. But bike rental is a hassle (get list at TI). Your best biking is likely up and down the traffic-free and people-filled Danube Island. Shops at two bridges—Floridsdörferbrücke (€3.60/hr, €18/day, near tram #31 stop, tel. 01/278-8698) and Reichsbrücke (tel. 01/263-5242)—each rent from about 9:30 until dusk, weather permitting, March through October. American Rick Watts runs Pedal Power, and will deliver your bike to your hotel and pick it up when you're done (€32/day including delivery, Ausstellungsstrasse 3, tel. 01/729-7234, www.pedalpower.at). There are no bike-rental options in the center, except for...

Citybikewien: The bikes you'll see parked in public racks all over town are part of a clever system that works fine for locals and technically works for tourists (but the complexity of the credit-card forms befuddled me). The bikes lock in their stalls (50 of which are scattered through the city center) and are released when you insert your credit card and log on. Figure it out, and you have a bike for €2 per hour (first hour free, fliers explain the process in English, www.citybikewien.at).

By Buggy: Rich romantics get around by traditional horse and buggy. These buggies, called *Fiakers*, clip-clop visitors on tours lasting 20 minutes (€40—old town), 40 minutes (€65—old town and the Ring), or one hour (€95—all of the above, but more thorough). You can share the ride and cost with up to five people. Because it's a kind of guided tour, before settling on a carriage, talk to a few drivers and pick one who's fun and speaks English.

TOURS

Walking Tours—The TI's *Walks in Vienna* brochure describes Vienna's many guided walks. The basic 90-minute "Vienna First Glance" introductory walk is offered daily throughout the summer (€12, leaves at 14:00 from near the Opera, in English and German, tel. 01/894-5363, www.wienguide.at). Various specialized tours go once a week and are listed on their Web site.

Hop-On, Hop-Off Bus Tours—Vienna Sightseeing operates hop-on, hop-off tours (departures from Opera at top of each hour 10:00–17:00, recorded commentary). The schedule is posted curbside (three different routes, €13 for one, €16 for two). You could pay much more for 24 hours of hop-on and -off privileges, but given the city's excellent public transportation and this outfit's meager one-bus-per-hour frequency, I'd take this not to hop on and off, but only to get the narrated orientation drive through town.

City Bus Tour—Vienna Sightseeing offers a basic three-hour city tour including a tour of Schönbrunn Palace (€35; daily at 10:30 from the Opera, live guide speaks German and English). While they advertise several departures daily "starting from the Opera House," only the 10:30 tour really starts at the Opera (others shuttle you through various pick-ups to start elsewhere 30 minutes later; call 01/7124-6830 to reserve or get info on their many other tours).

Local Guides—The tourist board Web site (www.vienna.info) has a long list of local guides with their specialties and contact information. Lisa Zeiler is an excellent English-speaking guide (two-hour walks for €130—if she's booked up, she can set you up with another guide, tel. 01/402-3688, lisa.zeiler@gmx.at). Ursula Klaus, an art scholar specializing in turn-of-the-century Vienna, music, art, and architecture, also offers two-hour tours for €130 (tel. 01/522-8556, mobile 0676-421-4884, ursula.klaus@aon.at). Lisa and Ursula are both top-notch, bring art museums to life masterfully, and can tailor tours to your interests.

SELF-GUIDED TRAM TOUR

Around the Ringstrasse

In the 1860s, Emperor Franz Josef had the city's ingrown medieval wall torn down and replaced with a grand boulevard 190 feet wide. The road, arcing nearly three miles around the city's core, predates all the buildings that line it—so what you'll see is very "neo": Neoclassical, Neo-Gothic, and Neo-Renaissance. On Europe's great streets, the Ringstrasse is lined with man city's top sights. Trams #1 and #2 and a great bike pa whole route—and so should you.

Vienna

This self-guided tram tour, rated ▲▲, gives you a fun orientation and a ridiculously quick glimpse of the major sights as you glide by (€1.50, €2 if bought on tram, 30-min circular tour). Tram #1 goes clockwise; tram #2, counterclockwise. Most sights are on the outside... se tram #2 (sit on the ... the front seat of the ... mmediately across ... e Opera. You can ... n and off as you go ... min). Read ahead ... ese sights can fly

🔾 Immediately on the left: The city's main pedestrian drag, Kärntner Strasse, leads to the zigzag-mosaic roof of **St. Stephen's Cathedral.** This tram tour makes a 360-degree circle around the cathedral, staying about this same distance from it.

🔾 At first bend (before first stop): Look right, toward the tall fountain and the guy on a horse. Schwarzenberg Platz shows off its **equestrian statue** of Prince Charles Schwarzenberg, who fought Napoleon. Behind that is the Russian monument (behind the fountain with the Soviet soldier holding a flag), which was built in 1945 as a forced thanks to the Soviets for liberating Austria from the Nazis. Formerly a sore point, now it's just ignored. Beyond that (out of sight, on tram D route) is Belvedere Palace (see page 777).

🔾 Going down Schubertring, you reach the huge **Stadtpark** (City Park) on the right, which honors many great Viennese musicians and composers with statues. At the beginning of the park, the gold-and-cream concert hall behind the trees is the **Kursalon,** opened in 1867 by the Strauss brothers, who directed many waltzes here. The touristy Strauss concerts are held in this building (see "Music Scene," page 784). If you'd like, hop off here for a stroll in the park.

🔾 Immediately after next stop, look right: In the same park, the gilded statue of "Waltz King" **Johann Strauss** holds a violin as he did when he conducted his orchestra, whipping his fans into a three-quarter-time frenzy.

🔾 Just after the next stop, at end of park: On the left, a green statue of **Dr. Karl Lueger** honors the popular man who was mayor of Vienna until 1910. Coming up, on the right, the big red-brick building is the **Museum of Applied Art** (MAK, showing furniture and design through the ages; described on page 781).

🔾 At next bend: On the right, the quaint white building with military helmets decorating the windows was the **Austrian Ministry of War**—back when that was a big operation. Field Marshal Radetzky, a military big shot in the 19th century under Franz Josef, still sits on his high horse. He's pointing toward the post office, the only Art Nouveau building facing the Ring.

The architecture along the Ring is known as **"historicism"** because it's all Neo-this and Neo-that—generally fitting the purpose of the particular building. For example, farther along the Ring, we'll see a Neoclassical parliament building—celebrating ancient Greek notions of democracy; the Neo-Gothic City Hall—recalling when medieval burghers ran the city government in Gothic days; Neo-Renaissance museums—celebrating learning; and the Neo-Baroque National Theater—recalling the age when opera and theater flourished.

🔾 At next corner: The white-domed building over your right shoulder as you turn is the Urania, Franz Josef's 1910 **observatory.**

Lean forward and look behind it for a peek at the huge red cars of the giant 100-year-old Ferris wheel in Vienna's Prater Park (fun for families, described on page 783).

❏ Now you're rolling along the **Danube Canal.** This "Baby Danube" is one of the many small arms of the river that once made up the Danube at this location. The rest have been gathered together in a mightier modern-day Danube, farther away. This neighborhood was thoroughly bombed in World War II. The buildings across the canal are typical of postwar architecture (1960s). They were built on the cheap, and are now being replaced by sleek, futuristic buildings. On your left was the site of the original Roman town, Vindobona.

In three long blocks, on the left (opposite the BP station, be ready—it passes fast), you'll see the ivy-covered walls and round Romanesque arches of St. Ruprecht's, the oldest church in Vienna (built in the 11th century on a bit of Roman ruins). Remember, medieval Vienna was defined by that long-gone wall that you're tracing on this tour. Across the river is an OPEC headquarters, where oil ministers often meet to set prices. Relax for a few stops (or marvel at the public-transit infrastructure Vienna enjoys) until the corner.

❏ Leaving the canal, turning left up Schottenring, at first corner: A block down on the right, you can see a huge red-brick **castle**—actually high-profile barracks built here at the command of a nervous Emperor Franz Josef (who found himself on the throne as an 18-year-old in 1848, the same year people's revolts against autocracy were sweeping across Europe).

❏ At next stop: On the left, the orange-and-white, Neo-Renaissance temple of money—the **Börse**—is Vienna's stock exchange.

❏ Next stop, at corner: The huge, frilly, Neo-Gothic church on the right is a **"votive church,"** built to thank God when an 1853 assassination attempt on Emperor Franz Josef failed. Ahead on the right (in front of tram stop) is the **Vienna University** building (established in 1365, it has no real campus as the buildings are scattered around town). It faces (on the left, behind a gilded angel across the Ring) a chunk of the old **city wall.** Beethoven lived and composed in the building just above the piece of wall.

❏ At next stop, on right: The Neo-Gothic **City Hall** (Rathaus), flying the flag of Europe, towers over Rathaus Platz. This square is a festive site in summer, with a huge screen showing outdoor movies, operas, and concerts and a thriving food circus (see page 791—or, if you're hungry and it's thriving, hop off now). In the winter, the City Hall becomes a huge Advent calendar, with 24 windows opening—one each day—as Christmas approaches.

Immediately across the street (on left) is the **Burgtheater,**

Austria's national theater. Behind that is the Landtmann Café (the only café built with the Ringstrasse buildings, and one of the city's finest).

➔ At next stop, on right: The Neo-Greek temple of democracy houses the **Austrian Parliament.** The lady with the golden helmet is Athena, goddess of wisdom. Across the street (on left) is the imperial park called the **Volksgarten,** with a fine rose garden (free and open to the public).

➔ After the next stop on the right is the **Natural History Museum,** the first of Vienna's huge twin museums. It faces the **Kunsthistorisches Museum,** containing the city's greatest collection of paintings (see page 761). The **MuseumsQuartier** behind them completes the ensemble with a collection of mostly modern art museums (see page 770). A hefty statue of Empress Maria Theresa squats between the museums, facing the grand gate to the **Hofburg,** the emperor's palace (on left, across the Ring, described on page 747). Of the five arches, only the center one was used by the emperor. (Your tour is essentially finished. If you want to jump out here, you're at many of Vienna's top sights.)

➔ Fifty yards after the next stop, on the left through a gate in the black-iron fence, is a statue of Mozart. It's one of many charms in the **Burggarten,** which until 1918 was the private garden of the emperor. Vienna had more than its share of intellectual and creative geniuses. A hundred yards farther (on left, just out of the park), the German philosopher Goethe sits in a big, thought-provoking chair playing trivia with Schiller (across the street on your right). Behind the statue of Schiller is the **Academy of Fine Arts** (and next to it is the Burg Kino, which plays the movie *The Third Man* three times a week in English—see page 791).

➔ Hey, there's the **Opera** again. Jump off the tram and see the rest of the city.

SELF-GUIDED WALK

Welcome to Vienna

This walk connects the top three sights in Vienna's old center: the Opera, St. Stephen's Cathedral, and the Hofburg Palace. Along the way, you'll get a glimpse of Vienna past and present. The total trip takes about an hour, not counting sightseeing stops (which could be lengthy).

• *Begin by standing on the square in front of Vienna's landmark Opera.*

Opera: This is regarded by music-lovers as one of the planet's premier houses of music. If you're a fan, consider taking a guided tour of the Opera, or spring for a performance (standing-room tickets are surprisingly cheap; for information on all your Opera options, see page 743). The U-Bahn station in front of the Opera is

Vienna at a Glance

▲▲▲Opera Dazzling, world-famous opera house. **Hours:** Visit by guided 35-min tour only, daily in English; generally July–Aug at 11:00, 13:00, 14:00, 15:00, and often at 10:00 and 16:00; Sept–June fewer tours, afternoon only; call ahead to confirm tour times or check out daily schedule in red on door.

▲▲▲Hofburg Imperial Apartments Lavish main residence of the Hapsburgs. **Hours:** Daily 9:00–17:00.

▲▲▲Hofburg Treasury The Hapsburgs' collection of jewels, crowns, and other valuables—the best on the Continent. **Hours:** Wed–Mon 10:00–18:00, closed Tue.

▲▲▲Kunsthistorisches Museum World-class exhibit of the Hapsburgs' art collection, including Raphael, Titian, Caravaggio, Bosch, and Brueghel. **Hours:** Tue–Sun 10:00–18:00, Thu until 21:00, closed Mon.

▲▲▲Schönbrunn Palace Spectacular summer residence of the Hapsburgs, similar in grandeur to Versailles. **Hours:** Daily July–Aug 8:30–18:00, April–June and Sept–Oct 8:30–17:00, Nov–March 8:30–16:30, reservations recommended.

▲▲St. Stephen's Cathedral Enormous, historic Gothic cathedral in the center of Vienna. **Hours:** Church doors open Mon–Sat 6:00–22:00, Sun 7:00–22:00; nave open for tourists only Mon–Sat 8:30–11:30 & 13:00–16:30, Sun 13:00–16:30.

▲▲Hofburg New Palace Museums Uncrowded collection of armor, musical instruments, and ancient Greek statues, in the elegant halls of a Hapsburg palace. **Hours:** Armor and music—Tue–Sun 10:00–18:00, closed Mon; Greek—Wed–Mon 10:00–18:00, closed Tue.

▲▲Albertina Museum Hapsburg residence with decent apartments and world-class permanent and temporary exhibits. **Hours:** Daily 10:00–18:00, Wed until 21:00.

▲▲Kaisergruft Crypt for the Hapsburg royalty. **Hours:** Daily 9:30–16:00.

▲▲Haus der Musik Modern musuem with interactive exhibits on Vienna's favorite pastime. **Hours:** Daily 10:00–22:00.

▲▲**Belvedere Palace** Elegant palace of Prince Eugene of Savoy, with a collection of 19th- and 20th-century Austrian art (including Klimt). **Hours:** Tue–Sun 10:00–18:00, closed Mon.

▲**Monument Against War and Fascism** Powerful four-part statue remembering victims of the Nazis. **Hours:** Always open.

▲**Lipizzaner Museum** Displays dedicated to the regal Lipizzaner stallions; horse-lovers should check out their practice sessions. **Hours:** Museum open daily 9:00–18:00; stallions practice across the street roughly Feb–June and Sept–Oct Tue–Sat 10:00–12:00 when the horses are in town—call to confirm.

▲**Augustinian Church** Hapsburg marriage church, now hosting an 11:00 Sunday Mass with wonderful music. **Hours:** Open long hours daily.

▲**Imperial Furniture Collection** Eclectic collection of Hapsburg furniture. **Hours:** Tue–Sun 10:00–18:00, closed Mon.

▲**Natural History Museum** Big building facing Kunsthistorisches Museum, featuring the ancient *Venus of Willendorf*. **Hours:** Wed–Mon 9:00–18:30, Wed until 21:00, closed Tue.

▲**Dorotheum** Vienna's highbrow auction house. **Hours:** Mon–Fri 10:00–18:00, Sat 9:00–17:00, closed Sun.

▲**Academy of Fine Arts** Small but exciting collection with works by Bosch, Botticelli, Rubens, Guardi, and Van Dyck. **Hours:** Tue–Sun 10:00–18:00, closed Mon.

▲**Secession** A great chance to see Klimt *in situ*. **Hours:** Tue–Sun 10:00–18:00, Thu until 20:00, closed Mon.

▲**Naschmarkt** Sprawling, lively, people-filled outdoor market. **Hours:** Mon–Fri 6:00–18:30, Sat 6:00–17:00, closed Sun, closes earlier in winter.

▲**Liechtenstein Museum** Impressive Baroque collection. **Hours:** Fri–Mon 10:00–17:00, closed Tue–Thu.

▲**KunstHausWien** Modern art museum dedicated to zany local artist/environmentalist Hundertwasser. **Hours:** Daily 10:00–19:00.

Vienna Self-Guided Walk

U - U-Bahn Stop
T - Tram Stop

100 YDS.
100 METERS

DCH

1 Opera
2 Sacher Café
3 Monument Against War & Fascism
4 Albertina Museum
5 Kaisergruft
6 Kärntner Strasse

7 Stephansplatz
8 Graben
9 Plague Monument
10 Kohlmarkt
11 Demel Bakery & Café
12 Carriage Courtyard
13 Michaelerplatz

actually a huge underground shopping mall with fast food, news-stands, lots of pickpockets, and even an Opera Toilet Vienna experience (€0.60, *mit Musik*).

• *Walk behind the Opera to find the famous...*

Sacher Café: This is the home of every chocoholic's fantasy, the *Sachertorte*. While locals complain that the cakes have gone downhill (and many tourists are surprised by how dry they are), a coffee and slice of cake here can be €8 well invested. For maximum elegance, sit inside (daily 8:00–23:30, Philharmoniker Strasse 4, tel. 01/51456). While the café itself is grotesquely touristy, the adjacent Sacher Stube has ambience and natives to spare.

• *Near the Sacher Café (turn right as you exit) is a square called Albertinaplatz, where you'll find the TI, as well as the evocative...*

Monument Against War and Fascism: This powerful, thought-provoking, four-part statue merits ▲. The split white monument, *The Gates of Violence,* remembers victims of all wars and violence, including the 1938–1945 Nazi rule of Austria. Standing directly in front of it, you're at the gates of a concentration camp. Step into a montage of wartime images: clubs and WWI gas masks, a dying woman birthing a future soldier, and chained slave laborers sitting on a pedestal of granite cut from the infamous quarry at Mauthausen Concentration Camp (just up the Danube from Vienna). The hunched-over figure on the ground behind is a Jew forced to scrub anti-Nazi graffiti off a street with a toothbrush. The statue with its head buried in the stone (Orpheus entering the underworld) reminds Austrians (and the rest of us) of the consequences of not keeping their government on track. Behind that, the 1945 declaration of Austria's second republic—with human rights built into it—is cut into the stone. The experience gains emotional impact when you realize this monument stands on the spot where several hundred people were buried alive when the cellar they were hiding in was demolished during a WWII bombing attack (see photo to right of park, English description of memorial on the left).

Austria was pulled into World War II by Germany, which annexed the country in 1938, saying Austrians were wannabe Germans anyway. But Austrians are not Germans—never were, never will be. They're quick to tell you that while Austria was founded in the 10th century, Germany wasn't born until 1870. For seven years during World War II (1938–1945), there was no Austria. In 1955, after 10 years of joint occupation by the victorious Allies, Austria regained total independence on the condition that it would be forever neutral (and never join NATO or the Warsaw Pact). To this day, Austria is outside of NATO (and Germany).

• *Across the square from the TI is the...*

Albertina Museum: Overlooking Albertinaplatz is what

looks like a big terrace. This was actually part of Vienna's original defensive rampart. Later, it was the home to Empress Maria Theresa's daughter Maria Christina. And today, it's topped by a sleek, controversial titanium canopy (called the "diving board" by critics) that welcomes visitors into a recently restored museum. For details on the Albertina Museum, see page 758.

• *Across Albertinaplatz from the Albertina Museum (beyond the memorial photo plaque) is the street called Tegetthoffstrasse. Walk down this street a block to the square called Neuer Markt. Fronting the square is the...*

Kaisergruft: This church has a crypt filled with the fancy coffins of the Hapsburgs. Before moving on, consider paying your respects here (described on page 759).

• *After visiting the Kaisergruft, cross to the center of the square.*

The **fountain,** with the "four rivers" of the Hapsburg Empire (only the Danube is famous), dates from the mid-1700s. The original nude statues were replaced with more modest versions by Maria Teresa (originals are in the Lower Belvedere Palace). The buildings all around you were rebuilt after World War II, when half of the first district was intentionally destroyed by Churchill to demoralize the Viennese, who were disconcertingly enthusiastic about the Nazis.

• *Atop the fountain is a statue of Providence. Her one bare breast points to Kärntner Strasse (50 yards away). Go there and turn left.*

Kärntner Strasse: This grand, mall-like street (traffic-free since 1974) is the people-watching delight of this in-love-with-life city. While it's mostly a crass commercial pedestrian mall with its famed elegant shops now long gone, locals know it's the same road Crusaders marched down as they headed off for the Holy Land in the 12th century. Its name indicates that it points south, in the direction of the region of Kärnten (Carinthia, today divided between Austria and Slovenia).

Along this drag, you'll find lots of action: shops, street music, the city casino (at #41), the venerable Lobmeyr Crystal shop (#26—climb up the classic Old World interior to the glass museum), American Express (#21), the minimalism of the Loos American Bar (see sidebar; dark, plush, small, great €8 cocktails, no shorts, Kärntnerdurchgang 10, tel. 01/512-3283), and then, finally, the cathedral. Where Kärntner Strasse hits Stephansplatz (at #3), the Equitable Building (filled with lawyers, bankers, and insurance agents) is a fine example of historicism from the turn of the 20th century. Look up and imagine how slick Vienna must have felt in 1900.

Across the street on the corner, facing St. Stephen's, is the sleek concrete-and-glass **Haas Haus** by noted Austrian architect Hans Hollein (finished in 1990). The curved facade is supposed to

Adolf Loos
(1870–1933)

Adolf Loos—Vienna's answer to Frank Lloyd Wright—famously condemned needless ornamentation, declaring in his treatise *Ornament and Crime* that ornamentation needs a function. You can see two good examples of his work (each c. 1900 and described in this chapter) as you stroll the old center. Just off Kärntner Strasse is the Loos American Bar (Kärntnerdurchgang 10). And facing Michaelerplatz, in front of the Hofburg entrance, is the Loos House (a.k.a. the "house without eyebrows").

echo the Roman fortress of Vindobona (whose ruins were found near here)...but the Viennese, who protested having this stark modern tower right next to their beloved cathedral, were not convinced. Since then, it's become a fixture of Vienna's main square. Notice the way the smooth, rounded glass reflects St. Stephen's pointy Gothic architecture, providing a great photo opportunity. The café and pricey restaurant inside offer a nice perch, complete with a view of Stephansplatz below.

• *At the end of Kärntner Strasse, you'll wander into...*

Stephansplatz: Vienna's fun and colorful main square is also home to its cathedral, St. Stephen's. Now's the time to visit this massive church (see page 744).

• *When you're finished on Stephansplatz, head for the Hofburg. At the bottom of the square (near the start of Kärntner Strasse) is the street called...*

Graben: This was once a *Graben*, or ditch—originally the moat for the Roman military camp. In the middle of this pedes-

trian zone (at the intersection with Bräuner Strasse), top-notch street entertainers dance around an extravagant **plague monument,** officially called the Trinity Column (step back to notice the wonderful gilded "Father, Son, and Holy Ghost" at its top). In the Middle Ages, people didn't understand the causes of plagues, and figured they were a punishment from God. It was common for survivors to bribe or thank God with a monument like this one (c. 1690). One-third of Vienna died—so this column is thanks from the other two-thirds. Find Emperor Leopold, who ruled during the plague and made this statue in gratitude. (Hint: The typical inbreeding of royal families left him with a gaping underbite.) Below Leopold, Faith (with the help of a disgusting little cupid) tosses an old naked woman—symbolizing the plague—into the abyss.

Just before the plague monument is Dorotheergasse, leading to the Dorotheum auction house (see page 772). Just beyond the monument, you'll pass a fine set of **public WCs.** Around 1900, a local chemical-maker needed a publicity stunt. He purchased two wine cellars under the Graben and had classy WCs built in the Modernist style (complete with chandeliers and finely crafted mahogany) to prove that his chemicals really got things clean. The restrooms remain clean to this day—in fact, they're so inviting that they're used for poetry readings. Locals and tourists happily pay €0.50 for a quick visit.

• *The Graben dead-ends at the aristocratic supermarket Julius Meinl am Graben (see "Eating," page 803). At the end of Graben, turn left onto...*

Kohlmarkt: This is Vienna's most elegant shopping street (except for "American Catalog Shopping" at #5, second floor), with the emperor's palace at the end. Strolling Kohlmarkt, daydream about the edible window displays at **Demel** (#14, daily 10:00–19:00). Demel is the ultimate Viennese chocolate shop. The room is filled with Art Nouveau boxes of Empress Sisi's choco-dreams come true: *Kandierte Veilchen* (candied violet petals), *Katzenzungen* (cats' tongues), and so on. The cakes here are moist (compared to the dry *Sachertortes*). The delectable window displays change about monthly, reflecting current happenings in Vienna. Inside, an impressive cancan of cakes is displayed to tempt visitors into springing for the €10 cake-and-coffee deal (point to the cake you want). You can sit inside, with a view of the cake-making, or outside, with the street action. (Upstairs is less crowded.) Shops like this boast "K. u. K."—good enough for the *König und Kaiser* (king and emperor—same guy).

Next to Demel, the Manz bookstore has a Loos-designed facade. Just beyond Demel and across the street, at #1152, you can pop into a charming little Baroque **carriage courtyard,** with the surviving original carriage garages.

• *Kohlmarkt ends at...*

Michaelerplatz: In the center of this square, a scant bit of Roman Vienna lies exposed. On the left are the fancy Loden Plankl shop, with traditional formal wear, and the stables of the Spanish Riding School. Study the grand entry facade to the Hofburg Palace—it's Neo-Baroque from around 1900. The four heroic giants illustrate Hercules wrestling with his great challenges (much like the Hapsburgs, I'm sure). Opposite the facade, notice the modern Loos House (now a bank), which was built at about the same time. It was nicknamed the "house without eyebrows" for the simplicity of its windows. An anti–Art Nouveau statement (inspired by Frank Lloyd Wright and considered Vienna's first "modern" building), this was actually shocking at the time. To quell some of the outrage, the architect added flower boxes (or, some would say, moustaches).

• *You've made it to the Hofburg Palace. To get to the sights inside, simply walk through the gate, under the dome, and into the first square (In der Burg). For details on all the sights here, see page 747.*

SIGHTS

For a self-guided walk connecting these first three landmark sights, see page 735.

Opera (Staatsoper)

The Opera, facing the Ring and near the TI, is a central point for any visitor—easily worth ▲▲▲. While the critical reception of the building 130 years ago led the architect to commit suicide, and though it's been rebuilt since being destroyed by WWII bombs, it's still a sumptuous place.

Tours: Unless you're attending a performance, you can enter the Opera only with a guided 35-minute tour, offered daily in English (€6.50, generally July–Aug at 11:00, 13:00, 14:00, 15:00, and often at 10:00 and 16:00; Sept–June fewer tours, afternoons only, tel. 01/514-442-606). Tour times are often changed or cancelled due to rehearsals and performances. The opera posts a monthly schedule (blue, on the wall), but the more accurate schedule is the daily listing (red, posted on the door on the Operngasse side of building, farthest from St. Stephen's Cathedral). Tour tickets include the tiny and disappointing Opera Museum (across the street toward the Hofburg), except on Monday, when the museum is closed.

Opera Museum: New and included in your Opera tour ticket (whether you like it or not), the Opera Museum is a let-down, with descriptions only in German and rotating six-month-long special exhibits—2007 features Gustav Mahler, then Herbert von Karajan (€3, or included in the €6.50 tour ticket, Tue–Sun 10:00–18:00, closed Mon, a block away from the Opera, near Albertina Museum).

Performances: The Vienna State Opera—with musicians provided by the Vienna Philharmonic Orchestra in the pit—is one of the world's top opera houses. There are 300 performances a year, but in July and August the singers rest their voices (or go on tour). Since there are different operas nearly nightly, you'll see big trucks out back and constant action backstage—all the sets need to be switched each day. Even though the expensive seats normally sell out long in advance, the opera is perpetually in the red and subsidized by the state.

Opera Tickets: To buy tickets in advance, call 01/513-1513 (phone answered daily 10:00–21:00, www.wiener-staatsoper.at). The theater's box office is open from 9:00 until two hours before each performance. Unless Placido Domingo is in town, it's easy to get one of 567 **standing-room tickets** (*Stehplätze*, €2 at the top or €3.50 downstairs). While the front doors open one hour before the show starts, a side door (middle of building, on the Operngasse side) opens 80 minutes before curtain time, giving those in the know an early grab at standing-room tickets. Just walk in straight, then head right until you see the ticket booth marked *Stehplätze* (tel. 01/514-442-419). If fewer than 567 people are in line, there's no need to line up early. If you're one of the first 160 in line, try for the "Parterre" section and you'll end up directly under the Emperor's Box. You can even buy standing-room tickets after the show has started—in case you want only a little taste of opera. Dress is casual (but do your best) at the standing-room bar. Locals save their spot along the rail by tying a scarf to it.

Rick's Crude Tips: For me, three hours is a lot of opera. But just to see and hear the Opera in action for half an hour is a treat. You can buy a standing-room spot and just drop in for part of the show. Ushers don't mind letting tourists with standing-room tickets in for a short look. Ending time is posted in the lobby—you could stop by for just the finale. If you go at the start or finish, you'll see Vienna dressed up. Of the 567 people with cheap standing-room tickets, invariably many will not stand through the entire performance. You can drop by at about 21:30, ask for standing-room tickets, and if none are available, just wait for tourists to leave and bum their tickets off them. Guards don't care. Even those with standing-room tickets are considered "ticket-holders," and are welcome to explore the building. As you leave, wander around the first floor (fun if leaving early, when halls are empty) to enjoy the sumptuous halls (with prints of famous stage sets and performers) and the grand entry staircase. The last resort (and worst option) is to drop into the Opera Café and watch the opera live on TV screens (reasonable menu and drinks).

St. Stephen's Cathedral (Stephansdom)

This massive church, worth ▲▲, is the Gothic needle around which Vienna spins. According to the medieval vision, it stands like a giant jeweled reliquary, offering praise to God from the center of the city. It has survived Vienna's many wars and today symbolizes the city's freedom.

Cost: Entering the church is free (except July–mid-Oct, when it's €3 to get past the rear of the nave). Going up the towers costs €3 (by stairs, south tower) or €4 (by elevator, north tower). For more information, see "Towers".

Hours: The church doors are open Mon–Sat 6:00–22:00, Sun 7:00–22:00, but the nave is only open for tourists Mon–Sat 8:30–11:30 & 13:00–16:30, Sun 13:00–16:30. During services, you can't enter the main nave (unless you're attending Mass), but you can go into the back of the church to reach the north tower elevator (daily April–Oct 8:30–17:30, Nov–March 8:30–16:30). The stairs up to the south tower (enter from outside) are open daily 9:00–17:30.

Tours: The €4 tours in English are entertaining (daily April–Oct at 15:45, check information board inside entry to confirm schedule). Audioguides may be available.

➔ **Self-Guided Tour:** This is the third church to stand on this spot. The church survived the bombs of World War II, but, in the last days of the war, fires from the ruins leapt to the rooftop. The original timbered Gothic rooftop burned, and the cathedral's huge bell crashed to the ground. With a financial outpouring of civic pride, the roof was rebuilt in its original splendor by 1952. The ceramic tiles are purely decorative (locals who contributed to the postwar reconstruction each "own" one for their donation). Dramatic photos show WWII damage (with bricks neatly stacked and ready).

The **grounds** around the church were a cemetery until Josef II emptied it as an "anti-plague" measure in 1780. All the tombs were removed, and the remains were dumped into mass graves outside of town (as was the case when Mozart died here in 1791). A few of the most important tombstones decorate the church walls (see west facade flanking entry). You can still see the footprint of the old cemetery church in the pavement, today ignored by the buskers and human statues. Remains of the earlier Virgil Chapel (dating from the 13th century) are immediately under this (actually on display underground, in the U-Bahn station).

Study the church's **main entrance** (west end). You can see the original Romanesque facade (c. 1240) with classical Roman statues embedded in it. Above are two stubby towers nicknamed "pagan towers" because they're built with a few Roman stones (flipped over to hide the inscriptions and expose the smooth sides). The two 30-foot-tall columns flank the main entry. If you stand back and look at the tops, you'll see that they symbolize creation (one's a penis, the other's a vagina).

Stepping inside, you'll find a Gothic nave with a Baroque

overlay. While the columns support the roof, they also tell a story. Richly populated with statues, the columns make a saintly parade leading to the high altar. Near the church's right rear, find the "Madonna with the Protective Mantle"—showing people of all walks of life seeking and finding refuge in the holy mother. The Tupperware-colored glass windows date from 1950. Before World War II, the entire church was lit with windows like the richly colored ones behind the altar. Those, along with the city's top art treasures, were hidden safely from the Nazis in cellars and mines. The altar painting of the stoning of St. Stephen is early Baroque, painted on copper.

St. Stephen's is proud to be Austria's national church. A **plaque** (10 feet up, three pillars in front of the main altar) explains how each region contributed to the rebuilding after World War II: windows from Tirol, furniture from Vorarlberg, the floor from Lower Austria, and so on.

The Gothic sandstone **pulpit** in the rear of the nave (on left) is a realistic masterpiece carved from three separate blocks (find the seams). A spiral stairway winds up to the lectern, surrounded and supported by the four Latin Church fathers: Saints Ambrose, Jerome, Gregory, and Augustine. The railing leading up swarms with symbolism: lizards (animals of light) and toads (animals of darkness). The "Dog of the Lord" stands at the top, making sure none of those toads pollutes the sermon. Below the toads, wheels with three parts (the Trinity) roll up, while wheels with four parts (the four seasons, symbolizing mortal life) roll down. This work, attributed by most scholars to Anton Pilgram, has all the elements of the Flamboyant Gothic style—in miniature. Gothic art was done for the glory of God. Artists were anonymous. But this was around 1500, and the Renaissance was going strong in Italy. While Gothic persisted in the North, the Renaissance spirit had already arrived. In the more humanist Renaissance, man was allowed to shine—and artists became famous. So Pilgram included a rare self-portrait bust in his work (the guy with sculptor's tools, in the classic "artist observing the world from his window" pose under the stairs). A few steps farther ahead on the left wall, you'll see a similar self-portrait of Pilgram in color (symbolically supporting the heavy burden of being a master builder of this huge place).

Towers: You can ascend both towers—the south (outside right transept, by spiral staircase) and the north (via crowded elevator inside on the left). The 450-foot-high south tower, called

St. Stephen's Tower, offers the far better view, but you'll earn it by hiking 343 tightly wound steps up the spiral staircase (€3, daily 9:00–17:30, this hike burns about 1 *Sachertorte* of calories). From the top, use your city map to locate the famous sights. The north tower elevator takes you to a mediocre view and a big bell: the 21-ton Pummerin, cast from the cannon captured from the Ottomans in 1683, and supposedly the second biggest bell in the world that rings by swinging (locals know it as the bell that rings in the Austrian New Year; elevator-€4, daily April–Oct 8:30–17:30, Nov–March 8:30–16:30).

Cathedral Museum (Dom Museum): This forlorn museum (outside left transept, past the horses) gives a close-up look at piles of religious paintings, statues, and a treasury (€5, Tue–Sat 10:00–17:00, closed Sun–Mon, Stephansplatz 6, tel. 01/515-523-560).

Hofburg Palace

The complex, confusing, and imposing Imperial Palace, with 640 years of architecture, demands your attention. This first Hapsburg residence grew with the family empire from the 13th century until 1913, when the last "new wing" opened. The winter residence of the Hapsburg rulers until 1918, it's still the home of the Spanish Riding School, the Vienna Boys' Choir, the Austrian president's office, 5,000 government workers, and several important museums.

Rather than lose yourself in its myriad halls and courtyards, focus on three sections: the Imperial Apartments, Treasury, and Neue Burg (New Palace). Note that Hapsburg sights not actually inside the Hofburg (including the Lipizzaner stallions, the Augustinian Church, and the Albertina Museum) are covered on pages 757–758.

Orientation from In der Burg: Begin at the square called In der Burg (enter through the gate from Michaelerplatz). The statue is of Emperor Franz II, grandson of Maria Theresa, grandfather of Franz Josef, and father-in-law of Napoleon. Behind him is a tower with three kinds of clocks (the yellow disk shows the stage of the moon tonight). On the right, a door leads to the Imperial Apartments. Franz faces the oldest part of the palace. The colorful gate (behind you), which used to have a drawbridge, leads to the 13th-century Swiss Court (named for the Swiss mercenary guards once stationed here), the Treasury (Schatzkammer), and the Imperial Chapel (Hofburgkapelle, where the Boys' Choir sings the Mass—see page 784). For the Heroes' Square and the New Palace, continue opposite the way you entered In der Burg, passing through the left-most tunnel.

Eating at the Hofburg: Down the tunnel to Heroes' square (described above) is a tiny but handy sandwich bar called **Hofburg**

Vienna's Hofburg Palace

① In der Burg Square
② Imperial Apartments
③ Schweizerhof (Entrances to Treasury & Imperial Chapel)
④ New Palace Museums
⑤ Lipizzaner Museum
⑥ Lipizzaner Stallions Ticket Line
⑦ Augustinian Church
⑧ National Library
⑨ Butterfly Exhibit
⑩ Rest. Zum Alten Hofkeller
⑪ Hofburg Stüberl (Snacks)
⑫ Café Rest. Palmenhaus

Stüberl (same €2/sandwich price whether you sit or go, Mon–Fri 7:00–18:00, Sat–Sun 10:00–16:00). For a cheap, quick meal, duck into the **Restaurant zum Alten Hofkeller** in a cellar under the palace (€5 plates, Mon–Fri 11:00–13:30, closed Sat–Sun, breakfast from 7:30, cafeteria-style, mod and efficient, Schauflergasse 7).

▲▲▲**Imperial Apartments (Kaiserappartements)**—These lavish, Versailles-type, "wish-I-were-God" royal rooms are the downtown version of the grander Schönbrunn Palace. If you're rushed and have time for only one palace, do this (€9, daily 9:00–17:00, last entry 30 min before closing; from courtyard through St. Michael's Gate, just off Michaelerplatz; tel. 01/533-7570, www .hofburg-wien.at). Palace visits are a one-way romp through 20 rooms. You'll find some helpful posted English information, and the included audioguide brings the exhibit to life. With those tools and the following description, you won't need the €8 *Imperial Apartments and Sisi* museum guidebook. Your ticket also gets you into the royal silver and porcelain collection *(Silberkammer)* near the turnstile. If touring the silver and porcelain, do it first to save walking.

➋ **Self-Guided Tour:** Get your ticket, tour the silver and porcelain collection, climb the stairs, go through the turnstile, consider the WC, and use the big model of the palace complex to understand the complex lay of the imperial land. Then head into the...

Sisi Museum: The first six rooms tell the life story of Empress Elisabeth's fancy world—her luxury homes and fairy-tale existence (see sidebar). While Sisi's life story is the perfect stuff of legends, the exhibit tries to keep things from getting too giddy, and doesn't add to the sugary, kitschy image that's been created. The exhibit starts with her assassination (see her death mask) and traces the development of her legend, analyzing how her fabulous but tragic life could create a 19th-century Princess Diana from a rocky start (when she was disdained for abandoning Vienna and her husband, the venerable Emperor Franz Josef). You'll read bits of her poetic writing, see exact copies of her now-lost jewelry, and learn about her escapes, dieting mania, and chocolate bills. Admire Sisi's hard-earned thin waist (20 inches at age 16, 21 inches at age 50...after giving birth to four children). The black statue in the dark room represents the empress after the suicide of her son—aloof, thin, in black, with her back to the world. At the end, ponder the crude knife that killed Sisi.

A special exhibit that opened in August 2006 celebrates the 50th anniversary of the films that made Sisi a household name (at least in Austria): *Sisi* (1955); *Sisi: The Young Empress* (1956); *Sisi: Fateful Years of an Empress* (1957); and the condensed English version, *Forever My Love* (1962). The exhibition showcases the

Sisi
(1837–1898)

Empress Elisabeth—Franz Josef's mysterious, narcissistic, and beautiful wife—is in vogue. Sisi was mostly silent. Her main goals in life seem to have been preserving her reputation as a beautiful empress, maintaining her Barbie Doll figure, and tending to her fairy-tale, ankle-length hair. In spite of severe dieting and fanatic exercise, age took its toll. After turning 30, she allowed no more portraits to be painted and was generally seen in public with a delicate fan covering her face (and bad teeth).

Complex and influential, Sisi was adored by Franz Josef, whom she respected. Her personal mission and political cause was promoting Hungary's bid for nationalism. Her personal tragedy was the death of her son Rudolf, the crown prince, an apparent suicide (an incident often dramatized as "The Mayerling Affair," after the royal hunting lodge where it happened).

Disliking Vienna and the confines of the court, Sisi traveled more and more frequently. Over the years, the restless Sisi and her hardworking husband became estranged. In 1898, while visiting Geneva, Switzerland, she was murdered by an Italian anarchist.

Sisi has been compared to Princess Diana because of her beauty, bittersweet life, and tragic death. Her story is wonderfully told in the new Sisi Museum, now part of the Hofburg Imperial Apartments tour.

furniture borrowed from the palace for the movies, along with photographs and props from the filming.

After the Sisi Museum, a one-way route takes you through a series of royal rooms. The first room—as if to make clear that there was more to the Hapsburgs than Sisi—shows a family tree tracing the Hapsburgs from 1273 to their messy WWI demise. From here you enter the private apartments of the royal family (Franz Josef's first, then Sisi's).

Waiting Room for the Audience Room: A map and mannequins from the many corners of the Hapsburg realm illustrate the multi-ethnicity of the vast empire. Every citizen had the right to meet privately with the emperor. Three huge paintings entertained guests while they waited. They were propaganda, showing crowds of commoners enthusiastic about their Hapsburg rulers. On the right: an 1809 scene of the emperor returning to Vienna, celebrating news that Napoleon had begun his retreat. Left: the return of the emperor from the 1814 Peace of Paris, the treaty that ended the

Emperor Franz Josef
(1830–1916)

Franz Josef I—who ruled for 68 years (1848–1916)—was the embodiment of the Hapsburg Empire as it finished its six-century-long ride. Born in 1830, Franz Josef had a stern upbringing that instilled in him a powerful sense of duty and—like so many men of power—a love of things military.

His uncle, Ferdinand I, was a dimwit. As the revolutions of 1848 were rattling royal families throughout Europe, the Hapsburgs replaced Ferdinand, putting 18-year-old Franz Josef on the throne. FJ put down the revolt with bloody harshness and spent the first part of his long reign understandably paranoid as social discontent simmered.

FJ was very conservative. But worse, he figured wrongly that he was a talented military tactician, leading Austria into catastrophic battles against Italy (which was fighting for its unification and independence) in the 1860s. As his army endured severe, avoidable casualties, it became clear: FJ was a disaster as a general.

Wearing his uniform to the end, he never saw what a dinosaur his monarchy was becoming, and never thought it strange that the majority of his subjects didn't even speak German. He had no interest in democracy and pointedly never set foot in Austria's parliament building. But, like Queen Victoria, his contemporary, he was the embodiment of his empire—old-fashioned but sacrosanct. His passion for low-grade paperwork earned him the nickname "Joe Bureaucrat." Mired in these petty details, he missed the big picture. In 1914, he helped start a Great War that ultimately ended the age of monarchs. The year 1918 marked the end of Europe's big royal families: Hohenzollerns (Prussia), Romanovs (Russia), and Hapsburgs (Austria).

Napoleonic wars. (The 1815 Congress of Vienna that followed was the greatest assembly of diplomats in European history. Its goal: to establish peace through a "balance of power" among nations. While rulers ignored nationalism in favor of continued dynastic rule, it worked for about a century, until a colossal war—World War I—wiped out the Hapsburgs and the rest of Europe's royal families.) Center: Less important, the emperor makes his first public appearance to adoring crowds after recovering from a life-threatening illness (1826). The chandelier—considered the best in the palace—is Baroque, made of Bohemian crystal.

Audience Room: Suddenly, you were face-to-face with the emp. The portrait on the easel shows Franz Josef in 1915, when he was over 80 years old. Famously energetic, he lived a spartan life dedicated to duty. He'd stand at the high table here to meet with commoners, who came to show gratitude or make a request. (Standing kept things moving.) On the table, you can read a partial list of 56 appointments he had on January 3, 1910 (three columns: family name, meeting topic, and *Anmerkung*—the emperor's "action log").

Conference Room: The emperor presided here over the equivalent of cabinet meetings. After 1867, he granted Hungary some authority over his sprawling and suddenly unruly lands (creating the "Austro-Hungarian Empire")—so Hungarians also attended these meetings. The paintings on the wall show the military defeat of a popular Hungarian uprising...subtle.

Emperor Franz Josef's Study: This room evokes how seriously the emperor took his responsibilities as the top official of a vast empire. The desk was originally between the windows. Franz Josef could look up from his work and see his lovely, long-haired, tiny-waisted Empress Elisabeth's reflection in the mirror. Notice the trompe l'oeil paintings above each door, giving the believable illusion of marble relief. Notice also all the family photos—the perfect gift for the dad/uncle/hubby who has it all.

The walls between the rooms are wide enough to hide servants' corridors (the hidden door to his valet's room is in the back left corner). The emperor lived with a personal staff of 14: "three valets, four lackeys, two doormen, two manservants, and three chambermaids."

Emperor's Bedroom: Franz Josef famously slept on this no-frills iron bed, and used the portable washstand until 1880 (when the palace got running water). While he had a typical emperor's share of mistresses, his dresser was always well-stocked with photos of Sisi. Franz Josef lived here after his estrangement from Sisi. An etching shows the empress—a fine rider and avid hunter—riding sidesaddle while jumping a hedge.

Large Salon: This room was for royal family gatherings, and went unused after Sisi's death. The big, ornate stove in the corner was fed from behind. Through the 19th century, this was a standard form of heating.

Small Salon: This is dedicated to the memory of the assassinated Emperor Maximilian of Mexico (bearded portrait, Franz Josef's brother, killed in 1867). This was also a smoking room—necessary in the early 19th century, when smoking was newly fashionable (but only for men—never in the presence of women). Left of the door is a small button the emperor had to buzz before entering his estranged wife's quarters. You, however, can go right in.

Empress' Bedroom and Drawing Room: This was Sisi's, refurbished Neo-Rococo in 1854. She lived here—the bed was rolled in and out daily—until her death in 1898.

Sisi's Dressing/Exercise Room: Servants worked two hours a day on Sisi's famous hair here. She'd exercise on the wooden structure. You can psychoanalyze Sisi from the people and photos she hung on her walls. It's mostly her favorite dogs, her Bavarian family, and several portraits of the romantic and anti-monarch poet Heinrich Heine. Her infatuation with the liberal Heine caused a stir in royal circles.

Sisi's Bathroom: Detour into the behind-the-scenes palace. In the narrow passageway, you'll walk by Sisi's hand-painted-porcelain, dolphin-head WC (on the right). In the main bathroom, you'll see her huge copper tub (with the original wall coverings behind it). Sisi was the first Hapsburg to have running water in her bathroom (notice the hot and cold faucets). You're walking on the first linoleum ever used in Vienna (c. 1880).

Servants' Quarters: Next, enter the servants' quarters, with tropical scenes painted by Bergl in 1766. Take time to enjoy Bergl's playful details. As you leave these rooms and re-enter the imperial world, look back to the room on the left.

Empress' Great Salon: The room is painted with Mediterranean escapes, the 19th-century equivalent of travel posters. The statue is of Elisa, Napoleon's oldest sister (by the Neoclassical master Canova). A print shows how the emperor and Sisi would share breakfast in this room. Turn the corner and pass through the anterooms of Alexander's apartments.

Small Salon: The portrait is of Crown Prince Rudolf, Franz Josef and Sisi's son, who supposedly committed suicide at age 30. The mysterious circumstances around his death at Mayerling hunting lodge have been dramatized in numerous movies, plays, opera—and even a ballet.

Red Salon: The Gobelin wall hangings were a 1776 gift from Marie-Antoinette and Louis XVI in Paris to their Viennese counterparts.

Dining Room: It's dinnertime, and Franz Josef has called his extended family together. The settings are modest...just silver. Gold was saved for formal state dinners. Next to each name card was a menu with the chef responsible for each dish. (Talk about pressure.) While the Hofburg had tableware for 4,000, feeding 3,000 was a typical day. The cellar was stocked with 60,000 bottles of wine. The kitchen was huge—50 birds could be roasted on the hand-driven spits at once. (Drop off your audioguide in this room.)

Zip through the shop, go down the stairs, and you're back on the street. Two quick lefts take you back to the palace square (In der Burg), where the treasury awaits just past the black, red, and gold gate on the far side.

▲▲▲**Treasury (Weltliche und Geistliche Schatzkammer)**—
This "Secular and Religious Treasure Room" contains the best
jewels on the Continent. Slip through the vault doors and reflect
on the glitter of 21 rooms filled with scepters, swords, crowns,
orbs, weighty robes, double-headed eagles, gowns, gem-studded
bangles, and a unicorn horn (€8, Wed–Mon 10:00–18:00, closed
Tue, follow *Schatzkammer* signs to the Schweizerhof, tel. 01/5252-
4486, www.hofburg-wien.at).

○ **Self-Guided Tour:** While no English descriptions are
provided within the treasury, the well-produced, €2 audioguide
provides a wealth of information and is worth renting. Here's an
insufficient rundown of the highlights (the audioguide is much
more complete).

Room 2: The personal crown of Rudolf II has survived
since 1602—it was considered too well-crafted to cannibalize for
other crowns. It's a big deal because it's the adopted crown of the
Austrian Empire, established in 1806 after Napoleon dissolved
the Holy Roman Empire (an alliance of Germanic kingdoms so
named because it wanted to be considered the continuation of the
Roman Empire). Pressured by Napoleon, the Austrian Francis
II—who had been Holy Roman Emperor—became Francis I,
Emperor of Austria. Francis I/II (the stern guy on the wall, near
where you entered) ruled from 1792 to 1835. Look at the crown. Its
design symbolically merges the typical medieval king's crown and
a bishop's miter.

Rooms 3 and 4: These contain some of the coronation vestments and regalia needed for the new Austrian emperor.

Room 5: Ponder the Throne Cradle. Napoleon's son was born
in 1811 and made king of Rome. The little eagle at the foot is symbolically not yet able to fly, but glory-bound. Glory is symbolized
by the star, with dad's big *N* raised high.

Room 8: The eight-foot-tall, 500-year-old unicorn horn (possibly a narwhal tusk), was considered incredibly powerful in the
old days, giving its owner the grace of God. This was owned by the
Holy Roman Emperor—clearly a divine monarch.

Room 11: The collection's highlight is the 10th-century crown
of the Holy Roman Emperor (HRE). The imperial crown swirls
with symbolism "proving" that the emperor was both holy and
Roman. The jeweled arch over the top is reminiscent of the parade
helmet of ancient Roman emperors whose successors the HRE
claimed to be. The cross on top says the HRE ruled as Christ's representative on earth. King Solomon's portrait (on the crown, right
of cross) is Old Testament proof that kings can be wise and good.
King David (next panel) is similar proof that they can be just. The
crown's eight sides represent the celestial city of Jerusalem's eight
gates. The jewels on the front panel symbolize the 12 apostles.

The nearby 11th-century Imperial Cross preceded the emperor in ceremonies. Encrusted with jewels, it carried a substantial chunk of *the* cross and *the* holy lance (supposedly used to pierce the side of Jesus while on the cross; both items displayed in the same glass case). This must be the actual holy lance, as Holy Roman Emperors actually carried this into battle in the 10th century. Look behind the cross to see how it was a box that could be clipped open and shut, used for holding holy relics. You can see bits of the "true cross" anywhere, but this is a prime piece—with the actual nail hole.

The other case has jewels from the reign of Karl der Grosse (Charlemagne), the greatest ruler of medieval Europe. Notice Charlemagne modeling the crown (which was made a hundred years after he died) in the tall painting adjacent.

Room 12: The painting shows the coronation of Maria Theresa's son Josef II in 1764. In a room filled with the literal big wigs of the day, Josef is wearing the same crown and royal garb you've just seen.

Room 16: Most tourists walk right by perhaps the most exquisite workmanship in the entire treasury, the royal vestments (15th century). Look closely—they're painted with gold and silver threads.

▲Heroes' Square (Heldenplatz) and the New Palace (Neue Burg)—This last grand addition to the palace, from the early 20th century, was built for the Hapsburg heir Franz Ferdinand (it was

tradition for rulers not to move into their predecessor's quarters). But—while he was waiting politely for his long-lived uncle, Emperor Franz Josef, to die so he could move into his new digs— Franz Ferdinand was assassinated in Sarajevo in 1914, sparking the beginning of World War I.

The palace's grand facade arches around **Heroes' Square.** Notice statues of two great Austrian heroes on horseback: Prince Eugene of Savoy (who defeated the Ottomans that had earlier threatened Vienna) and Archduke Charles (first to beat Napoleon in a battle, breaking Nappy's image of invincibility and heralding the end of the Napoleonic age). The frilly spires of Vienna's Neo-Gothic City Hall break the horizon, and a line of horse-drawn carriages await their customers.

▲▲New Palace Museums: Armor, Music, and Ancient Greek Statues—The Neue Burg—technically part of the Kunst-historisches Museum across the way—houses three fine museums (same ticket): an armory (with a killer collection of medieval weapons), historical musical instruments, and classical statuary from ancient Ephesus. The included audioguide brings the exhibits to life and lets you actually hear the collection's fascinating old instruments being played. An added bonus is the chance to wander all alone among those royal Hapsburg halls, stairways, and painted ceilings (€8; armor and music—Tue–Sun 10:00–18:00, closed Mon; Greek—Wed–Mon 10:00–18:00, closed Tue; almost no tourists, tel. 01/5252-4484).

More Hapsburg Sights near the Hofburg

Central Vienna has plenty more sights associated with the Hapsburgs. With the exception of the last one (on Mariahilfer Strasse), these are all near the Hofburg. Remember that the biggest Hapsburg sight of all, Schönbrunn Palace, makes a great half-day trip (four miles from the center—see page 779).

Palace Garden (Burggarten)—This greenbelt, once the back yard of the Hofburg and now a people's park, welcomes people to loiter on the grass. On nice days, it's lively with office workers enjoying a break. The statue of Mozart facing the Ringstrasse is popular. The iron-and-glass pavilion now houses the recommended Palmenhaus Restaurant (see page 804) and a small but fluttery butterfly exhibit (€5; April–Oct Mon–Fri 10:00–16:45, Sat–Sun 10:00–18:15; Nov–March daily 10:00–15:45). The

butterfly zone is delightfully muggy on a brisk off-season day, but trippy any time of year. If you tour it, notice the butterflies hanging out on the trays with rotting slices of banana. They lick the fermented banana juice as it beads, and then just hang out there in a stupor...or fly giddy loop-de-loops.

▲**Lipizzaner Museum**—While the famous court horses of the Hapsburg emperors were originally from Spain, by the 16th century they were moved closer to Vienna (to the Slovenian town of Lipica—described on page 555). For four centuries, the Lipizzaner stallions have been bred, raised, and trained in Lipica. They actually have "surnames" that can be traced to the original six 16th-century stallions that made the trip from Spain. A must for horse-lovers, this tidy museum in the Renaissance Stallburg Palace shows (and tells in English) the 400-year history of the famous Spanish Riding School and the Lipizzaner stallions (€5, €15 combo-ticket includes practice session—see "Seeing the Lipizzaner Stallions", daily 9:00–18:00, between Josefsplatz and Michaelerplatz at Reitschulgasse 2, tel. 01/5252-4583, www.lipizzaner.at). Any time of day, you can see the horses prance on video in the museum's window.

➋ **Self-Guided Tour:** This commentary will make your visit more meaningful.

First Room: This room shows the family tree for one horse, Conversano Toscana (born 1984), tracing his father's line (Conversano) back to 1767. Paintings show how horses were bred for small heads and legs, but massive bodies. The three-minute video is quite graphic, starting with a horse worked up and ready to "joust," followed by a horse giving birth, then a wobbly baby—just minutes old—taking its first steps.

Second Room: Videos clearly illustrate the evolution of the traditional moves so appreciated today. After horses were antiquated on the battlefield, dressage morphed from no-nonsense military moves to court entertainment. The "dancing" originated as battle moves: *pirouette* (quick turns for surviving in the thick of battle) and *courbette* (on hind legs, to make a living shield for the knight). The *capriole* is a strong back-kick that could floor any enemy.

Third Room: Each of the main movements is illustrated on video.

Basement Theater: A 45-minute movie with great horse footage runs constantly (showings alternate between German and English, ask upon arrival about the next English showing).

Upstairs: Here an exhibit retells the dramatic WWII Lipizzaner rescue story. Lipizzaner fans have a warm spot in their hearts for General Patton, who, at the end of World War II—knowing that the Soviets were about to take control of Vienna—ordered a raid on the stable to save the horses and ensure the survival of their fine old bloodlines.

If all this horse information gets you fired up for more, consider...

Seeing the Lipizzaner Stallions—Seats for performances by Vienna's prestigious Spanish Riding School book up months in advance, but standing room is often available the same day (tickets-€45–160, standing room-€28, Feb–June and Sept–Oct Sun at 11:00, sometimes also Fri at 18:00, no shows July–Aug, fewer Nov–Jan, tel. 01/533-9031, www.srs.at). Luckily for the masses, training sessions with music in a chandeliered Baroque hall are open to the public (€12 at the door, roughly Feb–June and Sept–Oct Tue–Sat 10:00–12:00—but only when the horses are in town).

Tourists line up early at Josefsplatz, gate 2. Save money and avoid the wait by buying the €15 combo-ticket that covers both the museum and the training session (and lets you avoid that ticket line). If you want to hang out with Japanese tour groups, get there early and wait for the doors to open at 10:00. Better yet, simply show up late. Almost no one stays for the full two hours—except for the horses. As people leave, new tickets are printed continuously, so you can just waltz in with no wait at all. Don't have high expectations, as the horses often do little more than trot and warm up.

With the riding school enduring financial problems, other ways to see the horses and their stables are now possible (pricey, but for some a good value, details on the Web—www.lipizzaner.at).

▲**Augustinian Church (Augustinerkirche)**—This is the Gothic and Neo-Gothic church where the Hapsburgs latched, then buried, their hearts (weddings took place here, and the royal hearts are in the vault). Don't miss the exquisite, tomb-like Canova memorial (Neoclassical, 1805) to Maria Theresa's favorite daughter, Maria Christina, with its incredibly sad white-marble procession. The church's 11:00 Sunday Mass is a hit with music-lovers—both a Mass and a concert, often with an orchestra accompanying the choir. To pay, contribute to the offering plate and buy a CD afterwards.

Programs are available at the table by the entry all week (church open long hours daily, Augustinerstrasse 3).

The church faces Josefsplatz, with its statue of the great reform emperor Josef II. The **National Library** (€5, Tue–Sun 10:00–18:00, Thu until 21:00, closed Mon, next to the Augustinian Church) is impressive.

▲▲**Albertina Museum**—This building, at the southern tip of the Hofburg complex (near the Opera), was the residence of Maria Teresa's favorite daughter: Maria Christina, who was the only one allowed to marry for love rather than political strategy. Her many sisters were jealous. (Marie-Antoinette had to marry the French king...and lost her head over it.) Maria Christina's husband, Albert of Saxony, was a great collector of original drawings. He amassed an enormous assortment of works by Dürer, Rembrandt, Rubens, and others. Today the Albertina presents wonderful exhibitions of these fine works and allows visitors to tour its elegant state rooms and enjoy temporary exhibits of other artists (€9, price can vary based on special exhibits, €3.50 audioguide also available for both permanent and temporary exhibits, daily 10:00–18:00, Wed until 21:00, overlooking Albertinaplatz across from TI and Opera, tel. 01/534-830, www.albertina.at).

The Albertina consists of three components. First, stroll through the Hapsburg state rooms (French Classicism—lots of white marble). Top-quality facsimiles of the collection's greatest pieces hang in these rooms. Then browse the modern gallery, featuring special exhibitions. Finally, the Albertina also displays selections from its own spectacular collection of works by Michelangelo, Rubens, Rembrandt, and Raphael, plus a huge sampling of precise drawings by Albrecht Dürer. Of 400 original Dürer drawings that survived, Albert collected 300. Most were sold or stolen over the ages, and today the collection is down to about 100. Since these fragile sketches and exquisite drawings are very sensitive to light, they're kept mostly in darkness and shown only rarely, in rotation. The collection is vast, so you'll always see exciting originals, thoughtfully described in English.

▲▲**Kaisergruft: The Remains of the Hapsburgs**—Visiting the imperial remains is not as easy as you might imagine. These original organ donors left their bodies—about 150 in all—in the unassuming Kaisergruft (Capuchin Crypt), their hearts in the Augustinian Church (described above; church open long hours daily, but to see the goods you'll have to talk to a priest), and their entrails in the crypt below St. Stephen's Cathedral. Don't tripe.

Upon entering the Kaisergruft (€4, daily 9:30–16:00, last entry at 15:40, behind Opera on Neuer Markt), buy the €0.50 map with a Hapsburg family tree and a chart locating each coffin.

The double coffin of **Maria Theresa** (1717–1780) and her husband, **Franz I** (1708–1765), is worth a close look for its artwork. Maria Theresa outlived her husband by 15 years—which she spent in mourning. Old and fat, she installed a special lift enabling her to get down into the crypt to be with her dear, departed Franz (even though he had been far from faithful). The couple recline— Etruscan-style—atop their fancy lead coffin. At each corner are the crowns of the Hapsburgs—the Holy Roman Empire, Hungary, Bohemia, and Jerusalem. Notice the contrast between the Rococo splendor of Maria Theresa's tomb and the simple box holding her more modest son, **Josef II** (at his parents' feet; for more on Maria Theresa and Joe II, see the sidebar on page 760).

Franz Josef (1830–1916) is nearby, in an appropriately austere military tomb. Flanking Franz Josef are the tombs of his son,

the archduke **Rudolf,** and Empress Elisabeth. Rudolf and his teenage mistress supposedly committed suicide together in 1889 at Mayerling hunting lodge and—since the Church figured he forced her and was therefore a murderer—it took considerable legal hairsplitting to win Rudolf this spot (after examining his brain, it was determined that he was physically retarded and therefore incapable of knowingly killing himself and his girl). *Kaiserin* Elisabeth (1837–1898), a.k.a. **Sisi,** always gets the "Most Flowers" award.

In front of those three is the most recent Hapsburg tomb. **Empress Zita** was buried in 1989. Her burial procession was

Empress Maria Theresa (1717–1780) and Her Son, Emperor Josef II (1741–1790)

Maria Theresa was the only woman to officially rule the Hapsburg Empire in that family's 640-year reign. She was a strong and effective empress (r. 1740–1780). People are quick to remember Maria Theresa as the mother of 16 children (10 survived). Imagine that the most powerful woman in Europe either was pregnant or had a newborn for most of her reign. Maria Theresa ruled after the Austrian defeat of the Ottomans, when Europe recognized Austria as a great power. (Her rival, the Prussian emperor, said, "When at last the Hapsburgs get a great man, it's a woman.")

The last of the Baroque imperial rulers, and the first of the modern rulers of the Age of Enlightenment, Maria Theresa marked the end of the feudal system and the beginning of the era of the grand state. She was a great social reformer. During her reign, she avoided wars and expanded her empire by skillfully marrying her children into the right families. For instance, after daughter Marie-Antoinette's marriage into the French Bourbon family (to Louis XVI), a country that had been an enemy became an ally. (Unfortunately for Marie, her timing was off. Arriving in time for the Revolution, she lost her head.)

Maria Theresa was a great reformer and in tune with her age. She taxed the Church and the nobility, provided six years of obligatory education to all children, and granted free health care to all in her realm. Maria Theresa also welcomed the boy genius Mozart into her court.

The empress' legacy lived on in her son, Josef II, who ruled as emperor himself for a decade (1780–1790). He was an even more avid reformer, building on his mother's accomplishments. An enlightened monarch, Josef mothballed the too-extravagant Schönbrunn Palace, secularized the monasteries, established religious tolerance within his realm, freed the serfs, made possible the founding of Austria's first general hospital, and promoted relatively enlightened treatment of the mentally ill. Josef was a model of practicality (for example, reusable coffins à la *Amadeus,* and no more than six candles at funerals)—and very unpopular with other royals. But his policies succeeded in preempting the revolutionary anger of the age, enabling Austria to avoid the turmoil that shook so much of the rest of Europe.

probably the last such Old Regime event in European history. The monarchy died hard in Austria.

While it's fun to chase down all these body parts, remember that the real legacy of the Hapsburgs is the magnificence of this city. Step outside. Pan up. Watch the clouds glide by the ornate gables of Vienna.

▲**Imperial Furniture Collection (Kaiserliches Hofmo-biliendepot)**—Bizarre, sensuous, eccentric, or precious, this is your peek at the Hapsburgs' furniture—from grandma's wheel-chair to the emperor's spittoon—all thoughtfully described in English. The Hapsburgs had many palaces, but only the Hofburg was permanently furnished. The rest were furnished on the fly—set up and taken down by a gang of royal roadies called the "Depot of Court Movables" (Hofmobiliendepot). When the monarchy was dissolved in 1918, the state of Austria took possession of the Hofmobiliendepot's inventory—165,000 items. Now this royal storehouse is open to the public in a fine and sprawling museum. Don't go here for the *Jugendstil* furnishings. The older Baroque, Rococo, and Biedermeier pieces are the most impressive and tied most intimately to the royals. Combine a visit to this museum with a stroll down the lively shopping boulevard, Mariahilfer Strasse (€7, Tue–Sun 10:00–18:00, closed Mon, Mariahilfer Strasse 88, U-3: Zieglergasse, tel. 01/5243-3570).

Kunsthistorisches Museum

This exciting museum, across the Ring from the Hofburg Palace, is worth ▲▲▲. It showcases the grandeur and opulence of the

Hapsburgs' collected artwork in a grand building (built as a museum in 1888). There are European masterpieces galore, all well-hung on one glorious floor, plus a fine dis-play of Egyptian, classical, and applied arts.

Cost, Hours, Location: €10, audio-guide–€2, Tue–Sun 10:00–18:00, Thu until 21:00, closed Mon, on the Ringstrasse at Maria-Theresien-Platz, U-2 or U-3: Volkstheater/Museumsplatz, tel. 01/525-240, www.khm.at.

❍ **Self-Guided Tour:** Thanks to Gene Openshaw for writing the following tour.

The Kunsthistorwhateveritis Museum—let's just say "Koonst"—houses some of the most beautiful, sexy, and fun-loving art from two centuries (c. 1450–1650). The collection reflects the joie de vivre of Austria's luxury-loving Hapsburg rulers. At their peak of power in the 1500s, the Hapsburgs ruled Austria, Germany, northern Italy, the Netherlands, and Spain—and you'll

Kunsthistorisches Museum

see a wide variety of art from all these places and beyond.

Of the museum's many exhibits, we'll tour only the Painting Gallery (Gemäldegalerie) on the first floor. Climb the main staircase, featuring Antonio Canova's statue of *Theseus Clubbing the Centaur*. Italian Art is in the right half of the building (as you face Theseus), and Northern Art to the left. Notice that the museum labels the largest rooms with Roman numerals (Saal I, II, III), and the smaller rooms around the perimeter with Arabic (Rooms 1, 2, 3).

• *Enter Saal I and walk right into the High Renaissance.*

Venetian Renaissance (1500–1600)—Titian, Veronese, Tintoretto: Around the year 1500, Italy had a Renaissance, or "rebirth," of interest in the art and learning of ancient Greece and Rome. In painting, that meant that ordinary humans and Greek gods joined saints and angels as popular subjects.

Saal I spans the long career of **Titian** the Venetian (that rhymes)—who seemed particularly intimate with the pre-Christian gods and their antics. In *Mars, Venus, and Amor*, a busy cupid oversees the goddess of love making her case that war is not the answer. Mars—his weapons blissfully discarded—sees her point.

Danae with Nursemaid, also in Saal I, features more pre-Christian mythology. Zeus, the king of the gods, was always zooming to earth in the form of some creature or other to fool around with mortal women. Here, he descends as a shower of gold to consort with the willing Danae. You can almost see the human form of Zeus within the cloud. Danae is helpless with rapture, opening her legs to receive him, while her servant tries to catch the heavenly spurt with a towel. Danae's rich, luminous flesh on the left of the canvas is set off by the dark servant at right and the threatening sky above. The white sheets beneath her make her glow even more. This is more than a classic nude—it's a Renaissance Miss August. How could ultra-conservative Catholic emperors have tolerated such a downright pagan and erotic painting? Apparently, without a problem.

In *Ecce Homo* (just to the right), Titian tackles a Christian theme. A crowd mills about, when suddenly there's a commotion. They nudge each other and start to point. Follow their gaze diagonally up the stairs to a battered figure entering way up in the corner. "Ecce Homo!" says Pilate. "Behold the man." And he presents Jesus to the mob. For us, as for the unsympathetic crowd, the humiliated Son of God is not the center of the scene, but almost an afterthought.

In the next large galleries (Saal II and Saal III), the colorful

works by **Paolo Veronese** and **Tintoretto** reflect the wealth of Venice, the funnel where luxury goods from the exotic East flowed into northern Europe. In Veronese's *Adoration of the Magi (Anbetung der Könige)*, these Three-Kings-from-Orient-are dressed not in biblical costume, but in the imported silks of Venetian businessmen. Tintoretto's many portraits give us a peek at the movers and shakers of the Venetian Empire.

• *Find the following paintings in Rooms 1–4, the smaller rooms that adjoin Saals I, II, and III.*

Italian Renaissance and Mannerism: In **Correggio's** *Jupiter and Io,* the king of the gods appears in a cloud—see his foggy face and hands?—to get a date with a beautiful nymph named Io. ("Io, Io, it's off to earth I go.") Correggio tips Renaissance "balance"—the enraptured Io may be perched vertically in the center of the canvas right now, but she won't be for long.

Find the little round painting nearby. In his *Self-Portrait in a Convex Mirror (Selbstbildnis im Konvexspiegel)*, 21-year-old **Parmigianino**

(like the cheese) gazes into a convex mirror and perfectly reproduces the curved reflection on a convex piece of wood. Amazing.

Mantegna's *St. Sebastian (Der Hl. Sebastian)*, shot through with arrows, was an early Christian martyr, but he stands like a Renaissance statue—on a pedestal, his weight on one foot, and displaying his Greek-god anatomy. Mantegna places the three-dimensional "statue" in a three-dimensional setting, using floor tiles and roads that recede into the distance to create the illusion of depth.

The 22-year-old **Raphael** (roff-eye-EL) captured the spirit of the High Renaissance, combining symmetry, grace, beauty and emotion. His *Madonna of the Meadow (Die Madonna im Grünen)* is a mountain of motherly love—Mary's head is the summit and her flowing robe is the base—enfolding baby Jesus and John the Baptist. The geometric perfection, serene landscape, and Mary's adorable face make this a masterpiece of sheer grace...but then you get smacked by an ironic fist: The cross the little tykes play with foreshadows their gruesome deaths.

• *Find Caravaggio in Saal V.*

Caravaggio: Caravaggio (karra-VAH-jee-oh) shocked the art world with brutally honest reality. Compared with Raphael's super-sweet *Madonna of the Meadow*, Caravaggio's *Madonna of the Rosary (Die Rosenkranzmadonna*, the biggest canvas in the room) looks perfectly ordinary, and the saints kneeling around her have dirty feet.

In *David with the Head of Goliath (David mit dem Haupt des Goliath)*—in the corner near the window—Caravaggio turns a

third-degree-interrogation light on a familiar Bible story. David shoves the dripping head of the slain giant right in our noses. The painting, bled of color, is virtually a black-and-white crime-scene photo, slightly underexposed. Out of the deep darkness shine only a few crucial details. This David is not a heroic Renaissance Man like Michelangelo's famous statue, but a homeless teen that Caravaggio paid to portray God's servant. And the severed head of Goliath is none other than Caravaggio himself, an in-your-face self-portrait.

• *Find Room 10, in the corner of the museum.*

Velázquez: When the Hapsburgs ruled both Austria and Spain, cousins kept in touch through portraits of themselves and their kids. Diego Velázquez (veh-LOSS-kehs) was the greatest of Spain's "photo-journalist" painters:

heavily influenced by Caravaggio's realism, capturing his subjects without passing judgment, flattering, or glorifying them.

Watch little Margarita Hapsburg grow up in three different *Portraits of Margarita Theresa (Die Infantin Margarita Teresa)*, from age two to age nine. Margarita was destined from birth to marry her Austrian cousin, the future Emperor Leopold I. Pictures like these, sent from Spain every few years, let her

pen-pal/fiancé get to know her. Also see a portrait of Margarita's little brother, *Philip Prosper*, looking like a tiny priest. The kids' oh-so-serious faces, regal poses, and royal trappings are contradicted by their cuteness. No wonder Velázquez was so popular.

• *Complete the Italian Art wing by passing through several rooms of Baroque art, featuring large, colorful canvases showcasing over-the-top emotions and the surefire mark of Baroque art—pudgy winged babies. Northern Art is in the east wing, opposite the Titian room.*

Early Northern Art: The "Northern Renaissance," brought on by the economic boom of Dutch and Flemish trading, was more secular and Protestant than Catholic-funded Italian art. We'll see fewer Madonnas, saints, and Greek gods and more peasants, landscapes, and food. Paintings are smaller and darker, full of down-to-earth objects. Northern artists sweated the details, encouraging the patient viewer to appreciate the beauty in everyday things.

In the three sections of Room 14 are three early Northern

painters. **Rogier Van Der Weyden**'s *Triptych: The Crucifixion (Kreuzigungsaltar)* strips the Crucifixion down to the essential characters, set in a sparse landscape. The agony is understated, seen in just a few solemn faces and dramatically creased robes. Just to the left, in the painstakingly detailed *Portrait of Cardinal Niccolo Albergati*, **Jan van Eyck** refuses to airbrush out the jowls and wrinkles, showcasing the quiet dignity of an ordinary man. And **Hieronymous Bosch**'s *Christ Carrying the Cross (Kreutzragning)* is crammed with puny humans, not supermen.

• *Room X contains the largest collection of Bruegels in captivity. Linger. If you like it, linger longer.*

Pieter Bruegel (c. 1525–1569)—the Norman Rockwell of the 16th Century: The undisputed master of the slice-of-life village scene was Pieter Bruegel the Elder. (His name is pronounced "BROY-gull," and is sometimes spelled *Brueghel*. Don't confuse Pieter Bruegel the Elder with his sons, Pieter Brueghel the Younger and Jan Brueghel, who added luster and an "h" to the family name.) Despite his many rural paintings, Bruegel was actually an urban metrosexual who liked to wear peasants' clothing to observe country folk at play (a trans-fest-ite?). He celebrated their simple life, but he also skewered their weaknesses—not to single them out as hicks, but as universal examples of human folly.

The Peasant Wedding (Bauernhochzeit), Bruegel's most famous work, is less about the wedding than the food. It's a farmers' feeding frenzy as the barnful of wedding guests scramble to get their share of free eats. Two men bring in the next course, a tray of fresh pudding. The bagpiper pauses to check it out. A guy grabs bowls and passes them down the table, taking our attention with them. Everyone's going at it, including a kid in an oversized red cap who licks the bowl with his fingers. In the middle of it all, look who's been completely forgotten—the demure bride sitting in front of the blue-green cloth. (One thing: The guy carrying the front end of the food tray—is he stepping forward with his right leg, or with his left, or with...all three?)

Speaking of two left feet, Bruegel's *Peasant Dance (Bauerntanz)* shows peasants happily clogging to the tune of a lone bagpiper who wails away while his pit crew keeps him lubed with wine. The three Bruegel landscape paintings are part of an original series of six "calendar" paintings, depicting the seasons of the year. *The Gloomy Day* opens the cycle,

as winter turns to spring...slowly. The snow has melted, flooding the distant river, the trees are still leafless, and the villagers stir, cutting wood and mending fences. We skip ahead to autumn *(The Return of the Herd)*—still sunny, but winter's storms are fast approaching. We see the scene from above, emphasizing the landscape as much as the people. Finally, in *The Hunters in Snow (Die Jäger im Schnee)* it's the dead of winter, and three

dog-tired hunters with their tired dogs trudge along with only a single fox to show for their efforts. As they crest the hill, the grove of bare trees opens up to a breathtaking view—they're almost home, where they can join their mates playing hockey. Birds

soar like the hunters' rising spirits—emerging from winter's work and looking ahead to a new year.

• *Linger among the Breugels, then head for the nearby Room 16.*

Albrecht Dürer: As the son of a goldsmith and having traveled to Italy, Dürer (DEW-rer) combined meticulous Northern

detail with Renaissance symmetry. So his *Landauer Altarpiece of the Trinity (Allerheiligenbild)* may initially look like a complex pig-pile of saints and angels, but it's perfectly geometrical. The crucified Christ forms a triangle in the center, framed by triangular clouds and flanked by three-sided crowds of people—appropriate for a painting about the Trinity. Dürer practically invented the self-portrait as an art form, and he included him-

self, the lone earthling in this heavenly vision (bottom right), with a plaque announcing that he, Albrecht Dürer, painted this in 1511.

• *Locate these paintings scattered through Rooms 17–21.*

More Northern Art: Contrast Dürer's powerful Renaissance Christ with **Lucas Cranach**'s all-too-human *Crucifixion (Die Kreuzigung)*—twisted, bleeding, scarred and vomiting blood, as the storm clouds roll in.

Albrecht Altdorfer's garish *Resurrection (Die Auferstehung Christi)* looks like a poster for a bad horror film: "Easter Sunday III. He's back from the dead...and he's ticked!" A burning Christ ignites the dark cave, tingeing the dazed guards.

Hans Holbein painted *Jane Seymour,* wife number III of the VI wives of Henry VIII.

The former lady in waiting—timid and modest—poses stiffly, trying very hard to look the part of Henry's queen. Next.

Giuseppe Arcimboldo's *Summer*—a.k.a "Fruit Face"—is one of four paintings the Hapsburg court painter did showing the seasons (and elements) as people. With a pickle nose, pear chin, and corn-husk ears, this guy literally is what he eats.

In *The Big Flower Bunch (Der Grosse Blumentraub),* **Jan Brueghel,** the son of the famous Bruegel, puts meticulously painted flowers from different seasons together in one artfully arranged vase.

• *Leaving the simplicity of Northern Art—small canvases, small themes, attention to detail—re-enter the big-canvased, bright-colored world of Baroque in Saal XIII.*

Peter Paul Rubens: Stand in front of Rubens' *Self-Portrait (Selbstbildnis)* and admire the darling of Catholic-dominated Flanders (Belgium) in his prime: famous, wealthy, well-traveled, the friend of kings and princes, an artist, diplomat, man about town, and—obviously—confident. Rubens' work

runs the gamut, from realistic portraits to lounging nudes, Greek myths to altarpieces, from pious devotion to violent sex. But, can we be sure it's Baroque? Ah yes, I'm sure you'll find a pudgy winged baby somewhere.

The 53-year-old Rubens married Hélène Fourment (*The Little Fur,* or *Das Pelzchen*), this dimpled girl of 16. She pulls the fur around her ample flesh, simultaneously covering herself and exalting her charms. Rubens called both this painting and his young bride "The Little Fur." Hmm. Hélène's sweet cellulite was surely an inspiration to Rubens—many of his female figures have Hélène's gentle face and dimpled proportions.

In the large *Ildefonso Altarpiece,* a glorious Mary appears (with her entourage of p.w.b.'s) to reward the grateful Spanish saint with a chasuble (priest's smock).

• *Saal XIV features more big Rubens canvases.*

How could Rubens paint all these enormous canvases in one lifetime? He didn't. He kept a workshop of assistants busy painting backgrounds and minor figures, working from Rubens' small sketches (often displayed in Room 14 or nearby). Then the master stepped in to add the finishing touches.

• *From there, find Room 23.*

Jan Steen: In *The World Upside-Down (Die Verkehrte Welt),* Steen (1626–1679) gives us an intimate look into Dutch life. Not everyone could afford a masterpiece, but even the poorer people wanted works of art for their own homes (like a landscape from Sears for over the sofa). Steen, the Norman Rockwell of his day, painted humorous scenes from the lives of the lower classes. As a tavern owner, he observed society firsthand. In this scene, everything's going wrong.

• *In the adjoining Room 22:*

Jan Vermeer: In his small canvases, the Dutch painter Jan Vermeer quiets down the world to where we can hear our own heartbeat, letting us appreciate the beauty in common things.

The curtain opens and we see *The Artist's Studio (Allegorie der Malerei),* a behind-the-scenes look at Vermeer at work. He's painting a model dressed in blue, starting with her laurel-leaf headdress. The studio is its own little dollhouse world framed by a chair in the foreground and the wall in back. Then Vermeer fills this space with the few gems he wants us to focus on—the chandelier, the map, the painter's costume. Everything is lit by a crystal-clear light, letting us see these everyday items with fresh eyes.

The painting is subtitled *An Allegory of Painting.* The model has the laurel leaves, trumpet, and book that symbolize fame. The artist—his back to the public—earnestly tries to capture fleeting fame with a small sheet of canvas.

• *Finish your tour in the corner room.*

Rembrandt van Rijn: Rembrandt got wealthy painting portraits of Holland's upwardly mobile businessmen, but his greatest subject was himself. In *The Large Self-Portrait (Das Grosse Selbstbildnis)* we see the hands-on-hips, defiant, open-stance determination of a man who will do what he wants, and if they don't like it, tough.

In typical Rembrandt style, most of the canvas is a dark, smudgy brown, with only the side of his face glowing from the darkness. (Remember Caravaggio? Rembrandt did.) Unfortunately, the year this was painted, Rembrandt's fortunes changed. Looking at the *Small Self-Portrait 1657 (Kleines Selbstbildnis 1657)*, consider Rembrandt's last years. His wife died, his children died young, and commissions for paintings dried up as his style veered from the common path. He had to auction off paintings to pay debts and died a poor man. Rembrandt's numerous self-portraits painted from youth until old age show a man always changing—from wide-eyed youth, to successful portraitist, to this disillusioned but still defiant old man.

The Rest of the Kunst: We've seen only the "Kunst" (art) half of the Kunst-"Historisches" (history) Museum. The collections on the ground floor are among Europe's best, filled with ancient treasures and medieval curios. Highlights include a statue of the Egyptian pharaoh Thutmosis III, and the Gemma Augustea, a Roman cameo kept by Julius Caesar on his private desk. Happily, one of the jewels in the museum's crown (recently stolen) is now back. Cellini's *Salt Cellar*, a divine golden salt bowl, will be the centerpiece of a new "Kunstkammer"—a section dedicated to Hapsburg medieval and Renaissance jeweled wonders.

Near the Kunsthistorisches Museum

▲**Natural History Museum**—In the twin building facing the Kunsthistorisches Museum, you'll find moon rocks, dinosaur stuff, and a copy of the fist-sized *Venus of Willendorf*—at 30,000 years old, the world's oldest sex symbol, found in the Danube Valley (the original is in the museum's vault). This museum is a hit with children (€8, Wed–Mon 9:00–18:30, Wed until 21:00, closed Tue, tel. 01/521-770).

MuseumsQuartier—The vast grounds of the former imperial stables now corral several impressive, cutting-edge museums. Walk into the complex from the Hofburg side, where the main entrance (with visitors center) leads to a big courtyard with cafés, fountains, and ever-changing "installation lounge furniture," all surrounded by the quarter's various museums (behind Kunsthistorisches Museum, U-2 or U-3: Volkstheater/Museumsplatz). Various combo-tickets are available for those interested in more than just the Leopold and Modern Art museums (visit www.mqw.at).

The **Leopold Museum** features modern Austrian art, including the largest collection of works by Egon Schiele (1890–1918; many Americans are offended by Schiele's relaxed comfort with human nudity) and a few paintings by Kokoschka and Klimt (€9, €2.50 audioguide, Wed–Mon 10:00–19:00, Thu until 21:00, closed Tue, tel. 01/525-700, www.leopoldmuseum.org). Note that for these three artists, you'll do better in the Belvedere Palace (described on page 777).

The **Museum of Modern Art** (Museum Moderner Kunst Stiftung Ludwig, a.k.a. "Mumok") is Austria's leading modern-art gallery. It's the striking lava-paneled building—three stories tall and four stories deep, offering seven floors of far-out art hard for most to appreciate. This huge, state-of-the-art museum displays revolving exhibits showing off art of the last generation—including Klee, Picasso, and Pop (€8, Tue–Sun 10:00–18:00, Thu until 21:00, closed Mon, tel. 01/525-001-440, www.mumok.at).

Rounding out the sprawling MuseumsQuartier are an architecture museum, Transeuropa, Electronic Avenue, children's museum, and the Kunsthalle Wien—an exhibition center for contemporary art (€7.50, Thu–Tue 10:00–19:00, Thu until 22:00, closed Wed, tel. 01/521-8933, www.kunsthallewien.at).

Central Vienna, Inside the Ring

▲▲**Haus der Musik**—Vienna's "House of Music" has a small first-floor exhibit on the Vienna Philharmonic, and upstairs you'll enjoy fine audiovisual exhibits on each of the famous hometown boys (Haydn, Mozart, Beethoven, Strauss, and Mahler). But the museum is unique for its effective use of interactive touch-screen computers and headphones to actually explore the physics of sound. You can twist, dissect, and bend sounds to make your own musical language, merging your voice with a duck's quack or a city's traffic roar. Wander through the "sonosphere" and marvel at the amazing acoustics—I could actually hear what I thought only a piano tuner could hear. Pick up a virtual baton to conduct the Vienna Philharmonic Orchestra (each time you screw up, the musicians put their instruments down and ridicule you). Really experiencing the place takes time. It's open late and makes a good evening activity (€10, daily 10:00–22:00, last entry 1 hour before closing, 2 blocks from Opera at Seilerstätte 30, tel. 01/51648, www.hdm.at).

Mozart Haus Museum—Opened in 2006 for Wolfgang's 250th birthday, this museum is easy to get excited about, but disappoints. Exhibits fill the only surviving Mozart residence in Vienna (where he lived from 1784 to 1787, when he had lots of money). You'll learn his life story, with an emphasis on his most creative years...when he lived here. Included is a rundown on the Vienna music scene during the Mozart years, a quirky look at his gambling habits and his interest in crudely erotic peep shows, and a four-minute montage of his most famous arias in a mini-theater. Unfortunately, visiting the museum is like reading a book standing up—rather than turning pages, you climb stairs. There are almost no real artifacts. Wolfie would have found the audio-guide dreadful. While the museum might be worth the time and money for Mozart enthusiasts, the Mozart sights in Salzburg are more gratifying. In Vienna, I enjoy the Haus der Musik (above) much more (€9, daily 10:00–20:00, a block behind the cathedral, go through arcade at #5 and walk 50 yards to Domgasse 5, tel. 01/512-1791, www.mozarthausvienna.at).

▲**Vienna's Auction House, the Dorotheum**—For an aristocrat's flea market, drop by Austria's answer to Sotheby's, the Dorotheum. Its five floors of antique furniture and fancy knickknacks have been put up either for immediate sale or auction, often by people who inherited old things they don't have room for. Wandering through here, you feel like you're touring a museum with exhibits you can buy (Mon–Fri 10:00–18:00, Sat 9:00–17:00, closed Sun, classy little café on second floor, between Graben and Hofburg at Dorotheergasse 17, tel. 01/515-600, www.dorotheum.com). The info desk at the ground floor has a building map and schedule of upcoming auctions. Labels on each item predict the auction value. Continue your hunt for the perfect curio on the streets around the Dorotheum, lined with many fine antique shops.

Judenplatz Memorial and Museum—The square called Judenplatz marks the location of Vienna's 15th-century Jewish community, one of Europe's larg-est at the time. The square, once filled with a long-gone synagogue, is now dominated by a blocky memorial to the 65,000 Austrian Jews killed by the Nazis. The memorial—a library turned inside out—symbolizes Jews as "people of the book" and causes viewers to ponder the huge loss of culture, knowledge, and humanity that took place between 1938 and 1945.

The Judenplatz Museum, while sparse, has displays on medi-eval Jewish life and a well-done video re-creating community scenes from five centuries ago. Wander the scant remains of the medieval synagogue below street level—discovered during the construction of the Holocaust memorial. This was the scene of a medieval massacre. Since Christians weren't allowed to lend money, Jews were Europe's moneylenders. As so often happened in Europe, when Viennese Christians fell too deeply into debt, they found a convenient excuse to wipe out the local ghetto—and their debts at the same time. In 1421, 200 of Vienna's Jews were burned at the stake. Others who refused a forced conversion committed mass suicide in the synagogue (€3, €7 combo-ticket includes synagogue and Jewish Museum of the City of Vienna—see page 782, Sun–Thu 10:00–18:00, Fri 10:00–14:00, closed Sat, Judenplatz 8, tel. 01/535-0431, www.jmw.at).

Near Karlsplatz

These sights cluster around Karlsplatz, just southeast of the Ringstrasse (U-1, U-2, or U-4: Karlsplatz).

Karlsplatz—This picnic-friendly square, with its Henry Moore sculpture in the pond, is ringed with sights. The Art Nouveau station pavilions—from the late-19th-century municipal train system *(Stadtbahn)*—are textbook *Jugendstil* by Otto Wagner, with iron frames, decorative marble slabs, and painted gold ornaments. One of Europe's first subway systems, this precursor to today's U-Bahn was built with a military purpose in mind: to move troops quickly in time of civil unrest—specifically, out to Schönbrunn Palace. One of the pavilions is open as an exhibit on Otto Wagner (€2, June–Oct Tue–Sun 9:00–18:00, closed Mon and Nov–May).

Charles Church (Karlskirche)—Charles Borromeo, a 16th-century bishop from Milan, was an inspiration during plague times. This "votive church" was dedicated to him in 1713, when an epidemic spared Vienna. The church offers the best Baroque in Vienna, with a unique combination of columns (showing scenes from the life of Charles Borromeo, à la Trajan's Column in Rome), a classic pediment, and an elliptical dome. But this church is especially worthwhile for the chance (probably through mid-2007) to see restoration work in progress and up close (€6 includes a skippable one-room museum, audioguide, and visit to renovation site; Mon–Sat 9:00–12:30 & 13:00–18:00, Sun 13:00–18:00, last entry 30 min before closing). The entry fee may seem steep, but remember that it funds the restoration.

Visitors ride the industrial lift to a platform at the base of the dome. (Consider that the church was built and decorated with a scaffolding system essentially the same as this one.) Once up there, you'll climb stairs to the steamy lantern at the extreme top of the church. At that dizzying height, you're in the clouds with cupids and angels. Many details that appear smooth and beautiful from ground level—such as gold leaf, rudimentary paintings, and fake marble—look rough and sloppy up close. It's surreal to observe the 3-D figures from an unintended angle. Faith, Hope, Charity, and Borromeo triumph and inspire— while Protestants and their stinkin' books are trashed. Borromeo lob- bies heaven for plague relief. At

the very top, you'll see the tiny dove representing the Holy Ghost, surrounded by a cheering squad of nipple-lipped cupids.

Historical Museum of the City of Vienna (Wien Museum Karlsplatz)—This under-appreciated museum walks you through the history of Vienna with fine historic artifacts. You'll work your way up, chronologically: The ground floor exhibits Roman arti- facts and original statues from St. Stephen's Cathedral (c. 1350), with various Hapsburgs showing off the slinky hip-hugging fash- ion of the day. The first floor features old city maps, booty from an Ottoman siege, and an 1850 city model showing the town just before the wall was replaced by the Ring. Finally, the second floor displays a city model from 1898 (with the new Ringstrasse), sen- timental Biedermeier paintings and objets d'art, and early-20th- century paintings (including some by Gustav Klimt). The museum is worth the €4 admission (free Sun and Fri morning, open Tue– Sun 9:00–18:00, closed Mon, www.wienmuseum.at).

▲Academy of Fine Arts (Akademie der Bildenden Künste)— This small but exciting collection includes works by Bosch, Botticelli, and Rubens (quick, sketchy cartoons used to create his giant canvases); a Venice series by Guardi; and a self-portrait by a 15-year-old van Dyck. It's all magnificently lit and well-described by the €2 audioguide, and comes with comfy chairs (€5, Tue–Sun 10:00–18:00, closed Mon, 3 blocks from Opera at Schillerplatz 3, tel. 01/5881-6225, www.akademiegalerie.at). The fact that this is a working art academy gives it a certain realness. As you wander the halls of the academy, ponder how history might have been dif- ferent if Hitler—who applied to study architecture here but was rejected—had been accepted as a student. Before leaving, peek into the ground floor's central hall—textbook historicism, the Ringstrasse style of the late 1800s.

▲The Secession—This little building, behind the Academy of Fine Arts, is nicknamed the "golden cabbage" today. It was created by the Vienna Secession movement, a group of non-conformist artists led by Gustav Klimt, Otto Wagner, and friends. The Secession, whose slogan was "To each age its art, and to art its liberty," first exhibited their "liberty-style" art here in 1897. The

Art Nouveau Sights

Vienna gave birth to its own curvaceous brand of Art Nouveau around the early 1900s: *Jugendstil* ("youth style"). The TI has a brochure laying out Vienna's 20th-century architecture. The best of Vienna's scattered *Jugendstil* sights: the gilded, cabbage-domed Secession building at the Ring end of the Naschmarkt; the Belvedere Palace collection; and the clock on Hoher Markt (which does a musical act at noon). This clock honors 12 great figures from Vienna's history, from Marcus Aurelius to Joseph Haydn. While each gets his own top-of-the-hour moment, all parade by at high noon. A plaque on the left names each figure. Notice the novel way to mark the time.

young trees carved into the walls and its bushy "cabbage" rooftop are symbolic of renewal cycle. Today, the Secession continues to showcase cutting-edge art, as well as one of Gustav Klimt's most famous works, the *Beethoven Frieze* (€6, Tue–Sun 10:00–18:00, Thu until 20:00, closed Mon, Friedrichstrasse 12, tel. 01/587-5307, www.secession.at).

While the staff hopes you take a look at the temporary exhibits (which the ticket includes whether you like it or not), most tourists head directly for the basement, home to a small exhibit about the history of the building and the museum's highlight: Klimt's classic *Beethoven Frieze* (a.k.a. the "Searching Souls"). One of the masterpieces of Viennese Art Nouveau, this 105-foot-long fresco was a centerpiece of a 1902 "homage to Beethoven"

exhibition. Sit down and read the free flier, which explains Klimt's still-powerful work. The theme, inspired by Beethoven's *Ninth Symphony*, features floating female figures "yearning for happiness." They drift and weave and search—like most of us do—through internal and external temptations and forces, falling victim to base and ungodly temptations, and losing their faith. Then, finally, they become fulfilled by poetry, music, and art as they reach the "Ideal Kingdom" where "True Happiness, Pure Bliss, and Absolute Love" are found in a climactic embrace.

Glass cases show sketches Klimt did in preparation for this work. The adjacent room tells the history of this masterpiece, and how the building was damaged in WWII.

▲**Naschmarkt**—In 1898, the city decided to cover up its Vienna River. The long, wide square they created was filled with a lively produce market that still bustles most days (closed Sun). It's long been known as *the* place to get exotic far-away foods. In fact, locals say, "From here starts the Balkans."

From near the Opera, the Naschmarkt (roughly, "Munchies Market") stretches along Wienzeile Street. This "Belly of Vienna" comes with two parallel lanes—one lined with fun and reasonable eateries, and the other featuring the town's top-end produce and gourmet goodies. This is where top chefs like to get their ingredients. At the gourmet vinegar stall, you sample the vinegar like perfume—with a drop on your wrist. Farther from the center, the Naschmarkt becomes likeably seedy and surrounded by sausage stands, Turkish *Döner Kebab* stalls, cafés, and theaters. At the market's far end is a line of buildings with fine Art Nouveau facades. Each Saturday, the Naschmarkt is infested by a huge flea market where, in olden days, locals would come to hire a monkey to pick little critters out of their hair (Mon–Fri 6:00–18:30, Sat 6:00–17:00, closed Sun, closes earlier in winter, U-4: Kettenbruckengasse). For a picnic in the park, pick up your grub here and walk over to Karlsplatz (described earlier).

Beyond the Ring

▲**Liechtenstein Museum**—The noble Liechtenstein family (who own only a tiny country, but whose friendship with the Hapsburgs goes back generations) amassed an incredible private art collection. Their palace was long a treasure for Vienna art-lovers. Then, in 1938—knowing Hitler was intent on plundering artwork to create an immense "Führer Museum"—the family fled to their tiny homeland with their best art. Since the museum reopened in 2004, attendance has been disappointing, and each year the museum cuts back its hours. The problem is its location...not its worthiness.

The Liechtensteins' "world of Baroque pleasures" includes the family's rare French Rococo carriage (which was used for their grand entry into Paris; it had to be carted to the edge of town and assembled, as nearly all such carriages were destroyed in the French Revolution), a plush Baroque library, an inviting English Garden, and an impressive collection of paintings including a complete cycle of early Rembrandts (€10, €4 audioguide, Fri–Mon 10:00–17:00, closed Tue–Thu, tram D to Bauernfeldplatz, Fürstengasse 1, tel. 01/319-5767-252, www.liechtensteinmuseum.at).

▲**KunstHausWien: Hundertwasser Museum**—This "make yourself at home" museum is a hit with lovers of modern art. It mixes the work and philosophy of local painter/environmentalist Friedensreich Hundertwasser (1928–2000). Stand in front of the colorful checkerboard building and consider Hundertwasser's

style. He was against "window rac-
ism": Neighboring houses allow only
one kind of window, but $100H_2O$'s
windows are each different—and he
encouraged residents to personalize
them. He recognized "tree tenants"
as well as human tenants. His buildings are spritzed with a forest and
topped with dirt and grassy little
parks—close to nature...good for
the soul. Floors and sidewalks are
irregular—to "stimulate the brain"
(although current residents complain

it just causes wobbly furniture and sprained ankles). Thus $100H_2O$
waged a one-man fight—during the 1950s and 1960s, when
concrete and glass ruled—to save the human soul from the city.
(Hundertwasser claimed that "straight lines are godless.") Inside
the museum, start with his interesting biography. His fun-loving
paintings are half *Jugendstil* ("youth style") and half just kids' stuff.
Notice the photographs from his 1950s days as part of Vienna's
bohemian scene. Throughout the museum, notice the fun philo-
sophical quotes from an artist who believed, "If man is creative,
he comes nearer to his creator" (€9 for Hundertwasser Museum,
€12 combo-ticket includes special exhibitions, half-price on Mon,
open daily 10:00–19:00, extremely fragrant and colorful garden
café, Weissgerberstrasse 13, U-3: Landstrasse, tel. 01/712-0491,
www.kunsthauswien.com).

Hundertwasserhaus: The KunstHausWien provides by far the
best look at Hundertwasser. For an actual lived-in apartment complex by the green master, walk five minutes to the one-with-nature
Hundertwasserhaus (free, at Löwengasse and Kegelgasse). This
complex of 50 apartments, subsidized by the government to provide
affordable housing, was built in the 1980s as a breath of architectural
fresh air in a city of boring, blocky apartment complexes. While not
open to visitors, it's worth visiting for its fun-loving and colorful
patchwork exterior and the Hundertwasser festival of shops across
the street. Don't miss the view from Kegelgasse to see the "tree
tenants" and the internal winter garden residents enjoy.

Hundertwasser detractors—of which there are many—remind
visitors that $100H_2O$ was a painter, not an architect. They describe
the Hundertwasserhaus as a "1950s house built in the 1980s," and
colorfully painted with no real concern about the environment,
communal living, or even practical comfort. Nearly all the original
inhabitants got fed up with the novelty and moved out.

▲▲**Belvedere Palace**—This is the elegant palace of Prince
Eugene of Savoy (1663–1736), the still-much-appreciated conqueror

of the Ottomans. Eugene, a Frenchman considered too short and too ugly to be in the service of Louis XIV, offered his services to the Hapsburgs. While he was short and ugly indeed, he became the greatest military genius of his age. When you conquer cities, as Eugene did, you get really rich. He had no heirs, so the state got his property and Emperor Josef II established the Belvedere as Austria's first great public art gallery. Today, his palace boasts sweeping views and houses the Austrian gallery of 19th- and 20th-century art (€9, €3 audioguide, Tue–Sun 10:00–18:00, closed Mon, entrance at Prinz-Eugen-Strasse 27, tel. 01/7955-7134, www .belvedere.at). To get here from the center, catch tram D at the Opera (direction Südbahnhof, it stops at the palace gate).

The palace is actually two grand buildings separated by a fine garden. For our purposes, the **Upper Belvedere Palace** is what matters. The Upper Palace was Eugene's party house. Today, like the Louvre in Paris (but much easier to enjoy), this palace contains a fine collection of paintings. The collection is arranged chrono- logically: On the first floor, you'll find historicism, Romanticism, Impressionism, Realism, tired tourism, Expressionism, Art Nouveau, and early modernism. Each room tries to pair Austrian works from that period with much better-known European works. It's fun to see the original work of artists like van Gogh, Munch, and Monet hung with their lesser-known Austrian contemporaries. As Austria becomes a leader in art around 1900, the collection gets stronger, with fine works by Gustav Klimt, Oskar Kokoschka, and Egon Schiele. The Klimt room (facing the city center, on the far right) shows how even in his early work, the face was vivid and the rest dissolved into decor. During his "golden period," this background became his trademark gold leaf studded with stones. The highlight is Klimt's most famous (and often-replicated) work, *The Kiss*. (Some Klimt paintings formerly in this collection have been returned to their rightful owners—see sidebar.) The corner room shows a small exhibit on Prince Eugene, Archduke Franz Ferdinand, and the signing of the state treaty in 1955. Don't miss the poignant Schiele family portrait from 1918—his wife died while he was still working on it. (Schiele and his child were soon taken by the influenza epidemic that swept through Europe after WWI.)

The upper floor shows off early-19th-century Biedermeier paintings (hyper-sensitive, super-sweet, uniquely Viennese Romanticism—the poor are happy, things are lit impossibly well, and folk life is idealized). Your ticket also includes the Austrian Baroque and Gothic art in the Lower Belvedere Palace. Prince Eugene lived in that palace, but he's long gone and I wouldn't bother to visit.

View: *Belvedere* means "beautiful view." Sit at the top palace

Restitution of Art Stolen by Nazis

The Austrian government has worked diligently to fairly reimburse victims of the Nazis, whose buildings, businesses, personal belongings, and art were taken after the 1938 *Anschluss* (when Germany annexed Austria).

A fund of over $200 million was established by both the Austrian government and corporations who profited through their collaboration with the Nazis. Surviving locals (mostly Jews) who paid a *Reichsfluchtsteuer* ("tax for fleeing the country") were located and given some money. Former slave laborers were also tracked down and given €5,000 each. (Imagine what an amazing windfall that would be for an 80-year-old Romanian peasant woman.)

Most significantly for sightseers, great art was returned to its rightful owners. The big news for the Vienna art world was the return of several Gustav Klimt paintings, most notably his *Golden Adele,* from Vienna's Belvedere Palace collection to a Jewish woman in California. In 2006, *The Golden Adele* was auctioned off for $135 million, the highest price ever paid for a painting. While the Austrian government wanted to buy it back, it figured she was asking too much for the art and refused to get into a bidding war. Fortunately for art-lovers, the most famous Klimt *(The Kiss)* was not involved in the restitution and remains in Vienna's Belvedere Palace.

and look over the Baroque gardens, the mysterious sphinxes (which symbolized solving riddles and the finely educated mind of your host, Eugene), the lower palace, and the city. The spire of St. Stephen's Cathedral is 400 feet tall, and no other tall buildings are allowed inside the Ringstrasse. The hills—covered with vineyards—are where the Viennese love to go to sample the new wine. You can see Kahlenberg, from where you can walk down to several recommended *Heurigen* (wine gardens) beyond the spire (see page 788). These are the first of the Alps, which stretch from here all the way to Marseilles, France. The square you're overlooking was filled with people on May 15, 1955, as local leaders stood on the balcony of the Upper Palace (behind you) and proclaimed Austrian independence following a decade-long Allied occupation after World War II.

Schönbrunn Palace (Schloss Schönbrunn)

Among Europe's palaces, only Schönbrunn rivals Versailles. Worth ▲▲▲, this summer residence of the Hapsburgs is located four miles from the center. It's big (1,441 rooms), but don't worry—only 40 rooms are shown to the public. (Today the families of

260 civil servants rent simple apartments in the rest of the palace, enjoying rent control and governmental protections so they can't be evicted.)

Getting There: Take U-4 to Schönbrunn and walk 400 yards (just follow the crowds). The main entrance is in the left side of the palace as you face it.

Royal Apartments—While the exterior is Baroque, the interior was finished under Maria Theresa in let-them-eat-cake Rococo. The chandeliers are either of hand-carved wood with gold-leaf gilding or of Bohemian crystal. Thick walls hid the servants as they ran around stoking the ceramic stoves from the back, and attending to other behind-the-scenes matters. Most of the public rooms are decorated in Neo-Baroque, as they were under Franz Josef (r. 1848–1916). When WWII bombs rained on the city and the palace grounds, the palace itself took only one direct hit. Thankfully, that bomb, which crashed through three floors—including the sumptuous central ballroom—was a dud.

Cost: The admission price is based on which route you select (each one includes an audioguide): the **Imperial Tour** (22 rooms, €9, 45 min, Grand Palace rooms plus apartments of Franz Josef and Elisabeth—mostly 19th-century and therefore least interesting) or the **Grand Tour** (40 rooms, €11.50, 60 min, includes Imperial tour plus Maria Theresa's apartments—18th-century Rococo). A combo-ticket called the **Schönbrunn Pass Classic** includes the Grand Tour, as well as other sights on the grounds: the Gloriette viewing terrace, maze, privy garden, and court bakery—complete with *Apfelstrudel* demo and tasting (€15, available April–Oct only). I'd go for the Grand Tour.

Hours: Daily July–Aug 8:30–18:00, April–June and Sept–Oct 8:30–17:00, Nov–March 8:30–16:30. Information: www .schoenbrunn.at.

Crowd-Beating Tips: Schönbrunn suffers from crowds. It can be a jam-packed sauna in the summer. It's busiest from 9:30 to 11:30, especially on weekends and in July and August; it's least crowded from 12:00 to 14:00 and after 16:00, when there are no groups. To avoid the long delays in summer, make a reservation by telephone (tel. 01/8111-3239, answered daily 8:00–17:00, wait through the long message for the operator). You'll get an appointment time and a ticket number. Check in at least 30 minutes early. Upon arrival, go to the "Group and Reservations" desk (immediately inside the gate on the left at the gate house—long before the actual palace), give your number, pick up your ticket, and jump in ahead of the masses. If you show up in peak season without calling first, you deserve the frustration. (In this case, you'll have to wait in line, buy your ticket, and wait until the listed time to enter—which could be tomorrow.) If you have any time to kill, spend it exploring the gardens or Coach Museum.

Palace Gardens—After strolling by the Hapsburgs tucked neatly into their crypts, a walk through the emperor's garden with countless commoners is a celebration of the evolution of civilization from autocracy into real democracy. As a civilization, we're doing well.

Most of the park itself is free, as it has been since the 1700s (open daily sunrise to dusk, entrance on either side of the palace). The small side-gardens are the most elaborate. The Kammergarten on the left was a fancy private garden for the Hapsburgs (now restored and with a fee). The so-called Sisi Gardens on the right are free. Inside are several other sights, including a **palm house** (€3.50, daily May–Sept 9:30–18:00, Oct–April 9:30–17:00), Europe's oldest **zoo** (*Tiergarten*, built by Maria Theresa's husband for the entertainment and education of the court in 1752; €12, May–Sept daily 9:00–18:30, less off-season, tel. 01/877-9294), and—at the end of the gardens—the **Gloriette,** a purely decorative monument celebrating an obscure Austrian military victory and offering a fine city view (viewing terrace-€2, included in €15 Schönbrunn Pass Classic, daily April–Sept 9:00–18:00, July–Aug until 19:00, Oct 9:00–17:00, closed Nov–March). A touristy choo-choo train makes the rounds all day, connecting Schönbrunn's many attractions.

Coach Museum Wagenburg—The Schönbrunn coach museum is a 19th-century traffic jam of 50 impressive royal carriages and sleighs. Highlights include silly sedan chairs, the death-black hearse carriage (used for Franz Josef in 1916, and most recently for Empress Zita in 1989), and an extravagantly gilded imperial carriage pulled by eight Cinderella horses. This was rarely used other than for the coronation of Holy Roman Emperors, when it was disassembled and taken to Frankfurt for the big event (€4.50; April–Oct daily 9:00–18:00; Nov–March Tue–Sun 10:00–16:00, closed Mon; last entry 30 min before closing, 200 yards from palace, walk through right arch as you face palace, tel. 01/877-3244).

"Honorable Mentions": More Vienna Museums

These museums, scattered around the city, are worth a peek if you have a special interest.

Museum of Applied Art—The Österreichisches Museum für Angewandte Kunst, or MAK, is Vienna's answer to London's Victoria and Albert collection. It shows off the fancies of local aristocratic society, including a fine *Jugendstil* collection. The MAK is more than just another grand building on the Ringstrasse. It was built to provide models of historic design for Ringstrasse architects, and is a delightful space in itself (many locals stop in to enjoy a coffee on the plush couches in the main lobby). Each wing is dedicated to a different era. Exhibits, well-described in English, come with a playful modern flair—notable modern designers were assigned various spaces (€8, €10 includes a big English guidebook, free on Sat, open Tue–Sun 10:00–18:00, Tue until 24:00, closed Mon, Stubenring 5, tel. 01/711-360, www.mak.at).

The associated **Restaurant Österreicher im MAK** is named for a chef renowned for his classic and modern Viennese cuisine. Classy and mod, it's trendy for locals (daily, reserve for evening, €10–15 plates).

Sigmund Freud Museum—Freud enthusiasts travel to Vienna just to see this humble apartment and workplace of the man who fundamentally changed our understanding of the human psyche. Freud established his practice here in 1891, and it was here that he wrote his work on the interpretation of dreams. Freud, who was Jewish, fled with the rise of Nazism, and took most of his furniture with him. You won't see "the couch," but you will see his waiting room, along with three rooms packed with papers, photos, mementos, and documents. These, along with a family video from the 1930s, give an intimate peek at Freud's life. The old-fashioned exhibit is tediously described in a three-ring info binder loaned to visitors, which complements the more general audioguide (€6, daily 9:00–17:00, July–Sept until 18:00, cool shop, half a block from a tram D stop at Berggasse 19, tel. 01/319-1596, www.freud -museum.at).

And More Museums—There's much, much more. The city map lists everything. If you're into Esperanto, undertakers, tobacco, clowns, firefighting, or the homes of dead composers, you'll find them all in Vienna.

These good museums try very hard but are submerged in the greatness of Vienna: **Jewish Museum of the City of Vienna** (€5, or €7 combo-ticket includes synagogue and Judenplatz Museum—described on page 772, Sun–Fri 10:00–18:00, Thu until 20:00, closed Sat, Dorotheergasse 11, tel. 01/535-0431, www .jmw.at), **Folkloric Museum of Austria** (Tue–Sun 10:00–17:00, closed Mon, Laudongasse 15, tel. 01/406-8905), and **Museum of Military History,** one of Europe's best if you like swords and shields (Heeresgeschichtliches Museum, €5.10, includes audioguide, Sat–Thu 9:00–17:00, closed Fri, Arsenal district, Objekt 18, tel. 01/795-610).

ACTIVITIES

People-Watching and Strolling

These activities allow you to take it easy and enjoy the Viennese good life.

▲**City Park (Stadtpark)**—Vienna's City Park is a waltzing world of gardens, memorials to local musicians, ponds, peacocks, music in bandstands, and Viennese escaping the city. Notice the *Jugendstil* entrance at the Stadtpark U-Bahn station. The Kursalon, where Strauss was the violin-toting master of waltzing ceremonies, hosts daily touristy concerts in three-quarter time.

▲**Prater**—Since the 1780s, when the reformist Emperor Josef II gave his hunting grounds to the people of Vienna as a public park, this place has been Vienna's playground. While tired and a bit run-down these days, Vienna's sprawling amusement park still tempts visitors with its huge 220-foot-tall, famous, and lazy Ferris wheel *(Riesenrad)*, roller coaster, bumper cars, Lilliputian railroad, and endless eateries. Especially if you're traveling with kids, this is a fun, goofy place to share the evening with thousands of Viennese (daily 9:00–24:00 in summer, but quiet after 22:00, U-1: Praterstern). For a local-style family dinner, eat at Schweizerhaus (good food, great Czech "Budweiser" beer, classic conviviality).

Danube Island (Donauinsel)—In the 1970s, the city dug a canal parallel to the mighty Danube River, creating both a flood barrier and a much-loved island escape from the city (easy U-Bahn access on U-1 to Donauinsel). This skinny, 12-mile-long island provides a natural wonderland. All along the traffic-free, grassy park you'll find Viennese—especially immigrants and those who can't afford their own cabin or fancy vacation—at play. The swimming comes tough, though, with rocky entries rather than sand. The best activity here is a bike ride (see "By Bike," page 730). Be careful—if you venture too far from the crowds, you're likely to encounter nudists on inline skates.

A Walk in the Vienna Woods (Wienerwald)—For a quick side-trip into the woods and out of the city, catch the U-4 to Heiligenstadt, then bus #38A to Kahlenberg, where you'll enjoy great views and a café overlooking the city. From there, it's a peaceful 45-minute downhill hike to the *Heurigen* of Nussdorf or Grinzing to enjoy some new wine (see "Vienna's Wine Gardens," page 788). Your free TI-produced city map can be helpful...just go downhill. For the very best views, stay on bus #38A to Leopoldsberg, where you'll find a lovely Baroque church, a breezy *Weinstube* (pub), and shady tables with expansive panoramas of the city and the Danube. While it seems like a long way to go for a big view, buses are cheap (or free with a transit pass) and go twice an hour until 22:00.

Naschmarkt—Vienna's busy produce market is a great place for people-watching (see page 776).

Shopping for Traditional Austrian Clothing—Two famous shops are fun to visit if you're interested in picking up a classy felt suit or dirndl. Most central is the fancy **Loden Plankl** shop (across from the Hofburg, at Michaelerplatz 6). But the **Tostmann Trachten** shop is the ultimate for serious shopping. Mrs. Tostmann powered the resurgence of this style. Her place is like a shrine to traditional Austrian and folk clothing—handmade and very expensive

(Schottengasse 3A, 3-min walk from Am Hof, tel. 01/533-5331, www.tostmann.at).

Fast Boat to Bratislava—The generally overlooked capital of Slovakia is suddenly on the radar screen for Vienna travelers for three reasons: its newly lively economy (thanks to its recent EU membership and intense foreign investment); its popular discount airport (see page 179); and the new fast catamaran day trip. The DDSG line offers several daily boat trips from Schwedenplatz (where Vienna's old town hits the canal) to Bratislava in 75 minutes with good views (€23 each way, cheaper at less convenient times). For a fine day trip, you can depart at 8:30, arrive at 9:45 in Bratislava's Old Town, explore Bratislava, and return to Vienna at 14:15 or 18:15 (departures daily June–Oct only, they also offer a day tour with guide and lunch for €60, tel. 01/58880, www.ddsg-blue -danube.at). The train makes the trip a bit faster and much cheaper (hourly, 1-hour trip). For more on Bratislava, see page 176.

EXPERIENCES

Music Scene

As far back as the 12th century, Vienna was a mecca for musicians—both sacred and secular (troubadours). The Hapsburg emperors of the 17th and 18th centuries were not only generous supporters of music, but fine musicians and composers themselves. (Maria Theresa played a mean double bass.) Composers like Haydn, Mozart, Beethoven, Schubert, Brahms, and Mahler gravitated to this music-friendly environment. They taught each other, jammed together, and spent a lot of time in Hapsburg palaces. Beethoven was a famous figure, walking—lost in musical thought—through Vienna's woods. In the city's 19th-century belle époque, "Waltz King" Johann Strauss and his brothers kept Vienna's 300 ballrooms spinning.

This musical tradition continues into modern times, leaving some prestigious Viennese institutions for today's tourists to enjoy: the Opera (see page 743), the Boys' Choir, and the great Baroque halls and churches, all busy with classical and waltz concerts. As you poke into churches and palaces, you may hear groups practicing. You're welcome to sit and listen.

Vienna is Europe's music capital. It's music *con brio* from October through June, reaching a symphonic climax during the Vienna Festival each May and June. Sadly, in July and August, the Boys' Choir, the Opera, and many more music companies are—like you—on vacation. But Vienna hums year-round with live classical music. Except for the Boys' Choir, the musical events listed below are offered in summer.

Vienna Boys' Choir—The boys sing (from a high balcony, where they are heard but not seen) at the 9:15 Sunday Mass from September through March in the Hofburg's Imperial Chapel (Hofburgkapelle; entrance at Schweizerhof, from Josefsplatz go through tunnel). Reserved seats must be booked two months in advance (€5–29, reserve by fax, e-mail, or mail: fax from the US 011-431-533-992-775, hmk@aon.at, or write Hofmusikkapelle, Hofburg-Schweizerhof, 1010 Wien; call 01/533-9927 for information only—they can't book tickets at this number). Much easier, standing room inside is free and open to the first 60 who line up. Even better, rather than line up early, you can simply swing by and stand in the narthex just outside, where you can hear the boys and see the Mass on a TV monitor. Boys' Choir concerts (on stage at the Musikverein) are also given Fridays at 16:00 in May, June, September, and October (€35–48, standing room goes on sale at 15:30 for €15, Karlsplatz 6, U-1, U-2, or U-4: Karlsplatz, tel. 01/5880-4141). They're nice kids, but, for my taste, not worth all the commotion. Remember, many churches have great music during Sunday Mass. Just 200 yards from the Boys' Choir chapel, Augustinian Church has a glorious 11:00 service each Sunday (see page 758).

Touristy Mozart and Strauss Concerts—If the music comes to you, it's touristy—designed for flash-in-the-pan Mozart fans. Powdered-wig orchestra performances are given almost nightly in

grand traditional settings (€25–50). Pesky wigged-and-powdered Mozarts peddle tickets in the streets. They rave about the quality of the musicians, but you'll get second-rate chamber orchestras, clad in historic costumes, performing the greatest hits of Mozart and Strauss. These are casual, easygoing concerts with lots of tour groups. While there's not a Viennese person in the audience, the tourists generally enjoy the evening. To sort through all your options, check with the ticket office in the TI (same price as on the street, but with all venues to choose from). Savvy locals suggest getting the cheapest tickets, as no one seems to care if cheapskates move up to fill unsold pricier seats. Critics explain that the musicians are actually very good (often Hungarians, Poles, and Russians working a season here to fund an entire year of music studies back home), but that they haven't performed much together so aren't "tight." Of the many fine venues, the Mozarthaus is a small room richly decorated in Venetian Renaissance style with intimate chamber-music concerts (€35–42, almost nightly at 19:30, near St. Stephen's Cathedral at Singerstrasse 7, tel. 01-911-9077).

Strauss Concerts in the Kursalon—For years, Strauss concerts have been held in the Kursalon, where the "Waltz King" himself directed wildly popular concerts 100 years ago (€38–54, concerts nightly generally at 20:30, tel. 01/512-5790 to reserve). Shows last 1.75 hours and are a mix of ballet, waltzes, and a 15-piece orchestra. It's touristy—tour guides holding up banners with group numbers wait out front after the show. Even so, the performance is playful, visually fun, fine quality for most, and with a tried-and-tested, crowd-pleasing format. The conductor welcomes the crowd in German (with a wink) and English; after that...it's English only.

Serious Concerts—These events, including the Opera, are listed in the monthly *Wien-Programm* (available at TI, described on page 726). Tickets run from €36 to €75 (plus a stiff 22 percent booking fee when booked in advance or through a box office like the one at the TI). While it's easy to book tickets online long in advance, spontaneity is also workable, as there are invariably people with tickets they don't need selling them at face value or less outside the door before concert time. If you call a concert hall directly, they can advise you on the availability of (cheaper) tickets at the door. Vienna takes care of its starving artists (and tourists) by offering cheap standing-room tickets to top-notch music and opera (generally an hour before each performance).

Theater an der Wien—Considered the oldest theater in Vienna, this was designed in 1801 for Mozart operas—intimate, with just a thousand seats. Reopened in 2006 for Mozart's 250th birthday, it treats Vienna's music-lovers to a different opera every month—generally Mozart with a contemporary setting and modern interpretation—with the top-notch Vienna Radio Orchestra in the pit. With the reopening of Theater an der Wien, Vienna now supports three opera companies. This one is the only company playing through the summer (facing the Naschmarkt at Linke Wienzeile 6, tel. 01/5818-1110 for information, tickets available at www.theater -wien.at).

Summer of Music Festival (a.k.a. "KlangBogen")—This annual festival assures that even from June through September, you'll find lots of great concerts, choirs, and symphonies (special *KlangBogen* brochure at TI; get tickets at Wien Ticket pavilion off Kärntner Strasse next to Opera, or go directly to location of particular event; Summer of Music tel. 01/42717, www.klangbogen.at).

Musicals—The Wien Ticket pavilion sells tickets to contemporary American and British musicals done in German language (€10–95, €2.50 standing room), and offers these tickets at half price from 14:00 until 17:00 the day of the show. Or you can reserve (full-price) tickets for the musicals by phone (call combined office for the three big theaters at tel. 01/58885).

Films of Concerts—To see free films of great concerts in a lively, outdoor setting near City Hall, check "Nightlife," page 790.

Dance Evening—If you'd like to actually dance (waltz and ballroom), or watch people who are really good at it, consider the Dance Evening at the Tanz Café in the Volksgarten (€5–10, May–Aug Fri–Sun from 19:00, www.volksgarten.at).

Classical Music to Go—To bring home Beethoven, Strauss, or the Wiener Philharmoniker on a top-quality CD, shop at Gramola on the Graben, EMI on Kärntner Strasse, or Virgin Megastore on Mariahilfer Strasse.

Vienna's Cafés

In Vienna, the living room is down the street at the neighborhood coffeehouse. This tradition is just another example of Viennese expertise in good living. Each of Vienna's many long-established (and sometimes even legendary) coffeehouses has its individual character (and characters). These classic cafés are a bit tired, with a shabby patina and famously grumpy waiters who treat you like an uninvited guest invading their living room. Still, it's a welcoming place. They offer newspapers, pastries, sofas, quick and light workers' lunches, elegance, smoky ambience, and "take all the time you want" charm for the price of a cup of coffee. Order it *melange* (like a cappuccino), *brauner* (strong coffee with a little milk), or *schwarzer* (black). Americans who ask for a latte are mistaken for Italians and given a cup of hot milk. Rather than buy the *Herald Tribune* ahead of time, spend the money on a cup of coffee and read the paper for free, Vienna-style, in a café.

These are my favorites:

Café Hawelka has a dark, "brooding Trotsky" atmosphere, paintings by struggling artists who couldn't pay for coffee, a saloon-wood flavor, chalkboard menu, smoked velvet couches, an international selection of newspapers, and a phone that rings for regulars. Mrs. Hawelka died just a couple weeks after Pope John Paul II. Locals suspect the pontiff wanted her much-loved *Buchteln* (marmalade-filled doughnuts) in heaven. Mr. Hawelka, now alone and understandably a bit forlorn, still oversees the action (Wed–Mon 8:00–2:00, Sun from 16:00, closed Tue, just off Graben, Dorotheergasse 6).

Café Sperl dates from 1880, and is still furnished identically to the day it opened—from the coat tree to the chairs (Mon–Sat 7:00–23:00, Sun 15:00–20:00 except closed Sun July–Aug, just off Naschmarkt near Mariahilfer Strasse, Gumpendorfer 11, tel. 01/586-4158).

Café Braunerhof, between the Hofburg and the Graben, offers a classic ambience with no tourists, live music on weekends (light classics, no cover, Sat–Sun 15:00–18:00), and a practical menu with daily specials (open long hours daily, Stallburgasse 2).

Other Classics in the Old Center: All of these places are

open long hours daily: **Café Pruckel** (at Dr.-Karl-Lueger-Platz, across from the City Park at Stubenring 24); **Café Tirolerhof** (2 blocks from the Opera, behind the TI on Tegetthoffstrasse, at Führichgasse 8); and **Landtmann Café** (directly across from the City Hall on the Ringstrasse at Dr.-Karl-Lueger-Ring 4). The Landtmann is unique, as it's the only grand café built along the Ring with all the other grand buildings.

Vienna's Wine Gardens *(Heurigen)*

The *Heuriger* (HOY-rih-gur; plural is *Heurigen*, HOY-rih-gehn) is a uniquely Viennese institution. When the Hapsburgs let Vienna's vintners sell their own new wine (called *Sturm*) tax-free, several hundred families opened *Heurigen* (wine-garden restaurants clustered around the edge of town)—and a tradition was born. Today they do their best to maintain the old-village atmosphere, serving the homemade new wine (the last vintage, until November 11, when a new vintage year begins) with light meals and strolling musicians. Most *Heurigen* are decorated with enormous antique presses from their vineyards. Wine gardens might be closed on any given day; always call ahead to confirm, if you have your heart set on a particular place. (For a near-*Heuriger* experience right downtown, drop by Gigerl Stadtheuriger—see page 800.)

At any *Heuriger*, fill your plate at a self-serve cold-cut buffet (€6–9 for dinner). Food is sold by the *"10 dag"* unit. (A *dag* is a decigram, so *10 dag* is 100 grams...about a quarter-pound.) Dishes to look for...or look out for: *Stelze* (grilled knuckle of pork), *Fleischlaberln* (fried ground-meat patties), *Schinkenfleckerln* (pasta with cheese and ham), *Schmalz* (a spread made with pig fat), *Blunzen* (black pudding...sausage made from blood), *Presskopf* (jellied brains and innards), *Liptauer* (spicy cheese spread), *Kornspitz* (whole-meal bread roll), and *Kummelbraten* (crispy roast pork with caraway). Waitresses will then take your wine order (€2.20 per quarter-liter, about 8 oz). Many locals claim it takes several years of practice to distinguish between the *Sturm* wine and vinegar.

There are more than 1,700 acres of vineyards within Vienna's city limits, and countless *Heuriger* taverns. For a *Heuriger* evening, rather than go to a particular place, take a tram to the wine-garden district of your choice and wander around, choosing the place with the best ambience.

Getting to the *Heurigen:* You have three options: a 15-minute taxi ride, trams and buses, or a goofy tourist train.

Trams make a trip to the Vienna Woods quick and affordable. The fastest way is to ride U-4 to its last stop, Heiligenstadt, where trams and buses in front of the station fan out to the various neighborhoods. Ride tram D to its end point for Nussdorf. Ride bus #38A for Grinzing and on to the Kahlenberg viewpoint—#38A's end station. (Note that tram #38—different from bus #38A—starts at the Ring and finishes at Grinzing.) To get to Neustift am Walde, ride U-6 to Nussdorfer Strasse and catch bus #35A. Connect Grinzing and Nussdorf with bus #38A and tram D (transfer at Grinzinger Strasse).

The **Heurigen Express** tourist train is tacky but handy and relaxing, chugging you on a hop-on, hop-off circle from Nussdorf through Grinzing and around the Vienna Woods with light narration (€7.30, buy ticket from driver, 1 hour, daily April–Oct 12:00–19:00, departs from end station of tram D in Nussdorf at the top of the hour, tel. 01/479-2808).

Here are a couple of good *Heuriger* neighborhoods:

Grinzing—Of the many *Heuriger* suburbs, Grinzing is the most famous, lively...and touristy. Many people precede their visit to Grinzing by riding tram #38 from Schottentor (on the Ring) to its end (up to Kahlenberg for a grand Vienna view), and then ride 20 minutes back into the *Heuriger* action. From the Grinzing tram stop, follow Himmelgasse uphill toward the onion-top dome. You'll pass plenty of wine gardens—and tour buses—on your way up. Just past the dome, you'll find the heart of the *Heurigen*.

Heiligenstadt (Pfarrplatz)—Between Grinzing and Nussdorf, this area features several decent spots, including the famous and touristy Mayer am Pfarrplatz (a.k.a. **Beethovenhaus**, Mon–Sat 16:00–23:00, Sun 11:00–23:00, bus #38A stop: Fernsprechamt/Heiligenstadt, walk 5 min uphill on Dübling Nestelbachgasse to Pfarrplatz 2, tel. 01/370-1287). This place has a charming inner courtyard with an accordion player and a sprawling backyard with a big children's play zone. Beethoven lived—and composed his *Sixth Symphony*—here in 1817. He hoped the local spa would cure his worsening deafness. **Weingut and Heuriger Werner Welser,** a block uphill from Beethoven's place, is lots of fun, with music nightly from 19:00 (open daily 15:30–24:00, Probusgasse 12, tel. 01/318-9797).

Nussdorf—A less-touristy district, characteristic and popular with the Viennese, Nussdorf has plenty of *Heuriger* ambience. Right at the end station of tram D, you'll find three long and skinny places side by side: **Schübel-Auer Heuriger** (Tue–Sat 16:00–24:00, closed Sun–Mon, Kahlenberger Strasse 22, tel. 01/370-2222) is my favorite. Also consider **Heuriger Kierlinger** (daily 15:30–24:00, Kahlenberger Strasse 20, tel. 01/370-2264) and **Steinschaden** (daily 15:00–24:00, Kahlenberger Strasse 18, tel. 01/370-1375). Walk through any of these and you pop out on Kahlenberger Strasse, where a walk 20 yards uphill takes you to some more eating and drinking fun: **Bamkraxler** ("Tree Jumper"), the only beer garden amid all these vineyards. It's a fun-loving, youthful place with fine keg beer and a regular menu—traditional, ribs, veggie, kids' menu—rather than the *Heuriger* cafeteria line (€6–10 meals, kids' playground, Tue–Sat 16:00–24:00, Sun 11:00–24:00, closed Mon, Kahlenberger Strasse 17, tel. 01/318-8800).

Sirbu Weinbau Heuriger—This option is actually in the vine-yards, high above Vienna with great city and countryside views, a top-notch buffet, a glass veranda, and a traditional interior for cool weather. It's a bit more touristy, since it's more upmarket and famous as "the ultimate setting" (April–Oct Mon–Sat from 15:00, closed Sun, big children's play zone, Kahlenberger Strasse 210, tel. 01/320-5928). It's high above regular transit service, but fun to incorporate into a little walking. Ideally, ride bus #38A to the end at Kahlenberg, and ask directions to the *Heuriger* (a 20-min walk downhill).

NIGHTLIFE

If old music and new wine aren't your thing, Vienna has plenty of alternatives. For an up-to-date rundown on fun after dark, get the TI's free *Vienna Hype* booklet.

Open-Air Classical Music Cinema and Food Circus—A thriving scene erupts each evening in July and August at the park in front of City Hall (Rathaus, on the Ringstrasse). Thousands of people keep a food circus of 24 simple stalls busy. There's not a paper plate or plastic cup anywhere, just real plates and glasses—Vienna wants the quality of eating to be as high as the music that's about

to begin. About 3,000 folding chairs face a 60-foot-wide screen up against the City Hall's Neo-Gothic facade. When darkness falls, an announcer explains the program, and then the music starts. The program is different every night—mostly movies of opera and classical concerts, with some films. The schedule is at the TI (programs generally last around two hours, starting when it's dark—between 9:30 in July and 8:30 in August).

Since 1991, the city has paid for 60 of these summer event nights each year. Why? To promote culture. Officials know the City Hall Music Festival is mostly a "meat market" where young people come to hook up. But they believe many of these people will develop a little appreciation of classical music and the high culture on the side.

Bermuda Triangle (Bermuda Dreieck)—The area known as the "Bermuda Triangle"—north of St. Stephen's Cathedral, between Rotenturmstrasse and Judengasse—is the hot local nightspot.

You'll find lots of music clubs and classy pubs, or *Beisl* (such as Krah Krah, Salzamt, Bermuda Bräu, and First Floor—for cocktails with live fish). The serious-looking guards have nothing to do with the bar scene—they're guarding the synagogue nearby.

Gürtel—The Gürtel is Vienna's outer ring road. The arches of a lumbering viaduct (which carries a train track) are now filled with trendy bars, sports bars, dance clubs, strip clubs, antique shops, and restaurants. To experience—or simply see—the latest scene in town, head out here. The people-watching—the trendiest kids on the block—makes the trip fun even if you're looking for exercise rather than a drink. Ride U-6 to Nussdorfer Strasse or Thaliastrasse and hike along the viaduct.

English Cinema—Two great theaters offer three or four screens of English movies nightly (€6–9): **English Cinema Haydn,** by my recommended hotels on Mariahilfer Strasse (Mariahilfer Strasse 57, tel. 01/587-2262, www.haydnkino.at); and **Artis International Cinema,** right in the town center a few minutes from the cathedral (Schultergasse 5, tel. 01/535-6570).

The Third Man **at Burg Kino**—This movie, voted the best British film ever by the British Film Institute, takes place in 1949 Vienna—when it was divided like Berlin between the four victorious Allies. With a dramatic Vienna cemetery scene, coffeehouse culture surviving amid the rubble, and Orson Welles being chased through the sewers, the tale of a divided city about to fall under Soviet rule and rife with smuggling is an enjoyable two-hour experience while in Vienna (€8, in English with German subtitles; three showings weekly: Fri at 23:00, Tue and Sun around 15:30 depending on other film times; Opernring 19, tel. 01/587-8406, www.burgkino.at).

SLEEPING

As you move out from the center, hotel prices drop. My listings are in the old center (figure at least €100 for a decent double), along the likeable Mariahilfer Strasse (around €80), and near the Westbahnhof (around €60). While few accommodations in Vienna are air-conditioned (they are troubled by the fact that, per person, Las Vegas expends more energy keeping people cool than arctic Norway does to keep people warm), you can generally get fans on request. Places with elevators often have a few stairs to climb, too.

These hotels lose big and you pay more if you find a room through Internet booking sites. Book direct by phone, fax, or e-mail and save. The city has deliberately created an expensive hell for cars in the center. Don't even try. If you must bring a car into Vienna, leave it at an expensive garage.

Sleep Code

(€1 = about $1.20, country code: 43, area code: 01)
S = Single, **D** = Double/Twin, **T** = Triple, **Q** = Quad, **b** = bathroom,
s = shower only. English is spoken at each place. Unless otherwise noted, credit cards are accepted and breakfast is included.

To help you sort easily through these listings, I've divided the rooms into three categories, based on the price for a standard double room with bath:

$$$ **Higher Priced**—Most rooms €120 or more.
$$ **Moderately Priced**—Most rooms between €75–120.
$ **Lower Priced**—Most rooms €75 or less.

Within the Ring, in the Old City Center

You'll pay extra to sleep in the atmospheric old center, but if you can afford it, staying here gives you the best classy Vienna experience.

$$$ **Hotel am Stephansplatz** is a four-star business hotel with 56 rooms. It's plush but not over-the-top, and reasonably priced for its incredible location—literally facing the cathedral—and sleek comfort. Every detail is modern and quality, breakfast is superb with a view of the city waking up around the cathedral, and the staff is always ready with a friendly welcome (Db-€205–245, Tb-€245, €20 less July–Aug and in winter, €15 less Fri–Sat, children free or very cheap, elevator, Stephansplatz 9, U-1 or U-3: Stephansplatz, tel. 01/534-050, fax 01/5340-5710, www.hotelamstephansplatz.at, office@hotelamstephansplatz.at).

$$$ **Pension Pertschy,** circling an old courtyard, is bigger and more hotelesque than the options that follow. Its 50 rooms are huge, but well-worn and a bit musty. Those on the courtyard are quietest (Sb-€90–105, small Db-€133, large Db-€151, cheaper off-season, extra bed-€32, non-smoking rooms, elevator, Habsburgergasse 5, U-1 or U-3: Stephansplatz, tel. 01/534-490, fax 01/534-4949, www.pertschy.com, pertschy@pertschy.com).

$$$ **Pension Aviano** is another peaceful place, with 17 comfortable rooms on the fourth floor above lots of old center action (Sb-€93, Db-€136–143 depending on size, 15 percent cheaper Nov–March, extra bed-€32, non-smoking rooms, fans, elevator, between Neuer Markt and Kärntner Strasse at Marco d'Avianogasse 1, tel. 01/512-8330, fax 01/5128-3306, www.pertschy.com, aviano@pertschy.com). In July and August, they offer four nights for the price of three.

Hotels in Central Vienna

① Hotel am Stephansplatz
② Pension Pertschy
③ Pension Neuer Markt
④ Pension Aviano
⑤ Hotel Schweizerhof
⑥ To Pension Dr. Geissler
⑦ Hotel zur Wiener Staatsoper
⑧ Pension Nossek
⑨ Pension Suzanne
⑩ To Schweizer Pension

$$$ Hotel Schweizerhof is classy, with 55 big rooms, all the comforts, shiny public spaces, and a more formal ambience. It's centrally located midway between St. Stephen's Cathedral and the Danube Canal (Sb-€84–95, Db-€111–140, extra bed-€32, low prices are for July–Aug and slow times, with cash and this book get your best price and then claim a 10 percent discount in 2007, elevator, Bauernmarkt 22, U-1 or U-3: Stephansplatz, tel. 01/533-1931, fax 01/533-0214, www.schweizerhof.at, office@schweizerhof.at). Since this is in the "Bermuda Triangle" nightclub area, it can be noisy on weekends. Ask for a quiet room when you reserve.

$$$ Hotel zur Wiener Staatsoper, the Schweizerhof's sister hotel, is quiet, with a more traditional elegance. Its 22 tidy rooms come with high ceilings, chandeliers, and fancy carpets on parquet floors (tiny Sb-€85, Db-€111–128, Tb-€133–150, extra bed-€22, cheaper prices are for July–Aug and Dec–March, fans on request, elevator, a block from Opera at Krugerstrasse 11, U-1, U-2, or U-4: Karlsplatz, tel. 01/513-1274, fax 01/513-127-415, www.zurwienerstaatsoper.at, office@zurwienerstaatsoper.at, manager Claudia).

$$ At Pension Nossek, an elevator takes you above any street noise into Frau Bernad's and Frau Gundolf's world, where the children seem to be placed among the lace and flowers by an interior designer. With 30 rooms right on the wonderful Graben, this is a particularly good value (S-€46–54, Ss-€58, Sb-€69–73, Db-€115, €28 extra for sprawling suites, extra bed-€35, cash only, elevator, Graben 17, U-1 or U-3: Stephansplatz, tel. 01/5337-0410, fax 01/535-3646, www.pension-nossek.at, reservation@pension-nossek.at).

$$ Pension Suzanne, as Baroque and doily as you'll find in this price range, is wonderfully located a few yards from the Opera. It's small, but run with the class of a bigger hotel. The 25 rooms are packed with properly Viennese antique furnishings (Sb-€77, Db-€96–117 depending on size, 4 percent discount if you pay cash, extra bed-€30, spacious apartment for up to 6 also available, discounts in winter, fans on request, elevator, free Internet access, a block from Opera, Walfischgasse 4, U-1, U-2, or U-4: Karlsplatz and follow signs for Opera exit, tel. 01/513-2507, fax 01/513-2500, www.pension-suzanne.at, info@pension-suzanne.at, manager Michael).

$$ Pension Neuer Markt is family-run, with 37 quiet, comfy rooms in a perfectly central locale. Its hallways have the ambience of a cheap cruise ship (Ss-€85, Sb-€90–115, smaller Ds-€80–96, Db-€110–135, prices vary with season and room size, extra bed-€20, request a quiet room when you reserve, elevator, Seilergasse 9, tel. 01/512-2316, fax 01/513-9105, www.hotelpension.at/neuermarkt, neuermarkt@hotelpension.at).

$$ Schweizer Pension has been family-owned for three generations. The current owners, Anita and Gerhard, run an extremely tight ship, offering 11 homey rooms for a great price, with parquet floors and lots of tourist info (S-€40–45, big Sb-€55–65, D-€58–68, Db-€78–89, Tb-€102–112, Qb-€126–131, prices depend on season and room size, cash only, entirely non-smoking, elevator, laundry-€14/load, Heinrichsgasse 2, U-2 or U-4: Schottenring, tel. 01/533-8156, fax 01/535-6469, www.schweizerpension.com, schweizer.pension@chello.at).

$$ Pension Dr. Geissler has 23 comfortable rooms on the eighth floor of a modern, nondescript apartment building about 10 blocks northeast of St. Stephen's, near the canal (S-€48, Ss-€68, Sb-€76, D-€65, Ds-€77, Db-€95, 20 percent less in winter, elevator, Postgasse 14, U-1 or U-4: Schwedenplatz, tel. 01/533-2803, fax 01/533-2635, www.hotelpension.at/dr-geissler, dr.geissler@hotelpension.at).

Hotels and Pensions Along Mariahilfer Strasse

Lively Mariahilfer Strasse connects the Westbahnhof (West Train Station) and the city center. The U-3 line, starting at the Westbahnhof, goes down Mariahilfer Strasse to the cathedral. This very Viennese street is a tourist-friendly and vibrant area filled with shopping malls, simpler storefronts, and cafés. Its smaller hotels and private rooms are generally run by people from the non-German-speaking part of the former Hapsburg Empire (i.e., Eastern Europe). Most hotels are within a few steps of a U-Bahn stop, just one or two stops from the Westbahnhof (direction from the station: Simmering). The nearest place to do laundry is **Schnell & Sauber Waschcenter** (wash-€6 for small load or €9 for large load, plus a few euros to dry, daily 9:00–21:00, a few blocks north of Westbahnhof on Urban-Loritz-Platz).

$$$ NH Hotels, a Spanish chain, runs two stern, passionless business hotels a few blocks apart on Mariahilfer Strasse. Both rent ideal-for-families suites, each with a living room, two TVs, bathroom, desk, and kitchenette (rack rate: Db suite-€155, going rate usually closer to €100, plus €14 per person for optional breakfast, apartments for 2–3 adults, kids under 12 free, non-smoking rooms, elevator). The 78-room **NH Atterseehaus** is at Mariahilfer Strasse 78 (U-3: Zieglergasse, tel. 01/5245-6000, fax 01/524-560-015, nhatterseehaus@nh-hotels.com), and the **NH Wien** has 106 rooms at Mariahilfer Strasse 32 (U-3: Neubaugasse, tel. 01/521-720, fax 01/521-7215, nhwien@nh-hotels.com). The Web site for both is www.nh-hotels.com.

$$ Pension Corvinus is bright, modern, and warmly run by a Hungarian family: Miklós, Judit, and Zoltan. Its 12 comfortable rooms are spacious, with small, compact bathrooms (Sb-€58,

Db-€91, Tb-€105, these prices promised with this book in 2007, extra bed-€26, non-smoking rooms, portable air-con-€10/day, elevator, free Internet access and Wi-Fi, parking garage-€11/day, on the third floor at Mariahilfer Strasse 57–59, U-3: Neubaugasse, tel. 01/587-7239, fax 01/587-723-920, www.corvinus.at, hotel @corvinus.at).

$$ Pension Mariahilf offers a clean, aristocratic air in an affordable and cozy pension package. Its 12 rooms are spacious but outmoded, with an Art Deco flair. Book direct and ask for a Rick Steves discount in 2007 (Sb-€59–66, Db-€95–102, Tb-€124, lower prices are for longer stays, elevator, Mariahilfer Strasse 49, U-3: Neubaugasse, tel. 01/586-1781, fax 01/586-178-122, www.mariahilf -hotel.at, office@mariahilf-hotel.at).

$$ Haydn Hotel is big and more formal, with masculine public spaces and 50 spacious rooms (Sb-€70–80, Db-€110, suites and family apartments, extra bed-€30, ask for a Rick Steves discount in 2007, non-smoking rooms, air-con, elevator, free Internet access, Mariahilfer Strasse 57–59, U-3: Neubaugasse, tel. 01/587-44140, fax 01/586-1950, www.haydn-hotel.at, info@haydn-hotel .at, Nouri).

$$ Hotel Admiral is huge, quiet, and practical, with 80 large, comfortable rooms (Sb-€66, Db-€91, extra bed-€23, manager Alexandra promises these prices with cash and this book in 2007, cheaper in winter, breakfast-€5 per person, free Internet access, limited free parking, a block off Mariahilfer Strasse at Karl-Schweighofer-Gasse 7, U-2 or U-3: Volkstheater, tel. 01/521-410, fax 01/521-4116, www.admiral.co.at, hotel@admiral.co.at).

$$ Hotel Kugel is run with pride and attitude. "Simple quality and good value" is the motto of the hands-on owner, Johannes Roller. It's a big 34-room hotel with simple Old World charm, offering a fine value (S-€35, Sb-€55, D-€48, Db-€83, supreme Db with canopy beds-€100, Siebensterngasse 43, at corner with Neubaugasse, U-3: Neubaugasse, tel. 01/523-3355, fax 01/5233-3555, www.hotelkugel.at, office@hotelkugel.at). Herr Roller is happy to offer his cheaper rooms for backpackers.

$ Pension Hargita rents 24 generally small, bright, and tidy rooms (mostly twins) with Hungarian decor. This spick-and-span, well-located place is a good value (S-€38, Ss-€45, Sb-€55, D-€52, Ds-€58, Db-€66, Ts-€73, Tb-€80, Qb-€110, extra bed-€12, breakfast-€5, reserve with credit card but pay with cash to get these rates, corner of Mariahilfer Strasse and Andreasgasse, Andreasgasse 1, U-3: Zieglergasse, tel. 01/526-1928, fax 01/526-0492, www.hargita.at, pension@hargita.at, Erika and Tibor). As the pension has some street noise, request a room in the back.

$ K&T Boardinghouse is a top value, renting four big, bright, airy, and comfortable rooms facing the bustling Mariahilfer

Strasse (Db-€65, Tb-€85, Qb-€105, 2-night minimum, no breakfast, air-con-€10/day, cash only, non-smoking, free Internet access in lobby, coffee in rooms, 3 flights up, no elevator, Mariahilfer Strasse 72, U-3: Neubaugasse, tel. 01/523-2989, fax 01/522-0345, www.kaled .at, kaled@chello.at, Tina).

$ Pension Lindenhof rents 19 worn but clean rooms. It's a dark and mysteriously dated time-warp filled with plants (S-€30, Sb-€37, D-€51, Db-€67, cash only, elevator, Lindengasse 4, U-3: Neubaugasse, tel. 01/523-0498, fax 01/523-7362, pensionlindenhof @yahoo.com, Gebrael family, Keram and his father speak English).

$ *Private Rooms:* If you're on a tight budget and wish you had a grandmother to visit in Vienna, stay with English-speaking **Budai Ildiko.** She rents high-ceilinged rooms with Old World furnishings out of her dark and homey apartment. Two cavernous rooms, which sleep two to four, and a skinny twin room all share one bathroom (S-€32, D-€45, T-€64, Q-€79, cash only, no breakfast but free coffee, lots of tourist information, classic old elevator, laundry-€4, Lindengasse 39, apartment #5, U-3: Neubaugasse, tel. 01/523-1058, tel. & fax 01/526-2595, www.wienwien.at, budai @hotmail.com).

Near the Westbahnhof (West Station)

$$$ Hotel Mercure Wien Europaplatz offers high-rise modern efficiency and comfort in 210 air-conditioned rooms, directly across from the Westbahnhof (Db-€130–150 depending on season, online deals as cheap as Db-€80 if you book well in advance, breakfast-€13, elevator, Matrosengasse 6, U-3: Westbahnhof, tel. 01/599-010, fax 01/597-6900, www.mercure.com, h1707@accor.com).

$$ Hotel Ibis Wien, a modern high-rise hotel with American charm, is ideal for anyone tired of quaint old Europe. Its 340 cookie-cutter rooms are bright, comfortable, and modern, with all the conveniences (Sb-€71, Db-€86, Tb-€101, €5 cheaper in July, breakfast-€9, non-smoking rooms, air-con, elevator, parking garage-€11/day, exit Westbahnhof to the right and walk 400 yards, Mariahilfer Gürtel 22–24, U-3: Westbahnhof, tel. 01/59998, fax 01/597-9090, www.ibishotel.com, h0796@accor.com).

$ Pension Fünfhaus is big, clean, and stark—almost institutional. The neighborhood is run-down (with a few ladies loitering late at night) and the staff can be grouchy, but this 47-room pension offers the best doubles you'll find for around €50 (S-€32, Sb-€40, D-€44, Db-€54, T-€66, Tb-€78, 4-person apartment-€92, prices

Hotels and Restaurants Outside the Ring

1. Hotel NH Atterseehaus
2. Hotel NH Wien
3. Hotel Ibis Wien
4. Hotel Mercure Wien Europaplatz
5. Pension Corvinus & Haydn Hotel
6. Pension Mariahilf
7. Hotel Admiral
8. Pension Hargita
9. Pension Lindenhof
10. K&T Boardinghouse
11. Budai Ildiko Rooms
12. Hotel Kugel
13. To Pension Fünfhaus, Wombat's City Hostel & Hostel Ruthensteiner
14. Westend City Hostel
15. Jugendherberge Myrthengasse
16. Lauria Rooms & Hostel
17. Spittelberg Quarter Restaurants
18. Schnitzelwirt
19. Café Sperl
20. City Hall Food Circus
21. Landtmann Café

promised with this book in 2007, cash only, closed mid-Nov–Feb, Sperrgasse 12, U-3: Westbahnhof, tel. 01/892-3545 or 01/892-0286, fax 01/892-0460, www.pension5haus.at, pension5haus@tiscali.at, Frau Susi Tersch). Half the rooms are in the main building and half are in the annex, which has good rooms but is near the train tracks and a bit scary on the street at night. From the station, ride tram #52 or #58 two stops down Mariahilfer Strasse away from center, and ask for Sperrgasse.

Cheap Dorms and Hostels near Mariahilfer Strasse

$ Jugendherberge Myrthengasse is your classic huge and well-run youth hostel, with 260 beds (€15–19 per person in 4- to 6-bed rooms, includes sheets and breakfast, non-members pay €3.50 extra, always open, no curfew, lockers and lots of facilities, Myrthengasse 7, tel. 01/523-6316, fax 01/523-5849, hostel@chello.at).

$ Westend City Hostel, just a block from the Westbahnhof and Mariahilfer Strasse, is well-run and well-located, with 180 beds in 4- to 12-bed dorms (€17–25 per person, depending on how many in the room; includes sheets, breakfast, and locker; cash only, Internet access, laundry, Fügergasse 3, tel. 01/597-6729, fax 01/597-672-927, www.westendhostel.at, westendcityhostel @aon.at).

$ Lauria Rooms and Hostel is a creative little place run by friendly Gosha, with two 10-bed coed dorms with lockers for travelers ages 17 to 30 (€13.50/bed), plus several other rooms sleeping two to six each (any age, €24/bed, D-€48; Kaiserstrasse 77, tram #5 or a 10-min walk from Westbahnhof, tel. 01/522-2555, lauria_vienna@hotmail.com).

$ *More Hostels:* Other hostels with €16 beds and €40 doubles near Mariahilfer Strasse are **Wombat's City Hostel** (near tracks behind the station at Grangasse 6, tel. 01/897-2336, www .wombats-hostels.com, office@wombats-vienna.at) and **Hostel Ruthensteiner** (Robert-Hamerling-Gasse 24, tel. 01/893-4202, www.hostelruthensteiner.com, info@hostelruthensteiner.com).

EATING

The Viennese appreciate the fine points of life, and right up there with waltzing is eating. The city has many atmospheric restaurants. As you ponder the Eastern European specialties on menus, remember that Vienna's diverse empire may be gone, but its flavor lingers.

While cuisines are routinely named for countries, Vienna claims to be the only *city* with a cuisine of its own: Vienna soups come with fillings (semolina dumpling, liver dumpling, or pancake slices). *Gulasch* is a beef ragout of Hungarian origin (spiced with onion and paprika). Of course, Viennese schnitzel *(Wiener Schnitzel)* is traditionally a breaded and fried veal cutlet (though pork is more common these days). Another meat specialty is boiled beef *(Tafelspitz)*. While you're sure to have *Apfelstrudel*, try the sweet cheese strudel, too *(Topfenstrudel—*wafer-thin strudel pastry filled with sweet cheese and raisins). The *dag* you see in some prices stands for "decigram" (10 grams). Therefore, *10 dag* is 100 grams, or about a quarter-pound.

On nearly every corner, you can find a colorful *Beisl* (BYE-zul). These uniquely Viennese taverns are a characteristic cross between an English pub and a French brasserie—filled with poetry teachers and their students, couples loving without touching, housewives on their way home from cello lessons, and waiters who enjoy serving hearty food and good drink at an affordable price. Ask at your hotel for a good *Beisl*.

Near St. Stephen's Cathedral

Each of these eateries is within about a five-minute walk of the cathedral.

Gigerl Stadtheuriger offers a friendly near-*Heuriger* experience (à la Grinzing—see "Vienna's Wine Gardens," page 788), often with accordion or live music, without leaving the city center. Just point to what looks good. Food is sold by the weight; 100 grams *(10 dag)* is about a quarter-pound (cheese and cold meats cost about €3 per 100 grams, salads are about €2 per 100 grams; price sheet is posted on the wall to right of buffet line). The *Karree* pork with herbs is particularly tasty and tender. They also have menu entrées, spinach strudel (€2), quiche, *Apfelstrudel,* and, of course, casks of new and local wines (sold by the *Achtel*). Meals run €7 to €11 (daily 15:00–24:00, indoor/outdoor seating, behind cathedral, a block off Kärntner Strasse, a few cobbles off Rauhensteingasse on Blumenstock, tel. 01/513-4431).

Am Hof Eateries: The square called Am Hof (U-3: Herrengasse) is surrounded by a maze of atmospheric medieval lanes; the following eateries are all within a block of the square. **Restaurant Ofenloch** serves good, old-fashioned Viennese cuisine with friendly service, both indoors and out. This 300-year-old eatery, with great traditional ambience, is dressy (with white tablecloths) but intimate and woodsy. It's central but not overrun with tourists (€12–18 main dishes, Tue–Sat 11:30–24:00, Mon 18:00–24:00, closed Sun, Kurrentgasse 8, tel. 01/533-8844). **Brezel-Gwölb,** a Tolkien-esque wine cellar with outdoor dining on a quiet square, serves delicious light meals, fine *Krautsuppe* (cabbage soup), and old-fashioned Viennese dishes. It's ideal for a romantic late-night glass of wine (daily 11:30–1:00, leave Am Hof on Drahtgasse, then

Restaurants in Central Vienna

U – U-BAHN STOP
T – TRAM STOP
★ – STEPHANS-PLATZ

100 YDS.
100 METERS

1. Gigerl Stadtheuriger
2. Restaurant Ofenloch
3. Brezel-Gwölb
4. Beisl Zum Scherer
5. Esterhazykeller
6. To Melker Stiftskeller
7. To Zu den Drei Hacken
8. Zum Schwarzen Kameel
9. Wrenkh Vegetarian Restaurant & Bar
10. Buffet Trzesniewski
11. Julius Meinl am Graben Deli
12. Café Hawelka & Reinthaler's Beisl
13. Gyros
14. To Plachutta Restaurant
15. Zanoni & Zanoni Gelateria
16. Café Rest. Palmenhaus
17. Rosenberger Markt Rest.
18. Ruckenbauer (in Underpass)
19. Kurkonditorei Oberlaa & Le Bol Patisserie Bistro
20. Danieli Ristorante
21. Starbucks
22. Sacher Café
23. Café Braunerhof
24. To Café Pruckel
25. Café Tirolerhof
26. Loos American Bar

take first left to Ledererhof 9, tel. 01/533-8811). Around the corner, **Beisl "Zum Scherer"** is untouristy and serves traditional plates for €10. Sitting outside, you'll face a stern Holocaust memorial. Inside comes with a soothing woody atmosphere and intriguing decor (Mon–Sat 11:30–22:00, closed Sun, Judenplatz 7, tel. 01/533-5164). Just below Am Hof, the ancient and popular **Esterhazykeller** has traditional fare deep underground. For a cheap and sloppy buffet, climb down to the lowest cellar. For table service on a pleasant square, sit outside (Mon–Fri 11:00–23:00, Sat–Sun 16:00–23:00, Haarhof 1, tel. 01/533-3482).

Wine Cellars: These wine cellars are fun and touristy but typical, in the old center, with reasonable prices and plenty of smoke: **Melker Stiftskeller,** less touristy, is a *Stadtheuriger* in a deep and rustic cellar with hearty, inexpensive meals and new wine (Tue–Sat 17:00–24:00, closed Sun–Mon and most of July, between Am Hof and Schottentor U-Bahn stop at Schottengasse 3, tel. 01/533-5530). **Zu den Drei Hacken** is famous for its local specialties (€10 plates, Mon–Sat 11:00–23:00, closed Sun, indoor/outdoor seating, Singerstrasse 28, tel. 01/512-5895).

Zum Schwarzen Kameel ("The Black Camel") is popular for its two classy but very different scenes: a tiny, elegant restaurant and a trendy wine bar. The small, dark-wood, 12-table, Art Nouveau restaurant serves fine gourmet Viennese cuisine (three-course dinner–€43 plus pricey wine). The wine bar is filled with a professional local crowd enjoying small plates from the same kitchen at a better price. This is *the* place for horseradish and thin-sliced ham (*Beinschinken mit Kren*, €7 a plate). I'd order the *Vorspeisenteller* (a great antipasti dish that comes with ham and horseradish) and their *Tafelspitz* (boiled ham and vegetable, €15). Stand, grab a stool, or sit anywhere you can—it's customary to share tables in the wine-bar section. Fine Austrian wines are sold by the *Achtel* (eighth-liter glass) and listed on the board. They also have a buffet of tiny €1–2 sandwiches (daily 11:00–23:00, Bognergasse 5, tel. 01/533-8125).

Wrenkh Vegetarian Restaurant and Bar is well-liked for its high vegetarian cuisine. Chef Wrenkh offers daily €8 fixed-price meals at lunch and €8–13 dinner plates in a bright, mod bar or in a dark, fancier restaurant (Mon–Sat 11:30–23:00, closed Sun, can be smoky, Bauernmarkt 10, tel. 01/533-1526).

Buffet Trzesniewski is an institution—justly famous for its elegant and cheap finger sandwiches and small beers (€1 each). Three different sandwiches and a *kleines Bier (Pfiff)* make a fun, light lunch. Point to whichever delights look tasty (or grab the English translation sheet and take time to study your 21 sandwich options). The classic favorites are *Geflügelleber* (chicken liver), *Matjes mit Zwiebel* (herring with onions), and *Speck mit Ei* (bacon and eggs). Pay for your sandwiches and a drink. Take your drink tokens to the lady on the right. Sit on the bench and scoot over to a tiny table when a spot opens up. Trzesniewski has been a Vienna favorite for a century...and many of its regulars seem to have been here for the grand opening (Mon–Fri 8:30–19:30, Sat 9:00–17:00, closed Sun, 50 yards off Graben, nearly across from brooding Café Hawelka, Dorotheergasse 2, tel. 01/512-3291). In the fall, this is a good opportunity to try the fancy grape juices—*Most* or *Traubenmost*. Their other location, at Mariahilfer Strasse 95, serves the same sandwiches with the same menu in the same ambience, and is near many recommended hotels.

Reinthaler's Beisl is a time-warp serving simple, traditional *Beisl* fare all day. It's handy for its location (a block off the Graben, across the street from Buffet Trzesniewski) and because it's a rare restaurant in the center that's open on Sunday. Its fun, classic interior winds way back (use the handwritten daily menu rather than the printed English one, €6–10 plates, daily 11:00–23:00, at Dorotheergasse 4, tel. 01/513-1249).

Julius Meinl am Graben, a posh supermarket right on the Graben, has been famous since 1862 as a top-end delicatessen with all the gourmet fancies. Along with the picnic fixings on the shelves, there's a café with light meals and great outdoor seating, a stuffy and pricey restaurant upstairs, and a take-away counter (shop open Mon–Fri 8:30–19:30, Sat 9:00–18:00, closed Sun; restaurant open Mon–Sat until 24:00, closed Sun; Am Graben 19, tel. 01/532-3334).

Akakiko Sushi: If you're just schnitzeled out, this small chain of Japanese restaurants with an easy sushi menu may suit you. The €9 bento box meals are a tasty value. Three locations have no charm but are fast, reasonable, and convenient (€7–10 meals, all open daily 10:30–23:30): Singerstrasse 4 (a block off Kärntner Strasse near the cathedral), Heidenschuss 3 (near other recommended eateries just off Am Hof), and Mariahilfer Strasse 42–48 (fifth floor of Kaufhaus Gerngross, near many recommended hotels).

Gyros is a humble little Greek/Turkish joint run by Yilmaz, a fun-loving Turk from Izmir. He simply loves to feed people—the food is great, the price is cheap, and you almost feel like you took a quick trip to Turkey (daily 10:00–23:30, a long block off Kärntner Strasse at corner of Fichtegasse and Seilerstätte, tel. 01/228-9551).

Plachutta Restaurant, with a stylish green-and-cream, elegant-but-comfy interior and breezy covered terrace, is famous for the best beef in town. You'll find an enticing menu with all the classic Viennese beef dishes, fine desserts, attentive service, and an enthusiastic and sophisticated local clientele. They've developed the art of beef to the point of producing popular cookbooks. Their specialty is a page-long list of *Tafelspitz*—a traditional copper pot of boiled beef with broth and vegetables. Treat the broth as your

Wieners in Wien

For hardcore Viennese cuisine, drop by a *Würstelstand*. The local hot-dog stand is a fixture on city squares through the old center, serving a variety of hot dogs and pickled side dishes with a warm corner-meeting-place atmosphere. The *Wiener* we know is named for Vienna, but the guy who invented the weenie studied in Frankfurt. Out of nostalgia for his school years, he named his fun fast food for that city...a *Frankfurter*. Only in Vienna are *Wieners* called *Frankfurters*. (Got that?)

Explore the fun menus. Be adventurous. The many varieties of sausage cost €2–3 each. Key words: *Weisswurst*—boiled white sausage, *Bosna*—with onions and curry, *Käsekrainer*—with melted cheese inside, *Debreziner*—spicy Hungarian, *Frankfurter*—our weenie, *frische*—fresh ("eat before the noon bells"), *Kren*—horseradish, and *Senf*—mustard (ask for *süss*—sweet or *scharf*—sharp). Generally, the darker the weenie, the spicier it is. Only a tourist puts the sausage in a bun like a hot dog. Munch alternately between the meat and the bread ("that's why you have two hands"), and you'll look like a native.

You'll find particularly good stands on Hoher Markt, Graben, and in front of the Albertina Museum.

soup course. A chart on the menu lets you choose your favorite cut. Make a reservation for this high-energy Vienna favorite (€16–21 per pot, daily 11:30–23:00, 10-min walk from St. Stephen's Cathedral, Wollzeile 38, U-3: Stubentor, tel. 01/512-1577).

Ice Cream!: **Zanoni & Zanoni** is a very Italian *gelateria* run by an Italian family. They're mobbed by happy Viennese hungry for their huge €2 cones to go. Or, to relax and watch the thriving people scene, lick your gelato in their fun outdoor area (daily 7:00–24:00, 2 blocks up Rotenturmstrasse from cathedral at Lugeck 7, tel. 01/512-7979).

Near the Opera

Café Restaurant Palmenhaus overlooks the Palace Garden (Burggarten—see page 756). Tucked away in a green and peaceful corner two blocks behind the Opera in the Hofburg's back yard, this is a world apart. If you want to eat modern Austrian cuisine with palm trees rather than tourists, this is it. And, since it's at the edge of a huge park, it's great for families. Their fresh fish with generous vegetables specials are on the board (€8 two-course lunches available Mon–Fri, €15–18 entrées, open daily 10:00–24:00, serious vegetarian dishes, fish, extensive wine list, indoors in greenhouse or outdoors, tel. 01/533-1033).

Rosenberger Markt Restaurant is mobbed with tour groups. Still, if you don't mind a freeway cafeteria ambience in the center of the German-speaking world's classiest city, this self-service eatery is fast and easy. It's just a block toward the cathedral from the Opera. The best cheap meal here is a small salad or veggie plate stacked high (daily 10:30–23:00, lots of fruits, veggies, fresh-squeezed juices, addictive banana milk, ride the glass elevator downstairs, Maysedergasse 2, tel. 01/512-3458).

Ruckenbauer, a fast-food kiosk in a transit underpass (under the street in front of the Opera), is a favorite for a quick bite (daily 6:00–20:00). Their €1.50 *Tramezzini* sandwiches and fine pastries make a classy, quick picnic lunch or dinner before the opera (just 100 yards away).

Kurkonditorei Oberlaa may not have the royal and plush fame of Demel (see page 742), but this is where Viennese connoisseurs serious about the quality of their pastries go to get fat. With outdoor seating on Neuer Markt, it's particularly nice on a hot summer day (€10 daily three-course lunches, great selection of cakes, daily 8:00–20:00, Neuer Markt 16, tel. 01/5132-9360). Next door, **Le Bol Patisserie Bistro** satisfies your need for something French. The staff speaks to you in French, serving fine €8 salads, baguette sandwiches, and fresh croissants (daily 8:00–22:00, Neuer Markt 14).

Danieli Ristorante is your best classy Italian bet in the old center. White-tablecloth dressy, but not at all stuffy, it has reasonable prices (€8–12 pizza and pastas, fresh fish, open daily, 30 yards off Kärntner Strasse opposite Neuer Markt at Himmelpfortgasse 3, tel. 01/513-7913).

City Hall (Rathaus) Food Circus: During the summer, scores of outdoor food stands and hundreds of picnic tables are set up in the park in front of the City Hall. Local mobs enjoy mostly ethnic meals on disposable plates for decent-but-not-cheap prices. The fun thing here is the energy of the crowd, and a feeling that you're truly eating as the Viennese do...not schnitzel and quaint traditions, but trendy "world food" with young people out having fun in a fine Vienna park setting (July–Aug daily from 11:00 until late, in front of City Hall on the Ringstrasse).

Spittelberg Quarter

A charming cobbled grid of traffic-free lanes and Biedermeier apartments has become a favorite neighborhood for Viennese wanting a little dining charm between the MuseumsQuartier and Mariahilfer Strasse (handy to many recommended hotels; take Stiftgasse from Mariahilfer Strasse, or wander over here after you close down the Kunsthistorisches Museum). Tables tumble down sidewalks and into breezy courtyards filled with appreciative natives enjoying dinner or a relaxing drink. It's only worth the trip on a balmy summer evening, as it's dead in bad weather. Stroll Spittelberggasse, Schrankgasse, and Gutenberggasse and pick your favorite. Don't miss the vine-strewn wine garden at Schrankgasse 1.

Amerlingbeisl, with a casual atmosphere both on the cobbled street and in its vine-covered courtyard, is a great value (€7 plates, €6–8 daily specials, salads, veggie dishes, traditional specialties, daily 9:00–24:00, Stiftgasse 8, tel. 01/526-1660).

Plutzer Bräu, next door, is also good (ribs, burgers, traditional dishes, Tirolean beer from the keg, daily 11:00–2:00, food until 22:30, Schrankgasse 4, tel. 01/526-1215).

Witwe Bolte is classier and a good choice for uninspired Viennese cuisine with tablecloths. Its tiny square has wonderful leafy ambience (daily 11:30–15:00 & 17:30–23:30, Gutenberggasse 13, tel. 01/523-1450).

Zu Ebener Erde and Erster Stock is a charming little restaurant with a near-gourmet menu. The upstairs is Biedermeier-style, with violet tablecloths and seating for about 20. The downstairs is more casual and woody. Reservations are smart (modern Viennese seasonal fixed-price meal-€40, traditional three-course fixed-price meal-€28, Tue–Sat from 18:00, closed Sun–Mon, Burggasse 13, tel. 01/523-6254).

Near Mariahilfer Strasse

Mariahilfer Strasse is filled with reasonable cafés serving all types of cuisine. For a quick yet traditional bite, consider the venerable **Buffet Trzesniewski** sandwich bar at Mariahilfer Strasse 95 (described in "Near St. Stephen's Cathedral").

Schnitzelwirt is an old classic with a 1950s patina and a clientele to match. In this smoky, working-class place, no one finishes their schnitzel ("to go" for the dog is wrapped in newspaper, "to go" for you is wrapped in foil). You'll find no tourists, just cheap €6 schnitzel meals (Mon–Sat 11:00–22:00, closed Sun, Neubaugasse 52, tel. 01/523-3771).

Naschmarkt (described on page 776) is Vienna's best Old World market, with plenty of fresh produce, cheap local-style eateries, cafés, *Döner Kebab* and sausage stands, and the best-value sushi in town (Mon–Fri 6:00–18:30, Sat 6:00–17:00, closed Sun, closes earlier in winter, U-4: Kettenbrückengasse). Survey the lane of eateries at the end of the market nearest the Opera. The circa-1900 pub is inviting. Picnickers can buy supplies at the market and eat on nearby Karlsplatz (plenty of chairs facing the Charles Church).

TRANSPORTATION CONNECTIONS

Vienna has two main train stations: the Westbahnhof (West Station), serving Munich, Salzburg, and some Budapest-bound trains; and the Südbahnhof (South Station), serving the Czech Republic, Poland, Slovenia, Croatia, other Budapest-bound trains, and usually Italy (though some Italy-bound trains go from the Westbahnhof). A third station, Franz Josefs, serves Austria's Danube Valley (including Krems, but Melk is served by the Westbahnhof). There are exceptions, so always confirm which station your train leaves from. Metro line U-3 connects the Westbahnhof with the center, tram D takes you from the Südbahnhof and the Franz Josefs station to downtown, and tram #18 connects West and South stations. Train info: tel. 051-717 (to get an operator, dial 2, then 1).

Vienna is a handy springboard for a trip to Prague or Budapest—it's three hours by train from Budapest (€40 one-way; covered by any railpass that includes both Austria and Hungary) and four hours from Prague (€44 one-way, €88 round-trip; Eurailpass-holders need only a ticket from the Czech border into Prague: €28 one-way, €56 round-trip).

From Vienna by Train to: Bratislava (about hourly, 1 hr; or try the boat trip described on page 784), **Budapest** (6/day, 3 hrs), **Prague** (6/day, 4.5 hrs), **Český Krumlov** (5/day, 6–7 hrs, up to 3 changes), **Kraków** (4/day, 6–9 hrs, 2 direct including a night train departing at about 22:00, arriving around 6:00), **Warsaw** (4/day, 7–10 hrs, 2 direct including a night train), **Ljubljana** (7/day, 6–7 hrs, convenient early-morning direct train, others change in Villach or Maribor), **Zagreb** (8/day, 6–10 hrs, 3 direct, others with up to 3 changes including Villach and Ljubljana), **Krems** (hourly, 1 hr), **Melk** (2/hr, 1 hr, some with change in St. Pölten), **Salzburg** (hourly, 3 hrs), **Innsbruck** (every 2 hrs, 5.5 hrs), **Munich** (3/day direct, 4 hrs; otherwise about hourly, 5 hrs, transfer in Salzburg), **Berlin** (5/day, 10 hrs, longer on night train), **Zurich** (3/day, 9 hrs), **Rome** (1/day, 13 hrs), **Venice** (3/day, 7 hrs, longer on night train), **Frankfurt** (8/day, direct every 2 hours, 7 hrs, more with up to 2 changes, usually in Munich and Salzburg), **Amsterdam** (1/day, 14 hrs).

Excursions by Car with Driver: Those wishing they had wheels may consider hiring Johann (see page 730) for Danube excursions from Vienna or en route to Salzburg (particularly economical for groups of 3–4).

UNDERSTANDING YUGOSLAVIA

Americans struggle to understand the complicated breakup of Yugoslavia (especially when visiting countries that rose from its ashes, such as Croatia and Slovenia). During the Yugoslav era, it was no less confusing. As the old joke went, Yugoslavia had eight distinct peoples in six republics, with five languages, three religions (Orthodox, Catholic, and Muslim), and two alphabets (Roman and Cyrillic), but only one Yugoslav—Tito.

Everyone you talk to in the former Yugoslavia will have a different version of events. A very wise Bosnian Muslim told me, "Listen to all three sides—Muslim, Serb, and Croat. Then decide for yourself what you think." That's the best advice I can offer. But since you likely won't have time for that on your brief visit, here's an admittedly oversimplified, as-impartial-as-possible history to get you started.

Who's Who

For starters, it helps to have a handle on the Balkans—the southeastern European peninsula between the Adriatic and the Black Sea, stretching from Hungary to Greece. The Balkan Peninsula has always been a crossroads of cultures. The Illyrians, Greeks, and Romans had settlements here before the Slavs moved into the region from the north around the seventh century. During the next millennium and a half, the western part of the peninsula—which would become Yugoslavia—was divided by a series of cultural, ethnic, and religious fault lines.

The most important influences were three religions: **Western Christianity** (i.e., Roman Catholicism, primarily brought to the western part of the region by Charlemagne, and later reinforced by the Austrian Hapsburgs), **Eastern Orthodox Christianity** (brought to the east from the Byzantine Empire), and **Islam** (in

Yugoslav Succession

AUSTRIA
HUNGARY
SLOVENIA
ITALY ★Ljub.
SLOVENE
★ Zagreb
HUNGARIAN
ROMANIA
VOJVODINA
SERBO
BOSNIA-
HERZ.
★ Belgrade
SERBIA
CROATIA
CROATIAN
★
Sarajevo
ADRIATIC
SEA
★ Podgorica
KOSOVO
BULG
MONTE-
NEGRO
ALBANIAN
★ Skopje
MACEDONIA
50 MILES
100 KM
ALBANIA
GREECE

〰 Former Yugoslavia Border

／／／ "Serbian Krajina"
(Serb-controlled 1991-1995)

— Current Political Borders

⌐‿⌐ Minority-Dominated
Provinces Within Serbia

SLOVENE
Languages

the south, from the Ottomans).

Two major historical factors made the Balkans what they are today: The first was the **split of the Roman Empire** in the fourth century A.D., dividing the Balkans down the middle into Roman Catholic (west) and Byzantine Orthodox (east)—roughly along today's Bosnian-Serbian border. The second was the **invasion of the Islamic Ottomans** in the 14th century. The Ottoman victory at the Battle of Kosovo (1389) began five centuries of Islamic influence in Bosnia-Herzegovina and Serbia, further dividing the Balkans into Christian (north) and Muslim (south).

Because of these and other events, several distinct ethnic identities emerged. Confusingly, the major "ethnicities" of Yugoslavia are all South Slavs—they're descended from the same ancestors, and speak essentially the same language, but they practice different religions. Catholic South Slavs are called **Croats** or **Slovenes** (mostly west of the Dinaric Mountains: Croats along the Adriatic coast, and Slovenes farther north, in the Alps); Orthodox South Slavs are called **Serbs** (mostly east of the Dinaric range); and Muslim South Slavs are called **Bosniaks** (who converted to Islam under the Ottomans, mostly living in the Dinaric Mountains). To complicate matters, the region is also home to several non-Slavic groups, including **Hungarians** (in the northern province of Vojvodina) and **Albanians,** concentrated in the southern province of Kosovo (descended from the Illyrians, who lived here long before the Greeks and Romans).

Of course, these geographic divisions are extremely general. The groups overlapped a lot—which is exactly why the breakup of Yugoslavia was so contentious. For example, one of the biggest causes of this ethnic mixing came in the 16th century. The Ottomans were threatening to overrun Europe, and the Austrian Hapsburgs wanted a buffer zone—a "human shield." The Hapsburgs encouraged Serbs who were fleeing from Ottoman invasions to settle along today's Croatian-Bosnian border (known as *Vojna Krajina,* or "Military Frontier"). The Serbs stayed after the Ottomans had left, establishing homes in predominantly Croat communities.

After the Ottoman threat subsided in the late 17th century, some of the Balkans (basically today's Slovenia and Croatia) became part of the Austrian Hapsburg Empire. The Ottomans stayed longer in the south and east (today's Bosnia-Herzegovina and Serbia)—making the cultures in these regions even more different. Serbia finally gained its independence from the Ottomans in the mid-19th century, but it wasn't too long before World War I started...after a disgruntled Bosnian Serb nationalist killed the Austrian archduke.

South Slavs Unite

When the Austro-Hungarian Empire fell at the end of World War I, the European map was redrawn for the 20th century. After centuries of being governed by foreign powers, the South Slavs began to see their shared history as more important than their minor differences. A tiny country of a few million Croats or Slovenes couldn't have survived. Rather than be absorbed by a non-Slavic power, the South Slavs decided that there was safety in numbers, and banded together as a single state—first called the "Kingdom of the Serbs, Croats, and Slovenes" (1918), later known as Yugoslavia ("Land of the South Slavs"—*yugo* means "south"). "Yugoslav unity" was in the air, but this new union was artificial and ultimately bound to fail (not unlike the partnership between the Czechs and Slovaks, formed at the same time and for much the same reasons).

From the very beginning, the various ethnicities struggled for power within the new union. Croats in particular often felt they were treated as lesser partners under the Serbs. (For example, many Croats objected to naming the country's official language "Serbo-Croatian"—why not "Croato-Serbian?") Serbia already had a very strong king, Alexander Karađorđević, who immediately made attempts to give his nation a leading role in the federation. A nationalistic Croatian politician named Stjepan Radić, pushing for a more equitable division of powers, was shot by a Serb during a parliament session in 1928. Karađorđević abolished the parliament and became dictator. Six years later, infuriated Croatian separatists killed him.

Many Croat nationalists sided with the Nazis in World War II in the hopes that it would be their ticket to independence from Serbia. The Nazi puppet government in Croatia (called the Ustaše) conducted an extermination campaign, murdering many Serbs (along with Jews and Roma) living in Croatia; other Serbs were forced to flee the country or convert to Catholicism. Most historians consider the Ustaše concentration camps to be the first instance of "ethnic cleansing" in the Balkans...and the Serbs' long memory of it may go far in explaining their own ethnic cleansing of the Croats in the 1990s.

At the end of World War II, the rest of Eastern Europe was "liberated" by the Soviets—but the Yugoslavs regained their independence on their own, as their communist partisan army forced out the Nazis. After the short but rocky Yugoslav union between the World Wars, it seemed that no one could hold the southern Slavs together in a single nation. But there was one man who could, and did: Tito.

Tito

Communist Party president and war hero Josip Broz—who dubbed himself with the simple nickname Tito—emerged as a political leader after World War II. With a Slovene for a mother, a Croat for a father, a Serb for a wife, and a home in Belgrade, Tito was a true Yugoslav. Tito had a compelling vision that this fractured union of the South Slavs could function. And it did. For the next three decades, Tito managed to keep Yugoslavia intact, essentially by the force of his own personality.

Tito's new incarnation of Yugoslavia aimed for a more equitable division of powers. It was made up of six republics, each with its own parliament and president: **Croatia** (mostly Catholic Croats), **Slovenia** (mostly Catholic Slovenes), **Serbia** (mostly Orthodox Serbs), **Bosnia-Herzegovina** (the most diverse—mostly Muslim Bosniaks, but with very large Croat and Serb populations), **Montenegro** (mostly Serb-like Montenegrins), and **Macedonia** (with about 25 percent Albanians and 75 percent Macedonians—who are claimed variously by Bulgarians and Serbs). There were also two autonomous provinces, each one dominated by an ethnicity that was a minority in greater Yugoslavia: Albanians in **Kosovo** (to the south) and Hungarians in **Vojvodina** (to the north). Tito hoped that by allowing these two provinces some degree of independence—including voting rights—they could balance the political clout of Serbia, preventing a single republic from dominating the union.

Each republic managed its own affairs...but always under the watchful eye of president-for-life Tito, who said that the borders between the republics should be "like white lines in a marble column."

Tito was unquestionably a political genius, carefully crafting a workable union. For example, every Yugoslav had to serve in the National Army, and Tito made sure that each unit was a microcosm of the complete Yugoslavia—with equal representation from each ethnic group. (Allowing an all-Slovene unit, stationed in Slovenia, would be begging for trouble.) There was also a dark side to Tito, who resorted to violent, strong-arming measures to assert his power, especially early in his reign. He staged brutal, Stalin-esque "show trials" to intimidate potential dissidents, and imprisoned church leaders, such as Alojzije Stepinac (see page 703). Nationalism was strongly discouraged, and this tight control—though sometimes oppressive—kept the country from unraveling. In retrospect, most former Yugoslavs forgive Tito for governing with an iron fist, believing that this was necessary for keeping the country strong and united. Today, most of them consider Tito more of a hero than a villain, and usually speak of him with reverence.

Tito's Yugoslavia was communist, but it wasn't Soviet communism; you'll find no statues of Lenin or Stalin here. Despite strong pressure from Moscow, Tito refused to ally himself with the Soviets—and therefore received good will (and $2 billion) from the United States. Tito's vision was for a "third way," where Yugoslavia could work with both East and West, without being dominated by either. Yugoslavia was the most free of the communist states: While large industry was nationalized, Tito's system allowed for small businesses. This experience with market economy benefited Yugoslavs when Eastern Europe's communist regimes eventually fell. And even during the communist era, Yugoslavia remained a popular tourist destination, keeping its standards more in line with the West than the Soviet states.

Things Fall Apart

With Tito's death in 1980, Yugoslavia's six constituent republics gained more autonomy, with a rotating presidency. But before long, the delicate union Tito had held together began to unravel. In the late 1980s, Serbian politician Slobodan Milošević took advantage of ethnic-motivated conflicts in the province of Kosovo to become president of Serbia and grab more centralized power. Other republics (especially Slovenia and Croatia) feared that he would gut their nation to create a "Greater Serbia," instead of a friendly coalition of diverse Yugoslav republics. Some of the leaders—most notably Milan Kučan of Slovenia—tried to avoid warfare by suggesting a plan for a loosely united Yugoslavia, based on the Swiss model of independent yet confederated cantons. But other parties, who wanted complete autonomy, refused. Over the next decade, Yugoslavia broke apart, with much bloodshed.

The Slovene Secession

Slovenia was the first Yugoslav republic to hold free elections, in the spring of 1990. The voters wanted the communists out—and their own independent nation. Along with being the most ethnically homogeneous of the Yugoslav nations, Slovenia was also the most Western-oriented, most prosperous, and most geographically isolated—so secession just made sense. But that didn't mean that there was no violence.

After months of stockpiling weapons, Slovenia closed its borders and declared independence from Yugoslavia on June 25, 1991. Belgrade sent in the Yugoslav National Army to take control of Slovenia's borders with Italy and Austria, figuring that whoever controlled the borders had a legitimate claim on sovereignty. Fighting broke out around these borders. Because the Yugoslav National Army was made up of soldiers from all republics, many Slovenian soldiers found themselves fighting their own countrymen. (The army had cut off communication between these conscripts and the home front, so they didn't know what was going on—and often didn't realize they were fighting their friends and neighbors until they were close enough to see them.)

Slovenian civilians bravely entered the fray, blockading the Yugoslav barracks with their own cars and trucks. Most of the Yugoslav soldiers—now trapped—were young and inexperienced, and were terrified of the ragtag (but relentless) Slovenian militia even though their own resources were far superior.

After 10 days of fighting and fewer than a hundred deaths, Belgrade relented. The Slovenes stepped aside and allowed the Yugoslav National Army to take all of the weapons with them back into Yugoslavia, and destroy all remaining military installations. When the Yugoslav National Army had cleared out, they left the Slovenes with their freedom.

The Croatian Conflict

In April of 1990, a historian named Franjo Tuđman—and his highly nationalistic, right-wing party, the HDZ (Croatian Democratic Union)—won Croatia's first free elections (for more on Tuđman, see page 612). Like the Slovenian reformers, Tuđman and the HDZ wanted more autonomy from Yugoslavia. But Tuđman's methods were more extreme than that of the gently progressive Slovenes. Tuđman immediately invoked the spirit of the last group that led an "independent" Croatia—the Ustaše, who had ruthlessly run Croatia's puppet government under the Nazis. Tuđman reintroduced the Ustaše's red-and-white checkerboard flag and their currency (the *kuna*). The 600,000 Serbs living in Croatia, mindful of their grandparents who had been massacred by the Ustaše, saw the writing on the wall and began to rise up.

The first conflicts were in the Serb-dominated Croatian city of Knin. Among Tuđman's reforms was the decree that all of Croatia's policemen wear a new uniform, which bore a striking resemblance to Nazi-era Ustaše uniforms. Infuriated by this slap in the face, and inspired by Slobodan Milošević's rhetoric, Serb police officers in Knin refused. Over the next few months, tense negotiations ensued. Serbs from Knin and elsewhere began the so-called "tree trunk revolution"—blocking important tourist roads to the coast with logs and other barriers. Meanwhile, the Croatian government—after being denied support from the United States—illegally purchased truckloads of guns from Hungary. Tensions escalated, and the first shots of the conflict were fired on Easter Sunday of 1991 at Plitvice Lakes National Park, between Croatian policemen and Serb irregulars from Knin.

By the time Croatia declared its independence (on June 25, 1991—the same day as Slovenia), it was already embroiled in the beginnings of a bloody war. Croatia's more than half-million Serb residents immediately declared their own independence from Croatia. The Serb-dominated Yugoslav National Army swept in, supposedly to keep the peace between Serbs and Croats—but it soon became obvious that they were there to support the Serbs. The ill-prepared Croatian resistance, made up mostly of policemen and a few soldiers who defected from the Yugoslav National Army, were quickly overwhelmed. The Serbs gained control over a large swath of inland Croatia, mostly around the Bosnian border (including Plitvice) and in Croatia's inland panhandle (the region of Slavonia). They called this territory—about a quarter of Croatia—the **Republic of Serbian Krajina** (*krajina* means "border"). This new "country" (hardly recognized by any other nations) minted its own money and had its own army, much to the consternation of Croatia—which was now worried about the safety of Croats living in Krajina.

As the Serbs advanced, hundreds of thousands of Croats fled to the coast and lived as refugees in resort hotels. The Serbs began a campaign of ethnic cleansing, systematically removing Croats from their territory—often by murdering them. The bloodiest siege was at the town of **Vukovar,** which the Yugoslav army surrounded and shelled relentlessly for three months. At the end of the siege, thousands of Croat soldiers and civilians mysteriously disappeared. Many of these people were later discovered in mass graves; hundreds are still missing, and bodies are still being found. In a surprise move, Serbs also attacked the tourist resort of **Dubrovnik** (see page 620). By early 1992, both Croatia and the Republic of Serbian Krajina had established their borders, and a tense ceasefire fell over the region.

The standoff lasted until 1995, when the now well-equipped Croatian Army retook the Serbian-occupied areas in a series of two offensives—**"Lightning"** *(Blijesak),* in the northern part of the country, and **"Storm"** *(Oluja),* farther south. Some Croats retaliated for earlier ethnic cleansing by doing much of the same to Serbs—torturing and murdering them, and dynamiting their homes. Croatia quickly established the borders that exist today, and the Erdut Agreement brought peace to the region—but most of the 600,000 Serbs who once lived in Croatia/Krajina were forced into Serbia or were killed. Today, only a few thousand Serbs remain in Croatia. While Serbs have long since been legally invited back to their ancestral Croatian homes, few have returned—afraid of the "welcome" they might receive from the Croat neighbors who killed their relatives or blew up their houses just a few years ago.

The War in Bosnia-Herzegovina

Bosnia-Herzegovina declared its independence from Yugoslavia four months after Croatia and Slovenia did. But Bosnia-Herzegovina was always at the crossroads of Balkan culture, and therefore even more diverse than Croatia—predominantly Muslim Bosniaks (mostly in the cities), but also with large Serb and Croat populations (often farmers), as well as Albanian Kosovars.

In the spring of 1992, Serbs within Bosnia-Herzegovina (with the support of Serbia) began a campaign of ethnic cleansing against the Bosniaks and Croats. Before long, the Croats did the same against the Serbs. A three-way war (between the Bosniaks, Serbs, and Croats) raged for years. Even the many mixed families were forced to choose sides. If you had a Serb mother and a Croat father, you were expected to pick one ethnicity or the other—and your brother might choose the opposite. As families and former neighbors trained their guns on each other, proud and beautiful cities such as Sarajevo and Mostar were turned to rubble, and people throughout Bosnia-Herzegovina lived in a state of constant terror.

Serb sieges of Bosnian Muslim cities—such as the notorious siege of Srebrenica in July of 1995, which ended with a massacre of about 7,000 Bosniak civilians—brought the ongoing atrocities to the world's attention. Perhaps most despicable was the establishment of so-called "rape camps"—concentration camps where Bosniak women were imprisoned and systematically raped by Serb soldiers.

The United Nations Protection Force (UNPROFOR)—dubbed "Smurfs" both for their light-blue helmets and for their ineffectiveness—exercised their limited authority to try to suppress the violence. This ugly situation was brilliantly parodied in the film *No Man's Land* (which won the Oscar for Best Foreign Film in 2002), a very dark comedy about the absurdity of the Bosnian war.

Finally, in 1995, the Dayton Peace Accords carefully divided Bosnia-Herzegovina among the different ethnicities. Today, Bosnia-Herzegovina continues to work on its tenuous peace, rebuild its devastated country, and bring its infrastructure up to its neighbors' standards.

Kosovo

The ongoing Yugoslav crisis finally reached its peak in the Serbian province of Kosovo. After years of poor treatment by the Serbs, Kosovars rebelled in 1998. Milošević sent in the army, and in March 1999, they began a campaign of ethnic cleansing. Thousands of Kosovars were murdered, and hundreds of thousands fled into Albania and Macedonia. NATO planes, under the command of US General and Supreme Allied Commander Wesley Clark, bombed Serb positions for two months, forcing the Serb army to leave Kosovo in the summer of 1999.

The Fall of Milošević

After years of bloody conflicts, Serbian public opinion had decisively swung against their president. The transition began gradually in early 2000, spearheaded by Otpor and other nonviolent, grass-roots, student-based opposition movements. These organizations used clever PR strategies to gain support and convince Serbians that real change was possible. As anti-Milošević sentiments gained momentum, opposing political parties banded together and got behind one candidate, Vojislav Koštunica. Public support for Koštunica mounted, and when the arrogant Milošević called an early election in September 2000, he was soundly defeated. Though Milošević tried to claim that the election results were invalid, determined Serbs streamed into their capital, marched on their parliament, and—like the Czechs and Slovaks a decade before—peacefully took back their nation.

In 2001, Milošević was arrested and sent to The Hague, in

the Netherlands, to stand trial before the International Criminal Tribunal for the Former Yugoslavia (ICTY). Milošević served as his own attorney as his trial wore on for five years, frequently delayed due to his health problems. Then, on March 11, 2006—as his trial was coming to a close—Milošević was found dead in his cell. Ruled a heart attack, Milošević's death, like his life, was controversial. Supporters claimed that Milošević was denied suitable medical care while on trial, some speculated that he was poisoned, and others suspected that he'd intentionally worsened his heart condition to avoid the completion of his trial. Whatever the cause, it seems that in the end Milošević avoided coming to justice—he was never found guilty of a thing.

Finding Their Way: The Former Yugoslav Republics

Today, Slovenia and Croatia are as stable as Western Europe, Bosnia-Herzegovina is slowly putting itself back together, Macedonia feels closer to Bulgaria than to Belgrade, and the last two united parts of "Yugoslavia"—Serbia and Montenegro—have peacefully parted ways, leaving six independent countries where once there was one.

It's important to remember that there were no "good guys" and no "bad guys" in these wars—just a lot of ugliness on all sides. If there were any victims, they were the Bosniaks and the Kosovars—but even they were not blameless. When considering specifically the war between the Croats and the Serbs, it's tempting for Americans to take Croatia's "side"—because we saw them in the role of victims first; because they're Catholic, so they seem more "like us" than the Orthodox Serbs; and because we admire their striving for an independent nation. But in the streets and the trenches, it was never that clear-cut. When Croatians retook Serb-occupied areas in 1995, they were every bit as brutal as the Serbs had been a few years before. Both sides resorted to ethnic cleansing, both sides had victims, and both sides had victimizers.

Perhaps the only "easy" villains in this conflict were Serbian President Slobodan Milošević and Croatian President Franjo Tuđman. Even after the deaths of both men, information continually emerges that makes these two leaders out to be even more ruthless than once thought. It's increasingly clear that Tuđman and Milošević secretly orchestrated the whole brutal war in close association with each other, using their citizens as pawns in a giant war game. (Their ultimate plan was to partition Bosnia-Herzegovina between their newly independent countries, much as Hitler and Stalin secretly plotted to divide Poland.)

It's easy to blame these conflicts on some deep-seated, inevitable cultural hatred among the Yugoslav ethnic groups. But this is an oversimplification, and ignores the fact that Serbs, Croats, Bosniaks, and Kosovars coexisted more or less peacefully and happily during the Tito era. While some long-standing tensions and misunderstandings did exist, it wasn't until Milošević and Tuđman expertly colluded to manipulate them that the country fell into war. By vigorously fanning the embers of ethnic grudges, and carefully controlling media coverage of the escalating violence, these two leaders turned a healthy political debate into a holocaust.

Tension still exists throughout the former Yugoslavia—especially areas that were most war-torn. When Serbs or Croats encounter other Yugoslavs in their travels, they immediately evaluate each other's accent to determine: Are they one of us, or one of them?

But, with time, these hard feelings are fading. The younger generations don't look back—teenaged Slovenes no longer learn Serbo-Croatian, can't imagine not living in an independent little country, and get bored (and a little irritated) when their old-fashioned parents wax nostalgic about the days of a united Yugoslavia. A middle-aged Slovene friend of mine thinks fondly of his months of compulsory service in the Yugoslav National Army, when his unit was made up of Slovenes, Croats, Serbs, Bosniaks, Macedonians, and Montenegrins—all of them countrymen, and all good friends. To these young Yugoslavs, minor ethnic differences didn't matter. He still often visits with his army buddy from Dubrovnik—600 miles away, not long ago part of the same nation—and wishes there had been a way to keep it all together. But he says, optimistically, "I look forward to the day when the other former Yugoslav republics also join the European Union. Then, in a way, we will all be united once again."

APPENDIX

Let's Talk Telephones

To make international calls, you need to break the codes: the international access codes and country codes (see below). For specifics on making local, long-distance, and international calls, please see the "European Calling Chart" on the next page. You'll find more information on telephones in the Introduction on page 34.

Country Codes

After you've dialed the international access code (011 if you're calling from the US or Canada; 00 if you're calling from virtually anywhere in Europe), dial the code of the country you're calling.

Austria—43	Ireland—353
Belgium—32	Italy—39
Bosnia-Herzegovina—387	Montenegro—382
Britain—44	Morocco—212
Canada—1	Netherlands—31
Croatia—385	Norway—47
Czech Rep.—420	Poland—48
Denmark—45	Portugal—351
Estonia—372	Slovakia—421
Finland—358	Slovenia—386
France—33	Spain—34
Germany—49	Sweden—46
Gibraltar—350	Switzerland—41
Greece—30	Turkey—90
Hungary—36	US—1

European Calling Chart

Just smile and dial, using this key:
AC = Area Code, LN = Local Number.

European Country	Calling long distance within ...	Calling from the US or Canada to ...	Calling from a European country to ...
Austria	AC + LN	011 + 43 + AC (without the initial zero) + LN	00 + 43 + AC (without the initial zero) + LN
Belgium	LN	011 + 32 + LN (without initial zero)	00 + 32 + LN (without initial zero)
Britain	AC + LN	011 + 44 + AC (without initial zero) + LN	00 + 44 + AC (without initial zero) + LN
Croatia	AC + LN	011 + 385 + AC (without initial zero) + LN	00 + 385 + AC (without initial zero) + LN
Czech Republic	LN	011 + 420 + LN	00 + 420 + LN
Denmark	LN	011 + 45 + LN	00 + 45 + LN
Estonia	LN	011 + 372 + LN	00 + 372 + LN
Finland	AC + LN	011 + 358 + AC (without initial zero) + LN	999 + 358 + AC (without initial zero) + LN
France	LN	011 + 33 + LN (without initial zero)	00 + 33 + LN (without initial zero)
Germany	AC + LN	011 + 49 + AC (without initial zero) + LN	00 + 49 + AC (without initial zero) + LN
Greece	LN	011 + 30 + LN	00 + 30 + LN
Hungary	06 + AC + LN	011 + 36 + AC + LN	00 + 36 + AC + LN
Ireland	AC + LN	011 + 353 + AC (without initial zero) + LN	00 + 353 + AC (without initial zero) + LN
Italy	LN	011 + 39 + LN	00 + 39 + LN

European Country	Calling long distance within ...	Calling from the US or Canada to ...	Calling from a European country to ...
Netherlands	AC + LN	011 + 31 + AC (without initial zero) + LN	00 + 31 + AC (without initial zero) + LN
Norway	LN	011 + 47 + LN	00 + 47 + LN
Poland	LN	011 + 48 + LN (without initial zero)	00 + 48 + LN (without initial zero)
Portugal	LN	011 + 351 + LN	00 + 351 + LN
Slovakia	AC + LN	011 + 421 + AC (without initial zero) + LN	00 + 421 + AC (without initial zero) + LN
Slovenia	AC + LN	011 + 386 + AC (without initial zero) + LN	00 + 386 + AC (without initial zero) + LN
Spain	LN	011 + 34 + LN	00 + 34 + LN
Sweden	AC + LN	011 + 46 + AC (without initial zero) + LN	00 + 46 + AC (without initial zero) + LN
Switzerland	LN	011 + 41 + LN (without initial zero)	00 + 41 + LN (without initial zero)
Turkey	AC (if no initial zero is included, add one) + LN	011 + 90 + AC (without initial zero) + LN	00 + 90 + AC (without initial zero) + LN

- The instructions above apply whether you're calling a land line or mobile phone.
- The international access codes (the first numbers you dial when making an international call) are 011 if you're calling from the US or Canada, or 00 if you're calling from virtually anywhere in Europe (except Finland, where it's 999).
- To call the US or Canada from Europe, dial 00, then 1 (the country code for the US and Canada), then the area code and number. In short, 00 + 1 + AC + LN = Hi, Mom!

US Embassies

Austria: Boltzmanngasse 16, Vienna, tel. 01/313-390, www
.usembassy.at
Croatia: Ulica Thomasa Jeffersona 2, Zagreb, tel. 01/661-2200,
consular services tel. 01/661-2300, www.usembassy.hr
Czech Republic: Tržiště 15, Prague, tel. 257-022-000, www
.usembassy.cz
Hungary: Szabadság tér 12, Budapest, tel. 1/475-4400, after-hours
emergency tel. 1/475-4703 or 1/475-4924, www.usembassy.hu
Poland: Aleja Ujazdowskie 29/31, Warsaw, tel. 022/504-2000,
www.usinfo.pl; also a US Consulate in Kraków at ulica Stolarska
9, tel. 012/424-5100
Slovakia: Bratislava, tel. 02/5443-3338, www.usembassy.sk
Slovenia: Prešernova 31, Ljubljana, tel. 01/200-5500, www
.usembassy.si

Eastern European Festivals and Holidays

Note that this isn't a complete list; holidays strike without warning. Catholic holidays are celebrated in Poland, Slovakia, Croatia,
and Slovenia (and to a lesser extent in Hungary and the Czech
Republic). For more details on holidays, check with each country's
tourist office (see page 9).

Jan 1	New Year's Day, all countries
Jan 6	Epiphany, Catholic countries
Jan 19	Anniversary of Jan Palach's Death, Prague, Czech Republic (flowers in Wenceslas Square)
Feb 8	National Day of Culture, Slovenia (cel-ebrates Slovenian culture and national poet France Prešeren)
Feb 28–March 8	One World International Human Rights Film Festival, Prague, Czech Republic (www.oneworld.cz)
March 15	National Day, Hungary (celebrates 1848 Revolution)
March 16–April 1	Budapest Spring Festival, Budapest, Hungary (www.festivalcity.hu)
March 22–25	Ski Flying World Championships, Planica, Slovenia (www.planica.info)
April 8–9	Easter Sunday and Monday, all countries
April 27	National Resistance Day, Slovenia
April 30	Witches' Night, Czech Republic (similar to Halloween, with bonfires)
May	Vienna Festival of Arts and Music
May 1	Labor Day, all countries

2007

JANUARY
S	M	T	W	T	F	S
	1	2	3	4	5	6
7	8	9	10	11	12	13
14	15	16	17	18	19	20
21	22	23	24	25	26	27
28	29	30	31			

FEBRUARY
S	M	T	W	T	F	S
				1	2	3
4	5	6	7	8	9	10
11	12	13	14	15	16	17
18	19	20	21	22	23	24
25	26	27	28			

MARCH
S	M	T	W	T	F	S
				1	2	3
4	5	6	7	8	9	10
11	12	13	14	15	16	17
18	19	20	21	22	23	24
25	26	27	28	29	30	31

APRIL
S	M	T	W	T	F	S
1	2	3	4	5	6	7
8	9	10	11	12	13	14
15	16	17	18	19	20	21
22	23	24	25	26	27	28
29	30					

MAY
S	M	T	W	T	F	S
		1	2	3	4	5
6	7	8	9	10	11	12
13	14	15	16	17	18	19
20	21	22	23	24	25	26
27	28	29	30	31		

JUNE
S	M	T	W	T	F	S
					1	2
3	4	5	6	7	8	9
10	11	12	13	14	15	16
17	18	19	20	21	22	23
24	25	26	27	28	29	30

JULY
S	M	T	W	T	F	S
1	2	3	4	5	6	7
8	9	10	11	12	13	14
15	16	17	18	19	20	21
22	23	24	25	26	27	28
29	30	31				

AUGUST
S	M	T	W	T	F	S
			1	2	3	4
5	6	7	8	9	10	11
12	13	14	15	16	17	18
19	20	21	22	23	24	25
26	27	28	29	30	31	

SEPTEMBER
S	M	T	W	T	F	S
						1
2	3	4	5	6	7	8
9	10	11	12	13	14	15
16	17	18	19	20	21	22
23/30	24	25	26	27	28	29

OCTOBER
S	M	T	W	T	F	S
	1	2	3	4	5	6
7	8	9	10	11	12	13
14	15	16	17	18	19	20
21	22	23	24	25	26	27
28	29	30	31			

NOVEMBER
S	M	T	W	T	F	S
				1	2	3
4	5	6	7	8	9	10
11	12	13	14	15	16	17
18	19	20	21	22	23	24
25	26	27	28	29	30	

DECEMBER
S	M	T	W	T	F	S
						1
2	3	4	5	6	7	8
9	10	11	12	13	14	15
16	17	18	19	20	21	22
23/30	24/31	25	26	27	28	29

May 3	Constitution Day, Poland (celebrates Europe's first constitution)
May 8	Liberation Day, Czech Republic and Slovakia
May 12–June 3	"Prague Spring" Music Festival, Prague, Czech Republic (www.festival.cz)
May 13	Prague International Marathon, Prague, Czech Republic (www.pim.cz)
May 17	Ascension Day, Catholic countries
May 27	Pentecost, Catholic countries
May 28	Whitmonday, Hungary
Early June	Dance Week Festival, Zagreb, Croatia (www.danceweekfestival.com)
June 7	Corpus Christi, Catholic countries
June 22	Antifascist Struggle Day, Croatia

June 22–24	Celebration of the Rose, Český Krumlov, Czech Republic (medieval festival, music, theater, dance, knights' tournament)
June 23–24	Floating of the Wreaths Midsummer Festival, Kraków, Poland (wreaths on rafts in Vistula River, fireworks, music)
June 23–July 1	Jewish Culture Festival, Kraków, Poland (www.jewishfestival.pl)
June 25	National Day, Slovenia; Statehood Day, Croatia
Late June	Midsummer Eve Celebrations, Austria
July 5	Sts. Cyril and Methodius Day, Czech Republic and Slovakia
July 6	Jan Hus Day, Czech Republic
July 10–Aug 25	Dubrovnik Summer Festival, Croatia (www.dubrovnik-festival.hr)
Early July–late Aug	Ljubljana Summer Festival, Slovenia (www.festival-lj.si)
July 20–22	Marco Polo Festival, Korčula, Croatia (www.marcopolofest.hr)
July 20–Aug 25	International Music Festival, Český Krumlov, Czech Republic (www.czechmusicfestival.com)
Late July	International Folklore Festival, Zagreb, Croatia (costumes, songs, dances from all over Croatia; www.msf.hr)
Aug 5	National Thanksgiving Day, Croatia; Formula 1 races, Budapest, Hungary (www.hungaroinfo.com/formel1)
Aug 8–15	Sziget Festival, Budapest, Hungary (rock and pop music, www.sziget.hu)
Aug 15	Assumption of Mary, Catholic countries
Aug 20	Constitution Day and St. Stephen's Day, Hungary (fireworks, celebrations)
Aug 29	National Uprising Day, Slovakia (commemorates uprising against Nazis)
Late Aug–early Sept	Jewish Summer Festival, Budapest, Hungary (www.jewishfestival.hu)
Early Sept	Marco Polo Naval Battle Reenactment, Korčula, Croatia
Sept 1	Constitution Day, Slovakia
Sept 12–Oct 1	Prague Autumn Music Festival, Czech Republic (www.pragueautumn.cz)

Sept 28	St. Wenceslas Day, Czech Republic (celebrates national patron saint and Czech statehood)
Oct 8	Independence Day, Croatia
Oct 23	Republic Day, Hungary (remembrances of 1956 Uprising)
Oct 28	Independence Day, Czech Republic
Oct 31	Reformation Day, Slovenia
Late Oct	Budapest Autumn Festival, Budapest, Hungary (music, www.festivalcity.hu)
Nov 1	All Saints' Day/Remembrance Day, Catholic countries (religious festival, some closures)
Nov 11	Independence Day, Poland; St. Martin's Day (official first day of wine season), Slovenia and Croatia
Nov 17	Velvet Revolution Anniversary, Czech Republic and Slovakia
Dec 5	St. Nicholas Eve, Prague, Czech Republic (St. Nick gives gifts to children in town square)
Dec 24–25	Christmas Eve and Christmas Day, all countries
Dec 26	Boxing Day/St. Stephen's Day, all countries; Independence and Unity Day, Slovenia
Dec 31	St. Sylvester's Day, Prague, Czech Republic (fireworks)

Numbers and Stumblers

- Europeans write a few of their numbers differently than we do: 1 = 1, 4 = 4 7 = 7. Learn the difference or miss your train.
- Europeans write dates as day/month/year (Christmas is 25/12/07).
- Commas are decimal points, and decimals are commas. A dollar and a half is 1,50. There are 5.280 feet in a mile.
- When counting with fingers, start with your thumb. If you hold up your first finger to request one item, you'll probably get two.
- What we Americans call the second floor of a building is the first floor in Europe.
- Europeans keep the left "lane" open for passing on escalators and moving sidewalks. Keep to the right.

Climate

Here is a list of average temperatures (first line—average daily low; second line—average daily high; third line—days of rain). This can be helpful in planning your itinerary, but I have never found European weather to be particularly predictable, and these charts ignore humidity.

J	F	M	A	M	J	J	A	S	O	N	D

AUSTRIA • Vienna

25°	28°	30°	42°	50°	56°	60°	59°	53°	44°	37°	30°
34°	38°	47°	58°	67°	73°	76°	75°	68°	56°	45°	37°
15	14	13	13	13	14	13	13	10	13	14	15

CROATIA • Dubrovnik

42°	43°	57°	52°	58°	65°	69°	69°	64°	57°	51°	46°
53°	55°	58°	63°	70°	78°	83°	82°	77°	69°	62°	56°
13	13	11	10	10	6	4	3	7	11	16	15

CZECH REPUBLIC • Prague

23°	24°	30°	38°	46°	52°	55°	55°	49°	41°	33°	27°
31°	34°	44°	54°	64°	70°	73°	72°	65°	53°	42°	34°
13	11	10	11	13	12	13	12	10	13	12	13

HUNGARY • Budapest

25°	28°	35°	44°	52°	58°	62°	60°	53°	44°	38°	30°
34°	39°	50°	62°	71°	78°	82°	81°	74°	61°	47°	39°
13	12	11	11	13	13	10	9	7	10	14	13

POLAND • Kraków

22°	22°	30°	38°	48°	54°	58°	56°	49°	42°	33°	28°
32°	34°	45°	55°	67°	72°	76°	73°	66°	56°	44°	37°
16	15	12	15	12	15	16	15	12	14	15	16

SLOVENIA • Ljubljana

25°	25°	32°	40°	48°	54°	57°	57°	51°	43°	36°	30°
36°	41°	50°	60°	68°	75°	80°	78°	71°	59°	47°	39°
13	11	11	13	16	16	12	12	10	14	15	15

Temperature Conversion: Fahrenheit and Celsius

FOR WEATHER   FOR HEALTH

Europe takes its temperature using the Celsius scale, while we opt for Fahrenheit. For weather, remember that 28°C is 82°F—perfect. For health, 37°C is just right.

Metric Conversion (approximate)

1 inch = 25 millimeters   32°F = 0°C
1 foot = 0.3 meter   82°F = about 28°C
1 yard = 0.9 meter   1 ounce = 28 grams
1 mile = 1.6 kilometers   1 kilogram = 2.2 pounds
1 centimeter = 0.4 inch   1 quart = 0.95 liter
1 meter = 39.4 inches   1 square yard = 0.8 square meter
1 kilometer = 0.62 mile   1 acre = 0.4 hectare

Making Your Hotel Reservation

Most hotel managers know basic "hotel English." Faxing or e-mailing are the preferred methods for reserving a room. They're more accurate than telephoning and much faster than writing a letter. Use this handy form for your fax or find it online at www.ricksteves.com/reservation. Photocopy and fax away.

One-Page Fax

To: _____ @ _____
       hotel   **fax**

From: _____@ _____
        name   **fax**

Today's date: _____ / _____ / _____
              day   **month**   **year**

Dear Hotel _____ ,
Please make this reservation for me:

Name: _____

Total # of people:_____ # of rooms: _____ # of nights: _____

Arriving: _____ / _____ / _____   My time of arrival (24-hr clock): _____
          day **month** **year**   (I will telephone if I will be late)

Departing: ____ / ____ / ____
           day **month** **year**

Room(s): Single _____ Double ____ Twin _____ Triple ____ Quad _____

With: Toilet _____ Shower _____ Bath _____ Sink only _____

Special needs: View ____ Quiet ____ Cheapest ____ Ground Floor ____

Please fax, mail, or e-mail confirmation of my reservation, along with the type of room reserved and the price. Please also inform me of your cancellation policy. After I hear from you, I will quickly send my credit-card information as a deposit to hold the room. Thank you.

_____
Signature

_____
Name

_____
Address

_____
City   *State*   *Zip Code*   *Country*

_____
E-mail Address

INDEX

Travel smart...carry on!

The latest generation of Rick Steves' carry-on travel bags is easily the best—benefiting from two decades of on-the-road attention to what really matters: maximum quality and strength; practical, flexible features; and no unnecessary frills. You won't find a better value anywhere!

Rick Steves' Convertible Carry-On

This is the classic "back door bag" that Rick Steves lives out of for three months every summer. It's made of rugged, water-resistant 1000-denier nylon. Best of all, it converts easily from a smart-looking suitcase to a handy backpack with comfortably-curved shoulder straps and a padded waistbelt.

This roomy, versatile 9" x 21" x 14" bag has a large 2500 cubic-inch main compartment, plus three outside pockets (small, medium and huge) that are perfect for often-used items. And the cinch-tight compression straps will keep your load compact and close to your back—not sagging like a sack of potatoes.

Wishing you had even more room to bring home souvenirs? Pull open the full-perimeter expando-zipper and its capacity jumps from 2500 to 3000 cubic inches. When you want to use it as a suitcase or check it as luggage (required when "expanded"), the straps and belt hide away in a zippered compartment in the back. Choose from five great traveling colors: black, navy, blue spruce, evergreen or merlot.

Rick Steves' 21" Roll-Aboard

At 9" x 21" x 14" our sturdy 21" Roll-Aboard is rucksack-soft in front, but the rest is lined with a hard ABS-lexan shell to give maximum protection to your belongings. We've spared no expense on moving parts, splurging on an extra-long button-release handle and big, tough inline skate wheels for easy rolling on rough surfaces.

Wishing you had even more room to bring home souvenirs? Pull open the full-perimeter expando-zipper and its capacity jumps from 2500 to 3000 cubic inches.

Rick Steves' 21" Roll-Aboard features exactly the same three-outside-pocket configuration and rugged 1000-denier nylon fabric as our Convertible Carry-On, plus a full lining and a handy "add-a-bag" strap.

Choose from five great traveling colors: black, navy, blue spruce, evergreen or merlot.

For great deals on a wide selection of travel goodies, begin your next trip at the Rick Steves Travel Store!

Visit the Rick Steves Travel Store at
www.ricksteves.com

Start your trip at
www.ricksteves.com

Rick Steves' Web site is packed with over 3,000 pages of timely travel information. It's also your gateway to getting FREE monthly travel news from Rick— and more!

Free Monthly European Travel News

Fresh articles on Europe's most interesting destinations and happenings. Rick will even send you an e-mail every month (often direct from Europe) with his latest discoveries!

Timely Travel Tips

Rick Steves' best money-and-stress-saving tips on trip planning, packing, transportation, hotels, health, safety, finances, hurdling the language barrier…and more.

Travelers' Graffiti Wall

Candid advice and opinions from thousands of travelers on everything listed above, plus whatever topics are hot at the moment (discount flights, packing tips, scams…you name it).

Rick's Annual Guide to European Railpasses

The clearest, most comprehensive guide to the confusing array of rail-pass options out there, and how to choo-choose the railpass that best fits your itinerary and budget. Then you can order your railpass (and get a bunch of great freebies) online from us!

Great Gear at the Rick Steves Travel Store

Enjoy bargains on Rick's guidebooks, planning maps and TV series DVDs, and on his custom-designed carry-on bags, roll-aboard bags, day packs and light-packing accessories.

Rick Steves Tours

This year more than 10,000 lucky travelers will explore Europe on a Rick Steves tour. Learn more about our 25 different one-to-three-week itineraries, read uncensored feedback from our tour alums, and sign up for your dream trip online!

Rick on Radio and TV

Download free podcasts of our weekly *Travel with Rick Steves* public radio show; read the scripts and see video clips from public television's *Rick Steves' Europe*.

Respect for Your Privacy

Ordering online from us is secure. When you buy something from us, join a tour, or subscribe to Rick's free monthly travel news e-mails, we promise to never share your name, information, or e-mail address with anyone else. You won't be spammed!

Have fun raising your Travel I.Q. at
www.ricksteves.com

Rick Steves®

More *Savvy*. More *Surprising*. More *Fun*.

COUNTRY GUIDES 2007

Croatia & Slovenia
England
France
Germany & Austria
Great Britain
Ireland
Italy
Portugal
Scandinavia
Spain
Switzerland

CITY GUIDES 2007

Amsterdam, Bruges & Brussels
Florence & Tuscany
Istanbul
London
Paris
Prague & The Czech Republic
Provence & The French Riviera
Rome
Venice

BEST OF GUIDES

Best of Eastern Europe
Best of Europe

PHRASE BOOKS & DICTIONARIES

French
French, Italian & German
German
Italian
Portuguese
Spanish

MORE EUROPE FROM RICK STEVES

Easy Access Europe
Europe 101
Europe Through the Back Door
Postcards from Europe

RICK STEVES' EUROPE DVDs

All 43 Shows 2000-2005
Britain
Eastern Europe
France & Benelux
Germany, The Swiss Alps & Travel Skills
Ireland
Italy
Spain & Portugal

PLANNING MAPS

Britain & Ireland
Europe
France
Germany, Austria & Switzerland
Italy
Spain & Portugal

CREDITS

Contributor

Gene Openshaw

Gene is the co-author of eight Rick Steves books. For this book, he wrote material on Europe's art, history, and contemporary culture. When not traveling, Gene enjoys composing music, recovering from his 1973 trip to Europe with Rick, and living everyday life with his wife and daughter.

IMAGES

Title Page: Széchenyi Baths, Budapest, Hungary	Cameron Hewitt
1st Full-Page Color: Ulica Długa, Gdańsk, Poland	Cameron Hewitt
2nd Full-Page Color: Ljubljana, Slovenia	Cameron Hewitt
Czech Republic (full-page image): Charles Bridge, Prague	Cameron Hewitt
Prague: Vltava River, Charles Bridge, and Prague Castle	Cameron Hewitt
Český Krumlov: View of City	David C. Hoerlein
Slovakia (full-page image): St. Michael's Gate, Bratislava	Cameron Hewitt
Bratislava: Bratislava Castle	Cameron Hewitt
The Spiš Region: Spiš Castle	Cameron Hewitt
Poland (full-page image): Old Town Square, Warsaw	Cameron Hewitt
Kraków: Main Market Square	Cameron Hewitt
Auschwitz-Birkenau: Birkenau Guard Tower	Rick Steves
Warsaw: Castle Square and the Old Town	Rick Steves
Gdańsk: Artus Court on Ulica Długa	Cameron Hewitt
Pomerania: Malbork Castle	Cameron Hewitt
Hungary (full-page image): Parliament, Budapest	Cameron Hewitt
Budapest: Chain Bridge Panorama	Cameron Hewitt
The Danube Bend: View from Visegrád Citadel	Cameron Hewitt
Eger: Minorite Church and Eger Castle	Cameron Hewitt

Slovenia (full-page image):
Soča River Valley — Cameron Hewitt

Ljubljana: Ljubljana Castle overlooking
Prešeren Square — Cameron Hewitt

The Karst: Predjama Castle — Rick Steves

Bled: Pletna Boat on Lake Bled — Cameron Hewitt

The Julian Alps: Mountain Hut — Cameron Hewitt

Croatia (full-page image): Dubrovnik — Cameron Hewitt

Dubrovnik: View of Old Town — Cameron Hewitt

Korčula: Korčula Old Town — Cameron Hewitt

Split: Riva Promenade and Old Town — Cameron Hewitt

Zagreb: Jelačić Square — Cameron Hewitt

Plitvice Lakes National Park: Plitvice — Rick Steves

Austria (full-page image):
St. Peter's Church, Vienna — Cameron Hewitt

Vienna: Schönbrunn Palace — Cameron Hewitt

Annibale Caracci
Venus findet Adonis

Paolo Veronese
Venus und Adonis

Jacobo Chimenti
Jgen. Empolo

Susanna im Bade.

Perseus befreit Andromeda

Michiel Coxcie
The Fall of Man
The Expulsion from Paradise

Rubens
The Infant Christ w/ John the
Baptist & 2 Angels.

Rick Steves' Guidebook Series

Country Guides

Rick Steves' Best of Europe
Rick Steves' Best of Eastern Europe
Rick Steves' Croatia & Slovenia (new in 2007)
Rick Steves' England
Rick Steves' France
Rick Steves' Germany & Austria
Rick Steves' Great Britain
Rick Steves' Ireland
Rick Steves' Italy
Rick Steves' Portugal
Rick Steves' Scandinavia
Rick Steves' Spain
Rick Steves' Switzerland

City and Regional Guides

Rick Steves' Amsterdam, Bruges & Brussels
Rick Steves' Florence & Tuscany
Rick Steves' Istanbul (new in 2007)
Rick Steves' London
Rick Steves' Paris
Rick Steves' Prague & the Czech Republic
Rick Steves' Provence & the French Riviera
Rick Steves' Rome
Rick Steves' Venice

Rick Steves' Phrase Books

French
German
Italian
Spanish
Portuguese
French/Italian/German

Other Books

Rick Steves' Europe Through the Back Door
Rick Steves' Europe 101: History and Art for the Traveler
Rick Steves' Easy Access Europe
Rick Steves' Postcards from Europe
Rick Steves' European Christmas

(Avalon Travel Publishing)

Handwritten notes at top:
Zechariah 3, 4
Sof S 5:11-16
Isaiah 54:17 . .
Dame in Gab
Max Kurzweil

el Publishing
treet, Suite 250
CA 94608
vel Publishing
t of Avalon Publishing Group
07 by Rick Steves
2007 by Avalon Travel Publishing, Inc. All rights reserved.
2007 by Europe Through the Back Door
in the USA by Worzalla. First printing February 2007.

thanks to Ian Watson for his innumerable contributions. Many thanks also to
Vihan, the co-author of *Rick Steves' Prague & the Czech Republic*, for his help with
ngs Czech. *Danke* to Gene Openshaw for his *wunderbar* tour of the Kunsthistorisches
um in Vienna.

ions of this book were originally published in *Rick Steves' Germany & Austria* © 2007,
6, 2005, by Rick Steves; in *Rick Steves' Germany, Austria & Switzerland* © 2004, 2003,
02, 2001, 2000, 1999, by Rick Steves; and in *Rick Steves' Prague & the Czech Republic*
2007, 2006, 2005, by Rick Steves and Honza Vihan.

or the latest on Rick Steves' lectures, guidebooks, tours, public radio show, and public
television series, contact Europe Through the Back Door, Box 2009, Edmonds, WA 98020,
tel. 425/771-8303, fax 425/771-0833, www.ricksteves.com, rick@ricksteves.com.

ISBN (10) 1-56691-806-5
ISBN (13) 978-1-56691-806-0
ISSN 1547-8505

Europe Through the Back Door Managing Editor: Risa Laib
ETBD Editors: Gretchen Strauch, Jennifer Madison Davis, Cathy McDonald
Avalon Travel Publishing Editor and Series Manager: Madhu Prasher
Avalon Travel Publishing Project Editor: Patrick Collins
Copy Editor: Ellie Behrstock
Proofreader: Kay Elliott
Indexer: Stephen Callahan
Production & Typesetting: McGuire Barber Design
Cover Design: Kari Gim, Laura Mazer
Interior Design: Laura Mazer, Jane Musser, Amber Pirker
Maps & Graphics: David C. Hoerlein, Laura VanDeventer, Lauren Mills, Barb Geisler,
Mike Morgenfeld
Photography: Cameron Hewitt, Rick Steves, David C. Hoerlein
Front Matter Color Photos: page i: Széchenyi Baths, Budapest, Hungary © Cameron
Hewitt; page ii: Ulica Długa, Gdańsk, Poland © Cameron Hewitt; page xii: Ljubljana,
Slovenia © Cameron Hewitt
Cover Photos: front: Wawel Cathedral, Kraków, Poland © Cameron Hewitt; back: Soča
River Valley, Slovenia © Cameron Hewitt

Distributed to the book trade by Publishers Group West, Berkeley, California